MUNDO)real

MEDIA edition

Teacher's Edition

3

© Editorial Edinumen, 2016

Authors:
Julia Caballero, María Carmen Cabeza, Francisca Fernández, Patricia Fontanals,
Luisa Galán, Amelia Guerrero, Peter Hearn, Debra L. King, Emilio José Marín, Celia Meana, Liliana Pereyra
and Francisco Fidel Riva.
Coordination Team: Celia Meana.

ISBN - Teacher's Edition: 978-1-107-47272-3

Printed in the United States of America

Editorial Coordination:
Mar Menéndez

Cover Design:
Juanjo López

Design and Layout:
Juanjo López, Analia García y Carlos Yllana

Cambridge University Press
32 Avenue of the Americas
New York, NY 10013

Editorial Edinumen
José Celestino Mutis, 4. 28028 Madrid. España
Telephone: (34) 91 308 51 42
Fax: (34) 91 319 93 09
e-mail: edinumen@edinumen.es
www.edinumen.es

MUNDO)real
MEDIA edition

TABLE OF CONTENTS

INTRODUCTION TO THE PROGRAM

STUDENT BOOK

APPENDIX

TE3

PROGRAM AT A GLANCE

Mundo Real Media Edition is a three-level Spanish language program designed for high school students that uses lively and compelling content, images, and video to teach the language that learners need to succeed in and outside the classroom.

Each level of *Mundo Real Media Edition* provides a complete curriculum of instruction for one year of high school Spanish.

COMPONENTS AT A GLANCE: PRINT + TECHNOLOGY

Mundo Real Media Edition offers a communicative approach that focuses on functional, real-life language. The program's guided and manageable content encourages students to begin speaking the language immediately. With real-life themes, high-interest content, and natural speech, *Mundo Real* teaches the language relevant to students' lives.

| Student Book | Online Workbook | Teacher's Edition | DVD |

| eBooks | Digital Master Guide | Cuaderno para hispanohablantes |

ELEteca, Cambridge / Edinumen's educational platform (**www.cambridge.org/eleteca**), offers **additional material** for teachers and students which expands and complements all three levels of the program.

STUDENT RESOURCES

STUDENT'S BOOK

Mundo Real Media Edition uses lively and compelling content, images, and video to teach real-world language. The student book's experiential format encourages the development of strong communicative skills, which will increase your comfort level in real-world settings.

EBOOK

Mundo Real Media Edition eBooks are fully interactive and fully integrated with the Learning Management System ELEteca. Integrated audio and a seamless connection to online video content, as well as online and offline modes for Mac, PC, iOS, and Android, make using your eBook simple.

ONLINE WORBOOK

The *Mundo Real Media Edition* online workbook features a wide variety of activity types and exercises, and includes embedded video, a video note-taking feature, and speech recognition technology.

CUADERNO PARA HISPANOHABLANTES

The *Mundo Real Media Edition* Cuaderno para hispanohablantes is written exclusively for native speakers who have grown up speaking conversational Spanish, and includes sophisticated activities and lessons that expand on the Student's Book.

ELETECA

Mundo Real Media Edition features a wealth of digital resources designed to supplement and enhance the Student's Book. All are available in the rich, interactive world of *Mundo Real Media Edition* ELEteca—in one place, with one password.

Interactive Activities

Online Workbook and eBook Integration

The *Mundo Real Media Edition* Online Workbook and eBook are accessible through ELEteca, so you can access all of your digital resources in one place, using one password.

Gamification

"La Pasantía," a game that allows you to engage with the Spanish language in a fun context, as you compete to win a spot on the staff of a Spanish newspaper.

Mundo Real Media Edition contains a wealth of video content, which:
- highlights both the unit theme and the culture of the Spanish-speaking world
- clarifies difficult grammar points and language skills
- models authentic language and a wide variety of accents and dialects

¡Acción!

Mundo Real Media Edition features a brand new narrative video series that aligns with each chapter of the Student's Book, modeling and synthesizing the communicative skills of the text.

Video segments are connected but episodic, and set in and around a Latin American university. Real-life situations and activities —navigating a new city, shopping, playing and watching sports— model relevant language in context, building a student's ability to communicate outside the classroom.

Voces Latinas

Cultural video segments expand upon the cultural sections of the text, inviting students to explore the traditions and histories of different areas of the Spanish-speaking world.

Grammar Tutorials

These short clips can be used to introduce new grammar concepts, or to reinforce and review difficult skills. Explanations and examples are all in Spanish, encouraging critical thinking in the target language.

Casa del Español

These street interviews model the target grammar and vocabulary skills in an authentic and engaging context, and feature a wide range of language varieties and dialects.

ELETECA FOR TEACHERS

The **ELEteca** is an online learning management platform that provides additional teaching options with the following technology resources:

DIGITAL MASTER GUIDE

The Digital Master Guide is a Digital Teacher's Edition including related resources that allows teachers to access and use the materials dynamically anywhere, using any kind of device (iPad and Android tablets, PC and Apple computers), or in the classroom with a computer and an interactive whiteboard to engage students.

IMPORTANT: To download and install the Digital Master Guide, the teacher should first enter and register in ELEteca and follow the instructions to complete the process.

Assessments
A comprehensive bank of downloadable, editable assessments.

Appendix and extra resources
Downloadable documents with all the material needed to get the best experience from the course: audioscripts, videoscripts for *¡Acción!* Section, Workbook answer keys and audioscripts, User's Guide for the cooperative activities suggested for students on ELEteca.

Interactive Whiteboard Lessons
The Interactive Whiteboard Lessons are additional resources which are downloadable from ELEteca and inter-referenced throughout the Teacher's Guide, that provide additional opportunities for teachers to present new material and for students to practice in a dynamic way.

Extension Activities (Photocopiable)
The Extension Activities are downloadable from ELEteca and can be printed and distributed to students for classroom group activities that enhance learning.

ELEteca collects data for the teachers to help adapt their pedagogical approach, gathering information on student use of the online activities and tests and how well students have performed on these. Teachers can use ELEteca to generate reports on individual students and for the class as a whole.

Class Reports

These reports summarize data for the whole class collected by ELEteca, based on individual student responses, allowing teachers to make decisions about student grouping and inform further review, revision, practice, and instruction.

Individual Student Reports

• These reports provide information on what activities and tests an individual student has completed and their scores, including dates completed.
• Teachers can retrieve the tests completed by students to gain further insight into a student's level of command of the language and provide personalized, individual feedback.

ACTIVATING YOUR DIGITAL INSTRUCTOR ACCESS

MundoReal Media Edition includes a set of digital components and services for the teacher that enhance and complement the print material, providing what we think is the best teaching experience with the program. Please follow the instructions below to activate these digital components.

1. Visit www.cambridge.org/eleteca. If you are a new user, click "Create User Account" on the right side of your screen.

2. Fill out the necessary information. Please use a valid email address, as you will receive a confirmation email that you´ll need to access in order to activate your account. You can also use this email address to recover a lost or forgotten password.

IMPORTANT: Be sure to select "Teacher" at the bottom of your registration screen, or you will be unable to access your Teacher Resources.

3. Once you have created an account, scroll down and select the appropriate course (*Mundo Real Media Edition* Level 1, 2 or 3).

4. Enter the Digital Content Access Code printed in the front of your Teacher's Edition. Please note that this is a single-use code, and can be activated only once.

5. Congratulations! You can now access all Student Resources. To access your Teacher Resources, click on the "Teacher Resources" icon on the right side of your screen.

6. The system will ask you to enter your access code again. Enter the Digital Content Access Code printed in the front of your Teacher's Edition (the same code you entered in Step 4).

7. Congratulations! You can now access your Teacher Resources, including audio tracks, video scripts, answer keys, assessment tests, and instructions for the collaborative activities.

8. To access your Digital Master Guide –a full eBook of the Teacher's Edition, available online or offline on any tablet or computer– click on the "My eBooks" icon at the top of your screen.

9. For first time access, you'll need to activate your Digital Master Guide using the same code you used in steps 4 and 6. Click the "Redeem" button and once again enter your Digital Content Access Code.

10. Congratulations! You can now access your Digital Master Guide. The Digital Master Guide is available at any time, and on any device, through your ELEteca account. You can also download the free Cambridge Spanish Bookshelf app, which will allow you to access your Digital Master Guide offline on any computer or tablet.

The *Mundo Real Media Edition* testing program offers comprehensive means for evaluating student performance.

The Assessment Program Components include:

- Comprehensive ready-made test for each unit
- Additional Test Bank questions for customized assessment
- Midterm Exam
- Final Exam
- Integrated Performance Assessment Tests

Unit Tests measure vocabulary, grammar, and culture concepts and include specific sections for listening and reading comprehension, in addition to covering speaking and writing. The modules for speaking include three different kinds of activities: presentational, interactive (student-to-student) and communicative interaction between teacher and student.

Three editable Test Banks are included per unit: one for on-level assessment, one for advanced learners, and one for slower-paced learners.

Each unit also contains one Integrated Performance Assessment (IPA) Test. IPA is a classroom-based assessment model that is used for evaluating student's language use in the three communicative modes (interpersonal, interpretive, and presentational) that correspond to the ACTFL standards.

INTEGRATED PERFORMANCE ASSESSMENT

Interpretive Communication

▼

Interpersonal Communication

▼

Presentational Communication

USING THE SPECIAL FEATURES OF THE TEACHER'S EDITION

UNIT OPENER

Objectives for the Unit Opener
This section provides a quick summary of objectives for the unit opener and how it connects the unit's learning outcomes.

Objectives for the Unit
The unit's learning objectives are an organizational tool for both the teacher and the student. Teachers can use them to preview what students will learn, and they serve as a way to assess whether students have mastered the main ideas and skills.

Unit Resources at a Glance
All of the teacher's resources available for the unit are listed here for quick reference.

Instructional Strategies
These provide specific recommendations to the teacher for presenting and teaching the material to students.

Common Core Standards
A correlation to the four strands of the Common Core Standards is provided in the Unit Opener, listing which activities in each section of the unit correspond to each of these strands.

Core Resources

This lists the specific instructional resources *Mundo Real Media Edition* provides for each section of the unit.

Objectives for the Lessons

Each section starts with a list of learning objectives that teachers can use as an organizational tool. Teachers can use them to preview what students will learn in this section, and they serve as a way to assess whether students have mastered the main ideas and skills.

Extensions and Alternative Activities

These supplementary activities allow teachers to give students more practice, if needed.

Cultural Notes

These notes provide support for the teacher, with additional cultural information to share with students, bringing Hispanic culture alive for students and motivating them to learn.

Answers

An answer key is provided immediately below the activities for quick reference and to facilitate feedback to students.

Standards for Learning Languages

This lists the ACTFL Standards for Learning Languages covered in this section.

Activity-Specific Instructional Strategies

These instructional strategies provide specific recommendations to the teacher for teaching the unit content and for guiding students on how to carry out specific activities.

UNIT STRUCTURE

Each unit of *Mundo Real Media Edition* follows a consistent, clear sequence of instruction.

UNIT SECTION	PEDAGOGICAL PURPOSE
UNIDAD	**UNIT OPENER** • This is a visual introduction to the unit theme. Each unit focuses on a different real-world content area. • Discussion questions act as a springboard for students to begin using the language immediately, creatively adapting language they have learned previously to respond to new situations.
HABLAMOS DE...	**PREVIEWING LANGUAGE AND STRUCTURES** • A sample dialog, featuring engaging images related to the unit theme, previews important structures and vocabulary from the unit. • These dialogs immediately engage students in the language, improving their listening and reading comprehension skills.
COMUNICA	**COMMUNICATIVE FUNCTIONS** • Develops speaking skills and oral interaction using communicative structures and activities.
¡ACCIÓN!	**INTEGRATED LANGUAGE VIDEO** • Built around a video segment following the lives of students in Spain. This authentic language input not only strengthens comprehension and listening skills, but also acts as a model for speaking. • Before, during, and after viewing activities provide a structured approach to viewing the video. The video contextualizes the content of the unit in a familiar scenario.
PALABRA POR PALABRA	**LANGUAGE AND VOCABULARY** • Introduces high-frequency vocabulary, which is practiced and expanded throughout the unit.
GRAMÁTICA	**GRAMMAR IN CONTEXT** • Presents three to four grammar points in each unit. • *Gramática* allows students to examine and practice specific grammar points and language functions from the unit while enabling them to sharpen their listening and speaking skills. • Accessible and contextualized grammar charts and presentations provide students with added clarity.
DESTREZAS	**COMMUNICATIVE SKILLS** • Integrates key language skills (listening, reading comprehension, oral and written expression). • Provides guided strategies and activities related to the unit theme to further student comprehension and learning.
PRONUNCIACIÓN	**PRONUNCIATION** • Activities focus on the high-priority features of phonetics, stress, and intonation, to help students improve overall speech.
SABOR HISPANO	**CULTURE IN CONTEXT** • Presents different aspects of Hispanic cultures using images, maps, and other cultural realia to provide students a window into the Hispanic world.
RELATO	**COMPREHENSIVE PRACTICE** • Brings the unit's content together through a fictional text and encourages students to build their reading and listening comprehension skills.
EVALUACIÓN	**SELF-ASSESSMENT** • A built-in self-assessment for students to assess their knowledge of the content covered in each unit.
EN RESUMEN: VOCABULARIO/ GRAMÁTICA	**UNIT REVIEW** • A one-page glossary of the unit vocabulary and a one-page summary of grammar structures covered in each unit for easy reference and review. • Teacher's Edition models for students how to review vocabulary and grammar and provides instructional strategies to help students develop learning and studying skills.
AHORA COMPRUEBA	**CUMMULATIVE REVIEW** • A built-in cumulative self-assessment every two units for students to assess their knowledge of the content covered in the previous units. • Teachers can assign point value to each activity as a way for students to self-assess. If students achieve less than 80% on each activity, teachers can direct them to En resumen in the previous units for unit sections to review.

SCOPE AND SEQUENCE

 Pair icon: indicates that the activity is designed to be done by students working in pairs.

 Group icon: indicates that the activity is designed to be done by students working in small groups or as a whole class.

 Audio icon: indicates recorded material either as part of an activity or a reading text.

 Language icon: provides additional language and grammar support in presentations and activities.

 Regional variation icon: provides examples of regional variations in the language.

Recycling icon: provides a reminder of previously taught material that students will need to use in an activity.

EXPLORE A UNIT

A dynamic image provides a visual introduction to the unit theme. Each unit theme focuses on a different real-world content area.

A discussion question acts as a springboard for students to begin using the language immediately, creatively adapting language they have learned previously to respond to new situations.

Each unit of *Mundo Real Media Edition* contains eleven focused sections:

Hablamos de...	Destrezas / Pronunciación
Comunica	Sabor hispano
¡Acción!	Relato
Palabra por palabra	Evaluación
Gramática	En resumen

HABLAMOS DE..., a sample dialogue featuring engaging images related to the unit theme, previews important structures and vocabulary from the unit. These dialogues immediately engage students in the language, improving their listening and reading comprehension skills.

COMUNICA develops speaking skills and oral interaction using communicative structures and activities.

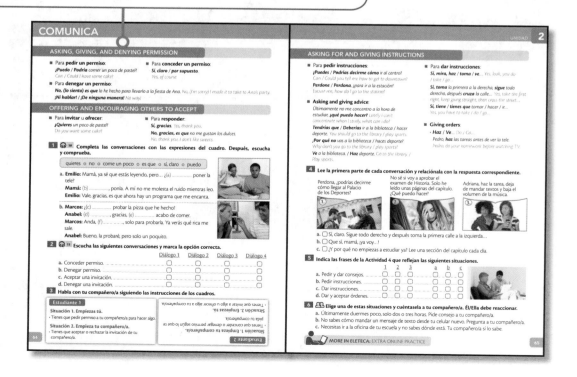

¡ACCIÓN! is built around a video segment following the lives of students in Spain. This authentic language input not only strengthens comprehension and listening skills, but also acts as a model for speaking.

Before, during, and after viewing activities provide a structured approach to viewing the video. The video contextualizes the content of the unit in a familiar scenario.

PALABRA POR PALABRA introduces high-frequency vocabulary, which is practiced and expanded throughout the unit.

GRAMÁTICA presents three to four grammar points in each unit. **Gramática** allows students to examine and practice specific grammar points and language functions from the unit while enabling them to sharpen their listening and speaking skills.

Accessible and contextualized grammar charts and presentations provide students with added clarity.

DESTREZAS integrates key language skills –listening and reading comprehension, oral and written expression– and provides guided strategies and activities related to the unit theme to further student comprehension and learning.

PRONUNCIACIÓN activities focus on the high-priority features of stress and intonation, to help students improve overall speech.

SABOR HISPANO presents different aspects of Hispanic cultures using images, maps, and other cultural realia to provide students with a window into the Hispanic world.

RELATO brings the unit's content together through a fictional text and encourages students to build their reading and listening comprehension skills.

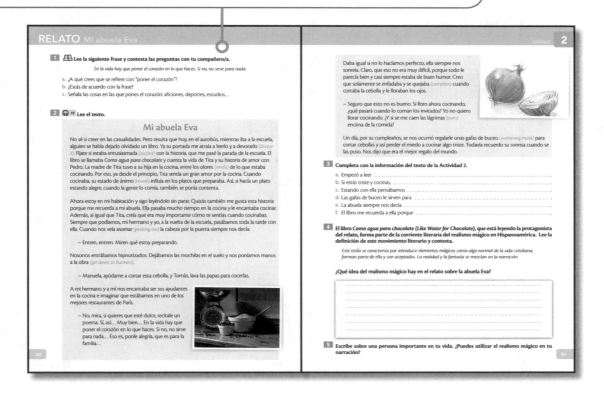

EVALUACIÓN is an integrated review for students to assess their knowledge of the content covered in each unit.

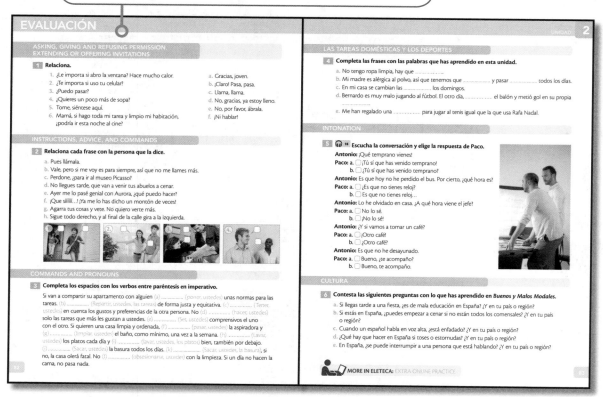

EN RESUMEN contains a glossary of the vocabulary and grammar structures covered in each unit for easy reference and review.

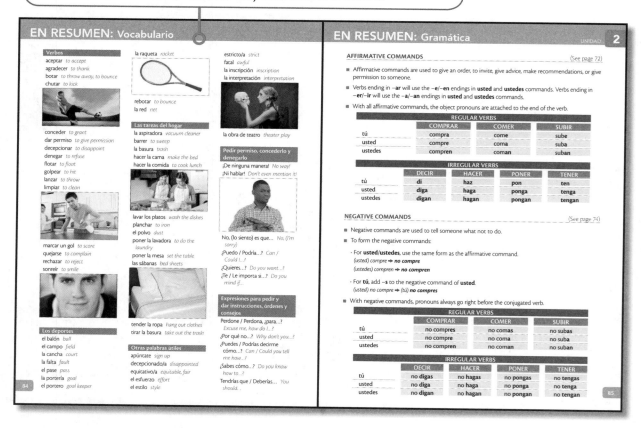

ACKNOWLEDGMENTS

The authors and publisher would like to thank the following teachers for their insight and comments during the development of *Mundo Real Media Edition*. The experience and intuition of these educators was crucial in the development of this course.

Jeremy Aldrich - Harrisonburg City Public Schools (VA), **Susan Allen** - Eastern High School (NJ), **Marilu Alvarado** - Academia Margarita Muniz (MA), **Jose M. Aviña** - Sunset High School (TX), **Vicki S. Baggia** - Phillips Exeter Academy (NH), **David Barkley** - George C. Marshall High School (VA), **Vanda Baughman** - Cascade High School (OR), **Emily A. Berry** - Irvington Preparatory Academy (IN), **Candace Blatt** - Kokomo High School (IN), **Pilar Blazey** - Wilson High School (WA), **Patricia Boyarizo** - Ragsdale High School (NC), **Sonia Brandon** - Fork Union Military Academy (VA), **Ariel Bueno** - Lake Ridge High School (TX), **Maria L. Cabra** - Ronald W. Reagan / Doral Senior High School (FL), **Lilian M. Castillo de Hutchinson** - The Loomis Chaffee School (CT), **John S. Coco** - Cocalico School District (CO), **Pamela Conte** - Nordonia Hills City Schools (OH), **Rita Morales Cooley** - The Madeira School (VA), **Deb Dargay** - Bloomington Jefferson High School (MN), **Jesús López Díez** - Dana Hall School (MA), **Maria Elena Downes** - NYOS Charter School (NY), **Marsha Dragonetti** - Latin School of Chicago (IL), **Yvonne Easaw** - Richland School District Two (SC), **Cristina Escotto** - Fredericksburg Academy (VA), **Margaret K. Esten** - South Portland High School (OR), **Calvin Feehan** - Redwood High School (CA), **Scott L. Fisher** - McGavock High School (TN), **Mary Jo Flood** - Royal High School (CA), **Alejandra Fonseca** - Wyandanch Memorial High School (NY), **William Frank** - Pinkerton Academy (NH), **Coleen Garcia** - La Serna High School (CA), **Ramón García-Tamaran** - Bloomington High School South (IN), **Angela Giffin** - Stevens High School (SD), **Jeanne Gilbert** - The Hawbridge School (NC), **Robert Giosh** - The Latin School of Chicago (IL), **Xiomara Gonzalez** - Barbara Goleman Senior High School (FL), **Adriana Gonzalez-Novello** - Trinity School (NY), **Catherine A. Haney** - Loudoun County Public Schools (VA), **Ana Hermoso** - The Hotchkiss School (CT), **Wilson R. Hernández** - Hightstown High School (NJ), **Lesley Hinson** - Churchill High School (TX), **Efila Jzar-Simpson** - Ben Davis University High School (IN), **Anne Karakash, M.A.** - Franklin Academy (NC), **Nora L. Kinney** - Montini Catholic High School (IL), **Ivonete Kinson-Blackwelder** - North Pole High School (AK), **Heather Kissel** - TechBoston Academy (MA), **Dr. Jean Robert Lainé** - Putnam City Public Schools (OK), **William A. Leheny** - Garces Memorial High School (CA), **Jacqueline Liebold** - Groton Dunstable Regional High School (MA), **Patricio Lopez** - Harborfields High School (NY), **Adrianna Madril** - Martin Luther High School (CA), **Amanda Mancilla** - Union County Public Schools (NC), **Alice Nan Mannix** - Brown County High School (IN), **Nilma M. Martin Antonetti** - Richard Montgomery High School (MD), **Amanda Marvin** - The Barstow School (MO), **Rubenm Mascarenas** - Teacher Summit High School (TX), **Maritza Massopust** - Adelson Educational Campus (NV), **Justin Vanlee McClain** - Bishop McNamara High School (MD), **Marcelina McCool** - West Philadelphia High School (PA), **Darcie McGee** - Minnesota Online High School (MN), **Jennifer Mitchell** - The Hun School of Princeton (NJ), **Kathleen Monks** - Holley Central School (NY), **Yolanda Montague** - Stuarts Draft High School (VA), **Weston Moody** - Manhattan-Ogden School (NY), **Sydney Munson** - All Saints' Episcopal School (TX), **Sergio Navarro** - Redondo Union High School (CA), **Carmen Neale** - Watkinson School (CT), **Valerie Neri** - Park Center Senior High - International Baccalaureate World School (MN), **Andrew Noelle** - Central Magnet School (TN), **Marie G. Nuzzi** - Garden City High School (NY), **Santa Olmedo** - Foothill High School (CA), **Joseph A. Parodi** - Marianapolis Preparatory School (CT), **Olga A. Pietrantonio** - Blaine High School (WA), **Tim Pillsbury** - Trinity-Pawling School (NY), **Viviana Planine** - Newton South High School (MA), **Sofia Catalina Pollock** - John Champe High School (VA), **Andrew Poolman** - The Haverford School (PA), **Gregory Prais** - Detroit Catholic Central High School (MI), **Ashleigh Marsh Prendable** - Montgomery County Public Schools (MD), **Cecilia Remeta** - Palos Verdes High School (CA), **Mary Beth Ricci** - Olathe South High School (OK), **Gimara Richards, M.A.T.** - Stonewall Jackson High School (VA), **Myra M. Rios, M.A.** - Lower Merion High School (PA), **Alison Robinson** - Fort Worth Country Day School (TX), **Norman Sargen** - Agnes Irwin School (PA), **David M. Sawyer** - The Covenant School (VA), **Carl A. Seese** - Twin Lakes High School (IN), **Rosana Serna** - Seven Lakes High School (TX), **Bertha Sevilla** - Notre Dame Academy (CA), **Jonathan L. Sirois** - Tabor Academy (MA), **Ellen J. Spitalli** - Naperville Central High School (IL), **Maribel Squibb** - Sharyland High School (TX), **Tamara Tamez** - Nimitz High School (TX), **Yamila Tamny** - River Ridge High School (FL), **Susan Tawney** - Ragsdale High School (NC), **Candida Thompson** - Academy of Richmond County (GA), **Lisa Todd** - Colorado Academy (CO), **Delia Topping** - Central Magnet School (TN), **Yari Torres** - Douglass High School (TN), **Rachel Torrie** - Woodinville High School (WA), **Rosanna Tucci** - Miami Beach Senior High (FL), **Karen Twyford** - Highland High School (IL), **Maria Vazquez** - Mother Seton Regional High School (NJ), **Janice Ventresco** - Avon High School (OH), **Barbara A. Volkman** - Lanphier High School (IL), **Michelle Warner** - East Muskingum Schools (OH), **Rhonda L. Wells** - DeKalb County School District (GA), **Rand Wiseman** - Gig Harbor High School (WA).

PROFESSIONAL ORGANIZATIONS AND RESOURCES

These organizations provide a wealth of teaching resources with online materials, conferences, and workshops.

American Association of Teachers of Spanish and Portuguese (AATSP)

AATSP's mission is to promote the study and teaching of the Spanish and Portuguese languages and their corresponding literatures and cultures at all levels of education.

http://www.aatsp.org/

The American Council on the Teaching of Foreign Languages (ACTFL)

ACTFL is an individual membership organization of more than 12,000 language educators and administrators, dedicated to the improvement and expansion of the teaching and learning of all languages at all levels of instruction.

www.actfl.org

In addition, ACTFL provides an "Alignment of the National Standards for Learning Languages with the Common Core Standards" at the following URL:

http://www.actfl.org/news/reports/alignment-the-national-standards-learning-languages-the-common-core-state-standards

Center for Applied Linguistics (CAL)

Language acquisition experts at the Center for Applied Linguistics focus on language education at all levels of instruction. They conduct language research, professional development for language teachers, information collection and dissemination, and program evaluation.

www.cal.org

National Capital Language Resource Center

NCLRC is a joint project of Georgetown University, The George Washington University, and the Center for Applied Linguistics. NCLRC is located in Washington, DC, and is one of fifteen nonprofit Language Resource Centers funded by the U.S. Department of Education.

http://www.nclrc.org

Partnership for 21st Century Skills (P21)

P21's mission is "To serve as a catalyst to position 21st century readiness at the center of US K12 education by building collaborative partnerships among education, business, community and government leaders." P21's focus includes the learning of foreign languages in K–12.

http://www.p21.org

Regional Foreign Language Conferences and Teacher Organizations

- The Central States Conference on the Teaching of Foreign Languages (CSCTFL)
  http://www.csctfl.org/
- The Greater Washington Association of Teachers of Foreign Languages http://www.gwatfl.org/
- Southern Conference on Language Teaching
  http://scolt.webnode.com/
- Southwest Conference on Language Teaching
  http://www.swcolt.org/
- Northeast Conference on the Teaching of Foreign Languages
  http://alpha.dickinson.edu/prorg/nectfl/index.html
- Pacific Northwest Council for Languages (PNCFL)
  http://www.pncfl.org

BIBLIOGRAPHICAL REFERENCES

Teaching Methods

Gattegno, C. (1976). *The Common Sense of Teaching Foreign Languages.* New York: Educational Solutions.

Holt, D. (1993). *Cooperative Learning: A Response to Linguistic and Cultural Diversity.* McHenry, IL, and Washington, DC: Delta Systems and Center for Applied Linguistics.

Johnson, K. (1982). *Communicative Syllabus Design and Methodology.* Oxford: Pergamon.

Krashen, S.D. (1981). *Second Language Acquisition and Second Language Learning.* Oxford: Pergamon.

Krashen, S.D., & Terrell, T.D. (1983). *The Natural Approach: Language Acquisition in the Classroom.* Englewood Cliffs, NJ: Prentice Hall.

Larsen-Freeman, D. (2000). *Techniques and Principles in Language Teaching* (2nd ed.). Oxford: Oxford University Press.

Littlewood, W. (1982). *Communicative Language Teaching: An Introduction.* Cambridge: Cambridge University Press.

Littlewood, W. (1992). *Teaching Oral Communication: A Methodological Framework.* Oxford: Blackwell.

Lozanov, G. (1978). *Suggestology and Outlines of Suggestopedy.* New York: Gordon and Breach.

Lozanov, G., & Gateva, E. (1988). *The Foreign Language Teacher's Suggestopedic Manual.* New York: Gordon and Breach.

National Standards in Foreign Language Education Project (1999, 2006). *Standards for Foreign Language Learning in the 21st Century (SFFLL)* (2nd & 3rd edns.). Lawrence, KS: Allen Press.

Nunan, D. (1999). Second Language Teaching and Learning. Boston: Heinle & Heinle.

Richards, J. C., & Rodgers, T.S. (2001). *Approaches and Methods in Language Teaching.* (2nd ed.). Cambridge: Cambridge University Press.

Stern, H.H. (1983). *Fundamental Concepts of Language Teaching.* Oxford: Oxford University Press.

Access for All Students / Differentiated Instruction

Downey, D.M. (1992, April). *Accommodating the foreign language learning disabled student.* Paper presented at the Foreign Language and Learning Disabilities Conference, The American University, Washington, DC.

Ganschow, L., Myer, B.J., & Roeger, K. (1989). Foreign language policies and procedures for students with specific learning disabilities. *Learning Disabilities Focus,* 5(1), 50-58.

Ganschow, L. and Schneider, E. (2006). *Assisting Students With Foreign Language Learning Difficulties in School. From Perspectives on Language and Literacy, Special Edition 2006.* Baltimore, MD:International Dyslexia Association.

Gardner, Howard E. (1993). *Multiple Intelligences: The Theory in Practice.* New York: Basic Books.

Teaching Spanish to Spanish Heritage Speakers

American Association of Teachers of Spanish and Portuguese. (2000). Volume I. *Spanish for native speakers: AATSP Professional Development Series Handbook for Teachers K-16. A handbook for teachers.* Fort Worth, TX: Harcourt College Publishers.

Jim Cummins "Beyond Curricular Scripts and Instructional Techniques: Implementing Classroom Interactions that Foster Power, Identity, Imagination, and Intellect Among Bilingual Students." NABE conference. Philadelphia, PA. March 2002.

Poey, Delia and Virgil Suárez. (1992) *Iguana Dreams.* New York, Harper Collins. Samaniego et al. (2002).

Webb, J.B., & Miller, B.L. (Eds.) (2000). *Teaching Heritage Language Learners: Voices from the Classroom.* Yonkers, NY: American Council on the Teaching of Foreign Languages.

Additional Bibliographical References

For additional reading suggestions and teaching materials, visit the following sites.

- **CAL Resource Guides Online**
  http://www.cal.org/resources/archive/rgos/methods.html
- **NCLRC Teaching Materials for Spanish**
  http://nclrc.org/teaching_materials/materials_by_language/spanish.html
- **Resource Publications from AATSP**
  http://www.aatsp.org/?page=RESOURCPUB

EL UNIVERSO HISPANO

Estados Unidos

Phoenix

Dallas

El Paso

Houston

Tijuana Mexicali

Chihuahua

Monterrey

Mazatlán

MÉXICO

Colima

México D.F.

Veracruz

Acapulco

GUATEMALA

MÉXICO, CENTROAMÉRICA Y CARIBE

EL SALVADOR

HONDURAS

Atlanta

CUBA

Miami

Bahamas

La Habana

Cienfuegos

Camagüey

Guantánamo

Mérida

Santiago de Cuba

Haití

Belice

San Pedro Sula

Ciudad de Guatemala

Tegucigalpa

San Salvador

León

Managua

Granada

San José

Puntarenas

Colón

Panamá

REPÚBLICA DOMINICANA

PUERTO RICO

Santo Domingo

San Juan

La Romana

Ponce

NICARAGUA

COSTA RICA

PANAMÁ

Caracas

Barranquilla

Medellín
Bogotá

Cali

Islas Galápagos

Quito

Iquitos

Trujillo

Lima

Cuzco

Arequipa

La Paz

Santa
Cruz

Sucre

Brasil

Asunción

Córdoba

Rosario

Santiago de
Chile

Buenos Aires

Montevideo

Bahía Blanca

Comodoro
Rivadavia

Río
Gallegos

Punta
Arenas

VENEZUELA

COLOMBIA

BOLIVIA

ECUADOR

PARAGUAY

PERÚ

URUGUAY

CHILE

ARGENTINA

SUDAMÉRICA Y ESPAÑA

La Coruña · Bilbao · Barcelona
Francia
Madrid
Portugal · Valencia
Sevilla

ESPAÑA

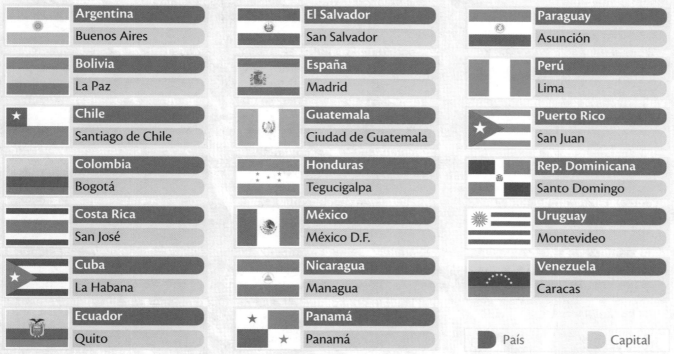

Argentina — Buenos Aires

Bolivia — La Paz

Chile — Santiago de Chile

Colombia — Bogotá

Costa Rica — San José

Cuba — La Habana

Ecuador — Quito

El Salvador — San Salvador

España — Madrid

Guatemala — Ciudad de Guatemala

Honduras — Tegucigalpa

México — México D.F.

Nicaragua — Managua

Panamá — Panamá

Paraguay — Asunción

Perú — Lima

Puerto Rico — San Juan

Rep. Dominicana — Santo Domingo

Uruguay — Montevideo

Venezuela — Caracas

País | Capital

EN SABOR HISPANO

CULTURE PHOTOS

Argentina *Glaciar Perito Moreno** (Perito Moreno Glacier). Located in the Glacier National Park in Patagonia, Argentina, it is a place of spectacular beauty and great glaciological and geomorphic interest.

Bolivia Salar de Uyuni. Situated in the southwest of Bolivia, it is the largest continuous salt flat in the world, covering an area of 10,582 km2 (4,085 square miles) and holds one of the biggest deposits of lithium in the world.

Chile Desierto de Atacama (Atacama Desert). Situated in the Norte Grande in Chile, it is the most arid desert on the planet and covers an area of approximately 105,000km2. It is considered to be one of the best places in the world for observing the skies and studying astronomy.

Colombia *Cartagena de Indias.** Located on the shores of the Caribbean Sea, the city was founded in 1533. It holds such historic sites as the San Felipe Castle, the Palace of the Inquisition, the Clock Tower, the city walls and the Colonial streets.

Costa Rica Río Celeste. Flowing through the Tenorio Volcano National Park, this river is famous for its sky blue color, an optical effect produced by the high concentration of aluminum silicates in its waters. According to a local legend, the river is this color because "when God finished painting the heavens, He washed his brushes in the waters of this river."

Cuba *La Habana** (Havana). Havana is the capital of the Republic of Cuba and its largest city, main port and cultural and economic center. Founded in 1519, the historic center is famed for its decadent beauty and atmosphere.

Ecuador *Islas Galápagos** (The Galapagos Islands). An archipelago in the Pacific Ocean, located 972 km off the coast of Ecuador. Apart from being a World Heritage Site, UNESCO declared the Galapagos Islands to be a Biosphere Reserve in 1985. The islands are the natural habitat of several species in danger of extinction, among them, the giant tortoises.

El Salvador El volcán Izalco (The Izalco Volcano). "Place in the dark sands" in the Nahuatl language, it is the youngest of the volcanoes in El Salvador and one of the youngest in the continent. The volcano erupted continuously for almost 200 years and the flames could be seen from the ocean – hence its nickname: *Lighthouse of the Pacific.*

España *La Alhambra** (The Alhambra). Situated in Granada, in the south of Spain, it is an elaborate complex of palaces and fortress where the sultans of the Moorish Kingdom of Granada lived during the XIIIth – XVth centuries. The interior decoration is striking, in andalusi style, and the palace stands in an incomparable natural setting.

Guatemala *Tikal.** Situated in the region of Petén, in what is today Guatemala, in the Tikal National Park, it is one of the largest archaeological sites and urban centers of the pre-Columbian Maya civilization.

Honduras *Ruinas de Copán** (Copán Ruins). An archaeological site located in the west of Honduras. It is famous for its magnificent Maya ruins, considered now to be the Paris of the Central American Maya world.

México *Pirámide de Kukulkán** (Kukulkán Pyramid). A pre-Hispanic building located in the Yucatan Peninsula, built in the XIIth century AD by the Mayas in the ancient city of Chichén Itzá. The Temple of Kukulkán shows the profound knowledge of mathematics, geometry, acoustics and astronomy of the Mayas.

Nicaragua Granada. Situated between Xalteva and Lake Nicaragua, it was founded in 1524 by the Spanish conquistador, Francisco Hernández de Córdoba. It is also known as *La Gran Sultana* because of its Andalusian Moorish appearance. The Colonial architecture of its historic center, as well as the surrounding natural setting, make it the main tourist destination in Nicaragua.

Panamá El canal de Panamá (The Panama Canal). It is an inter-oceanic channel between the Caribbean Sea and the Pacific Ocean, which cuts across the isthmus of Panama at its narrowest point. It opened in 1914 and had the effect of shortening maritime communications in distance and time between remote places of the world. The United States, China, Chile, Japan and South Korea are the five principal users of the canal.

Paraguay *Ruinas jesuíticas** (Jesuit Ruins). The Jesuit missions formed a group of thirty missionary settlements founded in the XVIIth century by the Company of Jesus among the Guaraní Indians, for the purpose of evangelizing them. These missions saved more than 100,000 Indians from slavery. At present all that is left are the imposing ruins of these villages, such as Jesús, Trinidad and Santa Rosa.

Perú *Machu Picchu.** A religious sanctuary and vacation residence of the Inca emperor Pachacútec, in the middle of the XVth century, it lies between the mountains of Machu Picchu and Huayna Picchu in the south of Peru. Machu Picchu is considered a masterpiece of both architecture and engineering. The site was recently declared one of the seven wonders of the modern-day world.

Puerto Rico *Castillo de San Felipe del Morro** (San Felipe del Morro Castle). A Spanish fortification built at the northern end of San Juan, Puerto Rico, in the XVIth century. Its purpose was to protect Puerto Rico and the Bay of San Juan from any invasion that might turn the fort into an enemy base from which to invade and attack other Spanish towns and ships.

República Dominicana Isla Saona (Saona Island). Situated in the south east of the Dominican Republic, it forms part of the Este National Park and is one of the largest of its islands. Its endless beaches of fine white sand are lined with coconut palms. Here, numerous species of birds and marine animals live. The island is protected officially and therefore there are no buildings on its shores.

Uruguay Punta del Este. It is a peninsular city situated on the southern end of Uruguay and one of the most important spa cities in Latin America. *Los Dedos, La Mano, Monumento al ahogado* or *Hombre emergiendo a la vida* are famous sculptures on the Brava Beach, which has become one of the best-known places in Uruguay.

Venezuela *Parque Nacional de Canaima** (Canaima National Park). Situated in the state of Bolívar, Venezuela, it stretches over 30,000 km2 as far as the border with Guyana and Brazil. Because of its size it is considered to be the sixth largest national park in the world. Almost 65% of the park is taken up with rock mesetas called *tepuyes*, a unique biological environment, of great interest to geologists. The steep cliffs and waterfalls are spectacular sights.

---

* All these places have been declared World Heritage Sites by UNESCO. **World Heritage Site** is the title granted by UNESCO (United Nations Educational, Scientific and Cultural Organization) to specific places on the planet (forests, mountains, lakes, caves, deserts, buildings, architectural complexes, cultural routes, cultural panoramas or cities) which have been proposed and confirmed for inclusion on this list. The aim of the program is to catalog, preserve and publicize places of exceptional cultural or natural interest for the common heritage of mankind.

UNESCO was founded on November 16, 1945, with the purpose of contributing to peace and safety in the world through education, science, culture and communications.

WHY STUDY SPANISH

WHY SPANISH?

Learning to communicate in Spanish can help you achieve a more vibrant and prosperous future, especially in today's globalizing world. As of 2014, **more than 450 million people speak Spanish** as a native language, making Spanish is the second most common native language in the world. According to a study by the Instituto Cervantes, **45 million people in the United States** speak Spanish as a first or second language. That's a Spanish-speaking community the size of the whole country of Spain!

Spanish is the most-spoken language in the Western Hemisphere, and the official language of the European Union, making it an important language for international business. By learning Spanish, you'll be joining 20 million other students worldwide who are learning to speak Spanish. You'll also be gaining a valuable professional skill on an increasingly bilingual continent. ¡Bienvenidos!

WHY COMMUNICATIVE EXPERIENTIAL LEARNING?

Mechanical learning doesn't work.

How did you learn to ride a bike? Did you sit in a chair while someone explained the fundamentals of bike riding to you, or did you go outside and give it a try yourself? Did you get better by memorizing a set of expert techniques, or did you suffer a few skinned knees until you improved?

If you're like most people, you learned by doing —and we don't think learning a language should be any different. When you learn out-of-context grammar and vocabulary skills, or complete exercises designed to perfect isolated language functions, it can be difficult to combine these skills when you want to express something new, or understand something that you've never heard before. Even more importantly, this kind of instruction can make us forget that Spanish is a living language that is spoken creatively and individually by people all over the world.

We need to feel, experience and reflect in order to learn.

When we learn by doing —by following our own initiative and self-direction— we associate the things we learn with specific feelings and experiences, which helps us comprehend and retain new language. Activities that connect with our emotions awaken our curiosity, and help us remember what we've learned years later.

Communicative Experiential Learning is self-directed, and constructed according to the unique styles and needs of each individual. Differences in learning style and speed are allowed for and embraced in the experiential classroom.

Learning is more rewarding as part of a community.

Communicative Experiential Learning also creates a supportive peer environment, in which learners are truly part of a classroom community. Learning by doing naturally encourages cooperative learning strategies, and rewards an open exchange of ideas and experiences.

Spanish is a vital, living language —which can be surprisingly easy to forget when you're conjugating endless strings of AR verbs! Communicative Experiential Learning reminds us that the purpose of language is to connect with ourselves and with our communities, both locally and globally.

MUNDO)real
MEDIA edition

Student Book

3

Cover Photograph:

Relieve azteca. *"América es un grandioso escenario donde se mezclan múltiples culturas y lenguas, muchas de ellas de considerable antigüedad, como la azteca, maya e inca. Estas grandes civilizaciones han constituido la base de una diversidad cultural americana de valor universal".* David Isa.

© Editorial Edinumen, 2016

Authors:
Eduardo Aparicio, Cecilia Bembibre, María Carmen Cabeza, Noemí Cámara, Francisca Fernández, Patricia Fontanals, Luisa Galán, Amelia Guerrero, Emilio José Marín, Celia Meana, Liliana Pereyra and Francisco Fidel Riva.
Coordination Team: David Isa, Celia Meana and Nazaret Puente.

ISBN - Student Book: 978-1-107-11022-9

Printed in the United States of America

Editorial Coordination:
Mar Menéndez

Cover Design:
Juanjo López

Design and Layout:
Juanjo López, Carlos Casado, Analia García,
Carlos Yllana and Lucila Bembibre

Illustrations:
Carlos Casado

Photos:
See page 270

Cambridge University Press
32 Avenue of the Americas
New York, NY 10013

Editorial Edinumen
José Celestino Mutis, 4. 28028 Madrid. España
Telephone: (34) 91 308 51 42
Fax: (34) 91 319 93 09
Email: edinumen@edinumen.es
www.edinumen.es

SCOPE AND SEQUENCE

 Pair icon: indicates that the activity is designed to be done by students working in pairs.

 Group icon: indicates that the activity is designed to be done by students working in small groups or as a whole class.

 xx **Audio icon:** indicates recorded material either as part of an activity or a reading text.

Language icon: provides additional language and grammar support in presentations and for activities.

Regional variation icon: provides examples of regional variations in the language.

 Recycling icon: provides a reminder of previously taught material that students will need to use in an activity.

ACKNOWLEDGMENTS

The authors and publisher would like to thank the following teachers for their insight and comments during the development of *Mundo Real Media Edition*. The experience and intuition of these educators was crucial in the development of this course.

Jeremy Aldrich - Harrisonburg City Public Schools (VA), **Susan Allen** - Eastern High School (NJ), **Marilu Alvarado** - Academia Margarita Muniz (MA), **Jose M. Aviña** - Sunset High School (TX), **Vicki S. Baggia** - Phillips Exeter Academy (NH), **David Barkley** - George C. Marshall High School (VA), **Vanda Baughman** - Cascade High School (OR), **Emily A. Berry** - Irvington Preparatory Academy (IN), **Candace Blatt** - Kokomo High School (IN), **Pilar Blazey** - Wilson High School (WA), **Patricia Boyarizo** - Ragsdale High School (NC), **Sonia Brandon** - Fork Union Military Academy (VA), **Ariel Bueno** - Lake Ridge High School (TX), **Maria L. Cabra** - Ronald W. Reagan / Doral Senior High School (FL), **Lilian M. Castillo de Hutchinson** - The Loomis Chaffee School (CT), **John S. Coco** - Cocalico School District (CO), **Pamela Conte** - Nordonia Hills City Schools (OH), **Rita Morales Cooley** - The Madeira School (VA), **Deb Dargay** - Bloomington Jefferson High School (MN), **Jesús López Díez** - Dana Hall School (MA), **Maria Elena Downes** - NYOS Charter School (NY), **Marsha Dragonetti** - Latin School of Chicago (IL), **Yvonne Easaw** - Richland School District Two (SC), **Cristina Escotto** - Fredericksburg Academy (VA), **Margaret K. Esten** - South Portland High School (OR), **Calvin Feehan** - Redwood High School (CA), **Scott L. Fisher** - McGavock High School (TN), **Mary Jo Flood** - Royal High School (CA), **Alejandra Fonseca** - Wyandanch Memorial High School (NY), **William Frank** - Pinkerton Academy (NH), **Coleen Garcia** - La Serna High School (CA), **Ramón García-Tamaran** - Bloomington High School South (IN), **Angela Giffin** - Stevens High School (SD), **Jeanne Gilbert** - The Hawbridge School (NC), **Robert Giosh** - The Latin School of Chicago (IL), **Xiomara Gonzalez** - Barbara Goleman Senior High School (FL), **Adriana Gonzalez-Novello** - Trinity School (NY), **Catherine A. Haney** - Loudoun County Public Schools (VA), **Ana Hermoso** - The Hotchkiss School (CT), **Wilson R. Hernández** - Hightstown High School (NJ), **Lesley Hinson** - Churchill High School (TX), **Efila Jzar-Simpson** - Ben Davis University High School (IN), **Anne Karakash, M.A.** - Franklin Academy (NC), **Nora L. Kinney** - Montini Catholic High School (IL), **Ivonete Kinson-Blackwelder** - North Pole High School (AK), **Heather Kissel** - TechBoston Academy (MA), **Dr. Jean Robert Lainé** - Putnam City Public Schools (OK), **William A. Leheny** - Garces Memorial High School (CA), **Jacqueline Liebold** - Groton Dunstable Regional High School (MA), **Patricio Lopez** - Harborfields High School (NY), **Adrianna Madril** - Martin Luther High School (CA), **Amanda Mancilla** - Union County Public Schools (NC), **Alice Nan Mannix** - Brown County High School (IN), **Nilma M. Martin Antonetti** - Richard Montgomery High School (MD), **Amanda Marvin** - The Barstow School (MO), **Rubenm Mascarenas** - Teacher Summit High School (TX), **Maritza Massopust** - Adelson Educational Campus (NV), **Justin Vanlee McClain** - Bishop McNamara High School (MD), **Marcelina McCool** - West Philadelphia High School (PA), **Darcie McGee** - Minnesota Online High School (MN), **Jennifer Mitchell** - The Hun School of Princeton (NJ), **Kathleen Monks** - Holley Central School (NY), **Yolanda Montague** - Stuarts Draft High School (VA), **Weston Moody** - Manhattan-Ogden School (NY), **Sydney Munson** - All Saints' Episcopal School (TX), **Sergio Navarro** - Redondo Union High School (CA), **Carmen Neale** - Watkinson School (CT), **Valerie Neri** - Park Center Senior High - International Baccalaureate World School (MN), **Andrew Noelle** - Central Magnet School (TN), **Marie G. Nuzzi** - Garden City High School (NY), **Santa Olmedo** - Foothill High School (CA), **Joseph A. Parodi** - Marianapolis Preparatory School (CT), **Olga A. Pietrantonio** - Blaine High School (WA), **Tim Pillsbury** - Trinity-Pawling School (NY), **Viviana Planine** - Newton South High School (MA), **Sofia Catalina Pollock** - John Champe High School (VA), **Andrew Poolman** - The Haverford School (PA), **Gregory Prais** - Detroit Catholic Central High School (MI), **Ashleigh Marsh Prendable** - Montgomery County Public Schools (MD), **Cecilia Remeta** - Palos Verdes High School (CA), **Mary Beth Ricci** - Olathe South High School (OK), **Gimara Richards, M.A.T.** - Stonewall Jackson High School (VA), **Myra M. Rios, M.A.** - Lower Merion High School (PA), **Alison Robinson** - Fort Worth Country Day School (TX), **Norman Sargen** - Agnes Irwin School (PA), **David M. Sawyer** - The Covenant School (VA), **Carl A. Seese** - Twin Lakes High School (IN), **Rosana Serna** - Seven Lakes High School (TX), **Bertha Sevilla** - Notre Dame Academy (CA), **Jonathan L. Sirois** - Tabor Academy (MA), **Ellen J. Spitalli** - Naperville Central High School (IL), **Maribel Squibb** - Sharyland High School (TX), **Tamara Tamez** - Nimitz High School (TX), **Yamila Tamny** - River Ridge High School (FL), **Susan Tawney** - Ragsdale High School (NC), **Candida Thompson** - Academy of Richmond County (GA), **Lisa Todd** - Colorado Academy (CO), **Delia Topping** - Central Magnet School (TN), **Yari Torres** - Douglass High School (TN), **Rachel Torrie** - Woodinville High School (WA), **Rosanna Tucci** - Miami Beach Senior High (FL), **Karen Twyford** - Highland High School (IL), **Maria Vazquez** - Mother Seton Regional High School (NJ), **Janice Ventresco** - Avon High School (OH), **Barbara A. Volkman** - Lanphier High School (IL), **Michelle Warner** - East Muskingum Schools (OH), **Rhonda L. Wells** - DeKalb County School District (GA), **Rand Wiseman** - Gig Harbor High School (WA).

ACTIVATING ELETECA

HOW TO ACCESS ELETECA

ELEteca is the Learning Management System that accompanies your *Mundo Real Media Edition* Student's Book. To learn more about ELEteca, please turn to page 17. To activate your ELEteca access code, follow the directions below.

1. Visit **cambridge.edinumen.es**. If you are a new user, click "Create User Account" on the right side of your screen.

2. Fill out the necessary information. Please use a valid e-mail address, as this will allow you to recover a lost or forgotten password.

3. Once you have created an account, scroll down and select the appropriate course (*Mundo Real Media Edition* Level 1, 2 or 3).

4. Enter your unique ELEteca access code. This code will either be printed on an access card accompanying your Student's Book, or you will receive it from your teacher.

5. Congratulations! You are now registered for ELEteca, and you can begin acccessing all of your online resources. To log in from any computer or tablet, simply visit **cambridge.edinumen.es** and enter your e-mail address and password.

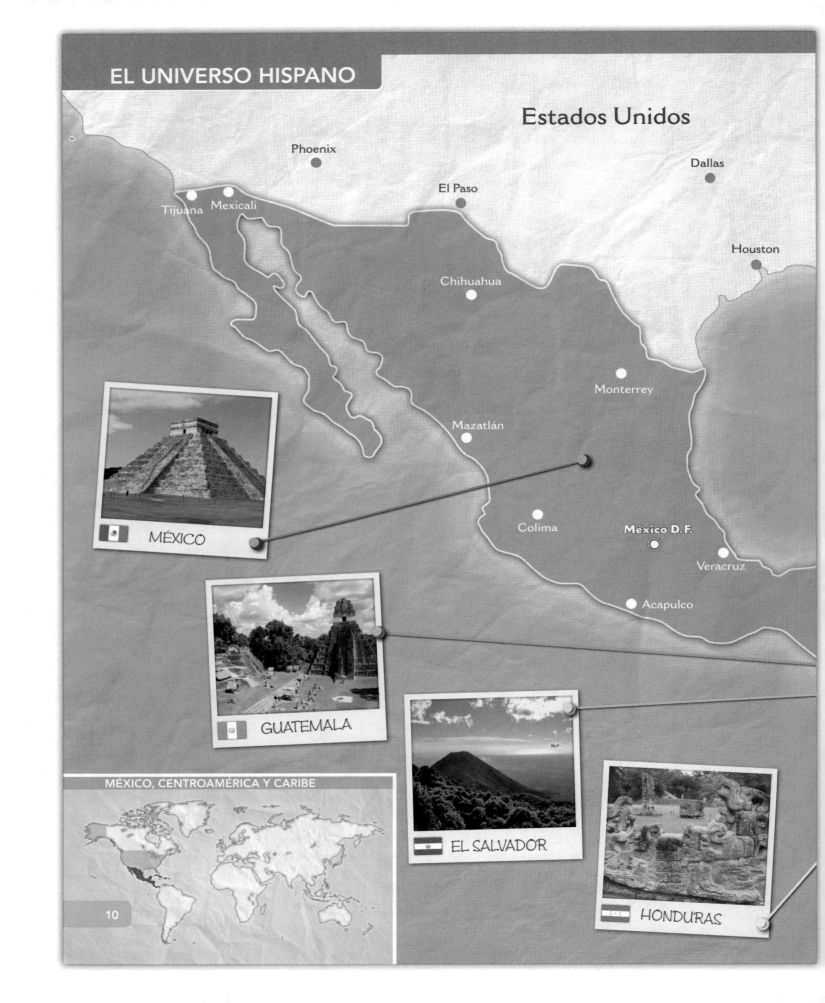

Estados Unidos

Phoenix

Dallas

El Paso

Tijuana Mexicali

Houston

Chihuahua

Monterrey

Mazatlán

MÉXICO

Colima

México D. F.

Veracruz

Acapulco

GUATEMALA

MÉXICO, CENTROAMÉRICA Y CARIBE

10

EL SALVADOR

HONDURAS

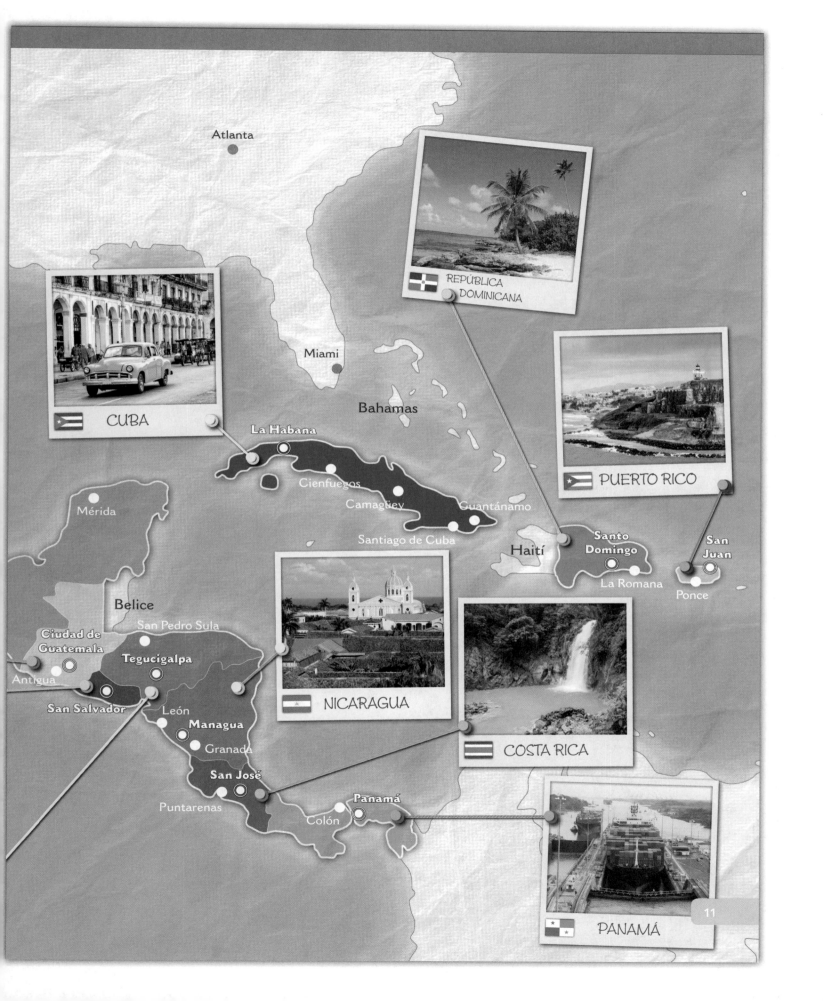

Atlanta

REPÚBLICA
DOMINICANA

CUBA

Miami

Bahamas

La Habana

Cienfuegos

Camagüey

Guantánamo

Santiago de Cuba

Haití

Santo
Domingo

La Romana

Ponce

San
Juan

PUERTO RICO

Mérida

Belice

San Pedro Sula

Ciudad de
Guatemala

Tegucigalpa

Antigua

San Salvador

León

Managua

Granada

San José

Puntarenas

NICARAGUA

COSTA RICA

Colón

Panamá

PANAMÁ

11

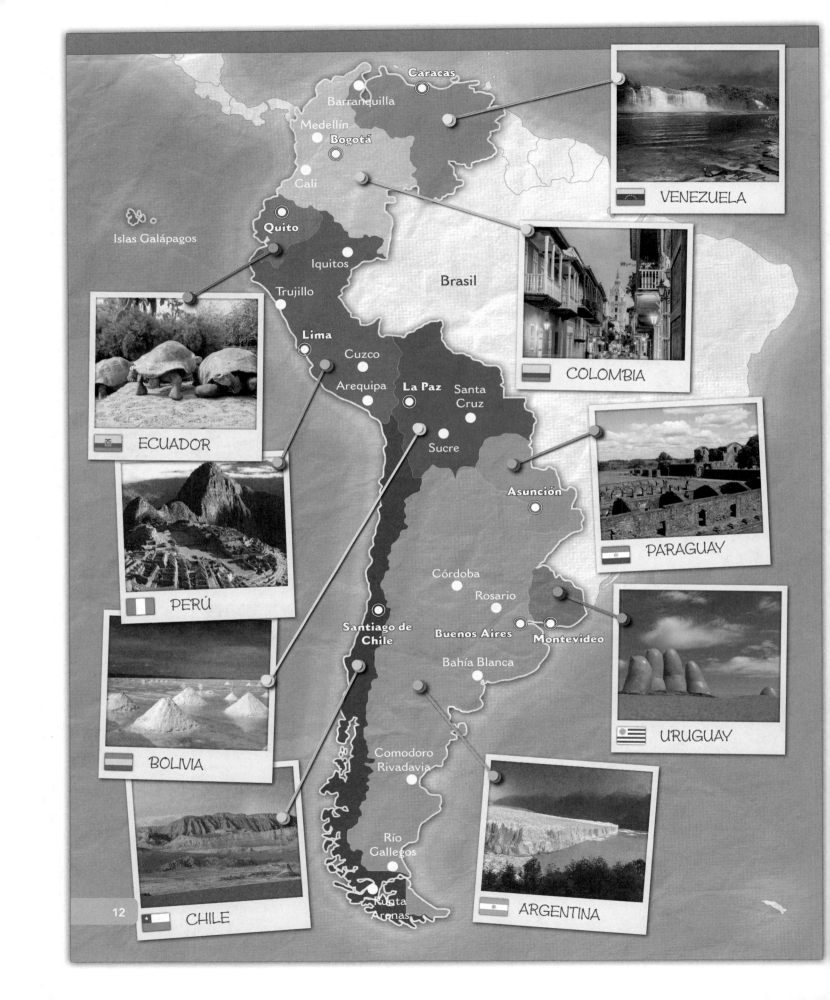

VENEZUELA

COLOMBIA

Caracas

Barranquilla

Medellín

Bogotá

Cali

Islas Galápagos

Quito

Iquitos

Brasil

Trujillo

ECUADOR

Lima

Cuzco

Arequipa

La Paz

Santa Cruz

PERÚ

Sucre

Asunción

PARAGUAY

Córdoba

Rosario

Santiago de Chile

Buenos Aires

Montevideo

BOLIVIA

Bahía Blanca

URUGUAY

Comodoro Rivadavia

Río Gallegos

Punta Arenas

CHILE

ARGENTINA

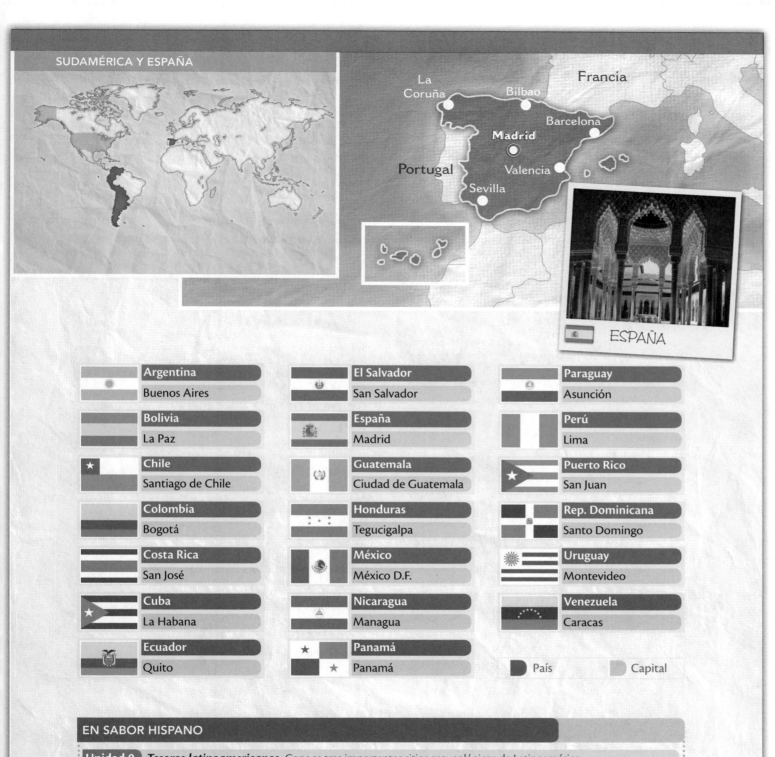

SUDAMÉRICA Y ESPAÑA

La Coruña
Bilbao
Francia
Barcelona
Madrid
Portugal
Valencia
Sevilla

ESPAÑA

Argentina
Buenos Aires

Bolivia
La Paz

Chile
Santiago de Chile

Colombia
Bogotá

Costa Rica
San José

Cuba
La Habana

Ecuador
Quito

El Salvador
San Salvador

España
Madrid

Guatemala
Ciudad de Guatemala

Honduras
Tegucigalpa

México
México D.F.

Nicaragua
Managua

Panamá
Panamá

Paraguay
Asunción

Perú
Lima

Puerto Rico
San Juan

Rep. Dominicana
Santo Domingo

Uruguay
Montevideo

Venezuela
Caracas

País   Capital

EN SABOR HISPANO

Argentina *Glaciar Perito Moreno (Perito Moreno Glacier). Located in the Glacier National Park in Patagonia, Argentina, it is a place of spectacular beauty and great glaciological and geomorphic interest.

Bolivia Salar de Uyuni. Situated in the southwest of Bolivia, it is the largest continuous salt flat in the world, covering an area of 10,582 km2 (4,085 square miles) and holds one of the biggest deposits of lithium in the world.

Chile Desierto de Atacama (Atacama Desert). Situated in the Norte Grande in Chile, it is the most arid desert on the planet and covers an area of approximately 105,000km2. It is considered to be one of the best places in the world for observing the skies and studying astronomy.

Colombia *Cartagena de Indias.** Located on the shores of the Caribbean Sea, the city was founded in 1533. It holds such historic sites as the San Felipe Castle, the Palace of the Inquisition, the Clock Tower, the city walls and the Colonial streets.

Costa Rica Río Celeste. Flowing through the Tenorio Volcano National Park, this river is famous for its sky blue color, an optical effect produced by the high concentration of aluminum silicates in its waters. According to a local legend, the river is this color because "when God finished painting the heavens, He washed his brushes in the waters of this river."

Cuba *La Habana** (Havana). Havana is the capital of the Republic of Cuba and its largest city, main port and cultural and economic center. Founded in 1519, the historic center is famed for its decadent beauty and atmosphere.

Ecuador *Islas Galápagos** (The Galapagos Islands). An archipelago in the Pacific Ocean, located 972 km off the coast of Ecuador. Apart from being a World Heritage Site, UNESCO declared the Galapagos Islands to be a Biosphere Reserve in 1985. The islands are the natural habitat of several species in danger of extinction, among them, the giant tortoises.

El Salvador El volcán Izalco (The Izalco Volcano). "Place in the dark sands" in the Nahuatl language, it is the youngest of the volcanoes in El Salvador and one of the youngest in the continent. The volcano erupted continuously for almost 200 years and the flames could be seen from the ocean – hence its nickname: *Lighthouse of the Pacific.*

España *La Alhambra** (The Alhambra). Situated in Granada, in the south of Spain, it is an elaborate complex of palaces and fortress where the sultans of the Moorish Kingdom of Granada lived during the XIIIth – XVth centuries. The interior decoration is striking, in andalusi style, and the palace stands in an incomparable natural setting.

Guatemala *Tikal.** Situated in the region of Petén, in what is today Guatemala, in the Tikal National Park, it is one of the largest archaeological sites and urban centers of the pre-Columbian Maya civilization.

Honduras *Ruinas de Copán** (Copán Ruins). An archaeological site located in the west of Honduras. It is famous for its magnificent Maya ruins, considered now to be the Paris of the Central American Maya world.

México *Pirámide de Kukulkán** (Kukulkán Pyramid). A pre-Hispanic building located in the Yucatan Peninsula, built in the XIIth century AD by the Mayas in the ancient city of Chichén Itzá. The Temple of Kukulkán shows the profound knowledge of mathematics, geometry, acoustics and astronomy of the Mayas.

Nicaragua Granada. Situated between Xalteva and Lake Nicaragua, it was founded in 1524 by the Spanish conquistador, Francisco Hernández de Córdoba. It is also known as *La Gran Sultana* because of its Andalusian Moorish appearance. The Colonial architecture of its historic center, as well as the surrounding natural setting, make it the main tourist destination in Nicaragua.

Panamá El canal de Panamá (The Panama Canal). It is an inter-oceanic channel between the Caribbean Sea and the Pacific Ocean, which cuts across the isthmus of Panama at its narrowest point. It opened in 1914 and had the effect of shortening maritime communications in distance and time between remote places of the world. The United States, China, Chile, Japan and South Korea are the five principal users of the canal.

Paraguay *Ruinas jesuíticas** (Jesuit Ruins). The Jesuit missions formed a group of thirty missionary settlements founded in the XVIIth century by the Company of Jesus among the Guaraní Indians, for the purpose of evangelizing them. These missions saved more than 100,000 Indians from slavery. At present all that is left are the imposing ruins of these villages, such as Jesús, Trinidad and Santa Rosa.

Perú *Machu Picchu.** A religious sanctuary and vacation residence of the Inca emperor Pachacútec, in the middle of the XVth century, it lies between the mountains of Machu Picchu and Huayna Picchu in the south of Peru. Machu Picchu is considered a masterpiece of both architecture and engineering. The site was recently declared one of the seven wonders of the modern-day world.

Puerto Rico *Castillo de San Felipe del Morro** (San Felipe del Morro Castle). A Spanish fortification built at the northern end of San Juan, Puerto Rico, in the XVIth century. Its purpose was to protect Puerto Rico and the Bay of San Juan from any invasion that might turn the fort into an enemy base from which to invade and attack other Spanish towns and ships.

República Dominicana Isla Salona (Saona Island). Situated in the south east of the Dominican Republic, it forms part of the Este National Park and is one of the largest of its islands. Its endless beaches of fine white sand are lined with coconut palms. Here, numerous species of birds and marine animals live. The island is protected officially and therefore there are no buildings on its shores.

Uruguay Punta del Este. It is a peninsular city situated on the southern end of Uruguay and one of the most important spa cities in Latin America. *Los Dedos, La Mano, Monumento al ahogado* or *Hombre emergiendo a la vida* are famous sculptures on the Brava Beach, which has become one of the best-known places in Uruguay.

Venezuela *Parque Nacional de Canaima** (Canaima National Park). Situated in the state of Bolívar, Venezuela, it stretches over 30,000 km2 as far as the border with Guyana and Brazil. Because of its size it is considered to be the sixth largest national park in the world. Almost 65% of the park is taken up with rock mesetas called *tepuyes*, a unique biological environment, of great interest to geologists. The steep cliffs and waterfalls are spectacular sights.

---

* All these places have been declared World Heritage Sites by UNESCO. **World Heritage Site** is the title granted by UNESCO (United Nations Educational, Scientific and Cultural Organization) to specific places on the planet (forests, mountains, lakes, caves, deserts, buildings, architectural complexes, cultural routes, cultural panoramas or cities) which have been proposed and confirmed for inclusion on this list. The aim of the program is to catalog, preserve and publicize places of exceptional cultural or natural interest for the common heritage of mankind.

UNESCO was founded on November 16, 1945, with the purpose of contributing to peace and safety in the world through education, science, culture and communications.

WHY STUDY SPANISH

WHY SPANISH?

Learning to communicate in Spanish can help you achieve a more vibrant and prosperous future, especially in today's globalizing world. As of 2014, **more than 450 million people speak Spanish** as a native language, making Spanish is the second most common native language in the world. And according to a study by the Instituto Cervantes, **45 million people in the United States** speak Spanish as a first or second language. That's a Spanish-speaking community the size of the whole country of Spain!

Spanish is the most-spoken language in the Western Hemisphere, and the official language of the European Union, making it an important language for international business. By learning Spanish, you'll be joining 20 million other students worldwide who are learning to speak Spanish. You'll also be gaining a valuable professional skill on an increasingly bilingual continent. ¡Bienvenidos!

WHY COMMUNICATIVE EXPERIENTIAL LEARNING?

Mechanical learning doesn't work.

How did you learn to ride a bike? Did you sit in a chair while someone explained the fundamentals of bike riding to you, or did you go outside and give it a try yourself? Did you get better by memorizing a set of expert techniques, or did you suffer a few skinned knees until you improved?

If you're like most people, you learned by doing —and we don't think learning a language should be any different. When you learn out-of-context grammar and vocabulary skills, or complete exercises designed to perfect isolated language functions, it can be difficult to combine these skills when you want to express something new, or understand something that you've never heard before. Even more importantly, this kind of instruction can make us forget that Spanish is a living language that is spoken creatively and individually by people all over the world.

We need to feel, experience and reflect in order to learn.

When we learn by doing —by following our own initiative and self-direction— we associate the things we learn with specific feelings and experiences, which helps us comprehend and retain new language. Activities that connect with our emotions awaken our curiosity, and help us remember what we've learned years later.

Communicative Experiential Learning is self-directed, and constructed according to the unique styles and needs of each individual. Differences in learning style and speed are allowed for and embraced in the experiential classroom.

Learning is more rewarding as part of a community.

Communicative Experiential Learning also creates a supportive peer environment, in which learners are truly part of a classroom community. Learning by doing naturally encourages cooperative learning strategies, and rewards an open exchange of ideas and experiences.

Spanish is a vital, living language —which can be surprisingly easy to forget when you're conjugating endless strings of AR verbs! Communicative Experiential Learning reminds us that the purpose of language is to connect with ourselves and with our communities, both locally and globally.

STUDENT RESOURCES

STUDENT'S BOOK

Mundo Real Media Edition uses lively and compelling content, images, and video to teach real-world language. The student book's experiential format encourages the development of strong communicative skills, which will increase your comfort level in real-world settings.

EBOOK

Mundo Real Media Edition eBooks are fully interactive and fully integrated with the Learning Management System ELEteca. Integrated audio and a seamless connection to online video content, as well as online and offline modes for Mac, PC, iOS, and Android, make using your eBook simple.

ONLINE WORBOOK

The *Mundo Real Media Edition* online workbook features a wide variety of activity types and exercises, and includes mbedded video, a video note-taking feature, and speech recognition technology.

CUADERNO PARA HISPANOHABLANTES

The *Mundo Real Media Edition* Cuaderno para hispanohablantes is written exclusively for native speakers who have grown up speaking conversational Spanish, and includes sophisticated activities and lessons that expand on the Student's Book.

ELETECA

Mundo Real Media Edition features a wealth of digital resources designed to supplement and enhance the Student's Book. All are available in the rich, interactive world of *Mundo Real Media Edition* ELEteca—in one place, with one password.

Interactive Activities

Audio and Video

• **¡Acción!** Narrative video that complements the student book.

• **Voces Latinas** Cultural clips to introduce the Spanish-speaking world.

• **Grammar Tutorials** Short grammar presentations to reinforce tricky skills.

• **Casa del Español** Street interviews that model authentic language.

Gamification

"La Pasantía," a game that allows you to engage with the Spanish language in a fun context, as you compete to win a spot on the staff of a Spanish newspaper.

Online Workbook and eBook Integration

The *Mundo Real Media Edition* Online Workbook and eBook are accessible through ELEteca, so you can access all of your digital resources in one place, using one password.

OBJECTIVES FOR UNIT OPENER

- Introduce unit theme: **Volvemos a vernos**, about activities in the past and vacation time
- Introduce culture for the unit: Learn about vacation time in Hispanic countries

STANDARDS

- 1.1 Interpersonal communication
- 1.2 Understand the language
- 2.1 Practices and perspectives

INSTRUCTIONAL STRATEGIES

- Introduce unit theme and objectives and explain to students that this unit is a review of vocabulary and grammatical functions from previous levels.
- Talk about the photo and have students state who these people are, where they are, what they are doing, how they feel, etc.
- Have the students discuss the questions and call on several students to respond. Help students recall verb forms and expressions from **Mundo real**, Levels 1 & 2 by modeling answers as necessary.
- Use the photographs to review vocabulary: **¿Dónde vas de vacaciones? ¿Con quién vas? ¿Cuál es tu lugar favorito? ¿Por qué? ¿Cuándo fue la última vez que fuiste? ¿Qué tiempo hizo? ¿Qué actividades hiciste?**
- Ask related questions: **¿Qué te gusta hacer cuando vas a la playa / a la montaña / al extranjero? ¿Por qué? ¿Cuál es tu actividad favorita? ¿Por qué?**
- Help students formulate their ideas using: **A mí me gusta hacer surf... porque me encanta el mar y el buen tiempo, no hay clases y me divierto mucho**, etc.

ANSWERS

Answers will vary. Possible answers are:
- Hola, ¿qué tal te fue?
- ¿Dónde fuiste de vacaciones? ¿Qué hiciste? ¿Cuánto tiempo estuviste? ¿Con quién fuiste? ¿Te gustó?, etc.
- Answers will vary.

ADVANCED LEARNERS

After answering the questions on the page, put students into pairs to write a dialogue between two friends who are seeing each other again after some time away. Then have students perform a role play with their dialogues in front of the class.

HERITAGE LANGUAGE LEARNERS

Discuss greetings between people in Hispanic culture. What traditions do they know about or follow? Do people hug, kiss (on one cheek or two), shake hands, etc.? Are the greetings the same or different between family members and friends? Are the greetings different if the people haven't seen each other for a longer period of time? Encourage them to compare and contrast these greetings customs with those in another culture.

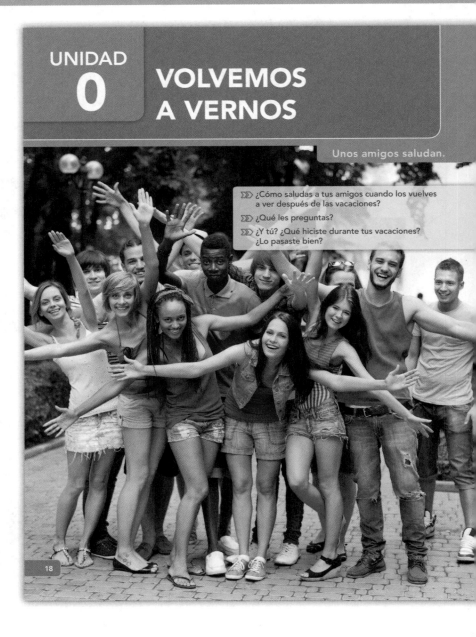

UNIDAD 0

VOLVEMOS A VERNOS

Unos amigos saludan.

>> ¿Cómo saludas a tus amigos cuando los vuelves a ver después de las vacaciones?

>> ¿Qué les preguntas?

>> ¿Y tú? ¿Qué hiciste durante tus vacaciones? ¿Lo pasaste bien?

18

ADDITIONAL UNIT RESOURCES

Extension Activities (EA) (Photocopiable)	Interactive Whiteboard Lessons (IWB)	Audio
EA: 0.1	IWB: 0.1, 0.2	🎧 1 to 3

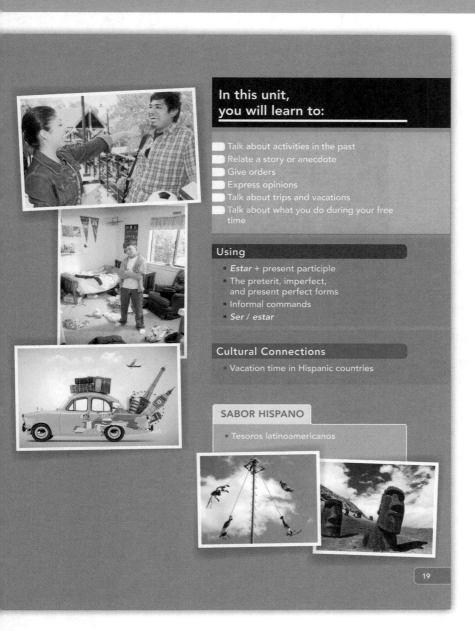

In this unit, you will learn to:

- ☐ Talk about activities in the past
- ☐ Relate a story or anecdote
- ☐ Give orders
- ☐ Express opinions
- ☐ Talk about trips and vacations
- ☐ Talk about what you do during your free time

Using

- *Estar* + present participle
- The preterit, imperfect, and present perfect forms
- Informal commands
- *Ser / estar*

Cultural Connections

- Vacation time in Hispanic countries

SABOR HISPANO

- Tesoros latinoamericanos

19

Learning Outcomes

- Talk about activities in the past
- Relate a story or anecdote
- Give orders
- Express opinions
- Talk about trips and vacations
- Talk about what you do during your free time

Instructional Strategies

- Explain to students that the purpose of this unit is to help them determine what they already know, and also help them focus on what they personally need to improve upon. Review the learning outcomes with students and then change them to questions. For example: *Are you able to talk about activities in the past?* and so on.
- Have students look at the images on this page and try to relate them to the objectives listed. Ask questions using the grammatical structures listed as prompts. Ask: *¿Cómo están los muchachos? ¿Por qué? ¿Qué tiene la muchacha en la mano? ¿Y el muchacho? ¿Por qué? ¿Qué crees que va a hacer? ¿Qué quieres decirle al muchacho de la segunda imagen? Describe su habitación. ¿Qué no ha hecho últimamente? ¿Por qué crees que no lo ha hecho? ¿Estaba de mal humor? ¿Tenía mucha tarea?* and so on.
- Invite students to read the topic for **Sabor hispano** and preview that section in the unit. Ask questions such as: *¿Cuáles son algunos tesoros de tu país? ¿Dónde están? ¿A cuántos has ido? ¿Cuál te gustó más?*

> **Note** Common Core State Standards (CCSS)
> The four strands of the *Common Core State Standards for English Language Arts (ELA) and Literacy in History/Social Studies, Science, and Technical Subjects* (Reading, Writing, Speaking and Listening, and Language) are represented in the National Standards for Learning Languages by the Communication standards: Interpersonal, Interpretive, and Presentational. The three modes of communication align with the goals in Reading, Writing, Speaking, and Listening by emphasizing the purpose behind the communication.

Slower-paced Learners

During the question-answer period in which you explore the images and unit topics, consider writing some of the students' responses and key words on the board to help students follow along. Alternatively, you may want to invite students to the board to write their responses and read them aloud to the class. This will slow down the pace of the back-and-forth and give others a chance to follow along more closely.

THREE MODES OF COMMUNICATION: UNIT 0			
	INTERPERSONAL	**INTERPRETIVE**	**PRESENTATIONAL**
Las vacaciones	3, 4, 7	1, 2, 5, 6, 7, 8, 9, 10, 11	
Recuerdos de la escuela	8	1, 2, 3, 4, 5, 6, 7	1, 4, 7, 9
Un poco más		1, 2, 3, 4, 5, 6	
Cultura		Sabor hispano	

LAS VACACIONES

Objectives for Las vacaciones

- Review vocabulary related to travel and free-time activities
- Review grammatical structures: Present progressive tense; preterit, and present perfect
- Talk about past vacations and what you did

Core Resources

- Audio Program: Track 1
- Interactive Whiteboard Lessons: IWB 0.1, 0.2

Standards

1.1 Engage in conversation
1.2 Understand the language
1.3 Present information
4.2 Compare cultures

Instructional Strategies

- Explain to students that **Unidad 0** is a brief review of vocabulary and grammatical structures. Content is grouped thematically by sections. The purpose is to guide students to begin at a similar point while providing practice before new material is presented. Remind students that none of the material should be new to them.

Activity 1

- Ask students to look at the image and ask: **¿Dónde están los muchachos que aparecen en la imagen? ¿Qué relación hay entre ellos? ¿De qué están hablando?**
- Have students write then say the sentences for each one.
- Tell students to expand upon the information and create a short conversation between Carlos and Lucía. Call on student volunteers to present their conversation for the class.

🎧 1 Activity 2

- Play the audio and have students listen to the conversation between Carlos and Lucía and fill in the missing words.
- Play the audio a second time and have students check their answers.

Answers

Activity 1

Carlos: Fui a Colorado y estuve haciendo senderismo.
Lucía: Fui a las playas de California y estuve haciendo surf.

Activity 2

a. ¡No me digas!; **b.** bastante bien; **c.** montón; **d.** Cuéntame; **e.** de miedo;
f. cansadísimo; **g.** peligrosa; **h.** No vuelvo a ir; **i.** ¡Vaya, hombre!; **j.** nada.

Slower-paced Learners

After listening to the conversation in Activity 2, have students take turns reading the different parts aloud with a partner for additional oral practice. Encourage them to help each other clarify meaning if there are any parts of the conversation that they haven't understood.

Advanced Learners

Challenge students to complete the conversation in Activity 2 before listening to it. Play the audio for them to check their answers.

LAS VACACIONES

1 Carlos y Lucía se reencuentran en la escuela después de sus vacaciones. ¿Qué ha hecho cada uno? Ordena las palabras para crear frases.

Carlos
estuve o haciendo o a o Fui o y o Colorado o senderismo

Lucía
surf o playas o haciendo o Fui o y o California o las o estuve o a o de

Carlos: Fui ....

Lucía: Fui ....

2 🎧 1 Completa la conversación entre Carlos y Lucía con las siguientes expresiones coloquiales. Después, escucha y comprueba.

> bastante bien o cansadísimo o cuéntame o de miedo o montón o nada
> no me digas o peligrosa o vaya, hombre o no vuelvo a ir

Carlos: ¡Hola, Lucía! ¿Qué tal tus vacaciones?
Lucía: ¡Genial! Estuve en las playas de California haciendo surf.
Carlos: ¡(a) ....! ¿Surf? No sabía que practicabas surf.
Lucía: Sí, estuvo (b) .... Las playas son fantásticas y lo mejor es que conocí a un (c) .... de gente joven de muchos países.
Carlos: ¡Qué suerte!
Lucía: ¿Y tú? (d) .... Fuiste a Colorado, ¿no? ¿Qué tal te fue?
Carlos: Bueno, ¡lo pasé (e) ....! Pero terminé (f) ....
Ya sabes que fui con Luis y Javier y no descansamos nada. Hacer senderismo con ellos fue una experiencia un poco (g) .... Incluso, nos perdimos una noche.
(h) .... con ellos.
Lucía: ¡(i) ....!, ¡qué aventura!
Carlos: Sí, creo que las próximas vacaciones las voy a pasar en las playas de California sin hacer (j) ....

20

3 ¿Cuál es la mejor forma de pasar las vacaciones? Lee los siguientes comentarios y elige la respuesta que mejor expresa tu opinión sobre cada uno. Después, comparte tus opiniones con tu compañero/a. ¿Están de acuerdo?

a. Ir a un hotel es mejor que ir de camping.
b. Pasar las vacaciones en la playa es la mejor manera de descansar.
c. Viajar en avión es la forma más fácil de viajar.
d. Visitar una ciudad y descubrir una cultura nueva es lo mejor de las vacaciones.
e. La montaña es mejor que la playa.
f. Los campamentos de verano son aburridos.

- A mí me parece que sí.
- A mí me parece que no.
- Yo creo que sí.
- Yo pienso que no.
- No sé qué decir.
- ¡Yo qué sé!
- No te puedo decir.

4 Y tú, ¿adónde fuiste de vacaciones? ¿Qué hiciste? ¿Dónde te alojaste? Habla con tu compañero/a.

5 Estas personas están disfrutando de sus vacaciones. Completa las frases como en el ejemplo y relaciónalas con su imagen correspondiente.

a. (leer) Está leyendo un libro.
b. (dormir) .... la siesta.
c. (entrar) .... a los servicios.
d. (vestirse) ....
e. (construir) .... un castillo.
f. (bañarse) ....
g. (comer) .... un helado.
h. (tomar) .... una foto.
i. (tomar) .... el sol.
j. (salir) .... del agua.

21

Instructional Strategies
Activity 3
- Have students first read through the sentences and ask questions about vocabulary. Then review the recycling box to practice expressions. Have students repeat after you. Use gestures and appropriate emphasis to help students access meaning. For example, shrug your shoulders as you review the last three expressions to indicate that you don't feel strongly either way.
- Put students in pairs so they can practice orally, taking turns reading the statements and reacting.
- Have students build conversations by giving a reason or explanation for their opinions. Encourage students to use appropriate intonation in their responses.

Activity 4
- Review typical vacation activities such as **bañarse, descansar, divertirse, hacer surf / senderismo, pasear, tomar el sol, ir en avión, alojarse en un hotel, hacer la maleta, llevar el pasaporte**, etc.
- Remind them how to talk about the past and review some of the most common verbs (**fui, estuve**, etc.).
- Ask students to share their experiences and offer details.
- Go around the class and help students to clarify questions they might have.
- Ask students to write about their vacations and collect them so you can assess their writing skills as well.

Activity 5
- Before doing the activity, call a student to the front of the room and ask him/her to mime something: reading a book, writing on the board, eating a banana, drinking a cup of coffee, etc.
- Ask the class what the student is doing. When they guess the sentence, write it on the board and remind them about the structure (**estar** + present participle) and its use: for actions that are happening at the moment.
- Have students complete the sentences with the progressive form and them match the sentences with the people in the picture.
- Project IWB 0.1, **En la playa** to review the answers. Encourage students to include additional comments about the scene.

Answers
Activity 5
a. 10, Está leyendo; **b.** 4, Está durmiendo; **c.** 9, Está entrando; **d.** 8, Está vistiéndose; **e.** 7, Está construyendo; **f.** 2, Está bañándose; **g.** 5, Está comiendo; **h.** 6, Está tomando; **i.** 1, Está tomando; **j.** 3, Está saliendo.

Heritage Language Learners
For students who have returned or traveled to a Hispanic country, encourage them to talk about those experiences in Activity 4, even if they were not their last vacations. Tell them to make comparisons with their experiences there and in the United States. Consider having students talk about these trips in front of the class instead of just in pairs.

INSTRUCTIONAL STRATEGIES

Activity 6

- Ask students to do this activity individually first.
- Working in pairs, students compare their answers.
- Call on students to share their answers and explain in Spanish what each of the boldface words mean. Get students started by providing cues such as: *lo/la usas para..., es una persona que..., es lo que haces...*
- Ask students to be creative and write two more sentences related to the topic.
- With another pair, students ask for the correct answers to the sentences they have created.

Activity 7

- Project IWB 0.2, **Actividades de tiempo libre** and review the situations with students with books closed. Brainstorm vocabulary students need to talk about these topics. Use the printed questions as a guide to prompt students, but without reading them aloud. Write the words and expressions in the spaces next to each situation.

- In pairs, ask students to choose one of the pastimes and talk about it with their partners. Each student should choose a different topic.
- As a follow-up, have students practice either the same topic or a new one with a different partner. In this round, students are encouraged to build a conversation by asking as many questions as possible of each other and giving as many details as possible.
- Have students volunteer to present to the class. Allow students to choose their topic to present, but ensure that all are represented. You may have student pairs compete to see which one conducted the most exchanges. You and the rest of the students can ask questions as well.

Alternative Activity

- After practicing with their partner, allow students to ask you questions on a topic, again to see how many exchanges they can conduct.
- Another option is to call on a student and ask him/her to respond to your questions.
- All or any variety of these options promote student oral interaction and encourage students to participate.

ANSWERS

Activity 6

a. pasaporte; **b.** los boletos; **c.** te alojas, reservación; **d.** propina; **e.** El guía del hotel; **f.** tarjeta de crédito.

SLOWER-PACED LEARNERS

Before they speak in Activity 7, give students time to write out two or three additional questions related to their chosen topic. Remind them to listen carefully to their partners' responses before asking follow-up questions. They may need to adjust their questions based on what their partners say. Encourage them to take notes on their partners' responses to focus their listening so they can report back to the class later.

LAS VACACIONES

6 Pedro va a hacer un viaje y sus padres le dan consejos. Escoge la palabra correcta en cada frase.

- **a.** Si vas a un país extranjero, necesitas tu **pasaporte** / **cuaderno**.
- **b.** No te olvides de **los boletos** / **las maletas** de avión.
- **c.** Si **entras** / **te alojas** en un hotel, necesitas hacer una **maleta** / **reservación**.
- **d.** Si tomas un taxi, no te olvides de darle una **propina** / **llave** al conductor.
- **e.** **El recepcionista** / **El guía del hotel** te puede dar información útil.
- **f.** Puedes pagar el hotel con **tarjeta de crédito** / **llave**.

7 Elige una de las actividades del cuadro y coméntala con tu compañero/a. Usa las preguntas como guía.

• Ir al cine	¿Qué tipo de películas te gusta ver? Comedias, dramas, horror, suspenso, documentales…
• Pasar tiempo con la familia	¿Qué te gusta hacer con tu familia? ¿Ir de vacaciones con ellos? ¿Por qué?
• Trabajar como voluntario	¿Dónde haces de voluntario?
• Jugar a los videojuegos	¿Cuál es tu videojuego favorito? ¿Con quién te gusta jugar? ¿Cuánto rato pasas jugando a los videojuegos?
• Tocar un instrumento	¿Tocas algún instrumento? ¿Solo o en grupo?
• Escuchar música e ir a conciertos	¿Qué tipo de música te gusta escuchar? ¿Por qué vas a conciertos?
• Leer	¿Qué te gusta leer? Novelas, noticias, poesía, revistas…
• Ir de compras	¿Dónde te gusta ir de compras? ¿Prefieres ir solo o acompañado?

HERITAGE LANGUAGE LEARNERS

Working in groups of three, have students convert the sentences in Activity 6 into a dialogue between Pedro and his parents before he takes a trip. Encourage students to make the conversation natural and add more specific information about Pedro's travel plans or aspirations. Have the groups perform their conversations in front of class.

8 Completa el crucigrama con el pretérito para descubrir la palabra secreta.

1. venir (yo)
2. traer (ustedes)
3. hacer (yo)
4. traducir (ella)
5. conducir (tú)
6. decir (tú)
7. dormir (él)
8. andar (nosotros)
9. leer (ellos)
10. ir (nosotros)

9 Completa las frases con el verbo en el pretérito perfecto.

a. Este verano (hacer, nosotros) .... muchas excursiones al campo.
b. Hace un rato (ver, yo) .... a Luis en la cafetería.
c. ¿(Estar, tú) .... alguna vez en México?
d. Este fin de semana (ponerse, yo) .... morena porque (ir, yo) .... a la playa.
e. Siempre (querer, ellos) .... viajar en barco pero nunca lo (hacer) ....
f. El viento (abrir) .... la ventana y (romperse) .... el cristal.
g. Este año (volver, ustedes) .... de vacaciones antes que el año pasado.

23

Instructional Strategies

Activity 8
- Ask students to do this activity individually first.
- Working in pairs, students compare their answers. Ask students to identify the secret word (**vacaciones**).
- In pairs, ask students to classify the verbs into regular and irregular. They should recognize all as being irregular. Then ask students to explain how they are irregular. For example: −**ir** stem-changing verbs (**dormir**), **i** ➡ **y** stem-changing verbs (**leer**), verbs with new stems (**venir**, **traer**, **hacer**, **traducir**, **decir**, **conducir**, **andar**), and completely irregular verbs (**ir**).
- Ask students to be creative and write a sentence with each of the verbs.
- Ask a couple of students to read two or three sentences they have created.

Activity 9
- Ask for volunteers to provide examples of the present perfect form in Spanish and write them on the board, making corrections as needed. Review the parts of the present perfect (**haber** + past participle).
- Ask if there are any irregulars and have students identify which verbs in the activity are irregular (**hacer**, **ver**, **ponerse**, **abrir**, **romperse**, **volver**).
- Give students five minutes to do the activity individually and then correct with the entire class.
- With a partner, ask students to discuss what they have done **este verano**, **hace un rato**, **alguna vez**, etc.

Answers

Activity 8
1. VINE; **2.** TRAJERON; **3.** HICE; **4.** TRADUJO; **5.** CONDUJISTE; **6.** DIJISTE; **7.** DURMIÓ; **8.** ANDUVIMOS; **9.** LEYERON; **10.** FUIMOS.
Palabra secreta: vacaciones.

Activity 9
a. hemos hecho; **b.** he visto; **c.** Has estado; **d.** me he puesto, he ido; **e.** han querido, han hecho; **f.** ha abierto, se ha roto; **g.** han vuelto.

Advanced Learners

As an extension to Activity 8, have students create their own crossword puzzles with preterit verbs (regular or irregular) and a secret word. They can make a smaller version with just five or six words. Then have them switch crossword puzzles with a partner, complete them, and correct each other's answers.

LAS VACACIONES

Activity 10

- Read the text with students and address any questions about vocabulary.
- Ask students if they remember the names of the two tenses highlighted in the reading: present perfect and preterit.
- Call on volunteers to explain their use.

Extension

Tell students to write back to Elena as if they were Sara and tell her what they have done during their vacation. Students should also include questions for Elena to demonstrate interest in her vacation.

Cultural Note

Las ferias son fiestas que tienen lugar en ciudades y pueblos de toda Hispanoamérica. Pueden ser un mercado que se celebra ciertos días del año para la venta de determinados productos, o también pueden ser las instalaciones recreativas que ponen para celebrar fiestas (circos, puestos de ventas, atracciones, lugares con música…).

Activity 11

- Have students read the text again carefully to themselves.
- Give students some minutes to do the activity individually and then correct with the entire class.
- Without looking at the book, challenge students to retell Elena's story using the verbs from their lists and in third person. Have them recreate as much as they can remember.
- In pairs, ask students to compare their texts to see who had the most details and correct information.

ANSWERS

Activity 10

The preterit is used to talk about actions that were completed at a fixed point in the past and have no relation with the present. The present perfect is used to say what a person has done.

Activity 11

Present perfect: lo he pasado (pasar); ha dicho (decir); he estado (estar); he vuelto (volver); he escrito (escribir); he hecho (hacer).

Preterit: decidieron (decidir); llegué (llegar); me gustó (gustar); me aburrí (aburrir); tuve (tener); conocí (conocer); nos hicimos (hacer); fuimos (ir); nos encontramos (encontrar); estuvimos (estar); nos divertimos (divertirse); pidió (pedir).

a. preterit; **b.** present perfect.

ADVANCED LEARNERS

Ask a couple of follow-up comprehension questions about the content of the postcard in Activity 10. Then ask students to write one or two comprehension questions of their own. Put students into small groups to ask and answer their questions about the postcard. Alternatively, collect the questions, and play a game as a class. Divide the class into two teams. One person from each team goes to the board at a time. Read the question and give them a limited amount of time to respond. Award points for correct answers. Challenge students but do not allow them to refer back to the postcard, responding only from memory.

LAS VACACIONES

10 Lee la postal que Elena escribió a su amiga Sara el último día de sus vacaciones. Fíjate en los verbos marcados. ¿Recuerdas lo que expresan y cuándo se usan?

¡Hola, Sara!

¿Qué tal tus vacaciones? ¡Este verano me lo he pasado genial!

Ya sabes que mis padres decidieron ir a visitar a mis abuelos en Montana.

El viaje en auto fue muy largo y aburrido, pero cuando llegué, me gustó mucho el sitio. Los primeros días me aburrí un poco y, además, tuve que ir con mis padres a visitar a toda la familia. Por suerte, hace dos semanas conocí a Fani, la nieta de los vecinos de mis abuelos, y desde ese día nos hicimos muy amigas. El viernes pasado fuimos a la feria del pueblo y nos encontramos a sus primos, estuvimos todo el rato con ellos y nos divertimos mucho. El mayor, Jorge, ¡es guapísimo! Creo que me gusta. Esta mañana Fani me ha dicho que yo también le gusto y que ayer le pidió mi correo electrónico. Hoy es mi último día aquí, así que he estado toda la mañana en la piscina con Fani y después he vuelto a casa y les he escrito a todos. Ahora te dejo porque quiero despedirme de todo el mundo y ¡todavía no he hecho la maleta! Me da lástima irme, pero también tengo ganas de empezar el curso para verles de nuevo a todos. ¡¡Muchos besos!!

¡Hasta pronto! _Elena_

SARA MARTÍNEZ
3333 Rock Avenue
Albuquerque,
New Mexico 33333

11 Escribe los verbos de la postal de Elena en su cuadro correspondiente según el tiempo del pasado y escribe su infinitivo al lado. Después, completa los espacios para describir el uso de cada tiempo.

PRESENT PERFECT	PRETERIT
lo he pasado ➡ pasar(lo)	decidieron ➡ decidir

a. Usamos el .... para hablar de acciones pasadas en un **tiempo terminado.**
b. Usamos el .... para hablar de acciones pasadas en un **tiempo no terminado o en relación con el presente.**

RECUERDOS DE LA ESCUELA

UNIDAD **0**

1 El abuelo de Elena, Gregorio Fernández, está recordando diferentes momentos de su vida. ¿En qué crees que está pensando? Observa la imagen y completa las frases con tu compañero/a.

- Cuando era niño ....
- A los 18 años ....
- Cuando cumplí los 30 ....
- Hoy ....

2 Escucha a Gregorio hablando de su vida y escribe los números de las frases en su lugar correspondiente.

a. Cuando era niño ....   **c.** Cuando cumplí los 30 ....
b. A los 18 años ....   **d.** Hoy ....

3 Escucha de nuevo y escribe los siguientes verbos en el tiempo en el que aparecen.

a. empezar ....   **d.** estar ....   **g.** aprender ....
b. jugar ....   **e.** tener ....   **h.** ir ....
c. casarme ....   **f.** trabajar .... **i.** afeitarse ....

25

OBJECTIVES FOR RECUERDOS DE LA ESCUELA

- Talk about activities in the past
- Relate a story or anecdote
- Describe physical characteristics and personality traits in the past

CORE RESOURCES

- Audio Program: Track 2
- Extension Activities: EA 0.1

STANDARDS

1.1   Engage in conversation
1.2   Understand the language
1.3   Present information
4.1   Compare cultures

INSTRUCTIONAL STRATEGIES

Activity 1

- Review the vocabulary and grammatical structures corresponding to activities in the past using the images as a guide. Ask students to look at the thought bubbles and brainstorm related words and expressions. For example, *ser estudiante*, *ir a la universidad*, *casarse*, *tener un hijo*, *jubilarse*, etc.
- Then tell students to work with a partner to complete the sentences about Gregorio's life. Remind them to think about what past tenses they should use with each.

2 Activity 2

- Play the audio and tell students to write the number of the statement that corresponds to when the action takes place. Point out that there will be more than one sentence per timeframe.
- Play the audio again and ask students to check their answers.
- Ask students to compare what they wrote in Activity 1 with what they heard in the audio. Did they use the correct tenses?

See audioscript on page APP3

2 Activity 3

- Play the audio one more time so students write the forms of each verb.
- Write all the forms on the board for students to check their answers.

Extension

Play the audio again and have students write the sentences they hear as a dictation. Pause the audio after each statement and remind students to use the verbs already listed on the board as a reference. This will help students review the use of the different tenses in context.

ANSWERS

Activity 2

a. 2, 7; **b.** 1, 5, 9; **c.** 3, 6; **d.** 4, 8.

Activity 3

a. empecé; **b.** jugaba; **c.** me casé; **d.** estoy; **e.** tenía; **f.** trabajaba; **g.** aprendí; **h.** he ido; **i.** me afeité.

SLOWER-PACED LEARNERS

If necessary, pause the audio after the key words or sentences to cue students and give them additional time to write the answers.

HERITAGE LANGUAGE LEARNERS

Using the phrases from Activity 1, but in the third person, have students write about an older family member of theirs. Encourage them to add more information, perhaps an additional sentence, about each time period. Then put students in pairs or small groups to share what they've written.

RECUERDOS DE LA ESCUELA

INSTRUCTIONAL STRATEGIES

Activity 4

- To introduce the activity, write the following sentence on the board: **Cuando pienso en mi infancia me vienen a la memoria muy buenos recuerdos**. Ask students: **¿Recuerdan algún momento especial de su infancia que quieran compartir con el resto de la clase?**
- With books closed, distribute copies of EA 0.1, **Mi primer día de la escuela** to student pairs. Tell students to put the images in order to recreate Gregorio's first day at school and to practice retelling what happened.
- Ask students to present their stories in class. You may also have students tape the images to the board as they present their version to the class. Ask the class if they agree with the order presented: **¿Están de acuerdo?**
- Correct vocabulary and grammar and review tenses if necessary.
- Have students open their books to confirm the correct order.

Activity 5

- Ask students to do the activity individually and correct with the entire class.
- Take opportunities to review tenses.

Extension

- For additional oral practice, string together the retelling of the story by having each student add the next line. Start with: **Cuando el señor Gregorio piensa en su época de estudiante le vienen a la memoria muy buenos recuerdos, bueno, menos el primer día de la escuela, porque...** To ensure that all students have a chance to participate, encourage them to go beyond the events presented in the images and provide additional details.
- Another option is to have students write out the story, this time describing the opposite experience. In this case, tell students to use the opposite meaning of the adjectives in the original story and verbs to turn the story around. Have students begin the story as follows: **Cuando pienso en mi época de estudiante vienen a mi memoria muy malos (en vez de buenos) recuerdos...**

ANSWERS

Activity 5

1. fue; **2.** han pasado; **3.** sentí; **4.** despertó; **5.** me levanté; **6.** me vestí; **7.** desayuné; **8.** decía; **9.** ayudó; **10.** agarré; **11.** salí; **12.** estaba; **13.** era; **14.** era; **15.** he sido; **16.** sentía; **17.** era; **18.** Fui; **19.** dejó; **20.** me puse; **21.** empecé; **22.** lloraban; **23.** vino; **24.** intentó; **25.** estuve; **26.** llamó; **27.** vino; **28.** me acostumbré; **29.** encantaba; **30.** fue; **31.** he tenido.

RECUERDOS DE LA ESCUELA

4 Gregorio tiene tan buena memoria que incluso se acuerda de su primer día de escuela. Mira los dibujos e intenta imaginar cómo fue ese día. Habla con tu compañero/a.

5 Comprueba tus hipótesis. Completa el texto con los verbos del pasado.

Cuando pienso en mi época de estudiante siempre vienen a mi memoria muy buenos recuerdos, bueno, menos el de mi primer día de escuela... Se puede decir que para mí (1) .... (ser) toda una experiencia y, aunque ya (2) .... (pasar) muchos años desde entonces, me acuerdo perfectamente de lo que (3) .... (sentir).

Recuerdo que ese día mi mamá me (4) .... (despertar) muy temprano. (5) .... (Levantarse), (6) .... (vestirse) yo solo y (7) .... (desayunar) muy bien, porque mi mamá siempre (8) .... (decir) que "antes de estudiar, tu barriga debes llenar". Después mi mamá me (9) .... (ayudar) a peinarme, yo (10) .... (agarrar) mi mochila nueva y (11) .... (salir) hacia la escuela. Yo (12) .... (estar) muy emocionado porque (13) .... (ser) mi primer día de escuela y ya (14) .... (ser) un niño mayor. Además, como toda mi vida (15) .... (ser) una persona muy curiosa e inquieta, (16) .... (sentir) mucha curiosidad por saber qué (17) .... (ser) eso de la escuela. (18) .... (Ir) todo el camino contento, iba a conocer la escuela, a mis compañeros, a mi maestra... Sin embargo, cuando mi mamá me (19) .... (dejar) en la puerta de la escuela junto a los demás niños, (20) .... (ponerse) tan nervioso que (21) .... (empezar) a llorar y, para mi desconsuelo, ¡los demás niños también (22) .... (llorar)!

Enseguida (23) .... (venir) mi maestra e (24) .... (intentar) consolarme, pero (25) .... (estar) todo el día triste y de mal humor, tanto, que al final la maestra (26) .... (llamar) a mi mamá por teléfono y ella (27) .... (venir) a buscarme a la escuela. Cuando (28) .... (acostumbrarse), la escuela me (29) .... (encantar) y la maestra Margarita (30) .... (ser) la mejor maestra que (31) .... (tener) nunca.

HERITAGE LANGUAGE LEARNERS

Give students a chance to be the "experts" on the different past tenses. Put them into small groups and assign each group one of the tenses from Activity 5. Tell them to plan how they would teach the tense to new learners of Spanish. Remind them to include information on both the form and the use of the tense. Encourage them to add a quick activity to check that students have understood. Tell them that each person in the group must speak during the presentation. Allow time for them to give their presentations in class.

6 Lee las siguientes frases sacadas del texto. Escribe la letra de cada una en el cuadro correspondiente según el uso del pasado.

a. Se puede decir que para mí fue toda una experiencia.
b. Ya han pasado muchos años desde entonces.
c. Recuerdo que ese día mi mamá me despertó muy temprano.
d. Mi mamá siempre decía que "antes de estudiar, tu barriga debes llenar".
e. Yo estaba muy emocionado porque era mi primer día de escuela y ya era un niño mayor.
f. Toda mi vida he sido una persona muy curiosa e inquieta.
g. Sentía mucha curiosidad por saber qué era eso de la escuela.
h. Enseguida vino mi maestra e intentó consolarme, pero estuve todo el día triste y de mal humor.
i. Margarita fue la mejor maestra que he tenido nunca.

Acción sin relación con el presente	Descripción de una situación	Acción en un pasado reciente o en relación con el presente	Acción habitual	Valoración
				a

7 Imagina cómo fue el primer día de escuela de uno de tus compañeros/as y escribe cuatro frases.

a. ....
b. ....
c. ....
d. ....

8 👥 ¿Recuerdas tu primer día de escuela? Intercambia experiencias con tu compañero/a. ¿Has acertado en alguna de las frases que escribiste sobre tu compañero/a en la actividad anterior?

Modelo: Yo tenía 6 años cuando empecé la escuela.

9 Ahora, escribe cómo fue el primer día de escuela de tu compañero/a.

Activity 7

- Give the students a few minutes to think about what their partner's first day of school was like. Tell students to write four sentences about their classmate's experience. Encourage them to be creative yet realistic in their descriptions.
- Explain to students that they will have an opportunity to share their version in the next activity.

Activity 8

- In pairs, ask students to retell their first day of school to their partner. Circulate around the room to check that students are on task and actively participating. Note down any errors to correct later as a class.
- Then have students share with their partners the sentences they prepared in Activity 7. How close were they?

Activity 9

- For this activity, students are asked to recall their partner's story and write about it.
- Collect all the texts and correct them to check vocabulary and grammar of this unit. You can also have students exchange papers with their partner for peer correction.

ANSWERS

Activity 6

Acción sin relación con el presente: c, h.
Descripción de una situación: e, g.
Acción en un pasado reciente o en relación con el presente: b.
Acción habitual: d, f.
Valoración: a, i.

SLOWER-PACED LEARNERS

Instead of focusing on their partners' experiences in Activity 7, give students time to think about and prepare to discuss their own first day of school. Encourage them to take notes about what they remember from that day and then organize the notes chronologically on a timeline. You may want to model this on the board for them. In Activity 8, students can refer to their timelines when speaking with their partners. Tell them to listen and take notes on their partners' first day of school. In Activity 9, they write a summary of what they heard from their partners. They can swap timelines to help each other with the writing task.

ADVANCED LEARNERS

As an extension to the lesson, have students talk to each other about their best, worst, or most memorable day at school. Before they speak, give them time to collect their thoughts. While they're speaking, encourage them to ask and answer questions with each other to make it more of a conversation. Finally, for homework, have students write out a short description of this experience more formally and post it on a class discussion forum. Tell students to read and post a response to one other classmate's story as well (someone who wasn't their partner in class).

INSTRUCTIONAL STRATEGIES

Activity 6

- Introduce the activity by asking students how many past tenses they know in Spanish (preterit, present perfect, imperfect). Call on volunteers to explain what they remember about the uses of these forms.
- Have students do this activity individually first.
- Ask them to compare their answers with a partner.
- Correct the activity with the entire class.
- While correcting, take the opportunity to review all the past tenses.

UN POCO MÁS

- Review verbs **ser** / **estar**
- Review informal commands

Standards

1.2 Understand the language

1.4 Present information

Instructional Strategies

Activity 1

- Ask students to describe the images to provide context for the activity.
- Then have students work individually and match the statements with the images.
- After you review answers, ask students what these expressions all have in common (they are giving instructions, advice, orders, and permission to do something).
- Ask students to tell you who they think is making the statements to the people in the images.

Activity 2

- Ask students to classify the commands according to their use.
- In pairs, have students compare their answers.

Activity 3

- Practice first with commands by telling students to do the following: **Carla, cierra el libro**; **Albert, sal a la pizarra**; **Emma, dame tu libro**. Call on volunteers to explain the formation of **tú** commands (**tú** form, drop the **s**). Ask others what happens to the pronoun (it's attached to the end of the command).
- Have students complete this activity individually and time it to see who finishes first.
- After completing the activity, ask a student to come to the front of the class and act out what his/her classmates tell him/her to do. Remind the student to do the action only if the command was properly stated.

Extension

Have students write two linked commands on a piece of paper (it must be possible to do them in the classroom). For example: **Quítate un zapato y métetelo en tu mochila**. Then divide the class into small groups and distribute commands. The first student reads the instructions, carries out the action, and the rest of the group writes what he/she did. The group who performs all the actions first and gets the forms correct is the winner.

Answers

Activity 1

1. e; **2.** a; **3.** d; **4.** c; **5.** b.

Activity 2

Dar órdenes: e; **Dar permiso:** b; **Invitar:** d; **Dar consejos:** c; **Dar instrucciones:** a.

Activity 3

a. Sal a la pizarra; **b.** Abre la ventana; **c.** Recoge el libro; **d.** Siéntate bien; **e.** Cierra la puerta; **f.** Quítate la gorra.

UN POCO MÁS

1 Relaciona las siguientes frases con la imagen correspondiente.

1. ☐ ¡Ordena tu cuarto!
2. ☐ Respire, por favor.
3. ☐ Coman ensalada.
4. ☐ Haz tu tarea.
5. ☐ Entra.

2 Clasifica las órdenes de la actividad anterior según su uso.

Dar órdenes	Dar permiso	Invitar	Dar consejos	Dar instrucciones

3 Observa las imágenes. Imagina que tú eres el profesor de estos alumnos. Dile a cada uno la orden correspondiente usando los siguientes verbos en imperativo.

- cerrar   • abrir   • salir   • recoger   • quitarse   • sentarse

a. Sal al pizarrón
b. _____
c. _____
d. _____
e. _____
f. _____

28

Advanced Learners

Have students add one or two more commands under each category in Activity 2.

Heritage Language Learners

As an extension to Activity 1, put students into small groups to search Spanish language print resources or later units in this book for other images. Have them write commands related to the images and then share them with the class.

4 Completa las frases con la forma correcta de *ser* o *estar*. Después, relaciona cada frase con su uso.

1. Mariela .... argentina.
2. La isla de Pascua ....parte de Chile.
3. Lola .... una muchacha muy antipática.
4. Roberto .... un muchacho muy guapo.
5. Pedro .... informático.
6. La puerta .... de cristal.
7. Carlos .... el primo de Lucía.
8. .... las diez de la mañana.
9. Laura .... enferma.

a. Decir el material de una cosa.
b. Describir características físicas.
c. Decir la nacionalidad.
d. Describir situaciones temporales.
e. Describir personalidad o rasgos de carácter.
f. Decir la hora.
g. Decir la profesión.
h. Identificar a personas.
i. Expresar localización.

5 Elige el verbo apropiado según el contexto.

a. Lima **es / está** la capital de Perú.
b. El avión **es / está** más rápido que el tren.
c. **Soy / Estoy** muy contento porque este año voy a ir de vacaciones a la playa.
d. En esta época del año siempre **es / está** nublado.
e. ¿**Eres / Estás** cansado?
f. Mi hermano **es / está** más alto que yo.
g. Los libros **son / están** encima de la mesa.

6 Completa las frases con *ser* o *estar* y un adjetivo apropiado de la lista.

> aburrido/a o abierto/a o listo/a o malo/a o rico/os

a. Pedro .... un muchacho muy ...., por eso habla con todo el mundo.
b. Hoy yo .... en casa, sin saber qué hacer, y he decidido preparar un pastel, por cierto, ... muy ....
c. Hoy, cuando he llegado a casa, he visto que la puerta ....
d. Ayer Laura no fue a clase porque ...., tenía un poco de fiebre y dolor de cabeza.
e. Los vecinos de mi padre ...., tienen mucho dinero, pero tienen un hijo que .... muy ...., y es que no se puede tener todo en esta vida.
f. ¡Muchachos! ¡A comer! La comida ....
g. Esta película .... muy ...., mejor la quitamos y hacemos otra cosa.
h. .... un muchacho muy ...., siempre tiene muy buenas notas en la escuela.

INSTRUCTIONAL STRATEGIES

Activity 4

- With books closed, read aloud the uses of **ser** and **estar** from the activity. Tell students to show one finger for **ser** and two fingers for **estar**. Explain that they should hold their hands in front of their chests to keep their answers private. In this way, the teacher can see individual responses to better assess how much students recall. You can correct answers now or after students complete the activity.
- Then have students work individually and match the sentences with the uses of verbs **ser** and **estar**.
- Ask students to compare their answers with another partner.

Activity 5

- Ask students to choose the appropriate verbs and add two more sentences.
- Have students compare their answers in pairs.

Activity 6

- Review the use of adjectives with **ser** and **estar**. Ask students to recall which adjectives change in meaning when used with both **ser** and **estar**. Use the adjectives in the word bank to prompt students.
- Have students complete this activity individually paying attention to the context.
- Project activity and review the answers together as a class. Be sure students used the correct forms of the adjectives to show agreement.

ANSWERS

Activity 4

1. es, c; **2.** está, i; **3.** es, e; **4.** es, b; **5.** es, g; **6.** es, a; **7.** es, h; **8.** Son, f; **9.** está, d.

Activity 5

a. es; **b.** es; **c.** Estoy; **d.** está; **e.** Estás; **f.** es; **g.** están.

Activity 6

a. es, abierto; **b.** estoy, aburrido; está, rico; **c.** estaba, abierta; **d.** estaba, mala; **e.** son, ricos; es, malo; **f.** está, lista; **g.** es, mala; **h.** Es, listo.

SLOWER-PACED LEARNERS

Consider allowing students to do Activity 6 with a partner so they can determine the correct options together.

OBJECTIVES FOR SABOR HISPANO

- Learn about Hispanic treasures
- Compare similarities

CORE RESOURCES

- Audio Program: Track 3

STANDARDS

2.1	Practices and perspectives
2.2	Products and perspectives
3.2	Acquire information
5.2	Using language for personal enjoyment and enrichment

INSTRUCTIONAL STRATEGIES

- Introduce the topic by asking what the students know about Hispanic treasures.
- Put students in pairs to discuss the questions in the **Antes de leer** box.
- Monitor their conversations and assist as needed.
- Call on volunteers to report back on their discussions.
- Focus students' attention on the images and their captions. Ask what they see, where the images are from, why they are famous. Tell students to talk about the images and elicit what they already know and can share.
- Before playing the audio, tell students to listen for the question posed at the beginning of the audio and be prepared to answer it. Either have students close their books while they listen or follow along with the text in the book.
- Elicit responses to the target question. For more detail, ask: **¿Qué tipo de lugares van a presentar?**
- To help build vocabulary, have students locate and underline any words from the glossary on the next page in the text. Then have them make and share new sentences with the words. You may choose to have them work individually or in pairs.

ADVANCED LEARNERS

Have students find an image of Teotihuacán or an artifact from the site that is on display at the National Anthropology Museum in Mexico City. Tell them to write a description of the image or artifact. They should do some additional research and provide background information about it in their paragraphs as well. Have students present their images and information to the class.

SABOR HISPANO

TESOROS

Turistas visitan una pirámide en Teotihuacán, México.

LATINOAMERICANOS

Antes de leer

¿Qué aspectos te atraen de los lugares que visitas o que quieres visitar? (la historia, las actividades, las compras, etc.).

¿Qué sabes de las culturas prehispánicas en México?

3 ¿Buscas hacer un viaje diferente? Te invitamos a conocer tres de los sitios más interesantes de Latinoamérica por su originalidad, historia y toque de misterio.

«Es como estar en la cima° del mundo. Es increíble. ¡Pero lleva zapatos cómodos!», dice Devyn, un turista de Nueva York, después de su visita al sitio arqueológico de Teotihuacán en México. Es un sitio donde los aztecas construyeron una gran ciudad entre los siglos II y VII. Armando, un visitante° de California, dice: «Era el lugar número uno que quería visitar en México. Recomiendo llegar bien

temprano y subir a la Pirámide del Sol y a la Pirámide de la Luna para tener un panorama completo», sugiere en el sitio de viajes Tripadvisor.

Hoy, Teotihuacán es el segundo sitio arqueológico con más visitas del mundo. Más de dos millones y medio de turistas llegan para admirar las pirámides, los templos y las avenidas.

También pueden ver la recreación de un antiguo ritual azteca, la Danza de los Voladores. Consiste en cinco personas (los voladores) que, a gran altura, hacen impresionantes acrobacias. Originalmente, se trataba de una ceremonia asociada a las cosechas° y a la fertilidad.

La Danza de los Voladores en Teotihuacán

Las líneas de Nazca

Estas líneas son dibujos en el suelo* hechos por la civilización prehispánica nazca. Se conservaron muy bien porque están en una zona donde casi nunca llueve. No se sabe exactamente cuál es la función de las líneas, aunque hay varias teorías. Este es un resumen numérico del lugar:

Están a **200** millas de Lima, capital de Perú.

Son Patrimonio de la Humanidad desde **1994**.

Hay cerca de **800** dibujos de animales y humanos.

Las líneas tienen **30** cm de profundidad*.

Se investigaron por primera vez en **1932**.

Rapa Nui

Rapa Nui, o Isla de Pascua, es parte del territorio de Chile en el Pacífico Sur. El atractivo turístico de la isla son las esculturas gigantes con forma de cabezas, creadas entre los siglos XII y XVII. No se conoce con certeza* por qué se construyeron.

① En la isla hay más de 800 estatuas. Se llaman **«moái»**.

② Las esculturas tienen entre **3,5** y **12** metros de alto.

③ Están **talladas*** en piedra de un volcán extinguido.

④ Se cree que representan a los **antepasados***.

⑤ Hoy viven en la isla **5.000** personas.

Los moáis de la isla de Pascua

¿COMPRENDISTE?

Decide si las siguientes frases son verdaderas (V) o falsas (F).

① Teotihuacán es el sitio arqueológico más visitado del mundo.   V ◯ F ◯

② Los turistas recomiendan ir a primera hora.   V ◯ F ◯

③ Los moáis están hechos de piedra volcánica.   V ◯ F ◯

④ La función de los moáis fue descubierta en 1932.   V ◯ F ◯

⑤ Las líneas de Nazca tienen poca profundidad.   V ◯ F ◯

Un colibrí* dibujado en Nazca, Perú

AHORA TÚ

¿Qué opinas? Contesta las siguientes preguntas y comenta tus ideas con otros/as compañeros/as.

① ¿Cuál fue el viaje más interesante que hiciste? ¿Por qué?

② ¿Qué consejo le puedes dar a alguien que quiere hacer ese mismo viaje?

③ ¿Cuál de estos tres sitios recomiendas a alguien interesado en la escultura? ¿Por qué?

④ ¿Cuál de estos tres sitios es ideal para alguien que quiere hacer ejercicio? ¿Por qué?

⑤ ¿Cuál de estos tres sitios te gustaría visitar a ti? ¿Por qué?

Glosario:

el antepasado – ancestor	**la profundidad** – depth
la certeza – certainty	**el suelo** – ground
la cima – top	**tallado/a** – carved
el colibrí – hummingbird	**el visitante** – visitor
la cosecha – harvest	

Fuentes: *El Cronista*, Tripadvisor, INAH.

31

OBJECTIVES FOR EN RESUMEN: VOCABULARIO

- Review unit vocabulary and expressions
- Practice communicative skills

STANDARDS

1.2 Understand the language

1.3 Present information

4.1 Evaluate similarities and differences in language

INSTRUCTIONAL STRATEGIES

- Encourage students to use index cards used as flashcards with the Spanish term on one side and the English term on the other, or a picture or drawing.
- Students work in pairs or groups, using vocabulary flashcards as they would the cards of a board game to help each other practice unit vocabulary.
- Encourage students to write labels or captions for the photos on this page. Remind them to use the vocabulary and expressions they have learned in this unit.
- For additional oral practice, put students into pairs. Tell them to take turns using the words in **Verbos** to make sentences. For example, Student A says, ***Me aburro con las películas largas***. Student B says, ***Después de un año en España, mi hermana se acostumbró al horario de las comidas***, and so on. When they get to the end of the list, have them go down the list again, this time with Student B beginning with ***aburrirse***. Then have students switch partners and do the same for the remaining two categories: ***Los viajes y las vacaciones*** and ***Ocio y tiempo libre***.

EN RESUMEN: Vocabulario

Verbos

aburrirse *to be bored*
acostumbrarse *to get used to*
agarrar *to take*
bañarse *to swim*
conocer *to know*
construir *to build*

decidir *to decide*
desayunar *to have breakfast*
descansar *to rest*
descubrir *to discover*
despertarse *to wake up*
divertirse *to have fun*
dormir *to sleep*
encontrar *to find*
entrar *to come in*
hacer senderismo *to hike*

hacer surf *to surf*
intentar *to try*
leer *to read*
levantarse *to get up*
ordenar *to clean up*
pasear *to walk*
pedir *to ask for*
relajarse *to relax*

respirar *to breathe*
sentir *to feel*
tener *to have*
tomar el sol *to sunbathe*
vestirse *to get dressed*
volver *to go back*

Los viajes y las vacaciones

el aeropuerto *airport*
el avión *plane*

el boleto / billete *ticket*

el campamento de verano *summer camp*

el extranjero *foreigner*
el hotel *hotel*
la llave *key*
la maleta *suitcase*

la montaña *mountain*
el paisaje *landscape*

el pasaporte *passport*
la propina *tip*
la tarjeta de crédito *credit card*

Ocio y tiempo libre

escuchar música *to listen to music*

hacer deporte *to do sports*
ir a museos o a eventos culturales *to go to museums or cultural events*

ir al cine *to go to the movies*
ir de compras *to go shopping*

jugar a los videojuegos *to play videogames*
leer *to read*
pasar tiempo con la familia *to spend time with family*
salir con amigos *to go out with friends*

tocar un instrumento *to play an instrument*

trabajar como voluntario *to work as a volunteer*
ver la televisión *to watch TV*

EN RESUMEN: Gramática

PRESENT PROGRESSIVE TENSE

(See page 21)

■ Use **estar** + present participle to express an action in progress or the continuity of an action.

Esta semana ***estoy estudiando*** *mucho.*
This week, I'm studying a lot.

Ahora mismo ***estoy comiendo****, te llamo luego.*
Right now I'm eating, I will call you later.

■ The present participle in Spanish is formed by removing the **–ar** ending and replacing it with **–ando** or by removing the **–er** or **–ir** ending and replacing it with **–iendo**.

PRESENT PARTICIPLE		
traba**jar** = traba**jando**	*to work*	*= working*
co**rrer** = co**rriendo**	*to run*	*= running*
escri**bir** = escri**biendo**	*to write*	*= writing*

USING THE PRETERIT, IMPERFECT AND PRESENT PERFECT

(See page 23)

Preterit	Imperfect	Present Perfect
■ The preterit tense is used to talk about actions that were **completed** at a fixed point in the past and have **no relation** with the **present**. · *Ayer* ***fui*** *en bici a clase.* · *El año pasado* ***fui*** *de vacaciones a Ecuador.*	■ Use the imperfect to describe **ongoing** or **habitual actions** in the past. · *Aquel día* ***llovía*** *mucho.* · *Antes yo siempre* ***iba*** *a Florida de vacaciones.*	■ We use the present perfect to say what a person **has done**. You generally use it in the same way you use its English equivalent. · *Ya* ***he hablado*** *con mi profesor de Matemáticas.* · *Luis y Rob* ***han comido*** *aquí.*

INFORMAL COMMANDS

(See page 28)

■ Use an imperative **tú** command when you want to order or tell someone to do something. Also it can be used to give advice or suggestions.

■ The affirmative **tú** commands are formed the same way as the present-tense forms that you use for **usted**, **él**, *or* **ella**.

Infinitive	Tú ➡ drop s	Affirmative *tú* commands
hablar	habla	*Habla más lentamente.* Speak more slowly.
comer	come	*Come la cena.* Eat dinner.
escribir	escribe	*Escribe la carta.* Write the letter.

The following verbs have irregular **tú** commands in the affirmative:

Infinitive	oír	tener	venir	salir	ser	poner	hacer	decir	ir
Imperative	oye	ten	ven	sal	sé	pon	haz	di	ve

33

OBJECTIVES FOR EN RESUMEN: GRAMÁTICA

• Review unit grammar
• Practice communication skills

STANDARDS

1.2 Understand the language
1.3 Present information

INSTRUCTIONAL STRATEGIES

• Model how to review grammar.
• Have the students review the Learning Outcomes in the unit opener to assess whether they feel they have mastered the main ideas and skills.
• Ask them if they can remember additional examples for each grammar topic.
• Model how to find and go back to the appropriate page in the unit to review any grammar topic they may need help with.
• Invite students to review the grammar activities they completed in this unit.
• Ask them what grammar activities they found easy and which they found challenging. Encourage them to rework any activities they found particularly challenging.
• To practice the present progressive tense as a class, play a game of charades. Ask for volunteers to come to the front of the room. Give them a verb or phrase to act out, such as ***jugar al tenis, comer pizza, hacer senderismo, hacer la maleta***, etc. Students have to guess or describe what he or she is doing using the present progressive tense.
• Put students into pair or small groups. Give each pair or group a few verbs, or allow them to choose verbs from the vocabulary list on page 32. Tell them to write three sentences for each verb, one for each of the past tenses: preterit, imperfect, and present perfect. Remind them to think about how the context of the sentences needs to change for the appropriate use of each past tense. Have the groups share their sentences with the class.
• Put students into pairs or small groups. Give each group a card with a different scenario on it. The scenario should be one in which informal commands are used, for example, a person is lost and asks for directions; a parent enters a child's messy room; a coach helps a student prepare for an important game; a teacher gives students tips to help them prepare for a test; etc. Have students work together to write three commands for the scenario they've been given. Have them share their ideas with the class. Then swap the lists of commands between the groups, and challenge each group to add one more command to each list. Continue until all groups have added a command to each of the scenarios.

OBJECTIVES FOR UNIT OPENER

- Introduce unit theme: *Construyendo un futuro*, about making plans for the future
- Introduce culture for unit: Learn about politics and the environment in Hispanic countries and compare cultural similarities

STANDARDS

1.1   Interpersonal communication
1.2   Understand the language
2.1   Practices and perspectives
4.2   Compare cultures

INSTRUCTIONAL STRATEGIES

- Introduce unit theme and objectives. Talk about the photo and have students make guesses about who the two people are: *Son compañeros de clase*, *El muchacho parece mayor*, *Tienen las mismas clases*, etc.
- Have the students discuss the questions and talk about themselves in the same context.
- Use the photograph to preview unit vocabulary: *¿Cuántos años crees que tienen? ¿Qué tipo de carrera crees que van a elegir? Y a ti, ¿qué carrera te gustaría hacer?*, etc.
- Ask related questions: *¿Tienes hermanos en la universidad? ¿Qué carrera estudian? ¿Te gustaría estudiar la misma carrera? ¿Te gustaría estudiar en otra ciudad/otro país?*, etc.
- Help students formulate their ideas using *Tengo un hermano que estudia arquitectura en Boston*, *Me gustaría estudiar contabilidad*, *No tengo ni idea*, etc.

SLOWER-PACED LEARNERS

Before having students answer the second and third questions, elicit names of different jobs or professions, and keep a list on the board. Put students in pairs to discuss their plans for the future. If they don't have specific plans, ask them to say whether or not they would like to do or would consider doing any of the jobs on the board. If they find one that interests them, have them discuss what they would have to do to prepare for it.

HERITAGE LANGUAGE LEARNERS

As a follow-up to the list of questions on the page, put students in pairs to discuss how their heritage and language skills do or don't affect their career aspirations for the future. Encourage them to share examples of Spanish-speaking members of the community whom they respect and consider role models.

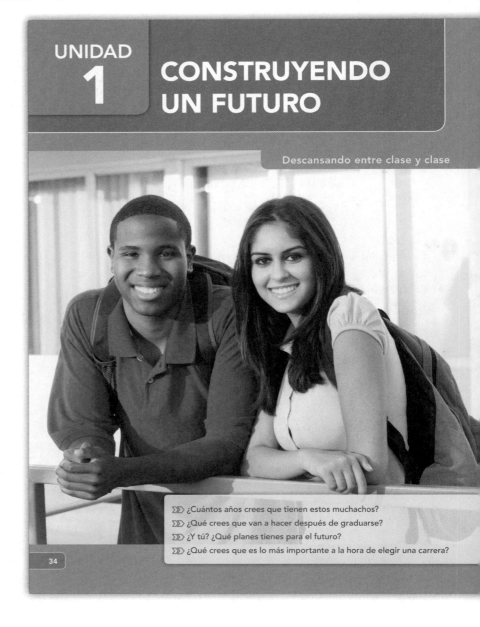

UNIDAD 1 CONSTRUYENDO UN FUTURO

Descansando entre clase y clase

▷▷ ¿Cuántos años crees que tienen estos muchachos?
▷▷ ¿Qué crees que van a hacer después de graduarse?
▷▷ ¿Y tú? ¿Qué planes tienes para el futuro?
▷▷ ¿Qué crees que es lo más importante a la hora de elegir una carrera?

34

ADDITIONAL UNIT RESOURCES

Extension Activities (EA) (Photocopiable)

EA: 1.1, 1.2, 1.3

Interactive Whiteboard Lessons (IWB)

IWB: 1.1, 1.2, 1.3

Audio

4 to 8

Video

Diálogo 1

Online ELEteca

EXTENSIÓN DIGITAL

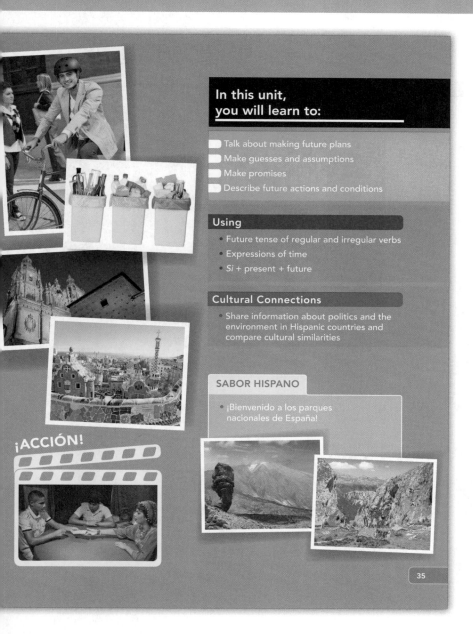

In this unit, you will learn to:

- Talk about making future plans
- Make guesses and assumptions
- Make promises
- Describe future actions and conditions

Using

- Future tense of regular and irregular verbs
- Expressions of time
- *Si* + present + future

Cultural Connections

- Share information about politics and the environment in Hispanic countries and compare cultural similarities

SABOR HISPANO

- ¡Bienvenido a los parques nacionales de España!

¡ACCIÓN!

35

INTRODUCTION TO LEARNING OUTCOMES

- The unit's learning objectives are an organizational tool for you and your students. Use them to preview what students will learn, and they serve as a way for you to assess whether your students have mastered the main ideas and skills. Encourage students to read the learning outcomes both before starting the unit and when they prepare for a test.

LEARNING OUTCOMES

- Talk about making future plans
- Make guesses and assumptions
- Make promises
- Describe future actions and conditions

INSTRUCTIONAL STRATEGIES

- Use unit opener to preview vocabulary and cultural topics for this unit.
- Have students look at the images on this page and relate them to the objectives listed. Ask questions such as: *¿Qué hace el hombre? ¿Por qué lleva casco? ¿Por qué va en bicicleta? ¿Cómo vienes a clase? ¿Tus padres usan la bici? ¿Qué hay en los contenedores? ¿En tu casa reciclan la basura? ¿En qué ciudades se encuentran estos sitios?*, etc.
- Invite students to read the topic for **Sabor hispano** and preview that section in the unit. Ask questions such as: *¿Hay parques nacionales cerca de aquí? ¿Qué se puede ver / hacer allí? ¿Conoces algún parque nacional en otro país?*
- Ask students to anticipate what they think the episode for **¡Acción!** will be about. Ask: *¿Qué hace esta mujer? ¿Dónde está?*
- Have students work in pairs to talk about the images using the questions you have modeled. Then ask for volunteers to present to the class what they understand this unit to be about.

Note Common Core State Standards (CCSS)

The four strands of the *Common Core State Standards for English Language Arts (ELA) and Literacy in History/Social Studies, Science, and Technical Subjects* (Reading, Writing, Speaking and Listening, and Language) are represented in the National Standards for Learning Languages by the Communication standards: Interpersonal, Interpretive, and Presentational. The three modes of communication align with the goals in Reading, Writing, Speaking, and Listening by emphasizing the purpose behind the communication.

ADVANCED LEARNERS

As a creative challenge, put students into pairs to create a story that relates to and connects at least five of the pictures of the page. Have each pair create an outline of their story. They can use their outlines either to present their stories to the class orally or to write out their stories, which they can share on a class discussion forum.

THREE MODES OF COMMUNICATION: UNIT 1			
	INTERPERSONAL	INTERPRETIVE	PRESENTATIONAL
HABLAMOS DE...	6	1, 2, 3, 4, 5	
COMUNICA	5, 6, 9	1, 2, 4, 7	3, 8, 9
¡ACCIÓN!	4	1, 2, 3	
PALABRA POR PALABRA	5, 6	1, 3, 4, 7, 8	2, 6, 9
GRAMÁTICA	2	1, 3, 4	5, 6
DESTREZAS		1, 2, 3	4
CULTURA		SABOR HISPANO	
RELATO	3, 5	1, 2, 3	4, 6

OBJECTIVES FOR HABLAMOS DE...

- Understand language in context
- Preview vocabulary: Talking about what people plan to do in the future
- Preview grammatical structures: Future of regular and irregular verbs; Time expressions; **Si** + present + future
- Read and listen to a conversation between two young people talking about their plans

CORE RESOURCES

- Audio Program: Track 4

STANDARDS

1.1 Engage in conversation
1.2 Understand the language
4.2 Compare cultures

INSTRUCTIONAL STRATEGIES

Activity 1

- Ask students to talk about the people in the photo and say what they are wearing, where they are or what they are holding. Ask if they are friends or a family and who they think each person is. Ask them what kind of job they think each one would like to have.
- Have the students cover the images of Víctor and Marta and do the activity without looking at the images.
- Have them decide which person each sentence refers to (some are for both and some for neither) and check the boxes, then have them compare their ideas with a partner and look at the images.
- Ask random students to read a sentence and other students to give the corresponding answer.
- Ask students when they think they are going to do all these things and remind them that the **ir a** + infinitive structure is used to talk about plans and intentions, usually in the near future.

Activity 2

- Have the students match the two parts of the sentences using what they already know about the two young people.
- Have them share their answers with a partner.
- Invite individual students to read one of the completed sentences and the rest of the class say who it refers to.

ANSWERS

Activity 1

a. Marta; **b.** Ninguno; **c.** Víctor; **d.** Los dos; **e.** Víctor; **f.** Víctor; **g.** Marta.

Activity 2

1. b; **2.** c; **3.** d; **4.** e; **5.** a.

ADVANCED LEARNERS

After Activity 2, ask students to write three more **ir a** + infinitive sentences about what Victor, Marta, both, or neither or them is going to do. Then put students into small groups to share their sentences without using Víctor or Marta's name. Their classmates have to identify who the sentences refer to.

HABLAMOS DE... El futuro

1 Observa las imágenes de Víctor y Marta e indica a quién se refiere cada frase.

VÍCTOR

MARTA

	Víctor	Marta	Los dos	Ninguno
a. Va a hacer deporte.	☐	☐	☐	☐
b. Va a pintar.	☐	☐	☐	☐
c. Va a tocar un instrumento.	☐	☐	☐	☐
d. Lleva una camiseta.	☐	☐	☐	☐
e. No va a jugar al tenis.	☐	☐	☐	☐
f. Va a practicar con su banda.	☐	☐	☐	☐
g. Va a ganar el partido.	☐	☐	☐	☐

2 Relaciona las dos columnas para saber qué actividades van a hacer Marta y Víctor.

1. Va a ponerse	**a.** el día.
2. Va a practicar su	**b.** protección solar.
3. Va a ir a clase	**c.** deporte favorito.
4. Va a tocar	**d.** de música.
5. Van a disfrutar	**e.** la guitarra.

36

3 🎧 4 **Escucha la conversación y completa.**

Marta: Todavía no sé qué quiero estudiar cuando empecemos (a) .... ¿Tú ya sabes qué vas a estudiar?
Víctor: Me encanta la música, así que me imagino que estudiaré (b) ...., como mi hermana mayor. Ella está muy contenta y dice que la universidad es genial.
Marta: Pero tu hermana estudia en (c) ...., ¿verdad?
Víctor: Sí, le encanta la ciudad y está muy contenta.
Marta: ¿Y tú también quieres irte a estudiar allí?
Víctor: Bueno, supongo que iré a Barcelona o quizás a (d) .... La universidad de Salamanca es preciosa y muy antigua y la ciudad tiene mucha marcha *(lively)*, porque hay mucha gente joven.
Marta: Yo creo que me quedaré aquí en Zaragoza y estudiaré (e) .... o Enfermería. Víctor, si te vas... ¡qué pena!
Víctor: Bueno, bueno, que solo estoy haciendo (f) .... Todavía no es nada seguro, ¡y faltan unos años! Además, si me voy, te prometo que vendré a verte cada fin de semana.
Marta: ¿Me lo prometes?
Víctor: ¡Prometido!

Casa de las Conchas, Salamanca

Parque Güell, Barcelona

Basílica del Pilar, Zaragoza

4 🎧 4 **Escucha otra vez y contesta verdadero (V) o falso (F), según lo que dicen Marta y Víctor.**

	V	F
a. Marta no tiene claro qué va a estudiar.	☐	☐
b. La hermana de Víctor estudia Bellas Artes.	☐	☐
c. Víctor ya sabe que va a estudiar en Salamanca.	☐	☐
d. Víctor y Marta viven en Zaragoza.	☐	☐
e. Víctor dice que en Barcelona hay mucha marcha.	☐	☐
f. A Marta le da igual si Víctor se va a estudiar a otra ciudad.	☐	☐
g. Víctor le hace una promesa a Marta.	☐	☐

37

Instructional Strategies

🎧 4 **Activity 3**

- Write the word ***universidad*** on the board and ask students to talk about college and what it means to them. Ask: ***Si vas a la universidad, ¿qué quieres estudiar? ¿Quieres ir a una universidad cerca de casa o en otro estado? ¿Qué universidades hay cerca de aquí? ¿Cómo son? ¿Quieres estudiar en el extranjero?***
- Inform the students that they are going to listen to a conversation between Marta and Víctor in which they talk about their plans for college.
- Have students close their books and listen to the audio.
- Ask how much they understood and have those who understood more explain what they understood.
- Play the audio again while the students follow in their books and fill in the missing words.

- Ask for volunteers to say the missing words and write them on the board.
- Have the students look at the photos and discuss them. Then find the cities on the map of Spain.

Cultural Note

Salamanca es una ciudad en la región de Castilla y León, muy famosa en España por sus monumentos y por su vida universitaria. Zaragoza es la capital de la Comunidad de Aragón, cerca de Cataluña. En ella, entre otros monumentos, se encuentra la Basílica de El Pilar, uno de los centros de peregrinación más importantes para los católicos.

🎧 4 **Activity 4**

- Have the students read the sentences and decide whether they are true or false as they listen one more time to the audio.
- Encourage students to cover the text and focus only on the audio.
- Invite volunteers to say the answers for the rest of the class.
- As a follow-up, ask students what they know of ***la Universidad de Salamanca*** based on their previous knowledge of the topic.
- You might ask students go online and visit the websites for these universities and report back on the types of degrees and programs offered at the university and what types of courses they offer foreign students. Or if time permits, visit these websites in class to find the equivalent in Spanish for common programs of studies.

ANSWERS

Activity 3
a. la universidad; **b.** Bellas Artes; **c.** Barcelona; **d.** Salamanca; **e.** Medicina; **f.** conjeturas.

Activity 4
a. T; **b.** T; **c.** F; **d.** T; **e.** F; **f.** F; **g.** T.

SLOWER-PACED LEARNERS

To guide students' listening for gist in Activity 3, pose one or two target questions for them to think about when listening to the conversation for the first time with their books closed. For example, you might ask: ***¿Quién tiene una hermana en la universidad? ¿Quién cree que va a quedarse en su ciudad para estudiar?*** Write the questions on the board, and take a class poll to check the answers after the first listening.

HERITAGE LANGUAGE LEARNERS

As an alternate approach to Activity 3, you might consider asking students to read the transcript and try to complete the conversation before listening to it. Have students share and compare their guesses as a class. Then play the audio to see if they're correct. After Activity 4, you might consider having students do more research about Salamanca, Barcelona, and Zaragoza, and post a comment on a class discussion board stating where among the three places they would prefer to study and why. Encourage them to write a response to at least one other student's post.

INSTRUCTIONAL STRATEGIES

Activity 5

- This activity previews the forms of the future and its use to make predictions.
- Have the students read the sentences and ask them if these statements refer to something that has already happened, is happening now, or hasn't happened yet. Ask students to identify the expressions that confirm their choice.
- Now ask them to match each sentence to an image.
- Have them compare answers with a partner.
- Ask one student to read a sentence and another to say which image it refers to.
- Point out that some of the expressions are followed by the future tense, which they will study later in the unit. For now, explain to students that they should just focus on becoming familiar with the form.
- If you like, you can ask students to describe what patterns they are beginning to see in this structure (infinitive form).

Activity 6

- Have the students read the questions and ask what other structure also refers to a future action (**ir a** + infinitive).
- Divide the students into pairs and have them take turns asking each other questions. Encourage students to make this activity as similar as possible to a real conversation.
- Circulate around the class as they work, providing assistance where required.
- Invite volunteers to say their answers aloud.

Extension

- Have student pairs present this activity to the class as a television or person-on-the-street type of interview. Tell students to create a "persona" for the interviewer and set up a context for the situation. For example, taking a survey, doing a show for Spanish language television about American students, as part of a comedy skit for a late-night talk show.
- Have the interviewer simulate a microphone and allow him/her to use note cards for the questions. The interviewer should react to the responses in a comical or serious way and ask follow-up questions as necessary.
- Have the class vote on the best interview, interviewer, or person on the street.
- The interviewer might also interview random students in the class without prior practice to see how well students think on their feet.

ANSWERS

Activity 5

1. e; **2.** b; **3.** h; **4.** g; **5.** c; **6.** a; **7.** f; **8.** d.

SLOWER-PACED LEARNERS

Before going over the sentences in the future form in Activity 5, focus students' attention on the images. As a class or in pairs, have students describe what they see and discuss the context of each scene. Then proceed with the matching.

HERITAGE LANGUAGE LEARNERS

As an extension to Activity 6, ask students to interview a native speaker of Spanish of their own age or younger outside of class. Have students ask him/her the same questions, and record the interview (audio only or video as well). Students can then share their interviews with the class or post them online. Have them comment on each other's interviews.

HABLAMOS DE... El futuro

5 Relaciona las frases con la imagen correspondiente.

- **a.** Me imagino que tendré que lavar los platos.
- **b.** Voy a subir a poner la lavadora.
- **c.** Te prometo que todo saldrá bien.
- **d.** Espero tener tiempo de verlo todo.
- **e.** Creo que este año sí aprobaré.
- **f.** Este verano tengo la intención de ponerme en forma.
- **g.** Te juro que te compraré otras.
- **h.** Para mi fiesta de cumpleaños, este año pienso ir a un karaoke.

6 Hazle las siguientes preguntas a tu compañero/a. Después, cambien de papel.

- **a.** ¿Ya sabes qué vas a hacer después de la escuela secundaria? ¿Qué?
- **b.** ¿Tienes claro qué vas a estudiar en la universidad o escuela técnica? ¿Qué?
- **c.** ¿Quieres ir a otra ciudad para estudiar o trabajar? ¿Por qué?
- **d.** ¿Has ido alguna vez a un karaoke? ¿Cómo fue?
- **e.** ¿Practicas algún deporte? ¿Cuál? ¿Con qué frecuencia?
- **f.** ¿Cuál fue la última ciudad que visitaste? ¿Y la próxima que quieres visitar?

38

COMUNICA

UNIDAD **1**

MAKING ASSUMPTIONS

■ Para **hacer suposiciones o conjeturas**:

Creo que *mañana lloverá.* I believe that it will rain tomorrow.

Me imagino que *no podremos ir a la playa.* I imagine that we won't be able to go the beach.

Supongo que *nos quedaremos en casa.* I guess that we will stay at home.

1 Indica qué han hecho las siguientes personas.

| a. Alicia (estudiar) | b. el abuelo Paco (pescar) | c. Iván (hacer excursiones) | d. el tío Pepe (tener un accidente) | e. Patricia (escalar montañas) |

Alicia ha estudiado mucho.

2 👥 Con tu compañero/a, relaciona las imágenes con las personas de la Actividad 1 según lo que van a hacer en el futuro.

1. 2. 3. 4. 5.

3 👥 ¿Qué actividades crees que van a hacer las personas de la Actividad 1? ¿Coinciden con las suposiciones que hicieron tu compañero/a y tú?

> Irá al mecánico ○ Irá de expedición a la selva ○ Subirá al Everest ○
> Irá a la universidad ○ Cocinará pescado a la plancha

a. Alicia _____
b. El abuelo Paco _____
c. Iván _____
d. El tío Pepe _____
e. Patricia _____

39

OBJECTIVES FOR COMUNICA

• Present communicative functions of the unit: Make assumptions or conjectures; Make promises

CORE RESOURCES

• Audio Program: Track 5
• Extension Activities: EA 1.1
• Interactive Whiteboard Lesson: IWB 1.1, 1.2
• Interactive Online Materials - ELEteca

STANDARDS

1.1   Engage in conversation
1.2   Understand the language
4.2   Compare cultures

INSTRUCTIONAL STRATEGIES FOR MAKING ASSUMPTIONS

• Project the conversation in Activity 3 (page 37) and ask students to identify the sentences that express assumptions or conjecture: ***Me imagino que estudiaré Bellas Artes***, ***Supongo que iré a Barcelona o quizás a Salamanca***, ***Yo creo que me quedaré aquí en Zaragoza***. Ask students: ***Cuando Víctor y Marta dicen estas cosas, ¿están seguros de lo que dicen o están haciendo una suposición?***

• Project IWB 1.1, ***Conjeturas***. With books closed, tell students to guess what they think the people in the images are going to do using the expressions ***Imagino / Supongo / Creo que***. Prompt students by asking, ***¿Quién es? ¿Dónde va?*** to elicit responses such as ***Me imagino que va a ir a la biblioteca porque lleva libros***.

• Then walk students through the sample sentences in the book, pointing out the forms of the future.

Activities 1 and 2

• In addition to recycling the present perfect tense, the purpose of this activity is to establish a context for students to see the relationship between actions and tenses, between what already happened and what might happen next.

• Have the students express what the people have already done using the verbs and the model provided.

• Have students look at the images and decide which one most likely correspond to the people in Activity 1.

Activity 3

Have students work with a partner to choose an activity from the list to describe what the people in Activity 1 are going to do next.

ANSWERS

Activity 1

a. Alicia ha estudiado mucho; **b.** El abuelo Paco ha pescado un pez grande; **c.** Iván ha hecho excursiones a las pirámides centroamericanas; **d.** El tío Pepe ha tenido un accidente; **e.** Patricia ha escalado una montaña.

Activity 2

1. c; **2.** e; **3.** d; **4.** a; **5.** b.

Activity 3

a. Alicia irá a la Universidad; **b.** El abuelo Paco cocinará el pescado a la plancha; **c.** Iván irá de expedición a la selva. **d.** El tío Pepe irá al mecánico; **e.** Patricia subirá al Everest.

SLOWER-PACED LEARNERS

Before writing sentences in Activity 1, review the form of the present perfect on the board. Remind them of regular and irregular past participles.

ADVANCED LEARNERS

Building upon Activity 3, challenge students to write an additional follow-up sentence about each person, making conjectures about what might happen next.

INSTRUCTIONAL STRATEGIES

Activity 4

- Call on students to read the statements aloud after you to ensure correct pronunciation. Help students put the stress on the last syllable of each verb.
- Read the model and remind students of other phrases they can use for conjectures: **Me imagino que**, **Creo que**, etc. Then put students into pairs to discuss their plans. Encourage them to ask each other for additional information or explanations.
- Circulate around the room as they work, providing assistance where required.

Activity 5

- Have students switch partners.
- Students talk to their new partner about what they think they may do in the future and ask about his/her plans. They should take note of each other's responses.
- Circulate around the room while they talk and provide corrections and assistance where required.
- When they finish, have them think about which one they have more in common with and share their conclusions with the class.

Extension

- If you feel your group is ready, expand the activity by introducing the **usted/él/ella** form of the future.
- Begin by asking students to reflect on the forms of the future they have seen so far. Ask what form of the verb (**yo**) and the ending (add *−é* to infinitive). Explain that to express the **usted/él/ella** form, students need to add *−á* instead of *−é*. For example: **Pedro cree que hablará español perfectamente**.
- Then call on students to report back on the information they gathered from their classmates.

INSTRUCTIONAL STRATEGIES FOR MAKING PROMISES

- Review the expressions for making promises. Then have students turn back to the conversation in Activity 3 of **Hablamos de...** on page 37 and pick out instances when these are used.
- Ask students to explain what the person is promising to do: **¿Qué promete hacer?** (**Te prometo que vendré a verte cada fin de semana**).
- For additional practice, have students take the last three lines of the conversation and substitute with a different expression.

ADVANCED LEARNERS

After reviewing the expressions for making promises, have students look back at the items they made plans for in Activity 4. With a partner, have them take turns combining those items with the new expressions and say them aloud.

COMUNICA

4 👥 En parejas, hablen sobre lo que creen que van o no van a hacer en su futuro. Completen las tres últimas frases según sus propios planes.

Modelo: E1: Supongo que viajaré a Argentina.
E2: Yo también. / Yo no. Creo que viajaré a Italia.

- Hablaré español perfectamente.
- Hablaré muchos idiomas.
- Seré un/a deportista profesional.
- Escribiré un libro.
- Viviré en el extranjero.
- Tocaré un instrumento.
- Correré maratones.
- Conoceré ....
- Iré a ....
- Estudiaré ....

Me imagino que viajaré por todo el mundo con mi mejor amiga.

5 👥 Ten la misma conversación con otro compañero/a. ¿Con cuál de ellos crees que tienes más en común? Explica tus razones a la clase.

MAKING PROMISES

■ Para **hacer promesas**:

- **Te prometo que...** I promise you that...
- **Te lo prometo / juro**. I promise / swear it...
- **Te doy mi palabra**. I give you my word.
- **Te juro que...** I swear that...
- **¡Prometido!** Promise!
- **Lo haré sin falta**. I will be sure to do it.

¡Prometido!

6 🎧 **5** Escucha y completa las conversaciones. Después, relaciónalas con sus imágenes.

(1.) → ☐

a. Madre: ¡El próximo fin de semana estás castigado (*punished*)! Ayer llegaste tardísimo.
Hijo: .... que no volverá a pasar, de verdad.
Madre: Siempre dices lo mismo y nunca haces caso. ¡No hay más que hablar!
Hijo: ¡Pero, mamá…!

(2.) → ☐

b. Luis: ¡Estuve media hora esperándote y la película ya ha empezado! La próxima vez entro yo solo al cine y no te espero.
Sandra: Anda, no te enfades. He llamado para avisarte… .... que no volverá a pasar.
Luis: ¡Pero si desde que te conozco siempre llegas tarde!

(3.) → 💬

c. Pedro: Tu fiesta ha estado genial. Nos hemos divertido muchísimo.
Daniel: Me alegro. A ver si celebramos otra para tu cumpleaños.
Pedro: ....

7 👥 Lee las siguientes promesas y comenta con tu compañero/a qué ha podido pasar para motivar cada promesa.

a. Te prometo que no me meteré en tu correo electrónico.
b. Te juro que tendré mucho cuidado con él.
c. De verdad que lo haré sin falta. ¡Prometido!

8 👥 Elige una de las promesas anteriores y prepara con tu compañero/a una conversación como las de la Actividad 6.

MORE IN ELETECA: EXTRA ONLINE PRACTICE

- Then play the audio with books closed and ask students to match each conversation to the correct illustration.
- Have the students open their books and listen to the audio again as they fill in the blanks with the missing expressions from the explanation above.
- Invite pairs of students to perform each exchange for the class.

Activity 7

- In pairs, students imagine what must have happened for the promises to have been made. Help students think of some possibilities by suggesting they identify who made the promise to whom and what the person has done.
- Have volunteers share their ideas with the class.

Extension

- To continue practice, distribute copies of EA 1.1, **Hacer promesas** to student pairs. Each student selects a role and writes a promise for each of the situations presented on his/her card.
- Then each student shares the promise with his/her partner. He/She will try to guess the situation.

Activity 8

- Read through the situations in Activity 8 again and have students in pairs choose one.
- Each pair prepares a conversation for the chosen situation, using Activity 7 as a model. Have the students practice their conversations in pairs.
- Circulate around the class as they talk, listening in and providing assistance and corrections where required.
- Invite volunteers to present to the class.

Answers

Activity 7

1. c: ¡Prometido!; **2.** a: Te juro; **3.** b: Te prometo.

Slower-paced Learners

You may want to have each pair focus on just one of the scenarios in Activity 7 instead of all three. To help structure their discussions, create a chart on the board that they can use to take notes. The first column can contain row headings like these: **La promesa, El/la que la ha dicho, A quién la ha dicho, Lo que pasó.**

Heritage learners

Have students make a promise to one of their classmates that they will keep for the week. Display the promises somewhere in the room or have students post them on an online forum. At the end of the week, students should confirm whether or not the promises were kept.

Instructional Strategies

🎧 **5** **Activity 6**

Project IWB 1.2, **¿Qué está pasando?** and ask students to predict what expression the person in the illustration will use according to the scene depicted. Prompt students by signalling which of the characters is making the promise. For more accelerated groups, ask them to complete the promise.

OBJECTIVES FOR ¡ACCIÓN!

- Provide students with a structured approach to viewing the video
- Contextualize the content of the unit in a familiar scenario

CORE RESOURCES

- Unit Video 1 - Una cita con Morgana
- Online Materials - ELEteca

STANDARDS

1.1 Interpersonal communication
1.2 Interpretive communication
2.1 Culture: Practices and perspectives

INSTRUCTIONAL STRATEGIES

Previewing: Antes del video

Activity 1

The purpose of this activity is to preview some of the vocabulary that will appear in the video. Have students work in pairs to match the words or phrases with the best definitions.

Activity 2

- Remind students to use all of the context clues available to them to make the best matches.
- Go over the answers as a class. Have students explain how they arrived at their decisions.

ANSWERS

Activity 1

1. d; **2.** j; **3.** a; **4.** k; **5.** b; **6.** l; **7.** e; **8.** f; **9.** c; **10.** g; **11.** i; **12.** h.

Activity 2

a. 5; **b.** 2; **c.** 1; **d.** 3; **e.** 6; **f.** 4.

ADVANCED LEARNERS

Challenge students to make sentences with the vocabulary in Activity 1 to demonstrate their ability to use them correctly in context.

¡ACCIÓN! Una cita con Morgana

1. 2. 3.
4. 5. 6.

ANTES DEL VIDEO

1 👥 **Todas estas palabras tienen relación con el episodio que vas a ver. Relaciónalas con su definición.**

1. adivina
2. confuso
3. ponerse nervioso
4. planes
5. medioambiente
6. candidato de un partido político
7. votos
8. guardabosques
9. ciencias de la naturaleza
10. parque nacional
11. especies salvajes
12. efecto invernadero

a. Cuando pierdes la tranquilidad y la calma.
b. Es el sistema formado por la naturaleza.
c. Disciplina científica que estudia los árboles, las plantas, etc.
d. Persona que conoce el futuro de las personas.
e. Expresión de las preferencias políticas de los ciudadanos.
f. Trabajador que cuida los bosques.
g. Lugar de la naturaleza protegido.
h. Subida de la temperatura de la atmósfera muy negativa para la vida natural.
i. Animales que viven en la naturaleza.
j. Cuando no tienes las ideas claras.
k. Cuando tienes una intención o un proyecto para el futuro.
l. Persona que se presenta a las elecciones.

2 **Fíjate en las imágenes y relaciónalas con las siguientes frases y conversaciones. Basa tu respuesta en lo que crees que puede ocurrir. Usa tu imaginación.**

a. "Harás un importante estudio sobre el efecto invernadero". Imagen ⃝
b. ≫ No sé qué estudiar y quiero aclarar mis planes de futuro. Imagen ⃝
   ≫ Divide la baraja en dos y deja que doña Morgana mire tu futuro. Imagen ⃝
c. "El futuro se mostrará a través de mis cartas. Abran la mente". Imagen ⃝
d. "Esta carta representa al árbol de la vida. Tu destino está muy claro". Imagen ⃝
e. ≫ Por fin ya tiene claro lo que va a estudiar. Imagen ⃝
   ≫ ¡Las cosas que se hacen por los amigos! Imagen ⃝
f. "Tendrás muchos votos por todo el país y ganarás unas elecciones".

DURANTE EL VIDEO

3 Mira el episodio y señala cuáles de las siguientes afirmaciones son verdaderas.

a. ☐ La adivina se llama Morgana.
b. ☐ Felipe pregunta por su futuro.
c. ☐ Sebas tiene dos caminos en su futuro.
d. ☐ Sebas prefiere ser guardabosques.
e. ☐ Sebas trabajará en economía.

f. ☐ Según las cartas, Sebas estudiará Ciencias de la Educación.
g. ☐ A Felipe le gustan los dos posibles destinos.
h. ☐ Morgana es una adivina falsa.

4 Ordena cronológicamente las frases de acuerdo a lo que ocurre en el episodio.

a. ① Los muchachos esperan impacientes en un sitio oscuro iluminado con velas.
b. ☐ Felipe y la adivina se quedan solos y se ríen.
c. ☐ Hay un posible futuro como político para Sebas.
d. ☐ Felipe dice que su amigo quiere saber cosas sobre su futuro.
e. ☐ La adivina pregunta qué quiere saber Sebas sobre el futuro.
f. ☐ La adivina echa las cartas.
g. ☐ Llega la adivina.
h. ☐ Sebas dice que no cree en los adivinos.
i. ☐ Hay un segundo posible futuro como guardabosques.

j. ☐ Sebas explica que tiene dudas sobre qué estudiar.
k. ☐ Aparecen dos posibles futuros para Sebas.
l. ☐ La adivina pide concentración.
m. ☐ A Sebas le gusta más el futuro como guardabosques.
n. ☐ La adivina pregunta quién quiere saber algo sobre su futuro.
ñ. ☐ Se va muy contento a contarle la novedad a sus padres.
o. ⊚ En realidad Morgana es una adivina disfrazada para ayudar a Sebas a tomar una decisión.

DESPUÉS DEL VIDEO

5 🗪 Contesta las preguntas y comenta tus respuestas con tu compañero/a.

	Sí	No	¿Por qué?
¿Has ido a visitar a una adivina?	☐	☐	
¿Crees en el tarot?	☐	☐	
¿Es necesario que alguien te ayude a tomar decisiones sobre tu futuro?	☐	☐	
¿Sabes ya qué vas a hacer en el futuro?	☐	☐	

6 🗪 Habla con tu compañero/a sobre las siguientes afirmaciones. Expresa tu opinión a favor o en contra.

a. Personalmente, puedo hacer poco por el medioambiente.
b. Si todos colaboramos podemos cambiar el futuro de la tierra.
c. Considero que hay personas que pueden adivinar el futuro.
d. Tengo muy claro lo que haré en el futuro.

MORE IN ELETECA: EXTRA ONLINE PRACTICE

43

INSTRUCTIONAL STRATEGIES

Viewing: Durante el video

📺 **Activity 3**

- Go over the instructions and give students time to read the statements before playing the video. Refer back to the images at the top of the lesson to point out who's who among the characters: Morgana (Image 1), Sebas (Images 4 and 5), and Felipe (the male in the center of Images 2 and 6).
- Play the video while students watch, listen, and check the correct statements.
- Before going over the answers one at a time, you may want to take a class poll to see how many true statements they checked. This will give you a sense of their comprehension after the first viewing.

Activity 4

- Before playing the video a second time, have students review the sentences that describe the events in the video. Point out that the first and last items are already given.
- Play the video again. Once it's over, give students a few minutes more to order the sentences on their own before comparing them with a partner. Confirm the correct order for the class.

Post-viewing: Después del video

Activity 5

Have students answer the questions individually first before putting them in pairs to ask and answer the questions with a partner. Alternatively, have students use the chart to take notes on their partners' responses and use them to report back to the class or another partner.

Activity 6

You may want to give students time to collect their thoughts and jot down notes about their ideas before they speak. For a more lively discussion, you might be students into small groups as opposed to pairs.

ANSWERS

Activity 3

a, c, d, g, h.

Activity 4

1. a; **2.** h; **3.** g; **4.** n; **5.** d; **6.** e; **7.** j; **8.** l; **9.** f; **10.** k; **11.** c; **12.** i; **13.** m; **14.** ñ; **15.** b; **16.** o.

SLOWER-PACED LEARNERS

To help students manage the long list of events in Activity 4, give them the correct number order for a few more of the statements so there are fewer to sort.

HERITAGE LANGUAGE LEARNERS

Have students take one of the sentences from Activity 6 and develop it into two paragraphs expressing their points of view.

OBJECTIVES FOR EL MEDIOAMBIENTE

- Present vocabulary needed to practice communicative and grammatical functions for the unit: The environment and the future
- Talk about ways to preserve natural resources

CORE RESOURCES

- Extension Activities: EA 1.2
- Interactive Whiteboard Lesson: IWB 1.3
- Interactive Online Materials - ELEteca

STANDARDS

1.1 Engage in conversation
1.2 Understand the language
1.3 Present information
3.2 Acquire information
4.1 Compare languages and cultures

INSTRUCTIONAL STRATEGIES

- Introduce the topic by projecting IWB 1.3, **El medioambiente**. With books closed, ask students to look at the images and draw conclusions about what they think the images represent. Ask students to describe some of the images. For example, **La muchacha lleva las botellas de plástico a reciclar**, **El hombre corta un árbol**…
- Then ask students to get into groups of four and distribute an equal number of cards from EA 1.2, **El medioambiente** to each group. Call on a student from each group to match their word to the correct image on the board. Ask the class, **¿Están de acuerdo? ¿Por qué?** Encourage students to justify their choices.
- Have students open their books and check their answers.

Activity 1

- Have the students decide which images show something with a negative impact on the environment and which show something positive, and write them in the correct column.
- Ask students to share their answers with a partner. Then call on volunteers to read from their lists and give examples or more information about the topics.
- Ask students to add other words connected with the topic.

Activity 2

- Tell students to think about the different labels on food, clothing, and other products that they buy. Elicit examples. Ask if any of the labels have to do with the environment and discuss how they relate.
- Have students look at the three logos and describe them in their own words. Ask them to explain what they stand for.
- Have students work individually to read the descriptions and match them to the logos.
- Go over the answers as a class.

PALABRA POR PALABRA El medioambiente

1 Observa las imágenes y separa los fenómenos y prácticas en positivos o negativos. Añade a la lista otras palabras que conozcas relacionadas con el medioambiente.

consumo responsable — reciclaje — contaminación

energía renovable — sequía — transporte ecológico

calentamiento global — deshielo — deforestación

 Positivos

 Negativos

2 Lean estas descripciones y relaciónenlas con su símbolo correspondiente. ¿Existen estos símbolos en Estados Unidos? ¿Significan lo mismo?

 (a.)
 (b.)
 (c.)

1. ➔ ☐ Esta ilustración invita al consumidor a ser cívico y dejar las botellas, latas o otra basura en un lugar adecuado para ello, como papeleras, basureros, etc. Lo encontrarás en casi todos los productos con el objetivo de responsabilizar al consumidor.

2. ➔ ☐ En este logo cada flecha representa uno de los pasos del proceso de reciclaje: recogida, el proceso mismo del reciclaje y la compra de los productos reciclados, de manera que el sistema continúa una y otra vez, como en un círculo.

3. ➔ ☐ El envase (container) que lleva este ícono garantiza que, al convertirse en basura, este envase se reciclará. Lo encontramos en envases de plástico, metálicos, cartón, papel…

ANSWERS

Activity 1

Positivo: a; b; d; f. **Negativo:** c; e; g; h; i.

Activity 2

1. b; **2.** c; **3.** a.

ADVANCED LEARNERS

Put students into groups to discuss examples of each of the environmental impacts in Activity 1. Encourage them to take notes to be able to report back to the class about their ideas. Alternatively, have students work individually to write sentences describing examples of each topic.

HERITAGE LANGUAGE LEARNERS

Have students find a recent article online from a Spanish language news source related to one of the topics in Activity 1. Tell them to show the article to the class, identify the theme it relates to, and briefly summarize it for the class.

3 👥 **Lee el siguiente artículo aparecido en una revista. Después, haz una lista de cuatro recomendaciones que hacen y compara tus respuestas con las de tu compañero/a.**

Ideas sencillas para salvar el planeta

El día a día nos ofrece muchas posibilidades para poner nuestro granito de arena en la protección y salvación del planeta. Si no sabes por dónde empezar, nosotros te damos algunas sugerencias *(suggestions)*.

Además de modificar los hábitos, se trata de que estos cambios sean sencillos de realizar *(easy to do)* para conseguir una repetición constante y resultados a largo plazo *(long term)*, los verdaderamente productivos.

Pero, ¿por dónde empezar? Podemos cambiar el chip sin esfuerzo en cuestiones cotidianas como la compra diaria, el uso de la computadora, nuestra basura, la publicidad comercial en papel que llena nuestro buzón *(mailbox)* o, entre muchos aspectos, la climatización de nuestro hogar.

Al ir a hacer la compra, infórmate del origen de los productos y las condiciones en que se elaboran, eso te ayudará a comprar con responsabilidad. Además, intenta consumir frutas y verduras orgánicas, mejorarás tu alimentación y ayudarás a mejorar el medioambiente.

Si utilizamos el portátil en lugar de una computadora ya estamos haciéndole un favor al medioambiente, y también a nuestro bolsillo *(pocket)* pues, por lo general, con él gastaremos aproximadamente la mitad de energía.

Otra idea es evitar *(avoid)* en nuestro buzón la publicidad en papel contactando con las empresas para que nos borren de sus listados. Si necesitamos ver algún catálogo, siempre podemos acudir a la versión *online* para consultarlo en un momento determinado. Piensa, además, que los recursos naturales no son infinitos y compara cuánto se tarda en cortar un árbol y cuánto tardará en crecer. Por eso, no malgastes el papel.

No gastar demasiado en climatización es otra cosa que podemos hacer teniendo un termostato programable y siguiendo consejos básicos para el aire acondicionado y la calefacción *(heating)*, así como evitar el transporte privado y preferir la bicicleta o el tren al coche o al avión.

También conviene revisar la temperatura a la que tenemos regulado el refrigerador, un par de puntos por encima de lo necesario supone un ahorro *(saving)* económico y eléctrico. Además, cambia tus electrodomésticos viejos por otros más modernos que causan un menor impacto medioambiental al consumir menos energía.

Un truco que nos ayudará a pensar qué hacer ante situaciones nuevas es recordar las famosas "tres erres" como propuesta de hábitos de consumo: Reducir, Reutilizar y Reciclar. Recicla los desechos domésticos de forma adecuada, separando los materiales; el reciclaje es básico para ayudar al planeta y son muchas las cosas y los materiales que pueden ser reutilizados.

Lógicamente, una sola persona no consigue cambios suficientes pero sí ayuda a hacerlos realidad si sus esfuerzos *(efforts)* se suman a los de otras muchas personas. El trabajo en equipo resulta totalmente imprescindible. Como ves, se pueden hacer más cosas de las que parece sin mucho esfuerzo. ¿Colaboras?

Texto adaptado de: *http://www.ecologiaverde.com/ideas-sencillas-para-ayudar-a-salvar-el-planeta/*

45

INSTRUCTIONAL STRATEGIES

Activity 3

- Have the students skim the text to pick out key words that explain what the text is about. For example: **salvar**, **protección**, **medioambiente**…
- Then have students read the text more carefully and write any words or expressions they do not understand.
- Read the text and pause after each section for a student to summarize or explain the main idea.
- Ask them to find four suggestions in the text and compare with a partner.
- Circulate around the room as they work providing assistance where required.
- Ask for volunteers to say the suggestions and ask if the others agree: **¿Están de acuerdo?**
- Ask for students to write the suggestions on the board for discussion.

> **Extension**
>
> - Have a class discussion and ask students to describe which of the suggestions listed on the board they and their families generally practice. Ask: **¿Qué hacen ya tú y tu familia? ¿Qué recomendaciones consideran las más fáciles de seguir? ¿Por qué? ¿Y las más difíciles? ¿Por qué? ¿Qué recomendación vas a intentar de seguir después de leer este artículo?**
> - Students may prepare their answers with a partner.

ANSWERS

Activity 3

Answers will vary. Possible answers include: consumir frutas y verduras orgánicas; usar el portátil en lugar de una computadora; borrarnos de los listados de la empresas para no recibir publicidad en papel; controlar el aire acondicionado y la calefacción para usar solo lo necesario; usar transporte público; cambiar los electrodomésticos antiguos por unos más modernos; recordar las tres erres: *Reducir, Reutilizar, Reciclar*.

SLOWER-PACED LEARNERS

As another approach to the reading in Activity 3, provide students with the suggestions from the article before they read it and have them match the suggestions to the correct paragraphs while they read. (Number the paragraphs as a class so everyone is referring to the content in the same way). This will help them focus on the main ideas and not get bogged down in unknown language or overwhelmed by the length of the article.

INSTRUCTIONAL STRATEGIES

Activity 4

- Have students look at the images and say a word or sentence to describe what they see and how it relates to the environment.
- Then have students read the statements and match each to an image.
- Have them share with a partner, before asking random students to give the correct answers.

Activity 5

- Students sit in pairs to discuss which ideas they already knew and which are new to them.
- Have them mark each idea with C (*conocida*) or N (*nueva*) in the margin.
- Ask for volunteers to report back to the class.

> **Extension**
>
> Have the class draw up a list of ideas, using the previous activities as a basis. Divide the class into small groups to write a few sentences and illustrate one of the ideas.
> Have the students make illustrated posters to show the results.

Activity 6

- Refer students to the questions and have them talk in small groups about what they already do to protect the environment and what new ideas they have gained from the text.
- Ask them to report back to the class.

> **Extension**
>
> As a follow-up, ask students to report on what environmental practices their school and community participate in. If students are unable to come up with many, encourage them to think about what the school and community can do based on some of the ideas discussed and ask students to draw up a list of recommendations. These should be bilingual so as to reach all members of the community and school staff. Tell students to use expressions such as ***hay que***, ***tener que*** and ***deber*** for their recommendations. Have students work in small groups of three.

ANSWERS

Activity 4

1. a; **2.** f; **3.** c; **4.** b; **5.** h; **6.** e; **7.** d; **8.** g.

ADVANCED LEARNERS

After discussing the questions in Activity 5, have students write a paragraph reacting to one of the suggestions from the article. They can write about whether or not they think the suggestion is a good one and why or why not. Challenge them to write at least five sentences in their comments.

HERITAGE LANGUAGE LEARNERS

As an extension to Activity 6, ask groups to discuss whether or not taking all of the measures in the article will save the planet. If not, what else do they think needs to happen? What environmental problems are not addressed by the suggestions in the article? Do any of those problems affect Hispanic communities more or less than other communities? How and why? What can be done about it?

PALABRA POR PALABRA

4 **Relaciona las frases sacadas del texto con la imagen correspondiente.**

a. Infórmate del origen de los productos y las condiciones en que se elaboran.

b. Intenta consumir frutas y verduras orgánicas.

c. Compara cuánto se tarda en cortar un árbol y cuánto tardará en crecer, no malgastes el papel.

d. Usa un termostato programable y sigue los consejos básicos para el aire acondicionado y la calefacción.

e. Prefiere la bicicleta o el tren al coche o al avión.

f. Si utilizamos el portátil en lugar de una computadora, ya estamos haciéndole un favor al medioambiente.

g. Cambia tus electrodomésticos viejos por otros más modernos que causan un impacto medioambiental menor al consumir menos energía.

h. Recicla los desechos domésticos de forma adecuada, separando los materiales.

5 👥 **Habla con tu compañero/a sobre la información del artículo. Usa las siguientes preguntas como modelo.**

- ¿Qué ideas prácticas de las que aparecen en el artículo ya conocías?
- ¿Qué información es nueva para ti?

6 👥 **En grupos pequeños, habla con tus compañeros/as sobre las cosas que haces para proteger el medioambiente.**

- ¿Qué cosas haces ya para proteger el medioambiente?
- ¿Crees que vas a hacer alguna más después de leer el artículo?

PALABRA POR PALABRA La política

7 Lee este artículo aparecido en un periódico.

Unas elecciones muy reñidas

Mañana se celebrarán las elecciones a la presidencia del país. Las encuestas de estos días señalan (*indicate*) que los dos principales partidos están muy igualados y que puede pasar cualquier cosa. Pablo Tomeu y Francisco Torres, los dos principales candidatos a presidente, están optimistas ante estas elecciones, aunque habrá que esperar hasta contar todos los votos para conocer el resultado final.

Los dos partidos (*parties*) han prometido hacer grandes cambios en el país si consiguen ganar las elecciones. El candidato Pablo Tomeu ha dicho que si gana, hará una gran reforma en educación. También ha dicho que mejorará (*will improve*) la salud pública y que abrirá varios hospitales nuevos.

El programa del partido de Francisco Torres apuesta por (*supports*) el medioambiente. Como ha dicho a lo largo de toda su campaña, este será un punto fundamental: si el partido de Torres sale elegido, aumentará el uso del transporte público, bajará el precio de los autos eléctricos, desarrollarán más energías renovables, etc.

Hasta mañana por la tarde no conoceremos quién será el futuro presidente del país y los cambios que viviremos en los próximos cuatro años.

> el candidato = el aspirante, el postulante
> la encuesta = el sondeo

8 Contesta verdadero (V) o falso (F).

	V	F
a. El partido de Tomeu es el favorito.	☐	☐
b. Los dos principales candidatos piensan que pueden obtener buenos resultados.	☐	☐
c. Se presentan más de dos partidos a estas elecciones.	☐	☐
d. El partido que quiere mejorar la sanidad, también quiere mejorar el transporte.	☐	☐
e. Las elecciones se celebran cada cinco años.	☐	☐

9 Se van a celebrar elecciones en tu ciudad y tú eres uno de los candidatos a alcalde. ¿Cuál es tu programa? Escribe un discurso usando el vocabulario que has aprendido y los siguientes temas.

> medioambiente ○ educación ○ trabajo ○ transporte ○ salud

> Estimados ciudadanos:
> Prometo que voy a construir más zonas verdes, así los niños podrán jugar en los parques. Además, si votan por mí, el transporte en la ciudad será más barato. Si mi partido gana, les prometo que...

👤💻 **MORE IN ELETECA:** EXTRA ONLINE PRACTICE

47

OBJECTIVES FOR LA POLÍTICA

- Present vocabulary needed to practice communicative and grammatical functions for the unit: Politics and elections
- Talk about candidates and campaign promises

STANDARDS

1.2 Understand the language
1.3 Present information
3.2 Acquire information

INSTRUCTIONAL STRATEGIES

Activity 7

- With books closed, draw 8 dashes on the board to represent the letters of the word **política**. Play Hangman with the students until they discover the word.
- Ask students what they know about politics in the U.S. Ask questions such as: **¿Qué partido lidera el Presidente? ¿Dónde se reúnen los senadores?**, etc.

- Ask what they know about politics in any of the countries in Latin America, for instance: **¿Quién es el Presidente del Gobierno? ¿Qué tipo de gobierno es? ¿Una democracia, una monarquía, una dictadura, un gobierno militar?**, etc. You might prepare ahead the names of the heads of state in these countries.
- Ask students to open their books and focus on the highlighted words in the text.
- Ask them to spell out the words while you write them on the board under the heading **Política**. Ask for volunteers to explain the meaning of the words.
- Have the students read quickly through the article and then read aloud in sections.

Activity 8

- Have the students read the statements and mark each as either true or false.
- When they have finished, they share their ideas with a partner.
- Ask for volunteers to give the correct answers.

Activity 9

- Ask for three students to volunteer to be candidates of their political party in the next mayoral elections. Select a team for each candidate to form political parties.
- Read the instructions and have the students write the rest of the speech in their groups, mentioning each of the topics in the box and using the expressions they have learned for making promises.
- Circulate around the room as they work offering assistance.
- When they have finished, have each candidate read their speech to the class, pretending to be a politician and exaggerating any gestures to make it more fun.
- Finally, have the students vote for the best speech and candidate.
- The winning speech can be put up on the classroom wall and the winner can become the class representative.

Extension

- Ask for a volunteer to come to the front and sit facing the rest of the class (unable to see the board).
- Write one of the words from the **Política** list in Activity 7 on the board.
- The other students attempt to define the word without saying it, until the first student guesses. He/she can ask questions such as: **¿Se mete en un sobre? ¿Se celebran cada cuatro años?**, etc.

ANSWERS

Activity 8
a. F; **b.** T; **c.** T; **d.** F; **e.** F.

SLOWER-PACED LEARNERS

After reading the article in Activity 7 together, elicit possible definitions of reñida. This will help students develop the ability to deduce meaning from context. Write their inferences on the board. Then have them find the definition in a dictionary and check their guesses. Finally, challenge them to write a new sentence with the word and share it with a partner.

HERITAGE LANGUAGE LEARNERS

Assign each student a Latin American country or let them pick one. Have students research and report back on its government, its main political leader and his/her title, the main political parties in the country, and one or two other details related to the country's government or politics that interest them. Have them prepare a poster with the information and present it to the class. Display the posters around the room.

GRAMÁTICA GRAMMAR IN CONTEXT

OBJECTIVES FOR GRAMÁTICA 1

- Present grammatical structures needed to practice communicative functions of the unit: The future tense of regular and irregular verbs
- Use the future tense to make predictions and talk about what will happen

CORE RESOURCES

- Interactive Online Materials - ELEteca

STANDARDS

1.1	Engage in conversation
1.2	Understand the language
1.3	Present information
4.1	Compare languages

INSTRUCTIONAL STRATEGIES

1. The Future Tense

- Write the following sentences on the board: **Te prometo que estaré allí a las ocho**, **Imagino que hablaré muy bien español**, **El próximo año estudiaré en la universidad**. Ask students to identify the sentence that expresses a promise, an assumption, and a future prediction. Then ask what they all have in common (use future tense).
- Walk students through the grammatical explanation in the book. Focus first on the regular forms. Point out that all verbs share the same endings and that all forms except **nosotros** have written accents on the last syllable.
- Provide practice by saying one of the verbs and asking students to say the correct future form of the person given. Say **hablar ➡ él** to elicit **hablará**.
- Focus attention next on the irregular verbs and point out that the endings are still the same, and it is the stem that is irregular. Review new verbs **caber** (to fit) and **valer** (to be worth).
- Again practice by saying an irregular verb and having the students say the correct future form for the person given.

Activity 1

- Have the students focus first on the verbs in parenthesis and say whether they are regular or irregular. If irregular they should give the correct stem for each.
- Have them read through the text and fill in the correct form of the future.
- Ask for volunteers to read the text aloud while you write the answers on the board, paying particular attention to accents.

Activity 2

- Look at the time expressions in the box with the students and have them provide examples using the future, such as: **Mañana vendré a clase pronto**.
- Have the students write the time expressions in the correct place on the timeline on the next page. Then ask them to compare answers with a partner.
- Ask for volunteers to say a sentence using an expression from the box and a verb in the future.

ANSWERS

Activity 1

Conocerás, será, Saldrán, querrá, dirás, Vendrás, tendrás, pedirás.

Activity 2

a. dentro de un rato; **b.** mañana; **c.** pasado mañana; **d.** el mes que viene; **e.** las próximas Navidades; **f.** el año que viene; **g.** dentro de dos años.

GRAMÁTICA

1. THE FUTURE TENSE

■ The future tense expresses what will happen. Regular verbs in the future tense are conjugated by adding the following endings to the infinitive form of the verb:

REGULAR VERBS			
	ESTUDIAR	COMER	VIVIR
yo	estudiaré	comeré	viviré
tú	estudiarás	comerás	vivirás
usted/él/ella	estudiará	comerá	vivirá
nosotros/as	estudiaremos	comeremos	viviremos
vosotros/as	estudiaréis	comeréis	viviréis
ustedes/ellos/ellas	estudiarán	comerán	vivirán

■ Irregular verbs in the future tense have irregular stems, but use the same endings as regular verbs.

IRREGULAR VERBS			
poder ➡ podr-			é
salir ➡ saldr-	tener ➡ tendr-		ás
caber ➡ cabr-	poner ➡ pondr-	hacer ➡ har-	á
haber ➡ habr-	venir ➡ vendr-	decir ➡ dir-	emos
saber ➡ sabr-	valer ➡ valdr-		éis
querer ➡ querr-			án

■ The future tense is often used with the following expressions of time:

- El año / el mes / la semana / la primavera **que viene**.
- **Dentro de** dos años / un rato / unos días.
- El / la **próximo/a** semana / mes / año.
- **Mañana / Pasado mañana**.

- **El año que viene** iré a España.
- **Dentro de** unos días vendrá a casa.
- **El próximo** año tendré 17 años.
- **Pasado mañana** tendré un examen.

1 Completa conjugando en futuro los verbos entre paréntesis. ¿Qué situación se describe?

Veo... que dentro de poco (conocer, tú) .... a una persona que (ser) .... muy importante para ti. (Salir, ustedes) .... juntos. Un día esta persona (querer) .... hacerte un regalo, pero tú le (decir) .... que no puedes aceptarlo. (Venir, tú) .... otra vez aquí porque (tener, tú) .... muchas dudas y me (pedir) .... consejo.

2 🗣 Ordena las siguientes expresiones en la línea de tiempo en la página siguiente. Empieza con la expresión más cercana al presente. Después, túrnate con tu compañero/a para decir qué harás en cada momento del futuro.

> el mes que viene ○ dentro de dos años ○ dentro de un rato ○ mañana
> pasado mañana ○ el año que viene ○ las próximas Navidades

ADVANCED LEARNERS

Put students into pairs. Using the expressions from Activity 2, have students write three sentences about their partners' future plans. Tell them to guess. Then have them share their sentences with their partners and find out if any of them are true or likely to be true.

2. SI + PRESENT + FUTURE

■ The sentence below describes an **action that depends on a certain condition** so that it can take place.
· **If I have** time (condition), **I will go** shopping. (action)

■ To talk about **future actions that depend on a condition**, in Spanish use:
Si + Present + Future
Si tengo tiempo, **iré** de compras.
Si no llueve, jugaremos al tenis. If it doesn't rain, we will play tennis.

3 Forma frases relacionando los elementos de las dos columnas.

1. Si el metro no funciona,
2. Si me invita a su cumpleaños,
3. Si me pongo enferma,
4. Si no nos vemos esta tarde,
5. Si piensas un poco,

a. te llamaré.
b. iré a pie.
c. no podré ir a la excursión.
d. sabrás la respuesta.
e. tendré que comprarle un regalo.

4 Completa el texto con los siguientes verbos.

castigan ○ llegaré ○ podré ○ vuelvo ○ veré ○ vemos ○ castigarán ○ salgo ○ aburriré

Si (a) .... la película de las 10 de la noche, (b) .... muy tarde a casa. Si (c) .... a llegar tarde, seguro que mis padres me (d) .... Si me (e) .... , no (f) .... salir el fin de semana con mis amigos. Si no (g) .... , no (h) .... a mis amigos y me (i) .... mucho.

5 Completa las siguientes frases con tu opinión. Después, habla de tus planes en grupos pequeños.
a. Si ...., daré la vuelta al mundo.
b. Si tengo suerte, ...
c. Si el sábado hace mal tiempo, ...
d. Si ...., aprenderé japonés.
f. Si me toca la lotería, ...

6 Escribe condiciones para conseguir estos propósitos.

estar en forma ○ ser feliz ○ ser rico ○ tener el mejor trabajo del mundo

Modelo: Si corro cada día, estaré en forma (be in shape).

MORE IN ELETECA: EXTRA ONLINE PRACTICE ● **GRAMMAR TUTORIALS** 1 AND 2   49

OBJECTIVES FOR GRAMÁTICA 2

• Present grammatical structures needed to practice communicative functions of the unit: **Si** + present + future
• Make predictions about what will happen under certain conditions

STANDARDS

1.1 Engage in conversation
1.5 Understand the language
1.6 Present information
4.1 Compare languages

INSTRUCTIONAL STRATEGIES

2. Si + Present + Future

• Walk the students through the explanation in the book. Point out that **si** is followed by the present tense and refers to the condition that needs to be met. The future tense refers to what will happen, just as in English.

Activity 3

• Have the students look at the sentences and find the correct ending for each.
• Ask them to share their answers with a partner. Then call on students to read out the answers.

Activity 4

• Have the students look at the image and say who they think the two people are and how they feel. Have them read quickly through the sentences to get a general idea.
• Then tell students to choose a verb from the list to fill each blank.
• Ask them to share their answers with a partner to see if they agree. Review correct answers.

Activity 5

• Have the students complete the sentences expressing their opinion.
• Circulate around the room as they work, checking that they are using the correct grammatical structure and providing assistance where required.
• When they have finished, ask them to sit in small groups to share their ideas. Ask some groups to share their ideas with the class.

Activity 6

• Tell students to create at least one sentence for each expression given. Ask for volunteers to read some of their ideas to the class.
• Tell the students they are going to link their sentences, with each person saying the next idea. Say: **Si quiero hablar español...** and invite a student to say: **Si quiero hablar español, tendré que estudiar mucho**. The next student takes the end of the last sentence and begins: **Si tengo que estudiar mucho, no podré salir con**..., etc. Continue round the room so that all the students can practice.

ANSWERS

Activity 3
1. b.; **2.** e; **3.** c; **4.** a; **5.** d.

Activity 4
a. vemos; **b.** llegaré; **c.** vuelvo; **d.** castigarán; **e.** castigan; **f.** podré; **g.** salgo; **h.** veré; **i.** aburriré.

SLOWER-PACED LEARNERS

Before students write their own sentences in Activity 6, you may want to elicit ideas from the class about the different ways to achieve each goal and take notes on the board. Then have students to write at least two sentences for each goal.

HERITAGE LANGUAGE LEARNERS

Have students do research on someone who is running for political office in a Spanish-speaking country or community. Using the structure of **Si** + present + future, tell students to report back to the class about two or three things that the candidate will do if he/she wins the election.

OBJECTIVES FOR DESTREZAS

- Scan for specific information
- Organize information in a logical order

STANDARDS

1.1 Interpersonal communication
1.2 Understand the language
1.3 Present information

Note

The design of the activities in this section is meant to simulate standardized testing formats students may encounter as part of international testing certificates as the DELE (*Diploma de Español como Lengua Extranjera*) or in preparation for other state and / or national assessments. For this reason, it is recommended you do not pre-teach any of the vocabulary. In addition, students should complete the tasks individually.

INSTRUCTIONAL STRATEGIES

Comprensión de lectura

Activity 1

- Have the students look at the images and use them to predict what the email is going to be about.
- Talk the students through the strategy, and have them read through the questions at the end. Have them write key words in the box.

Activity 2

- Ask the students to read the text and choose the best way to complete each statement.
- Ask for volunteers to say the correct answers.

ANSWERS

Activity 2

1. c; **2.** c; **3.** a; **4.** b; **5.** a.

SLOWER-PACED LEARNERS

If you think students will struggle with Activity 2, you can remove one of the possible answer choices for each question.

ADVANCED LEARNERS

For additional creative writing practice, have students write an email response to Teo from Luis.

DESTREZAS

COMPRENSIÓN DE LECTURA

1 Antes de leer el texto, repasa la estrategia en Destrezas y sigue las recomendaciones.

Destrezas

Scanning for specific information

Use the comprehension questions at the end of the activity to help you decide what information to search for as you read.

List some key words or phrases you should focus your attention on.

2 Lee el texto y elige la respuesta correcta.

1. Teo escribe un correo sobre…
   a. sus últimas vacaciones.
   b. sus exámenes.
   c. sus próximas vacaciones.

2. Teo tiene información sobre la isla…
   a. por sus amigos.
   b. porque se la ha dado Luis.
   c. porque se lo han contado y por Internet.

3. Teo pide información sobre…
   a. playas y alojamiento.
   b. playas y gastronomía.
   c. playas, gastronomía y alojamiento.

4. En el correo, Teo…
   a. solo pide información a su amigo.
   b. pide información a su amigo y le propone hacer actividades juntos.
   c. solo le propone a su amigo hacer actividades juntos.

5. Teo quiere practicar…

a.   b.   c.

Asunto: Mi viaje a Los Ángeles
De: teo@gmail.com   Para: luis@hotmail.com

Hola, Luis:

¿Qué tal va todo? Me imagino que seguirás de exámenes. ¡Con lo estudioso que eres, seguro que sacas unas notas increíbles!

Te escribo para decirte que el mes que viene tendré unos días de vacaciones y quiero ir a Los Ángeles. Supongo que estarás allí y que podremos hacer muchas cosas juntos. Por cierto, pienso llevarme mi tabla de surf. Me han dicho que allí hay unas olas fantásticas, ¿me puedes dar alguna información sobre las playas? También quiero ir un día a la isla Santa Catalina. He leído en Internet que es muy bonita y que se puede ir a ver delfines. ¿Vendrás conmigo? Me imagino que tú sabrás dónde están los botes que te llevan hasta allí. Por cierto, ¿conoces algún lugar para ir de acampada? Como ves, no pienso parar ni un solo día. Y por la tarde, supongo que me enseñarás los lugares donde va la gente joven…

¡Espero tu correo! Un abrazo,

Teo

50

Next Page

INSTRUCTIONAL STRATEGIES

Expresión e interacción escritas

Activity 3

- Read the information in the **Destrezas** box with the students and have them make their own notes, based on the information provided.
- Tell students to organize their ideas in logical order.

Activity 4

- Students write their email using the notes they made earlier. They should include all the information provided in the **Destrezas** box as well as their own ideas.
- Circulate around the room as they work, answering questions and providing assistance where required.
- Ask for volunteers to read their email to the class.
- The completed emails can be mounted for display on the classroom walls.

EXPRESIÓN E INTERACCIÓN ESCRITAS

3 Quieres pasar unos días en un parque nacional y necesitas información sobre qué se ofrece allí. Antes de empezar a escribir, lee la estrategia en Destrezas y sigue la sugerencia.

Destrezas

Organizing your information in a logical order
Think about the information you need and prepare your questions. Include the specific vocabulary you will need.
Information: availability for dates you want, access to pools and sports facilities included in price, pets allowed.
Vocabulary: plazas libres, wi-fi, restaurante, luz eléctrica…

4 Escribe tu email al camping para pedir la información.

PRONUNCIACIÓN La acentuación

As you know, all words in Spanish have a syllable that is pronounced with more stress than the other syllables in the word, and in some cases, a written accent is needed to identify the stressed syllable.

1 🎧 6 Escucha las siguientes palabras y subraya la sílaba en la que recae el acento en cada una de ellas.

• cuéntamelo	• historia	• ciudad	• lápiz	• aquí
• corazón	• carácter	• después	• verano	• rápido
• sábado	• música	• dáselo	• maravilla	• político
• pensar	• cómic	• devuélvemelo	• jardín	• casa
• salió	• fábrica	• gracias	• dímelo	• envíanoslas
• joven	• canción	• palo	• dificil	• genial

2 Ahora, clasifica las palabras de la Actividad 1 según la sílaba tónica.

• Palabras **agudas** ☐☐☐   • Palabras **esdrújulas** ☐☐☐

• Palabras **llanas** difícil ☐☑☐   • Palabras **sobreesdrújulas** ☑☐☐☐

3 Observa las palabras que tienen tilde (*written accent*) y completa las reglas de acentuación.
a. Las palabras agudas se acentúan cuando terminan en ...., ... o ....
b. Las palabras llanas se acentúan cuando terminan en una consonante distinta de .... o ....
c. Las palabras esdrújulas o sobreesdrújulas se acentúan ....
d. Recuerda que las palabras **qué**, **cómo**, **dónde**, **cuándo** y **cuánto** tienen tilde solamente en las frases .... y .... Por ejemplo: ¿De dónde eres? ¡Qué calor!

MORE IN ELETECA: EXTRA ONLINE PRACTICE

51

OBJECTIVES FOR PRONUNCIACIÓN

• Practice separating syllables and using stress correctly

CORE RESOURCES

• Audio Program: Track 6
• Interactive Online Materials - ELEteca

STANDARDS

1.2   Understand the language
3.2   Acquire information
4.1   Compare languages

INSTRUCTIONAL STRATEGIES

• Walk the students through the explanation and give them an example, such as **teléfono**. Have them clap or tap out the word on their desks, tapping louder on the stressed syllable.
• Do the same with a few more words to practice, for instance: **reciclaje**, **prometemos**, **escribiré**, etc.
• Point out that words that carry an accent are stressed on that syllable.

🎧 **6 Activity 1**

• Play the audio and have the students listen and repeat, raising their hand as they hear / say the stressed syllable.
• Repeat the audio and have the students underline the syllable in the word that carries the main stress.
• Ask random students to say each word and clap or tap out the syllables, indicating which syllable carries the main stress.

Activity 2

• Have students look at the four types of words in the activity. Tell students to clap or tap out the syllables for each type as indicated by the blanks and accents. Begin with the example: **difícil**.
• Have the students classify the words from Activity 1 according to where the stress falls as indicated by the white boxes that follow
• When they have finished, have them compare their answers with a partner.
• Ask individual students to give the correct answers.

Activity 3

• Have the students focus on the words that carry an accent.
• Students complete the rules for accents, referring back to the previous activities.
• Ask for volunteers to read the rules.

ANSWERS

Activity 1

Cuéntamelo, his**tor**ia, ciu**dad**, **lá**piz, a**quí**, cora**zón**, ca**rác**ter, des**pués**, ve**ra**no, **rá**pido, **sá**bado, **mú**sica, **dá**selo, mara**vi**lla, po**lí**tico, pen**sar**, **có**mic, de**vuél**vemelo, jar**dín**, **ca**sa, sa**lió**, **fá**brica, **gra**cias, **dí**melo, en**ví**anoslas, **jo**ven, can**ción**, **pa**lo, di**fí**cil, ge**nial**.

Activity 2

Agudas: corazón, pensar, salió, canción, ciudad, después, jardín, aquí, genial; **Llanas:** joven, historia, carácter, cómic, gracias, palo, lápiz, verano, maravilla, difícil, casa; **Esdrújulas:** sábado, música, fábrica, dáselo, dímelo, rápido, político; **Sobreesdrújulas:** cuéntamelo, devuélvemelo, envíanoslas.

Activity 3

a. *n*, *s* o vocal; **b.** *n* o *s*; **c.** siempre; **d.** interrogativas y exclamativas.

HERITAGE LANGUAGE LEARNERS

After the pronunciation activities, challenge students to find a poem written in Spanish that has a rhyming pattern. Have them identify whether the rhymes appear in **palabras llanas, agudas, esdrújulas,** or **sobreesdrújulas**. For example, in the poem "**Hombres necios**" by Sor Juana Ines de la Cruz, a Mexican nun who wrote during the Baroque period in the 17th century, there are verses with rhymes in both **palabras llanas** and **palabras agudas**. Some other poets you might invite students to investigate are Garcilaso de la Vega, Luis de Góngora, Francisco de Quevedo, Gertudis Gómez de Avellaneda, Gabriela Mistral, and Rubén Darío. You may invite them to prepare additional information about the poet and the poem as well.

OBJECTIVES FOR SABOR HISPANO
- Learn about Spanish national parks
- Activate vocabulary connected with the environment

CORE RESOURCES
- Audio Program: Track 7

STANDARDS
2.1   Culture: practices and perspectives
2.2   Products and perspectives
3.2   Acquire information
5.2   Using language for personal enjoyment and enrichment

INSTRUCTIONAL STRATEGIES

 7

- Introduce the topic by asking if the students know what a national park is and to explain what it means.
- Look at the images with them and elicit what they already know and can share.
- Have them look at the questions in **Antes de leer** and discuss them.
- Tell students to skim the reading and find different explanations of what a national park is and is not.
- Tell the students to look at the **Glosario** on the next page to help them with any vocabulary they may not know.
- Read the first section of the text and invite a volunteer to read after you. After each section, ask questions such as: ***¿Dónde está el volcán más grande del mundo? ¿Cómo se llama?***, etc.
- Ask what the students have understood and invite those who understood more to help those who understood less.
- You can also play the audio while students follow along with the text.

SLOWER-PACED LEARNERS

Working in groups, have them make a collage of at least seven images from one of the national parks in Spain. Encourage them to add captions to at least four of the images. Display the collages around the room.

SABOR HISPANO

¡BIENVENIDOS A LOS PARQUES

Parque Nacional del Teide, Tenerife, Islas Canarias

NACIONALES DE ESPAÑA!

Antes de leer
¿Hay parques nacionales en tu país?
¿Has visitado alguno?
¿Qué características tienen estos parques?

 7 **Naturaleza espectacular, flora única y fauna salvaje***. Estos son algunos de los elementos de los parques nacionales. ¡Visítalos!**

«Es nuestro mayor tesoro*», dice Humberto Gutiérrez, Jefe de Medioambiente de Tenerife, «el Parque Nacional del Teide es el que recibe más visitas de toda Europa y el segundo del mundo. Además, en él está el volcán más grande del mundo». El Parque Nacional del Teide, en las islas Canarias, España, es uno de los 15 parques nacionales de este país.

Los parques nacionales se caracterizan por su impresionante naturaleza y su fauna. A menudo están formados por cordilleras o montañas, volcanes, lagos, desiertos, cascadas*, bosques, rocas, barrancos*, calderas* o glaciares.

«No es suficiente con tener hectáreas de terreno. Para que una extensión sea declarada Parque Nacional, esta debe tener una belleza, fauna y flora especiales. El gobierno de un país la acota* y protege para que no se construya en ella», dicen desde el Ministerio de Agricultura, Alimentación y Medioambiente de España.

Otros parques nacionales importantes son el Parque Nacional de Doñana, el Parque Nacional de Sierra Nevada, el Parque Nacional Marítimo-Terrestre del Archipiélago de Cabrera y el Parque Nacional de los Picos de Europa.

Muchos de estos parques han sido declarados Patrimonio de la Humanidad por la UNESCO.

Parque Nacional de Ordesa y Monte Perdido, Aragón

52

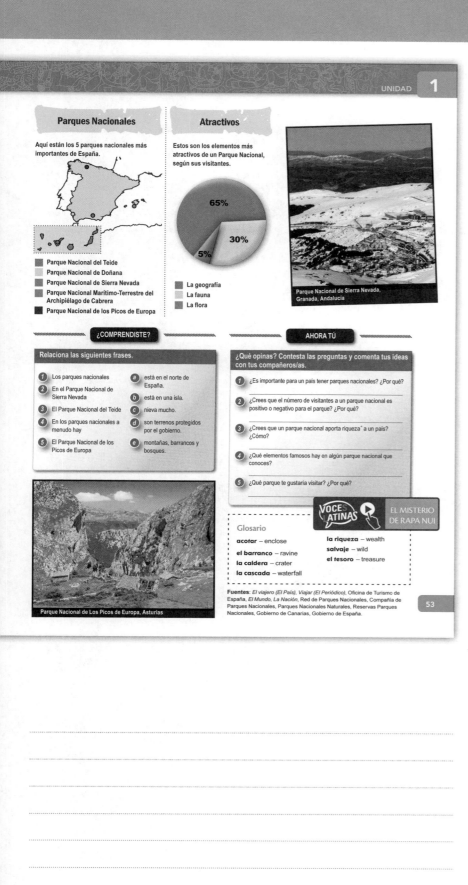

Parques Nacionales

Aquí están los 5 parques nacionales más importantes de España.

- ■ Parque Nacional del Teide
- ■ Parque Nacional de Doñana
- ■ Parque Nacional de Sierra Nevada
- ■ Parque Nacional Marítimo-Terrestre del Archipiélago de Cabrera
- ■ Parque Nacional de los Picos de Europa

Atractivos

Estos son los elementos más atractivos de un Parque Nacional, según sus visitantes.

65%
30%
5%

- ■ La geografía
- ■ La fauna
- ■ La flora

Parque Nacional de Sierra Nevada, Granada, Andalucía

¿COMPRENDISTE?

Relaciona las siguientes frases.

1. Los parques nacionales
2. En el Parque Nacional de Sierra Nevada
3. El Parque Nacional del Teide
4. En los parques nacionales a menudo hay
5. El Parque Nacional de los Picos de Europa

a. está en el norte de España.
b. está en una isla.
c. nieva mucho.
d. son terrenos protegidos por el gobierno.
e. montañas, barrancos y bosques.

AHORA TÚ

¿Qué opinas? Contesta las preguntas y comenta tus ideas con tus compañeros/as.

1. ¿Es importante para un país tener parques nacionales? ¿Por qué?
2. ¿Crees que el número de visitantes a un parque nacional es positivo o negativo para el parque? ¿Por qué?
3. ¿Crees que un parque nacional aporta riqueza* a un país? ¿Cómo?
4. ¿Qué elementos famosos hay en algún parque nacional que conoces?
5. ¿Qué parque te gustaría visitar? ¿Por qué?

VOCES LATINAS ▶ EL MISTERIO DE RAPA NUI

Glosario

acotar – enclose
el barranco – ravine
la caldera – crater
la cascada – waterfall
la riqueza – wealth
salvaje – wild
el tesoro – treasure

Fuentes: *El viajero (El País)*, *Viajar (El Periódico)*, Oficina de Turismo de España, *El Mundo*, *La Nación*, Red de Parques Nacionales, Compañía de Parques Nacionales, Parques Nacionales Naturales, Reservas Parques Nacionales, Gobierno de Canarias, Gobierno de España.

Parque Nacional de Los Picos de Europa, Asturias

53

INSTRUCTIONAL STRATEGIES

Call on students to interpret the information presented in the graphs and make statements about what they see.

Parques Nacionales

Ask questions about their location according to the map.

Atractivos

Have students make comparisons using the information in the pie chart. For example, ***A los visitantes les atrae más la geografía de los parques nacionales que la flora*** and so on.

¿Comprendiste?

- Have the students read the statements in the box and match the two parts of the sentences. Then have them check through the text to see if they are correct.
- Have them compare their answers with a partner.
- Invite individual students to share their answers with the class.

Ahora tú

- Read the questions with the students and have them think about the answers.
- Have the students answer the questions in pairs or small groups and then ask for volunteers to present to the class.

Extension

- Have the students make a list of the national parks in other Latin American countries (using the Internet).
- Divide the students into groups and have each group research one of the parks.
- Ask them to write a short article about the park and illustrate it with images from the Internet or from travel brochures.
- Invite each group to present their park to the class.
- The completed work can be mounted and displayed on the classroom walls.

ANSWERS

¿Comprendiste?

1. d; **2.** c; **3.** b; **4.** e; **5.** a.

ADVANCED LEARNERS

Have students prepare a presentation with a visual aid about one of the national parks in Spain besides ***el Parque Nacional del Teide***. Tell them to include information about its location, geography, flora, fauna, and visitors. Their visual aid should include at least three pictures of the park.

HERITAGE LANGUAGE LEARNERS

Tell students to design a travel brochure for a national park in Spain or elsewhere in Latin America. They should investigate travel costs, entrance fees, camping or lodging expenses, necessary clothing and equipment, and the ideal amount of days to visit. They should also write an itinerary with a detailed list of activities to do for each day recommended to visit the park. Have students present their travel brochures to the class.

OBJECTIVES FOR RELATO

- Revisit unit themes, grammar, vocabulary and culture in a new context
- Improve reading comprehension skills

CORE RESOURCES

- Audio Program: Track 8

STANDARDS

1.1 Engage in conversation
1.2 Understand the language
1.3 Present information
2.1 Practices and perspectives
5.3 Using language for personal enjoyment and enrichment

INSTRUCTIONAL STRATEGIES

Activity 1

- Have the students look at the image and title and guess what they think the text will be about.
- Ask them what changes they think may occur in the future, in 20 years, 100 years, for example.
- With a partner, have them look at the vocabulary and definitions and match them.
- Ask for volunteers to share their ideas with the class.

🎧 8 Activity 2

- Have the students look through the text to find and underline the words in Activity 1.
- Play the audio while the students follow in their books.
- Ask questions such as: **¿Alberto se sentó a la mesa? ¿Qué premio ha recibido la persona que da la entrevista?**, etc.
- Have those students who understood more help those who understood less.

ANSWERS

Activity 1

1. c; **2.** d; **3.** a; **4.** b.

HERITAGE LANGUAGE LEARNERS

In Latin American literature, there's a rich tradition of mixing elements of fantasy and reality, just as is done in this story. Encourage students to find out the **Vanguardista** movement, the "Boom", and the development of the genre **realismo mágico** in Latin American literature. Some authors from these periods that they might research include María Luisa Bombal and José Donoso (Chile), Juan Rulfo and Carlos Fuentes (Mexico), Guillermo Cabrera Infante and Severo Sarduy (Cuba), Julio Cortázar and Jorge Luis Borges (Argentina), Mario Vargas Llosa (Peru), Juan Carlos Onetti (Uruguay), and Gabriel García Márquez (Colombia). You might challenge students to present some brief biographical information about the author, some background about the historical context in which he or she wrote, and a brief description of his or her style or genre. Ideally, students will also provide an example of the author's work that includes a mix of fantasy and reality, such as the short story "La noche boca arriba" by Julio Cortázar or the novel *Cien años de soledad* by Gabriel García Márquez.

RELATO Viaje al futuro

1 Relaciona las siguientes expresiones con su definición correspondiente.

1. efecto invernadero
2. combustibles fósiles
3. vertedero
4. sensores

a. Lugar para depositar los residuos y la basura de una zona o ciudad.
b. Dispositivos que detectan una acción externa como la temperatura o la presión y que transmiten la información.
c. Calentamiento del planeta provocado por diversos gases.
d. Lo son el carbón, el petróleo y el gas natural.

2 🎧 8 **Lee el siguiente relato. Para ayudarte a comprenderlo, subraya antes las palabras de la Actividad 1 que aparecen en él.**

Viaje al futuro

Alberto llegó de la escuela, comió, encendió la tele, agarró el mando a distancia (*remote control*) y se tumbó en el sofá. ¡ZAP!

—Si quiere disfrutar de unas vacaciones de ensueño, Florida es su destino. ¡ZAP!

—Siempre te querré a ti, mi amor. ¡ZAP!

—Quiero hacerle una pregunta; usted, al recibir el Premio Nobel de Energía afirmó que el futuro que nos espera es mucho más negro de lo que pensamos —interesante, pensó Alberto.

—Sí, efectivamente. Las grandes ciudades del futuro provocarán el efecto invernadero y una megapolución si no hacemos algo. Habrá tanta superpoblación que tendremos que cultivar en grandes huertos urbanos para alimentarnos. Para no terminar con los combustibles fósiles, tendremos que reducir el número de carros y los kilómetros recorridos por los aviones. Habrá islas-vertedero para eliminar los residuos (*waste*). Se tendrá que ahorrar energía utilizando los elementos de la naturaleza como el sol, el viento o la lluvia. ¡ZAP!

—Buenos días, les presento a William Mitchell, del Instituto Tecnológico de Massachusetts. ¿Cómo piensa usted que serán las ciudades del futuro?

—Bueno, yo pienso que estarán diseñadas como organismos vivos, con inteligencia propia. Las calles y edificios tendrán luces inteligentes que cambiarán de color e intensidad dependiendo de la hora del día. Tanto dentro como fuera de la casa, habrá sensores que nos informarán de todo lo que sucede (*takes place*), como, por ejemplo, tener información de los edificios o monumentos de una ciudad solo con enfocarlos con un celular. ¡ZAP!

—Necesito montar en una nave para teletransportarme en una milésima de segundo a mi planeta, si no, se cerrarán los accesos y no podré entrar. ¡¡Necesito ayuda!! —gritó Alberto.

—Despierta, hijo. Has tenido una pesadilla.

Alberto miró primero a su madre, luego a su alrededor, y se sintió feliz de encontrarse en el siglo XXI.

3 👥 **Contesta las siguientes preguntas. Trabaja con tu compañero/a.**

a. ¿Qué cuenta el relato?
  - ☐ Un día en la vida de Alberto.
  - ☐ Un sueño.
  - ☐ Un viaje al futuro.

b. ¿Cuántos canales diferentes de televisión ve Alberto?

c. ¿Cuál de las visiones sobre el futuro te parece más optimista: la del primer científico o la del segundo?

d. ¿Cuál te parece más realista?

e. ¿Con cuál de los dos estás más de acuerdo?

f. ¿Por qué crees que Alberto se alegra cuando su madre lo despierta?

4 **Imagina cómo será la vida dentro de 100 años y escríbelo.**

Alimentación: ....

Vivienda: ....

Educación: ....

Transporte: ....

Trabajo: ....

Energías: ....

Familia: ....

Salud / Enfermedades: ....

5 👥 **Compara tu visión del futuro con la de tu compañero/a. ¿Comparten la misma visión?**

6 **Lee la siguiente frase: "Piensa globalmente, actúa localmente." ¿Qué crees que significa? Piensa en lo que puedes hacer para evitar un futuro negro.**

> **"Piensa globalmente, actúa localmente"**
>
> Prometo...
> - que intentaré no malgastar el papel que utilizo en clase y lo reciclaré.

INSTRUCTIONAL STRATEGIES

Activity 3

- Ask the students to answer the questions about the text without referring to the text.
- Have them compare their answers with a partner and check in the text.
- Ask different students to say the correct answers aloud.

Activity 4

- Ask students to look at the headings and write one sentence for each.
- Remind them to use the future tense.
- Have them share their sentences with a partner.
- Invite students to read one of their sentences to the class.
- Have the class make a poster for each heading and write their sentences on the posters.

Activity 5

Have the students discuss their ideas about the future with their partner and find out how much they agree or disagree.

Activity 6

- Read the quotation and ask the students what they think it means.
- Ask them to discuss the quotation in small groups and make a list of ideas of what they can do to help create a better future, following the model provided.
- Circulate around the room as they work, providing assistance where necessary.
- Have different groups present their ideas to the class.
- Students may vote for the best proposals.

ANSWERS

Activity 3

a. un sueño; **b.** 4; **c, d, e, f:** Answers will vary.

SLOWER-PACED LEARNERS

Before students write sentences in Activity 4, you may want to elicit and briefly review how to conjugate verbs in the future form. Write the forms on the board for easy reference. Consider allowing students to work with a partner to come up with these sentences, too. Alternatively, elicit some suggestions from the class first or make some of your own sentences so students have a few ideas to get them started.

ADVANCED LEARNERS

Using their ideas from Activity 4, have students imagine that someone from this point in history visits them in the future 100 years from now. They can write a dialogue, create a short story, or make a video about the interaction between them and their visitors.

OBJECTIVES FOR EVALUACIÓN

- Review grammar, vocabulary and culture from the unit
- Complete self-assessment

CORE RESOURCES

- Extension Activities: EA 1.3
- Interactive Online Materials - ELEteca

STANDARDS

1.2 Understand the language
2.1 Practices and perspectives
4.1 Compare cultures

INSTRUCTIONAL STRATEGIES

- Activities can be completed individually and then reviewed with the class. Vary by asking students if they agree with the answer given and then writing it on the board. Provide explanations as needed.
- You may wish to assign point value to each activity as a way for students to monitor their progress.
- Direct students to the indicated pages in **En resumen** if they make more than one or two mistakes in any one section.

Extension

- For additional practice with the forms of the irregular future, use EA 1.3, **Memory del futuro irregular** to play a memory game.
- Have students cut up the cards or have them ready ahead of time. Put students in groups of 4 and give each group a set of cards. Ask them to put all the cards face down but keep infinitive cards separate from conjugated forms. The first student draws an infinitive card and gives the correct **yo** form of the verb. He/she then picks a card from the conjugated side to find the match. The player with the most matched pairs wins.

ANSWERS

Activity 1

a. A; **b.** P; **c.** A; **d.** P; **e.** P; **f.** A.

Activity 2

a. tendré; **b.** cabrá; **c.** podrán; **d.** sabrán; **e.** vendremos; **f.** irán; **g.** saldrá; **h.** valdrán; **i.** seré; **j.** habrá; **k.** pondrás; **l.** harán; **m.** diré; **n.** querrás.

Activity 3

f, a, d, c, b, e.

Activity 4

a. va, iré; **b.** Llegaremos, perdemos **c.** llama, llamaré; **d.** Iré, vas.

EVALUACIÓN

MAKING ASSUMPTIONS AND PROMISES

1 Lee las frases e indica si son conjeturas (C) o promesas (P).

	C	P
a. Me imagino que mañana tendré que ir a hacer la compra.	☐	☐
b. Te prometo que no lo volveré a hacer.	☐	☐
c. Me imagino que no irá a la fiesta.	☐	☐
d. Mañana te traeré el libro sin falta.	☐	☐
e. Te juro que no lo contaré.	☐	☐
f. Supongo que esta tarde cenaremos en casa de Juan.	☐	☐

THE FUTURE TENSE

2 Escribe los siguientes verbos en el futuro.

a. Tener, yo ....
b. Caber, ella/él ....
c. Poder, Uds. ....
d. Saber, ellos ....
e. Venir, nosotros ....
f. Ir, Uds. ....
g. Salir, usted ....

h. Valer, ellos/ellas ....
i. Ser, yo ....
j. Haber, él/ella ....
k. Poner, tú ....
l. Hacer, Uds. ....
m. Decir, yo ....
n. Querer, tú ....

3 Ordena estas expresiones de más a menos cercanas en el futuro y escribe una frase con cada una.

a. ☐ Pasado mañana ....
b. ☐ El año que viene ....
c. ☐ El próximo verano ....
d. ☐ Dentro de poco ....
e. ☐ Dentro de 10 años ....
f. ☐ Mañana ....

SI + PRESENT + FUTURE

4 Completa las frases con el verbo entre paréntesis en el tiempo correspondiente.

a. Si todo (ir) .... bien, dentro de dos años (ir, yo) .... a la universidad.
b. (Llegar, nosotros) .... tarde si (perder, nosotros) .... el autobús.
c. Si no me (llamar) .... Juan, lo (llamar, yo) ....
d. (Ir, yo) .... a la fiesta si tú (ir) ....

EL MEDIOAMBIENTE Y LA POLÍTICA

5 **Completa el texto con las siguientes palabras.**

> sequía ○ deforestación ○ consumo responsable ○ energías renovables ○
> calentamiento global ○ contaminación ○ deshielo

a. Si no llueve, habrá ....
b. El .... del planeta está provocando el .... de los polos.
c. Los países deberían apostar por las .... y el .... para reducir la ....
d. Si no detenemos la ...., nos quedaremos sin selva.

6 **Completa las frases con las palabras entre paréntesis.**

a. Antes de ...., ... políticos presentan .... para dar a conocer sus proyectos. (los partidos, su programa, las elecciones)
b. Hasta que no se cuentan .... no se puede saber qué .... ha conseguido .... (candidato, la victoria, todos los votos)

WORD STRESS

7 **Encuentra el intruso y explica en qué se diferencia.**

a. café / amor / mesa / ratón / color ....
b. médico / fábula / manzana / sábado / fábrica ....
c. Jesús / comí / camión / reloj / salón ....
d. árbol / cárcel / mesa / cosa / azul ....
e. quien / que / como / cuesta / donde ....
f. dímelo / cuéntaselo / mecánica / recíbelo ....

CULTURA

8 **Contesta las preguntas según la información que has aprendido en** *¡Bienvenidos a los parques nacionales de España!*

a. ¿Qué aspectos necesitan tener los parques para clasificarlos como parques nacionales?
b. ¿Cuáles son los parques nacionales más importantes de España y dónde están?
c. Según los visitantes de los parques, ¿cuáles son los elementos más atractivos? ¿Y para ti?
d. ¿Cómo son los parques nacionales de tu estado? ¿Qué puedes hacer allí?

MORE IN ELETECA: EXTRA ONLINE PRACTICE

Activity 5
a. sequía; **b.** calentamiento global, deshielo; **c.** energías renovables, consumo responsable, contaminación; **d.** deforestación.

Activity 6
a. las elecciones, los partidos, su programa; **b.** todos los votos, candidato, la victoria.

Activity 7
a. mesa – llana entre agudas; **b.** manzana – llana entre esdrújulas; **c.** reloj – aguda sin tilde; **d.** azul – aguda entre llanas; **e.** cuesta – verbo entre pronombres interrogativos; **f.** cuéntaselo – sobreesdrújula entre esdrújulas.

Activity 8
Answers will vary. Possible answers include: **a.** Necesitan poseer una belleza, fauna y flora especiales además de una naturaleza impresionante; **b.** El Parque Nacional de Doñana que está en Huelva y Sevilla (Andalucía); el Parque Nacional de Sierra Nevada que está en Granada (Andalucía); el Parque Nacional Marítimo-Terrestre del Archipiélago de Cabrera que está en las Islas Baleares; el Parque Nacional de los Picos de Europa que está en Asturias; el Parque Nacional del Teide que está en la isla de Tenerife (islas Canarias); **c.** La geografía; **d.** Answers will vary.

Objectives for En resumen: Vocabulario
- Review unit vocabulary and expressions
- Practice communicative skills

Standards
1.2 Understand the language
1.3 Present information
4.1 Evaluate similarities and differences in language

Instructional strategies
- Encourage students to use self-adhesive notes to place on correct objects in their house.
- Index cards can be used as flashcards with the Spanish term on one side and the English term on the other, or a picture or drawing.
- Students work in pairs or groups, using vocabulary flashcards as they would the cards of a board game to help each other practice unit vocabulary.
- Encourage students to write labels or captions for the photos on this page. Remind them to use the vocabulary and expressions they have learned in this unit.
- Have students participate in an online scavenger hunt to find news articles in Spanish that use the vocabulary related to the environment and politics in context. Give points to students or teams who can find the most words in the shortest amount of time.

EN RESUMEN: Vocabulario

Verbos
aburrirse *to be bored*

aprobar *to pass (a test, a course)*
caber *to fit*
castigar *to punish*

dar igual *to care less*
diseñar *to design*
eliminar *to eliminate*
estar en forma *to be in shape*
prometer *to promise*

quedarse *to stay*
valer *to be worth*

Expresiones temporales
dentro de…. (periodo de tiempo) *within a (period of time)*
dentro de un rato *in a moment*
el mes que viene *next month*
pasado mañana *day after tomorrow*

Hacer conjeturas y promesas
Creo que… *I believe that…*
Lo haré sin falta. *I'll be sure to do it.*

Me imagino que… *I imagine that…*
¡Prometido! *Promised!*
Supongo que… *I guess that…*
Te juro que… *I promise you that…*
Te prometo que… *I promise you that…*
Te doy mi palabra. *I give you my word.*

El medioambiente
la basura *garbage*

el calentamiento global *global warming*

la climatización *heating and cooling systems*

los combustibles fósiles *fossil fuels*
consumir *to consume*
la contaminación *pollution*

la deforestación *deforestation*

los desechos *trash, waste*
el deshielo *melting*
el efecto invernadero *greenhouse effect*
la energía renovable *renewable energy*
malgastar *to waste*
reciclar *to recycle*
los recursos naturales *natural resources*
reducir *to reduce*
reutilizar *to reuse*
la sequía *drought*

el transporte ecológico *ecologically friendly transportation*
el vertedero *dumping site*

La política
el alcalde *mayor*
la campaña *campaign*
el candidato *candidate*
las elecciones *elections*
el partido político *political party*
el presidente *president*
el programa *platform*
la reforma *reform*
el voto *vote*

EN RESUMEN: Gramática

MAKING PROMISES

(See page 40)

- **Te prometo que**…
- **Te lo prometo / juro.**
- **Te doy mi palabra.**
- **Te juro que**…
- **¡Prometido!**
- **Lo haré sin falta.**

THE FUTURE TENSE

(See page 48)

- The future tense expresses what will happen. Regular verbs in the future tense are conjugated by adding the following endings to the infinitive form of the verb: **-é, -ás, -á, -emos, -éis, -án.**

	ESTUDIAR	COMER	VIVIR
yo	estudiar**é**	comer**é**	vivir**é**
tú	estudiar**ás**	comer**ás**	vivir**ás**
usted/él/ella	estudiar**á**	comer**á**	vivir**á**
nosotros/as	estudiar**emos**	comer**emos**	vivir**emos**
vosotros/as	estudiar**éis**	comer**éis**	vivir**éis**
ustedes/ellos/ellas	estudiar**án**	comer**án**	vivir**án**

- There are twelve common verbs that are irregular in the future tense. Their endings are regular, but their stems change.

IRREGULAR VERBS			
poder ➡ **podr-**			**é**
salir ➡ **saldr-**	tener ➡ **tendr-**		**ás**
caber ➡ **cabr-**	poner ➡ **pondr-**	hacer ➡ **har-**	**á**
haber ➡ **habr-**	venir ➡ **vendr-**	decir ➡ **dir-**	**emos**
saber ➡ **sabr-**	valer ➡ **valdr-**		**éis**
querer ➡ **querr-**			**án**

- The future tense is often used with the following expressions of time:

- El año / mes / la semana / primavera **que viene** *El año que viene iré a España.*
- **Dentro de** dos años / un rato / unos días *Dentro de unos días vendrá a casa.*
- El/la **próximo/a** semana / mes / año *El próximo año tendré 17 años.*
- **Mañana / Pasado mañana** *Pasado mañana tendré un examen.*

SI + PRESENT + FUTURE

(See page 49)

To talk about **future actions that depend on a condition**, use the following:

- **Si** + **present** + **future**
  Si   *no llueve,*   *iremos a la playa.*

OBJECTIVES FOR EN RESUMEN: GRAMÁTICA

- Review unit grammar
- Practice communication skills

STANDARDS

1.2   Understand the language

1.3   Present information

INSTRUCTIONAL STRATEGIES

- Model how to review grammar.
- Have the students review the Learning Outcomes in the unit opener to assess whether they feel they have mastered the main ideas and skills.
- Ask them if they can remember additional examples for each grammar topic.
- Model how to find and go back to the appropriate page in the unit to review any grammar topic they may need help with.
- Invite students to review the grammar activities they completed in this unit.
- Ask them what grammar activities they found easy and which they found challenging. Encourage them to rework any activities they found particularly challenging.
- Make sure that students have done all of the online grammar practice activities in ELEteca. Then have students search for other materials online that practice the future form in Spanish. After doing an activity online, have them swap websites with a classmate. Continue as time allows. You may want to recommend some sites to get the started so they don't all wind up on the same couple of websites.

OBJECTIVES FOR UNIT OPENER

- Introduce unit theme: **Cosas de casa**, about families and household chores
- Introduce culture for the unit: Learn about what is considered polite in Spanish culture and what is not

STANDARDS

1.1 Interpersonal communication	2.1 Practices and perspectives
1.2 Understand the language	4.2 Compare cultures

INSTRUCTIONAL STRATEGIES

- Introduce unit theme and objectives. Talk about the photo and have students state who they think the different people are and what they are doing. Ask what room of the house they are in, and invite students to name the different objects they see.
- Have the students discuss the questions and talk about themselves in the same context.
- Use the photograph to preview unit vocabulary: **¿Cuáles son tus responsabilidades en la casa? ¿Qué cosas haces para ayudar a tu familia?**
- Ask related questions to recycle vocabulary and structures: **¿Cuántas personas viven en tu casa? ¿Cenas con tu familia cada día? ¿Quién prepara la cena? ¿Comen juntos durante los fines de semana? ¿Quién hace la compra para la casa? ¿Qué comida casi siempre/nunca tienes en casa?**
- Help students formulate their ideas using **Hay (seis) personas en mi familia. Tengo (tres) hermanos. En general, cenamos juntos. Mis padres preparan la cena. A veces salimos para cenar en un restaurante los fines de semana.**

SLOWER-PACED LEARNERS

In pairs, have students review vocabulary by preparing lists of words related to the opening image. Some categories might be **La familia, La cocina, La ropa, Acciones** (verbos), **Descripciones físicas**, etc. Allow them access to a dictionary to refresh their memories. If time allows, have students take turns making sentences that use the words in context. Alternatively, have them write these sentences individually.

ADVANCED LEARNERS

Tell students to think about the different people in the opening image. What is each one thinking about? Have students write thought bubbles for each one of them expressing their thoughts in one or two sentences. Encourage them to be creative. Put students in pairs to share their ideas with a partner and elicit some of their favorites to be shared with the class.

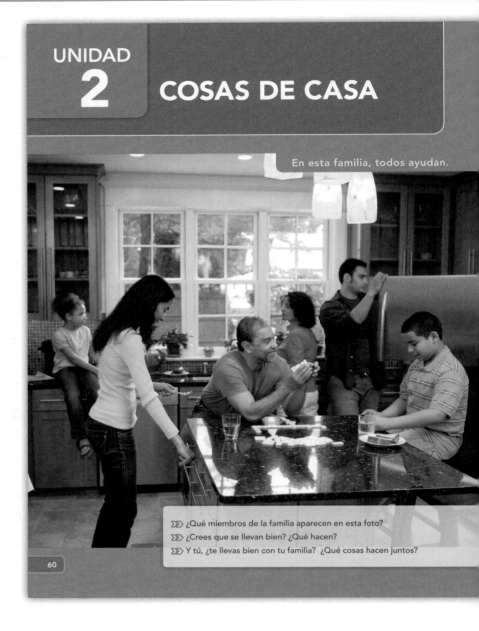

UNIDAD
2 COSAS DE CASA

En esta familia, todos ayudan.

⟫ ¿Qué miembros de la familia aparecen en esta foto?
⟫ ¿Crees que se llevan bien? ¿Qué hacen?
⟫ Y tú, ¿te llevas bien con tu familia? ¿Qué cosas hacen juntos?

60

ADDITIONAL UNIT RESOURCES

Extension Activities (EA) (Photocopiable)	Interactive Whiteboard Lessons (IWB)	Audio	Video	Online ELEteca
EA: 2.1, 2.2, 2.3	IWB: 2.1, 2.2	9 to 20	Diálogo 2	EXTENSIÓN DIGITAL

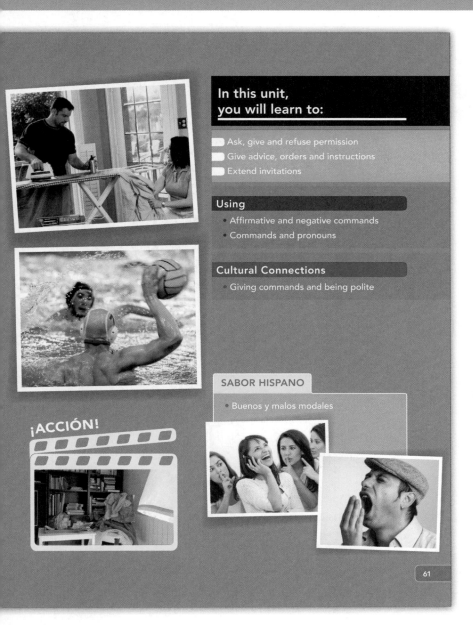

In this unit,
you will learn to:

- Ask, give and refuse permission
- Give advice, orders and instructions
- Extend invitations

Using
- Affirmative and negative commands
- Commands and pronouns

Cultural Connections
- Giving commands and being polite

SABOR HISPANO
- Buenos y malos modales

¡ACCIÓN!

61

LEARNING OUTCOMES
- Ask, give and refuse permission
- Give advice, orders and instructions
- Extend invitations

INSTRUCTIONAL STRATEGIES
- Use unit opener to preview vocabulary and cultural topics for this unit.
- Have students look at the images on this page and relate them to the objectives listed. Ask questions such as: *¿Qué hace el hombre? ¿Quién plancha en tu casa? ¿Ayudas en casa? ¿Qué haces para ayudar? ¿A qué deporte juegan? ¿Qué deportes haces tú? ¿Te gusta el deporte?*
- Invite students to read the topic for **Sabor hispano** and preview that section in the unit. Ask questions such as: *¿Qué hace la muchacha? ¿Qué hacen las otras muchachas? ¿Por qué abre la boca el hombre? ¿Crees que está bien visto hacer esto en público? ¿Por qué? ¿Crees que estará bien visto en los países hispanos?*
- Ask students to anticipate what they think the episode for **¡Acción!** will be about. Ask: *¿Qué ves en el cuarto? ¿Está ordenado? ¿En la casa de quién está este cuarto? ¿Qué piensas que va a pasar en el video?*
- Have students work in pairs to talk about the images using the questions you have modeled. Then have volunteers present to the class what they understand this unit to be about.

HERITAGE LANGUAGE LEARNERS

Invite students to share their own experiences about what's polite versus what's not in their cultures. Encourage students to make connections or compare and contrast what they know about customs related to politeness and courtesy in the US and other cultures.

THREE MODES OF COMMUNICATION: UNIT 2			
	INTERPERSONAL	**INTERPRETIVE**	**PRESENTATIONAL**
HABLAMOS DE...	4	1, 2, 3	4
COMUNICA	3, 6	1, 2, 4, 5	3, 6
¡ACCIÓN!	1, 4	2, 3	1
PALABRA POR PALABRA	5, 8	1, 2, 4, 6, 7, 9	3, 8, 10
GRAMÁTICA		1, 2, 3, 4, 5, 6, 7	
DESTREZAS		1, 2	3
CULTURA		SABOR HISPANO	
RELATO	1	2, 3, 4	4, 5

OBJECTIVES FOR HABLAMOS DE...

• Understand language in context
• Preview vocabulary: Talking about what people do in the family context
• Preview grammatical structures: Affirmative and negative commands; Commands and pronouns
• Read and listen to a conversation between two young people talking about their families

CORE RESOURCES

• Audio Program: Track 9

STANDARDS

1.1   Engage in conversation
1.2   Understand the language
4.2   Compare cultures

INSTRUCTIONAL STRATEGIES

Activity 1

• Ask students to talk about the people in the photos and say what they are doing and where students think they are. Ask students to predict the relationship between the people. Ask: **¿Son amigos o familia? ¿Quién creen que es Pilar?**, and so on.
• Read the text with the students and explain that not all the information has been provided. Tell students to use the information in the text and images to draw other conclusions in order to complete the chart accurately.
• Have them fill in the blanks in the chart with the profession, age and tastes or preferences of each person in the family.
• Ask individual students to give the class the information for one person. Ask the class if they agree. Then have the student explain how they arrived at the correct answer.

Activity 2

• To introduce the activity, ask students about typical family dynamics: **¿De qué cosas suelen discutir los hermanos? ¿Y los padres e hijos? ¿Con quién sueles discutir más en tu familia? ¿Por qué? ¿Quién se enfada más contigo?**
• Remind students that **discutir** in Spanish means to argue.
• Have the students complete the sentences using what they already know about the family.
• Have them share with a partner.
• To follow up, ask students what aspects in the Garrido family seem to be typical of most families: **¿Piensan que los Pérez-Garrido es una familia típica?**

ANSWERS

Activity 1

Juan: jubilado, 77, cantar; **Antonio:** médico, 43, música clásica; **Pilar:** pintora, 46, ir al cine; **Fernando:** recepcionista, 20, fútbol; **Daría:** estudiante, 16, música heavy; **Marcos:** estudiante, 11, videojuegos.

Activity 2

a. pintar; **b.** cantar; **c.** jugar; **d.** gustos.

HABLAMOS DE... Las tareas de la casa

1 Completa el cuadro con la información de las imágenes y la del texto.

Pilar

Antonio

Daría

Fernando

Marcos

Juan

Pilar Garrido, que es pintora, tuvo a Fernando con 26 años. Ella tiene tres años más que su marido, **Antonio Pérez**. A él le gusta la música clásica, pero a su hija Daría le gusta el heavy. **Daría** tiene cuatro años menos que Fernando y cinco más que su hermano Marcos. **Marcos** tiene 11 años y Juan, el abuelo, que está jubilado y le gusta cantar, tiene 77 años.

Nombre	Profesión	Edad	Gustos
Juan			
Antonio			
Pilar			ir al cine
Fernando	recepcionista		
Daría			
Marcos			

2 Completa las frases y descubre cómo es la convivencia en esta familia.

a. Antonio discute con su mujer porque usa sus camisas viejas para ....
b. Pilar se enfada con su padre porque se pone a .... mientras ella trabaja.
c. Fernando se enfada con su hermano porque nunca quiere .... con él.
d. Daría discute con su padre porque tienen .... musicales muy diferentes.

62

For additional listening practice, have students listen to you read the paragraph in Activity 1 aloud while they keep their books closed. Before you read, tell them to listen, take notes, and be prepared to look at pictures and identify the family members' by name. After you read the paragraph, project the images from Activity 1 one at a time, out of order, being sure to block out the captions. Have students identify each of the family members by name. As you go over the answers, ask students to share what else they remember or took notes on about the family members.

ADVANCED LEARNERS

Using one of the statements from Activity 2, have students write and then act out a conversation between two members of the Pérez-Garrido family in front of the class.

3 🎧 9 Escucha la conversación e indica si las frases son verdaderas (V) o falsas (F).

Ernesto: ¡Últimamente mis padres se quejan por todo!

Daría: ¿Por qué dices eso? Tus padres son encantadores.

E.: Pues ahora se han vuelto superestrictos con todo. Me han dicho que entre semana no puedo llegar a casa más tarde de las seis. Bueno, menos los días que tengo tenis, que tengo que estar en casa a las ocho de la noche. Me han dicho que si llego un minuto más tarde, me castigarán sin salir.

D.: ¡Pero si salimos de entrenar a las siete y media! ¡Tendrás que irte corriendo a casa! ¡Y sin ducharte!

E.: Además, ahora dicen que no hacemos nada en casa y que tenemos que colaborar más.

D.: ¡Uf! ¡Qué pesados! Mi madre el año pasado hizo una lista con las tareas que tenía que hacer cada uno, ¡y fue un desastre!

E.: ¿Y eso?

D.: Mi abuelo era el encargado de hacer la compra, pero lo que hacía era pagar 270 pesos a mi hermano Fernando si iba él. Él me pagaba 180 pesos a mí y mientras él "estaba haciendo la compra" se iba de paseo. Y como yo odio (*hate*) ir al supermercado, pues le pagaba 90 pesos a mi hermano Marcos, ¡y él encantado!

E.: ¿Y tus padres no se enteraban (*found out*)?

D.: Al principio no, pero un día vieron a Marcos salir del súper y lo descubrieron.

E.: ¿Y cómo reaccionaron?

D.: Pues decidieron que con los 270 pesos del abuelo, los 180 de Fernando y mis 90, podían pagar a alguien para limpiar la casa varias horas a la semana. ¡Pero nosotros tenemos que seguir haciendo nuestra parte!, ¡y además nos cuesta dinero!

E.: ¡Ja, ja! ¡Tus padres sí que saben!

	V	F
a. Ernesto no puede llegar a casa ningún día más tarde de las ocho.	☐	☐
b. Según la opinión de Daría, los padres de Ernesto son muy simpáticos.	☐	☐
c. Fernando conseguía 90 pesos por no hacer la compra.	☐	☐
d. La persona que limpia en la casa de Daría va una hora a la semana.	☐	☐
e. Los padres de Daría descubrieron la verdad porque el abuelo lo contó todo.	☐	☐

4 Escribe al lado de cada frase la persona correspondiente según la conversación de la Actividad 3.

a. Inicialmente tenía que encargarse de hacer la compra: ....

b. Repartió las tareas de la casa entre los miembros de la familia: ....

c. Fue descubierto por sus padres en la puerta del supermercado: ....

d. En lugar de hacer la compra se iba caminar: ....

e. No le gusta nada hacer la compra: ....

INSTRUCTIONAL STRATEGIES

🎧 9 Activity 3

- Inform the students that they are going to listen to a conversation between Daría and Ernesto in which they talk about their families.
- Project the True or False questions and review them with students before playing the audio. Have them listen first with books closed and complete the activity.
- Play the audio again while the students follow in their books and confirm their answers.
- Ask for volunteers to say whether each sentence is true or false.
- Ask for volunteers to make each sentence true.

Activity 4

- Working individually, have students review the text to match the sentences with the different characters in the story.
- Go over the answers as a class. Encourage students to refer back to the parts of the text where they found their answers.

Extension

- In small groups of three, have students talk about their own families. Put the following prompts on the boards as a guide: **¿Cómo son sus familias? ¿Qué tienen en común con la familia Pérez-Garrido? ¿Cuántos son en casa? ¿Qué aficiones tienen? ¿Tienen alguna hora de llegada o tareas domésticas asignadas?**
- You may also assign this as a written activity.

ANSWERS

Activity 3

a. T; **b.** T; **c.** F; **d.** F; **e.** F.

Activity 4

a. el abuelo de Daría; **b.** la madre de Daría; **c.** Marcos; **d.** Fernando; **e.** Daría.

HERITAGE LANGUAGE LEARNERS

Have students interview their family members to get each of their perspectives about the family dynamics at home. You may want to devise a list of potential questions as a class related to rules, routines, responsibilities, and relationships. Encourage students to create a slide show or bring in photos of their family members that they can show to the class while reporting back about their interviews.

OBJECTIVES FOR COMUNICA

- Present communicative functions of the unit:
  - Ask and give permission
  - Refuse permission
  - Offer and encourage others to accept

CORE RESOURCES

- Audio Program: Tracks 10 and 11
- Extension Activities: EA 2.1
- Interactive Whiteboard Lesson: IWB 2.1
- Interactive Online Materials - ELEteca

STANDARDS

- 1.1 Engage in conversation
- 1.2 Understand the language
- 4.2 Compare cultures

INSTRUCTIONAL STRATEGIES FOR ASKING, GIVING AND REFUSING PERMISSION, OFFERING AND ENCOURAGING OTHERS TO ACCEPT

- Distribute copies of EA 2.1, **Pedir permiso, invitar y ofrecer** to student pairs and tell them to list the expressions in the appropriate categories in the chart according to their function: **pedir permiso, concederlo, denegarlo, invitar u ofrecer** y **responder a una invitación**. The purpose is to have students decipher the meaning of these expressions before reading the chart in the book.

- Once students have completed the chart, have them check their work against the information in the book and ask how many listed the expressions in the correct category.
- Have students repeat chorally to ensure proper pronunciation and intonation. Then call on individual students to answer your prompts giving a thumbs up to indicate whether the student should respond affirmatively or deny permission.

🎧 10 Activity 1

- Focus attention on the photographs of people together. Then have students complete the conversation individually and fill in the blanks with words from the box.
- Play the audio while students listen and follow in the books to confirm their answers.
- Invite pairs of students to read the conversations aloud with their partner. Encourage students to use gestures and appropriate emotion in their presentations.

🎧 11 Activity 2

- Explain that this activity consists of four conversations and students choose the correct option for each.
- Play the audio while students listen and indicate the outcome of each conversation.
- Repeat the audio for students to confirm their answers.
- Ask students to give the answers for the class.

See audioscript on page APP4

COMUNICA

ASKING, GIVING, AND DENYING PERMISSION

- Para **pedir un permiso**:
  ¿Puedo / Podría comer un poco de pastel?
  Can / Could I have some cake?

- Para **conceder un permiso**:
  Sí, claro / por supuesto.
  Yes, of course.

- Para **denegar un permiso**:
  No, (lo siento) es que lo he hecho para llevarlo a la fiesta de Ana. *No, (I'm sorry) I made it to take to Ana's party.*
  ¡Ni hablar! / ¡De ninguna manera! *No way!*

OFFERING AND ENCOURAGING OTHERS TO ACCEPT

- Para **invitar** u **ofrecer**:
  ¿Quieres un poco de pastel?
  Do you want some cake?

- Para **responder**:
  Sí, gracias. *Yes, thank you.*
  No, gracias, es que no me gustan los dulces.
  No, thank you, I don't like sweets.

1 🎧 **10** Completa las conversaciones con las expresiones del cuadro. Después, escucha y comprueba.

> quieres ○ no ○ come un poco ○ es que ○ sí, claro ○ puedo

a. Emilio: Mamá, ya sé que estás leyendo, pero... ¿(a) .... poner la tele?
Mamá: (b) ...., ponla. A mí no me molesta el ruido mientras leo.
Emilio: Vale, gracias, es que ahora hay un programa que me encanta.

b. Marcos: ¿(c) .... probar la pizza que he hecho?
Anabel: (d) ...., gracias, (e) .... acabo de comer.
Marcos: Anda, (f) ...., solo para probarla. Ya verás qué rica me sale.
Anabel: Bueno, la probaré, pero solo un poquito.

2 🎧 **11** Escucha las siguientes conversaciones y marca la opción correcta.

	Diálogo 1	Diálogo 2	Diálogo 3	Diálogo 4
a. Conceder permiso.	○	○	○	○
b. Denegar permiso.	○	○	○	○
c. Aceptar una invitación.	○	○	○	○
d. Denegar una invitación.	○	○	○	○

3 Habla con tu compañero/a siguiendo las instrucciones de los cuadros.

Estudiante 1

Situación 1. Empiezas tú.
- Tienes que pedir permiso a tu compañero/a para hacer algo.

Situación 2. Empieza tu compañero/a.
- Tienes que aceptar o rechazar la invitación de tu compañero/a.

Estudiante 2

Situación 1. Empieza tu compañero/a.
- Tienes que conceder o denegar permiso según lo que te pida tu compañero/a.

Situación 2. Empiezas tú.
- Tienes que invitar a algo u ofrecer algo a tu compañero/a.

ANSWERS

Activity 1
a. Puedo; **b.** Sí, claro; **c.** Quieres; **d.** No; **e.** es que; **f.** come un poco.

Activity 2
a. diálogo 1; **b.** diálogo 3; **c.** diálogo 2; **d.** diálogo 4.

ADVANCED LEARNERS

Working in pairs, have students find an image from elsewhere in the book that they can use as a prompt to write a conversation that involves asking for permission or offering and encouraging others to accept something. Tell them to use the conversations in Activity 1 as models. Invite pairs to share their conversations in front of the class. After each conversation, have the rest of the class confirm the context of each conversation and the result.

ASKING FOR AND GIVING INSTRUCTIONS

■ Para **pedir instrucciones**:

¿Puedes / Podrías decirme cómo ir al centro?
Can / Could you tell me how to get to downtown?

Perdone / Perdona, ¿para ir a la estación?
Excuse me, how do I go to the station?

■ **Asking and giving advice**:

Últimamente no me concentro a la hora de estudiar, **¿qué puedo hacer?** *Lately I can't concentrate when I study, what can I do?*

Tendrías que / Deberías ir a la biblioteca / hacer deporte. *You should go to the library / play sports.*

¿Por qué no vas a la biblioteca / haces deporte? *Why don't you go to the library / play sports?*

Ve a la biblioteca. / **Haz** deporte. *Go to the library. / Play sports.*

■ Para **dar instrucciones**:

Sí, mira, haz / toma / ve... *Yes, look, you do / take / go...*

Sí, toma la primera a la derecha, **sigue** todo derecho, después **cruza** la calle... *Yes, take the first right, keep going straight, then cross the street...*

Sí, tiene / tienes que tomar / hacer / ir... *Yes, you have to take / do / go...*

■ **Giving orders**:

• **Haz / Ve**... *Do / Go...*

Pedro, **haz** las tareas antes de ver la tele. *Pedro, do your homework before watching TV.*

4 Lee la primera parte de cada conversación y relaciónala con la respuesta correspondiente.

Perdona, ¿podrías decirme cómo llegar al Palacio de los Deportes?

No sé si voy a aprobar el examen de Historia. Solo he leído unas páginas del capítulo. ¿Qué puedo hacer?

Adriana, haz la tarea, deja de mandar textos y baja el volumen de la música.

a. ☐ Sí, claro. Sigue todo derecho y después toma la primera calle a la izquierda…

b. ☐ Que sí, mamá, ¡ya voy…!

c. ☐ ¿Y por qué no empiezas a estudiar ya? Lee una sección del capítulo cada día.

5 Indica las frases de la Actividad 4 que reflejan las siguientes situaciones.

	1	2	3	a	b	c
a. Pedir y dar consejos.	☐	☐	☐	☐	☐	☐
b. Pedir instrucciones.	☐	☐	☐	☐	☐	☐
c. Dar instrucciones.	☐	☐	☐	☐	☐	☐
d. Dar y aceptar órdenes.	☐	☐	☐	☐	☐	☐

6 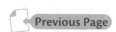 Elige una de estas situaciones y cuéntasela a tu compañero/a. Él/Ella debe reaccionar.

a. Últimamente duermes poco, solo dos o tres horas. Pide consejo a tu compañero/a.

b. No sabes cómo mandar un mensaje de texto desde tu celular nuevo. Pregunta a tu compañero/a.

c. Necesitas ir a la oficina de tu escuela y no sabes dónde está. Tu compañero/a sí lo sabe.

MORE IN ELETECA: EXTRA ONLINE PRACTICE

Previous Page

Cultural Note

Point out that in the second conversation Mario at first refuses the offer and gives a reason why. But at the end he does accept the offer with a condition. Explain to students that this is a very common social practice in Hispanic countries in that it's socially accepted to say no the first time and then allow yourself to be convinced or to convince others to do something.

Activity 3

• Have students work with a partner, with each student looking at a different set of instructions (one students holds the book upside down).

• Student 1 begins the conversation according to the instructions, and student 2 responds appropriately.

• Circulate around the room as they talk, checking pronunciation and assisting with vocabulary or expressions as required.

• Ask for volunteers to perform for the class.

INSTRUCTIONAL STRATEGIES FOR ASKING AND GIVING INSTRUCTIONS

• Use IWB 2.1, **Pedir y dar instrucciones, consejos o recomendaciones y órdenes** to introduce the next set of expressions. Project the chart and review the headings with students.

• Tell students to listen to the examples you provide and identify the correct function according to the chart. Ask the class if they agree with the answer. Then write the example in the chart. Use examples from the text such as: **Sí, mira, toma la primera a la derecha, ¿Por qué no vas a la biblioteca?**…

• Finally, ask students to confirm answers with the chart in the book.

Activity 4

• Tell the students to cover the text and look at the images. Ask them to describe who the people are and predict what they are saying.

• Explain to students that the text about the images is a speech bubble and that they have to match the best response for each.

• Ask them to compare with a partner. Have the students read each one as a conversation.

• Invite pairs of students to perform an exchange for the class.

Activity 5

• In this activity, students match the function listed with examples from Activity 4 that exemplify the function. Use the numbers to reference the first part of the conversation and the letters for the second part or response. Classify each according to its function in the conversation.

• Have the students share their answers with a partner.

• Ask individual students to say their answers aloud.

Activity 6

• Read through all the situations in the activity together. Ask students to brainstorm important vocabulary for each one. This will later provide linguistic support while students practice with their partners.

• Then have each student choose one situation and prepare what he/she will say and ask his/her partner. This should not be a scripted activity. Allow students to work only from notes or nothing at all.

• The partner responds appropriately. Then have them switch roles.

• Circulate around the class as they talk, listening in and providing assistance and corrections where required.

ANSWERS

Activity 4

1. a; **2.** c; **3.** b.

Activity 5

a. c, 2; **b.** 1; **c.** a, 1; **d.** b, 3.

OBJECTIVES FOR ¡ACCIÓN!

• Provide students with a structured approach to viewing the video
• Contextualize the content of the unit in a familiar scenario

CORE RESOURCES

• Unit Video 2 - El señor Don Limpio
• Online Materials - ELEteca

STANDARDS

1.1   Interpersonal communication
1.2   Interpretive communication
2.1   Culture: Practices and perspectives

INSTRUCTIONAL STRATEGIES

Previewing: Antes del video

Activity 1

• To get students thinking about the topic of the video, have them discuss the two statements with a partner. Encourage them to ask each other more questions related to their home environments and compare and contrast them to those of relatives and friends whom they visit.
• Invite pairs to share ideas from their discussions with the class.

Activity 2

• Direct students' attention to the six images from the video. Go over the instructions. Remind students that it's fine to guess the correct descriptions at this stage; they aren't expected to know the right answers yet. The idea is that by considering these options before they watch the video, they will be in a frame of mind that's more likely to grasp the main ideas when they do watch it.
• You may want to take a class poll to get a sense of how the students have guessed. Don't confirm or deny their guesses; help create a sense of mystery and anticipation.

ANSWERS

Activity 2 and 3

1. b; **2.** c; **3.** a; **4.** c; **5.** c; **6.** c.

HERITAGE LANGUAGE LEARNERS

As a continuation to the questions in Activity 1, have students think about any customs or traditions that might be involved in visiting someone's home for dinner. Invite them to share any experiences that they've had with people from their own culture or people from other cultures. If they haven't had any experiences having dinner at someone's house from another culture, encourage them to share what customs they may have read or heard about from others.

¡ACCIÓN! El señor Don Limpio

1.   2.   3.
4.   5.   6.

ANTES DEL VIDEO

1 ¿Con qué frases te identificas más? Coméntalo con tu compañero/a.

a. La casa refleja cómo somos y por eso siempre tiene que estar limpia y ordenada.
b. Solo limpio y ordeno mi casa cuando tengo visita.

2 Elige una frase para describir cada una de las imágenes y anticipa el contenido del episodio. Basa tu respuesta en lo que crees que puede ocurrir. Usa tu imaginación.

Imagen 1
a. El salón está muy desordenado, pero el resto de la casa está fenomenal.
b. El salón está como el resto de la casa, todo es un desastre.
c. El salón está muy limpio, solo hay que ordenar la mesa.

Imagen 2
a. Eli pide a Sebas ayuda para ordenar la casa.
b. Eli quiere ver el dormitorio de Sebas ordenado.
c. Eli comunica a Sebas que tiene tres invitados para cenar.

Imagen 3
a. A Sebas no le gusta la idea de tener invitados.
b. Sebas no quiere ayudar con las tareas de casa.
c. Sebas no quiere ordenar su habitación.

Imagen 4
a. Es Alba, una amiga universitaria de Eli.
b. Es Alba, una amiga de Felipe.
c. Es Alba, la hermana de un invitado a la cena.

Imagen 5
a. Sebas está feliz porque a Eli tampoco le apetece limpiar.
b. Sebas está feliz porque Eli le va a ayudar con la limpieza del salón.
c. Sebas está feliz porque Alba es una de las invitadas.

66

Imagen 6

a. Eli está enfadada porque Sebas no quiere ni ayudar en la casa ni ordenar el salón.

b. Eli está enfadada porque Sebas solo quiere limpiar ya que viene Alba a cenar.

c. Está enfadada porque Sebas, para impresionar a Alba, quiere organizar y limpiar toda la casa y a ella no le parece necesario.

DURANTE EL VIDEO

3 Mira el episodio completo y confirma tus hipótesis de la actividad anterior.

4 Vuelve a mirar el episodio y elige las frases que mejor se adaptan a cada una de las actitudes de los personajes. Después, para justificar tu respuesta, relaciona las frases con su explicación (a-f).

Eli	Felipe	Sebas

2c		

1. No quiere dar mala impresión a una de las invitadas.

2. No quiere limpiar.

3. Quiere invitar a unos amigos a su casa.

4. Le sorprende ver a su amigo tan preocupado por la limpieza.

5. No puede hacer ese favor.

6. Pide ayuda y da órdenes a todos.

a. Porque son sus compañeros de la universidad.

b. Porque no tienen perro.

c. Porque cree que la casa está limpia.

d. Para tener la casa perfecta.

e. Porque normalmente es algo que no le importa nada.

f. Porque esa persona le gusta.

DESPUÉS DEL VIDEO

5 Identifica las tareas de la casa que no mencionan en el episodio. Vuelve a verlo si es necesario.

a. limpiar el polvo
b. poner la lavadora
c. planchar
d. poner la mesa
e. hacer la cama

f. barrer
g. tender la ropa
h. poner el lavaplatos
i. limpiar el suelo
j. hacer la comida

k. sacar la basura
l. limpiar las ventanas
m. cambiar las sábanas
n. pasar la aspiradora
ñ. fregar los platos

6 ¿Con qué personaje te identificas más? Coméntalo con tus compañeros/as.

MORE IN ELETECA: EXTRA ONLINE PRACTICE

INSTRUCTIONAL STRATEGIES

Viewing: Durante el video

 Activity 3

Have students watch the video and check their guesses from Activity 2. Confirm the correct answers as a class.

Activity 4

• Explain that students will match the phrases and then associate them with the characters from the video. Give them some time to read the items and answer what they can based on what they remember from the first viewing.

• Play the video a second time so they can complete the activity.

Post-viewing: Después del video

Activity 5

• Working individually, have students identify which chores were not mentioned in the video.

• You may choose to replay the second half of the video (starting at 2:30) so they can listen again more closely for the specific information. Suggest that they strikethrough the chores as they hear them so only the correct answers (those that were not spoken) remain.

• Go over the correct answers as a class.

Activity 6

Give students some time to think about their own answers to the question and jot down notes before speaking with a partner. If they don't identify with either main character from the video, tell them to prepare to explain why not.

ANSWERS

Activity 4

Eli: 2c, 3a; **Felipe:** 4e, 5b; **Sebas:** 1f, 6d.

Activity 5

c, d, f, i, l, m, ñ.

SLOWER-PACED LEARNERS

After sharing their ideas in Activity 6, have students write an organized and detailed paragraph reflecting and clarifying their ideas.

ADVANCED LEARNERS

To extend their discussions in Activity 6, have students speculate about what would have happened in subsequent scenes if they video had continued. Will it be difficult for Eli and Sebas to get ready for the dinner party? How will it go? What will happen during it? What will happen after it?

OBJECTIVES FOR LAS TAREAS DOMÉSTICAS

- Present vocabulary needed to practice communicative and grammatical functions for the unit: Household chores
- Talk about how to organize family members to do household chores

CORE RESOURCES

- Audio Program: Track 12
- Extension Activities: EA 2.2
- Interactive Online Materials - ELEteca

STANDARDS

1.1	Engage in conversation	3.2	Acquire information
1.2	Understand the language	4.1	Compare languages and
1.3	Present information		cultures

INSTRUCTIONAL STRATEGIES

🎧 12 **Activity 1**

- Invite the students to look at the images and ask: **¿Dónde están las personas que aparecen en las imágenes? ¿Qué tipo de actividades están realizando, de tiempo libre, de trabajo...?**
- Ask students to make a sentence about each picture using the expression provided: **La muchacha hace la cama**, etc.
- Tell the students they are going to listen to a number of conversations about household chores and they will have to number each image.
- Play the audio while the students listen and number the images.
- Play the audio again for the students to confirm their answers.
- Ask different students to give their answers.

See audiosript on page APP4

Activity 2

- Have the students read the sentences and choose the correct verb for each.
- When they have finished, have them share with a partner. Ask individual students to read the complete sentences.

ANSWERS

Activity 1

a. 9; **b.** 11; **c.** 5; **d.** 3; **e.** 4; **f.** 2; **g.** 10; **h.** 6; **i.** 1; **j.** 12; **k.** 7; **l.** 8.

Activity 2

a. poner; **b.** cambiar; **c.** barro, friego; **d.** tender; **e.** limpiar; **f.** hago; **g.** planchas; **h.** pasar.

SLOWER-PACED LEARNERS

When listening to the audio in Activity 1 for a second time, encourage students to listen for and note the forms of the target verbs that they hear: **hacer**, **pon**, **pongo**, **lavar**, etc. Before doing Activity 2, point out that **fregar** is an **e ➡ ie** stem-changing verb.

PALABRA POR PALABRA Las tareas domésticas

1 🎧 12 Escucha las conversaciones y ordena las imágenes.

hacer la cama

tender la ropa

hacer la comida

lavar los platos

tirar la basura

poner la mesa

poner la lavadora / el lavaplatos

planchar

barrer

pasear al perro

fregar el suelo

pasar la aspiradora

- hacer la cama = tender la cama
- el suelo = el piso
- las tareas domésticas = los quehaceres (de la casa)

2 Completa las frases con los verbos del cuadro.

fregar o tender o poner o limpiar o hacer o planchar o barrer o cambiar o pasar

a. Lo contrario de *quitar la mesa* es .... la mesa.
b. A veces cuando haces la cama también .... las sábanas.
c. Si limpio el suelo sin agua, lo ....; si lo limpio con agua y jabón, lo ....
d. Después de poner la lavadora, tengo que .... la ropa.
e. Lo hago con el polvo, los cristales y el baño y es lo contrario de *ensuciar*: ....
f. Antes de comer, ... la comida.
g. Antes de ponerte la ropa, la ....
h. Es más fácil .... la aspiradora que barrer.

3 Pilar ha decidido repartir las tareas de casa entre los miembros de su familia. Observa las imágenes y escribe qué le dice cada uno usando el imperativo afirmativo y negativo.

a. Abuelo, *plancha la ropa, pero ten cuidado de no quemarla...*

b. Antonio...

c. Nerea...

d. Javier...

4 Lee este artículo sobre la organización de las tareas domésticas. Después, decide si las siguientes frases son verdaderas (V) o falsas (F).

Responsabilidades del hogar

Organizar un hogar y una familia no es fácil. Por eso, es importante organizarse para distribuir las tareas y conseguir la colaboración de todos:

1. Haz un cuadro de tareas de tres columnas. En la primera, escribe todas las tareas del hogar. Pon, en primer lugar, las que se hacen todos los días, como pasear al perro por las mañanas, y, luego, las tareas semanales, como barrer, a continuación de las anteriores.
2. Piensa cuánto tiempo necesita cada tarea y escríbelo al lado, en la segunda columna.
3. Escribe en la tercera columna los nombres de las personas de la casa que crees que pueden hacer cada tarea. Asigna tareas de acuerdo con (*according to*) la edad, para que no sean demasiado difíciles para la persona que la realizará, o los horarios de cada uno.
4. Asigna a cada persona una o dos tareas diarias y una o dos semanales.
5. Planifica un horario rotativo y así nadie tendrá siempre los peores trabajos, como limpiar el baño o planchar.

Texto adaptado de: *http://www.ehowenespanol.com/distribuir-tareas-del-hogar-semana-como_206328/*

	V	F
a. La organización de las tareas en un hogar es una labor complicada.	☐	☐
b. Es necesario organizarse por horas.	☐	☐
c. Hay que separar las tareas diarias de las semanales.	☐	☐
d. La distribución de las tareas se hace en función del tiempo que duran (*it takes*).	☐	☐
e. Cada tarea se asigna a cada miembro por sorteo (*randomly*).	☐	☐
f. La organización de las tareas debe ser siempre la misma.	☐	☐

5 Habla con tu compañero/a sobre las tareas domésticas.

¿Qué tareas domésticas hacen ustedes en casa? ¿Cuál de ellas les gusta menos? ¿Por qué?

69

Activity 4

- Read the text in sections and invite volunteers to repeat each section.
- Look at the statements below and have the students check True or False for each one. Have them share with a partner, before asking random students to give the correct answers.

Activity 5

Students sit in pairs to discuss the chores they do at home.

Extension

For additional practice with this vocabulary, use EA 2.2, **Memory de las tareas del hogar** to play a matching and memory game. Distribute photo and word cards to each group of 3 students and have them place the cards face down on separate sides. The object of the game is to identify the image in Spanish and match it to the corresponding expression. The student with the most matches wins.

ANSWERS

Activity 3

b. Antonio, pon la lavadora/lava la ropa, pero ten cuidado de no poner la ropa banca con la ropa de color; **c.** Nerea, haz/prepara la comida, pero ten cuidado de no quemarla; **d.** Javier, haz la cama, pero acuérdate de poner la manta.

Activity 4

a. T; **b.** F; **c.** T; **d.** T; **e.** F; **f.** F.

ADVANCED LEARNERS

As an extension to Activity 3, have students write a new round of commands and issue related warnings from Pilar to each family member. Tell students to use other verb phrases from Activity 1.

HERITAGE LANGUAGE LEARNERS

As an extension to the lesson, have students survey at least three Spanish-speaking friends or relatives about household chores. First create the surveys in class. Encourage students to find out information about what chores people do, how often they do them, how much time they take, and how they feel about each of them. They can use rating scales, but they should ask for additional information when conducting their interviews. Have students summarize the results in a chart, graph, or other organized way to give a summary presentation to the class.

INSTRUCTIONAL STRATEGIES

Activity 3

- Read the model with the students and ask them which of the following best describes the meaning: **El abuelo plancha la ropa** or **El abuelo tiene que planchar la ropa**. Ask students how they know this (Pilar is talking directly to the grandfather and telling him what to do). Ask them if they remember what form of the verb is used for cases like this (command form).
- Have students identify possible verbs they can use for each situation. Review **haz** for **hacer**. Ask student what **tener cuidado** means and ask them for the command form: **ten cuidado**. Have the students write the remaining sentences.
- Ask different students to say their answers aloud, while other students write them on the board to check.

Objectives for Los deportes

- Present vocabulary needed to practice communicative and grammatical functions for the unit: Sports
- Describe how to play certain sports and games

Standards

1.4	Engage in conversation
1.5	Understand the language
1.6	Present information
3.2	Acquire information
4.1	Compare languages and cultures

Instructional Strategies

Activity 6

- Have students look at the images and name the sports shown. If they are not sure, they should look at the vocabulary in the box or at the end of unit vocabulary list. Focus students' attention on **chutar** and ask them what they think it means (*to shoot*) and where they think it comes from (latinizing of *to shoot*). Explain that many sports terms, like technology terms, come from English. Then ask students which of these sports they play.
- Have them write the names of the sports at the top of each column and in the box below they write the words associated with each sport.
- Remind them that some words may be repeated. When they finish, have them share with a partner.
- Ask for volunteers to say a sport and the words associated with it.

Grammar Note

Share the following information with students about sports terms: *Red* corresponde a *tenis*, pero también se utiliza como sinónimo de *portería*; por otro lado, *balón* y *pelota* pueden usarse también como sinónimos, aunque se utiliza *balón* si su tamaño es más grande y *pelota* si es más pequeña; *golpear* podría clasificarse en todos los deportes, pero se prefiere para el tenis y el squash, ya que con fútbol se usa *chutar* y con balonmano y waterpolo se usa *lanzar*. *Cancha*, en algunos países de Hispanoamérica, se usa como sinónimo de *campo de fútbol*, pero no en España, que se refiere a un recinto cerrado.

Activity 7

- Have the students read the first set of rules with a partner and try to guess which sport is being described. When they finish, they do the same with the second card.
- Circulate around the room as they play, answering questions, checking pronunciation and helping with any vocabulary required.

Activity 8

- Each student chooses another sport and writes a set of rules, using ideas from Activity 7. They should not write the name of the sport.
- Have the students exchange sets of rules and guess which sport is being described. They can continue exchanging with other students until you feel they have practiced enough.

Answers

Activity 6

Fútbol: balón, falta, portería, red, portero, chutar, marcar un gol, campo, jugador, pase, botar; **Balonmano:** balón, falta, red, lanzar, cancha, jugador, pase, botar; **Tenis:** golpear, pelota, falta, red, raqueta, set, cancha, jugador, ventaja, botar; **Squash:** rebotar, golpear, pelota, falta, pared, raqueta, set, cancha, jugador, botar; **Waterpolo:** balón, falta, pase, portero, marcar un gol, lanzar, flotar, jugador.

PALABRA POR PALABRA Los deportes

6 Clasifica las siguientes palabras en la columna correspondiente. ¡*Atención!* Algunas palabras pueden aparecer en más de una columna. Si lo necesitas, usa el glosario.

> fútbol ○ golpear ○ tenis ○ balón ○ waterpolo ○ pelota ○ falta ○ portería ○ pared ○ red ○ squash ○ pase ○ raqueta ○ portero ○ chutar ○ marcar un gol ○ set ○ lanzar ○ cancha ○ campo ○ flotar ○ botar ○ ventaja ○ balonmano ○ jugador ○ rebotar

Deporte →	Fútbol				
Palabras asociadas →				pared	

7 Juega con tu compañero/a. Tienen que adivinar a qué deporte se refiere cada texto. Gana quien necesite leer menos reglas para adivinarlo.

A	B
· Consigue una raqueta y una pelota pequeña.	· Forma dos equipos. En cada uno tiene que haber un portero.
· Busca un adversario para jugar.	· Durante el partido, intenta marcar el mayor número de goles al equipo contrario.
· Si el jugador contrario te ha lanzado la pelota, no debes permitir que esta bote dos veces o más en el suelo o él conseguirá el punto.	· Para marcar un gol, lanza la pelota hacia la portería contraria. Si la metes dentro, habrás marcado.
· Para ganar puntos, intenta que el adversario no pueda responder a tus golpes.	· Intenta robar el balón al jugador del equipo contrario, pero no lo agarres porque cometerás falta. No cometas faltas porque podrás ser expulsado.
· Para poder jugar, encuentra un espacio cerrado rodeado de paredes.	· Para marcar gol, utiliza cualquier parte del cuerpo, pero si usas la mano, esta tiene que estar abierta.
· Golpea la pelota con la raqueta y haz que rebote en la pared frontal de la cancha.	· No pises el suelo de la piscina, está prohibido. Tienes que mantenerte flotando durante todo el partido.
Deporte:	**Deporte:** ....

8 Seguro que conoces bien otros deportes. Siguiendo el juego de la Actividad 7, escribe frases en imperativo sobre las reglas de un deporte y juega otra vez con otro/a compañero/a.

Activity 7

A: squash; **B:** waterpolo.

Heritage Language Learners

Have students research the three most popular sports in Spain or a Latin American country. Challenge them to find one other sport played there that is more unusual or at least not as popular. Have them report back to the class on the popular sports and explain the unusual sport, ideally with visual support.

9 Lee la siguiente entrevista a Vicky Alonso, una deportista española, y escribe las preguntas en su lugar correspondiente.

Preguntas:

1. ¿En estos tiempos están todos los pabellones (*sports centers*) adaptados?
2. ¿Cómo es jugar en un equipo en donde los compañeros son hombres?
3. ¿Cómo llegó al mundo del deporte?
4. ¿Qué es lo mejor que le ha dado el deporte?
5. ¿Practicar un deporte adaptado supone un gran trabajo?

Vicky Alonso (Vigo, 1982) es una de las internacionales del deporte español. Lleva diez años en la élite del baloncesto en silla de ruedas, jugando en el Amfiv, un equipo con hombres, y está a punto (*ready*) de iniciar su quinto campeonato de Europa con la selección femenina. Dice que el deporte le ha hecho más fácil su minusvalía (*disability*).

» (a) ....

» Llegué por casualidad. Cuando comencé a sacar el carné de conducir, mi profesor de la autoescuela, que era entrenador (*coach*), me lo propuso, fui a probar y me gustó...

» (b) ....

» Yo creo que todo lo contrario, creo que el hecho de hacer deporte te ayuda muchísimo a superar la minusvalía, es todo lo contrario que en la vida cotidiana (*everyday*).

» (c) ....

» En Vigo nunca hemos tenido dificultades, pero sí en alguna otra ciudad donde los pabellones no eran del todo accesibles...

» (d) ....

» Siempre he jugado sola entre hombres, pero la verdad es que es estupendo. Yo comencé a entrenar (*train*) con ellos y, la verdad, nunca he tenido ningún problema.

» (e) ....

» Lo mejor ha sido conocer a otras personas que están en la misma situación y que se han encontrado con las mismas dificultades que tú, gente que te hace pensar que no es tan trágico estar así y que tampoco es tan difícil salir adelante (*get ahead*).

Adaptado de Castro Vigo: *http://www.lavozdegalicia.es/coruna/2011/08/23/0003_201108H23P52991.htm*

---

10 Haz una presentación breve sobre Vicky Alonso ante tus compañeros/as. Describe qué ha conseguido y qué representa esta figura para ti.

MORE IN ELETECA: EXTRA ONLINE PRACTICE

INSTRUCTIONAL STRATEGIES

Activity 9

- Have students read the questions and explain that they have to place them in the correct place in the interview.
- Explain that it is a good idea to look at the words after the blank to obtain an idea of which question will fit best.
- Have the students read the interview and write in the questions, ensuring that the answer fits the question.
- Circulate around the room offering assistance, and when they have finished, have them share with a partner.
- Ask for volunteers to give the correct answers.

Activity 10

- Have the students work in pairs to think and write about Vicky Alonso and her accomplishments and what they mean.
- Circulate around the class, offering assistance where required.
- Invite students to share their ideas with the class.

Extension

- Have the students choose a well-known sportsperson and research them on the Internet.
- Have them write a short text about that person's life and achievements and illustrate it with images from the Internet as a poster.
- The completed poster can be displayed on the classroom walls.

ANSWERS

Activity 9

a. 3; **b.** 5; **c.** 1; **d.** 2; **e.** 4.

ADVANCED LEARNERS

Have students imagine that they were the ones interviewing Vicky Alonso. What other questions would they have asked her? Have them write two or three new questions and share them with with a partner or in a small group. Together, students speculate about the responses to the questions and / or do research to investigate likely or accurate answers.

OBJECTIVES FOR GRAMÁTICA 1

- Present grammatical structures needed to practice communicative functions of the unit: Affirmative commands of regular and irregular verbs
- Use affirmative command forms to tell different people what to do

CORE RESOURCES

- Extension activities EA 2.3
- Interactive Whiteboard Lesson: IWB 2.2
- Interactive Online Materials - ELEteca

STANDARDS

1.1 Engage in conversation
1.2 Understand the language
1.3 Present information
4.1 Compare languages

INSTRUCTIONAL STRATEGIES

1. Affirmative Commands

- Project the first chart of IWB 2.2, **El imperativo** to review affirmative commands. Have students fill in the empty spaces on the chart for the **tú** form of regular and irregular verbs. Then call on student volunteers to explain how they got the form (**tú** form of the present tense minus **s**). Call students up to fill in the blanks.
- To introduce the **usted** and **ustedes** forms, begin by filling in the forms of the present tense of regular verbs. As you do, ask students if they can explain the pattern (using the opposite endings). Continue practice with such verbs as: **lavar, limpiar, escribir, leer**, etc., for **usted** and **ustedes**. Then ask students to think of situation where these forms would be appropriate to use (formal and plural).
- Continue with the irregular forms and ask students to predict the forms. Then ask students to describe how the verbs went from **hacer** to **haga**, **tener** to **tenga** (begin with the **yo** form).

- Then have students open their books and review all the explanations.
- Go over the information in the box referring to the **vosotros** form. Explain that this is only used in Spain.
- Give extra practice by saying the beginning of a command and having the students complete it with their own ideas, for instance: **Ve al supermercado y...**, **Pon tu libro en la mesa y...**, etc., and then varying with **ustedes** form.
- Show students how pronouns are attached to the end of affirmative commands and explain that this often means an accent is required.

SLOWER-PACED LEARNERS

To further explore forming these commands in context, put students in pairs to write **tú** and **ustedes** commands using verb phrases for chores on page 68. Monitor their progress and assist as need. Go over common errors with the whole class.

GRAMÁTICA

1. AFFIRMATIVE COMMANDS

- Affirmative commands are used to give an order, to invite, give advice, make recommendations, or give permission to someone.
  *Marcos, **limpia** tu habitación y después, **haz** la tarea.*

- For **tú** or informal commands, drop the **–s** from the present tense form of the verb. There are some irregular verbs for the **tú** form (**decir, hacer, poner, tener**...).

	REGULAR VERBS			IRREGULAR VERBS			
	COMPRAR	COMER	SUBIR	DECIR	HACER	PONER	TENER
tú	compra	come	sube	di	haz	pon	ten

- For **usted** or formal commands and **ustedes** or plural commands, start with the **yo** form of the present tense, drop the **–o** and switch to the opposite **–ar** or **–er/–ir** endings of the verb. For example, verbs ending in **–ar** will use the **–e/–en** endings in **usted** and **ustedes** commands. Verbs ending in **–er/–ir** will use the **–a/–an** endings in **usted** and **ustedes** commands.

- The informal affirmative command for **vosotros/as** has a different ending formed by substituting the **–r** in the infinitive with a **–d**:
  Compra**d** / come**d** / subi**d** / deci**d** / hace**d** / pone**d** / tene**d**...
- This form is used in Spain to tell a group of people you normally address as individually **tú** to do something.
  *Niños, **tened** cuidado al cruzar la calle. Children, be careful when crossing the street.*

REGULAR VERBS			
INFINITIVE	yo FORM	usted	ustedes
comprar	compro	compre	compren
comer	como	coma	coman
subir	subo	suba	suban

***Compren** fruta fresca y **coman** una al día.*

IRREGULAR VERBS			
INFINITIVE	yo FORM	usted	ustedes
decir	digo	diga	digan
hacer	hago	haga	hagan
poner	pongo	ponga	pongan
tener	tengo	tenga	tengan

***Ponga** la lavadora y **haga** la cena.*

■ With all affirmative commands, object pronouns are attached to the end of the verb.

Pon la mayonesa y la mostaza en el refrigerador.
***Ponlas** allí.*
Put the mayonnaise and the mustard in the refrigerator.
Put them there.

*Compra el pan. **Cómpralo**.*
Buy the bread. Buy it.

1 **Completa las frases conjugando en imperativo afirmativo los verbos entre paréntesis.**

a. Por favor, (entrar, usted) ....
b. Muchachos, (guardar, ustedes) .... los libros.
c. (Mirar, ustedes) .... por la ventana.
d. (Escribir, ustedes) .... en el cuaderno.
e. Pedro, (leer, tú) .... este libro de poesía.
f. (Escuchar, usted) .... atentamente.
g. Por favor, (poner, tú) .... la mesa.
h. (Hacer, ustedes) .... las tareas para mañana.
i. (Decir, usted) .... lo que piensa.
j. (Tener, tú) .... cuidado al cruzar la calle.
k. (Hablar, tú) .... más alto, por favor, no te oigo bien.
l. (Estudiar, ustedes) .... mucho, mañana tienen un examen muy importante.
m. (Cerrar, usted) .... la ventana, por favor, hace mucho frío.
n. (Poner, ustedes) .... sus abrigos encima de la cama.

2 **Los padres de Daría se van de viaje. Lee la nota que ha dejado la madre al abuelo y a los hijos y escribe en imperativo afirmativo los verbos entre paréntesis.**

Fernando, (a) .... (poner) el despertador para no quedarte dormido por la mañana y (b) .... (tener) cuidado de no dejarte el fuego de la estufa encendido. Marcos, puedes jugar un poco a los videojuegos si quieres, pero antes (c) .... (hacer) la tarea. Y Daría, tú (d) .... (sacar) al perro a pasear después de la escuela. Papá, (e) .... (tener) cuidado si sales a la calle y (f) .... (agarrar) las llaves, que siempre te las olvidas. Y, por favor, (g) .... (dejar) la casa ordenada.

73

Activity 2

• Read the instructions and have the students read the text and write the correct form of the affirmative commands.
• Have them share their answers with a partner.
• Ask for volunteers to read each sentence with the correct command form.

Extension

Distribute copies of EA 2.3, ***Mira la vida de Dani Martín***. Explain to students that Dani Martín is a well-known singer in Spain. Share with them the following Cultural Note.

Cultural Note

Daniel Martín García (Madrid, 1977) es un cantante, compositor y actor español de gran éxito. Anteriormente, fue líder del grupo de *El Canto del loco*, muy famoso entre los jóvenes. Actualmente prosigue su carrera en solitario.

• Then have students review the song lyrics and answer the questions in pairs.
• Play the song from the internet and have students just listen. Then call on students to review answers.
• Play the song again and have students follow along with the lyrics. Encourage students to sing along as well.

ANSWERS

Activity 1

a. entre; **b.** guarden; **c.** Miren; **d.** Escriban; **e.** lee; **f.** Escuche; **g.** pon; **h.** Hagan; **i.** Diga; **j.** Ten; **k.** Habla; **l.** Estudien; **m.** Cierre; **n.** Pongan.

Activity 2

a. pon; **b.** ten; **c.** haz; **d.** saca; **e.** ten; **f.** agarra; **g.** deja.

ADVANCED LEARNERS

Working in pairs, have students choose one of the images on the page and write a dialogue that includes at least three commands. Have them practice the conversations together. Call on volunteers to present their conversations to the class.

HERITAGE LANGUAGE LEARNERS

Challenge students to find another song in Spanish that includes at least three commands. Have them prepare a brief description of the singer or band who wrote the song and post it on a class discussion board along with the title and lyrics of the song with the command structures called out.

INSTRUCTIONAL STRATEGIES

Activity 1

• Explain that they have to choose the correct command form of the verb (checking whether it is **tú**, **usted** or **ustedes**) and write it in the space provided.
• Do the first sentence with the class, asking for volunteers to say the correct form.
• Invite students to continue through the activity individually and then compare answers with a partner.
• Circulate while they work and answer any questions that may arise.
• When they have finished, ask for volunteers to call out the answers and write them on the board.
• If desired, ask them to change some of the commands to the **vosotros** form, for example b, c, d, h, l and n.

INSTRUCTIONAL STRATEGIES

Activity 3

- To review direct and indirect objects for students, write the model sentence on the board: **Pónganla en la estantería**. Ask students what **la** refers to (**la película**).
- Ask students what the correct order is when there are both a direct and an indirect object. Practice with **Dímelo**. Ask students what **lo** refers to (direct object pronoun taking the place of what is being said) and then **me** (person receiving the message).
- Tell them they have to use the correct affirmative command, checking which person is to be used, and then add the direct object pronoun to the end, which usually means adding an accent.
- Depending on the level of your students, you may want to have them underline the direct object in each sentence and prepare the corresponding pronoun as a middle step and ask individual students to say which pronouns they have chosen.
- Have the students work with a partner to choose the correct command form and then add the pronoun to the end, remembering to add an accent if necessary.
- Circulate as they work, answering questions and providing assistance where required.
- Ask for volunteers to read the answers and other volunteers to write them on the board. Ask the class where the accent should go if it is required.

OBJECTIVES FOR GRAMÁTICA 2

- Present grammatical structures needed to practice communicative functions of the unit: Negative commands of regular and irregular verbs
- Use negative command forms to tell different people what not to do

CORE RESOURCES

- Interactive Whiteboard Lesson: IWB 2.2

STANDARDS

1.1 Engage in conversation
1.2 Understand the language
1.3 Present information
4.1 Compare languages

INSTRUCTIONAL STRATEGIES

2. Negative Commands

- Project the second chart of IWB 2.2, **El imperativo** to introduce negative command forms. Begin by filling in the forms of regular verbs. As you do, ask students if they can explain the pattern (using the opposite endings). Then continue to complete the chart together. Next ask students to explain the forms for irregular verbs (originate with **yo** form).
- Then walk the students through the explanation in the book and say a command in the affirmative for them to say in the negative, for instance: **Compra pan – No compres pan; Haz la tarea – No hagas la tarea; Ponga las cosas en la mesa – No ponga las cosas en la mesa**. etc. For this last sentence, point out that with negative commands, the pronouns come before the conjugated verb, and ask students to substitute a pronoun (**No las ponga en la mesa**).
- Point out the note that explains the **vosotros** form.

GRAMÁTICA

3 **Transforma las siguientes frases en órdenes y sustituye las palabras por pronombres cuando sea posible.**

a. Poner la película en la estantería. (ustedes) .... Pónganla en la estantería.
b. Comprar la comida al perro. (tú) ....
c. Dejar las cosas en su sitio. (ustedes) ....
d. Meter los tamales en la nevera. (usted) ....
e. Poner el despertador a tu hermano. (tú) ....
f. Estudiar la lección para mañana. (ustedes) ....
g. Decir los verbos en imperativo. (tú) ....

2. NEGATIVE COMMANDS

- Negative commands are used to tell someone what not to do.
- To form the negative commands:
  - For **usted/ustedes**, use the same form as the affirmative command.
    - (usted) compre → **no compre**
    - (ustedes) compren → **no compren**
  - For **tú**, add **–s** to the negative command of **usted**.
    - (usted) no compre → (tú) **no compres**

REGULAR VERBS

	COMPRAR	COMER	SUBIR
tú	no compres	no comas	no subas
usted	no compre	no coma	no suba
ustedes	no compren	no coman	no suban

IRREGULAR VERBS

	DECIR	HACER	PONER	TENER
tú	no digas	no hagas	no pongas	no tengas
usted	no diga	no haga	no ponga	no tenga
ustedes	no digan	no hagan	no pongan	no tengan

- For **vosotros/as** (Spain) drop the **–ar**, **–er**, **–ir** ending of the infinitive and switch to **–éis** (for **–ar** verbs) or **–áis** (for **–er/–ir** verbs):
  - no **compréis** / no **comáis** / no **subáis** / no **digáis** / no **hagáis**...

74

Activity 3

b. Cómprasela; **c.** Déjenlas; **d.** Métalos; **e.** Pónselo; **f.** Estúdienla; **g.** Dilos.

HERITAGE LANGUAGE LEARNERS

Before going over the form of negative commands, encourage students to think about and discuss the contexts in which negative commands are used. When / In what circumstances do they use them? Why do they use them? Who do they say them to? How does the tone of their voice affect how the commands are received? Who do they hear negative commands from? How do they usually respond to them? What affects how they respond? You may invite them to discuss questions like these in groups and then report back to the class.

■ With negative commands, pronouns always go before the conjugated verb.
*No **lo** bebas / no **me lo** digas / no **las** comas / no **lo** pienses / no **te** olvides...*
Don't drink it / don't tell it to me / don't eat them / don't think about it / don't forget...

4 **Completa las frases conjugando en imperativo negativo los verbos entre paréntesis.**

a. Necesito silencio para estudiar. (Poner, tú) .... música.
b. No nos gustan los productos de ese supermercado. (Comprar, ustedes) .... aquí.
c. En la planta de arriba hace mucho calor. (Subir, ustedes) ....
d. Es un secreto. (Decirlo, usted) ....
e. El pastel está malo. (Probarlo, tú) ....

5 **El padre de Daría también ha escrito otra nota. Completa los espacios con los verbos del cuadro usando el imperativo negativo.**

> pelearse ○ comer ○ ensuciar ○ poner ○ olvidarse ○ quedarse ○ llegar

Marcos, no (a) .... solo pizzas, tienes que comer lo que cocine tu hermana.
Daría, tú eres la encargada de Hueso. No (b) .... de ponerle la comida y el agua todos los días, y ¡no (c) .... la cocina!
Fernando, no (d) .... tarde, ni (e) .... dormido viendo la tele en el sofá.
Abuelo, no (f) .... la radio muy alta, que después se quejan los vecinos.
Y a todos, por favor, no (g) ....

6 **Transforma en imperativo negativo estas frases usando los pronombres cuando sea posible.**

a. Poner la película en la estantería. (ustedes) ..... *No la pongan en la estantería.*
b. Comprar la comida al perro. (tú) ....
c. Dejar las cosas en su sitio. (ustedes) ....
d. Meter los tamales en la nevera. (usted) ....
e. Poner el despertador a tu padre. (tú) ....
f. Hacer la tarea a tu hermano. (tú) ....

7 **Ordena las palabras para formar frases en imperativo negativo.**

a. le / nada / mi / hermano. / a / No / digas ....
b. Dale / perro. / comida / la / al ....
c. pongas / te / No / ese / jersey. ....
d. Ponte / gafas / las / sol. / de ....
e. se / No / peleen / primos. / sus / con ....
f. compres. / lo / No / me ....

👤💻 **MORE IN ELETECA:** EXTRA ONLINE PRACTICE ● 🔲 **GRAMMAR TUTORIALS** 3 AND 4   75

INSTRUCTIONAL STRATEGIES

Activity 4

• Have students write the correct form of the negative command and then share with a partner. Remind them that any direct object pronouns are placed before the command in the negative.
• Invite students to read their sentences to the class in order to correct.

Activity 5

• Run through the list of verbs ensuring students understand them all.
• Students work in pairs to write the negative command form in the blank provided.
• When they have finished, ask for volunteers to read a sentence and write the negative commands on the board.
• Point out the need for the letter **u** in this form of **llegar**, and have the students think about which form will be used for the last command.

Activity 6

• Have the students look at the verbs and say the affirmative command form of each, according to the person in parenthesis.
• Read the model for the students and have half the class say the affirmative command form and the other half the negative.
• Have the students write the negative command for each sentence and change the direct object into a pronoun where possible.
• Have them compare answers with a partner.
• Invite students to say their answers aloud and write them on the board.

Activity 7

• Have the students work individually to put the words in the correct order.
• Ask them to share their answers with a partner.
• Have volunteers read their answers aloud.

ANSWERS

Activity 4

a. No pongas; **b.** No compren; **c.** No suban; **d.** No lo diga; **e.** No lo pruebes.

Activity 5

a. comas; **b.** te olvides; **c.** ensucies; **d.** llegues; **e.** te quedes; **f.** pongas; **g.** se peleen.

Activity 6

a. No la pongan en la estantería; **b.** No la compres; **c.** No las dejen desordenadas; **d.** No los meta en la nevera; **e.** No se lo pongas; **f.** No se la hagas.

Activity 7

a. No le digas nada a mi hermano; **b.** Dale la comida al perro; **c.** No te pongas ese jersey; **d.** Ponte las gafas de sol; **e.** No se peleen con sus primos; **f.** No me lo compres.

SLOWER-PACED LEARNERS

For additional practice, have students write the opposite commands for the sentences in Activity 7 with a partner. Go over common errors as a class.

ADVANCED LEARNERS

For some fun at the end of the lesson, put students in small groups to take turns acting out commands as the others say them. You may want to challenge one group to compete against another. Each group will have the same amount of time to give and act out commands. The group who can correctly say and act out the most commands within that time wins.

OBJECTIVES FOR DESTREZAS

- Learn to skim a brochure for information
- Asking the right questions

STANDARDS

1.1 Interpersonal communication
1.2 Understand the language
1.3 Present information

INSTRUCTIONAL STRATEGIES

Comprensión de lectura

Activity 1

- Have the students look at the image and ask if they can guess what the activity is going to be about.
- Talk the students through the strategy, and have them skim through the brochure.

Activity 2

- The students choose the correct ending for each statement.
- Have them compare answers with a partner.
- Ask for volunteers to give the correct answers.
- Ask questions about the information in the brochure, for instance: ***¿Cuándo empieza el curso? ¿Cuánto cuesta el curso?***, etc.

ANSWERS

Activity 2

1. c; **2.** c; **3.** b; **4.** a; **5.** c; **6.** c.

SLOWER-PACED LEARNERS

Suggest that the students circle, underline, or highlight the parts of the brochure that help them answer the questions in Activity 2. If possible, project the brochure so that students can mark it up for the class to see. Call on volunteers to point out where they found their answers and mark it. When the answer required more extrapolation, encourage students to explain how they arrived at it.

HERITAGE LANGUAGE LEARNERS

Have students investigate opportunities for Spanish-speaking amateur actors of their age either in their own communities or in a country of their choosing. Challenge them to find a brochure, website, or other promotional material that the theater company uses to recruit people. Have them share their findings with the class.

DESTREZAS

COMPRENSIÓN DE LECTURA

1 **Antes de realizar la lectura, repasa la estrategia en Destrezas y sigue la recomendación.**

> **Destrezas**
>
> **Asking yourself questions**
> It is helpful to ask yourself questions as you read. Skim through the brochure and ask yourself if you have read similar brochures to sign up for an activity you liked.

Si te gusta la interpretación o simplemente quieres conocer gente nueva y pasarlo bien, apúntate ya a nuestro taller de teatro. Puedes hacerlo de 8:00 a 20:30h en el teléfono (33) 3563-9184; en la recepción de la Casa Teatro El Caminante, C/ Marcos Castellanos, 26, Guadalajara; o a cualquier hora a través de nuestra web: *www.casateatroelcaminante.mx.*

El plazo de inscripción finaliza el 30 de septiembre.
- Inicio de curso: viernes 5 de octubre.
- Horario: todos los viernes de 18:00 a 20:00h.
- Lugar: Casa de la Cultura.
- Edad: sin límite de edad.
- Precio: 450 pesos al mes. (350 pesos para menores de 21 años y mayores de 55).
- Final de curso: 24 de junio. Ese día harán una representación para mostrar a sus amigos y familiares todo lo que aprendieron.

2 **Lee de nuevo el texto y elige la opción correcta en cada caso.**

1. El taller de teatro va dirigido a...
   a. personas que quieren ser actores profesionales.
   b. personas que tienen experiencia en el teatro.
   c. personas a las que les gusta el teatro.

2. El curso...
   a. es de una hora a la semana.
   b. dura un año.
   c. es un día a la semana.

3. El curso es para...
   a. mayores de 55 años.
   b. todas las edades.
   c. personas de entre 21 y 55 años.

4. La inscripción...
   a. puede hacerse a cualquier hora.
   b. puede hacerse solo los viernes de 18:00 a 20:00h.
   c. empieza el 30 de septiembre.

5. El precio del curso...
   a. es de 450 pesos.
   b. es gratis.
   c. depende de la edad.

6. El último día de curso...
   a. hay una clase gratis para los amigos y familiares de los alumnos.
   b. los alumnos van a ver una obra de teatro.
   c. los alumnos hacen una obra de teatro.

76

EXPRESIÓN E INTERACCIÓN ORALES

3 **Observa la imagen y habla durante 3 o 5 minutos siguiendo las instrucciones.**

a. Describe el lugar, las personas, los objetos y las acciones.
b. Habla sobre las características físicas de las personas y sobre su ropa o las cosas que llevan.

PRONUNCIACIÓN La entonación

■ Intonation refers to the pitch or the rising and falling of one's voice. Intonation is important because it can change the meaning of a sentence. In Spanish, statements end in a falling pitch.

- **Entonación enunciativa.** *Estudio español. Está duchándose.*

- **Entonación exclamativa.** *¡Qué interesante! ¡Ya he terminado!*

- **Entonación interrogativa.**   Abierta: *¿Dónde vives?*

                Cerrada: *¿Tienes un diccionario?*

- **Entonación suspendida.** *Pues si no lo sabe él... ¡Es tan lindo...!*

1 🎧 13 **Escucha los ejemplos y repite.**

2 🎧 14 **Escucha la entonación y elige la frase que oyes en cada caso.**

a. ☐ Ya ha venido.   b. ☐ No lo quiere.   c. ☐ Habla español.   d. ☐ Es que no puede.
☐ ¡Ya ha venido!   ☐ ¡No lo quiere!   ☐ ¡Habla español!   ☐ ¡Es que no puede!
☐ ¿Ya ha venido?   ☐ ¿No lo quiere?   ☐ ¿Habla español?   ☐ ¿Es que no puede?
☐ Ya ha venido...   ☐ No lo quiere...   ☐ Habla español...   ☐ Es que no puede...

3 🎧 15 **Escucha la conversación y pon los signos que faltan según la entonación que oyes.**

» Cuándo vendrá Marcos   » Acaso te viene mal   » Déjame que te explique
» Supongo que el domingo   » Cómo dices eso   » Pues habla ya
» Pues si viene el domingo   » Quieres hablar claro

🖥 **MORE IN ELETECA:** EXTRA ONLINE PRACTICE

77

INSTRUCTIONAL STRATEGIES

Expresión e interacción orales
Activity 3

- Have the students look at the image.
- Tell them to choose either option *a* or *b* and take a few minutes to think about what they will say.
- Divide them into pairs (one having prepared *a* and the other *b*), and have them take turns to talk for about 3 minutes each.
- Circulate as they prepare and talk, answering questions and providing assistance where required.

OBJECTIVES FOR PRONUNCIACIÓN

- Practice correct intonation
- Listen and identify meaning through pronunciation

CORE RESOURCES

- Audio Program: Tracks 13, 14 and 15
- Interactive Online Materials - ELEteca

STANDARDS

1.2   Understand the language
3.2   Acquire information
4.1   Compare languages

INSTRUCTIONAL STRATEGIES

- Walk the students through the explanation and go over the different intonations with them. Have them repeat each one.

🎧 **13** **Activity 1**

Play the audio and have the students listen and repeat.

🎧 **14** **Activity 2**

- Have students look briefly at the short sentences. Play the audio and have them check the statement that best matches the intonation they hear.
- Play the audio again while they confirm their answers. Ask for volunteers to give the correct answers.

Audioscript

a. ¡Ya ha venido!; **b.** ¿No lo quiere?; **c.** Habla español.; **d.** Es que no puede.

🎧 **15** **Activity 3**

- Have the students read the exchanges silently. Then play the audio pausing for them to add the missing punctuation.
- Invite different students to write a sentence on the board with the correct punctuation. Play the audio one more time while they listen and look at the corrected activity.

Audioscript

» ¿Cuándo vendrá Marcos?
» Supongo que el domingo.
» Pues si viene el domingo...
» ¿Acaso te viene mal?
» ¡Cómo dices eso!
» ¿Quieres hablar claro?
» Déjame que te explique...
» ¡Pues habla ya!

ADVANCED LEARNERS

For additional speaking practice, have students pick out another image from the book that they can talk about using the guidelines for **a** or **b** in Activity 3. Put students into pairs. Tell them to describe the image to their partner who has to draw it without looking it. This will challenge students to provide more detailed and accurate information in their descriptions. You may want to give students access to markers or crayons and allow more time for speaking and drawing.

OBJECTIVES FOR SABOR HISPANO
- Learn about manners in Spanish society
- Learn how other cultures have different norms

CORE RESOURCES
- Audio Program: Track 16

STANDARDS
2.1	Culture: Practices and perspectives
2.2	Products and perspectives
3.2	Acquire information
5.2	Using language for personal enjoyment and enrichment

INSTRUCTIONAL STRATEGIES

 16

- Introduce the topic by asking what the students know about what is considered polite or rude in Spanish society and in U.S. society.
- Talk about the images and elicit what they already know and can share.
- Ask if any of them have noticed examples of good/bad manners.
- Have them look at the questions in **Antes de leer**.
- Tell the students to look at the **Glosario** on the next page to help them with any vocabulary they may not know.
- Read the first section of the text and invite a volunteer to read after you. After each section, ask questions such as: **¿Es importante llegar en punto en Alemania? ¿De dónde es Sebastian Rohde?**, etc. Continue with the other sections.
- Ask what the students have understood and invite those who understood more to help those who understood less.

HERITAGE LANGUAGE LEARNERS

Give students a chance to react to the examples of good and bad manners in the text and draw any connections with their own experiences.

SABOR HISPANO

BUENOS Y MALOS MODALES

¿Hablas muy alto por teléfono?

Antes de leer
¿Qué son los buenos modales (*manners*), según tú?

¿Crees que la gente de tu país suele tener buenos modales?

¿Es importante ser educado? ¿Por qué?

16 Hablar alto, tocarse la nariz, empezar a comer antes que otros, llegar tarde... Mucha gente piensa que estos son malos modales pero, ¿son típicos de una persona maleducada o de una cultura?

«Cuando me mudé a España me invitaron a una fiesta. La fiesta era a las 8 de la tarde. En Alemania la puntualidad es importante así que llegué a las 8 en punto. Pero mis amigos españoles no llegaron hasta las 8 y media... ¡Qué vergüenza!», dice Sebastian Rohde, un muchacho de 21 años de Berlín.

La experiencia de Sebastian no es única. En España no se considera de mala educación llegar tarde a una fiesta. «Si quedo con amigos a una hora determinada, se sobreentiende* que llegar algo más tarde es lo normal», dice Marisa López, una chica de Valencia.

«Pero en el ambiente laboral la actitud es muy distinta: con cosas relacionadas con el trabajo, la gente es muy profesional», dice Marisa.

«La primera vez que visité el Reino Unido, me chocó* mucho que la gente empezara a cenar antes que el resto de comensales*. En España eso se considera de mala educación», dice Samantha Borrás, una estudiante de Madrid que vive en el Reino Unido. «Preferimos comer la comida cuando está caliente», dice su novio inglés.

«¿Que si los españoles son maleducados? A veces sí lo parecen», dice Soroya Conti, una chica argentina que vive en España, «En mi país la gente que trabaja de cara al público utiliza muchas palabras de cortesía. En España se habla de forma más directa. Por eso, a algunos extranjeros les puede parecer que los españoles son maleducados».

«Creo que los españoles hablan muy alto. En Finlandia hablamos mucho más bajo. Allí se considera de mala educación hablar alto. Por eso algunas personas pueden pensar que los españoles son groseros*», dice Karen Laatvala, una estudiante que vive en Salamanca.

Una muchacha llega tarde a una cita.

78

¿Qué suelen pensar los extranjeros del comportamiento social de los españoles?

- Que no son puntuales.
- Que hablan alto.
- Que no tienen muy buena atención al cliente.
- Que interrumpen mucho.

5 comportamientos de buena educación en España

- Utilizar expresiones de cortesía.
- No comer hasta que todos los comensales hayan recibido su comida.
- Taparse la boca al toser* o estornudar*.
- No abrir la boca al comer.
- Comer con cubiertos*.

Un muchacho bosteza en público.

¿COMPRENDISTE?

Decide si las siguientes frases son verdaderas (V) o falsas (F).

1. Sebastian y Karen hablan de los modales de los españoles. V ○ F ○
2. Soroya piensa que los españoles siempre hablan de forma cortés. V ○ F ○
3. Sebastian llegó tarde a la fiesta. V ○ F ○
4. Samantha prefiere esperar al resto de comensales. V ○ F ○
5. Comer con las manos es señal de buena educación en España. V ○ F ○

Un muchacho come muy rápido.

AHORA TÚ

¿Qué opinas? Contesta las siguientes preguntas y comenta tus ideas con tus compañeros/as.

1. ¿Qué comportamientos se consideran correctos en tu país?
2. ¿Qué expresiones corteses usarías en español para pedir información?
3. ¿Has tenido alguna experiencia con otras culturas en las cuales has observado alguna señal de mala educación?
4. ¿Qué comportamientos son de mala educación, según tú?
5. ¿Te has comportado de forma grosera alguna vez? ¿Cuándo?

Glosario

chocar – to be in shock
el comensal – dinner guest
el cubierto – cutlery
estornudar – to sneeze
grosero/a – rude
sobreentender – understand perfectly
toser – to cough

VOCES LATINAS
¿CÓMO SON TUS MODALES?

Fuentes: Entrevistas personales a estudiantes de Erasmus, Guía de Protocolo, Protocolo.org.

79

INSTRUCTIONAL STRATEGIES

- Look at the pie graph and have the students interpret the information they see and make statements about it. Prompt with: *¿Qué piensa la mayoría de los extranjeros sobre los españoles? ¿Qué aspecto les molesta menos?* Ask students to share their own perspectives about Spanish-speakers and people in their own culture and communities. What behaviors do they have in common?
- Have students do the same with the bar graph. Then in pairs, ask students to categorize five behaviors they consider important. Call on volunteers to present. Then together as a class choose which five from the ones suggested best reflect American culture.

¿Comprendiste?

- Have the students read the statements in the box and then check through the text to see if they are true or false.
- Have them compare their answers with a partner.
- Invite individual students to share their answers with the class.

Ahora tú

- Read the questions with the students and have them think about the answers.
- Have the students answer the questions in pairs and then ask for volunteers to present to the class.

ANSWERS

1. T; **2.** F; **3.** F; **4.** T; **5.** F.

ADVANCED LEARNERS

Working in groups, have students come up with a list of what they think people from other countries might consider bad manners by Americans. Encourage them to do some research to read about stereotypes and impressions of Americans around the world in terms of their social behavior.

OBJECTIVES FOR RELATO

- Revisit unit themes, grammar, vocabulary and culture in a new context
- Improve reading comprehension skills

STANDARDS

1.1 Engage in conversation
1.2 Understand the language
1.3 Present information
2.1 Practices and perspectives
5.3 Using language for personal enjoyment and enrichment

INSTRUCTIONAL STRATEGIES

Activity 1

- To introduce the activity, write the following quote on the board: **"En la vida hay que poner [el corazón] en lo que se hace. Si no, no sirve para nada"** leaving a blank for **corazón**. Ask students what word they think would complete the idea. Then have them read the quotation in the book.
- With a partner, have students answer and discuss the questions.
- Ask for volunteers to share their ideas with the class.

🎧 17 Activity 2

- Have the students read the title and look at the images to predict what they think the text will be about.
- Read the text in sections and ask individual students to repeat or play the audio.
- Ask questions about the text, such as: **¿Cómo se llama el libro encontrado? ¿Cuánto cuenta ese libro? ¿Por qué le gusta?**, etc.

Cultural Note

Tell students: *La novela* Como agua para chocolate *es de la escritora mexicana Laura Esquivel.* Encourage students to learn more about her at *http://www.epdlp.com/escritor.php?id=2484*

ANSWERS

Activity 1

a. Se refiere a poner mucho esfuerzo y hacerlo todo lo mejor posible.
b., c.: Answers will vary.

ADVANCED LEARNERS

In addition to having students look at the title and pictures before reading the story, invite them to share their own thoughts and experiences related to the idea of a grandmother's cooking, family recipes, and other family cooking traditions. Put students in pairs to discuss their associations and ideas. Then have them report back to the class about their partners' comments.

HERITAGE LANGUAGE LEARNERS

Have students do more research on Laura Esquivel and her novel **Como agua para chocolate**. Then have them write an essay that includes brief biographical information about the author, a summary of the story that includes the main characters, and reflections on the novel's success given the historical and literary context in which it was written.

RELATO Mi abuela Eva

1 👥 **Lee la siguiente frase y contesta las preguntas con tu compañero/a.**

En la vida hay que poner el corazón en lo que haces. Si no, no sirve para nada.

a. ¿A qué crees que se refiere con "poner el corazón"?
b. ¿Estás de acuerdo con la frase?
c. Señala las cosas en las que pones el corazón: aficiones, deportes, estudios…

2 🎧 **17 Lee el texto.**

Mi abuela Eva

No sé si creer en las casualidades. Pero resulta que hoy, en el autobús, mientras iba a la escuela, alguien se había dejado olvidado un libro. Ya su portada me atraía a leerlo y a devorarlo (*devour it*). Fíjate si estaba entusiasmada (*excited*) con la historia, que me pasé la parada de la escuela. El libro se llamaba *Como agua para chocolate* y cuenta la vida de Tita y su historia de amor con Pedro. La madre de Tita tuvo a su hija en la cocina, entre los olores (*smells*) de lo que estaba cocinando. Por eso, ya desde el principio, Tita sentía un gran amor por la cocina. Cuando cocinaba, su estado de ánimo (*mood*) influía en los platos que preparaba. Así, si hacía un plato estando alegre, cuando la gente lo comía, también se ponía contenta.

Ahora estoy en mi habitación y sigo leyéndolo sin parar. Quizás también me gusta esta historia porque me recuerda a mi abuela. Ella pasaba mucho tiempo en la cocina y le encantaba cocinar. Además, al igual que Tita, creía que era muy importante cómo te sentías cuando cocinabas. Siempre que podíamos, mi hermano y yo, a la vuelta de la escuela, pasábamos toda la tarde con ella. Cuando nos veía asomar (*peeking out*) la cabeza por la puerta siempre nos decía:

– Entren, entren. Miren qué estoy preparando.

Nosotros entrábamos hipnotizados. Dejábamos las mochilas en el suelo y nos poníamos manos a la obra (*get down to business*).

– Manuela, ayúdame a cortar esta cebolla, y Tomás, lava las papas para cocerlas.

A mi hermano y a mí nos encantaba ser sus ayudantes en la cocina e imaginar que estábamos en uno de los mejores restaurantes de París.

– No, mira, si quieres que esté dulce, recítale un poema. Sí, así… Muy bien… En la vida hay que poner el corazón en lo que haces. Si no, no sirve para nada… Eso es, ponle alegría, que es para la familia…

Daba igual si no lo hacíamos perfecto, ella siempre nos sonreía. Claro, que eso no era muy difícil, porque todo le parecía bien y casi siempre estaba de buen humor. Creo que solamente se enfadaba y se quejaba (complain) cuando cortaba la cebolla y le lloraban los ojos.

– Seguro que esto no es bueno. Si lloro ahora cocinando, ¿qué pasará cuando lo coman los invitados? Yo no quiero llorar cocinando. ¿Y si se me caen las lágrimas (tears) encima de la comida?

Un día, por su cumpleaños, se nos ocurrió regalarle unas gafas de buceo (swimming mask) para cortar cebollas y así perder el miedo a cocinar algo triste. Todavía recuerdo su sonrisa cuando se las puso. Nos dijo que era el mejor regalo del mundo.

3 Completa con la información del texto de la Actividad 2.

a. Empezó a leer ....
b. Si estás triste y cocinas, ...
c. Estando con ella pensábamos ....
d. Las gafas de buceo le sirven para ....
e. La abuela siempre nos decía ....
f. El libro me recuerda a ella porque ....

4 El libro *Como agua para chocolate (Like Water for Chocolate)*, que está leyendo la protagonista del relato, forma parte de la corriente literaria del realismo mágico en Hispanoamérica. Lee la definición de este movimiento literario y contesta.

Este estilo se caracteriza por introducir elementos mágicos como algo normal de la vida cotidiana; forman parte de ella y son aceptados. La realidad y la fantasía se mezclan en la narración.

¿Qué idea del realismo mágico hay en el relato sobre la abuela Eva?

....
....
....
....
....

5 Escribe sobre una persona importante en tu vida. ¿Puedes utilizar el realismo mágico en tu narración?

Extension

To help students understand magical realism and how it might be represented, share the following description from the movie version. Explain that Tita, as the youngest of the sisters and according to tradition, must remain unmarried to care for her mother. Yet she and Pedro have fallen in love. To stay a part of her life, Pedro decides to marry Tita's sister. Describe the following wedding scene for students to imagine.

Para la boda de su hermana, Tita, la protagonista de la historia, hace la torta de la boda para Pedro y su hermana Rosaura y después asiste a su boda. Tita no puede expresar las emociones por perder al amor de su vida que se casa con su hermana, pero sus lágrimas derramadas en la masa de la tarta de boda transmitirán sus emociones a todo aquel que la pruebe. El efecto del realismo mágico se ve en que toda la gente que come la tarta se pone enferma; sienten el dolor y la tristeza igual que si acabasen de perder a su amante.

ANSWERS

Activity 3

a. Empezó a leer un libro que alguien se había dejado olvidado en el autobús; **b.** Si estás triste y cocinas, transmitirás tu tristèza a las personas que coman lo que has cocinado; **c.** Estando con ella pensábamos que estábamos en uno de los mejores restaurantes de París; **d.** Las gafas de buceo le sirven para no tener que llorar mientras corta las cebollas y así evitar cocinar algo triste; **e.** La abuela siempre nos decía que en la vida hay que poner el corazón en lo que se hace porque si no, no sirve para nada; **f.** El libro me recuerda a ella porque también pasaba mucho tiempo en la cocina y le encantaba cocinar, además también creía que era muy importante cómo se sentía uno cuando cocinaba.

Activity 4

Answers will vary. Possible answer: Que el estado de ánimo que tenemos mientras cocinamos influye en los platos que preparamos y que estos lo transmiten a quien los come. Por ejemplo, en el texto aparece la idea de endulzar los platos recitando un poema o transmitir tristeza si se llora al cortar las cebollas.

SLOWER-PACED LEARNERS

Before writing their stories in Activity 5, help students gather their thoughts and plan their writing. As an overall strategy, encourage them to focus on one particularly strong memory or experience with the important person that they've chosen. Share your own example with the class as a model. Then discuss what characteristics make something magical or unreal. Jot down notes on the board as reminders. Refer them back to your memory and elicit how you can change parts of it or add details to make it more magical. Take suggestions from the class. Give students time to choose their people and memories. Then pair them up to strategize how to add elements of magic to their stories. After they write their first drafts, have students share them with their partners for corrections and additional suggestions.

INSTRUCTIONAL STRATEGIES

Activity 3

• Ask the students to complete the sentences with information from the text.
• Have them compare their answers with a partner.
• Ask different students to say the correct answers aloud.

Activity 4

• Ask students to read the definition of magical realism and look for examples of it in the story with a partner.
• Ask for students to report to the class and discuss any ideas that emerge.

Activity 5

• Have the students choose an important person in their life and think about how they could use magical realism to write about that person.
• Have them write some sentences about the person and share them with a partner.

OBJECTIVES FOR EVALUACIÓN

- Review grammar, vocabulary and culture from the unit
- Complete self-assessment

CORE RESOURCES

- Audio Program: Track 18
- Interactive Online Materials - ELEteca

STANDARDS

1.2 Understand the language
2.1 Practices and perspectives
4.1 Compare cultures

INSTRUCTIONAL STRATEGIES

- Activities can be completed individually and then reviewed with the class. Vary by asking students if they agree with the answer given and then writing it on the board. Provide explanations as needed.
- You may wish to assign point value to each activity as a way for students to monitor their progress.
- Direct students to the indicated pages in **En resumen** if they make more than one or two mistakes in any one section.

ANSWERS

Activity 1

1. e; **2.** c; **3.** b; **4.** d; **5.** a; **6.** f.

Activity 2

1. d, f; **2.** g, b; **3.** c, h; **4.** e, a.

Activity 3

a. pongan; **b.** Repártanlas; **c.** Tengan; **d.** hagan; **e.** Sean; **f.** pasen; **g.** limpien; **h.** Laven; **i.** lávenlos; **j.** Saquen; **k.** Sáquenla; **l.** se obsesionen.

EVALUACIÓN

ASKING, GIVING AND REFUSING PERMISSION. EXTENDING OR OFFERING INVITATIONS

1 Relaciona.

1. ¿Le importa si abro la ventana? Hace mucho calor.
2. ¿Te importa si uso tu celular?
3. ¿Puedo pasar?
4. ¿Quieres un poco más de sopa?
5. Tome, siéntese aquí.
6. Mamá, si hago toda mi tarea y limpio mi habitación, ¿podría ir esta noche al cine?

a. Gracias, joven.
b. ¡Claro! Pasa, pasa.
c. Llama, llama.
d. No, gracias, ya estoy lleno.
e. No, por favor, ábrala.
f. ¡Ni hablar!

INSTRUCTIONS, ADVICE, AND COMMANDS

2 Relaciona cada frase con la persona que la dice.

a. Pues llámala.
b. Vale, pero si me voy es para siempre, así que no me llames más.
c. Perdone, ¿para ir al museo Picasso?
d. No llegues tarde, que van a venir tus abuelos a cenar.
e. Ayer me lo pasé genial con Aurora, ¿qué puedo hacer?
f. ¡Que síííííí…! ¡Ya me lo has dicho un montón de veces!
g. Agarra tus cosas y vete. No quiero verte más.
h. Sigue todo derecho, y al final de la calle gira a la izquierda.

COMMANDS AND PRONOUNS

3 Completa los espacios con los verbos entre paréntesis en imperativo.

Si van a compartir su apartamento con alguien (a) .... (poner, ustedes) unas normas para las tareas. (b) .... (Repartir, ustedes, las tareas) de forma justa y equitativa. (c) .... (Tener, ustedes) en cuenta los gustos y preferencias de la otra persona. No (d) .... (hacer, ustedes) solo las tareas que más les gustan a ustedes. (e) .... (Ser, ustedes) comprensivos el uno con el otro. Si quieren una casa limpia y ordenada, (f) .... (pasar, ustedes) la aspiradora y (g) .... (limpiar, ustedes) el baño, como mínimo, una vez a la semana. (h) .... (Lavar, ustedes) los platos cada día y (i) .... (lavar, ustedes, los platos) bien, también por debajo. (j) .... (Sacar, ustedes) la basura todos los días. (k) .... (Sacar, ustedes, la basura), si no, la casa olerá fatal. No (l) .... (obsesionarse, ustedes) con la limpieza. Si un día no hacen la cama, no pasa nada.

LAS TAREAS DOMÉSTICAS Y LOS DEPORTES

4 **Completa las frases con las palabras que has aprendido en esta unidad.**

a. No tengo ropa limpia, hay que ....

b. Mi madre es alérgica al polvo, así que tenemos que .... y pasar .... todos los días.

c. En mi casa se cambian las .... los domingos.

d. Bernardo es muy malo jugando al fútbol. El otro día, ... el balón y metió gol en su propia ....

e. Me han regalado una .... para jugar al tenis igual que la que usa Rafa Nadal.

INTONATION

5 🎧 **18** **Escucha la conversación y elige la respuesta de Paco.**

Antonio: ¡Qué temprano vienes!

Paco: a. ☐ ¡Tú sí que has venido temprano!

b. ☐ ¿Tú sí que has venido temprano?

Antonio: Es que hoy no he perdido el bus. Por cierto, ¿qué hora es?

Paco: a. ☐ ¿Es que no tienes reloj?

b. ☐ Es que no tienes reloj...

Antonio: Lo he olvidado en casa. ¿A qué hora viene el jefe?

Paco: a. ☐ No lo sé.

b. ☐ ¡No lo sé!

Antonio: ¿Y si vamos a tomar un café?

Paco: a. ☐ ¡Otro café!

b. ☐ ¿Otro café?

Antonio: Es que no he desayunado.

Paco: a. ☐ Bueno, ¿te acompaño?

b. ☐ Bueno, te acompaño.

CULTURA

6 **Contesta las siguientes preguntas con lo que has aprendido en *Buenos y Malos Modales*.**

a. Si llegas tarde a una fiesta, ¿es de mala educación en España? ¿Y en tu país o región?

b. Si estás en España, ¿puedes empezar a cenar si no están todos los comensales? ¿Y en tu país o región?

c. Cuando un español habla en voz alta, ¿está enfadado? ¿Y en tu país o región?

d. ¿Qué hay que hacer en España si toses o estornudas? ¿Y en tu país o región?

e. En España, ¿se puede interrumpir a una persona que está hablando? ¿Y en tu país o región?

MORE IN ELETECA: EXTRA ONLINE PRACTICE

83

INSTRUCTIONAL STRATEGIES

🎧 **18** **Activity 5**

Audioscript

» ¡Qué temprano vienes!

» ¡Tú sí que has venido temprano!

» Es que hoy no he perdido el bus. Por cierto, ¿qué hora es?

» ¿Es que no tienes reloj?

» Lo he olvidado en casa. ¿A qué hora viene el jefe?

» No lo sé.

» ¿Y si vamos a tomar un café?

» ¿Otro café?

» Es que no he desayunado.

» Bueno, te acompaño.

ANSWERS

Activity 4

Answers may vary. Possible answers include: **a.** lavarla, poner la lavadora; **b.** barrer, la aspiradora; **c.** sábanas; **d.** chutó, portería; **e.** raqueta.

Activity 5

a. ¡Tú sí que has venido temprano!

b. ¿Es que no tienes reloj?

c. No lo sé.

d. ¿Otro café?

e. Bueno, te acompaño.

Activity 6

Answers will vary. **a.** En España no es de mala educación; **b.** En España tienes que esperar a todos los comensales; **c.** Cuando un español habla en voz alta no está necesariamente enfadado; **d.** En España, si toses o estornudas, tienes que taparte la boca con la mano; **e.** En España se puede interrumpir a una persona cuando está hablando.

OBJECTIVES FOR EN RESUMEN: VOCABULARIO

- Review unit vocabulary and expressions
- Practice communicative skills

STANDARDS

1.2 Understand the language
1.3 Present information
4.1 Evaluate similarities and differences in language

INSTRUCTIONAL STRATEGIES

- Encourage students to use self-adhesive notes to place on correct objects in their house.
- Index cards can be used as flashcards with the Spanish term on one side and the English term on the other, or a picture or drawing.
- Students work in pairs or groups, using vocabulary flashcards as they would the cards of a board game to help each other practice unit vocabulary.
- Encourage students to write labels or captions for the photos on this page. Remind them to use the vocabulary and expressions they have learned in this unit.
- Working in pairs, have students take turns giving each other informal affirmative and negative commands using the words and phrases in **Verbos** and **Las tareas del hogar**. Tell them to add on to the words or phrases to put them in more context.
- Encourage students to use graphic organizers such as word webs to link the words in **Los deportes** to individual sports.
- Give students prompts that involve asking for permission, giving directions, and making recommendations. Swap the prompts between pairs until they have practiced all of them in both roles.

EN RESUMEN: Vocabulario

Verbos

aceptar *to accept*
agradecer *to thank*
botar *to throw away, to bounce*
chutar *to kick*

conceder *to grant*
dar permiso *to give permission*
decepcionar *to disappoint*
denegar *to refuse*
flotar *to float*
golpear *to hit*
lanzar *to throw*
limpiar *to clean*

marcar un gol *to score*
quejarse *to complain*
rechazar *to reject*
sonreír *to smile*

Los deportes

el balón *ball*
el campo *field*
la cancha *court*
la falta *fault*
el pase *pass*
la portería *goal*
el portero *goal keeper*

la raqueta *racket*

rebotar *to bounce*
la red *net*

Las tareas del hogar

la aspiradora *vacuum cleaner*
barrer *to sweep*
la basura *trash*
hacer la cama *make the bed*
hacer la comida *to cook lunch*

lavar los platos *wash the dishes*
planchar *to iron*
el polvo *dust*
poner la lavadora *to do the laundry*
poner la mesa *set the table*
las sábanas *bed sheets*

tender la ropa *hang out clothes*
tirar la basura *take out the trash*

Otras palabras útiles

apúntate *sign up*
decepcionado/a *disappointed*
equitativo/a *equitable, fair*
el esfuerzo *effort*
el estilo *style*

estricto/a *strict*
fatal *awful*
la inscripción *inscription*
la interpretación *interpretation*

la obra de teatro *theater play*

Pedir permiso, concederlo y denegarlo

¡De ninguna manera! *No way!*
¡Ni hablar! *Don't even mention it!*

No, (lo siento) es que… *No, (I'm sorry)*
¿Puedo / Podría…? *Can / Could !…?*
¿Quieres…? *Do you want…?*
¿Te / Le importa si…? *Do you mind if…*

Expresiones para pedir y dar instrucciones, órdenes y consejos

Perdone / Perdona, ¿para…? *Excuse me, how do I…?*
¿Por qué no…? *Why don't you…?*
¿Puedes / Podrías decirme cómo…? *Can / Could you tell me how…?*
¿Sabes cómo…? *Do you know how to…?*
Tendrías que / Deberías… *You should…*

EN RESUMEN: Gramática

AFFIRMATIVE COMMANDS
(See page 72)

■ Affirmative commands are used to give an order, to invite, give advice, make recommendations, or give permission to someone.

■ Verbs ending in –**ar** will use the –**e**/–**en** endings in **usted** and **ustedes** commands. Verbs ending in –**er**/–**ir** will use the –**a**/–**an** endings in **usted** and **ustedes** commands.

■ With all affirmative commands, the object pronouns are attached to the end of the verb.

REGULAR VERBS			
	COMPRAR	COMER	SUBIR
tú	compra	come	sube
usted	compre	coma	suba
ustedes	compren	coman	suban

IRREGULAR VERBS				
	DECIR	HACER	PONER	TENER
tú	di	haz	pon	ten
usted	diga	haga	ponga	tenga
ustedes	digan	hagan	pongan	tengan

NEGATIVE COMMANDS
(See page 74)

■ Negative commands are used to tell someone what not to do.

■ To form the negative commands:

• For **usted/ustedes**, use the same form as the affirmative command.
(usted) compre ➡ **no compre**
(ustedes) compren ➡ **no compren**

• For **tú**, add –**s** to the negative command of **usted**.
(usted) no compre ➡ (tú) **no compres**

■ With negative commands, pronouns always go right before the conjugated verb.

REGULAR VERBS			
	COMPRAR	COMER	SUBIR
tú	no compres	no comas	no subas
usted	no compre	no coma	no suba
ustedes	no compren	no coman	no suban

IRREGULAR VERBS				
	DECIR	HACER	PONER	TENER
tú	no digas	no hagas	no pongas	no tengas
usted	no diga	no haga	no ponga	no tenga
ustedes	no digan	no hagan	no pongan	no tengan

OBJECTIVES FOR EN RESUMEN: GRAMÁTICA
• Review unit grammar
• Practice communication skills

STANDARDS
1.2 Understand the language
1.3 Present information

INSTRUCTIONAL STRATEGIES
• Model how to review grammar.
• Have the students review the Learning Outcomes in the unit opener to assess whether they feel they have mastered the main ideas and skills.
• Ask them if they can remember additional examples for each grammar topic.
• Model how to find and go back to the appropriate page in the unit to review any grammar topic they may need help with.
• Invite students to review the grammar activities they completed in this unit.
• Ask them what grammar activities they found easy and which they found challenging. Encourage them to rework any activities they found particularly challenging.
• Give students different scenarios for which they have to write a list of commands. Here are some possible scenarios: someone is going on vacation and leaving a note of reminders to a roommate; a doctor gives a patient tips; someone is lost and needs directions; a boss gives a list of assignments to an employee; a teacher gives a students corrections and feedback on an essay; etc. They can work individually, in pairs, or in groups. Monitor their work, and go over common errors as a class.

OBJECTIVES FOR AHORA COMPRUEBA

- Review and recycle grammar, vocabulary and culture from the last two units
- Complete self-assessment

CORE RESOURCES

- Audio Program: Tracks 19 and 20

STANDARDS

1.2 Understand the language
1.3 Present information
2.1 Practices and perspectives
4.1 Compare languages and cultures

INSTRUCTIONAL STRATEGIES

- Activities can be completed individually or in pairs and then reviewed with the class.
- When reviewing answers in class, expand by asking students if they agree with the answers given and then writing the correct answer on the board.
- You may wish to assign point value to each activity as a way for students to monitor their progress. If students achieve less than 80% on each activity, direct them to **En resumen** in the previous two units for page numbers to review.

Activity 1

Introduce the theme or topic for the activities in this section, studying aboard through an exchange program.

🎧 19 Activity 2

- Before playing the audio, have students read the column heads to know what to focus on as they listen. Explain that they will be listening to six, short conversations and that more than one function can be selected.
- Play the audio and repeat as needed to help students check off the correct function or to confirm answers.

Audioscript

a. » ¿Puedo bajar después de comer a la piscina?
   » No, lo siento, es que después de comer vamos a ir a comprar.

b. » ¿Qué te pasa, Andrés?
   » Es que esta noche hay una fiesta y me gustaría ir. ¿Puedo ir, mamá?

c. » ¿Quieres más papas?
   » No gracias, ¡estoy lleno!

d. » ¿Qué transporte es el mejor para moverme por la ciudad, papá?
   » Lo mejor es comprar el abono transporte. Cómpralo el primer día del mes, cuesta 40 euros. Puedes tomar el metro, el autobús y el tren todas las veces que quieras.

e. » ¡Andrés! ¡Sal ya de la piscina y ven a comer!
   » ¡Ya voy!

f. » Perdone, ¿para ir a la estación de Atocha?
   » Siga todo recto, al final de la calle gire a la derecha y después tome la primera a la izquierda.
   » Gracias.

g. » ¿Te importa si uso tu computadora? Es que quiero escribirles un email a mis amigos.
   » No, claro, hazlo.

h. » Andrés, ¿por qué no vamos a patinar esta tarde?
   » ¡Vale! ¡Buena idea!

AHORA COMPRUEBA

1 Leo, un estudiante americano, participa en un intercambio internacional. Va a pasar unos meses en Madrid en la casa de Andrés. Lee la carta que Andrés le escribió a Leo dándole algunos consejos para convivir con su familia y escribe los verbos entre paréntesis en futuro.

¡Hola, Leo! Hoy he recibido tu carta y la verdad es que me alegra mucho saber que finalmente (a) .... (venir, tú) a Madrid en agosto. En esas fechas (b) .... (hacer) mucho calor, pero no te preocupes porque entre semana (c) .... (poder, tú) estar todo el día en la piscina de mi casa. No es muy grande pero (d) .... (pasártelo, tú) muy bien. Los fines de semana mi familia y tú seguramente (e) .... (ir) a la sierra, a casa de mi tía. Allí ya (f) .... (ver, tú) cómo no (g) .... (pasar, tú) tanto calor; incluso por la noche probablemente (h) .... (necesitar, tú) ponerte una chaqueta. Mi hermana seguro que (i) .... (querer) hacer alguna excursión y, si van a La Pedriza, (j) .... (bañarse, ustedes) en el río. Yo creo que (k) .... (llevarse, tú) muy bien con mi hermana porque, aunque es un poco pesada, la verdad es que es muy divertida. Mi padre es muy hablador, así que te (l) .... (contar) muchas historias de cuando él era joven. Mi madre también habla mucho y, además, te (m) .... (preguntar) mil veces si quieres algo más de comer y le (n) .... (dar) igual si quieres más o no, porque ella siempre te (ñ) .... (poner) tanta comida ¡que te (o) .... (salir) por las orejas!

2 🎧 19 Escucha las diferentes conversaciones entre la familia de Andrés y di qué función tienen.

	Pedir permiso	Conceder permiso	Denegar o rechazar permiso	Dar órdenes	Dar consejos	Dar instrucciones	Invitar u ofrecer
a.	☐	☐	☐	☐	☐	☐	☐
b.	☐	☐	☐	☐	☐	☐	☐
c.	☐	☐	☐	☐	☐	☐	☐
d.	☐	☐	☐	☐	☐	☐	☐
e.	☐	☐	☐	☐	☐	☐	☐
f.	☐	☐	☐	☐	☐	☐	☐
g.	☐	☐	☐	☐	☐	☐	☐
h.	☐	☐	☐	☐	☐	☐	☐

3 🎧 20 Escucha las tareas que hay que hacer en casa de Andrés y clasifícalas en la columna correspondiente.

HACER	PONER	LIMPIAR	LAVAR	RECOGER

🎧 20 Activity 3

Point out to students that more than one possibility exists for arranging these chores.

Audioscript

Las ventanas, la compra, la mesa, los platos, el suelo, la cama, la habitación, la lavadora, el polvo de los muebles.

SLOWER-PACED LEARNERS

Have students make a list of the learning objectives noted in the opening spreads of the two previous units. Tell them to ask themselves: *How well can I do this: very well, well, or not well?* Then pair students who can't do an objective well with another student who can; that way, they can teach each other what they know and help each other review.

4 **¡Mira cómo ha dejado Andrés la habitación! Ayúdale a escribir un email a Leo para que ordene la habitación antes de que la vean sus padres. Completa las ordenes con imperativo y con los pronombres necesarios.**

Asunto: Ordenar la habitación

Para: leo@yamail.es

Leo, ¡ayúdame! ¡Con las prisas no me ha dado tiempo de ordenar la habitación! Esto es lo que hay que hacer:

a. Me dejé un vaso de agua al lado de la cama. Por favor, ...llévalo.... a la cocina.

b. No terminé de guardar la ropa en el armario. Por favor, ... tú.

c. Se me olvidó sacar la ropa de entrenar de la bolsa de deporte. .... de la bolsa y .... en la lavadora.

d. No me dio tiempo a hacer la cama. ....

e. No limpié el polvo de la estantería. ....

f. Dejé el escritorio muy desordenado. ....

g. Creo que, además, me dejé la computadora encendida. ....

¡Te prometo que te lo agradeceré toda la vida! :)

5 **Mira las imágenes y escribe qué va a hacer el fin de semana la familia de Andrés y cuándo.**

El fin de semana que viene ....

....

....

6 **Imagina que un estudiante de intercambio va a pasar un mes contigo. Explícale cómo es tu familia, lo que hacen normalmente, y cómo reparten las tareas. Dale consejos para vivir en tu casa y explícale lo que has planeado hacer durante esos días.**

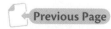

Previous Page

ANSWERS

Activity 1

a. vendrás; b. hará; c. podrás; d. te lo pasarás; e. irán; f. verás; g. pasarás; h. necesitarás; i. querrá; j. se bañarán; k. te llevarás; l. contará; m. preguntará; n. dará; ñ. pondrá; o. saldrá.

Activity 2

a. Pedir permiso y denegar o rechazar un permiso; b. Pedir permiso; c. Invitar u ofrecer; d. Dar consejos; e. Dar órdenes; f. Dar instrucciones; g. Pedir permiso y conceder un permiso; h. Invitar u ofrecer.

Activity 3

Answers may vary. Possible answers include: **Hacer:** la compra, la cama; **Poner:** la lavadora, la mesa; **Limpiar:** el polvo de los muebles, las ventanas; **Lavar:** los platos, el suelo; **Recoger:** la habitación.

INSTRUCTIONAL STRATEGIES

Activity 4

• Have the students read the text and choose the correct verb for each.

• When they have finished, have them share with a partner. Ask individual students to read the complete sentences.

Activity 5

Remind students to use the future tense in their description.

Activity 6

Remind students to use commands with and without pronouns, expressions for giving advice and instructions that they have learned in these two units.

ANSWERS

Activity 4

a. llévalo; b. guárdala; c. Sácala, ponla; d. Hazla; e. Límpialo; f. Arréglalo / Recógelo; g. Apágala.

Activity 5

Answers will vary. Possible answers include: El viernes estarán en Madrid y lloverá, por lo que irán al cine a la sesión de las ocho; El sábado irán de excursión a la Pedriza y hará buen tiempo. Allí pescarán y estarán al aire libre; El domingo estarán en Madrid y, como hará buen tiempo, irán por la mañana a la piscina y por la tarde al Museo del Prado.

ADVANCED LEARNERS

For those students who have a good handle on the vocabulary, grammar, and cultural content of the units, encourage them to focus on the development of their listening, speaking, reading, and writing skills prior to quizzes and tests. Challenge them to spend thirty minutes a night for four nights before the assessment focusing on one of each of the four skills each night. In addition to redoing the skills-based activities within the units, encourage them to seek new, related (and fun) material online to help them practice.

HERITAGE LANGUAGE LEARNERS

For students who already have a base of the language, challenge them to put themselves in the position of the teacher prior to assessments. How would they teach a non-native speaker the content of the previous two units? Have them develop worksheets, activities, games, presentations, and lesson plans that could be used to teach other students the material. By putting students in this new role, they will enhance their own knowledge and become masters of the content.

OBJECTIVES FOR UNIT OPENER

- Introduce unit theme: **De cine**, about movies and theater
- Introduce culture for the unit: Learn about movies and theater

STANDARDS

- 1.1 Interpersonal communication
- 1.2 Understand the language
- 2.1 Practices and perspectives
- 4.2 Compare cultures

INSTRUCTIONAL STRATEGIES

- Introduce unit theme and objectives. Talk about the photo and have students state who they think the people are: **Son fans del cine**, **Están esperando la llegada de gente famosa**, **Están muy contentos**, etc.
- Have the students talk about themselves in the same context. Then have students work individually to write answers to the three questions on the page.
- Put students into pairs to share and discuss their answers.
- Call on volunteers to report back on their responses and discussions.
- Use the photograph to preview unit vocabulary: **¿Cuántos años crees que tienen? ¿Qué crees que van a hacer?**, etc.
- Ask related questions: **¿Tienes una cámara de video? ¿Te gusta hacer fotos? ¿Te gusta ir al cine? ¿Qué tipo de película te gusta más?**, etc.
- Help students formulate their ideas using **Tengo una cámara / un celular / una videocámara**, **Puedo hacer videos con mi celular**, **Mando fotos a mis amigos**, **Me gustan las películas de terror**, etc.

SLOWER-PACED LEARNERS

Have students practice with descriptions so they can retrieve previous knowledge and practice subject / verb agreement, noun / adjective agreement, and word order.

ADVANCED LEARNERS

Have students come up with a list of adjectives, verbs, and nouns that can help them talk about movies and the experience of going to the movies.

HERITAGE LANGUAGE LEARNERS

Have students become aware that in Spanish, we don't go to the movies, but to the movie theater or to watch a movie: **Voy al cine todos los sábados. Voy a ver una película esta tarde.** You can also point out that video is pronounced **vídeo** in Spain.

¡Sonríe, que te están filmando!

UNIDAD 3

DE CINE

⏵⏵ ¿Has filmado algún video con tus amigos/as o compañeros/as de clase?
⏵⏵ ¿Alquilas películas en un videoclub o las miras en tu computadora?
⏵⏵ Cuando eras pequeño, ¿cuál era tu película favorita?

88

ADDITIONAL UNIT RESOURCES

Extension Activities (EA) (Photocopiable)

EA: 3.1, 3.2, 3.3

Interactive Whiteboard Lessons (IWB)

IWB: 3.1, 3.2

Audio

21 to 26

Video

Diálogo 3

Online ELEteca

In this unit, you will learn to:

- Express curiosity, surprise, and skepticism
- Give information, tell stories and anecdotes in inexact terms
- Express motive and purpose
- Talk about movies and theater

Using

- Imperfect and preterit (review)
- Pluperfect
- Time expressions
- Prepositions: *por* and *para*

Cultural Connections

- Share information about daily life in Hispanic countries and compare cultural similarities

SABOR HISPANO

- El cine mexicano... ¡está de moda!

¡ACCIÓN!

89

LEARNING OUTCOMES

- Express curiosity, surprise and skepticism
- Give information and tell stories
- Express motive and purpose
- Talk about movies and theater
- Learn about daily life in Hispanic countries

INSTRUCTIONAL STRATEGIES

- Use unit opener to preview vocabulary and cultural topics for this unit.
- Have students look at the images on this page and relate them to the objectives listed. Ask questions such as: *¿Quiénes son estas personas? ¿Son famosos? ¿Por qué? ¿Qué tiene en la mano? ¿Cómo se siente?*, etc.
- Invite students to read the topic for **Sabor hispano** and preview that section in the unit. Ask questions such as: *¿Has visto alguna película mexicana? ¿Qué tipo de película era? ¿De acción, de miedo, romántica? ¿Qué actores o directores mexicanos conocen?*, etc.
- Ask students to anticipate what they think the episode for **¡Acción!** will be about. Ask: *¿Quiénes son estos personajes? ¿Dónde están?*
- Have students work in pairs to talk about the images using the questions you have modeled. Then ask for volunteers to present to the class what they understand this unit to be about.

HERITAGE LANGUAGE LEARNERS

If students haven't seen any Mexican movies, ask about films from other countries. You can point out that many Spanish-speaking movies are co-productions, like **Cuento chino** (Argentina-Spain, 2011). Some Spanish-speaking actors are also featured in US movies. A list of Hollywood actors who speak fluently in Spanish can be found at http://www.latina.com/entertainment. Trailers from current movies can be found at http://www.ecartelera.com/videos/.

THREE MODES OF COMMUNICATION: UNIT 3		
	INTERPERSONAL	**INTERPRETIVE**	**PRESENTATIONAL**
HABLAMOS DE...		1, 2, 3, 4, 5, 6	1
COMUNICA	2, 4, 7	1, 5, 6	1, 3, 4, 7
¡ACCIÓN!	4	1, 2	3, 4
PALABRA POR PALABRA	1	2, 3, 4, 5, 6, 7	2, 4
GRAMÁTICA	4	1, 2, 3	4
DESTREZAS		1, 2, 3	
CULTURA		SABOR HISPANO	
RELATO		1, 2, 3	

OBJECTIVES FOR HABLAMOS DE...

- Understand language in context
- Preview vocabulary: Words and colloquial expressions relating to movies and theater
- Preview grammatical structures: Imperfect and preterit; Pluperfect; Time expressions; Prepositions **por** and **para**
- Read and listen to a conversation between two young people talking about a new theater workshop

CORE RESOURCES

- Audio Program: Track 21
- Interactive Whiteboard Lesson: IWB 3.1

STANDARDS

- 1.1 Engage in conversation
- 1.2 Understand the language
- 4.2 Compare cultures.

INSTRUCTIONAL STRATEGIES

Activity 1

- Ask students to talk about the people in the photos and describe what they see and what they think each represents. **¿Qué tipo de edificio creen que es? ¿Qué puede representar la estatua en número 3? ¿Qué están haciendo en número 4?**
- Have students work in pairs to answer and discuss the questions. Then ask: **¿Qué tienen todas las imágenes en común?** (**en todas hay un elemento relacionado con el cine o el teatro**). Guide students with questions to help them arrive at the same conclusion.

Activity 2

Have the students work individually to match the images to the correct description. Students will have an opportunity to confirm their answers in Activity 3.

Activity 3

- Explain to students that the headlines all appeared in the press and they should first try to match each headline to the appropriate image and then to a statement in Activity 2.
- Have students compare answers with a partner.
- Project IWB 3.1, **De cine y teatro** to review answers. Discuss each image and focus attention on the terms (**cine**, **teatro**, **director de cine**, **premio**, **taller de cine y teatro**). Make sure students understand the concept of **taller**. Explain as necessary in Spanish.

ANSWERS

Activity 2

a. 2; **b.** 1; **c.** 4; **d.** 3.

Activity 3

1. b; **2.** c; **3.** d; **4.** a.

HABLAMOS DE... Cines y teatros

1 👥 **Observa las imágenes y habla con tu compañero/a.**

- ¿Qué ves?
- ¿Reconoces a alguien?
- ¿Qué crees que pueden tener todas las imágenes en común?

2 **Relaciona estas frases con una de las imágenes de la Actividad 1.**

- **a.** ☐ Es la entrega de un Oscar a un famoso director de cine español.
- **b.** ☐ Es un teatro en la capital uruguaya, Montevideo, que lleva el nombre del descubridor del Río de la Plata.
- **c.** ☐ Es un taller de teatro.
- **d.** ☐ Es un Goya, el premio de cine más prestigioso del cine español.

3 **Ahora, relaciona cada titular con los enunciados de la Actividad 2.**

- **1.** ☐ Comienza el ciclo de teatro de vanguardia en el Solís.
- **2.** ☐ Este año las actividades extraescolares con más participación han sido los talleres de cine y teatro.
- **3.** ☐ La noche del cine español se viste de gala.
- **4.** ☐ Nunca antes un director español había pisado tantas veces la alfombra de Hollywood.

ADVANCED LEARNERS

As a follow-up activity to Activity 3, have students write more headlines. Point out that many headlines place the verb in front of the subject, as in item 1.

4 🎧 **21** **Escucha la conversación y completa.**

Ricardo: ¿Te has enterado de los talleres de este curso? (a) .... van a ser totalmente diferentes.
Daniela: ¿(b) ....?
R.: Pues (c) .... han contratado a dos famosos para organizar un taller con el Departamento de Literatura.
D.: ¡(d) ....! Dos famosos trabajando en una escuela…
R.: Ya, pero, (e) ...., a estos los han elegido por su relación con la cultura y por su carrera profesional. He oído que son amigos del nuevo profesor de Literatura, parece que se conocieron cuando trabajaban juntos en una escuela de idiomas, creo que enseñaban español.

D.: ¡(f) ....! Dos profesores famosos, ¡(g) ....! Pero, (h) ...., que (i) .... ¿De qué es el taller? ¿Quién lo va a impartir *(teach)*?
R.: (j) ...., es un taller de cine y teatro…
D.: ¡(k) ....!
R.: La parte de cine la va a impartir la directora y guionista Anamar Orson y la parte de teatro el actor Cristian Pascual.
D.: ¿(l) ....? Pero si los dos son conocidísimos… ¡Cristian Pascual en la escuela! ¡(m) ....! ¿(n) ....?
R.: Sí, Daniela, sí, hablo en serio, aunque si quieres, llamamos para preguntar al Departamento de Literatura, porque no estoy demasiado seguro.

5 🎧 **21** **Contesta verdadero (V) o falso (F). Después, escucha de nuevo y comprueba.**

	V	F
a. Daniela y Ricardo están hablando del nuevo profesor de Literatura.	☐	☐
b. Ricardo ha oído que este curso van a tener un taller de cine y teatro.	☐	☐
c. El taller lo va a impartir un importante director de cine.	☐	☐
d. El taller lo va a organizar el profesor de Literatura con dos amigos que son muy famosos.	☐	☐

6 **Clasifica ahora las expresiones que has escrito en la Actividad 4 según su significado. ¡Atención! Alguna puede tener más de una opción y no todos los significados tienen expresiones.**

1. Expresa sorpresa positiva o negativa. ➜ ....
2. Expresa seguridad. ➜ ....
3. No le interesa lo que le cuenta la otra persona. ➜ ....
4. Le parece difícil creer lo que le cuenta la otra persona. ➜ ....
5. Nunca dice quién le ha contado esa información. ➜ ...a...
6. Pide más información para continuar la conversación y expresa curiosidad. ➜ ...b...

91

Instructional Strategies

🎧 **21** Activity 4

- Inform the students that they are going to listen to a conversation between Daniela and Ricardo in which they talk about a new workshop.
- Tell students to close their books. Play the audio while the students listen.
- Ask how much they understood and have those who understood more explain what they heard.
- Play the audio again while the students follow in their books and fill in the missing words.
- Ask for volunteers to say the missing words and write them on the board.
- Explain vocabulary using examples in Spanish, for example: ***impartir** (**dar clase**)*, ***carrera** (**profesión**)*, ***guionista** (**la persona que escribe la historia para la película**)*, etc.

🎧 **21** Activity 5

- Have the students read the sentences and decide whether they are true or false.
- Remind them to refer to the conversation in Activity 4 for help.
- Play the audio again for students to check their answers and tell them to correct the statements that are false.
- Review together as a class. Call on student volunteers to summarize the conversation.

Activity 6

- Help students understand the use of the expressions in the conversation. Explain that these expressions, in general terms, are either reactions to what was said or report information from unidentified sources. Ask students to identify examples for both types.
- Then review the descriptions in the activity and have students sort the expressions.
- Review answers by categories and write the examples on the board.

Answers

Activity 4

a. He oído que; **b.** ¿Y eso?; **c.** parece que; **d.** ¡No me lo puedo creer!; **e.** según dicen; **f.** ¡Anda ya!; **g.** ¡imposible!; **h.** dime, dime; **i.** estoy intrigadísima; **j.** Al parecer; **k.** ¡Qué chévere!; **l.** ¿En serio?; **m.** ¡Qué fuerte!; **n.** ¿Hablas en serio?

Activity 5

a. falso (Están hablando sobre un nuevo taller de cine y teatro que se va a impartir en la escuela); **b.** verdadero; **c.** falso (La parte de cine la va a impartir la directora y guionista Anamar Orson y la parte de teatro el actor Cristian Pascual); **d.** verdadero.

Activity 6

1. d, k, l, m, n; **4.** d, f, g, l, n; **5.** a, c, e, j; **6.** b, h, i. (statements 2 and 3 do not have any examples).

Heritage Language Learners

Remind students that some expressions are more common in certain regions of the Spanish-speaking world than others. For instance, ***¡Qué chévere!*** is used mostly in the Caribbean, some countries in Central America, and the Andean Region. As with all colloquial expressions, they change with the time, and some new expressions may replace them. Ask students whether they know any other expressions of surprise, joy, apathy, etc. Additionally, you may want to have them discuss why colloquialisms change with time.

OBJECTIVES FOR COMUNICA

- Present communicative functions of the unit:
  - Express surprise, skepticism, curiosity and give information
  - React to information you hear

CORE RESOURCES

- Extension Activities: EA 3.1
- Interactive Online Materials - ELEteca

STANDARDS

1.1   Engage in conversation
1.2   Understand the language
4.2   Compare cultures

INSTRUCTIONAL STRATEGIES FOR EXPRESSING SURPRISE, SKEPTICISM, CURIOSITY, AND GIVING INFORMATION

- Walk students through the explanations and ask them to comment on how the expressions were used in the conversation between Ricardo and Daniela.
- Say all the expressions using appropriate intonation for exclamations and interrogative expressions. Have the students repeat as necessary.

Activity 1

- Focus attention on the images and have the students look at the accompanying statements said by one of the people in the images.
- Guide students through a description of each scene and have them focus on what is being communicated in each.
- In pairs, the students take turns reacting to the situations with an expression from the section above.
- Circulate around the room as they speak, listening in and correcting pronunciation and intonation, or offering assistance where required.
- Invite different pairs to role-play a situation for the class.

Activity 2

- Have students divide into groups of three to create two more situations similar to those in Activity 1.
- The students take turns to role-play their situations.
- Invite some groups to perform for the class.
- You may choose to point out and ask students about the different verb tenses without getting into too much detail as these will be addressed more thoroughly in **Gramática**.

SLOWER-PACED LEARNERS

To help students come up with ideas for Activity 2, suggest that they think about a time when something bad, strange, or unexpected happened to them as well as a time when they found out something very interesting about another person or thing. After going over the scenarios with the their groups, encourage them to classify each of the scenarios under the categories at the top of the page.

COMUNICA

EXPRESSING SURPRISE, SKEPTICISM, CURIOSITY, AND GIVING INFORMATION

- Para **dar una información** sin hablar de la fuente (source):
  - **Pues parece que**...
  - **Según dicen**...
  - **¿Te has enterado de**...?
  - **Al parecer**...
  - **He oído que**...

- Para expresar **sorpresa**:
  - **¿De veras?** (sorpresa positiva)
  - **¡Qué fuerte!**
  - **¡No me digas!**

- Para mostrar **interés** o **curiosidad** y pedir más información:
  - **Cuenta, cuenta**... / **Dime, dime**...
  - **Estoy intrigadísimo/a.**
  - **¿Y eso?**

- Para expresar **incredulidad** y extrañeza:
  - **¡Anda ya!**
  - **¡Imposible!**
  - **¡No me lo puedo creer!**
  - **¡Qué raro / extraño!**
  - **¿(Hablas) En serio?**

1 Fíjate en las imágenes y reacciona ante esas situaciones con las expresiones anteriores. Justifica tus reacciones ya que pueden ser varias.

Esta semana has llegado tarde cuatro veces.

a.

Tengo que contarles algo muy fuerte que me pasó ayer.

b.

Cuando mi abuela era joven ya usaba Internet.

c.

El año pasado nadie suspendió Matemáticas.

d.

¿Te has enterado de que este año no hay excursión de fin de curso?

e.

El sábado conocí a un muchacho superinteresante.

f.

2 Crea tres situaciones similares a las anteriores para que tu compañero/a reaccione.

3 Escribe dos experiencias o situaciones en dos hojas de papel sobre lo que crees que hicieron otros/as compañeros/as la semana pasada. Tu compañero/a leerá el comentario y reaccionará usando alguna de las expresiones que ya practicaste. Después, cambia de papel.

Modelo: El (writes): Juan finalmente le ganó a Rosario en la competencia de Ciencias.
E2 (reads and reacts): ¡No me lo puedo creer!

4 Elige una de las siguientes situaciones y preséntala a tus compañeros/as. Luego, túrnense escuchando y reaccionando a las situaciones presentadas.

Modelo: El: Al parecer…
E2: Cuenta, cuenta…

Situación 1
- Ayer alguien tomó tus apuntes, hizo fotocopias y ahora los está vendiendo en Internet.

Situación 2
- Esta mañana te han llamado de tu compañía telefónica para informarte de que has ganado una computadora.

Situación 3
- Anoche cuando estabas en la cama escuchaste ruidos extraños en una casa vecina en la que no vive nadie.

Situación 4
- Ayer te pasó algo muy fuerte y todavía no se lo has dicho a nadie…

Situación 5
- Hoy el director de la escuela ha comunicado que este año no van a poder usar las computadoras en ninguna clase.

Situación 6
- Mañana tienen que empezar la primera clase de la mañana dos horas antes.

Situación 7
- Las navidades pasadas todos los compañeros de tu madre se hicieron millonarios, pero ella no, porque olvidó comprar la lotería de su empresa.

Situación 8
- ¡Los boletos que has comprado para el concierto son falsos!

Situación 9
- El viernes, en la clase de español, nos van a poner una película.

Situación 10
- Alguien dice que te vio en un centro comercial en horario de clase.

93

INSTRUCTIONAL STRATEGIES

Activity 3
- Read the model with the students and explain what they are to do.
- On separate pieces of paper, students write two experiences or situations about other classmates.
- Their partner reacts to the situation with an expression from the list.
- Then they change roles and the partner reads a situation.
- Ask for volunteers to perform for the class.

Activity 4
- Have students read the situations in pairs or read them together as a class to ensure that students understand. See Cultural Note for more information about Situación 7.
- Then have student pairs choose one each to perform for the class.
- Tell students to practice their conversation and to make sure each situation includes four exchanges. So in addition to reacting to the situation selected, students must add more information or details to elicit another reaction from their partner.
- When they are ready, invite them to perform for the rest of the class.

Cultural Note
- Explain to students that in Spain, the Christmas lottery, the first prize of which is called **el Gordo**, is the largest one of the year. Lottery tickets are printed with 5-digit numbers. Many organizations buy tickets and divide them up and sell them as participations to their customers or employees. In this way, the winnings from the number drawn are often shared among many participants, increasing everyone's chances for winning.
- Encourage students to research more about this historical national lottery that has been in place since 1812 and is the second oldest lottery in the world.

Extension
- Cut up situation cards from EA 3.1, **Situaciones** and put them face down for student pairs to select at random. Give students about 2 minutes to prepare and then have them perform the situation for the class.
- Set up categories for students to vote for the best, such as: Most believable, Most unbelievable, Best acting and reacting, Most exchanges, etc. Present the winning pairs with photocopy cutouts of **Premios Goya** as prizes.

ADVANCED LEARNERS

For continued practice, have students switch partners and choose new scenarios to act out in Activity 4.

OBJECTIVES FOR COMUNICA

- Present communicative functions of the unit: Expressing purpose or motive of an action

STANDARDS

1.3 Engage in conversation

1.4 Understand the language

4.2 Compare cultures

INSTRUCTIONAL STRATEGIES FOR
EXPRESSING PURPOSE OR MOTIVE OF AN ACTION

- Introduce the topic by writing the following sentences on the board, leaving blanks as indicated: **_____ aprender español hay que viajar por países hispanos**, **Anoche cancelaron el concierto _____ la tormenta**. Ask students to fill in the blanks with **por** or **para**. Call on several students to give their answers without confirming which ones are correct. Ask students to try to explain why they chose **por** or **para**. In this way you introduce the general uses of **por** and **para**, motive for **por** and purpose, end goal for **para**.
- Point to **por** in the first sentence and explain that while the general rules are as stated, each preposition also can also have its own particular uses.
- Walk the students through the uses of **por** and **para** in the book.
- Ask a student to read the example in Spanish and another student to read the meaning in English.
- Focus attention on the extra information in the boxes.

Activity 5

- Students read the sentences and refer to the explanations above in order to fill in each blank with **por** or **para**.
- Ask for volunteers to say the correct answers and discuss any problems they may have encountered.
- Ask the students to point out which use of **por** or **para** from the explanation above was required in each case.

ANSWERS
Activity 5

a. para; **b.** por; **c.** Para; **d.** para; **e.** por.

SLOWER-PACED LEARNERS

Prepare flash cards with sentences that use **por** and **para**, leaving blanks where the prepositions should be. Distribute the cards and have students complete them following the tips in the book. Then have students check their answers with a partner.

ADVANCED LEARNERS

Have students work in two groups: each group writes a few sentences that use **por** and **para** but leaves blanks where the prepositions should be. Then have groups swap and complete each other's sentences. After a few minutes, have each group correct the answers provided by the other group.

HERITAGE LANGUAGE LEARNERS

You may want to introduce and discuss other expressions with **por**, such as **por suerte, por desgracia, por cierto, por supuesto, por lo general, por último, por fin, por eso, por ejemplo, por una / otra parte**, etc. Have students write sentences using the expressions.

COMUNICA

EXPRESSING PURPOSE OR MOTIVE OF AN ACTION

- Use **por** to express:
  - The **motive** behind an action

    *Los han elegido **por** su relación con la cultura y **por** su carrera profesional.* They were selected because of their association with culture and because of their professional careers.

- Other uses:
  - **Duration** of an event

    *Los Beatles triunfaron **por** los años sesenta.* The Beatles were successful in the seventies.
  - **Means** (teléfono, correo electrónico…)

    *Me enteré del premio de Ana **por** la tele.* I found out about Ana's prize on (by means of) television.
  - **Movement through**

    *Cuando miré **por** la ventana estaba lloviendo.* When I looked out (through) the window, it was raining.

    *Ana y Matilde han viajado **por** muchos países.* Ana and Matilde have traveled through many countries.
  - **Frequency**

    *Vamos al cine dos veces **por** semana (dos veces a la semana).* We go to the movies two times a week.

- Use **para** to express:
  - The **purpose**, **end goal** or **objective** behind an action

    *Han contratado a dos famosos **para** organizar un taller.* They have contracted two famous people to organize a workshop.

- Other uses:
  - **Deadline**

    *La tarea es **para** el próximo lunes.* The homework is due by next Monday.
  - **Recipient** of an action

    *Estos talleres son **para** estudiantes.* These workshops are for students.
  - **Opinion**

    Para mí, las películas románticas son muy aburridas. For me, romantic movies are very boring.

⚠ ■ Use an infinitive after **por**:

*Llegó tarde **por** estar en un atasco.* She arrived late due to being stuck in traffic.

■ Use a conjugated verb after **porque** and **como** (since):

*Llegó tarde **porque** estuvo en un atasco.* She arrived late because she was stuck in traffic.

***Como** estuvo en un atasco, llegó tarde.* Since she was stuck in traffic, she arrived late.

⚠ ■ Use an infinitive after **para**:

*Estudió **para** ser directora de cine.* She studied in order to be a director.

■ Other expressions that express **purpose**:

*Estudió **con el objetivo / el fin / la finalidad de** ser directora de cine* She studied for the purpose of being / in order to be a movie director.

5 Completa con *por* o *para*.

a. Esta carta no es .... mí, creo que ha habido un error.

b. Ayer el profesor de Matemáticas me riñó .... ser impuntual.

c. .... mi padre el cine comercial es de mala calidad.

d. Estudio español .... viajar por países hispanos.

e. Los documentos los enviaron .... correo electrónico.

6 Elige *por* o *para*. Luego, relaciona cada imagen con la frase correspondiente. ¡Atención! No todas las frases tienen imagen. Marca con una X la frase sin imagen.

1. ☐ Creo que el hotel está **por** / **para** el centro.
2. ☐ En vacaciones nos comunicamos **por** / **para** correo electrónico.
3. ☐ **Por** / **Para** los hispanos reunirse **por** / **para** comer es muy importante.
4. ☐ Tenemos que estar listos **por** / **para** las ocho.
5. ☐ Gracias **por** / **para** todo, estas flores son **por** / **para** ti.
6. ☐ Llamo **por** / **para** teléfono a mi abuela una vez **por** / **para** semana.
7. ☐ No me sonó el celular, es que estábamos pasando **por** / **para** un túnel.

7 👥 Completa el siguiente cuestionario con *por* o *para*. Después, hazle las preguntas a tu compañero/a.

Estudiante 1

a. ¿Qué haces .... mejorar tu español?
b. .... ti, ¿qué es mejor, ver una película en tu casa o en el cine?
c. ¿Has viajado mucho .... tu país?
d. ¿Cómo te comunicas más con tus amigos: .... Internet o .... teléfono?
e. ¿ .... quién piensas que deberían ser los descuentos en los teatros y los cines?

Estudiante 2

a. ¿Cuál es la mejor película .... ti?
b. ¿Cómo sueles entregar los trabajos de clase: .... correo electrónico o .... escrito?
c. ¿ .... quién piensas que se estrenan más obras de teatro?
d. ¿ .... qué países te gustaría viajar?
e. ¿Cuáles son los mejores consejos .... sacar buenas notas?

💻 **MORE IN ELETECA:** EXTRA ONLINE PRACTICE

INSTRUCTIONAL STRATEGIES

Activity 6

- Have students look at the images and read the sentences below.
- They choose **por** or **para** for each sentence.
- Then they decide which image is being referred to and write the number of the image in the box provided.
- The sentence that does not correspond with any image must be marked with an X.
- Have the students compare answers with a partner.
- Ask for volunteers to say the correct answers and identify the use for each.

Activity 7

- Have the students work in pairs and choose sentences in either **Estudiante 1** or **Estudiante 2**.
- Each student writes in **por** or **para** according to the meaning of the questions. Note that although each role has different questions, both sets contain the same uses so students can correct each other and discuss as needed.
- They interview each other using the completed questions.
- Circulate around the room as they talk, checking on correct usage of **por** and **para** and providing any assistance that may be required.
- Ask for volunteers to perform their interviews for the class.

ANSWERS

Activity 6

1. por, *movement through* (e); **2.** por, *means* (d); **3.** para, *opinion*, para, *purpose* (a); **4.** para, *deadline* (X); **5.** por, *motive*, para, *recipient* (c); **6.** por, *means*, por, *frequency* (f); **7.** por, *movement through* (b).

Activity 7

Estudiante 1: a. para; **b.** Para; **c.** por; **d.** por, por; **e.** Para.
Estudiante 2: a. para; **b.** por, por; **c.** Por; **d.** Por; **e.** para.

SLOWER-PACED LEARNERS

Continue to monitor students' use of **por** and **para**. You may want to have more advanced students work with slower-paced students in Activity 7.

ADVANCED LEARNERS

Have students write a summary of the dialogue in Activity 7. Ask them to describe what they learned about their fellow classmates.

HERITAGE LANGUAGE LEARNERS

Have students formulate questions based on the images in Activity 6: *¿Por dónde está el hotel? ¿Por qué medio nos comunicamos en vacaciones? ¿Para quién es importante reunirse para comer?*, etc.

OBJECTIVES FOR ¡ACCIÓN!

- Provide students with a structured approach to viewing the video
- Contextualize the content of the unit in a familiar scenario

CORE RESOURCES

- Unit Video 3 - La casa de las paredes negras
- Online Materials - ELEteca

STANDARDS

1.5 Interpersonal communication
1.2 Interpretive communication
2.1 Culture: Practices and perspectives

INSTRUCTIONAL STRATEGIES

Previewing: Antes del video

Activity 1

- To introduce the video, direct students' attention to the title and ask: **¿A qué se refiere el título?** Prompt them to look at the images for help, and encourage them to make guesses.
- Model a conversation with one of the students in class using the questions from this activity and adding your own follow-up questions.
- Put students in pairs to ask and answer the questions. Tell them to listen closely to their partners' responses and be prepared to report back.
- After their discussions, call on a few students to share what they learned about their partners.

Activity 2

- Explain that this activity is meant to preview vocabulary that they will hear in the video. Have them make their best guesses to the answers based on their prior knowledge, context clues, and process of elimination. You may want to also allow them access to a dictionary.
- Go over the answers as a class. Make sure everyone is clear on the meaning of the new vocabulary before watching the video.

Viewing: Durante el video

▶ Activity 3

- Let students read the sentences before you start the video.
- Play the first clip, pausing at the time indicated. Allow students to check their answers. Then go over the answers together, prompting students to correct the false sentences.

Activity 4

- Direct students' attention to the third image at the top of the lesson. Elicit students' ideas as to what they think is going to happen next. Have them guess what plan they think Sebas and Felipe might come up with.
- Play the next clip while students take notes on the actual plan that Sebas and Felipe come up with.
- At the end of the clip, call on a volunteer to explain their plan and compare it against any of the predictions that had been made by the class.

ANSWERS

Activity 2

1. d; **2.** c; **3.** f; **4.** a; **5.** b; **6.** e.

Activity 2

a. V; **b.** F; **c.** F; **d.** V.

¡ACCIÓN! La casa de las paredes negras

1. 2. 3. 4. 5. 6.

ANTES DEL VIDEO

1 **Mira la Imagen 1 y responde a las preguntas.**

a. ¿Vas mucho al cine?
b. ¿Cuál es la última película que has visto en el cine?
c. ¿Te gustó? ¿Por qué?
d. ¿Compras algo para comer o para beber cuando vas al cine?

2 **Relaciona.**

1. tráiler
2. taquilla
3. butaca
4. refresco
5. sala
6. palomitas

a. Puede ser de naranja, limón, cola...
b. Cada una de las habitaciones del cine.
c. Lugar donde compramos las entradas.
d. Publicidad de una película.
e. Comida de maíz que podemos comprar en el cine.
f. Silla en el cine.

DURANTE EL VIDEO

3 **Mira la Imagen 2 y marca verdadero (V) o falso (F).**
00:10 - 01:25

	V	F
a. Alba es nueva en la ciudad.	☐	☐
b. Las tres muchachas odian el cine de terror.	☐	☐
c. Van a ver una comedia con muchos efectos especiales.	☐	☐
d. Las muchachas creen que se reirán mucho.	☐	☐

4 **Mira la Imagen 3. Luego, mira la secuencia y toma nota del plan que tienen Felipe y Sebas. Escríbelo con tu compañero/a.**
01:30 - 03:50

96

Activity 4

Answers will vary. Possible answer. Felipe va a hablar con Lorena y Eli, mientras que Sebas va a hablar con Alba sobre la película que van a ver. De esta manera entran juntos a la sala de cine y Sebas se sienta junto a Alba para ver la película.

ADVANCED LEARNERS

Before watching the video, have students look at the images and predict the plot. Working with a partner, have them write a brief caption underneath each image explaining the sequence of events. Encourage them to think about what is not shown as well and make creative guesses about how the story progresses.

5 🔊 03:50 - 04:50 **Mira la Imagen 4. Clasifica estas frases. ¿Quién las dice, Alba o Sebas? Basa tu respuesta en lo que crees que puede ocurrir. Usa tu imaginación. Luego, mira la secuencia y comprueba tus respuestas.**

a. Yo sé que te encanta el cine de terror.

b. Pensé que no te gustaba el cine de terror.

c. A mí me encantan las comedias.

d. Me encanta pasar mucho miedo.

e. Una bolsa de palomitas y un refresco, por favor.

f. Algunas películas de terror sí me gustan.

Alba	Sebas

6 👥 **Fíjate en la Imagen 5 y habla con tu compañero/a. ¿Qué película crees que van a ver los muchachos? Basa tu respuesta en lo que crees que puede ocurrir. Usa tu imaginación. Después, continúa viendo el episodio y escribe el título de la película de terror que ponen en el cine.**

....

DESPUÉS DEL VIDEO

7 👥 **Mira la Imagen 6. ¿Por qué pone Felipe esa cara? ¿Qué pasó? Habla con tu compañero/a.**

8 **Escribe un texto en el que cuentas qué crees que va a pasar después de la película.**

....

....

9 **Marca si estas frases son verdaderas (V) o falsas (F) y, después, da tu opinión.**

	V	F	A mí me gustan	A mí no me gustan	Razones
a. A Eli le gustan las películas de terror.	☐	☐	☐	☐	
b. A Alba le gustan las películas con mucha fantasía.	☐	☐	☐	☐	
c. A Sebas le gustan las películas románticas.	☐	☐	☐	☐	
d. A Alba le gustan las palomitas.	☐	☐	☐	☐	

10 👥 **En grupos de tres, compartan sus gustos y opiniones, ¿están de acuerdo?**

💻 **MORE IN ELETECA:** EXTRA ONLINE PRACTICE

97

INSTRUCTIONAL STRATEGIES

Activity 5

- Before playing the next clip, direct students' attention to Image 4. Have students read the sentences aloud and anticipate whether Alba or Sebas will say them. Encourage them to justify their guesses.
- Play the clip so they can check and correct their guesses.

Activity 6

- Follow the instructions on the page. Encourage each pair to come up with a list of possible titles for the movie that the characters are going to see. Then have a volunteer from each pair come to the board to write their favorite possible title on the board.
- Play the remainder of the video and confirm the correct answer.

Post-viewing: Después del video

Activity 7

- With a partner, have students discuss their understanding of the end of the video and Felipe's reaction to what happens.

Activity 8

- Remind students that there are no right or wrong answers here. Nevertheless, they should make logical suggestions based on what they know about the characters and what has already happened in the video.

Activity 9

- The first part of this activity is a comprehension check. Confirm that students' have understood the correct opinions of the characters in the video.
- Then have students mark their own opinions and jot down notes that they can use later to help explain their preferences.

Activity 10

- Put students in groups of three to discuss their opinions about the different genres of movies and whether or not they like popcorn. Remind them to give reasons for their responses and ask each other follow-up questions for more information. Remind them to listen for points of agreement and disagreement amongst their responses.
- Call on volunteers to report back on any surprising or interesting information they learned about their classmates.

ANSWERS

Activity 5

Alba: a, d, e; **Sebas:** b, c, f.

Activity 6

La casa de las paredes negras.

Activity 9

a. F; **b.** V; **c.** F; **d.** F.

SLOWER-PACED LEARNERS

When students make their guesses in Activity 5, suggest that they write the names (or initials) of the characters next to the questions or on another sheet of paper. Tell them to wait until they watch the video to add the letters to the chart.

HERITAGE LANGUAGE LEARNERS

Have students write about their favorite Spanish language film or favorite movie with Hispanic actors or by a Hispanic director. Tell them to write one paragraph briefly summarizing the movie and a second paragraph providing their own opinions and commentaries about it.

OBJECTIVES FOR EL CINE Y EL TEATRO

- Present vocabulary needed to practice communicative and grammatical functions for the unit: Expressions relating to movies and theater
- Talk about the movie and theater industry and what people do

CORE RESOURCES

- Extension Activities: EA 3.2
- Interactive Online Materials - ELEteca

STANDARDS

1.1	Engage in conversation
1.2	Understand the language
1.3	Present information
3.2	Acquire information
4.1	Compare languages and cultures

INSTRUCTIONAL STRATEGIES

Activity 1

- Have students look at the images and express their preferences and routines regarding movies and plays. Ask the questions and have different students answer the question. It's important at this time to let students talk freely without correcting errors.
- Then have the students ask each other the questions in pairs.

Activity 2

- With books closed, write the following words on the board: **Cine**, **Teatro**, **Cine y teatro**.
- Have the students say words connected with these topics and classify them.
- Now have the students open their books and look at the vocabulary in the word bank. Tell them to add the new words to the headings on the board and discuss the meaning of any new words.
- The students copy the lists on the board into the columns in their books, using all the vocabulary in the box as well as any new words that may have been suggested.

Activity 3

- Have the students look at the activity and explain to them how words often come in 'families'.
- Read the model for them and show how **protagonizar** is connected with **protagonista**.
- Ask for a volunteer to do the second sentence and ask the class if they agree.
- Now have them continue to work individually.
- When they have finished, ask them to share with a partner.

ANSWERS

Activity 2

Cine: cámara, guion, película, efectos especiales; **Teatro:** escenario, decorado, obra, telón; **Cine y teatro:** actor, director/a, aplausos, interpretación, actriz, espectador/a, premio, escritor/a, taquilla, festival, argumento.

Activity 3

a. protagonizan; **b.** guion; **c.** telón; **d.** decorado; **e.** interpretación; **f.** aplausos.

ADVANCED LEARNERS

For continued development of vocabulary skills after Activity 3, have students make charts with word families: **protagonizar, protagonista; interpretar, intérprete, interpretación; decorar, decorador, decorado; actor, actuar, actuación; dirigir, director, dirección,** etc.

PALABRA POR PALABRA El cine y el teatro

1 👥 **Con tu compañero/a, habla de tus preferencias y experiencias sobre las películas y obras de teatro.**

- ¿Qué prefieres: el cine o el teatro?
- ¿Cuándo fuiste por última vez?
- ¿Qué obra de teatro o película viste?
- ¿Sobre qué trataba? ¿Te gustó?

2 **Clasifica las siguientes palabras en la columna correspondiente.**

> escenario o cámara o actor o director/a o guion o aplausos o interpretación actriz o decorado o espectador/a o premio o escritor/a o obra o taquilla o telón o película o efectos especiales o festival o argumento

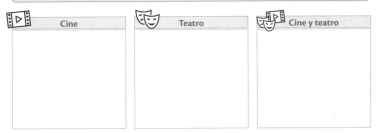

▶ Cine	🎭 Teatro	🎭 Cine y teatro

3 **Amplía tu vocabulario con las siguientes familias de palabras. Fíjate en el ejemplo.**

- **a.** Los protagonistas ...protagonizan... una obra o película.
- **b.** Los guionistas escriben el .... de una obra o película.
- **c.** El telonero abre el .... en el teatro.
- **d.** Los decoradores ganaron un premio por el .... de la obra.
- **e.** Javier Bardem, uno de los intérpretes de la película, *No es país para viejos*, ganó un Oscar por su .... como Anton Chigurh.
- **f.** Los espectadores aplaudieron a todos los actores de la obra, pero la actriz principal recibió los .... más fuertes.

PALABRA POR PALABRA Géneros de cine UNIDAD 3

4 Lee los siguientes títulos de películas en español. Con tu compañero/a, clasifícalas según su género. ¡Atención! Puede haber más de una opción. ¿Puedes poner más ejemplos?

- Rápido y furioso
- Star Trek: en la oscuridad
- Carrie
- Rescatando al soldado Ryan
- 12 años de esclavitud
- El gran Gatsby
- Pequeña señorita Sunshine
- El señor de los anillos
- Los juegos de hambre
- Diez cosas que odio de ti

 comedia drama terror romántica ciencia ficción

denuncia social | histórica | independiente | aventuras | acción

5 Completa estas opiniones sobre el cine con las palabras de la Actividad 4.

a. No me gusta ir al cine para ver historias de amor tontas. Odio (I hate) esas películas .... tan típicas del cine comercial como *Querido John*. Prefiero sufrir un poco con las historias tristes y realistas de los .... como *Lee Daniels, el mayordomo*. Bueno, y también me gustan las películas ...., como *Argo*, donde puedes aprender sobre lo que sucedió en la historia reciente.

b. A mí me encanta pasar miedo viendo una peli de ...., como *Destino final*, o imaginar mundos de fantasía con una película de ...., como *El hobbit*. Otra opción para un viernes por la noche es reírse con una buena ...., como *Ladrona de identidades*. La risa es muy buena para la salud, por eso no me gustan las películas tristes.

c. Cuando voy al cine prefiero no pensar demasiado y divertirme, por eso no entiendo a la gente que odia el cine comercial. Dicen que el cine .... es muy artístico, pero muchas personas creemos que es demasiado serio y aburrido. En general, me gusta mucho el cine comercial, excepto las películas de ...., como *The Avengers: los Vengadores*, creo que son demasiado violentas.

6 Relaciona las expresiones coloquiales con su significado.

1. » ¿Qué tal los exámenes?
   » **Me han ido de cine.**
   a. ◯ Me han ido muy bien y lo he aprobado todo.
   b. ◯ Los resultados han sido normales.

2. » ¿Vas a invitar a Matilde a tu fiesta?
   » Es muy **cómica**.
   a. ◯ Es muy famosa.
   b. ◯ Es muy graciosa y divertida.

3. » **¡No montes un drama!** Solo era un dólar.
   a. ◯ No exageres.
   b. ◯ No te preocupes.

4. Carlos es un **peliculero**.
   a. ◯ Filma películas.
   b. ◯ Es un poco mentiroso y exagerado.

MORE IN ELETECA: EXTRA ONLINE PRACTICE

99

OBJECTIVES FOR GÉNEROS DE CINE

- Present vocabulary needed to practice communicative and grammatical functions for the unit: Movie types
- Talk about the types of movies you prefer

STANDARDS

1.1	Engage in conversation	1.3	Present information
1.2	Understand the language	3.2	Acquire information

INSTRUCTIONAL STRATEGIES

Activity 4

- Write the word **género** on the board and explain that this refers to types of movie.
- Ask the students to suggest movie types and write any correct ones on the board.
- Ask them to say the titles of movies of each type.
- When students have exhausted their ideas, add any remaining words from the types under the movie images and explain them if necessary.
- Have the students look at the list of movie titles and say which type they are, using the images and the list on the board to help them.

- Have them discuss the types of movies in pairs and add more examples in Spanish if they can.
- Ask students to report back to the class. List their responses on the board under the appropriate categories.
- Have students go back to the cards from Activity 4 and fill in the missing piece of information. Call on student volunteers to share and ask the class if they agree.

Activity 5

- Have students read the three short texts and fill in the missing words.
- Ask for volunteers to read the completed texts.

Activity 6

- Explain that many expressions have come into the language from movies.
- Have the students look at the examples in bold in this activity and select the best definition according to the context.

ANSWERS

Activity 4

Answers may vary. Possible answers include: **Comedia:** *Pequeña señorita Sunshine, Diez cosas que odio de ti*; **Drama:** *Rescatando al soldado Ryan, El gran Gatsby, Diez cosas de odio de ti, 12 años de esclavitud*; **Terror:** *Carrie*; **Romántica:** *El gran Gatsby*; **Ciencia ficción:** *Star Trek: en la oscuridad*; **Denuncia social:** *12 años de esclavitud*; **Histórica:** *Rescatando al soldado Ryan, 12 años de esclavitud*; **Independiente:** *Pequeña señorita Sunshine*; **Aventuras:** *Los juegos de hambre, El señor de los anillos*; **Acción:** *Los juegos de hambre, Rápido y furioso*.

Activity 5

a. románticas, dramas, históricas; b. terror, aventuras, comedia; c. independiente, acción.

Activity 6

1. a; 2. b; 3. a; 4. b.

Extension

- Distribute individual cards at random to each student in the group using EA 3.2, **De película**. On the back of each card, have students jot down the following information about the movies they've been given: nacionalidad, **año de estreno, dirección, protagonistas, lugares donde se filmó, género**. Write the list on the board so they can copy it.
- Circulate around the room as they work, providing assistance where required.
- When they have finished, they take turns asking and answering questions about 'their' movie, using the chart they have already completed.
- Invite volunteers to come to the front to tell the class about one of the movies.

HERITAGE LANGUAGE LEARNERS

Have students investigate a recent Spanish-language film and report back to the class about it. They should identify what genre it is and explain how it fits that genre. Remind them that a film can reflect elements of more than one genre, which should be reflected in their descriptions.

GRAMÁTICA GRAMMAR IN CONTEXT

OBJECTIVES FOR GRAMÁTICA 1

- Present grammatical structures needed to practice communicative functions of the unit: Review of past tenses (preterit, imperfect and present perfect)
- Distinguish between the tenses and their uses

CORE RESOURCES

- Audio Program: Track 22
- Interactive Online Materials - ELEteca

STANDARDS

1.1 Engage in conversation
1.2 Understand the language
1.3 Present information
4.1 Compare languages

INSTRUCTIONAL STRATEGIES

1. Review of Past Tenses

- Have students go back to the conversation between Ricardo and Daniela on page 91 (Activity 4) and ask them to pick out all the verbs that refer to the past (**te has enterado**, **han contratado**, **han elegido**, **he oído**, **se conocieron**, **trabajaban**, **enseñaban**).
- Then have students say which tense is used for each verb and why. Provide cues to prompt their responses: does it refer to an action completed in the past, an ongoing or habitual action, or an action completed in the recent past?
- Walk students through the grammatical explanation in the book and review the sample sentences. Ask students what words or expressions help determine what tense to use (**anoche**, **cuando**, **este año**).

Activity 1

- Explain to students that most actions in stories are accompanied by time expressions so that we can understand when the action took place.
- Have the students read through the time expressions in the box and then the text. Ask them to explain what the message is about (**Cristian quiere hablar con Anamar sobre la posibilidad de colaborar en un taller de teatro con Paco**).
- Have them read through the text and fill in a correct time expression.
- Ask students to share their answers with a partner. Do not review answers with students yet.

🎧 22 Activity 2

- Play the audio for the students to correct their answers.
- Repeat the audio if necessary, pausing at each time expression.

ANSWERS

Activity 1

a. el otro día; **b.** entonces; **c.** En ese momento; **d.** luego; **e.** otra cosa.

OBJECTIVES FOR GRAMÁTICA 2

- Present grammatical structures needed to practice communicative functions of the unit: Time expressions associated with past tenses
- Sequence actions in the past

STANDARDS

1.1 Engage in conversation
1.2 Understand the language
1.3 Present information

GRAMÁTICA

1. REVIEW OF PAST TENSES

Preterit
- Use the preterit tense to talk about actions that were **completed** at a fixed point in the past.

  Anamar **volvió** de Madrid anoche. *Anamar returned from Madrid last night.*

Imperfect
- Use the imperfect to describe people, things or situations in the past, and to talk about ongoing or habitual actions in the past.

  Cuando **vivían** en Córdoba **estudiaban** juntos. *When they lived in Córdoba, they used to study together.*

Present Perfect
- Use the present perfect to say what a person **has done**. It describes actions completed in the recent past or in an unfinished period of time.

  Este año Anamar **ha ganado** dos premios. *This year Anamar has won two awards.*

1 Ayer Cristian llamó a Anamar y le dejó un mensaje en el contestador. Lee lo que le dijo y completa los espacios con los marcadores del cuadro.

> en ese momento ∘ otra cosa ∘ entonces ∘ luego ∘ el otro día

¡Anamar! Te he llamado mil veces esta semana. ¿Todavía no has vuelto de Berlín? Mira, te llamo para contarte que (a) .... quedé con Paco para tomar un café y me propuso colaborar en un taller de cine y teatro en su escuela. Yo acepté y (b) .... me pidió hablarlo contigo. (c) .... dije que estabas muy ocupada, pero (d) .... pensé: "Solo van a ser cuatro semanas y siempre te ha encantado trabajar con jóvenes..." Ah, (e) ...., la respuesta tiene que ser urgente. Paco necesita confirmar nuestra colaboración para empezar a organizarlo.

2 🎧 22 Ahora, escucha el mensaje y comprueba.

2. NARRATING IN THE PAST

3 Completa con los marcadores de la actividad anterior.

- To indicate when an action **approximately** takes place, use:
  - una vez
  - hace unos días / meses / minutos / años…
  - un día
  - ∘ ....
  - ∘ ....

- To indicate **continuity** or to **advance the story**, use:
  - al principio
  - después
  - a continuación
  - más tarde
  - unos momentos después
  - ∘ ....

- To **add detail or specify additional information**, use:
  - por cierto
  - ∘ ....

100

SLOWER-PACED LEARNERS

Review the main complications and difficulties with the preterite, the imperfect and the present perfect. For example, go over the most common irregularities for the preterite tense, the verbs that are irregular in the imperfect (**ser, ir, ver**), and how to build the participle for the present perfect. Refer them to online verb conjugators such as http://www.onoma.es/ if needed.

HERITAGE LANGUAGE LEARNERS

Have students take turns telling the class what they did yesterday. Tell them to use several different time expressions as they recount the events. Have other students listen and identify time expressions used.

4 🔀 **Prepara con tu compañero/a una conversación entre Anamar y Cristian con la siguiente información. Luego, túrnense representando la conversación.**

Anamar
a. Llama a Cristian para responder a su mensaje de voz.
b. Acepta la propuesta del taller y pide disculpas por no responder antes. Cuéntale que anoche perdieron tus maletas en el aeropuerto, y que tuviste que esperar tres horas hasta que las encontraron. Llegaste al hotel muy tarde y no escuchaste el mensaje hasta hoy por la mañana.
c. Después pregunta a Cristian por Paco y reacciona ante la información que Cristian te da sobre él.

Cristian
a. Contesta a la llamada de Anamar y muestra alegría por hablar con ella.
b. Acepta las disculpas y reacciona ante la información de Anamar.
c. Coméntale a Anamar que este año Paco tiene un nuevo trabajo en una escuela y que está muy contento porque el departamento lo ha elegido a él para organizar los talleres. Preséntale tu idea de organizar un taller de teatro y cine en esta escuela.

3. THE PLUPERFECT

■ We use the **pluperfect** or **past perfect** to talk about an action that took place before another action in the past. It is often referred to as the past within the past and corresponds to **had done** in English.

1.º Anamar llegó al aeropuerto a las 7:00h.

2.º Cristian dejó un mensaje a las 7:30h.

*Cuando Cristian dejó el mensaje, Anamar ya **había llegado** a casa.*
When Cristian left the message, Anamar had already arrived home.

■ The **pluperfect** is formed with the imperfect tense of **haber** and the past participle of the main verb.

		-AR	-ER	-IR
yo	había			
tú	habías			
usted/él/ella	había			
nosotros/as	habíamos	viajado	comido	dormido
vosotros/as	habíais			
ustedes/ellos/ellas	habían			

101

 Previous Page

INSTRUCTIONAL STRATEGIES

2. Narrating in the Past

Activity 3

Read the information with the students and have them complete the chart with the time expressions from Activity 1 according to the context described in each heading.

ANSWERS

Activity 3

el otro día, en ese momento; entonces, luego; otra cosa.

INSTRUCTIONAL STRATEGIES

Activity 4

- Have the students prepare a conversation between Anamar and Cristian, using the guidelines provided.
- Have the students work in pairs and explain that Anamar is responding to Cristian's message. Anamar starts the conversation using the information in **a**. Cristian responds with the information on his card for **a** and so on.
- Circulate around the room as they work, listening in and providing assistance or correction where required. When they have practiced, invite pairs to perform the conversation for the class.

OBJECTIVES FOR GRAMÁTICA 3

- Present grammatical structures needed to practice communicative functions of the unit: The pluperfect tense
- Describe actions that took place before other actions in the past

CORE RESOURCES

- Extension Activities: EA 3.3
- Interactive Whiteboard Lesson: IWB 3.2

STANDARDS

1.2   Understand the language

1.3   Present information

INSTRUCTIONAL STRATEGIES

3. The pluperfect

- Walk the students through the explanation of the pluperfect. Focus attention on the images and the time line between Anamar's arrival at the airport and Cristian leaving her a message. Ask students when both actions took place (in the past) and which one happened first (Anamar's arrival).
- Emphasize the fact that the pluperfect is used to represent an action before another action in the past, and is often introduced by the word ***ya*** in affirmative statements and ***todavía no*** in negative statements.

ADVANCED LEARNERS

Distribute cards with common verbs (***hacer, ser, tener, poner, ver, decir, escribir, ir, volver***, etc.) and ask them to say the participle. You can divide the class in groups and have a quick contest. Point out that infinitives derived from irregular root verbs keep the same structure when building the participle: ***prever-previsto, devolver-devuelto, rehacer-rehecho***, etc. Working in groups, have students develop a list of such verbs with irregular root verbs.

GRAMÁTICA GRAMMAR IN CONTEXT

INSTRUCTIONAL STRATEGIES

- Draw attention to the fact that the past participles are those the students used in the present perfect, including all the irregulars.
- Ask the students to remember the irregular past participles: say **romper** and have them respond **roto**, etc.
- Have them look at the irregular past participles in the recycle box to check and confirm their ideas.

Activity 5

- Have the students focus on the information about the career of Anamar Orson.
- Read the introduction and have different students read each of the subsequent points. Pause to explain any unfamiliar words or expressions.
- Have the students read the sentences below the information and fill in the blanks with the correct form of the verb given, in the preterit or pluperfect as required.
- Remind them that the pluperfect is always the first action in time, or the oldest action, and that is not necessarily the first action in the sentence.
- Write the following examples on the board: *When Annie had finished her work, she left the office. Mark opened the letter after the mailman had disappeared down the road.* Ask the students to underline the actions in both sentences and number them according which action came first and which came second.
- Now have them fill in the blanks in the sentences.
- Have them share their answers with a partner.
- Ask for volunteers to read the correct answers.
- If necessary, write the sentences on the board and underline and number the actions as above.

Extension

- Distribute cut up copies of EA 3.3, **El pluscuamperfecto** to student pairs and tell students to arrange the fragments into complete sentences. Help students get started by telling them the order of the cards: pink, green, blue.
- Project IWB 3.2, **El pluscuamperfecto** to review answers. Ask students to identify which action occurred first (in blue). Ask students to explain the expressions in red (time frame).

ANSWERS

Activity 5

a. escribió, había comenzado; b. había escrito; c. terminó, había dejado; d. se hizo, se había cambiado.

SLOWER-PACED LEARNERS

For additional practice with past tense verbs, have students rewrite the text in Activity 5 in the first person.

GRAMÁTICA

- To form the past participle of a verb, drop the ending of the infinitive and add **–ado** for **–ar** verbs and **–ido** for **–er** / **–ir** verbs.

- Some verbs have irregular past participles.

• abrir	➡ **abierto**	• morir	➡ **muerto**
• decir	➡ **dicho**	• poner	➡ **puesto**
• descubrir	➡ **descubierto**	• romper	➡ **roto**
• escribir	➡ **escrito**	• ver	➡ **visto**
• hacer	➡ **hecho**	• volver	➡ **vuelto**

5 Fíjate en la trayectoria de Anamar, una ponente del taller de teatro, y completa las frases con el pretérito indefinido o el pluscuamperfecto. ¡Atención! Piensa qué acciones precedieron a otras según su cronología.

Web: Anamar Orson

Anamar Orson

Sobre mí

Nació en Valencia, en 1970, donde vivió hasta que comenzó sus estudios universitarios en Barcelona.

- Terminó la carrera de Filología Clásica en 1992.
- Se mudó *(moved)* a Roma en 1993 y, dos años después, comenzó un máster en cine y televisión que terminó en 1998.
- En 1999 regresó a España, realizó un curso para enseñar español a extranjeros y comenzó a trabajar en una escuela de idiomas de Madrid.
- En el año 2001 escribió su primer guion para una miniserie de Telemadrid, lo firmó con el apellido de origen irlandés de su madre y, desde entonces, comenzó a llevar ese apellido.
- Filmó su primer corto *(short film)* en el año 2003, por el que recibió el premio del Festival de Cine de San Sebastián.
- En febrero de 2005 dejó la escuela. Un mes después, empezó a filmar *Laberinto*, su primera película premiada con dos goyas a la mejor película y al mejor actor revelación *(newcomer award)*.

🔍 Buscar

📋 **Archivo del blog**
  ⊞ Octubre
  ⊞ Septiembre
  ⊞ Agosto
  ⊞ Julio
  ⊞ Junio
  ⊞ Mayo

🐦 @anamar_O

📘 Sígueme

a. Cuando Anamar (escribir) .... su primer guion ya (comenzar) .... a trabajar en una escuela.
b. Antes de filmar su primera película, Anamar ya (escribir) .... un guion para Telecuatro.
c. Cuando (terminar) .... de filmar *Laberinto*, Anamar ya (dejar) .... la escuela de idiomas.
d. Cuando Ana se (hacerse) .... famosa por su primera película ya (cambiarse) .... el apellido.

MORE IN ELETECA: EXTRA ONLINE PRACTICE ◆ **GRAMMAR TUTORIALS** 5 AND 6

DESTREZAS

COMPRENSIÓN DE LECTURA

1 Antes de leer el texto, repasa la estrategia en Destrezas y sigue las recomendaciones.

Destrezas

Focusing on relevant information

When reading about a topic that may be unfamiliar to you, use the following steps.

1. Read the entire text to get a general idea of the topic.
2. Read each paragraph and highlight the main topic or subject as there could be more than one.
3. Look at each question. Is it asking about a topic or a person performing an action? Do you need a subject, a complement, a motive, a temporal expression, etc., to complete the sentence?
4. Go back to the highlighted text, look for information, and answer the question.
5. Remember that the question order follows the sequence of the information presented in the text.

2 Lee el texto y elige la opción correcta.

XII EDICIÓN DE JÓVENES TALENTOS CINEMATOGRÁFICOS
Una apuesta por el cine más actual

El pasado 4 de marzo se celebró el duodécimo certamen de jóvenes talentos cinematográficos. Al evento asistieron no solo directores y actores noveles, sino que contó con la presencia de un buen número de veteranos que acudieron a interesarse por el trabajo de las nuevas generaciones.

Este año la Academia de las Artes y las Ciencias Cinematográficas de España, organismo dependiente del Ministerio de Cultura, ha contado con un presupuesto mucho más bajo que en años anteriores, por lo que, después de unos meses de muchas dudas, ha conseguido celebrar su duodécima edición con la ayuda de la publicidad de empresas privadas.

En la apertura del acto, la presentadora, Amelia Guillén, agradeció la colaboración de estas empresas patrocinadoras y pidió al público un fuerte aplauso para los más de 300 candidatos a los diferentes premios.

Antes de entregar el primer premio, Amelia Guillén dedicó unas palabras a todos los profesionales anónimos del séptimo arte, técnicos de sonido, cámaras, maquilladores, decoradores… "todos ellos absolutamente imprescindibles, pero invisibles para la gran mayoría del público", señaló la presentadora.

1. Al certamen acudieron…
   a. actores y directores jóvenes únicamente.
   b. actores y directores de diferentes generaciones.
   c. actores y directores de diferentes partes del mundo.

2. Este año el certamen ha estado en peligro…
   a. por las pocas ayudas recibidas del Estado.
   b. porque había pocas empresas patrocinadoras.
   c. por la falta de candidatos.

OBJECTIVES FOR DESTREZAS
- Focus on relevant information

STANDARDS
1.1 Interpersonal communication
1.2 Understand the language
1.3 Present information

INSTRUCTIONAL STRATEGIES
Comprensión de lectura
Activity 1
- Talk the students through the strategy for focusing on relevant information.
- Answer any questions they may have at this stage.
- Have the students follow the instructions in the order they are set out. They should make notes.

Activity 2
- Ask the students to read the text and choose the best way to complete each statement.
- Have them use their notes and the instructions above to help them.
- When they have finished, have them compare answers with a partner.
- Ask for volunteers to say the correct answers.

ANSWERS
Activity 2
1. b (Al evento asistieron no solo directores y actores noveles, sino que contó con la presencia de un buen número de veteranos); **2.** a (Este año la Academia de las Artes y las Ciencias Cinematográficas de España, organismo dependiente del Ministerio de Cultura, ha contado con un presupuesto mucho más bajo que en años anteriores, por lo que, después de unos meses de muchas dudas, ha conseguido celebrar su duodécima edición con la ayuda de la publicidad de empresas privadas); **3.** c (En la apertura del acto, la presentadora, Amelia Guillén, agradeció la colaboración de estas empresas patrocinadoras); **4.** c (Antes de entregar el primer premio, Amelia Guillén dedicó unas palabras a todos los profesionales anónimos del séptimo arte, técnicos de sonido, cámaras, maquilladores, decoradores…).

ADVANCED LEARNERS

When reading the text in Activity 2, point out that names of months are not written in capital letters in Spanish while the names of festivals and awards are. Review ordinal numbers in Spanish (**primero, segundo, tercero**, etc.). Give them sample sentences with errors in capitalization or the usage of ordinal numbers to correct.

HERITAGE LANGUAGE LEARNERS

As an extension activity to the reading, you can have students write and deliver a version of the speech that Amelia Guillén might have given.

INSTRUCTIONAL STRATEGIES

Activity 3

- Have the students read the information in the **Destrezas** box again and have them make notes for the text in this activity.
- Ask for volunteers to read the text aloud and pause to explain any unfamiliar words or expressions.
- Have the students answer the questions below the text.
- When they have finished, have them share their answers with a partner.
- Ask for volunteers to say the answers aloud for the class to correct.

ANSWERS

Activity 3

1. b (El 11 de octubre de 1896, Eduardo Jimeno Correas filmó *Salida de la misa de doce de la iglesia* con la primera cámara Lumière que un año antes había comprado en Lyon, Francia); **2.** a (El siglo XX comenzó con una producción de cine experimental, representado por directores como Luis Buñuel que, con impactantes películas como *Un perro andaluz*, consiguió el prestigio internacional y cierto escándalo en España); **3.** c (Las películas contrarias a la dictadura se censuraban, o simplemente se prohibían); **4.** b (A partir de los años ochenta comienza un gran periodo para el cine español. Directores como Pedro Almodóvar, José Luis Garci y Montxo Armendáriz, entre otros, iniciaron en estos años sus carreras y las desarrollaron con éxito nacional e internacional).

SLOWER-PACED LEARNERS

Before reading the text, have students brainstorm what they already know about the history of film. You can ask them about the Lumière brothers, silent movies, color movies, etc. Ask them to think about how movies have been used for political purposes. Explain that Spain had a dictator for 40 years in the 20th century. Ask how they think that may have impacted the film industry and what they think happened after the dictatorship was over. (After his death, the cultural scene in Spain flourished).

ADVANCED LEARNERS

Have students notice that only the first word in the name of movies should be capitalized. Have them go back to page 99 so they can notice the same thing about the movie titles there. Then have students write a short summary of this text in their own words to consolidate its main ideas.

DESTREZAS

3. Amelia Guillén dio las gracias…
- **a.** a todos los participantes al certamen.
- **b.** al público que asistió a la ceremonia del certamen.
- **c.** a las empresas que colaboraron económicamente en el certamen.

4. La presentadora del certamen…
- **a.** pidió un gran aplauso a los profesionales anónimos.
- **b.** se emocionó al entregar el primer premio.
- **c.** reconoció el trabajo de profesionales del cine no conocidos por el público.

3 **Lee el texto y, aplicando la misma estrategia de la Actividad 1, contesta las preguntas.**

BREVE HISTORIA DEL CINE ESPAÑOL

El 11 de octubre de 1896, Eduardo Jimeno Correas filmó *Salida de la misa de doce de la iglesia* con la primera cámara Lumière que un año antes había comprado en Lyon, Francia. Un año después, el barcelonés Fructuós Gelabert filmó *Riña en un café*, la primera película española con argumento. El siglo XX comenzó con una producción de cine experimental, representado por directores como Luis Buñuel que, con impactantes películas como *Un perro andaluz*, consiguió el prestigio internacional y cierto escándalo en España.

Cuando en 1928 llegó el cine sonoro a España, pocas productoras habían desarrollado medios técnicos para realizar películas, esto provocó una crisis en la producción de trabajos cinematográficos.

Posteriormente, el cine producido durante la dictadura del General Francisco Franco fue, en general, un medio de propaganda de las ideas políticas, morales y religiosas oficiales. Las películas contrarias a la dictadura se censuraban, o simplemente se prohibían.

A partir de los años ochenta comienza un gran periodo para el cine español. Directores como Pedro Almodóvar, José Luis Garci y Montxo Armendáriz, entre otros, iniciaron en estos años sus carreras y las desarrollaron con éxito nacional e internacional. Además, en 1986 se fundó la Academia de las Artes y las Ciencias Cinematográficas, organismo encargado de la organización de los famosos premios Goya y que ha promocionado y difundido los méritos del cine producido en este país. En la actualidad son muchos los directores españoles con éxito y reconocimiento internacional.

1. La primera película española…
- **a.** fue de ficción.
- **b.** se filmó a la salida de una iglesia.
- **c.** se filmó con una cámara fabricada en España.

2. Las películas de Luis Buñuel tuvieron proyección internacional…
- **a.** pero no se entendieron muy bien en España.
- **b.** provocaron una crisis cinematográfica.
- **c.** fueron censuradas durante la dictadura de Franco.

3. El gobierno del dictador Francisco Franco…
- **a.** promocionó películas de cine experimental.
- **b.** estableció la Academia de las Artes y las Ciencias Cinematigráficas.
- **c.** prohibió películas contrarias a la dictadura.

4. El director Montxo Armendáriz inició su carrera profesional…
- **a.** durante la dictadura de Franco.
- **b.** en los años ochenta.
- **c.** en 1986 cuando fundó la Academia de las Artes y las Ciencias Cinematigráficas.

104

PRONUNCIACIÓN La letra *h*

1 Como ya sabes, en español la letra *h* no se pronuncia (*hola, hoy, hablar*). Lee la siguiente información sobre el uso de la *h* en la ortografía española.

Se escriben con *h*:

Grupo 1
Las palabras que empiezan por **hue–, hie–, hui–**: *huevo, hierba, huida.*

Grupo 2
Las palabras que empiezan por los prefijos **hidro–, hiper–, hipo–, homo–, hetero–, heli–**: *hidrógeno, hipermercado, hipopótamo, homogéneo, heterogéneo.*

Grupo 3
La mayoría de las palabras que empiezan por **hosp–, horm–, horn–, herm–, hern–**: *hospital, hormiga, horno, hermético, hernia...* Hay excepciones como: *Ernesto, ermita.*

Grupo 4
Otras palabras se escriben con *h* por derivación de palabras de la misma familia: *habitante, habitar, habitación...*

2 🎧 **23** Escucha esta serie de palabras y escribe el número en la columna adecuada.

Grupo 1	Grupo 2	Grupo 3	Grupo 4

■ In Spanish there is a group of words or expressions that sound the same, but have different meanings. Here are some examples of homophones.

a (preposition)	**ha** (verb **haber**)	
ay (exclamation)	**hay** (verb **haber**)	**ahí** (adverb)
haber (verb)	**a ver** (preposition + verb)	
hecho (verb **hacer**)	**echo** (verb **echar**)	
hola *(greeting)*	**ola** *(wave, noun)*	

3 🎧 **24** Completa con los homófonos anteriores. Después, escucha y comprueba.

a. Mónica .... vuelto .... Madrid.
b. ¿Ves estos libros de cine tan bonitos? Creo que los van .... vender todos y no va .... haber más hasta el próximo mes.
c. ¡ ...., Isaac! Quita la computadora de ...., ¿no ves que no .... espacio suficiente?
d. ¡ ...., Sergio! ¿Has visto qué .... tan buenas .... para hacer surf?
e. Otra vez he .... una tortilla horrible, siempre le .... demasiada sal.

👤💻 **MORE IN ELETECA:** EXTRA ONLINE PRACTICE

105

OBJECTIVES FOR PRONUNCIACIÓN

- Practice pronouncing and spelling words containing the letter **h**

CORE RESOURCES

- Audio Program: Tracks 23 and 24
- Interactive Online Materials - ELEteca

STANDARDS

1.2 Understand the language
3.2 Acquire information
4.1 Compare languages

INSTRUCTIONAL STRATEGIES

Activity 1

Walk the students through the explanation and ask them to think of more examples for each group. Write the words on the board in their groups and make a special note to one side of any more exceptions.

🎧 23 Activity 2

- Tell the students they are going to hear a series of words and they are to write them in the appropriate column according to which group they are in.
- Play the audio and have the students listen and repeat, and then write the word in the correct column.
- Repeat the audio and have the students confirm their answers.
- Repeat the audio if required.
- Ask random students to say which group each word is in.
- Read the note about homophones and have the students say the words so they can hear that they are pronounced the same in spite of being spelled differently.

Audioscript

1. habitual; **2.** helicóptero; **3.** había; **4.** hidroeléctrico; **5.** hiedra; **6.** hielo; **7.** hipersensible; **8.** homologar; **9.** honrado; **10.** hormonas; **11.** huele; **12.** huésped.

🎧 24 Activity 3

- Introduce homophones by writing the following sentence on the board: **El tren que llega _a las cuatro todavía no _a llegado**. Ask: **¿Cuál de las dos "a" lleva hache?** Review the examples in the box and clarify new vocabulary.
- Have the students read the sentences and fill in the missing homophones.
- Students work individually and then share their answers with a partner.
- Play the audio for students to confirm answers. Then ask for volunteers to read the completed sentences as you record them on the board.

ANSWERS

Activity 2

Grupo 1: 5, 6, 11, 12; Grupo 2: 2, 4, 7, 8; Grupo 3: 10, 9; Grupo 4: 1, 3.

Activity 3

a. ha, a; **b.** a, a; **c.** Ay, ahí, hay; **d.** Hola, olas, hay; **e.** hecho, echo.

HERITAGE LANGUAGE LEARNERS

Heritage Language Learners have a great challenge with this topic. Have them practice online or ask them to record a list of words with and without **hache** and use the list as a basis for dictations that they can make on their own. Other common mistakes are **habeces** (for **a veces**), **halla-allá, echo-hecho, echa-hecha, habra-abra,** and **habré-abre**.

OBJECTIVES FOR SABOR HISPANO

- Learn about the Mexican movie world
- Activate vocabulary connected with movies

CORE RESOURCES

- Audio program: Track 25

STANDARDS

2.1 Culture: practices and perspectives
2.2 Products and perspectives
3.2 Acquire information
5.2 Using language for personal enjoyment and enrichment

INSTRUCTIONAL STRATEGIES

🎧 25

- Introduce the topic by asking if the students know any Mexican actors / actresses / directors / movies.
- Look at the images with them and elicit what they already know and can share.
- Put students into pairs. Have them discuss the questions in the **Antes de leer** box. Encourage them to take notes about their partners' responses. Monitor their conversations and assist as needed.
- Have students switch partners and tell their new partners about their previous partners' responses. Monitor their conversations and assist as needed.
- Tell the students to look at the **Glosario** on the next page to help them with any vocabulary they may not know.
- Read the first section of the text and invite volunteers to read the questions.
- After each section, ask questions such as: **¿Qué tipo de películas le gustaban de niño? ¿Dónde estudió? ¿Cuándo filmó su primera película?**, etc.
- Ask what the students have understood and invite those who understood more to help those who understood less.
- Call on student volunteers to role-play the parts of interviewer and Guillermo del Toro.

ADVANCED LEARNERS

Have students watch trailers of the movies mentioned here. You can find a trailer for **El laberinto del fauno** on YouTube. Some of the images are frightening, so be sure that it's appropriate for your class before showing it. For additional information about Spanish movies and access to more trailers, visit: http://www.filmaffinity.com/es/main.html. When viewing trailers in class, direct students to listen different accents. Have them describe some of the images and ask some basic questions about what they've understood the story to be about, what predictions they might make about the film, and whether or not they would want to see it.

HERITAGE LANGUAGE LEARNERS

Have students write a short biography of Guillermo del Toro based on the information provided in the interview. If you give this as an assignment for homework, encourage them to do additional research online and include more details about his life.

SABOR HISPANO

EL CINE MEXICANO...

El actor mexicano Diego Luna atiende las entrevistas de los periodistas.

¡ESTÁ DE MODA!

Antes de leer
¿Qué tipo de películas te gustan?
¿Has visto alguna película en español? ¿Cuál?

🎧 25 El cine en español, y en especial el mexicano, tiene cada vez más presencia en los festivales y cines internacionales. Lee estos extractos de entrevistas al director Guillermo del Toro.

¿Cuándo supo que se quería dedicar al cine?
De niño crecí viendo películas de animación japonesas. Todas eran de monstruos japoneses y robots pilotados por humanos. Desde entonces quise contar historias a través de imágenes.

¿Cuándo comenzó?
Cuando estudiaba en el Instituto de Ciencias de Guadalajara comencé a filmar y a los 21 años filmé mi primera película. En esa época también fundé el Festival de Cine de Guadalajara.

¿Cuál es su especialidad?
La verdad es que no tengo ninguna. He filmado películas basadas en cómics, películas de terror, películas históricas, de fantasía, de ciencia ficción…

¿Cuáles son sus películas más importantes?
Sin duda, *El laberinto del fauno* y *El espinazo del diablo*.

¿Por qué?
Porque me dieron a conocer° en muchos países. A partir de ese momento comencé a trabajar en proyectos más ambiciosos e interesantes. Esas dos películas son muy queridas por mí… Tienen una temática que me interesa: en ellas hablo de la niñez° y de la política, y utilizo elementos fantásticos.

¿A qué otros directores mexicanos admira?
Admiro mucho a Luis Mandoqui porque tiene personalidad.

¿Dónde vive?
Ahora vivo en Los Ángeles, Estados

Unidos. México es mi hogar pero Los Ángeles es la cuna° del cine.

¿Qué proyectos futuros tiene?
Estoy estudiando una propuesta para desarrollar *El increíble Hulk*, una historia basada en los cómics de Marvel.

Guillermo del Toro, en la presentación de la película *Don't be Afraid of the Dark*

106

Estas son las películas más taquilleras¹ del cine moderno mexicano

- No se aceptan devoluciones
- Nosotros los nobles
- El crimen del padre Amaro
- El laberinto del fauno
- Como agua para chocolate

Estos son los 5 actores mexicanos más famosos

- Salma Hayek
- Gael García Bernal
- Diego Luna
- Paulina Rubio
- Camila Sodi

La actriz mexicana Salma Hayek, en la alfombra roja del Festival de Cannes

---

¿COMPRENDISTE?

Decide si las siguientes frases son verdaderas (V) o falsas (F).

1. Diego Luna y Luis Mandoqui trabajan en el cine. V ○ F ○
2. Guillermo del Toro está orgulloso de *El espinazo del diablo*. V ○ F ○
3. Los Ángeles es el centro de la industria cinematográfica. V ○ F ○
4. Salma Hayek es una directora de cine importante. V ○ F ○
5. La película mexicana que ha conseguido más dinero es *No se aceptan devoluciones*. V ○ F ○

El director mexicano Luis Mandoqui, en una entrevista

AHORA TÚ

¿Qué opinas? Contesta las siguientes preguntas y comenta tus ideas con tus compañeros/as.

1. ¿Has visto alguna película de Guillermo del Toro? ¿Qué te ha parecido?
2. ¿Qué cualidades piensas que son importantes para contar historias a través del cine?
3. ¿Qué otros medios son buenos para contar historias?
4. ¿Qué se necesita para ser un buen actor?
5. ¿Qué películas te han marcado¹? ¿Por qué?

Glosario

la cuna – cradle
dar a conocer – to become known
marcar – to influence
la niñez – childhood
taquillera – box office hit

VOCES LATINAS

EL MÉXICO DE FRIDA KALHO

Fuentes: *El País*, *La Vanguardia*, Prezi.com, Cineactual, *Fotogramas*, YouTube, *El Mundo*, Canal100.mx

107

OBJECTIVES FOR RELATO

- Revisit unit themes, grammar, vocabulary and culture in a new context
- Improve reading comprehension skills

CORE RESOURCES

- Audio Program: Track 26

STANDARDS

1.1. Engage in conversation
1.2 Understand the language
1.3 Present information
2.1 Culture: Practices and perspectives
5.3 Using language for personal enjoyment and enrichment

INSTRUCTIONAL STRATEGIES

Activity 1

- Have the students look at the image and title and guess what they think the text will be about. Ask them if they can name any other Hispanic poets or playwrights (or American ones).
- Introduce the poet and playwright, Federico García Lorca, and tell students that they are going to learn more about his life and works. Say to students: **Federico García Lorca nació en 1898 y murió en 1936. ¿Cuántos años tenía cuando murió?** (38 años), **¿Por qué creen que murió tan joven? ¿Estaba enfermo?** Then tell students they will find possible answers in the text, but to save their ideas for the end of the section when they will know more about Lorca.
- Before students begin to read, explain that the text is incomplete and that for now they should just read it for general understanding. Have students read through the text and write a summary statement and heading for each paragraph.
- Have them share their ideas with a partner.
- Discuss the themes and symbols in Lorca's works and share the following note with students.

Cultural Note

La simbología de Lorca es muy compleja y no tiene una sola interpretación, ya que depende del tema concreto de la obra. Dicho esto, se aceptan las siguientes interpretaciones: los elementos de la naturaleza y atmosféricos (el viento y el agua en movimiento, por ejemplo) como símbolo de libertad; el color verde: la muerte o la rebeldía; el negro: la represión, la falta de libertad y el fanatismo religioso; el caballo puede simbolizar la muerte, pero también la energía e incluso lo masculino; el rojo: la sangre, el dolor o la pasión; la luna representa la muerte, pero también la esterilidad; las flores: la felicidad; la sangre: los instintos; las palomas: la masculinidad…

Activity 2

- Have the students look through the text to find the numbers.
- Have them read the sentences and decide where each sentence should appear in the text. They write the number in the space provided.
- Have the students discuss their answers with a partner.

ANSWERS

Activity 2

a. 4; b. 1; c. 5; d. 3; e. 2.

SLOWER-PACED LEARNERS

After Activity 2, ask a series of general and specific questions about the text to exploit it further and aid students' comprehension.

RELATO Lorca y la Generación del 27

1 Lee el siguiente texto sobre el famoso poeta y dramaturgo español, Federico García Lorca.

Lorca y la Generación del 27

Federico García Lorca fue un escritor andaluz perteneciente a la Generación del 27, (1). La mayoría de los miembros del grupo estudió la obra de los clásicos españoles, publicó en las mismas revistas, vivió en la Residencia de Estudiantes y cultivó una literatura basada en la mezcla (*mixture*) de lo popular (*common*) y de lo culto (*cultured*), de lo tradicional y de lo moderno y miraba a su entorno (*surroundings*) español y al ámbito universal.

Lorca, como casi todos sus compañeros, apoyó (*supported*) públicamente las reformas democráticas de la Segunda República, en especial las dedicadas a la cultura y la educación, (2).

Cuando en 1939 Franco ganó la guerra civil muchos de estos escritores tuvieron que huir (*flee*) al extranjero por miedo a la represión del nuevo gobierno fascista. (3). Algún tiempo antes Lorca había recorrido España con *La Barraca* y había viajado a Nueva York y a Argentina, país en el que continuó con sus obras de teatro.

Sus poemas más conocidos son *Romancero Gitano* (1928), *Poeta en Nueva York* (1930) y *Poema del cante jondo* (1931). (4) (en todas se producen conflictos entre las normas establecidas y la libertad). Sus temas son el amor, la muerte, el destino, la soledad, la frustración, la tradición, el campo… Sus personajes favoritos, la mujer, los gitanos (*gypsies*), los niños y los marginados. Escribió con un cuidado estilo, tradicional y vanguardista al mismo tiempo, (5)…

2 Las siguientes frases están extraídas del texto que acabas de leer. Escribe al lado de cada una el número del lugar en el que deberían aparecer.

a. ☐ Sus obras de teatro más famosas son *Bodas de sangre* (1933), *Yerma* (1934) y *La casa de Bernarda Alba* (1936).

b. ☐ un grupo de escritores que compartieron experiencias y características literarias comunes.

c. ☐ y su lenguaje sigue siendo muy investigado por sus enigmáticos símbolos: la luna, el caballo, el agua, los gitanos.

d. ☐ Federico García Lorca no tuvo tanta suerte (*luck*) y murió asesinado en 1936, el mismo año en el que estalló (*broke out*) la guerra civil.

e. ☐ y fundó (*founded*) la compañía teatral *La Barraca* con la que estuvo dirigiendo e interpretando diversas obras de teatro por toda la geografía española.

3 🎧 **26** Lee estos fragmentos y relaciónalos con la obra de teatro de Federico García Lorca a la que pertenecen.

a
Bernarda: Niña, dame un abanico.   **Amelia:** Tome usted. *(Le da un abanico redondo con flores rojas y verdes).*   **Bernarda:** *(Tirando el abanico al suelo).* ¿Es este el abanico que se da a una viuda? Dame uno negro y aprende a respetar el luto de tu padre.   **Martirio:** Tome usted el mío.   **Bernarda:** ¿Y tú?   **Martirio:** Yo no tengo calor.   **Bernarda:** Pues busca otro, que te hará falta. En ocho años que dure el luto no ha de entrar en esta casa el viento de la calle. Haceros cuenta que hemos tapiado con ladrillos puertas y ventanas. Así pasó en casa de mi padre y en casa de mi abuelo.

b
(Mira hacia la puerta).   **Yerma:** ¡María! ¿Por qué pasas tan deprisa por mi puerta?   **María:** *(Entra con un niño en brazos).* Cuando voy con el niño, lo hago… ¡Como siempre lloras…!   **Yerma:** Tienes razón. *(Toma al niño y se sienta).*   **María:** Me da tristeza que tengas envidia *(envy). (Se sienta).*   **Yerma:** No es envidia lo que tengo; es pobreza.   **María:** No te quejes.   **Yerma:** ¡Cómo no me voy a quejar cuando te veo a ti y a las otras mujeres llenas por dentro de flores, y viéndome yo inútil en medio de tanta hermosura!

Yerma
Obra teatral de Federico García Lorca que narra la historia de Yerma, una joven campesina que sufre porque desea tener un hijo. La directora Pilar Távora adaptó la obra y en 1999 se estrenó en el cine.

La casa de Bernarda Alba
Fue la última obra de teatro de Lorca. En ella Bernarda, mujer tradicional y autoritaria, encierra a sus hijas jóvenes en casa tras la muerte de su marido. La obra se llevó al cine en 1987 en una película del director Mario Camus.

4 Contesta las siguientes preguntas acerca del estilo de Lorca según los textos que has leído.

a. ¿Qué características de la obra de Lorca observas en los textos?
b. ¿Qué tienen en común ambas obras?

INSTRUCTIONAL STRATEGIES

🎧 **26 Activity 3**

- Write the word **yerma** on the board and explain what it means: *inhabitado*, *incultivado*, *que no tiene cultivo ni labor* (*barren* in English). Project the image for the movie posters and point to the first one. Ask students, *¿A cuál de las dos creen que se refiere el título?*
- Next ask about the women in **La casa de Bernarda Alba** and ask: *¿Cuál es la relación entre esas mujeres? ¿Qué personalidades pueden tener?*
- Have the students read the brief information about the two plays, **Yerma** and **La casa de Bernarda Alba** below the excerpts to learn more about them.
- Tell students to read the passages from the two plays and decide which is which.
- Have them compare their answers with a partner.
- Play the audio while the students listen with books closed.
- Play the audio again as students follow in their books.
- Ask different students to say the correct answers aloud.

Activity 4

- Ask students to read the questions and discuss the answers in pairs.
- Ask for volunteers to express their ideas to the class.
- As a follow-up, ask students: *¿Cómo creen que se llaman los personajes presentados como "Señora" y "Chica joven y guapa"?* (*Bernarda Alba es la señora y Yerma es la chica joven y guapa*).

Extension

Go back to the question posed at the beginning of the lesson and ask students for their ideas regarding his death. Entertain different versions without confirming any just yet. Instead, encourage students to research online to learn what happened.

ANSWERS

Activity 3

a. *La casa de Bernarda Alba*; **b.** *Yerma*.

Activity 4

a. Personajes femeninos, la frustración, las tradiciones (como el luto), la falta de libertad…; **b.** Las dos son obras de teatro de Lorca, tienen personajes femeninos y han sido adaptadas al cine. También tienen argumentos de historias duras de falta de libertad y represión y ambas muestran un lenguaje lleno de símbolos.

ADVANCED LEARNERS

Explain that many works by García Lorca are based on real events. For instance, **La casa de Bernarda Alba** was inspired by a real story that happened in a small village not far away from Granada, called Valderrubio. Ask students to share examples of of other literary works or movies that are based on real events.

HERITAGE LANGUAGE LEARNERS

Have students investigate whether or not there have been or will be any productions of Federico García Lorca's plays nearby. Encourage them to look for and watch clips of productions of his work that can be found online. As a potential group project, you might have students select a short scene from one of his plays and act out in class or make a movie of it.

OBJECTIVES FOR EVALUACIÓN

- Review grammar, vocabulary and culture from the unit
- Complete self-assessment

CORE RESOURCES

- Interactive Online Materials - ELEteca

STANDARDS

1.2	Understand the language
2.1	Practices and perspectives
4.1	Compare cultures

INSTRUCTIONAL STRATEGIES

- Activities can be completed individually and then reviewed with the class. Vary by asking students if they agree with the answer given and then writing it on the board. Provide explanations as needed.
- You may wish to assign point value to each activity as a way for students to monitor their progress.
- Direct students to the indicated pages in **En resumen** if they make more than one or two mistakes in any one section.

ANSWERS

Activity 1

1. c; **2.** a; **3.** d; **4.** b.

Activity 2

a. Como no sonó el despertador, llegué a clase tarde; **b.** El partido se canceló porque llovía; **c.** La película tuvo muy mala crítica por su violencia; **d.** Para mejorar las instalaciones, la biblioteca estará cerrada una semana.

Activity 3

a. por; **b.** por; **c.** por; **d.** por; **e.** para.

Activity 4

Answers will vary. Possible answer:

El otro día Daniela me llamó por teléfono para ir al cine. Pero media hora antes había hablado con Ricardo para ver una película en mi casa, entonces, le comenté el plan y, al final, quedamos en mi casa.

EVALUACIÓN

EXPRESSING SURPRISE, SKEPTICISM, CURIOSITY, AND GIVING INFORMATION

1 **Relaciona cada frase con su respuesta.**

1. Los materiales del taller son gratis
2. ¡Han robado las cámaras del taller!
3. Han publicado las notas del examen de español
4. Te aseguro que te envié el correo. ¿De verdad que no lo has recibido?

a. ¡Qué fuerte! Las compraron ayer.
b. No, ¡qué raro
c. ¿De veras?
d. ¡Anda ya!, si lo hicimos ayer

EXPRESSING PURPOSE OR MOTIVE OF AN ACTION

2 **Escribe de nuevo las siguientes frases usando las palabras entre paréntesis. Haz los cambios necesarios.**

a. Llegué tarde a clase porque no sonó el despertador. (como) ....

b. El partido se canceló por la lluvia. (porque) ....

c. La película tuvo muy mala crítica debido a su violencia. (por) ....

d. Con el objetivo de mejorar las instalaciones, la biblioteca estará cerrada una semana. (para) ....

USING *POR* AND *PARA*

3 **Completa con *por* o *para*.**

a. El estreno de su primera película fue .... mayo.
b. Mis padres van al cine una vez .... semana.
c. Mi sueño es poder viajar .... el mundo.
d. Gracias .... todo.
e. Es una película muy fuerte, no es adecuada .... todas las edades.

NARRATING IN THE PAST

4 **Observa la siguiente cronología y escribe un relato sobre lo que ocurrió. Usa las expresiones temporales y esta información para ayudarte a desarrollarlo. ¡*Atención!* Hoy es lunes.**

media hora antes ○ y entonces ○ al final ○ El otro día

- Había hablado con Ricardo para ver una película en mi casa (viernes, 5:00h)
- Le comenté el plan (viernes, 5:35h)
- Quedamos en mi casa (viernes, 8:00h)
- Daniela me llamó para ir al cine (viernes, 5:30h)

Modelo: El otro día Daniela me llamó...

REVIEW OF PAST TENSES

5 Escribe los verbos entre paréntesis en el tiempo pasado correcto.

Cristian (a) .... (nacer) en 1971 en Cartagena, ciudad en la que (b) .... (realizar) sus estudios de Bellas Artes (*Fine Arts*). Tres meses antes de terminar la carrera (*degree*), (c) .... (decidir) que quería ser actor y (d) .... (mudarse) a Nueva York para perfeccionar su inglés y estudiar interpretación. Durante el tiempo en que (e) .... (vivir) en Nueva York, por las mañanas (f) .... (estudiar) Arte Dramático y por las tardes (g) .... (enseñar) español. Encontró ese trabajo con la ayuda de Paco, un profesor de español que (h) .... (conocer) de antes. En 1999 (i) .... (trasladarse) a Buenos Aires, donde (j) .... (continuar) trabajando como profesor de español, de nuevo con Paco, que ya (k) .... (regresar) a Argentina un año antes. En la escuela (l) .... (conocer) a Anamar y en el año 2002 (m) .... (actuar) por primera vez en una serie de televisión que (n) .... (escribir) su compañera Anamar el verano anterior. Por esta serie se hizo muy famoso y desde entonces no (ñ) .... (parar) de trabajar en cine, televisión y teatro. De hecho, se rumorea que últimamente (o) .... (recibir) varias ofertas de algunos de los directores más prestigiosos del mundo del cine.

EL CINE Y EL TEATRO

6 Completa estas frases con una palabra o expresión relacionada con el cine y el teatro.

a. Un tipo de cine más relacionado con el arte que con la taquilla es el cine ....
b. Cuando he tenido un gran día o todo me ha salido bien digo que me ha ido ....
c. Cuando vamos al cine para ver una .... podemos escuchar muchas carcajadas de risa.
d. Para comprar los boletos de una peli o una obra tienes que pasar por la ....

THE LETTER *H*

7 Elige la opción correcta.

a. Quita el bolso de **hay / ahí / ay**, no es un lugar seguro.
b. Esta semana hemos **hecho / echo** muchos exámenes.
c. Hoy es un poco peligroso bañarse en el mar con estas **holas / olas**.
d. Corren porque creen que no va a **ver / haber** boletos.

CULTURA

8 Contesta las siguientes preguntas con la información aprendida en *El cine mexicano*.

a. ¿Quién es Guillermo del Toro y cuál ha sido su trayectoria?
b. ¿Qué tipo de películas captó su imaginación como niño? ¿Tiene alguna especialidad?
c. ¿Qué actores mexicanos ya conocías de la lista que se presentó? Y de las películas, ¿conocías alguna?
e. ¿Crees que los directores mexicanos están de moda? Explica.

 MORE IN ELETECA: EXTRA ONLINE PRACTICE

ANSWERS

Activity 5

a. nació; **b.** realizó; **c.** decidió; **d.** se mudó; **e.** vivió; **f.** estudiaba; **g.** enseñaba; **h.** había conocido; **i.** se trasladó; **j.** continuó; **k.** había regresado; **l.** conoció; **m.** actuó; **n.** había escrito; **ñ.** ha parado; **o.** ha recibido.

Activity 6

a. independiente; **b.** de cine; **c.** comedia; **d.** taquilla.

Activity 7

a. ahí; **b.** hecho; **c.** olas; **d.** haber.

Activity 8

Answers may vary. **a.** Guillermo del Toro es director de cine. Nació en México y filmó su primera película a los 21 años. Sus películas más taquilleras son *No se aceptan devoluciones* y *Nosotros los nobles*; **b.** De niño le gustaban mucho las películas japonesas de animación.

OBJECTIVES FOR EN RESUMEN: VOCABULARIO

- Review unit vocabulary and expressions
- Practice communicative skills

STANDARDS

1.2   Understand the language

1.3   Present information

4.1   Evaluate similarities and differences in language

INSTRUCTIONAL STRATEGIES

- Encourage students to use self-adhesive notes to place on correct objects in their house.
- Index cards can be used as flashcards with the Spanish term on one side and the English term on the other, or a picture or drawing.
- Students work in pairs or groups, using vocabulary flashcards as they would the cards of a board game to help each other practice unit vocabulary.
- Encourage students to write labels or captions for the photos on this page. Remind them to use the vocabulary and expressions they have learned in this unit.
- Have students write sentences or conversations using the vocabulary in context. Then have them convert the sentences and conversations into a worksheet by removing the target vocabulary and placing them in an answer key. (When creating their worksheets, suggest that they change the order of the sentences and conversations so they don't follow the order of the vocabulary lists on the page). Have them swap worksheets with another classmate and try to complete the sentences and conversations with the correct words. Finally, have them correct each other's work.

EN RESUMEN: Vocabulario

Cine y teatro

la alfombra de Hollywood *the red carpet*
el aplauso *applause*
el argumento *plot, story line*
la cámara *camera*
el cámara *cameraman*
el cineasta *filmmaker*
la comedia *comedy*
el corto *short film*
el decorado *set*
el decorador *set designer*
el director de cine *film director*
el drama *drama*
los efectos especiales *special effects*
la escena *scene*
el escenario *stage*
el escritor *writer*
el espectador *spectator*
el estreno *premiere*
el guionista *scriptwriter*
la obra *work*
la obra de teatro *play*
la película de aventuras *adventure*
la película de ciencia ficción *science fiction*
la película de denuncia social *social protest*
la película de terror *horror movie*
la película histórica *historical film*
la película independiente *indie*
el premio *award*
el protagonista *leading actor*

el rodaje *film shoot*
el taller de teatro *performing arts workshop*
la taquilla *box office*
el telón *curtain*
la trayectoria *career*

Verbos

abrir *to open*
escribir *to write*
estrenar *to release*
filmar *to shoot*
interpretar *to perform*
protagonizar *to have the leading role*
rodar *to shoot*
vestirse de gala *to dress for a special event*

Marcadores temporales

a continuación *next*
al principio *in the beginning*
después *after*
el otro día *(the) other day / another day*
en ese momento *at that time*
entonces *then*
hace unos días / meses / años... *days / months / years ago...*
luego *then*
más tarde *later*
por cierto *by the way*
un día *one day*
una vez *once*
unos momentos después *moments later*

Para dar una información

Pues parece que... *Well, it seems that...*
Al parecer... *Apparently...*
Según dicen... *According to what they are saying...*
He oído que... *I have heard that...*

¿Te has enterado de...? *Have you noticed / realized that...*

Para mostrar interés o curiosidad

Dime, dime... *Tell me, tell me...*
Estoy intrigadísimo/a. *I'm so intrigued.*
¿Y eso? *What's that about?*

Para expresar sorpresa

¿De veras? *Really?*
¡Qué fuerte! *pretty rough*
¡No me digas! *You must be kidding!*

Para expresar incredulidad

¡Anda ya! *Go on now!*
¡No me lo puedo creer! *I can't believe it!*
¡Qué raro / extraño! *How weird / strange!*
¿(Hablas) En serio? *Are you serious?*

Coloquialismos

de cine *Awesome, amazing*
montar un drama *to make a fuss*
ser peliculero/a *to be a show off*
ser muy protagonista *to be self centered*
ser cómica *to be funny*

EN RESUMEN: Gramática

PAST TENSES (REVIEW)

(See page 100)

INTERPRETAR			
	PRETERIT	**IMPERFECT**	**PRESENT PERFECT**
yo	interpreté	interpretaba	he interpretado
tú	interpretaste	interpretabas	has interpretado
usted/él/ella	interpretó	interpretaba	ha interpretado
nosotros/as	interpretamos	interpretábamos	hemos interpretado
vosotros/as	interpretasteis	interpretabais	habéis interpretado
ustedes/ellos/ellas	interpretaron	interpretaban	han interpretado

Preterit

■ Use the preterit tense to talk about actions that were **completed** at a fixed point in the past.
*Anamar **volvió** de Venecia anoche. Anamar returned from Venice last night.*

Imperfect

■ Use the imperfect to describe people, things or situations in the past, and to talk about ongoing or habitual actions in the past.
*Cuando **vivían** en Madrid **estudiaban** juntos. When they lived in Madrid, they used to study together.*

Present Perfect

■ Use the present perfect to say what a person **has done**. It describes actions completed in a recent past or in an unfinished period of time.
*Este año Anamar **ha ganado** dos premios. This year Anamar has won two awards.*

PLUPERFECT OR PAST PERFECT TENSE

(See page 101)

■ Use the pluperfect to talk about an action that took place before another past action.
■ To form the pluperfect tense:

	IMPERFECT TENSE OF *HABER*	PAST PARTICIPLE	IRREGULAR PAST PARTICIPLES	
yo	había		abierto	muerto
tú	habías		dicho	puesto
usted/él/ella	había	viajado	descubierto	roto
nosotros/as	habíamos	comido	escrito	visto
vosotros/as	habíais	dormido	hecho	vuelto
ustedes/ellos/ellas	habían			

OBJECTIVES FOR EN RESUMEN: GRAMÁTICA

• Review unit grammar
• Practice communication skills

STANDARDS

1.2 Understand the language
1.3 Present information

INSTRUCTIONAL STRATEGIES

• Model how to review grammar.
• Have the students review the Learning Outcomes in the unit opener to assess whether they feel they have mastered the main ideas and skills.
• Ask them if they can remember additional examples for each grammar topic.
• Model how to find and go back to the appropriate page in the unit to review any grammar topic they may need help with.
• Invite students to review the grammar activities they completed in this unit.
• Ask them what grammar activities they found easy and which they found challenging. Encourage them to rework any activities they found particularly challenging.
• Have students describe a favorite scene from a film that they've seen. Tell them to write it in the past tense, and challenge them to use each of the past tenses reviewed here. Have them swap descriptions with a partner to correct each other's grammar.

OBJECTIVES FOR UNIT OPENER

- Introduce unit theme: **¡Superespacio!**, about healthy lifestyles and giving advice
- Introduce culture for the unit: Learn about pop culture and teen magazines in the Hispanic world

STANDARDS

1.1 Interpersonal communication
1.2 Understand the language
2.1 Practices and perspectives
4.2 Compare cultures

INSTRUCTIONAL STRATEGIES

- Introduce unit theme and objectives. Talk about the photo and have students state who they think the people are: **Son compañeras de clase, Una de ellas tiene una revista, Están mirando la revista,** etc.
- Have the students discuss the questions and talk about themselves in the same context.
- Use the image to preview unit vocabulary: **¿Cuántos años crees que tienen? ¿Qué crees que van a hacer?,** etc.
- Ask related questions: **¿Compran alguna revista regularmente? ¿Les gustan las revistas? ¿Qué tipo de artículos hay en las revistas que leen?,** etc.
- Help students formulate their ideas using **A veces / todas las semanas / cada dos semanas compro una revista, Me gustan los artículos sobre la moda joven,** etc.

ADVANCED LEARNERS

Consider bringing in a few magazines in Spanish so students can take a look at the different sections and headlines. Are these magazines very different to the ones they read in English?

HERITAGE LANGUAGE LEARNERS

Have students share their experience reading magazines in Spanish, both printed and online. What do they like to read? If they do not read magazines, ask them why not. They can also share their experiences seeing friends or family members reading magazines.

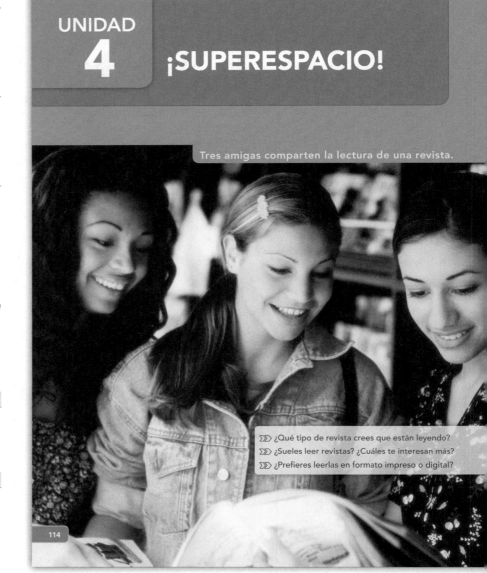

UNIDAD 4

¡SUPERESPACIO!

Tres amigas comparten la lectura de una revista.

>>> ¿Qué tipo de revista crees que están leyendo?
>>> ¿Sueles leer revistas? ¿Cuáles te interesan más?
>>> ¿Prefieres leerlas en formato impreso o digital?

114

ADDITIONAL UNIT RESOURCES

Extension Activities (EA) **(Photocopiable)**	**Interactive Whiteboard Lessons (IWB)**	**Audio**	**Video**	**Online ELEteca**
EA: 4.1, 4.2, 4.3	IWB: 4.1, 4.2	27 to 34	Diálogo 4	

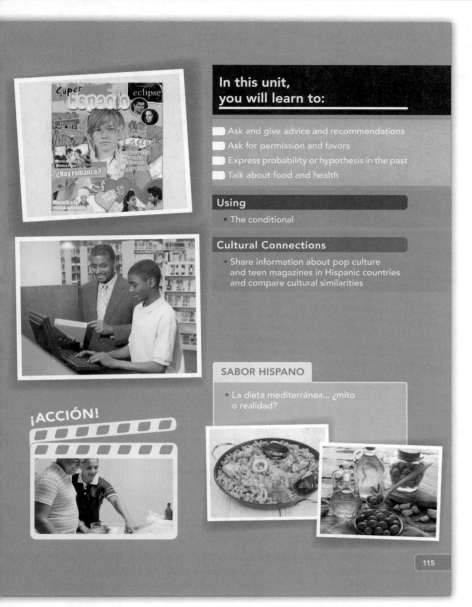

**In this unit,
you will learn to:**

- Ask and give advice and recommendations
- Ask for permission and favors
- Express probability or hypothesis in the past
- Talk about food and health

Using

- The conditional

Cultural Connections

- Share information about pop culture and teen magazines in Hispanic countries and compare cultural similarities

SABOR HISPANO

- La dieta mediterránea... ¿mito o realidad?

¡ACCIÓN!

115

LEARNING OUTCOMES

- Ask and give advice and recommendations
- Ask for permission and favors
- Express probability or hypothesis in the past
- Talk about food and health
- Share information about pop culture and teen magazines in Hispanic countries

INSTRUCTIONAL STRATEGIES

- Use unit opener to preview vocabulary and cultural topics for this unit.
- Have students look at the images on this page and relate them to the objectives listed. Ask questions such as: *¿Qué tipo de revista es esta? ¿Ven a alguna persona famosa? ¿Qué hace este muchacho en la segunda imagen? ¿Dónde está?*, etc.
- Invite students to read the topic for **Sabor hispano** and preview that section in the unit. Ask questions such as: *¿Qué tipo de comida les gusta más? ¿Qué ingredientes ven aquí? ¿Cómo se llama este plato? ¿Qué ven en la botella?*, etc.
- Ask students to anticipate what they think the episode for **¡Acción!** will be about. Ask: *¿Quiénes son? ¿Dónde están? ¿Creen que van a comer o que ya han comido?*, etc.
- Have students work in pairs to talk about the images using the questions you have modeled. Then ask for volunteers to present to the class what they understand this unit to be about.

SLOWER-PACED LEARNERS

Have students write and share the different things they have eaten in the last five days. Consider dividing the class in two groups: one says the name of a food, and the second group decides whether it is healthy (*sano/a*) or not. If relevant, encourage students to add how the food was prepared (*huevos fritos, huevos cocidos, bistec asado,* etc.). Ask whether or not they used sauces (*salsas*). Finally, ask them whether the foods was prepared at home, frozen, or prepared at a restaurant (*preparadas en casa, congeladas o precocinadas, preparadas en un restaurante*).

THREE MODES OF COMMUNICATION: UNIT 4			
	INTERPERSONAL	**INTERPRETIVE**	**PRESENTATIONAL**
HABLAMOS DE...		1, 2, 3, 4, 5	6
COMUNICA	4	1, 2, 3, 5, 6, 7	4, 6, 8
¡ACCIÓN!	1, 4	2, 3	3
PALABRA POR PALABRA	4, 7	1, 2, 3, 5, 6	4, 7
GRAMÁTICA	8	1, 3, 4, 5, 6	2, 7, 8
DESTREZAS		1, 2	
CULTURA		SABOR HISPANO	
RELATO		1, 2, 3, 4	2, 5

OBJECTIVES FOR HABLAMOS DE...

- Understand language in context
- Preview vocabulary: Talking about pop culture, food and health
- Preview grammatical structures: The conditional
- Read and listen to a conversation between two girls talking about the latest issue of a teen magazine

CORE RESOURCES

- Audio Program: Track 27

STANDARDS

1.1 Engage in conversation
1.2 Understand the language
4.2 Compare cultures

INSTRUCTIONAL STRATEGIES

Activity 1

- Tell students to talk about the people in the photos on the magazine cover and say what they are doing and where they are or who they are. Ask students for the name of these types of magazines in Spanish (**revistas del corazón**, **la prensa rosa**, **los cotilleos**). Ask if they are famous and what kind of TV program or movie they think each one appears in.
- Then ask: **¿Leen este tipo de revistas? ¿Quiénes suelen aparecer en ellas? ¿Qué temas suelen tratar?**, etc.
- Have students complete the activity individually.

Activity 2

- Have the students look at the images from the magazine cover and match each one to a description.
- Ask random students to read a sentence and other students to give the corresponding answer.

Extension

Go online and project other teen magazine covers in Spanish. Discuss the topics on the cover. You may choose to use some of these magazines to motivate students to read more about topics that interest them.

Cultural Note

En gran cantidad de revistas, tanto de adultos como de jóvenes, se especula bastante sobre las relaciones amorosas de la gente famosa. Ejemplos de revistas españolas para adolescentes son la revista *SuperPop* y la revista *Bravo*. *People en español*, en Estados Unidos.

ANSWERS

Activity 1

1. c; **2.** b; **3.** a; **4.** a.

Activity 2

b; d; c; e; a; no le corresponde ninguna imagen.

ADVANCED LEARNERS

Have students imagine what the first paragraph might be for any of the articles that have been advertised on the outside of this magazine and write it. Then have them share the paragraphs in small groups. Group members have to guess which story or headline the introduction refers to.

HABLAMOS DE... Revistas juveniles

1 Fíjate en la imagen y elige la opción correcta.

1. La imagen representa…
   a. ☐ una revista de moda.
   b. ☐ una revista de cocina.
   c. ☐ una revista para jóvenes.

2. Maruchi es…
   a. ☐ actriz.
   b. ☐ cocinera.
   c. ☐ bailarina.

3. ¿Qué tipo de programa crees que es *Amor en directo*? Un programa…
   a. ☐ para encontrar pareja (*partner*).
   b. ☐ de canciones de amor.
   c. ☐ de chismes (*gossip*) de amor.

4. Mónica Pérez es…
   a. ☐ una famosa actriz.
   b. ☐ una cocinera.
   c. ☐ la participante de un concurso para encontrar pareja.

2 Relaciona el texto con su imagen correspondiente de la portada. ¡*Atención*! No todos los textos tienen imagen.

☐ Parece ser que el amor está en el aire. Varios rumores circularon días atrás sobre la famosa pareja, aunque esta foto parece confirmar que se aman.

☐ Una receta infalible: descúbrela con nuestra cocinera favorita.

☐ "De pequeño ya sabía que quería ser actor", confiesa.

☐ Josefa y Benjamín se conocen en el estudio, ¿habrá flechazo?

☐ Escenas de la película más romántica del año.

☐ Define tu estilo de verano.

116

3 🎧 **27** Escucha la conversación entre Lucía y Carla y contesta las preguntas.

	Carla	Lucía
a. ¿Quién está muy "enamorada" de Maxi Castro?	☐	☐
b. ¿Quién sabe más sobre la vida de Mónica Pérez?	☐	☐
c. ¿A quién no le gusta la comida sana?	☐	☐
d. ¿Quién pide ayuda para contestar un test?	☐	☐
e. ¿Quién cree que la entrevista tiene mucha información sobre la vida de Maxi?	☐	☐

4 Lee la conversación y contesta verdadero (V) o falso (F). Corrige las afirmaciones falsas.

Lucía: Mira, Carla, las fotos que trae esta semana *SuperEspacio*. Hay una entrevista a Maxi Castro.

Carla: ¡Maxi Castro? ¡Ay!, Lucía, déjame ver… Yo estoy enamoradísima de ese actor… Es tan guapo y tan simpático.

Lucía: Mira… también viene un test para saber si conoces bien la vida de Maxi… Y si aciertas *(answer correctly)* todas las preguntas, participas en el sorteo *(sweepstake)* de un viaje a París, la ciudad del amor. ¿Podrías ayudarme?

Carla: Claro, yo conozco todos los secretos de la vida de Maxi. De todos modos, yo que tú primero leería la entrevista y después contestaría el test. Seguro que esa entrevista contiene mucha información.

Lucía: ¿Has visto que parece que Mario Medina y Mónica Pérez están juntos?

Carla: ¿Mónica Pérez es la actriz de la película *La soga*?

Lucía: Carla, deberías estar más informada… Es la actriz de la serie *Sombras*. Es la que hace el papel *(role)* de mala.

Carla: Bueno, vale. También sale la cocinera esa de *Salud al día*, el programa de televisión… A mi madre le encanta y en casa nos lo pone todos los días.

Lucía: A mí no me saques de las hamburguesas y las papas fritas. Odio las verduras.

Carla: ¿En serio? No me lo puedo creer. Pues deberías comer más verdura. Es muy buena para la salud.

	V	F
a. Maxi Castro es un cantante muy famoso.	☐	☐
b. *Salud al día* es un programa de cocina sana.	☐	☐
c. La actriz Mónica Pérez es protagonista en una serie de televisión.	☐	☐
d. La cocinera y el actor tienen un romance.	☐	☐

117

INSTRUCTIONAL STRATEGIES

🎧 **27** **Activity 3**

- Tell the students they are going to listen to a conversation between Lucía and Carla about the latest issue of *SuperEspacio*.
- Have the students read the questions and tell them they have to decide which of the two girls is speaking for each question.
- Play the audio with books closed.
- Have the students open their books and play the audio again while they check the boxes.
- Ask for volunteers to give the correct answers.

Activity 4

- Now have the students look at the true or false statements in their books.
- Have them read the dialogue and check the boxes.
- Ask them to compare their answers with a partner.
- Play the audio again as they follow in their books, pausing at the answers to the questions for them to confirm.

ANSWERS

Activity 3

  a. Carla; **b.** Lucía; **c.** Lucía; **d.** Lucía; **e.** Carla.

Activity 4

  a. falso (Maxi Castro no es cantante, es actor); **b.** verdadero; **c.** verdadero; **d.** falso (El actor Mario Medina tiene un romance con la actriz Mónica Pérez, y no con la cocinera Maruchi).

SLOWER-PACED LEARNERS

Remind students that although the general rule is that words ending in *-a* are feminine, there are many words that don't follow the rule. Have them scan the conversation in Activity 4 to look for an example: ***programa*** (which is masculine) and notice the articles. Point out that ***protagonista*** can be feminine or masculine.

HERITAGE LANGUAGE LEARNERS

Have students write a short summary of the text in Activity 4.

INSTRUCTIONAL STRATEGIES

Activity 5

- Have the students focus on the sentences marked in bold in the conversation.
- Tell them that they contain a new tense: the conditional.
- Have them connect the expressions with the uses of the conditional on the right.
- Remind them to refer to the conversation in Activity 4 for help.
- Ask for volunteers to say the correct answers.

Activity 6

- Provide context for students before they discuss the questions with a partner. Engage students in a conversation about these magazines and ask: *¿Qué piensan de las personas que salen en estas revistas? ¿Por qué creen que reciben tanta atención? ¿Es por su talento, su comportamiento, su apariencia física? ¿Es fácil hacerse famoso? ¿Les gustaría ser famosos? ¿Qué ventajas o desventajas creen que tiene la fama?* Note answers on the board as necessary to guide students in their discussion later.
- Have the students look at the magazine covers illustrated.
- Ask questions such as: *¿Reconocen a esta persona? ¿Cómo se llama?*
- Now have them ask and answer the questions in pairs.
- Circulate around the room to check that students are on task, provide support, and correct students as needed.

Cultural Note

Letizia, cuyo nombre completo es Letizia Ortiz Rocasolano y que aparece en la portada de la revista *¡Hola!* en la actividad 4, es reina desde no hace mucho tiempo. Ella es la reina de España. Su esposo es el rey Felipe VI de España. Antes de casarse con él, ella era periodista y presentadora de informativos.

Extension

Have students go online and research some of the people on the covers and report back to the class on what they discovered. Who is the person, what does he/she do, why is he/she famous, why is he/she appearing in this issue.

ANSWERS

Activity 5

1. b; **2.** a; **3.** a; **4.** a.

SLOWER-PACED LEARNERS

When going over the questions in Activity 6, point out that the verb *interesar* is like *gustar*: the thing that interests you is the subject of the sentence. Also remind students about the first person of *soler* (*suelo*) and other possible forms to say the same: *normalmente*, *generalmente*, and *usualmente*. Also, they may need extra practice with *parecer*.

ADVANCED LEARNERS

Have students prepare some headlines for magazines like these. Have them reflect on these or similar questions to get ideas: What celebrities would they choose? What type of information is interesting to the readers? Do they remember any celebrities from previous chapter (*De cine*)?

HABLAMOS DE... Revistas juveniles

5 En la conversación anterior aparecen frases destacadas con un nuevo tiempo: el condicional. ¿Para qué crees que se usa este tiempo en cada caso? Relaciona.

1. ¿Podrías ayudarme?
2. Yo que tú leería la entrevista y después contestaría el test.
3. Deberías estar más informada…
4. Deberías comer más verdura.

a. Para dar una recomendación o un consejo.

b. Para pedir un favor.

6 Observa las siguientes portadas de revistas. Después, con tu compañero/a, contesta las preguntas.

a. ¿Qué tipo de revistas son?
b. ¿A qué tipo de público piensas que va dirigida cada una?
c. ¿Sueles leer algunas de estas revistas? ¿Qué contenidos te gustan más?
d. ¿Te interesan las revistas del corazón?
e. ¿Qué tipos de famosos suelen aparecer en ellas?
f. ¿Te parece que han ganado la fama de una manera justa?
g. ¿Piensas que es fácil hacerse famoso?
h. ¿Te gustaría llegar a ser famoso?
i. ¿Qué ventajas o desventajas crees que tiene la fama?

COMUNICA

ASKING FOR AND GIVING ADVICE

■ Para **pedir consejos**:

¿Qué puedo hacer? *What can I do?*

¿Tú qué harías? *What would you do?*　　**¿Podrías** aconsejarme? *Could you advise me?*

■ Para **dar consejos** o recomendaciones:

Yo / Yo que tú / Yo en tu lugar, comería de una manera más saludable. *If I were you, I would eat healthier.*

Deberías / podrías acostarte. Es tarde. *You should / could go to sleep. It´s late.*

■ Otras formas:

¿Por qué no vas al médico? *Why don't you go to the doctor?*

Toma un taxi, llegarás más rápido. *Take a taxi, you'll get there faster.*

¿Y si comes menos fritos? *And if you eat less fried food?*

Juan y tú **tienen que** ir a ver esa película. *Juan and you have to go see that movie.*

No fumes. Te hace daño. *Don't smoke. It's harmful.*

---

1 Maxi Castro va a rodar una nueva película y los productores han organizado un *casting* para encontrar a una muchacha "actual" que participe con él. Carla se ha apuntado a las pruebas pero ahora está muy nerviosa y cree que lo hará fatal. ¿Puedes ayudarla dándole algunos consejos?

a. .... me aprendería muy bien el papel.

b. ¿Y si ....? Van a ser muchos en el casting.

c. .... me tomaría un té de hierbas relajante antes de la prueba.

d. Deberías ....

e. ¿Por qué no ....? Tú lo haces muy bien y eso es un punto extra a tu favor.

2 La chef Maruchi da a sus telespectadores algunos consejos para llevar una alimentación rica y saludable. Completa las conversaciones con los siguientes verbos.

> podrías o practicaría o tomaría o deberías o comería o harías o disminuiría o prepararía

Carlos: Maruchi, te veo todos los días en la tele y me encanta tu programa. Mi problema es que últimamente estoy engordando mucho, ¿tú qué (a) .... para adelgazar?

Maruchi: Yo que tú (b) .... con moderación y (c) .... las comidas con aceite de oliva, preferentemente crudo. También (d) .... el consumo de azúcar y de sal.

Carlos: ¡Uf!... todo eso ya lo hago, pero engordo...

Maruchi: A lo mejor consumes más calorías de las que necesitas. En ese caso, yo en tu lugar, (e) .... ejercicio diariamente.

Alicia: Hola, Maruchi, me encanta tu programa. Mira, mi problema es que últimamente me encuentro muy cansada y, a veces, me duele la cabeza. El médico dice que estoy sanísima, pero yo me siento sin energías, ¿(f) .... darme algunos consejos?

Maruchi: Alicia, querida, ¿seguro que te alimentas bien? En primer lugar, (g) .... incluir legumbres y frutos secos en tu dieta. Para el dolor de cabeza, yo que tú (h) .... abundante cantidad de agua durante todo el día.

3 🎧 28 Ahora, escucha y comprueba tu respuesta de la Actividad 2.

119

OBJECTIVES FOR COMUNICA

- Present communicative functions of the unit: Ask for and give advice

CORE RESOURCES

- Audio Program: Track 28
- Extension Activities: EA 4.1
- Interactive Online Materials - ELEteca

STANDARDS

1　Engage in conversation

2　Understand the language

4.2　Compare cultures

INSTRUCTIONAL STRATEGIES FOR ASKING FOR AND GIVING ADVICE

- Tell the class you have a problem and would like some advice from them, for instance: **Mis hijos no ayudan en las tareas de la casa. ¿Qué puedo hacer?**
- Have the students make recommendations and give advice. They may need help at first with structures, so suggest: **¿Por qué no...?** or **¿Podrías...,?** etc.
- Once they have made some recommendations, walk them through the explanations on this page to learn how to ask for and give advice.

Activity 1

- Explain to students that many of the activities in **Comunica** expand on the topics presented in *SuperEspacio*. Ask students to describe the fictitious Maxi Castro to provide context for the activity.
- Explain that there are several possible answers. Have the students complete the sentences and then share their answers with a partner.
- Ask for volunteers to say the correct sentences and have the rest of the class say any alternative answers.

Activity 2

- Review the words from this list: **podría, practicaría, tomaría, deberías, comería, harías, disminuiría, prepararía** to make sure students recognize the infinitive. For now, have students repeat after you to become familiar with the form and sound of these verbs.
- Have students read the first conversation and fill each blank with the correct verb. Have them share their answers with a partner.
- Ask them to continue on to the second conversation and do the same.
- Invite pairs to read the completed conversations for the class.

🎧 28 Activity 3

- Play the audio and have the students follow in order to correct the completed conversations from Activity 2.

ANSWERS

Activity 1

Answers will vary. **a.** Yo / Yo que tú / Yo en tu lugar; **b.** inventas algo original; **c.** Yo / Yo que tú / Yo en tu lugar; **d.** ser tú misma; **e.** cantas una canción.

Activity 2

a. harías; **b.** comería; **c.** prepararía; **d.** disminuiría; **e.** practicaría; **f.** podrías; **g.** deberías; **h.** tomaría.

SLOWER-PACED LEARNERS

If students struggle to come up with the words to use in Activity 1, consider writing a list of possible answers on the board that they can choose from.

HERITAGE LANGUAGE LEARNERS

After doing Activity 3, have students reenact the conversation in Activity 2 with a partner but in their own words. Call on volunteers to perform their variations of the dialogue in front of the class.

INSTRUCTIONAL STRATEGIES

Activity 4

- Have the students work in pairs, with each of them looking at a different card (one holds the book upside down).
- Each student reads through the information and asks the other for advice, taking turns. Their partner reacts to the situation with an expression of advice.
- Circulate around the room as they work, providing assistance and answering questions as required.
- Ask for volunteers to perform for the class.

Alternative Activity

Distribute two sets of cards from EA 4.1, **Tengo un problema** to student pairs. Explain to students that their partner is going to choose a card and give them advice about a problem they have. They in turns have to guess what that problem is based on the advice they receive. Partners must continue giving advice until the student guesses the problem. Then they switch roles.

OBJECTIVES FOR COMUNICA

- Present communicative functions of the unit: Ask for favors and permission

STANDARDS

1.1	Engage in conversation
1.2	Understand the language
4.2	Compare cultures

INSTRUCTIONAL STRATEGIES FOR
ASKING FOR FAVORS AND PERMISSION

- Pretend to feel cold and ask a student: **¿Podrías dejarme tu chaqueta? Es que tengo frío.** Use mime and exaggeration to help convey the meaning.
- Ask similar questions, such as: **¿Podrías acercarme una silla? Es que quiero sentarme, ¿Podrías prestarme tu lápiz? Es que necesito apuntar algo**, etc.
- Walk the students through the expressions presented in the book for asking for favors and permission. Point out that in this context **dejar** and **prestar** have similar meanings.

Activity 5

- Remind students that **Amor en directo** is the program presented in the magazine, *SuperEspacio*.
- Have them combine the two halves of the sentences. When they have finished, ask them to share with a partner.
- Ask for volunteers to say the completed sentences.

ANSWERS

Activity 5

1. b; **2.** e; **3.** c; **4.** d; **5.** f; **6.** a.

COMUNICA

4 👥 Con tu compañero/a, pide consejos para las siguientes situaciones.

Estudiante 1

a. ¡No soy popular en Facebook!
b. Siempre que tengo un examen me pongo muy nervioso y no me puedo concentrar.
c. Tengo muchos granos *(pimples)* pero no puedo dejar de comer chocolate.
d. Lloro viendo todas las películas.
e. Mis padres quieren que salga con el hijo / la hija de sus amigos, pero a mí no me gusta.

Estudiante 2

a. Necesito ver mi celular constantemente.
b. Creo que en mi casa hay un fantasma pero nadie me cree.
c. El muchacho / La muchacha que me gusta me ha invitado a una fiesta pero bailo fatal.
d. No puedo dormir por las noches.
e. Me encanta la ropa de mi hermano/a mayor pero no me la deja.

ASKING FOR FAVORS AND PERMISSION

- Para **pedir permiso** decimos:
  ¿Te importa si me llevo estos libros? *Do you mind if I take these books?*
  ¿Puedo cerrar la puerta? *Can I close the door?*
  ¿Podría salir un poco antes de clase? *Could I leave class a little early?*
  ¿Me dejas usar tu teléfono? *Will you allow me to use your phone?*

- Para **pedir favores** decimos:
  ¿Me prestas un boli? *Will you lend me a pen?*
  ¿Te importaría llevar estos libros a la biblioteca? (formal) *Would you mind taking these books to the library?*
  ¿Podrías prestarme tu diccionario de español? (formal) *Could you lend me your Spanish dictionary?*
  ¿Sería tan amable de decirme la hora? (muy formal) *Would you be so kind as to tell me the time?*

- Para **explicar** o **justificar** el porqué de la petición se utiliza **es que**...:
  Es que he perdido mi boli. *It's just that I lost my pen.*

5 **Amor en directo** es un programa popular con personas que buscan un romance. Benjamín, el siguiente participante, está buscando novia. Quiere dar una buena impresión en su primera cita. Mientras espera en el camerino antes del programa, prepara lo que podría decirle. Relaciona para formar las frases en las que ha pensado.

1. ¿Te importa si	a. pasarme la sal?
2. ¿Podría	b. te llamo para vernos otro día?
3. ¿Puedo	c. invitarte a cenar?
4. ¿Me dejas	d. acompañarte a casa?
5. ¿Le importaría	e. aconsejarnos en la comida?
6. ¿Podrías	f. tomarnos una foto juntos?

HERITAGE LANGUAGE LEARNERS

Have students write other possible sentences for Activity 5 based on things they usually do or ask at school: **¿Te importa si abro la ventana? ¿Podría salir al baño? ¿Me dejas tu cuaderno? ¿Puedo contestar la pregunta yo? ¿Podrías dejar de hablar con tu compañero?** You can also have them write sentences that a teacher says: **¿Podrías contestar esta pregunta? ¿Te importa si te respondo mañana?** Ask them to provide an appropriate context, if needed.

6 Escribe el número de las frases de la Actividad 5 al lado de la situación en la que Benjamín las diría.

a. ☐ Están cenando y la comida está sosa *(bland)*.

b. ☐ Acaban de salir del restaurante.

c. ☐ Se acaban de sentar en la mesa del restaurante y piden ayuda al camarero.

d. ☐ Se están despidiendo después de la cita.

e. ☐ Han salido del plató *(set)* de *Amor en directo* y están pensando qué hacer.

f. ☐ Están pasando una buena noche y le pide al camarero un recuerdo de ella.

EXPRESSING PROBABILITY IN THE PAST

■ Si queremos **expresar probabilidad** en el pasado, decimos:

*Anoche **cenaría** sobre las 7.* (Serían aproximadamente las siete, pero no estoy seguro).
Last night I must have had dinner around seven.

***Tendría** unos 15 años cuando conocí a Sara.* (No recuerdo con exactitud la edad que tenía).
I must have been about 15 when I met Sara.

7 Fíjate en las imágenes y adivina qué pudo pasarles a estas personas. Utiliza las expresiones del cuadro.

> estar nervioso/a por el examen de Historia ○ perder la cartera ○ quedarse dormido/a ○
> perder el metro o el autobús ○ quedarse chateando por Internet hasta tarde

a. Ayer Pepe llegó tarde a clase… *Perdería el autobús.*

b. Hoy Carlos se ha dormido en clase…

c. Ayer María tenía la luz de la habitación encendida a las 4 de la mañana…

d. Ayer llamé a Laura por teléfono y estaba muy rara…

e. Ayer estaba en la cafetería y un cliente muy bien vestido se fue sin pagar…

8 La muchacha que tenía que encontrarse con Benjamín no ha venido al programa. En parejas, hablen sobre los posibles motivos.

Sería…   Se quedaría…
Tendría…   Estaría…

👤💻 **MORE IN ELETECA:** EXTRA ONLINE PRACTICE

121

STANDARDS

1.1   Engage in conversation
1.2   Understand the language
4.2   Compare cultures

INSTRUCTIONAL STRATEGIES FOR EXPRESSING PROBABILITY IN THE PAST

Read the explanation with the class and focus on the form of the verb for expressing probable cause in the past (what must have happened).

Activity 7

• Project IWB 4.1, **¡Qué raro!** and say to students, **Ayer Pepe llegó tarde a clase. ¿Por qué creen que llegó tarde?** Tell students to look at the images and read the captions. Ask them to come up with possible explanations for the situation. Help students with the forms as necessary.

• Have the students complete the activity individually.
• Circulate around the room as they work and provide assistance where required.
• Ask for volunteers to read the completed sentences to the class.

Activity 8

• Have the students work in pairs to conjecture about why the girl did not show up to meet Benjamin on the program.
• Ask for volunteers to read out their suggestions while you record them on the board. Vote on the best and worst excuse for what must have happened to her.

ANSWERS

Activity 6

a. 6a; **b.** 4d; **c.** 2e; **d.** 1b; **e.** 3c; **f.** 5f.

Activity 7

a. Perdería el autobús; **b.** Se quedaría chateando por Internet hasta tarde; **c.** Se quedaría dormida; **d.** Estaría nerviosa por el examen de Historia; **e.** Perdería la cartera.

INSTRUCTIONAL STRATEGIES

Activity 6

• Have students connect the expressions in Activity 5 with the situations given here.
• They write the number of the favor requested in the box.
• Have them share their answers with a partner.
• Ask for volunteer pairs to read the requests and situations for the class.

OBJECTIVES FOR COMUNICA

• Present communicative functions of the unit: Express probability in the past

CORE RESOURCES

• Interactive Whiteboard Lesson: IWB 4.1

SLOWER-PACED LEARNERS

Remind students to place the pronoun in front of pronominal verbs when conjugated: **Se quedaría**… Have them practice with other pronouns if needed: **Te quedarías**…, **Nos quedaríamos**…, etc.

ADVANCED LEARNERS

Challenge students to write an additional guess related to each image and situation in Activity 7.

OBJECTIVES FOR ¡ACCIÓN!

• Provide students with a structured approach to viewing the video
• Contextualize the content of the unit in a familiar scenario

CORE RESOURCES

• Unit Video 4 - Paella con curry
• Interactive Online Materials - ELEteca

STANDARDS

1.3 Interpersonal communication
1.2 Interpretive communication
2.1 Culture: Practices and perspectives

INSTRUCTIONAL STRATEGIES

Previewing: Antes del video

Activity 1

Focus students' attention on the images. Have them answer both questions in writing about each image. Then put them in small groups to discuss their interpretations of the story.

Activity 2

• To better deduce the answer the first question, have students analyze Images 4–6 more closely. **¿Qué expresión lleva Sebas en el imagen 4? ¿Parece contento y con confianza, o parece preocupado y dudoso? ¿Qué piensas está pasando mientras que Sebas y Felipe juegan a videojuegos? ¿A quién está llamando Alba y por qué?**
• Put students in pairs to come up with two essential aspects of teamwork. Encourage them to draw on their own experiences with good and bad teamwork.

Viewing: Durante el video

Activity 3 and 4

• Before playing the video, direct students' attention to the list of food. Point out the names of the seafood, and ask students if they recognize them: **camarones** (shrimp, also known as **gambas**) and **mejillones** (mussels). In the video, they will also see a picture of **paella** with **cigalas** (prawns), too. You may want to show images of shrimp, prawns, and lobster so students can get a sense of how they are similar and different.
• Have students read the instructions for Activity 4 before playing the video as well.
• Play the video while students complete Activities 3 and 4.
• Have students compare answers with a partner and then confirm them as a class.
• Ask some general comprehension questions to see what else they have understood. How would they revise their interpretations and explanations of the images now?

Activity 5

• Challenge students to remember and identify who said each of the lines from the video. Then play the video from the beginning up until 4:30 so they can check their answers.
• Go over the correct answers with the class.

ANSWERS

Activity 3

a. tomate; **d.** pimiento; **f.** cebolla; **g.** ajo; **h.** aceite de oliva; **i.** arroz; **l.** camarones.

¡ACCIÓN! Paella con curry

1. 2. 3.
4. 5. 6.

ANTES DEL VIDEO

1 Observa las imágenes y responde a las preguntas. Basa tu respuesta en lo que crees que puede ocurrir. Usa tu imaginación.

a. ¿Qué hacen los muchachos?   b. ¿Por qué?

2 Los muchachos están trabajando en equipo. ¿Crees que les saldrá bien? Comenta con tu compañero/a dos aspectos necesarios para hacer un buen trabajo en equipo.

DURANTE EL VIDEO

3 ¿Qué ingredientes lleva la paella de los muchachos? Marca todos los que veas durante el episodio.

a. ☐ tomate   f. ☐ cebolla   k. ☐ mejillones
b. ☐ carne picada   g. ☐ ajo   l. ☐ camarones
c. ☐ aceitunas   h. ☐ aceite de oliva m. ☐ pollo
d. ☐ pimiento   i. ☐ arroz   n. ☐ pescado
e. ☐ huevos   j. ☐ pasta   ñ. ☐ jamón

4 ¿Qué otros ingredientes extra añade Felipe? Escríbelos.

_____

5 ¿Quién de los dos muchachos, Felipe (Imagen 3) o Sebas (Imagen 4) dice las siguientes frases?

a. Yo nunca he hecho una paella.   ....
b. Tenemos que hacerlo todo en su orden. ....
c. Tienes que impresionarla con algo fuera de lo normal. ....

122

Activity 4

mantequila, frijoles, curry y otra especia más.

Activity 5

a. Sebas; **b.** Felipe; **c.** Felipe; **d.** Sebas; **e.** Felipe; **f.** Felipe.

SLOWER-PACED LEARNERS

You may want to start the discussion about teamwork as a class, eliciting examples from different students and writing key phrases or vocabulary on the board. Then put students in pairs to choose the two most important aspects of teamwork in their opinion.

ADVANCED LEARNERS

Before watching the video, have each student find two different recipes for **paella**. With a partner or in small groups, have students compare the recipes and discuss any similarities or differences between the ingredients, cooking methods, or other aspects of the recipes.

d. Preferiría los tacos, porque me salen muy ricos. ....

e. Una paella es mucho más sorprendente. ....

f. Hay que ser creativo. ....

6 ▭▭▭ **Mira esta secuencia y elige la opción correcta en cada uno de los casos.**
04:30 - 06:00

a. Los muchachos están jugando a videojuegos porque **ya han terminado** / **la paella está todavía cocinándose**.

b. Sebas quiere ir a la cocina a ver la paella pero Felipe le dice que **continúe jugando** / **es demasiado pronto**.

c. Cuando llega Alba, en la casa huele **muy bien** / **a quemado**.

d. Alba decide pedir unas **hamburguesas** / **pizzas** para cenar.

7 **Di si estas afirmaciones son verdaderas (V) o falsas (F).**

	V	F
a. Sebas quiere preparar una paella para impresionar a Alba.	☐	☐
b. Sebas y Felipe miran la receta en un libro.	☐	☐
c. Sebas ha gastado sus ahorros en los ingredientes.	☐	☐
d. Felipe cree que los frijoles están buenos con todo.	☐	☐
e. La paella de Sebas y Felipe no lleva marisco.	☐	☐
f. Los muchachos se ponen a jugar a videojuegos cuando han terminado de comer.	☐	☐
g. Cuando Alba llega, la mesa ya está preparada.	☐	☐
h. Alba es la invitada a la cena pero ella paga las pizzas.	☐	☐

DESPUÉS DEL VIDEO

8 👥 **¿Por qué la receta no salió bien? Marca con tu compañero/a todas las opciones posibles.**

a. No siguieron la receta punto por punto.

b. Añadieron ingredientes fuera de la receta.

c. No vigilaron la paella hasta el final.

d. No conocían el plato previamente.

e. Improvisaron mucho.

f. Compraron ingredientes caros.

g. No estaban supervisados por un adulto.

9 **¿Alguna vez has preparado algún plato? Escribe brevemente qué preparaste, cuándo, con quién estabas y cómo salió el plato.**

....

....

....

👤💻 **MORE IN ELETECA:** EXTRA ONLINE PRACTICE

INSTRUCTIONAL STRATEGIES

Activity 6

• Have students read the sentences and possible answer choices before playing the clip.

• After watching the segment, call on volunteers to share their answers with the class.

Activity 7

• Working individually, have students identify whether the sentences are true or false.

• Have students check their work with a partner. Circulate, and help them clarify any discrepancies in their answers.

Post-viewing: Después del video

Activity 8

Have students work with a different partner to identify and discuss the reasons why the *paella* didn't come out very good. Encourage them to explain their choices and make comparisons with their own experiences.

Activity 9

• Suggest that students jot down their ideas before they write. Model how they can use a chart, list, word web, or other graphic organizer to collect and organize their thoughts.

• Students may write about their experiences in class or for homework.

ANSWERS

Activity 6

a. la paella está todavía cocinándose; **b.** continúe jugando; **c.** a quemado; **d.** pizzas.

Activity 7

a. V; **b.** F; **c.** V; **d.** V; **e.** F; **f.** F; **g.** V; **h.** V.

Activity 8

Answers will vary. Likely answers: a, b, c, d, e.

HERITAGE LANGUAGE LEARNERS

To help develop students' writing skills, have them exchange their writing from Activity 9 with a partner for peer review. Then have them write a second draft. Finally, have them switch papers with a new partner and write a comment or reaction in response. Give them a target word count for their responses.

OBJECTIVES FOR LA COMIDA

- Present vocabulary needed to practice communicative and grammatical functions for the unit: Foods and healthy eating
- Talk about foods and following a healthy diet

CORE RESOURCES

- Audio Program: Track 29
- Interactive Whiteboard Lessons: IWB 4.2
- Extension Activities: EA 4.2
- Interactive Online Materials - ELEteca

STANDARDS

1.1 Engage in conversation
1.2 Understand the language
3.1 Knowledge of other disciplines
3.2 Acquire information

INSTRUCTIONAL STRATEGIES

🎧 29 Activity 1

- Invite the students to look at the images and name any items they already know.
- Have the students look at the categories and discuss what they mean.
- Now have them categorize the foodstuffs and write the letter of the image next to the correct word. Have them share the results with a partner.
- Play the audio for the students to check their answers. Check that students understand **entera** and **desnatada**. Ask students if they recognize a cognate in **entera** (entire) and think what kind of milk it can refer to. Tell students that **nata** means cream and what they think **desnatada** refers to.
- Ask questions to practice the new vocabulary, such as: **¿Comes sano? ¿Qué tipo de comida te gusta más? ¿Con qué frecuencia comes carne / pescado / dulces...? ¿Cuántas veces a la semana comes carne / pescado / dulces...?**, etc.

Audioscript

a. aceite de girasol	**i.** cereza	**p.** magdalena
b. berenjena	**j.** chorizo	**q.** mantequilla
c. espinacas	**k.** carne picada	**r.** pechuga de pollo
d. piña	**l.** guisantes	**s.** yogur natural / desnatado / con futas
e. aceite de oliva	**m.** kiwi	**t.** salchichón
f. calabacín	**n.** lentejas	**u.** bistec
g. bizcocho	**ñ.** chuleta de cerdo	**v.** leche entera / desnatada
h. garbanzos	**o.** frijoles	

ANSWERS

Activity 1

1. e; **2.** a; **3.** g; **4.** p; **5.** b; **6.** f; **7.** c; **8.** i; **9.** d; **10.** m; **11.** l; **12.** n; **13.** o; **14.** h; **15.** k; **16.** ñ; **17.** r; **18.** u; **19.** t; **20.** j; **21.** v; **22.** q; **23.** s.

HERITAGE LANGUAGE LEARNERS

Students will probably come up with different names for some of the items on this page. Use this opportunity to talk about the variety in the Spanish language. For instance, **guisante, arveja**, and **chícharo**; **calabacín, calabacita,** and **zapallito**; **aceituna** and **oliva**; **bizcocho** and **queque**; **piña** and **ananá**; **plátano** and **banana**; **crema (de leche)** and **nata**, etc.

PALABRA POR PALABRA La comida

1 🎧 29 Relaciona los alimentos con las siguientes imágenes. Luego, escucha el audio y verifica tus respuestas.

Aceites	Azúcares, dulces y pastelerías	Verduras y vegetales	Frutas
1. aceite de oliva ⬜	3. bizcocho ⬜	5. berenjena ⬜	8. cereza ⬜
2. aceite de girasol ⬜	4. magdalena ⬜	6. calabacín ⬜	9. piña ⬜
		7. espinacas ⬜	10. kiwi ⬜

Legumbres	Carnes y derivados	Lácteos y derivados de la leche
11. guisantes ⬜	15. carne picada ⬜	21. leche entera / desnatada ⬜
12. lentejas ⬜	16. chuleta de cerdo ⬜	22. mantequilla ⬜
13. frijoles ⬜	17. pechuga de pollo ⬜	23. yogur natural / desnatado / con futas ⬜
14. garbanzos ⬜	18. bistec ⬜	
	Embutidos (cold cuts)	
	19. salchichón ⬜	
	20. chorizo ⬜	

2 Relaciona las palabras de las dos columnas para formar combinaciones frecuentes.

1. pescado
2. ensalada
3. pan
4. leche
5. trozo de
6. agua
7. fruta
8. yogur
9. papas

a. entera
b. fritas
c. del tiempo
d. multicereales
e. desnatado
f. mixta
g. mineral
h. pastel
i. a la plancha

3 Mónica Pérez, la actriz, y Maruchi, la famosa chef, están hablando de cómo mejorar los hábitos alimenticios de Mónica. Lee la conversación y completa con las palabras de la Actividad 2.

Maruchi: Primero, vamos a analizar qué es lo que comes habitualmente. A ver, ¿qué sueles desayunar?

Mónica: Tomo un vaso de (a) ....

Maruchi: ¿Y qué más?

Mónica: Pues, nada más.

Maruchi: ¿Solo eso? Bueno, ¿y luego? ¿A la hora de la comida?

Mónica: Como una hamburguesa con (b) .... y un refresco.

Maruchi: ¿Tomas postre?

Mónica: Sí, un (c) .... de chocolate.

Maruchi: ¿Y para cenar?

Mónica: Para cenar tomo (d) .... como salmón o sardinas con una (e) .... y de postre, un (f) ....

Maruchi: Bien. En realidad, creo que tenemos que hacer algunos cambios, sobre todo en el desayuno y la comida. Para desayunar, yo tomaría café o té, con leche desnatada, pero lo acompañaría con (g) .... y mermelada. Lo que yo cambiaría bastante es la comida. Para empezar, la haría más variada, incorporando verduras y legumbres de todo tipo. Por otro lado, yo en tu lugar abandonaría completamente los dulces y tomaría una (h) .... de postre. ¡Ah! y olvídate también de las bebidas con gas, mucho mejor beber (i) ....

4 👥 Túrnate con tu compañero/a y hazle preguntas sobre sus hábitos alimenticios. Después, dale los consejos necesarios según sus respuestas.

Estudiante 1

a. ¿En qué consiste tu dieta?
b. ¿Te gusta la comida rápida?
c. ¿Te interesa comer de forma saludable?
d. ¿Has cambiado algo de tu alimentación en los últimos años?

Estudiante 2

a. ¿Con qué frecuencia comes verdura?
b. ¿Vas mucho a restaurantes de comida rápida?
c. ¿Dónde crees que tienes una alimentación más sana: en casa o en la escuela?
d. ¿Crees que comes bien?

125

- Now have them continue to work individually.
- When they have finished, ask them to share with a partner.
- Ask for volunteers to read out the correct answers.

Activity 4

- Divide the students into pairs. Each student looks at a different card (one of them holds the book upside down).
- They take turns to ask and answer the questions on the cards.
- Invite volunteers to interview each other in front of the class.

Extension

- For additional practice and to wrap up this section, distribute copies of IWB 4.2 y EA 4.2, *La pirámide de los alimentos* to student pairs. Have them place the food items in the correct location on the food pyramid.

- Then project the pyramid and remind students that good nutrition includes the following: *Una alimentación básicamente sana debe incluir alimentos de los siguientes grupos: cereales, verduras, frutas frescas, leche y sus derivados, carnes, pescados, huevos y legumbres secas y azúcares y grasas (estos últimos lo menos posible). La buena alimentación es básica en la adolescencia y juventud.*
- Call on students to say the word for the food item and stick it on the board. Ask the class: *¿Están de acuerdo?*
- Encourage students to visit websites to learn more about nutrition.

ANSWERS

Activity 2

1. i; **2.** f; **3.** d; **4.** a; **5.** h; **6.** g; **7.** c; **8.** e; **9.** b.

Activity 3

a. leche entera; **b.** papas fritas; **c.** trozo de pastel; **d.** pescado a la plancha; **e.** ensalada mixta; **f.** yogur desnatado; **g.** pan multicereales; **h.** fruta del tiempo; **i.** agua mineral.

SLOWER-PACED LEARNERS

For additional oral practice, have students practice and act out the conversation in Activity 3.

HERITAGE LANGUAGE LEARNERS

Have students realize that the Spanish spoken in the US incorporates some words from English that most speakers understand but may be not understood in other Spanish-speaking countries: *vegetales* instead of *verduras*; *sodas* instead of *bebidas gaseosas*; etc. Also, remind students that *hora de la comida* (Activity 3) in Spain is the same as *hora del almuerzo* in other Spanish-speaking countries, although it is usually a little bit later.

INSTRUCTIONAL STRATEGIES

Activity 2

- Have the students look at the images and match the words on the left to the words on the right.
- Read the example with them and have them continue individually.
- When they finish, have them share their answers with a partner.
- Ask for volunteers to say the correct combinations.
- Ask the students to name the items illustrated. Encourage students to say as much as possible about each.

Activity 3

- Have the students read the conversation between Mónica Pérez the actress and Maruchi the chef. Ask students to explain who these people are.
- Ask for a volunteer to suggest the word for the first blank.
- Ask for a volunteer to fill the second blank and ask the class if they agree.

OBJECTIVES FOR ¡A COCINAR!

• Present vocabulary needed to practice communicative and grammatical functions for the unit: Cooking
• Talk about food preparation and recipes

CORE RESOURCES

• Extension Activities: EA 4.3

STANDARDS

1.1 Engage in conversation
1.2 Understand the language
1.3 Present information
3.2 Acquire information

INSTRUCTIONAL STRATEGIES

Begin by asking students: **¿Les gusta cocinar? ¿Saben preparar algún plato o alguna receta? ¿Qué saben preparar?** Then tell students they are going to learn some tricks of the trade in cooking.

Activity 5

• Introduce the verbs on the left and act them out as in charades to provide context for students before they begin the activity. Then have the students match the verbs with their definitions on the right.
• When they have finished, have them share with a partner.
• Ask for volunteers to say the correct answers and provide assistance if necessary.

Activity 6

• Have the students look at the images and say what they can see.
• Ask them to use the verbs from the previous activity to fill in the blanks in the cooking tips while they look at the images which illustrate the actions.
• When students finish, have them share their answers with a partner.
• Ask for volunteers to say the correct answers.

Extension

Distribute cut up questions and texts of EA 4.3, **Curiosidades culinarias** so that some students have questions and others have answers. Have students search out their match among the other students. Then call on student pairs to read and answer the question. Encourage students to share their own **curiosidades** about food and health.

Activity 7

• Divide the class into small groups and have them discuss how to prepare a simple dish.
• Student groups can present their recipe to the class orally or in writing.

PALABRA POR PALABRA ¡A cocinar!

5 Relaciona las siguientes palabras, que se utilizan habitualmente en la preparación de comidas, con su correspondiente definición. Trabaja con tu compañero/a. Fíjate en las pistas que aparecen en las definiciones para ayudarte.

1. añadir
2. escurrir
3. aliñar
4. poner en remojo
5. lavar
6. cocer
7. congelar
8. triturar

a. Poner un alimento en agua durante un tiempo para poder cocinarlo bien el día siguiente.
b. Quitar el agua de un alimento después de cocinar.
c. Limpiar con agua un alimento.
d. Cortar un alimento en trozos más pequeños. Hay máquinas que lo hacen muy bien y muy rápido.
e. Poner alimentos a temperaturas muy frías para conservarlos frescos.
f. Poner un alimento, como la verdura, en agua caliente durante un tiempo determinado.
g. Poner sal, aceite y vinagre a la ensalada.
h. Poner ingredientes adicionales poco a poco o al final.

6 Maruchi también prepara diferentes platos para la revista *SuperEspacio* y nos enseña algunos trucos para preparar una comida saludable y sabrosa. Utiliza los verbos de la Actividad 5 para completar los trucos de Maruchi.

1. Para conseguir unos garbanzos tiernos (tender), los tienes que (a) .... la noche anterior. Para las lentejas no es necesario, pero las tendrás que (b) .... lentamente.
2. Si has comprado mucha carne y no la vas a comer en el mismo día, la puedes (c) ...., así conservará todas sus propiedades.
3. Después de cocer la pasta, la tendrás que (d) .... antes de (e) .... la salsa de tomate.
4. Para cambiar la consistencia de la sopa de verduras, la puedes (f) .... y hacer un puré de verduras.
5. Antes de comer fruta, la deberás (g) ....
6. Para darle más sabor a la ensalada, la puedes (h) .... con aceite de oliva.

7 ¿Te gusta cocinar? En grupos pequeños, túrnense para describir lo que saben preparar. Usen las expresiones aprendidas para explicar cómo lo preparan. Luego decidan quién es la persona del grupo que mejor sabe cocinar.

126 **MORE IN ELETECA:** EXTRA ONLINE PRACTICE

ANSWERS

Activity 5

1. h; **2.** b; **3.** g; **4.** a; **5.** c; **6.** f; **7.** e; **8.** d.

Activity 6

a. poner en remojo; **b.** cocer; **c.** congelar; **d.** escurrir; **e.** añadir; **f.** triturar; **g.** lavar; **h.** aliñar.

ADVANCED LEARNERS

Have students share recipes from the countries their families are from or from countries they have visited. Have them discuss the ingredients and why some of them are more popular in some countries than in others, such as rice, beans, bread, tortillas, potatoes, etc.

GRAMÁTICA
UNIDAD **4**

1. THE CONDITIONAL TENSE: REGULAR VERBS

	CANTAR	COMER	ESCRIBIR
yo	cantaría	comería	escribiría
tú	cantarías	comerías	escribirías
usted/él/ella	cantaría	comería	escribiría
nosotros/a	cantaríamos	comeríamos	escribiríamos
vosotros/as	cantaríais	comeríais	escribiríais
ustedes/ellos/ellas	cantarían	comerían	escribirían

Note that all endings have a written accent on the **í**.

The simple conditional is used to:

■ Give **advice** and make recommendations:

> **Yo / Yo que tú / Yo en tu lugar, comería** más fruta y verdura. *If I were you, I would eat more fruit and vegetables.*
> **Deberías / Podrías dejarle** un mensaje. Creo que está preocupado. *You should / could leave him a message. I think he's worried.*

■ Ask for **favors** and **permission**:

> ¿**Te importaría** hacerme un favor? Es que mañana tengo un examen… *Would you mind doing me a favor? It's just that tomorrow I have a test…*

■ Express **probability** or **hypothesis** in the past:

> En aquella época yo **ganaría** unos 1.000 euros al mes. *Back then I was probably earning some 1.000 euros a month.*

1 Josefa, la muchacha que iba a quedar con Benjamín en *Amor en directo*, ha decidido ir finalmente al programa porque la convenció su amiga Diana, pero, ahora, está hecha un mar de nervios. Lee la conversación entre las dos amigas y completa con los verbos entre paréntesis.

Josefa: ¡Qué vergüenza! ¿Y qué hago si me hace una pregunta indiscreta?
Diana: Yo le (a) .... (responder) con otra pregunta.
Josefa: ¿Y si lo veo y no me gusta?
Diana: Pues yo que tú le (b) .... (dar) una oportunidad y (c) .... (cenar, yo) con él. Si después de la cena no te gusta, no (d) .... (participar, yo) más en el programa.
Josefa: ¿Y si me gusta?
Diana: Pues entonces (e) .... (seguir) conociéndolo y sobre todo (f) .... (quedar) con él fuera de las cámaras, ya sabes que la televisión engaña (*misleads*) mucho… Si no que te lo digan a ti, que no querías ni ir…
Josefa: Tienes razón, (g) .... (deber, yo) conocerlo mejor. Pero, igual me enamoro de él y él no de mí, ¿te imaginas?
Diana: ¡Ay, Josefa! Yo no lo (h) .... (pensar) más, ¡solo es un concurso! (i) .... (Ir), (j) .... (divertirse) un rato, (k) .... (conocer) a gente nueva y quién sabe…, igual es el hombre de tu vida…
Josefa: ¿Y si lo es?
Diana: Pues entonces yo (l) .... (casarse) con él, y (m) .... (ser, yo) muy feliz.
Josefa: Y entonces… ¿me (n) .... (ayudar, tú) a elegir vestido de novia?
Diana: ¡¡Grrrrrr!! Que sí, ¡¡pesada!!

127

OBJECTIVES FOR GRAMÁTICA 1

- Present grammatical structures needed to practice communicative functions of the unit: The conditional tense of regular verbs
- Use the conditional to give advice

CORE RESOURCES

- Interactive Online Materials - ELEteca

STANDARDS

1.1	Engage in conversation
1.2	Understand the language
1.3	Present information
4.1	Compare languages

INSTRUCTIONAL STRATEGIES

1. The Conditional Tense: Regular Verbs

- Explain to students that the form of the verb they have been using is called the conditional tense. Explain that the tense is formed by adding **-ía**, **-ías**, **-ía**, **-íamos**, **-íais**, **-ían** endings to the infinitive. Ask students what other tense is formed by adding endings to the infinitive (future).
- Have students turn back to the conversation between Mónica and Maruchi in Activity 3 (page 125) and underline the verbs in the conditional in the section on the left (Maruchi's recommendations). Then ask students to explain one of the uses of the conditional (give advice and recommendations).
- Walk students through the grammatical explanation of this tense and the uses that follow.
- Provide practice by saying a verb and asking students to say the form of the conditional for the person given. For instance, say **hablar – él**. Students should respond: **hablaría**, etc.

Activity 1

- Have the students focus on the images and identify the two girls. Remind students again of who the characters in the conversation are and ask them to provide background information on the show: **Amor en directo**.
- Have students read through the text and fill in the blanks with a form of the conditional of the verb in parenthesis.
- Ask students to share their answers with a partner. Ask questions to check comprehension: **¿Qué siente Josefa? ¿Qué consejos le da su amiga para el primer encuentro? ¿Qué haría Diana por Josefa?**
- Ask for two volunteers to read the completed conversation.

ANSWERS

Activity 1

a. respondería; **b.** daría; **c.** cenaría; **d.** participaría; **e.** seguiría; **f.** quedaría; **g.** debería; **h.** pensaría; **i.** Iría; **j.** me divertiría; **k.** conocería; **l.** me casaría; **m.** sería; **n.** ayudarías.

SLOWER-PACED LEARNERS

Help students realize that the conditional sentence is built similarly to the future tense. In fact, as they will discover on page 128, verbs that have irregular future forms, also have irregular conditional forms.

HERITAGE LANGUAGE LEARNERS

Have students share other expressions that can be used instead of **pesada** at the end of the conversation in Activity 1: **petardo**, **pelma**, **fastidioso**, **cargante**, **machacón**, **latoso**, **plomo**, etc. Have them think about situations in which they could use them.

INSTRUCTIONAL STRATEGIES

Activity 2

- Have the students look at the image of Benjamin and read the information.
- Remind students to use the previous activity as a model and the expressions in **Comunica** to give Benjamin advice.
- Circulate around the room as they work, ensuring they are using the conditional correctly. Invite volunteers to read their advice aloud.

OBJECTIVES FOR GRAMÁTICA 2

- Present grammatical structures needed to practice communicative functions of the unit: The conditional tense of irregular verbs
- Use the conditional to ask for favors and express probability

CORE RESOURCES

- Audio Program: Track 30

STANDARDS

1.1	Engage in conversation	1.3	Present information
1.2	Understand the language	4.1	Compare languages

INSTRUCTIONAL STRATEGIES

2. The Conditional Tense: Irregular Verbs

- Ask students to recall the irregular stems used in the future tense and write them on the board, prompting students as necessary. Explain to students that these verbs are also irregular in the conditional and use the same stem.
- Read through the explanation in the book and point out that the endings for irregular verbs are the same as those for regular verbs.
- Practice the irregular verbs in the conditional by saying a person an irregular verb and having the students say the correct form of that verb.

Activity 3

- Have the students read the sentences and fill in the blanks with the conditional of one of the verbs in the box.
- Remind them to check which verbs are irregular and underline them before they begin to answer. When they have finished, have them share with a partner.
- Ask for volunteers to report back to the class.

Activity 4

- Have the students look at the images taken from the *SuperEspacio* magazine and identify the characters and give as much background information as they remember. Have them match them with the sentences in the previous activity.
- Ask for volunteers to say the answers for the class.

ANSWERS

Activity 3

a. Tendría; **b.** pondría; **c.** sabría; **d.** diría; **e.** animaría.

Activity 4

1. b; **2.** c; **3.** a; **4.** d; **5.** e.

SLOWER-PACED LEARNERS

Students may need some extra practice with irregular forms. Have more advanced students invent sentences and situations (**Con un millón de dólares**…, **Con más tiempo**…, etc.) and have them ask slower-paced students to complete the sentences.

GRAMÁTICA

2 | El pobre Benjamín también está muy nervioso. Como ya sabes qué opina Josefa, ¿qué consejos le darías? Escríbele una nota.

Modelo: *Querido Benjamín, yo en tu lugar…*

2. THE CONDITIONAL TENSE: IRREGULAR VERBS

- For all irregular verbs in the conditional, the endings remain the same as with regular verbs, only the stem changes as follows:

IRREGULAR VERBS				
poder → **podr-**				ía
salir → **saldr-**	tener → **tendr-**			ías
caber → **cabr-**	poner → **pondr-**	hacer → **har-**		ía
haber → **habr-**	venir → **vendr-**	decir → **dir-**		íamos
saber → **sabr-**	valer → **valdr-**			íais
querer → **querr-**				ían

What other tense uses these same stems?

3 | Completa los espacios con el verbo adecuado del cuadro en condicional.

poner ○ saber ○ decir ○ tener ○ animar

a. .... unos cuatro años cuando empecé a dar mis primeros pasos como actor.
b. No tengo nada que decir respecto a mi relación con Mario Medina. Yo que tú .... en la revista que solo somos buenos amigos.
c. Yo no .... qué hacer sin los consejos de mi amiga Diana.
d. Yo .... a todos los jóvenes que una alimentación con muchas verduras es una garantía de salud para el futuro.
e. Yo .... a los jóvenes tímidos a buscar pareja a través de *Amor en directo*.

4 | Piensa otra vez en los relatos de la revista *SuperEspacio*. ¿Quién dijo qué? Relaciona las frases de la Actividad 3 con la persona correspondiente.

Mónica Pérez	Josefa	Maxi Castro	Maruchi	Benjamín

5 🎧 30 Escucha las entrevistas e identifica a la persona entrevistada en cada caso.

> Benjamín ○ Maruchi ○ Maxi ○ Mónica

a. .... b. .... c. .... d. ....

6 🎧 30 Escucha las entrevistas de nuevo y completa con el verbo adecuado en condicional.

	Uso
» ¿Qué .... si a tu hijo no le gusta el sabor de casi ninguna?	ⓒ
» .... usar tu imaginación.	○
» .... la primera vez que venía a la tele.	○
» ¿Y tú qué .... entonces, Luz?	○
» Mira, yo	○
» Sí, ... decir que sí.	○
» Creo que no .... hacer otra cosa.	○
» ¿Te .... firmarme un autógrafo para mi hija?	○
» ¿ .... decirnos cuándo nació esa bonita amistad?	○
» Reconoces que Mario Medina .... parte de tu vida privada.	○
» .... limitarte a escribir lo que digo.	○
» Yo que tú lo .... claro de una vez.	○

7 👥 Con tu compañero/a, comprueba tus respuestas de la Actividad 6. Luego, identifiquen cuál de los siguientes usos del condicional corresponde a cada frase. Fíjate en el ejemplo.

a. dar consejo
b. expresar probabilidad o hipótesis en el pasado

c. pedir consejo
d. pedir un favor

8 👥 Con tu compañero/a, comprueba tus respuestas en la Actividad 6. ¿Cómo reaccionarías en las siguientes situaciones? Prepara dos respuestas para cada una. Luego, en grupos pequeños, compartan las reacciones. ¿Quién tiene las mejores respuestas?

a. Vas al programa de Maruchi, *Salud al día*, y como siempre, invita a algunos espectadores a probar el plato que acaba de preparar. Te escoge a ti, pero cuando lo pruebas (*taste*), ¡sabe fatal! ¿Qué harías?
b. Ahora vas a la grabación del programa *Amor en directo*. Presentan al primer concursante y ves que sale tu novio/a al escenario. ¿Qué harías?
c. Ya no puedes más, y necesitas tomar un café. Estás esperando en cola en uno de esos cafés de moda y ves a la actriz Mónica Pérez con Maxi Castro sentados en una mesa. Parece que están enamorados. Se levantan y salen por una puerta de atrás, tomados por la mano. ¿Qué harías?

💻 MORE IN ELETECA: EXTRA ONLINE PRACTICE ⬢ 🖥 GRAMMAR TUTORIALS 7 AND 8   129

INSTRUCTIONAL STRATEGIES

🎧 **30 Activity 5**

- Tell the students they are going to hear some interviews and need to identify the person being interviewed.
- Play the audio.
- Repeat the audio for the students to confirm their answers.
- Have the students write the names in the spaces provided.
- Ask for volunteers to say the correct answers.

See audioscript on page APP7

Activity 6

- Have the students read over the interviews and play the audio again while they fill in the blanks with an appropriate verb in the conditional.
- Tell them not to do anything as yet with the last column.

Activity 7

- Have the students check their answers to the previous activity with a partner.
- Now have them identify the uses of the conditional from the list provided.
- They write the letter of the use in the box in the previous activity using the list provided.
- Ask for volunteers to say the correct uses.

Activity 8

- Have the students read quickly through the situations and identify which image matches which situation.
- Read the first situation and ask for reactions from the class.
- Now have the students divide into small groups and read the other situations and react to them in at least two ways.
- Ask for volunteers to read a situation and react to it.

ANSWERS

Activity 5

a. Maruchi; **b.** Benjamin; **c.** Maxi; **d.** Mónica.

Activities 6 and 7

harías (c); deberías (a); Sería (b); harías (c); esperaría (a); podríamos (b); sabría (b); importaría (d); Podrías (d); formaría (b); Deberías (a); dejaría (a).

ADVANCED LEARNERS

Have students write new situations for Activity 8. Then put them in groups and have them swap their situations. Together they discuss what they would do in the new situations.

HERITAGE LANGUAGE LEARNERS

If students show proficiency in using the conditional, have them practice writing complete conversations for Activity 8. One of the main challenges of heritage language learners is spelling and by having them write the exercise, they will focus on writing strategies.

OBJECTIVES FOR DESTREZAS

• Identify the format of a text

STANDARDS

1.1 Interpersonal communication

1.2 Understand the language

1.3 Present information

INSTRUCTIONAL STRATEGIES

Comprensión de lectura

Activity 1

• Talk the students through the strategy for identifying the format of a text.

• Answer any questions they may have at this stage.

• Have the students follow the instructions in the order they are set out, filling in the boxes for each of the texts in Activity 2.

Activity 2

• Ask the students to read each short text and the corresponding question on the next page.

• Have them use their notes and the instructions above to help them.

• When they have finished, have them compare answers with a partner.

• Ask for volunteers to say the correct answers.

Cultural Note

Share the following information about Madrid:

La Puerta del Sol es el centro neurálgico de Madrid. A pesar de su nombre, en el lugar donde se encuentra no hay ninguna puerta, pero en sus orígenes fue uno de los accesos de la cerca que rodeaba Madrid en el siglo XV. Esta cerca recogía en su perímetro los arrabales medievales que habían ido creciendo extramuros, en torno a la muralla cristiana del siglo XII. El nombre de la puerta proviene de un sol que adornaba la entrada, colocado ahí por estar orientada la puerta hacia el este.

El Oso y el Madroño es una estatua que se encuentra en la Puerta del Sol y que es el símbolo de Madrid.

El Madroño es un árbol típico de la Comunidad de Madrid y con sus frutos se hace el licor de madroño.

La chocolatería San Ginés es un lugar típico de Madrid para ir a tomar chocolate con churros. Es tradición tomar esta bebida en la madrugada de Año Nuevo.

ANSWERS

Activity 2

1. b; **2.** b; **3.** b.

SLOWER-PACED LEARNERS

Have students notice the different verb forms used in the texts and their functions: recommendations, future events, etc. Have them list the verbs that indicate an order or recommendation and those that express things that will happen in the future.

ADVANCED LEARNERS

Have students write a paragraph about a city located in any other Spanish-speaking country. What would they recommend to visit? Why? What city would they like to visit if they won a contest?

DESTREZAS

COMPRENSIÓN DE LECTURA

1 Antes de empezar a leer, repasa la estrategia en Destrezas y sigue las recomendaciones.

Destrezas

Identifying the format of a text

Look at the images, headings, and layout to help you understand the purpose of the text. Then follow these steps:

	Texto 1	Texto 2	Texto 3
1. Read the text and the question connected to this text for a general sense of the content.			
2. Highlight the most important word or phrase in the question or write it in the column to the right.			
3. Go back to the main text and look for related nouns or verbs.			
4. Read the supporting details. Do they answer what is asked?			

2 Lee los textos y contesta las preguntas en la página siguiente.

La revista para jóvenes a partir de 15 años.

Suscripción a la revista

Ahora podrás disfrutar de las más interesantes noticias sobre actualidad, videojuegos, música, cine, deportes, literatura; propuestas de escapadas de fin de semana, salir por tu ciudad, talleres, concursos; entrevistas a tus ídolos, los consejos de Maruchi… ¡Todo esto y mucho más en la puerta de tu casa!

No te lo pienses más y aprovecha la oferta: si te suscribes este mes, ¡recibirás gratis la revista durante 6 meses!

Participa en el sorteo y ¡gana un viaje a París, la ciudad del amor!

¿Cómo puedes participar?

Es muy fácil, tan solo tienes que leer la entrevista a Maxi Castro y responder al cuestionario sobre su vida que encontrarás en el interior de la revista. Después envíanos tus respuestas, bien por correo ordinario o por Internet a través de nuestra revista digital. Entre los participantes que acierten todas las preguntas se realizará un sorteo ante notario. El nombre del ganador se dará a conocer en la publicación del mes de febrero. No lo dudes, participa y ¡gana!

¿Qué ver en Madrid?

El paseo comienza en la Puerta del Sol, centro de Madrid. No olvides fotografiarte junto al Oso y el Madroño, uno de los símbolos de la ciudad. Después, dirige tus pasos a la calle Arenal y busca la chocolatería San Ginés, donde puedes desayunar un chocolate con churros.

1. Si quieres suscribirte a la revista *SuperEspacio*…
   a. debes tener más de 15 años.
   b. no necesitarás bajar al quiosco a comprarla.
   c. no tendrás que abonar ningún importe.

2. Podrás participar en el sorteo…
   a. tan solo con contestar el cuestionario y enviar tus respuestas a la revista.
   b. si has contestado correctamente al cuestionario.
   c. si acudes a la celebración del sorteo que se realizará ante notario.

3. El texto sobre Madrid recomienda…
   a. recorrer la calle Arenal.
   b. encontrar la chocolatería en la calle Arenal.
   c. evitar ir a la calle Arenal.

PRONUNCIACIÓN Las letras y y x

- To form the plural of a word ending in **y**, add **-es: rey / reyes**. Notice that the **y** is now pronounced as a consonant.

- Verbs like **oír**, **caer**, **creer** and those ending in **-uir** like **construir**, **destruir**, and **huir** (to flee) will have a **y** in the **usted/él/ella** and **ustedes/ellos/ellas** form in the preterit.

  oír → o**y**ó   caer → ca**y**eron   creer → cre**y**ó
  construir → constru**y**ó   destruir → destru**y**eron   huir → hu**y**eron

1 **Completa con la forma correcta de los verbos entre paréntesis.**

   a. Ayer Juan (oír) .... un ruido extraño y (creer) .... que era un ladrón. Salió corriendo para atraparlo, (caerse) .... y el ladrón (huir) .... con todo el dinero.
   b. El pueblo maya consiguió muchos avances tecnológicos y (construir) .... un gran imperio.
   c. El huracán (destruir) .... la casa de mis tíos en Santo Domingo.

- The letter **x** is used in place of s before the consonant pairs **pl-** and **pr-**: **explorar, exprimir.**

2 **Completa con x o s, según la regla que acabas de aprender.**

   a. e ☐ plotar   c. e ☐ timado   e. e ☐ tupidez   g. e ☐ presar
   b. e ☐ plicar   d. e ☐ presión   f. e ☐ tatuto   h. e ☐ tirar

   MORE IN ELETECA: EXTRA ONLINE PRACTICE

OBJECTIVES FOR PRONUNCIACIÓN
- Practice pronouncing and spelling words containing the letters **y** and **x**

CORE RESOURCES
- Interactive Online Materials - ELEteca

STANDARDS
  1.2   Understand the language
  3.2   Acquire information
  4.1   Compare languages

INSTRUCTIONAL STRATEGIES
Walk the students through the explanation and ask them to think of more examples for each group. Write the words on the board in their groups.

Activity 1
- Have the students fill the blanks with the correct form of the verbs in parenthesis. Remind them to check the list above to verify spellings.
- Have the students share their answers with a partner.
- Invite students to come to the front and write the correct sentences on the board.
- Ask for volunteers to read the sentences to the class.

Activity 2
- Have the students read the note about the use of **x** or **s**.
- Students work individually to fill in the missing letter according to the information above and then share their answers with a partner.
- Ask for volunteers to read the completed words.
- Have the students comment on any difficulties and discuss these with the class.
- The first group to complete their dictation correctly is declared the winner.

ANSWERS
Activity 1
   a. oyó, creyó, se cayó, huyó; **b.** construyó; **c.** destruyó.

Activity 2
   a. explotar; **b.** explicar; **c.** estimado; **d.** expresión; **e.** estupidez; **f.** estatuto; **g.** expresar; **h.** estirar.

HERITAGE LANGUAGE LEARNERS
Have students compile a list of similar words with **y** and **ll**. You can also dictate a few: **cayó**, **calló**; **haya**, **halla**; **apoyo**, **pollo**, etc. Have them notice that the pronunciation of **y** and **ll** is the same except for a limited number of regions, and that is why native speakers have trouble with the spelling of words that use them. Explain that, in general, only practice writing and reading can help people become good spellers. The rules included on this page will help, but students have to make an effort to practice on their own as much as they can.

OBJECTIVES FOR SABOR HISPANO

- Learn about the Mediterranean diet and healthy eating
- Activate vocabulary connected with food and cooking

CORE RESOURCES

- Audio Program: Track 31

STANDARDS

2.1	Culture: practices and perspectives	3.2	Acquire information
2.2	Products and perspectives	5.2	Using language for personal enjoyment and enrichment

INSTRUCTIONAL STRATEGIES

 31

- Introduce the topic by asking the students to look at the images and say any words they already know.
- Put students in pairs to discuss the questions in the **Antes de leer** box.
- Before playing the audio, tell students to listen for the question posed at the beginning of the audio and be prepared to answer it. Either have students close their books while they listen or follow along with the text in the book.
- Elicit responses to the target question. Ask for different opinions and explanations.
- Play the audio of the text in sections as students follow along. After each section, ask questions such as: **¿De dónde es típica la dieta mediterránea? ¿Cuál es el factor más importante? ¿Qué ingredientes tienen en común muchos de los platos típicos?**, etc.
- Ask what the students have understood and invite those who understood more to help those who understood less.
- To help build vocabulary, have students locate and underline any words from the glossary on the next page in the text. Then have them make and share new sentences with the words. You may choose to have them work individually or in pairs.

SLOWER-PACED LEARNERS

Before having students discuss the questions in **Antes de leer**, focus their attention on the captions to the images. Ask them to share what they already know or have heard about the Mediterranean diet and to give other examples of fast food.

ADVANCED LEARNERS

Invite students to give examples of how climate affects people's diet in other regions around the world and how it affects their own diet. Ask them why they think junk food is so popular among young people and what the consequences are of eating that food.

SABOR HISPANO

LA DIETA MEDITERRÁNEA...

¿MITO O REALIDAD?

Vegetales, queso, aceitunas, sal, pimienta y aceite de oliva, ingredientes típicos de la dieta mediterránea

Antes de leer

¿Qué tipo de comida sueles comer?

¿Te gusta la comida rápida? ¿Por qué?

¿Qué ingredientes son sanos?

31 **La comida mediterránea es típica de los países que rodean° el mar Mediterráneo. España es uno de ellos. Pero, ¿esta dieta existe o es un mito?**

«El clima es el factor más importante de la dieta mediterránea, ya que produce una serie de ingredientes típicos de esta gastronomía», dice el Doctor José Ordovas.

Hay muchos platos típicos de los países mediterráneos que tienen ingredientes en común, como los vegetales, las aceitunas°, el pescado, el marisco, las frutas, el aceite de oliva y algunos condimentos.

«Culturalmente, los países del Mediterráneo pueden ser muy distintos. Y, claro, su gastronomía también puede

diferir, pero los ingredientes son los mismos», dice el doctor.

España es uno de estos países. Sin embargo, solo una parte del país está en el Mediterráneo y disfruta de° este clima cálido. El norte de España, por ejemplo, tiene un clima más frío y lluvioso.

«En España, al hablar de los hábitos alimentarios, no se puede generalizar. El clima y la dieta varían mucho de norte a sur, o de este a oeste. En el norte se come marisco, pero también mucha carne y patatas. En el centro son típicos los guisos°», asegura Mariona Coslada, nutricionista.

Además, la dieta está cambiando. Las familias ya no tienen tanto tiempo para cocinar y suelen preparar platos rápidos, a menudo no muy saludables.

Una encuesta° reciente reveló que muchos jóvenes ahora prefieren la comida rápida, o comida basura, a la dieta mediterránea. «A mí me encanta la comida rápida, la verdad. Hamburguesas, papas fritas, aros de cebolla... », dice Mario Velázquez, un estudiante de 20 años.

La hamburguesa se considera un ejemplo de comida rápida en España.

Glosario

aceitunas – olives
disfrutar de – to enjoy
encuesta – poll
el guiso – stew
rodear – surround

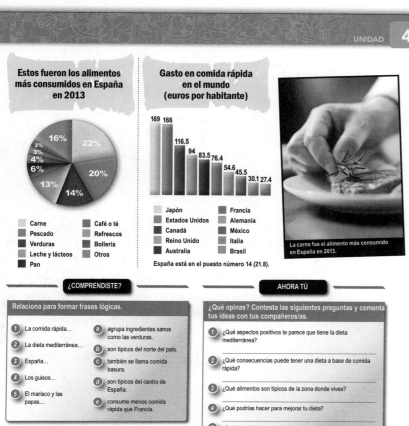

Estos fueron los alimentos más consumidos en España en 2013

16%
22%
2%
3%
4%
6%
20%
13%
14%

- Carne
- Pescado
- Verduras
- Leche y lácteos
- Pan
- Café o té
- Refrescos
- Bollería
- Otros

Gasto en comida rápida en el mundo (euros por habitante)

169 166
116.5
94 83.5 76.4
54.6 45.5
30.1 27.4

- Japón
- Estados Unidos
- Canadá
- Reino Unido
- Australia
- Francia
- Alemania
- México
- Italia
- Brasil

España está en el puesto número 14 (21.8).

La carne fue el alimento más consumido en España en 2013.

¿COMPRENDISTE?

Relaciona para formar frases lógicas.

1. La comida rápida…
2. La dieta mediterránea…
3. España…
4. Los guisos…
5. El marisco y las papas…

a. agrupa ingredientes sanos como las verduras.
b. son típicos del norte del país.
c. también se llama comida basura.
d. son típicos del centro de España.
e. consume menos comida rápida que Francia.

La paella, un plato típico de la dieta mediterránea

AHORA TÚ

¿Qué opinas? Contesta las siguientes preguntas y comenta tus ideas con tus compañeros/as.

1. ¿Qué aspectos positivos te parece que tiene la dieta mediterránea?
2. ¿Qué consecuencias puede tener una dieta a base de comida rápida?
3. ¿Qué alimentos son típicos de la zona donde vives?
4. ¿Qué podrías hacer para mejorar tu dieta?
5. ¿Qué ingredientes sueles comer de la dieta mediterránea?

VOCES LATINAS
LA DIETA MEDITERRÁNEA, ¿MITO O REALIDAD?

Fuentes: *El País*, Ministerio de Agricultura, Pesca y Alimentación de España, EAE Business School, Unitedexplanations.org, *ABC*, Friedman School of Nutrition.

133

INSTRUCTIONAL STRATEGIES

Alimentos más consumidos

- Call on a volunteer to read the caption and chart data aloud.
- Elicit examples of food items that belong to some of the categories to recycle unit vocabulary.
- Review any common errors with the class, eliciting the corrections.
- Put students into pairs to discuss whether or not they consume similar percentages of food as the people in Spain. Have them come up with their own percentages for each category and add any new categories of their own.
- Call on volunteers to report back on their similarities or differences with the data from Spain.

Gasto en comida rápida

- Call on a volunteer to read the title. Then call on others to describe the information that follows.
- Check students' understanding of the information by asking questions, such as: **¿En qué puesto está Estados Unidos? ¿Hay algún dato que les sorprende? ¿Qué tipo de comida consideran comida rápida en Estados Unidos?**
- Help students calculate the equivalent spent in dollars by providing the current exchange rate. Ask students for their impressions of the dollar amounts spent.
- Have students write three questions about the data.
- Put them into pairs to take turns asking and answering the questions.
- Monitor their conversations and assist as needed. Take note of any common errors that you hear in their discussions.

¿Comprendiste?

- Have the students combine the phrases in the box. Then have them check through the text to see if they are correct.
- Have them compare their answers with a partner.
- Invite individual students to share their answers with the class.

Ahora tú

- Read the questions with the students and have them think about the answers.
- Have the students answer the questions in pairs or small groups and then ask for volunteers to present to the class.

ANSWERS

1. c; 2. a; 3. e; 4. d; 5. b.

HERITAGE LANGUAGE LEARNERS

Have students work in groups to write an article for the school newspaper about the food students eat and how it relates to the eating habits of the US population. Have them write some recomemndations, such as: **Deberíamos comer menos comida basura, Deberíamos beber más agua, Deberíamos cocinar la comida en casa…**

OBJECTIVES FOR RELATO

- Revisit unit themes, grammar, vocabulary and culture in a new context
- Improve reading comprehension skills

CORE RESOURCES

- Audio Program: Track 32

STANDARDS

1.1 Engage in conversation
1.2 Understand the language
1.3 Present information
2.1 Practices and perspectives
5.3 Using language for personal enjoyment and enrichment

INSTRUCTIONAL STRATEGIES

Activity 1

- Have the students look at the photo and introduce José Lezama Lima as an internationally recognized Hispanic author and poet of the twentieth century.
- Ask them if they can name any other Cuban poets or writers (or American poets).
- Explain to students that Lezama's works exemplify a baroque style of writing. Ask students if they have ever heard of this term and can explain what it means. Share the Cultural Note below with students to set the tone for the fragment they will be reading.
- Read the questions with the students and remind them that reading the questions often provides useful information about the text.
- Have them read through the biography and answer the questions together with a partner. Invite volunteers to share their answers with the class.

Cultural Note

Los escritores barrocos hispanoamericanos usaban un lenguaje muy decorado, abundante, complicado, cargado de adornos literarios como la metáfora y el hipérbaton en el cual el autor juega con el orden lógico de las palabras para producir otro efecto. Su objetivo era el de complicar el significado del texto.

Extension

Project images of different styles of baroque architecture from Spain and Latin America. Include images of pre-Columbian art, which also factored into the baroque expression of Latin-American writers.

Activity 2

- Have the students look at the words taken from the next text and guess their meaning.
- Now have them read quickly through the text in Activity 3 and locate and underline the words in the text.
- Have the students discuss their answers with a partner.
- Have those students who understood more help those who understood less.
- Offer a dictionary for students to check any words still unknown.
- Ask for volunteers to give the correct answers.

ANSWERS

Activity 1

a. Se le reconoce internacionalmente por su obra *Paradiso* que tuvo mucho éxito; **b.** La obra no fue bien vista por las autoridades cubanas porque

---

1 Lee el siguiente texto sobre José Lezama Lima, poeta, ensayista y novelista cubano. Después, contesta las preguntas.

José Lezama Lima nació en Cuba en 1910 y murió en 1976.

Aunque se dedicó principalmente a la poesía y al ensayo, se le recuerda sobre todo por su faceta de novelista, en concreto por su obra *Paradiso*, publicada en 1966 y de gran repercusión internacional.

De estilo barroco, y considerado uno de los autores más importantes de la literatura hispanoamericana, ha influido en una gran cantidad de escritores de su época y posteriores *(later)*.

El argumento de su principal novela se centra en la infancia y juventud de José Cemí, el protagonista, a través del cual *(through which)* el autor construye todo un mundo poético en el que se mezclan la realidad, el mito y la fantasía, escritos con un excelente dominio de la lengua española.

Tras su publicación, en 1971, el hecho de abordar *(tackle)* temas controvertidos hizo que su novela no fuera bien vista por las autoridades cubanas, que acusaron al autor de participar en actividades contrarrevolucionarias, algo que actualmente han rectificado.

Para muchos, Lezama fue el reinventor del lenguaje cuando parecía que todo estaba ya dicho, describiendo una nueva realidad a través de la metáfora y la imagen.

a. ¿Por qué obra se reconoce internacionalmente a Lezama Lima? ¿Tuvo éxito?
b. ¿Fue entendida en su época la obra por parte de las autoridades cubanas? ¿Por qué?
c. ¿Esa misma situación continúa actualmente?
d. ¿Qué tipo de estilo desarrolló Lezama Lima en *Paradiso*?
e. ¿En qué personaje se centra la novela?
f. ¿Qué etapas de la vida del protagonista desarrolla?
g. ¿Qué tipo de mundo construye Lezama Lima en *Paradiso*?

2 Las siguientes palabras se tomaron de un capítulo de la novela *Paradiso*, de Lezama Lima. Con tu compañero/a, selecciona la definición correcta de las palabras, usando el diccionario si hace falta.

a. lascas del pavo: patas / trozos / plumas
b. garzones: adultos / niñas / jóvenes
c. refinamiento: elegancia, buen gusto / calidad de estrecho / mal sabor
d. pachorra: nombre de persona / tranquilidad excesiva / de broma
e. acatar: ordenar / saborear la comida / obedecer
f. paladar: parte interior de la boca, fundamental para el sentido del gusto / parte interior de la boca que sirve para morder y triturar los alimentos / parte interior de la boca, fundamental para el sentido del olfato

---

abordaba temas controvertidos; **c.** No, actualmente las autoridades cubanas han rectificado su postura; **d.** Un estilo barroco, con el que describe una nueva realidad a través de la metáfora y la imagen; **e.** Se centra en el personaje de José Cemí; **f.** Se centra en su infancia y juventud; **g.** Lezama Lima construye un mundo poético donde se mezclan realidad, mito y fantasía.

Activity 2

a. trozos; **b.** jóvenes; **c.** elegancia, buen gusto; **d.** tranquilidad excesiva; **e.** obedecer; **f.** parte interior de la boca, fundamental para el sentido del gusto.

HERITAGE LANGUAGE LEARNERS

Have students chose a poem written by José Lezama Lima to read and interpret for the class: http://www.los-poetas.com.

3 🎧 32 **Lee el texto.**

(1) Los mayores solo probaron algunas lascas del pavo, (2) pero no perdonaron el relleno que estaba elaborado con unas almendras que se deshacían y con unas ciruelas que parecían crecer de nuevo con la provocada segregación del paladar.

(3) Los garzones, un poco huidizos aún al refinamiento del soufflé, crecieron su gula habladora en torno al almohadón de la pechuga, **donde comenzaron a lanzarse tan pronto el pavón** (peacock) dio un corto vuelo de la mesa de otra lata de leche condensada, y llega entonces el hada, es decir, más rápidamente querían ver al pavón todo plumado, con su pachorra (sluggishness) en el corralón.

Al final de la comida, doña Augusta quiso mostrar una travesura (prank) en el postre. Presentó en las copas de champagne la más deliciosa crema helada. Después que la familia mostró su más rendido acatamiento (acceptance) al postre sorpresivo, doña Augusta regaló la receta: "(4) Son las cosas sencillas, que podemos hacer en la cocina cubana, (5) la repostería más fácil, y que enseguida el paladar declara incomparables. Un coco rallado en conserva, más otra conserva de piña rallada, unidas a la mitad de otra lata de leche condensada, y llega entonces el hada, es decir, la viejita Marie Brizard, para rociar con su anisete la crema olorosa. Al refrigerador, se sirve cuando está bien fría".

Luego la vamos saboreando, recibiendo los elogios de los otros comensales que piden con insistencia el bis (encore), como cuando oímos alguna pavana de Lully.

Al mismo tiempo que se servía el postre, doña Augusta le indicó a Baldovina que trajese el frutero, (6) donde mezclaban sus colores las manzanas, peras, mandarinas y uvas.

4 **Busca la frase enumerada del texto correspondiente a cada descripción.**

a. ☐ El relleno del pavo estaba compuesto por almendras muy tiernas y buenas y con ciruelas muy ricas.
b. ☐ En el frutero había frutas de diferentes colores.
c. ☐ Los postres cubanos son de fácil preparación pero exquisitos.
d. ☐ Los jóvenes no estaban acostumbrados a esa comida tan refinada y se dedicaron a comer pollo.
e. ☐ Los adultos probaron un poco de pavo.
f. ☐ La señora habla de la sencillez de la comida cubana.

5 👥 **Busca más información sobre Lezama Lima y su obra, *Paradiso*, y contesta las preguntas. Después, habla con tu compañero/a y comparen sus respuestas.**

a. ¿En qué lugar pasó José Cemí, el protagonista de *Paradiso*, su primera infancia?
b. ¿Qué tipo de niño era José Cemí?
c. ¿Qué importante papel juega Oppiano Licario en la vida de José Cemí?
d. ¿Quién lo inicia en el mundo de la poesía?
e. ¿A qué corriente o periodo literario pertenece la obra de Lezama Lima?
f. Además de Lezama Lima, ¿qué otros autores pertenecen a este movimiento?

INSTRUCTIONAL STRATEGIES

🎧 32 **Activity 3**

- To introduce the reading have the students talk about Thanksgiving and the types of food which are prepared especially for that festivity. Then play the audio while the students listen with books closed.
- Play the audio again as students follow in their books.
- Discuss any vocabulary or expressions that may still give difficulty.

Activity 4

Ask students to read the sentences and look for the corresponding numbered sentences in the text. Have them share their answers with a partner.

Activity 5

- Read the questions with the students and have them research the answers on the Internet.
- Once they have some information, they report to the class and compile more complete answers to the questions.

ANSWERS

Activity 4

a. 2; **b.** 6; **c.** 5; **d.** 3; **e.** 1; **f.** 4.

Activity 5

Answers will vary. Possible answers include:

a. José Cemí pasó su primera infancia en un campamento militar adonde su padre, coronel de artillería, se había trasladado con toda la familia; **b.** José Cemí era un niño asmático, mimado por las mujeres de la familia y la servidumbre; **c.** Oppiano Licario es una extraña figura que aparece como maestro, precursor y protector espiritual de José Cemí; **d.** De niño, su tío Alberto Olaya lo inicia en los misterios de la poesía y a través de él conoce a Oppiano Licario, personaje fundamental en su historia futura; **e.** La obra de Lezama Lima pertenece al movimiento de la novela hispanoamericana del siglo XX y se la suele clasificar dentro de la narrativa metafísica; **f.** Borges, Alejo Carpentier, Miguel Ángel Asturias…

SLOWER-PACED LEARNERS

To familiarize students with Lezama Lima's baroque style, have students notice how long the sentences are and how many adjectives are used. Have them underline verbs and explain why the different past tenses are used (preterite to introduce actions and events, imperfect for descriptions, etc.). Also have them notice that Lezama Lima changes the expected location of some sentence components, which makes the text more difficult to understand.

ADVANCED LEARNERS

Tell students to imagine that they were writing their own essay or poem with the title **Paradiso**. What would their work be about? Have them write a draft of it to share with a partner. After a round of revision, have them share their final drafts with the class.

OBJECTIVES FOR EVALUACIÓN

- Review grammar, vocabulary and culture from the unit
- Complete self-assessment

CORE RESOURCES

- Interactive Online Materials - ELEteca

STANDARDS

1.2 Understand the language
2.1 Practices and perspectives
4.1 Compare cultures

INSTRUCTIONAL STRATEGIES

- Activities can be completed individually and then reviewed with the class. Vary by asking students if they agree with the answer given and then writing it on the board. Provide explanations as needed.
- You may wish to assign point value to each activity as a way for students to monitor their progress.
- Direct students to the indicated pages in **En resumen** if they make more than one or two mistakes in any one section.

ANSWERS

Activity 1

Answers will vary. **a.** Podrías guardar un poco para después; **b.** Yo que tú ordenaría un poco la ropa; **c.** Yo en tu lugar haría la cama nada más levantarme; **d.** Deberías conducir más despacio; **e.** Yo que tú me olvidaría de ese muchacho; **f.** Deberíais comprar menos cosas.

Activity 2

1. d; **2.** a; **3.** e; **4.** b; **5.** c.

Activity 3

a. saldría; **b.** pondría; **c.** Tendrían; **d.** vendría; **e.** sabría; **f.** diría; **g.** Podríamos.

Activity 4

Carnes: solomillo de ternera, pechuga de pollo, salchichón; **Frutas:** piña, manzana, cerezas; **Legumbres:** frijoles, lentejas, garbanzos; **Verduras:** calabacín, guisantes, espinacas, berenjena.

EVALUACIÓN

GIVING ADVICE OR RECOMMENDATIONS

1 Fíjate en las personas de las imágenes y dales un consejo.

THE CONDITIONAL TENSE

2 Relaciona las frases con su uso correspondiente del condicional.

1. Estoy hecho un lío, ¿tú que harías?
2. Yo que tú, cortaría la relación con ese muchacho.
3. ¿Podría hacer una llamada?
4. Ayer Nacho llegó muy tarde. Regresaría sobre las cuatro de la mañana.
5. ¿Podrías dejarme tu boli azul?

a. Dar consejos o recomendaciones.
b. Expresar probabilidad o hipótesis en el pasado.
c. Pedir un favor.
d. Pedir consejo.
e. Pedir permiso.

3 Completa las frases con los verbos en condicional.

a. Yo que tú, no (salir) .... a la calle sin abrigo, hace mucho frío.
b. Yo, no (poner) .... tanto peso en la estantería, creo que no lo va a resistir.
c. (Tener, ustedes) .... que tener más cuidado con el mando de la tele, ¡siempre se les cae al suelo!
d. Yo creo que ayer (venir, él) .... sobre las dos. Yo estaba ya en la cama.
e. No (saber, yo) .... qué decirte. Por un lado, te entiendo, pero por otro creo que él también tiene razón.
f. Yo en tu lugar, le (decir, yo) .... realmente lo que pienso.
g. ¿(Poder, nosotros) .... entregar el trabajo la semana que viene?

LA COMIDA

4 Clasifica estas palabras en la columna correspondiente.

piña ○ frijoles ○ calabacín ○ solomillo de ternera ○ lentejas ○ pechuga de pollo salchichón ○ guisantes ○ manzana ○ espinacas ○ cerezas ○ berenjena ○ garbanzos

CARNES Y DERIVADOS	FRUTAS	LEGUMBRES	VERDURAS Y HORTALIZAS

5 **Completa la receta de cocina con las siguientes palabras.**

> lavar ○ añadir ○ poner en remojo ○ guisar ○ cocer ○ escurrir (2)

Necesitas medio kilo de garbanzos. Para ablandarlos, los tendrás que (a) .... el día anterior. Pasado ese tiempo, los deberás (b) .... bien, quitándoles el agua sobrante. Las espinacas, si son frescas, se deben (c) .... muy bien para eliminar la tierra que pueden traer; también se pueden usar las espinacas congeladas.

En primer lugar, debemos (d) .... las espinacas cubriéndolas de agua, a fuego lento durante unos diez minutos. Después de retirarlas del fuego, para quitarles el agua, las tenemos que (e) .... y dejar a un lado.

A continuación, por separado, tenemos que (f) .... los garbanzos con agua, aceite, ajo, cebolla y pimienta. Una vez tiernos los garbanzos, ya podemos (g) .... las espinacas. Lo dejamos todo en el fuego durante unos dos minutos y ya tendremos listo ¡un delicioso guiso de garbanzos con espinacas!

THE LETTERS Y AND X

6 **Pon las letras que faltan. Después, usa las palabras para completar las frases.**

> ca ☐ ó ○ e ☐ plotar ○ re ☐ es ○ hu ☐ ó ○ e ☐ presionista ○ le ☐ es

a. Las .... de mi país son muy estrictas.
b. El periódico *El País* publicó una noticia sobre los .... de España.
c. Si sigues comiendo así, vas a ....
d. La semana pasada mi hermano se .... en la ducha y se golpeó la cabeza.
e. El ladrón .... por los edificios con la famosa obra de arte *La Gioconda*.
f. El estilo .... pertenece al siglo XX.

CULTURE

7 **Contesta las siguientes preguntas con la información que has aprendido en *La dieta mediterránea… ¿mito o realidad?***

a. ¿Cuáles son algunos de los ingredientes típicos de la gastronomía mediterránea?
b. ¿Cómo es el clima de estos países? ¿Qué parte de España no está incluida en este clima? ¿Por qué?
c. ¿De qué manera está cambiando la dieta y cuál es el resultado?
d. Últimamente, ¿qué prefieren comer los jóvenes? ¿Y tú?
e. ¿Qué alimento consumen más los españoles? ¿Crees que es igual en Estados Unidos?
f. ¿Qué alimento se consume menos en España? ¿Crees que es igual en Estado Unidos?

 MORE IN ELETECA: EXTRA ONLINE PRACTICE

ANSWERS

Activity 5

a. poner en remojo; **b.** escurrir; **c.** lavar; **d.** cocer; **e.** escurrir; **f.** guisar; **g.** añadir.

Activity 6

a. leyes; **b.** reyes; **c.** explotar; **d.** cayó; **e.** huyó; **f.** expresionista.

Activity 7

Answers may vary.

a. Los ingredientes típicos son los vegetales, el queso, las aceitunas, la sal, la pimienta y el aceite de oliva; **b.** El clima de estos países es cálido, pero el norte de España es diferente porque tiene un clima más frío y lluvioso; **c.** Las familias ya no tienen tanto tiempo para cocinar y suelen preparar platos rápidos, a menudo no muy saludables; **d.** Últimamente los jóvenes prefieren comer comida rápida; **e.** El alimento que más se consume en España es la carne; **f.** El alimento que menos se consume en España es la bollería.

- Review unit vocabulary and expressions
- Practice communicative skills

STANDARDS

1.2 Understand the language

1.3 Present information

4.1 Evaluate similarities and differences in language

INSTRUCTIONAL STRATEGIES

- Encourage students to use self-adhesive notes to place on correct objects in their house.
- Index cards can be used as flashcards with the Spanish term on one side and the English term on the other, or a picture or drawing.
- Students work in pairs or groups, using vocabulary flashcards as they would the cards of a board game to help each other practice unit vocabulary.
- Encourage students to write labels or captions for the photos on this page. Remind them to use the vocabulary and expressions they have learned in this unit.
- Working with a partner, have students take turns describing the verbs on the page without naming them while their partners guess which verb they are describing: **Quitar el agua de las verduras después de hervirlas** (**escurrir**).
- Have students discuss their food preferences and eating habits with the items in **Los alimentos** and **Descripciones**.

EN RESUMEN: Vocabulario

Verbos

adelgazar *to lose weight*
aliñar *to dress (salad)*
añadir *to add*
cocer *to boil, cook*
congelar *to freeze*
consumir *to consume*
engordar *to gain weight*
escurrir *to drain*
estar enamorado/a de *to be in love with*
lavar *to rinse*

poner en remojo *to soak*
triturar *to grind*

Descripciones

a la plancha *grilled*
crudo *raw*
desnatado/a *skimmed*
entero/a *whole*
saludable *healthy*
sano/a *healthy*
soso/a *bland*

Pedir y dar consejos

Deberías… *You should…*
Es que… *It's just that…*
Para pedir permiso. *Asking for permission.*
¿Me dejas…? *Will you allow me to…?*
¿Podría…? *Could I…?*
¿Podrías…? *Could you…?*
¿Puedo…? *Can I…?*
¿Qué puedo hacer? *What can I do?*

¿Sería tan amable de…? *Would you be so kind as to…?*
¿Te importaría…? *Would you mind…?*
¿Te importa si…? *Do you mind if…?*
¿Tú qué harías? *What would you do?*
Yo que tú / Yo en tu lugar… *If I were you…*

Los alimentos

el aceite de girasol *sunflower oil*
el aceite de oliva *olive oil*

la berenjena *eggplant*

el bistec *steak*
el bizcocho *cake*

el calabacín *zucchini*
la carne picada *ground beef*

las cerezas *cherries*
el chorizo *sausage*

la chuleta de cerdo *pork chop*
los dulces *sweets*
los embutidos *cold cuts*
las espinacas *spinach*
los frijoles *beans*
los garbanzos *chick peas*

los guisantes *peas*
las lentejas *lentils*
la magdalena *muffin*

la mantequilla *butter*

la pechuga de pollo *chicken breast*
la piña *pineapple*
el sabor *taste, flavor*
la sal *salt*
el salchichón *salami*
la salsa *sauce*
el trozo de *piece of*
el vinagre *vinegar*

EN RESUMEN: Gramática

ASKING FOR AND GIVING ADVICE

(See page 119)

■ Para **pedir consejos**:

¿Qué puedo hacer? **¿Tú qué harías?** **¿Podrías** aconsejarme?

■ Para **dar consejos** o recomendaciones:

Yo / Yo que tú / Yo en tu lugar, comería de una manera más saludable.

Deberías / podrías acostarte. Es tarde.

■ Otras formas:

¿Por qué no vas al médico? Juan y tú **tienen que** ir a ver esa película.

Toma un taxi, llegarás más rápido. **No fumes**. Te hace daño.

¿Y si comes menos fritos?

THE CONDITIONAL TENSE

(See pages 127 and 128)

■ Regular verbs.

REGULAR VERBS			
	CONGELAR	**COCER**	**ESCURRIR**
yo	congelaría	cocería	escurriría
tú	congelarías	cocerías	escurrirías
usted/él/ella	congelaría	cocería	escurriría
nosotros/as	congelaríamos	coceríamos	escurriríamos
vosotros/as	congelaríais	coceríais	escurriríais
ustedes/ellos/ellas	congelarían	cocerían	escurrirían

■ Irregular verbs.

IRREGULAR VERBS			
poder ➡ **podr-**			ía
salir ➡ **saldr-**	tener ➡ **tendr-**		ías
caber ➡ **cabr-**	poner ➡ **pondr-**	hacer ➡ **har-**	ía
haber ➡ **habr-**	venir ➡ **vendr-**	decir ➡ **dir-**	íamos
saber ➡ **sabr-**	valer ➡ **valdr-**		íais
querer ➡ **querr-**			ían

■ The conditional is used to:

• Give **advice** or **recommendations**:

Yo / yo que tú / yo en tu lugar, comería más fruta y verdura. Comes fatal.

Deberías escribirle un mensaje. Creo que está preocupado.

Podrías dedicarte al deporte a nivel profesional. Eres muy bueno.

• Ask for **favors** or **permission**:

¿Te importaría hacerme un favor? Es que mañana tengo un examen...

• Express **probability** or **hypothesis** in the past:

En aquella época yo ganaría unos 1.000 euros al mes.

OBJECTIVES FOR EN RESUMEN: GRAMÁTICA

• Review unit grammar
• Practice communication skills

STANDARDS

1.2 Understand the language
1.3 Present information

INSTRUCTIONAL STRATEGIES

• Model how to review grammar.
• Have the students review the Learning Outcomes in the unit opener to assess whether they feel they have mastered the main ideas and skills.
• Ask them if they can remember additional examples for each grammar topic.
• Model how to find and go back to the appropriate page in the unit to review any grammar topic they may need help with.
• Invite students to review the grammar activities they completed in this unit.
• Ask them what grammar activities they found easy and which they found challenging. Encourage them to rework any activities they found particularly challenging.
• Have students write and perform mini-skits with the target expressions in **Pedir y dar consejos** from the vocabulary summary and incorporate the grammar reviewed here.

AHORA COMPRUEBA

OBJECTIVES FOR AHORA COMPRUEBA

- Review and recycle grammar, vocabulary and culture from the last two units
- Complete self-assessment

CORE RESOURCES

- Audio Program: Tracks 33 and 34

STANDARDS

1.2 Understand the language

4.1 Compare languages

INSTRUCTIONAL STRATEGIES

To introduce the theme, ask students what sections they would include in a monthly magazine at their school. Encourage students to think back to the content presented in the previous units.

Activity 1

- As a warm-up, tell students to react to the following: **Un famoso director de cine ha aceptado ser entrevistado para la revista de la escuela pero todavía no les puedo decir quién es.** Prompt as needed to elicit reactions of surprise, incredulity, and curiosity. Record student responses on the board.
- Have students match the responses in the activity.

Activity 2

- Have students select the appropriate response.
- As a follow-up, ask students to provide additional reactions and turn back to the section in the unit where these were presented.

Activity 3

In this activity students practice with **por** and **para** plus the uses of all past tenses including the pluperfect.

ANSWERS

Activity 1

1. b; **2.** c; **3.** a.

Activity 2

a. 3; **b.** 1; **c.** 2.

Activity 3

había regresado; para; para; conocí; conoció; han ganado; filmé; recibí; por; había ganado.

SLOWER-PACED LEARNERS

Have students make a list of the learning objectives noted in the opening spreads of the two previous units. Tell them to ask themselves: *How well can I do this: very well, well, or not well?* Then pair students who can't do an objective well with another student who can; that way, they can teach each other what they know and help each other review.

ADVANCED LEARNERS

For those students who have a good handle on the vocabulary, grammar, and cultural content of the units, encourage them to focus on the development of their listening, speaking, reading, and writing skills prior to quizzes and tests. Challenge them to spend thirty minutes a night for four nights before the assessment focusing on one of each of the four skills each night. In addition to redoing the skills-based activities within the units, encourage them to seek new, related (and fun) material online to help them practice.

AHORA COMPRUEBA

LA REVISTA DE LA ESCUELA

Los estudiantes de la escuela han decidido crear su propia revista. En ella incluirán entrevistas, una sección de consejos, se hablará de cine, teatro y literatura, o se informará de los últimos talleres o actividades impartidas en el centro.

1 Relaciona los comentarios de algunos estudiantes sobre la nueva revista con lo que expresan.

1. Cuenta, cuenta, ¿de quién ha sido la idea de crear la revista?
2. ¡Qué fuerte! ¿Has visto? ¡Entrevistan a la directora de cine Anamar Orson!
3. ¡Imposible! ¡Anamar Orson entrevistada por estudiantes de la escuela!

a. Incredulidad.
b. Interés y curiosidad.
c. Sorpresa.

2 Contesta a los comentarios de otros estudiantes con un comentario de la actividad anterior.

a. Cuando me dijeron que los creadores de la revista habían hablado personalmente con ella, me sorprendí muchísimo. Lo primero que dije al escucharlo fue:

b. Cuando estaba desayunando en la cafetería con Lucía, escuchamos a Dani contar que unos alumnos le habían propuesto a Paco, el profe de Literatura, crear una revista para la escuela, y en ese momento yo le interrumpí:

c. Ayer en la puerta de la escuela estaban repartiendo ejemplares del primer número de la revista. Agarré uno y solo ver la portada ¡me quedé alucinada!, ¡no me lo podía creer! ¿Cómo lo habían conseguido? Así que fui corriendo a buscar a Carla y le dije:

3 Algunos estudiantes han hablado con Anamar Orson. Lee parte de la entrevista y elige la forma correcta de los verbos y las preposiciones: *por* o *para*.

Entrevistador: Pero, entonces, Anamar, ¿usted y el actor Cristian Pascual se conocen desde hace mucho tiempo?

Anamar Orson: Sí, somos viejos amigos. Nos conocemos desde el 99, yo **regresé / había regresado** a España **por / para** hacer un curso **por / para** enseñar español y fue entonces cuando **conocí / había conocido** a Cristian.

E.: Y fue en esa misma época cuando **conoció / había conocido** también a Paco, nuestro profesor de Literatura, ¿no?

A.O.: Efectivamente.

E.: Por lo que sabemos, sus trabajos **han ganado / habían ganado** un total de tres premios cinematográficos.

A.O.: Sí, así es. En el año 2005 **filmé / he filmado** mi primera película y **recibí / había recibido** dos premios Goya. Pero este no fue mi primer premio **para / por** mi trabajo en el cine. Dos años antes **había ganado / ha ganado** la Concha de Oro del Festival de San Sebastián al mejor corto español.

140

4 🎧 **33** Escucha los comentarios relacionados con la nueva revista de la escuela y escribe su número al lado del consejo o recomendación correspondiente.

a. ☐ ¿Por qué no hablas sinceramente con ellos? Seguro que te entenderán.

b. ☐ ¿Y si le pedimos una suya? Es tan maja que seguro que nos da alguna.

c. ☐ Deberías organizarte, estudiar un poco todos los días y hacerte resúmenes y esquemas, porque si lo dejas todo para antes del examen, te agobiarás más.

d. ☐ ¿Por qué no echas un vistazo a las sugerencias para el finde de la revista? Proponen un montón de planes alternativos: desde rutas turísticas por la ciudad, hasta intercambios de idiomas, excursiones a la sierra… Seguro que encuentras algo interesante.

e. ☐ No te preocupes, tu problema tiene solución. Es evidente que te esfuerzas, pero creo que no estás dando los pasos acertados. Yo en tu lugar buscaría un profesor particular.

f. ☐ Eso se llama pánico escénico. Yo que tú intentaría aprender algunas técnicas de relajación y centraría mis esfuerzos en prepararme bien el guion.

5 🎧 **34** Escucha los diálogos completos y comprueba las respuestas de la actividad anterior.

6 Lee los siguientes consejos o recomendaciones extraídos de la revista. Después, relaciónalos con el texto correspondiente.

1. ¿Por qué no haces el siguiente test de compatibilidad?
2. Yo que tú esperaría un poco más y aclararía antes mis ideas.
3. Deberías contactar con la gente del lugar a pesar del miedo.
4. Trata de alcanzar una velocidad de cuatro a nueve kilómetros por hora.

a. ☐ Imaginemos que viajas para hacer un curso de español a España. Aterrizas y te das cuenta de que todos tus miedos son reales. Te cuesta entender a la gente, entras en pánico y tomas el camino fácil: te juntas con personas de tu país de origen y hablas todo el tiempo tu lengua materna. ¡¡¡Error!!!

b. ☐ ¡Sorpresa! Maxi Castro, nuestro actor favorito, se está dejando de nuevo el pelo largo, eso ya lo veíamos venir, ¿verdad? Pero lo que no sabíamos es que se volvería a dejar el pelo como en sus inicios. Si quieres saber si eres compatible con Maxi,…

c. ☐ Caminata rápida. Este ejercicio es uno de los más recomendables. El único equipo necesario es calzado cómodo y un camino. Alarga el paso y ve a un ritmo bastante rápido.

d. ☐ Querida Alicia: Sé que estás pasando por un mal momento y que tal vez piensas que ese muchacho es el apoyo que necesitas, pero ahora mismo no te conviene empezar una relación.

7 La nueva revista de la escuela aún está en periodo de pruebas. Sus creadores necesitan buscarle un título y algunas sugerencias de los alumnos. Escribe una carta a la revista y:

a. propón un título para esta;

b. da algunas sugerencias y recomendaciones sobre sus contenidos;

c. pide algún consejo;

d. envía una receta de cocina para su próximo concurso de recetas.

INSTRUCTIONAL STRATEGIES

🎧 33 Activity 4

- To introduce the listening activity and in keeping with the theme about creating a school magazine, tell students that they are going to listen to excerpts of students talking about their school magazine either as part of the editorial team that put the publication together, the students in charge of the advice section, or students reading the magazine.
- Have students read through the statements and ask them to think about which might be the logical context for each.
- Play the audio. Students will have the opportunity to confirm their answers in the next activity.

Audioscript

1. He suspendido otra vez Matemáticas…, no sé cómo voy a aprobar esta asignatura, estudio un montón pero es que soy muy malo para los números.
2. ¡Qué horror! ¡¡¡Esta fotografía queda fatal!!! Se la ve desde muy lejos y borrosa, casi no se reconoce que es ella.
3. No sé qué hacer… Por un lado, quiero seguir con la tradición familiar de ser médico y no quitarles la ilusión a mis padres, pero por otro pienso que es mi futuro lo que está en juego y que a mí lo que me apasiona es el periodismo.
4. Estoy aburrida de hacer siempre lo mismo el fin de semana: o película o discoteca. ¿Es que a nadie se le ocurre algún plan más interesante?
5. Nunca conseguiré que me seleccionen para el papel, cuando estoy en el escenario se me olvida todo y no me salen ni las palabras.
6. No sé qué hacer para aprobar Historia: es demasiada información y no retengo nada.

🎧 34 Activity 5

- Here students will have the opportunity listen to the entire conversations for each of the statements in Activity 4.
- Play the audio and have students confirm their answers.

See audioscript on page APP8

Activity 6
Students may work in pairs or individually.

Activity 7

- Remind students that the letter they are composing is directed to the students on the editorial team of the magazine so they should choose their approach accordingly.
- Tell students that they must address all four points.

ANSWERS

Activity 4
a. 3; **b.** 2; **c.** 6; **d.** 4; **e.** 1; **f.** 5.

Activity 6
a. 3; **b.** 1; **c.** 4; **d.** 2.

HERITAGE LANGUAGE LEARNERS

For students who already have a base of the language, challenge them to put themselves in the position of the teacher prior to assessments. How would they teach a non-native speaker the content of the previous two units? Have them develop worksheets, activities, games, presentations, and lesson plans that could be used to teach other students the material. By putting students in this new role, they will enhance their own knowledge and become masters of the content.

OBJECTIVES FOR UNIT OPENER

- Introduce unit theme: *¡Ojalá!* about expressing wishes and emotional reactions to events
- Introduce culture for unit: Learn about opportunities for volunteering in Hispanic countries

STANDARDS

1.1 Engage in conversation

2.1 Practices and culture

INSTRUCTIONAL STRATEGIES

- Before students open their books, write **Tareas solidarias** on the board. Elicit a definition and examples. If students struggle to understand or contribute, consider giving them examples of two different actions, one that exemplifies volunteer work and one that doesn't. Have them guess which one is an example of a **tarea solidaria**. Then ask them for more examples of their own.
- Have students open their books. Focus their attention on the photo. Invite them to share things they see or notice. You can prompt them to provide simple and obvious statements as well, such as: **Hay cuatro personas**, **Son amigos**, **Están sonriendo**, **Llevan guantes y tienen bolsas de plástico**, etc.
- Have students work individually to write answers to the three questions on the page.
- Put students into pairs to share and discuss their answers.
- Call on volunteers to report back on their responses and discussions.
- Help students formulate their ideas using **Van a recoger basura**, **Creo que están en su comunidad o cerca de su escuela**, **Sí, he participado en una campaña solidaria, he cocinado para personas sin hogar**.

HERITAGE LANGUAGE LEARNERS

Have students prepare a list of adjectives, nouns, and verbs related to voluntary work, such as **generoso/a, gratificante/a, construir, limpiar, enseñar, cocinar, profesor/a, tutor/a, jardinero**, etc. Have students dictate the words to the class. If students don't come up with enough words, encourage them to think of professions, activities, and people they have seen doing voluntary work.

UNIDAD 5 ¡OJALÁ!

Cuatro amigos comparten su tiempo realizando tareas solidarias.

≫ ¿Qué van a hacer los muchachos?

≫ ¿Dónde crees que están desarrollando su tarea?

≫ ¿Has participado alguna vez en campañas solidarias? ¿Qué has hecho?

142

ADDITIONAL UNIT RESOURCES

Extension Activities (EA) (Photocopiable)

EA: 5.1, 5.2, 5.3

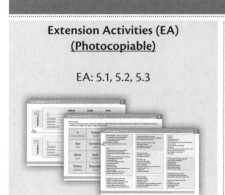

Interactive Whiteboard Lessons (IWB)

IWB: 5.1, 5.2, 5.3, 5.4

Audio

🎧 35 to 41

Video

Diálogo 5

Online ELEteca

EXTENSIÓN DIGITAL

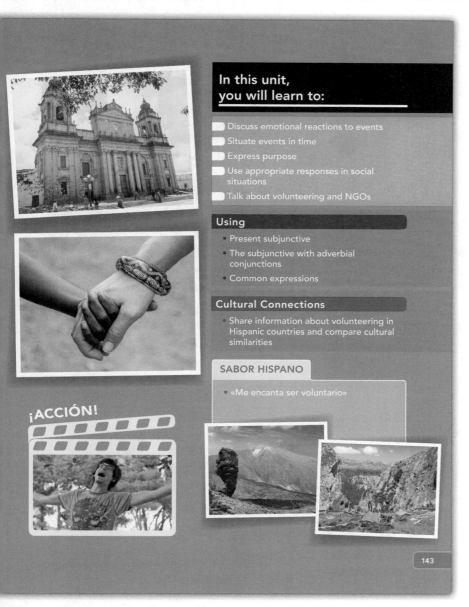

In this unit, you will learn to:

- Discuss emotional reactions to events
- Situate events in time
- Express purpose
- Use appropriate responses in social situations
- Talk about volunteering and NGOs

Using

- Present subjunctive
- The subjunctive with adverbial conjunctions
- Common expressions

Cultural Connections

- Share information about volunteering in Hispanic countries and compare cultural similarities

SABOR HISPANO

- «Me encanta ser voluntario»

¡ACCIÓN!

143

LEARNING OUTCOMES

- Discuss emotional reactions to events
- Situate events in time
- Express purpose
- Use appropriate responses in social situations
- Talk about volunteering and NGOs

INSTRUCTIONAL STRATEGIES

- Use the unit opener to preview vocabulary and cultural topics for this unit.
- Have students look at the images on this page and try to relate them to the objectives listed.
- Exploit the two main photos a bit further: **Miren la foto del edificio: ¿En qué país creen que está? ¿Por qué? ¿Qué tipo de edificio creen que es?** (It's a church in the Plaza de la Constitución in Guatemala City). **Miren la foto de las dos manos: ¿Quiénes son? ¿Cuál es su historia? ¿Cómo se sienten cuando ven esta foto?**
- Invite students to read the topic for **Sabor hispano** and preview that section in the unit. Ask questions, such as: **¿Te gusta ser voluntario? ¿Por qué?**
- Ask students to anticipate what they think the episode for **¡Acción!** will be about.

SLOWER-PACED LEARNERS

Have students write down the words dictated by their heritage language classmates and the sentences dictated by the advanced learners. Encourage them to ask for clarification if they do not understand a word or sentence.

ADVANCED LEARNERS

Have students write down the words dictated by their heritage language classmates and ask them to write a sentence using at least at least two of the words. Have them dictate their sentences to the class.

THREE MODES OF COMMUNICATION: UNIT 5			
	INTERPERSONAL	**INTERPRETIVE**	**PRESENTATIONAL**
HABLAMOS DE...	6	1, 2, 3, 4, 5	6
COMUNICA	4, 7	1, 2, 3, 5, 6	3
¡ACCIÓN!		1, 2, 3, 4	
PALABRA POR PALABRA	1, 9	1, 2, 3, 4, 5, 6, 7, 8	
GRAMÁTICA	3, 6, 8	1, 2, 4, 5, 7	6, 8
DESTREZAS		1, 3	2, 4
CULTURA		SABOR HISPANO	
RELATO		1, 2, 3, 4	5

OBJECTIVES FOR HABLAMOS DE...

- Understand language in context
- Preview vocabulary: Expressing wishes
- Preview grammatical structures: The present subjunctive
- Read and listen to a conversation between Paula and Irene about their summer plans

CORE RESOURCES

- Audio Program: Track 35

STANDARDS

1.2 Understand the language
1.3 Present the language

INSTRUCTIONAL STRATEGIES

Activity 1

- Have students look at the illustrations. Ask: **¿Qué tipo de relación creen que tienen los personajes de las imágenes?** Discuss their ideas until they reach agreement. Guide them to the conclusion that the first scene is between a father and his son, and the second scene is between an ill, older man and his neighbor.
- Put students into pairs to ask and answer the questions.
- Call on volunteers to report back. You might to challenge student responses to encourage discussion.

Activity 2

- Working in the same pairs as Activity 1, have students match the speech bubbles to the correct scene.
- Go over the answers as a class and ask for student volunteers to present.
- Once the answers are reviewed, ask students: **¿En qué situación se utiliza la expresión "¡Que aproveche!"?** (se dice antes de empezar a comer o cuando ves a alguien que está comiendo). You can also point out to students that these are phrases and expressions that people use frequently to express wishes and social courtesies. Tell students to note that these expressions use a new form of the verb that they are going to learn in this unit: the present subjunctive.

🎧 35 Activity 3

- Have students close their books. Tell the students that they are going to listen to a phone call between two friends, Paula and Irene. Write two question on the board to focus their attention on the first listening: **¿Por qué llamó Irene a Paula? ¿Qué va a hacer Paula este verano?**
- Play the audio. Call on volunteers to offer answers to the target questions.
- Have students open their books. Tell them they are going to listen again to determine whether the sentences are true or false.

ANSWERS

Activity 1

Escena 1: Lo está acostando; **Escena 2:** Estar un poco enfermo.

Activity 2

Escena 1: ¡Que duermas bien! **Escena 2:** ¡Que se mejore!

Activity 3

a. F; **b.** F; **c.** T; **d.** T; **e.** T; **f.** F; **g.** F.

HABLAMOS DE... Expresar deseos

Escena 1

Hasta mañana, papi.

¿Cómo está hoy, don Eduardo?

Un poco pachucho... me duele la cabeza y tengo mucha tos...

Escena 2

1 👥 Observa las imágenes, contesta las preguntas y justifica tu respuesta. Trabaja con tu compañero/a.

Escena 1: ¿El padre está acostado o despertando al niño?
Escena 2: ¿Pachucho es un tipo de enfermedad o significa "estar un poco enfermo"?

2 👥 Lee las siguientes expresiones y, con tu compañero/a, completa los bocadillos de las imágenes anteriores con dos de ellas.

a. ¡Que se mejore!
b. ¡Que tengas suerte!
c. ¡Que aproveche!
d. ¡Que duermas bien!

3 🎧 **35** Escucha la conversación y marca verdadero (V) o falso (F).

	V	F
a. Paula va a Guatemala a un colegio que han construido allí.	☐	☐
b. Va a estar en Guatemala dos semanas en julio.	☐	☐
c. Va a hacer un curso para aprender a convivir y trabajar en equipo.	☐	☐
d. Quiere dormir durante el viaje en avión.	☐	☐
e. Irene le desea buena suerte en su viaje.	☐	☐
f. El viaje de Paula es unos días después de terminar las clases.	☐	☐
g. Paula le contará muchas cosas a Irene desde Guatemala.	☐	☐

144

ADVANCED LEARNERS

Students may ask why in expressions such as **¡Que te mejores!** and **¡Que duermas bien!** the word **que** doesn't have an accent mark. Point out that these sentences really shortened ways of saying something like **Deseo que te mejores**, and for that reason no accent mark is necessary on **que**. **Deseo** is implied and left off the sentence.

HERITAGE LANGUAGE LEARNERS

Point out that **pachucho** is a colloquial word used in Spain. Have students brainstorm other words that they may use to express they are not feeling well: **indispuesto/a**, **mareado/a**, **debilitado/a**, **griposo/a**, **fastidiado/a**, etc.

4 Lee la conversación y comprueba tus respuestas.

Irene: ¡Hola, Paula! Oye, ¿has hablado ya con Ana? Es que esta mañana me ha dicho que (a) quiere que vayamos este verano a la casa que tienen sus tíos en la Costa Brava y que si queremos podemos pasar todo el mes de julio allí. Ellos ya no van nunca y la casa está vacía.

Paula: Sí, precisamente te llamo por eso. Es que me han ofrecido la posibilidad de ir a Guatemala para ayudar a construir un colegio. Así que yo no podré ir con ustedes.

I.: ¡Qué me dices! Eso es estupendo, Paula. ¿Y vas tú sola?

P.: Bueno, voy a través de una ONG que se llama *Ayuda en Acción*. La verdad es que no conozco mucho a la gente pero, (b) antes de irnos, nos van a dar un curso durante dos semanas para saber lo que tenemos que hacer allí, conocer la situación, su cultura… y también para que nos conozcamos entre nosotros. ¡Vamos a estar un mes conviviendo y trabajando! (c) Espero llevarme bien con todos.

I.: Ya verás como sí. ¿Y cuándo te vas?

P.: (d) En cuanto terminemos las clases. De hecho, el avión sale el mismo día por la noche. ¡Ay, Irene! Son doce horas de avión y ¡odio

volar *(to fly)*! ¡(e) Ojalá me quede dormida pronto en el avión!

I.: ¡Uf! ¡Doce horas! Bueno, tú llévate el libro que nos ha recomendado el profesor de Filosofía y seguro que te duermes enseguida. Yo lo intenté empezar el otro día pero, en cuanto lo abrí, me quedé dormida *(fell asleep)*. Oye, ahora en serio, me parece genial tu idea de ir a Guatemala, creo que va a ser toda una experiencia y (f) te deseo de todo corazón que te vaya muy bien y (g) ojalá tu esfuerzo sirva para que esos niños puedan vivir mejor.

P.: Muchas gracias. Ya te contaré (h) cuando vuelva. ¡Ah! y yo también (i) espero que se lo pasen muy bien en la Costa Brava. Dense un bañito en la playa por mí.

I.: ¡Eso seguro! Pero, bueno, nos veremos (j) antes de que te vayas para despedirnos, ¿no?

P.: ¡Claro! ¡Faltaría más!

5 Clasifica las expresiones marcadas en la conversación anterior.

Alguien expresa un deseo para otra persona	Alguien desea algo para sí mismo	Se habla del futuro
a,		

6 Dos compañeros/as y tú han decidido ir de voluntarios a un proyecto en América Latina. Elige un país y el tipo de proyecto: social, educativo o medioambiental. Usa las siguientes expresiones para presentar tu plan a la clase.

- antes de irnos…
- mientras estemos…
- después de estar…
- esperamos…
- deseamos…
- ojalá…

145

Activity 4

- Have students read the conversation individually. Monitor their progress and assist with vocabulary as needed.
- Then put students into pairs and have them check their answers to Activity 3 with a partner. Encourage them to use the transcript to correct any mistakes.
- Go over the answers as a class. Once again, point out the new form of the verb and ask students if they recognize the form (same as **usted** command) and if they can begin to figure out when it is used.

Activity 5

- Working individually or in pairs, have the students sort the highlighted expressions from the transcript into the correct categories. The first one has been done for them.
- After reviewing the answers, ask students what sentences a, g, h, j have in common with d, i, k (they all use the subjunctive form of the verb). Explain that these are some of the functions that they're going to be focusing on in this unit.

Activity 6

- Put students into small groups. Write categories on the board: **País** and **Proyecto**. Elicit examples of different countries in Latin America and possible volunteer projects. Write a few examples on the board under the appropriate categories.
- Give students two minutes to decide in their groups on the country and project they want to focus on. Monitor their progress and assist as needed.
- Focus students' attention back on the board. Add the categories: **antes de irnos**, **mientras estemos**, **después de estar**. Ask students to think of things that they would need or want to do before, during, and after the project. Take note of their ideas on the board under the appropriate categories and ask if these actions refer to the present, past, or future (future).
- Then, write the category **deseamos**, **esperamos**, **ojalá** on the board. Continue eliciting examples of wishes or aspirations related to the volunteer project. Take notes on the board using infinitive expressions. For example, **Deseamos ayudar a los niños**, etc. For now, tell students to try to use the new verb form after **ojalá**. Provide some examples, **Ojalá que ayude a mucha gente**, **Ojalá que tenga una experiencia inolvidable**, etc.
- Give students five minutes to use their notes and the expressions in the book to write their own sentences for their presentation. Suggest that they divide up responsibilities so each person in the group writes a few sentences and prepares to share them. Monitor their progress and assist as needed, especially with the writing of sentences that might require the subjunctive.
- Finally, have each group present their volunteer project to the rest of the class.

Activity 5

Alguien expresa un deseo para otra persona: a, g, h, j; Alguien desea algo para sí mismo: c, e; Se habla del futuro: b, d, i, k; Se habla del pasado: f.

Eliminate **ojalá** from the prompts in Activity 6. Remind students to use **ir a + infinitivo** or the future tense to talk about plans and intentions.

OBJECTIVES FOR COMUNICA

• Present communicative functions of the unit:
  – Expressing the moment when an action takes place
  – Expressing purpose or objective
  – Expressing wishes and desires
  – Other expressions of wishes and social responses

CORE RESOURCES

• Interactive Whiteboard Lesson: IWB 5.1, 5.2
• Audio Program: Track 36 and 37
• Interactive Online Materials - ELEteca

STANDARDS

1.1	Engage in conversation	3.2	Acquire information
1.2	Understand the language	4.1	Compare languages

INSTRUCTIONAL STRATEGIES FOR EXPRESSING THE MOMENT WHEN AN ACTION TAKES PLACE

• To introduce the topic, project IWB 5.1, **Cuando...** and go over it as a class.
• Have students look at the images. Call on volunteers to read the sentences in number 1, and match them with the appropriate images. Ask students to think about when the actions take place as you review answers.
• Then tell students to match each of the sentences in number 1 with the correct time periods in number 2.
• Use the answers from number 2 to elicit the correct formulas in number 3. Encourage them to write the formulas in the chart in their notebooks for future reference. Then have students open their books, and walk them through the examples.
• Note that the examples **Antes de que** and **Después de que** are not modeled in the category for **pasado** because they require the past/imperfect subjunctive (**Salí antes de que / después de que cenaras**), which students haven't studied yet.

🎧 36 Activity 1

• Have students work on their own to complete the conversation with the phrases in the box.
• Play the audio to allow them to go over their answers. Ask if they need any clarification; offer to play the audio again, if necessary.
• Put the students in pairs, and have them practice the conversations. Have them practice both roles.

ANSWERS

IWB 5.1

Futuro: *Cuando* + verbo en subjuntivo: Cuando llegue a la portería, no lo dudaré, chutaré y meteré un gol (Imagen 3); **Pasado:** *Cuando* + verbo en indicativo: Cuando llegué a la portería, no lo dudé, chuté y metí el gol (Imagen 1); **Acción habitual:** *Cuando* + verbo en indicativo: Qué suerte, yo cuando llego a la portería, me pongo tan nervioso que no consigo ni chutar (Imagen 2).

COMUNICA

EXPRESSING THE MOMENT WHEN AN ACTION TAKES PLACE

■ Para relacionar dos acciones en el **futuro**:

Al llegar a casa, **cenaré**. *Upon arriving home, I will have dinner.*
Cuando / En cuanto llegue a casa, **cenaré**. *When / As soon as I get home, I will have dinner.*
Saldré antes de / después de cenar. *I'll leave before / after having dinner.*
Saldré antes de que / después de que vengan mis padres. *I'll leave before / after my parents come.*
Veré la tele hasta que cene. *I'll watch TV until I have dinner.*

■ Para hablar de verdades universales o **hábitos**:

Al llegar a casa, **hago** la tarea. *Upon arriving home, I do my homework.*
Cuando / En cuanto llego a casa, **hago** la tarea. *When / As soon as I get home, I do my homework.*
Siempre hago la tarea antes de / después de salir de clase. *I always do my homework before / after getting home.*
A veces escucho música hasta que llego a casa. *Sometimes I listen to music until I get home.*

1 🎧 36 **Completa las conversaciones con una expresión del cuadro. Luego, escucha el audio y comprueba.**

> al ○ después de ○ en cuanto ○ hasta que

» ¡Que tengas buen viaje, cariño! ¡No te olvides de llamarme (a) .... llegar al hotel!
» Descuida. Te llamaré (b) .... llegue.
» Eso espero, porque la última vez no me llamaste.
» ¡Cómo que no! Sí te llamé.
» Sí, me llamaste, pero tres días (c) .... llegar.
» No, también te llamé antes, pero no contestaste. De todas formas, no te preocupes, esta vez no dejaré de llamarte (d) .... me contestes.

EXPRESSING PURPOSE OR OBJECTIVE

2 **Lee los usos de *para* y *para que*. Después, busca más ejemplos de cada caso en la conversación de la página 145.**

■ Para expresar la finalidad (*purpose*) o el motivo por el que se hace algo se usa **para** o **para que**.

• **Para** + infinitivo ➡ Si los dos sujetos (*subjects*) de la oración son los mismos, o uno de los dos no está especificado.

(Yo) he hecho muchas fotos **para** (yo) **colgarlas** en Facebook.
(a) ....

• **Para que** + subjuntivo ➡ Si hay sujetos diferentes.

(Yo) he traído las fotos de las vacaciones **para que** (tú) las **veas**.
(b) ....

146

---

a. al; **b.** en cuanto; **c.** después de; **d.** hasta que.

INSTRUCTIONAL STRATEGIES FOR EXPRESSING PURPOSE OR OBJECTIVE

Activity 2

• Walk students through the explanations and examples on the page.
• Have students find examples of **para** and **para que** from the conversation on page 145 to complete the chart.
• In preparation for the next activity, elicit the subjunctive conjugations of the forms of **ver**. Do the same with an –**ar** verb, such as **hablar**. Ask what they notice about the endings for the –**er** verb versus the –**ar** verb..

Extension

• For additional practice, project 5.2, **¿Para qué...?**
• Put students into pairs to discuss their ideas for each scene. Have them write down their descriptions so they are prepared to share them with the class.

EXPRESSING WISHES AND DESIRES

3 👥 **Estos son los deseos de diferentes alumnos. ¿Cuáles compartes? ¿Tienes otros deseos? Habla con tu compañero/a.**

- **Ojalá** que algún día dejen de existir los exámenes.
- Este año **espero** no recibir menos de C en ninguna asignatura.
- El año que viene **quiero** ir a España a estudiar español.
- **Deseo** que mis amigos me hagan una fiesta sorpresa para mi cumpleaños.
- **Espero** que este curso no sea tan difícil como nos han contado.
- **Deseo** hacer un safari por África.

⚠️ The expression **ojalá** comes from an Arabic expression meaning "God (Allah)" and is used as the equivalent of "I hope that, let's hope that". It may be used with or without **que**.

4 👥 **Mira de nuevo las expresiones marcadas en la Actividad 4 y completa con** *desear, esperar, infinitivo, querer* **y** *subjuntivo*.

(a)		verbo en (d) .... (si el sujeto de las dos acciones es el mismo).
(b)	+	**(Yo) Quiero (yo) ir mañana** a la playa.
(c)		**que** + verbo en (e) .... (si el sujeto de las dos acciones es diferente).
		(Yo) Quiero que (tú) me compres un helado.

OTHER EXPRESSIONS AND SOCIAL RESPONSES

5 🎧 37 **Escucha las conversaciones y completa.**

- A alguien que se va a dormir.
  Que duermas bien. (a) ....
- A alguien que va a empezar a comer o está comiendo. (b) ....
- A alguien que tiene un examen o una entrevista de trabajo.
  Que tengas suerte. (c) ....
- A alguien que está enfermo.
  Que te mejores.

- A alguien que va a hacer algo divertido.
  Que disfrutes. (d) ....
  Que (te) lo pases bien.
- A alguien que ha tenido una mala noticia. (e) ....
- A alguien que ha tenido una buena noticia.
  Enhorabuena. (f) ....
- A alguien que se va por mucho tiempo. (g) ....

6 👥 **En parejas, y por turnos, responde a lo que te dice tu compañero/a.**

Estudiante 1

Dices:
1. ¡Ana / Juan y yo nos casamos!
2. Me voy a dormir.
3. Esta noche voy a un concierto.

Estudiante 2

Dices:
1. El partido va a comenzar.
2. ¡Van a quitar los exámenes!
3. Me voy a estudiar al extranjero seis meses.

 MORE IN ELETECA: EXTRA ONLINE PRACTICE

⬅ **Previous Page**

- Call on volunteers to offer their descriptions for each picture. Ask questions such as **¿Para qué ha llamado por teléfono?** (**Para preguntarle qué tal está**) to encourage students to offer different examples with **para** and **para que**. Help students self-correct, if necessary.

ANSWERS

IWB 5.2

Possible answers might include the following: **a.** La muchacha le llama por teléfono para preguntarle cómo está; **b.** Anima a su amigo para que sople las velas; **c.** Quedaron para comer juntas; **d.** Mira al cielo para ver si llueve; **e.** Va a la estación para despedirse

y para que tengan buen viaje; **f.** Se acercan a los novios para desearles que sean muy felices; **g.** Van al centro para pasear un rato; **h.** Le compraron una colección de libros de su autora favorita para que los lea este verano.

Activity 2

a. Es que me han ofrecido la posibilidad de ir a Guatemala para ayudar a construir un colegio; nos van a dar un curso durante dos semanas para saber lo que tenemos que hacer allí...; nos veremos antes de que te vayas para despedirnos...; **b.** también para que nos conozcamos entre nosotros; ojalá tu esfuerzo sirva para que esos niños puedan vivir mejor.

FOR EXPRESSING WISHES AND DESIRES

Activity 3

- Read the first sentence and focus students' attention on **ojalá** and the language note. Call on students to read the remaining sentences to discuss any vocabulary.
- Then individually, have students select the ones that are true for them.
- Take a class poll for each wish on the list. Have students give a thumbs up for each wish they selected. Discuss which ones are the most popular.

Activity 4

- Put students into pairs to complete the chart. Remind students to use the examples in Activity 3 to get them started and then, to focus on what happens to the rest of the sentence after these verbs.
- Have student pairs compare their answers with another pair.

ANSWERS

Activity 4

a. Querer; **b.** Esperar; **c.** Desear; **d.** infinitivo; **e.** subjuntivo.

INSTRUCTIONAL STRATEGIES FOR OTHER EXPRESSIONS AND SOCIAL RESPONSES

🎧 37 **Activity 5**

- Explain to the students that they are going to listen to a series of conversations. Each conversation contains an expression appropriate to the social context presented. Give them a few minutes to skim the different contexts presented.
- Play the audio and repeat as necessary. Have students compare their answer with a partner. Confirm the correct responses as a class.

See audioscript on page APP9

Activity 6

- Tell student pairs to first choose a role and then read the sentence on the card to elicit an appropriate response from their partner.
- To correct the activity together assign half the class to **Estudiante 1** and the other to **Estudiante 2**. One student from the first group says one of the sentences to one of the students in the other group, who responds appropriately and continues in the same way choosing to whom he/she directs the comments until all responses are reviewed.

ANSWERS

Activity 5

a. Querer; **b.** Esperar; **c.** Desear; **d.** infinitivo; **e.** subjuntivo.

Activity 6

a. Que descanses; **b.** Que aproveche; **c.** Que te vaya bien; **d.** Que te diviertas; **e.** Lo siento mucho; **f.** Felicidades; **g.** Cuídate.

OBJECTIVES FOR ¡ACCIÓN!

- Provide students with a structured approach to viewing the video
- Contextualize the content of the unit in a familiar scenario

CORE RESOURCES

- Unit Video 5 - Casting en Somalia
- Online Materials - ELEteca

STANDARDS

1.3 Interpersonal communication

1.2 Interpretive communication

2.1 Culture: Practices and perspectives

INSTRUCTIONAL STRATEGIES

Previewing: Antes del video

Activity 1

- Have students write responses to the questions on their own. Challenge them to write full sentences. Point out that for Image 6 they will be writing a question, not an answer.
- Then put them in pairs to discuss their ideas. Encourage them not to read their responses to each other but to make eye contact and speak more freely and naturally with each other.

Activity 2

If it seems like not many students have acting experiences to share or discuss, you may want to conduct this activity as a class rather than in pairs.

Viewing: Durante el video

Activities 3 and 4

- Point out that both Activities 3 and 4 relate to the first clip that you will show. While watching it, tell students to focus their attention on the main events so they can summarize them afterward in Activity 3. Encourage them to take notes to help them remember. You may want to give students a chance to read over the sentences and options in Activity 4 before playing the clip as well. That way, they'll be better prepared for what they might see and hear.
- Play the clip while students watch and take notes. Then given them time to write their descriptions and select the correct options. Play the clip again, if necessary.
- Go over the answers as a class.

ANSWERS

Activity 4

1. c; **2.** b; **3.** b.

SLOWER-PACED LEARNERS

Rather than writing responses individually and discussing answers in pairs in Activity 1, you can ask and answer these questions as a class so they can benefit from the ideas of others and you can guide the discussion.

¡ACCIÓN! Casting en Somalia

1. 2. 3.
4. 5. 6.

ANTES DEL VIDEO

1 Observa las imágenes y responde a las preguntas. Usa tu imaginación sobre lo que crees que puede ocurrir. Después, compara tus respuestas con las de tu compañero/a.

Imagen 1. ¿Dónde se desarrolla el episodio?

Imagen 2. ¿De qué crees que están hablando Juanjo y Alfonso en esta imagen?

Imagen 3. ¿Cómo describirías el estado de ánimo de Juanjo en esta escena?

Imagen 4. ¿Qué crees que hace Juanjo en esta imagen?

Imagen 5. ¿Le gusta a Alfonso lo que está viendo?

Imagen 6. Escribe una pregunta para hacer a tu compañero/a sobre esta imagen. ....

2 ¿Alguna vez has actuado o participado en alguna obra? Cuéntaselo a tu compañero/a.

DURANTE EL VIDEO

3 00:30 - 01:40 Describe con tus propias palabras qué ocurre en esta secuencia.

....

....

....

4 Elige las opciones correctas para describir la escena.

1. Han llamado a Juanjo para que...	2. Tiene que prepararse para...
a. done dinero.	a. hacer un examen.
b. venda cursos *online*.	b. hacer un *casting*.
c. haga un prueba para un comercial.	c. hacer una película.

148

3. **Están haciendo una campaña por televisión para...**

  a. buscar personas desaparecidas.
  b. buscar voluntarios.
  c. cantar en televisión.

5 🎞 01:40 - 03:25   **Observa esta secuencia. Escribe el consejo que Alfonso le da a Juanjo para actuar mejor. Escribe otros dos consejos más para él, incluyendo un adjetivo diferente en cada caso.**

Es importante que ....
Es .... que ....
Es .... que ....

6 👥 **Observa cómo Juanjo expresa un deseo en la misma escena y escríbelo. Después, comenta con tu compañero/a cuál es tu deseo imposible.**

....

7 🎞 03:25 - 06:15   **Termina de ver el episodio hasta el final. Luego, señala las palabras que están relacionadas con el mundo de las ONG.**

☐ audición	☐ proyectos	☐ hospital	☐ memorizar
☐ solidario	☐ viaje	☐ colegios	☐ ensayar
☐ guion	☐ nativo	☐ alojamiento	☐ voluntario
☐ comercio justo	☐ ¡acción!	☐ humanitaria	☐ campaña

8 👥 **¿Tienes marcadas las mismas palabras que tu compañero/a? Comparen y expliquen las que tengan diferentes.**

DESPUÉS DEL VIDEO

9 👥 **Comenta con tu compañero/a si crees que finalmente Juanjo tendrá éxito en la audición y explica por qué.**

10 👥 **Escribe brevemente las ventajas y desventajas de participar en un proyecto con una ONG y debatan en clase sobre si es productivo ser solidario.**

Ventajas	Desventajas

🖥 **MORE IN ELETECA:** EXTRA ONLINE PRACTICE

circumstance and based on his performance in the video. Steer them in the right direction without getting into detailed explanations about the forms of the subjunctive. (They'll learn more later in **Gramática**; this is meant to be a preview and to familiarize them with more contexts in which the subjunctive is used.)

• Call on volunteers to share their advice. Gently correct them while keeping the focus on the content of their suggestions as opposed to the grammar at this stage.

• Finally, have students write their own wishes in Activity 6. You may want to have them imagine what they would wish for if they were in Juanjo's shoes and mock up an example of something else he might say. Have them share their wishes with a partner.

Activity 7

• Explain or remind students of the meaning of ONG (**Organización no gubernamental**), and elicit examples of such organizations. (Note that the topic and examples will be explored in more detail in **Palabra por palabra**). Tell them that there are several possible answers for this activity and that their answers may vary. Point out that they will discuss and defend their choices in the next activity.

• Play the remainder of the video while students note the words they hear and any others that relate to the topic.

• As a follow-up and to check their overall comprehension, you may want to ask them some of your own questions about the details of the script for the commercial and the conclusion of the video.

Activity 8

Encourage students to discuss, debate, justify their choices and work together to brainstorm other words that relate to ONGs. You may want to allow them access to bilingual dictionaries to expand their lists of related vocabulary.

Post-viewing: Después del video
Activity 9

To explain their answers, students can refer to specific moments in the video or what they know about Juanjo from past videos. They might also draw conclusions based on their own knowledge and experiences of acting auditions.

Activity 10

Put students in groups to discuss their ideas. Challenge them to rank them. Then elicit their ideas and create a class list.

ANSWERS
Activity 5

Es importante que pronuncies bien.

Activity 6

Ojalá me den el papel.

Activity 7

solidario, comercio justo, proyectos, nativo, hospital, humanitaria, voluntario.

ADVANCED LEARNERS

Have students make their own commercials for an ONG. Tell them that they can use some of the ideas from the script that Juanjo is practicing or come up with their own ideas.

HERITAGE LANGUAGE LEARNERS

After preparing their lists in Activity 10, have students expand upon the ideas in the form of an essay.

INSTRUCTIONAL STRATEGIES
Activities 5 and 6

• The point of the next two activities is to have students notice the use of the subjunctive in context. Before completing these activities, though, you may want to have students watch the next clip for gist and general comprehension first. Ask: **¿Cómo va la práctica? ¿Qué opina Alfonso de la interpretación de Juanjo? ¿Qué opinas tú?**

• Tell students that you are going to play the same clip again. This time they should listen for two particular expressions: one is a piece of advice from Alfonso using the structure **Es + adjetivo + que**; the other is wish expressed by Juanjo using **Ojalá**.

• Play the clip while students listen for and jot down the expressions. Afterward, review the advice Alfonso gives Juanjo and the wish that Juanjo expresses.

• Then move on to the creative portions of the two activities. To complete their own advice for Juanjo, first brainstorm or provide them with a list of adjectives that could be used with **Es + adjetivo + que** structure to give advice, such as **necesario**, **menester**, **esencial**, **imprescindible**, etc. Encourage students to be creative and consider what additional advice they would give to Juanjo in his

OBJECTIVES FOR LAS ONG

- Present vocabulary needed to practice communicative and grammatical functions for the unit: Non-governmental organizations or NGOs
- Identify and discuss different causes for which people often volunteer

CORE RESOURCES

- Interactive Whiteboard Lesson: IWB 5.3
- Interactive Online Materials - ELEteca

STANDARDS

1.2 Understand the language
3.1 Knowledge of other disciplines

INSTRUCTIONAL STRATEGIES

Activity 1

- Before students open their books, project IWB 5.3, **Las ONG**. Hide the phrases beneath the images. Look at the images one at a time.
- Ask students to describe what they see. Ask questions, such as: **¿Dónde están? ¿Qué están haciendo? ¿Cuál es el problema? ¿Qué tienen todos en común?**

Activity 2

- Review the first item with the class. Put students into pairs and have them work together on the remaining items.
- Project IWB 5.3, **Las ONG** again to review answers as a class. Check their understanding of the phrases by asking for definitions or additional examples.

Activity 3

- Take a class poll to find out how many students recognize each organization.
- Elicit basic explanations of what each organization does.
- Give examples of different scenarios and see if they can correctly identify which of the three organizations helps in each situation.

Activity 4

Put students into pairs. Tell them to read statements about the Red Cross. Have them work together to decide if the statements are true or false based on what they may already know about this organization. Tell them to guess if they are unsure of the answers. Do not review answers until you review Activity 5.

Review noun-adjective agreement using the words in Activity 2. Help students realize that **voluntario** may function as both and adjective and a noun.

ADVANCED LEARNERS

For extra practice, have students say or write sentences using the vocabulary in Activity 2.

PALABRA POR PALABRA Las ONG y el voluntariado

1 Observa las siguientes imágenes y describe lo que están haciendo las personas. ¿Qué tienen todos en común?

2 Con tu compañero/a, relaciona las imágenes de la Actividad 1 con las siguientes expresiones. ¡Atención! A cada expresión le corresponde más de una letra o imagen. Después, haz una lista de otras expresiones que sepas en español referentes a las ONG (Organizaciones No-Gubernamentales).

1. catástrofes naturales ➡ ...a....
2. conflictos bélicos (armed) ➡ ....
3. labores humanitarias ➡ ....
4. protección del medioambiente ➡ ....
5. comercio justo ➡ ....
6. donativo ➡ ....
7. voluntario ➡ ....
8. labor social ➡ ....

3 Observa estos logotipos. ¿Sabes a qué pertenecen?

4 Decide si las siguientes afirmaciones sobre la Cruz Roja son verdaderas (V) o falsas (F). Compara tus respuestas con tu compañero/a.

	V	F
a. La Cruz Roja nació después de un viaje de su fundador por los países del tercer mundo.	☐	☐
b. La Cruz Roja es una organización que atiende a personas de todo el planeta.	☐	☐
c. La mayoría de los países dan parte de su Producto Interior Bruto o PIB (Gross Domestic Producto or GDP) a las ONG para ayudarlas a financiarse.	☐	☐
d. Las personas que trabajan en las ONG son todas voluntarias.	☐	☐

HERITAGE LANGUAGE LEARNERS

Have students talk about one of the topics in Activity 2 without saying what it is. They can use definitions, examples, or synonyms. The other members of the group guess the target word or phrase. To make it more competitive, students can earn points for each correct guess.

5 Lee el siguiente texto y comprueba tus respuestas de la Actividad 4.

Las siglas ONG significan **Organización No Gubernamental**. La primera ONG que se conoce como tal es la Cruz Roja, que fue fundada en 1864 por el suizo (Swiss) Henry Dunant. El 8 de mayo de 1859, Dunant, que era un hombre de negocios, se encontraba en el norte de Italia. Allí fue testigo de una cruel batalla y de cómo las víctimas quedaban desatendidas en medio de las calles. Fueron las mujeres de los pueblos cercanos quienes se hacían cargo de aquellos pobres hombres.

Le impactó tanto aquella experiencia que pensó en la necesidad de crear organizaciones, **sin ánimo de lucro** e independientes de poderes (power) políticos e ideologías, para atender a las víctimas en los **conflictos bélicos** o en caso de **catástrofes naturales**. Así nació la Cruz Roja Internacional que hoy en día está presente en los cinco continentes.

Desde entonces el número de ONG ha aumentado en todo el mundo y también han ampliado su campo de trabajo. Algunas están enfocadas más a las **labores humanitarias** y otras a la **protección del medioambiente.** La mayoría de países aportan parte de su **PIB** a la **financiación** de las ONG. Otra forma de **recaudar fondos** son las **campañas de sensibilización** para captar socios (partners) o la venta de artículos de **comercio justo**, aunque hay algunas que prefieren, para mantener su libertad, financiarse solo con **donativos**.

La mayoría de personas que trabajan en las ONG son **voluntarios**, es decir, personas que combinan sus responsabilidades diarias, estudios o trabajos con ofrecer una **ayuda desinteresada** a otras personas. Sin embargo, también cuentan con trabajadores asalariados (salaried), ya que, sobre todo (especially) las grandes ONG, requieren de personal cualificado y dedicado a tiempo completo (full time) para su buen funcionamiento.

6 Estos son algunos de los trabajos que realizan las ONG. Relaciona las dos columnas para averiguarlo. ¡Atención! Debes crear un total de 10 frases.

a. Luchar por
b. Luchar en
c. Luchar a favor
d. Luchar contra
e. Trabajar por
f. Ofrecer
g. Organizar

1. ☐ campañas de sensibilización.
2. ☐ la protección del medioambiente.
3. ☐ la explotación infantil.
4. ☐ de los derechos humanos.
5. ☐ actos benéficos para recaudar fondos.
6. ☐ la pobreza.
7. ☐ el comercio justo.
8. ☐ orientación laboral.
9. ☐ la defensa de los animales.
10. ☐ el calentamiento global.

151

INSTRUCTIONAL STRATEGIES

Activity 5

- The goal of this activity is for students to learn vocabulary associated with NGOs in an appropriate context so that they will be able to discuss NGOs and what they do.
- Explain to students that the abbreviation of NGOs in Spanish is **las ONG** (**o-ene-ge**) and that unlike English, acronyms in Spanish are never pluralized. Only the article will indicate number.
- Call on a volunteer to read the first paragraph. Go over the answer to the first question from Activity 4. Have a student correct the false statement.
- Have another volunteer read the second paragraph, and check students' answers to the second questions from Activity 4.
- Continue with another volunteer and the third paragraph. Encourage students to explain their answers and find the related lines in the text.
- Finally, have a volunteer read the fourth paragraph and answer the last question from Activity 4. Have him/her correct the false statement.

Activity 6

- The purpose of this activity is to help students recognize the prepositions that are used with these verbs. You may want to review them first with students. For example: **luchar por** (on behalf of), **luchar en** (in), **luchar a favor** (followed by preposition **de**), **luchar contra** (against), **trabajar por** (on behalf of).
- Have students work individually to match the phrases.
- Monitor their progress and assist as needed.
- Go over the answer as a class.

ANSWERS

Activities 4 and 5

a. F (Surgió después de un viaje a Italia); **b.** T; **c.** T; **d.** F (Aunque la mayoría son voluntarios, las ONG también cuentan con trabajadores asalariados).

Activity 6

1. f, g; **2.** a, e; **3.** d; **4.** c; **5.** g; **6.** d; **7.** a, e; **8.** f; **9.** a, b, c; **10.** d.

SLOWER-PACED LEARNERS

Have students write a sentence for each of the verb phrases in Activity 6. Tell them to vary the tenses and forms they use and to adjust the noun phrases to make them more specific. For example: **Mi prima luchará en defensa de los animales en los tribunales después de graduarse**.

🔖 **Previous Page**

ANSWERS

Activity 1

Todos son voluntarios de distintas ONG.

Activity 2

1. a, d; **2.** b; **3.** b, c; **4.** a, d; **5.** b; **6.** b; **7.** a, b, c, d; **8.** b, c.

Activity 3

a. Unicef (Fondo de Naciones Unidas para la Infancia, encargado de ayudar a los niños y proteger sus derechos); **b.** Cruz Roja (movimiento humanitario mundial, que realiza campañas de ayuda humanitaria, de intervención en casos de desastres, prevención de enfermedades, etc.); **c.** WWF (organización independiente para la conservación de la naturaleza, cuya misión es detener la degradación del ambiente natural del planeta).

INSTRUCTIONAL STRATEGIES

Activity 7

- Go over the instructions and sample answer. Point out that **Países subdesarrollados** are also referred to as **Países en vías de desarrollo**. Then have students continue working individually to sort their sentences from Activity 6 under the correct NGO.
- Monitor their progress and assist as needed. Encourage students to add at least one more action or task in each NGO.

Extension

- Divide the class into groups and assign each group one of the NGOs.
- Have the groups research their NGO on the Internet to determine its main functions, actions, and tasks. Websites: *www.ecologistasenaccion.org; www.redacoge.es; www.globalhumanitaria.org; www.once.es; www.sin-techo.es; www.fundacionmujeres.es.*
- Then put the students into new groups, each person from a different NGO, to share their findings and add to their lists.

Activity 8

- Have three volunteers read each of the volunteer experiences aloud. Ask a comprehension question or two after each description to check students' understanding, for example: ***¿Para qué fue a Malawi Inés? ¿A qué edad se fue allí? ¿Dónde vive Walter? ¿Él piensa que es necesario dedicar mucho tiempo a las tareas solidarias? ¿De dónde es Rocío? ¿Para qué organizan un mercadillo en Sevilla?***
- Put the students into pairs to match the definitions with the correct phrases from the text. Go over the answers as a class.

Activity 9

- Call on a volunteer. Model a conversation based on the questions provided.
- Put students into pairs, and have them take turns asking and answering the questions on the page. Monitor their conversations and assist as needed.
- Call on students to report back on interesting details from their conversations.

ANSWERS

Activity 7

Medioambiente: trabajar por la protección del medioambiente, luchar en defensa de los animales, trabajar por el comercio justo; **Países subdesarrollados:** luchar contra la pobreza, trabajar por el comercio justo, luchar contra la explotación infantil, luchar a favor de los derechos humanos, organizar actos benéficos para recaudar fondos; **Discapacitados:** Organizar campañas de sensibilización, organizar actos benéficos para recaudar fondos, ofrecer orientación laboral; **Personas sin hogar:** luchar a favor de los derechos humanos, organizar campañas de sensibilización de la población, ofrecer orientación laboral, organizar actos benéficos para recaudar fondos; **Inmigrantes:** ofrecer orientación laboral, organizar campañas de sensibilización de la población, luchar contra la pobreza. **Mujeres y niños:** luchar contra la explotación infantil, ofrecer orientación laboral, luchar a favor de los derechos humanos, organizar campañas de sensibilización de la población.

Activity 8

1. c; **2.** a; **3.** b; **4.** f; **5.** d; **6.** e.

PALABRA POR PALABRA Las ONG

7 Estos son algunos colectivos o causas apoyados por las ONG. Clasifica las frases que creaste en la Actividad 6 en el lugar más adecuado. Piensa en otras acciones o tareas que se pueden realizar para estos colectivos o causas.

Medioambiente	Países subdesarrollados	Discapacitados
ECOL**☉**GISTAS Trabajar por la protección del medioambiente,...		**△**ONCE

Personas sin hogar	Inmigrantes	Mujeres y niños
sintecho	acoge	mujeres

8 Lee los testimonios de estos voluntarios y relaciona las expresiones marcadas con su significado.

Inés, 35 años, Malawi
Cuando terminé Arquitectura intenté encontrar trabajo en Colombia, pero no lo conseguí, así que decidí empezar mi carrera profesional como voluntaria en África. Hace 10 años llegué a Malawi para colaborar en la construcción de un hospital y sigo aquí. Lo mejor es que (a) trabajamos codo con codo con la población de aquí. Así, todos aprendemos de todos y esperamos que en el futuro no nos necesiten, porque eso significará que ellos tendrán los medios para (b) salir adelante. Es una manera de tener un (c) trabajo satisfactorio y (d) ser solidario al mismo tiempo.

Walter, 15 años, Buenos Aires
Yo soy voluntario porque quiero que el mundo sea mejor cada día. Todos podemos hacer algo por los demás, no tienen que ser grandes gestos, porque si cada uno (e) pone su granito de arena, al final se pueden hacer cosas muy importantes.

Rocío, 22 años, Sevilla
Cada año organizamos un mercadillo benéfico. La gente trae las cosas que ya no necesita pero que están en buen estado.
Nosotros no ponemos precio, sino que la gente (f) da la voluntad. La verdad es que se recoge bastante dinero.

1. ☐ Realizar un trabajo que te hace feliz.
2. ☐ Realizar un trabajo en colaboración con otra persona.
3. ☐ Superar una situación difícil.
4. ☐ Dar el dinero que tú quieres.
5. ☐ Ser generoso.
6. ☐ Colaborar.

9 Con tu compañero/a, comenta los siguientes temas.
- ¿Qué ONG de tu país conoces?
- ¿Colaboras con alguna ONG o conoces a alguien que lo haga?
- Habla sobre el tipo de trabajo que haces o que hace esa persona.

MORE IN ELETECA: EXTRA ONLINE PRACTICE

HERITAGE LANGUAGE LEARNERS

After discussing the questions in Activity 9, tell students to imagine that they have $100 to donate to an NGO (or divide between multiple NGOs). Working with their partners, have them debate and decide which organizations will get their money. Have them report back using the conditional forms they learned in the previous unit.

GRAMÁTICA

UNIDAD **5**

1. THE PRESENT SUBJUNCTIVE: REGULAR VERBS

- In this unit you have learned to express wishes, hopes, and desires as well as goals for the future using a new form of the verb. This form is called the subjunctive mood. Unlike the indicative, which states facts, the subjunctive describes reality from the point of view of the speaker.

  » *Quiero un helado.* vs. *Quiero que me compres un helado.*
  » *Este curso es muy difícil.* vs. *Espero que este curso no sea muy difícil.*
  » *Cuando llegué a casa, cené.* vs. *Cuando llegue a casa, cenaré.*

- Here are the forms of the present subjunctive.

	–AR HABLAR	–ER COMER	–IR VIVIR
yo	hable	coma	viva
tú	hables	comas	vivas
usted/él/ella	hable	coma	viva
nosotros/as	hablemos	comamos	vivamos
vosotros/as	habléis	comáis	viváis
ustedes/ellos/ellas	hablen	coman	vivan

1 Completa estas frases con infinitivo o subjuntivo.

a. ¡Ojalá que me (llamar) .... Juanjo!
b. Cuando (hablar, tú) .... en español, intenta abrir más la boca.
c. ¡Te quedas sentada a la mesa hasta que te (terminar) .... todo el pescado!
d. Mario y Sara han venido para (presentar) .... su nuevo disco.
e. Susana nos va a explicar una receta muy sencilla para que (aprender, nosotros) .... a hacer paella.
f. Cuando (independizarse, yo) ...., espero que mis amigos (vivir) .... cerca de mí.
g. ¡Que la fuerza te (acompañar) .... !
h. Quiero (cambiar, yo) .... mi número de teléfono.

2 Relaciona las frases de la Actividad 1 con la imagen adecuada. Explica por qué.

153

OBJECTIVES FOR GRAMÁTICA 1

- Present grammatical structures needed to practice communicative functions of the unit: The present subjunctive: regular verbs
- Learn to conjugate regular verbs in the present subjunctive

CORE RESOURCES

- Extension Activities: EA 5.1
- Interactive Online Materials - ELEteca

STANDARDS

1.1 Engage in conversation
1.1 Understand the language
4.1 Compare languages

INSTRUCTIONAL STRATEGIES

1. The Present Subjunctive: Regular Verbs

- Before presenting the grammar, distribute copies of EA 5.1, ***Presente de subjuntivo: verbos regulares***, giving half the class the chart for ***Estudiante A*** and the other half the chart for ***Estudiante B***. The purpose is to have students work out the forms of the subjunctive based on examples they have already seen and patterns they recognize.
- Have students work individually to try to complete their charts.
- Then put students into A/B pairs. Explain that ***Estudiante A*** has the answers to ***Estudiante B***'s chart, and vice versa. Have the students ask each other and answer questions of each other to check their answers.
- Then have students open their books to check their answers. Go over the uses of the present subjunctive and the sample sentences on the page.

Activity 1

- Have students work individually to complete the sentences.
- Go over the answers as a class. Ask students to reflect on the use of the subjunctive in each case (wishes, hopes, and future actions) and why the infinitive is needed in the other cases (no change of subject).

Activity 2

Have students work individually to match the sentences from Activity 2 to the images. Put the students in small groups to compare and explain their answers.

Extension

Have each student write a sentence on a piece of paper using the present subjunctive expressing a wish or hope that students in class can associate with him/her. Collect all the sentences. Read a few of them aloud, and have the class guess which student wrote each one.

ANSWERS

Activity 1

a. llame; **b.** hables; **c.** termines; **d.** presentar; **e.** aprendamos; **f.** me independice, vivan; **g.** acompañe; **h.** cambiar.

Activity 2

1. g; **2.** e; **3.** d; **4.** b; **5.** c; **6.** a; **7.** f; **8.** h.

ADVANCED LEARNERS

Have students find three images from the book and write a sentence about each one. Then students show the pictures and share their sentences with a partner, who has to correctly match them as in Activities 1 and 2.

OBJECTIVES FOR GRAMÁTICA 2

- Present grammatical structures needed to practice communicative functions of the unit: The present subjunctive: irregular verbs
- Learn to conjugate irregular verbs in the present subjunctive.

CORE RESOURCES

- Extension Activities: EA 5.2

STANDARDS

1.1	Engage in conversation	4.1	Compare languages
1.1	Understand the language		

INSTRUCTIONAL STRATEGIES

2. The Present Subjunctive: Irregular Verbs

- Explain that there are three different kinds of irregularities in the present subjunctive:
    1. **Stem-changing verbs.** Almost all verbs that stem change in the **yo** form of the present indicative also stem-change in the present subjunctive in all forms except in *–ar/–er nosotros/vosotros* forms. Note other exceptions such as **dormir** and **morir**.
    2. **Irregular yo form verbs.** Verbs with irregular **yo** forms in the indicative are also irregular in the present subjunctive in all forms.
    3. **Completely irregular.** Some verbs have unique irregular forms in the present subjunctive.
- Go over the charts one at a time, doing Activity 3 after presenting the chart of stem-changing verbs and Activity 4 after presenting the chart of irregular **yo** form verbs.

Stem-changing verbs

Remind students again of the rule: Stem-changing verbs ending in *–ar* and *–er* will stem-change in the present subjunctive in all forms except *nosotros/vosotros*.

Activity 3

- Put students in pairs to complete the chart.
- Monitor their progress and assist as needed.
- Go over the answers as a class, eliciting corrections from other students as needed.

ANSWERS

Activity 3

Entender: entienda, entiendas, entienda, entendamos, entendáis, entiendan;
Encontrar: encuentre, encuentres, encuentre, encontremos, encontréis, encuentren; **Repetir:** repita, repitas, repita, repitamos, repitáis, repitan.

INSTRUCTIONAL STRATEGIES

Stem-changing –ir verbs and dormir / morir

- For stem-changing verbs ending in *–ir*, it may be simpler to have students remember the forms of **dormir** and **morir** then to explain the type of stem-change that occurs as there are very few *–ir* verbs students are likely to use in the present subjunctive form that stem-change *e* ➡ *ie* (and that would therefore change to only *i* in the *nosotros/vosotros* forms.) For example: *preferir* ➡ *prefiera*, *prefiramos*.

Irregular yo form verbs

- Remind students again of the general rule for forming the present subjunctive form: Begin with the **yo** form of the present indicative, drop the **o** and switch to the opposite endings. In this way, verbs with irregular **yo** forms will also have irregular forms in the present subjunctive.

GRAMÁTICA

2. THE PRESENT SUBJUNCTIVE: IRREGULAR VERBS

- Almost all **irregular verbs** in the present indicative are also irregular in the present subjunctive.

Stem-changing verbs

	QUERER	VOLVER	JUGAR	PEDIR
	e ➡ ie	o ➡ ue	u ➡ ue	e ➡ i (en todas las personas)
yo	quiera	vuelva	juegue	pida
tú	quieras	vuelvas	juegues	pidas
usted/él/ella	quiera	vuelva	juegue	pida
nosotros/as	queramos	volvamos	juguemos	pidamos
vosotros/as	queráis	volváis	juguéis	pidáis
ustedes/ellos/ellas	quieran	vuelvan	jueguen	pidan

3 Conjuga en presente de subjuntivo los siguientes verbos irregulares.

ENTENDER	ENCONTRAR	REPETIR

- The verbs **dormir** and **morir** have two stem changes in the present subjunctive: o ➡ ue and o ➡ u as follows:

	DORMIR	MORIR
yo	duerma	muera
tú	duermas	mueras
usted/él/ella	duerma	muera
nosotros/as	durmamos	muramos
vosotros/as	durmáis	muráis
ustedes/ellos/ellas	duerman	mueran

Irregular yo form verbs

- The present subjunctive of verbs with irregular **yo** forms is as follows:

TENER	SALIR	TRAER
tenga	salga	traiga
tengas	salgas	traigas
tenga	salga	traiga
tengamos	salgamos	traigamos
tengáis	salgáis	traigáis
tengan	salgan	traigan

SLOWER-PACED LEARNERS

Have students create flashcards for the irregular subjunctive verb forms, assigning each students a different verb or two. Then collect and shuffle the cards. Put students in pairs, and give each pair a batch of cards to practice together. Swap the batches between pairs for continued practice.

HERITAGE LANGUAGE LEARNERS

Before going over the irregular forms in the book, see if you can elicit them from the class. Then challenge students to use the irregular subjunctive forms in a sentence. Review the contexts in which the present subjunctive is used.

4 Conjuga en presente de subjuntivo los siguientes verbos irregulares en la primera persona del presente de indicativo.

PONER	DECIR	CONSTRUIR

■ The following verbs have irregular subjunctive forms:

HABER	IR	SABER	ESTAR	SER	VER	DAR
haya	vaya	sepa	esté	sea	vea	dé
hayas	vayas	sepas	estés	seas	veas	des
haya	vaya	sepa	esté	sea	vea	dé
hayamos	vayamos	sepamos	estemos	seamos	veamos	demos
hayáis	vayáis	sepáis	estéis	seáis	veáis	deis
hayan	vayan	sepan	estén	sean	vean	den

5 Lee esta conversación entre Beatriz y Luis e identifica los verbos en presente de subjuntivo.

Beatriz: Toma, Luis, aquí tienes algunas cosas para el mercadillo benéfico. Oye, ¿cuándo es?
Luis: Es el sábado que viene.
Beatriz: ¿Estás bien preparado?
Luis: Sí, espero que la gente compre de todo para que podamos recaudar los fondos necesarios para la Cruz Roja.
Beatriz: ¿Quieres que te ayude con algo más?
Luis: No, gracias. Solo deseo que todos colaboren con su tiempo o con donativos.
Beatriz: Pues, que tengas suerte.
Luis: Gracias. Ya te contaré cuando te vea.

155

INSTRUCTIONAL STRATEGIES

Activity 4
- Put students in pairs to complete the chart.
- Monitor their progress and assist as needed.
- Go over the answers as a class, eliciting corrections from other students as needed.

Completely irregular verbs
Tell students that these are the last category of irregular verbs in the present subjunctive. Point out that as in most other forms, these verbs are irregular here too.

Extension

After reviewing the charts, put students in groups of three and distribute a copy of EA 5.2, **Tres en raya** to each group. Explain that they will take turns choosing a square and correctly conjugating the verb in the present subjunctive form. If the conjugation is correct, they write their name in the square. The first person to get three squares in a row correct, wins.

Activity 5
Have students read the conversation and identify the verbs in the present subjunctive form. Then have them confirm their answers with a partner and practice the dialogue together.

ANSWERS

Activity 4
Poner: ponga, pongas, ponga, pongamos, pongáis, pongan; **Decir:** diga, digas, diga, digamos, digáis, digan; **Construir:** construya, construyas, construya, construyamos, construyáis, construyan.

Activity 5
compre, podamos, ayude colaboren, tengas, vea.

ADVANCED LEARNERS

Working in pairs, have students use the dialogue in Activity 5 as a variation of their own version of a similar conversation about a different NGO-based activity or fundraising benefit. Then have them present the conversations to the class.

INSTRUCTIONAL STRATEGIES

Activity 6

- Looking back at the present subjunctive verbs they found in the previous activity, have students determine whether they are regular or irregular with a partner. Then have them analyze the structure of each sentence that necessitated the use of the present subjunctive and add it to the chart, as in the **Modelo**. Finally, have students indicate the correct function of each use of the subjunctive.

Activity 7

- Elicit the rest of the first sentence from the class and write it on the board. Have students complete the rest of the sentences individually before comparing answers with a partner.

Activity 8

- Have students work individually to complete the sentences with their own ideas.
- Put students into small groups to share and compare their ideas.
- Have groups report back on any interesting aspects of their discussions.

Activity 9

- Have students work individually to complete the sentences.
- Monitor their progress and assist as needed.
- Put the students in pairs to share their sentences.
- Go over the answers as a class. Then ask a series of comprehension questions about the story to switch the focus from the grammar to the content.

ANSWERS

Activity 6

a. Espero que + verbo en subjuntivo: Expresa deseos / esperanzas; **b.** para que + verbo en subjuntivo: Expresa finalidad; **c.** Quieres que + verbo en subjuntivo: Expresa deseos / esperanzas; **d.** Deseo que + verbo en subjuntivo: Expresa deseos/esperanzas; **e.** Que + verbo en subjuntivo: Expresa deseos / esperanzas; **f.** Cuando + verbo en subjuntivo: Relaciona dos acciones en el futuro.

Activity 7

a. Beatriz espera que Luis esté contento; **b.** Luis desea que Beatriz vaya al mercadillo; **c.** Ojalá que la gente sea generosa; **d.** Esperamos que el sábado no llueva. / Esperamos que no llueva el sábado; **e.** Luis quiere que vengan muchas personas al mercadillo; **f.** Ojalá que Luis organice más actividades benéficas en el futuro.

Activity 8

Answers will vary but should all include correct present subjunctive forms.

Activity 9

a. sea; **b.** sepa; **c.** compres; **d.** den; **e.** pongan; **f.** llamen; **g.** digan; **h.** haga; **i.** crezcas; **j.** viva; **k.** duermas; **l.** sueñes.

SLOWER-PACED LEARNERS

For additional oral practice, have students record themselves telling the story in Activity 9 outside of class.

HERITAGE LANGUAGE LEARNERS

Have students write a summary of the story in Activity 9 in their own words.

GRAMÁTICA

6 👥 Comenta con tu compañero/a si son regulares o irregulares los verbos que anotaron en Actividad 5. Después, escribe las estructuras en las que se encuentran estos verbos e indica su función.

	Expresa deseos / esperanzas	Expresa finalidad (purpose)	Relaciona dos acciones en el futuro
a. Modelo: Espero que + verbo en subjuntivo			
b.			
c.			
d.			
e.			

7 Transforma estas frases.

a. **Luis está contento.** Beatriz espera que Luis…
b. **Beatriz irá al mercadillo.** Luis desea que Beatriz…
c. **La gente es generosa.** Ojalá que…
d. **El sábado no lloverá.** Esperamos que…
e. **Muchas personas vendrán al mercadillo.** Luis quiere que…
f. **Luis organizará más actividades benéficas en el futuro.** Ojalá que…

8 👥 Completa las frases con tus propias ideas. Luego, en grupos pequeños, túrnense para compartir su información. ¿Tuvieron todos respuestas similares?

a Cuando tenga 20 años…
b. Quiero que mis padres me compren…
c. Ojalá que mañana…
d. Mi profesor espera que yo…
e. Cuando mis amigos se van de vacaciones les digo que…
f. Pienso vivir en casa hasta que…
g. Cuando seamos mayores,…

9 Completa la historia de *Antoñito el fantasioso* con los verbos entre paréntesis.

Antoñito era un niño que se pasaba el día soñando.

– Cuando (a) ....(ser) mayor, me iré a vivir a Australia –decía siempre.
– Sí, te irás a Australia, pero tendrás que saber inglés –le respondía su madre.
– Bueno, estudiaré y cuando (b) ....(saber, yo) hablarlo bien, me iré. Por cierto, mamá, quiero que me (c) ....(comprar, tú) un buen diccionario, que me hará falta. Ojalá me (d) ....(dar) una beca (*scholarship*) para ir a estudiar a Australia… –pensaba siempre Antoñito–. Eso sí, espero que no me (e) ....(poner, los profesores) tantas

tareas como aquí y que no (f) ....(llamar) a mi madre y le (g) ....(decir) que no estoy estudiando mucho. ¡Ay! pronto…! –suspiraba Antoñito–. ¡Ojalá me (h) ....(hacer) mayor

Los padres de Antoñito, que ya sabían que a su hijo le encantaba construir castillos en el aire, le decían:

– Sí, Antoñito, pero tú, hasta que no (i) ....(crecer, tú), estudia, hijo, estudia…

Antes de dormir, Antoñito le preguntaba a su madre:

– Mamá, cuando (j) ....(vivir, yo) en Australia, vendrás a verme, ¿no?

– Sí, hijo, sí, buenas noches, que (k) ....(dormir) bien y que (l) ....(soñar) con los angelitos, perdón, con los canguritos –se corregía su madre.

Lo curioso es que hoy Antoñito es uno de los principales importadores de café en Australia, porque, aunque no siempre es bueno construir castillos en el aire, también es verdad que quien quiere, puede.

10 **Piensa en tus objetivos para el futuro. Compártelos con tu compañero/a y pregúntale por los suyos.**

Modelo: Cuando termine los estudios en la secundaria, iré a estudiar a una universidad fuera de mi ciudad. Cuando esté en la universidad, estudiaré Periodismo. Cuando termine Periodismo, me haré corresponsal y cuando…

11 **Contesta a lo que te pregunte tu compañero/a.**

Estudiante 1
Dices:
a. "Soy el genio de la lámpara maravillosa: pide tres deseos y te serán concedidos".
b. Te vas de vacaciones dentro de una semana, ¿qué quieres hacer?
c. Imagina que es fin de año. ¿Qué deseos pides para el año que empieza?
d. ¿Qué le pides al muchacho/a ideal?
e. Piensa en ti dentro de quince años. ¿Qué le pides a la vida?

Estudiante 2
Dices:
a. Estás en una isla desierta y al parecer el resto del mundo se ha olvidado de ti. ¿Qué desearías?
b. Se acerca tu cumpleaños, ¿cuáles son tus deseos?
c. Imagina que vas a conocer al presidente de tu país, ¿qué le pides?
d. Mañana empieza el curso y tenéis nuevo profesor de español. ¿Cómo quieres que sea?
e. ¿Qué le pides a la ciudad ideal?

 MORE IN ELETECA: EXTRA ONLINE PRACTICE   GRAMMAR TUTORIALS 9 AND 10   157

Activity 10

- Review the instructions and read the model aloud. Give students some time to jot down notes about their own goals for the future.
- Then put students into pairs. Tell them to listen closely to what their partners say, because they will be asked to report back (orally or in writing) about their partner's goals to the rest of the class. Encourage students to take notes.
- Monitor their conversations and assist as needed.
- Either call on students to orally relay their partner's goals or have them submit them to you in writing. If the students write their summaries, read them to the class, and have students guess whose goals they are.

Activity 11

Put students into pairs. Have them choose who is **Estudiante 1** and who is **Estudiante 2**. Explain that they are going to take turns reading the statements on their cards, and their partners are going to respond appropriately using the present subjunctive. Model a conversation with a volunteer.

Extension

- Have students write down three wishes for themselves, e.g. **Deseo aprobar esta asignatura.**
- Then have them pass those wishes to another classmate. That classmate must respond to each wish, e.g. **Espero que apruebes esta asignatura.**
- Have the students return their papers to the original writers and check or correct the usage of the present subjunctive.

ANSWERS

Activities 10 and 11

Answers will vary but should all include correct present subjunctive forms.

ADVANCED LEARNERS

Have students swap their paragraphs from Activity 10 with a partner. Have them rewrite each other's material, converting the perspective from the **yo** form to the **él / ella** form.

OBJECTIVES FOR DESTREZAS

- Develop writing skills by learning how to use a chart to organize information
- Learn strategies for writing an email

CORE RESOURCES

- Interactive Whiteboard Lesson: IWB 5.4

STANDARDS

1.3   Present information
5.1   Spanish in the community

INSTRUCTIONAL STRATEGIES

Expresión e interacción escritas (1)

Activity 1

- Review the instructions and **Destrezas** box aloud.
- Point out that the categories in the chart were generated from the survey below. Have students find the corresponding questions or sections in the survey. Explain that *motivos* refers to reasons why they are traveling to Ecuador and why they like to travel in general.
- Give students time to complete the chart with a few of their own details related to each category. Encourage them to use notes, not sentences, at this stage.
- Monitor their progress and assist as needed.

Activity 2

- Read (or have a student read) the instructions and the situation. Explain that students are going to use their notes to complete the survey.
- Have students work individually to complete the survey.
- Put students into pairs to interview each other so they can share and compare their responses.

Extension

- For additional practice with the survey or just for fun, have students answer the questions imagining that they are a famous person.
- Then put students into pairs to interview each other once again, but this time they should not reveal their fictitious names. The partners need to guess who they are based on their responses to the questions.

DESTREZAS

EXPRESIÓN E INTERACCIÓN ESCRITAS (1)

1 En esta actividad vas a completar una encuesta. Antes de empezar, repasa la estrategia en **Destrezas** y sigue las recomendaciones.

Destrezas

Using a personal chart

Create a chart to organize your personal information. Review the form and identify major categories of information you will need to provide. Decide which categories require more thought and preparation. Select those to include in your chart.

Categoría	Detalles
trabajo	
estudios	
tiempo libre (aficiones, deporte, viajes)	
motivos	

2 Lee la siguiente situación y completa la tarea asignada.

Acabas de llegar a Guayaquil, Ecuador, y has ido a la oficina de turismo de la ciudad para solicitar información. Antes de marcharte, la dirección te pide que rellenes este formulario para un estudio que están haciendo sobre las características de los jóvenes turistas de la ciudad.

OFICINA DE TURISMO DE GUAYAQUIL

1. DATOS PERSONALES
NOMBRE: ....
APELLIDO(S): ....
NACIONALIDAD: ....
EDAD: ....
SEXO: [V] [M]
DOMICILIO: ....
¿CON QUIÉN VIVES?: ....
TELÉFONO: ....
CORREO ELECTRÓNICO: ....

2. TRABAJO/ESTUDIOS
¿ESTUDIA O TRABAJA? ¿QUÉ ESTUDIA O EN QUÉ CONSISTE SU TRABAJO?
....
....

3. OCIO
¿QUÉ HACE NORMALMENTE EN SU TIEMPO LIBRE?

¿SUELE VIAJAR MUCHO? ¿POR QUÉ? ¿CON QUÉ FRECUENCIA?

¿CUÁLES SON SUS AFICIONES? ¿PRACTICA ALGÚN DEPORTE?

LUGARES QUE LE GUSTARÍA CONOCER:
....
....

UNIDAD 5

EXPRESIÓN E INTERACCIÓN ESCRITAS (2)

3 Antes de empezar a escribir, repasa la estrategia en Destrezas y sigue las recomendaciones.

Destrezas

Strategies for writing an email

a. Keep in mind that 10 words are generally 1 sentence. Do not count the opening or the greeting as a sentence.

b. Divide the sentences by the number of topics you are required to write about -in this case, 5. Now you know how to organize your writing.

c. Choose the opening: formal (*Estimado/a...*) or informal (*Querido/a..., Hola, Juan...*).

d. The conditional tense also expresses courtesy. Use it!

e. Choose the greeting: formal (*Reciba un cordial saludo, Me despido de usted*), or informal (*Cuídate mucho, Un abrazo, Hasta pronto*).

4 Escribe un email de entre 80 y 100 palabras de acuerdo con esta situación.

Escribe a un amigo ecuatoriano para invitarle a pasar un fin de semana en tu ciudad. Explícale qué cosas van a hacer, qué van a visitar, cómo es la ciudad y qué tiempo hace. Dile también cómo esperas que sea el fin de semana.

PRONUNCIACIÓN Los diptongos e hiatos: acentuación

■ In addition to representing their own vowel sounds, the letters **i** and **u** may also represent glides, which are brief, weak sounds that combine with a vowel to form a single syllable (**diptongo**):
• *nue-vo, sie-te, vein-te, gua-po, eu-ro.*
In these cases, remember to follow the rules for written accents in general:
• *ha-céis, can-ción, pen-sáis, des-pués, cuí-da-lo.*

■ However, the letters **i** and **u** are not always glides when next to other vowels. When they are vowels and not glides, a written accent mark is used (**hiato**):
• *dí-a, rí-o, pa-ís, Ra-úl.*

1 🎧 **38** Escucha el audio y escribe las palabras que oyes.

2 🎧 **38** Escucha de nuevo las palabras que escribiste en la Actividad 1. Después, sepáralas por sílabas.

3 Clasifica las palabras que tienen diptongos o hiatos y coloca las tildes donde sea necesario.

Diptongos:
Hiatos:

MORE IN ELETECA: EXTRA ONLINE PRACTICE

159

INSTRUCTIONAL STRATEGIES

Expresión e interacción escritas (2)

Activity 3

• Have students think about how they organize their email messages. Elicit the parts of an email from students. Project IWB 5.4, **Querido/a** to give them a visual example of the form of an email message. Elicit alternative phrases or sentences they might use in each of the parts on display.

• Call on a student to read the instructions and the strategies in the book. Elicit an example of a sentence with the conditional tense to confirm their understanding. Quickly review the form, if necessary.

Activity 4

• Encourage students to use the organizational chart in Activity 1 with the pertinent categories to organize their email. Have them number their notes and the chart categories so they can determine the best order and necessary number of paragraphs for their email.

• After they've written their first drafts, have students exchange papers and correct each other's work.

OBJECTIVES FOR PRONUNCIACIÓN

• Practice the correct pronunciation of diphthongs and hiatuses

CORE RESOURCES

• Audio Program: Track 38
• Interactive Online Materials - ELEteca

STANDARDS

1.2 Understand the language   4.1 Compare languages

INSTRUCTIONAL STRATEGIES

• Walk students through the notes and examples on the page. Focus their attention on the use of accent marks when *i* and *u* do not combine with other vowel sounds.

• Elicit one or two more examples of Spanish words with two consecutive vowels. Determine as a class whether there is a glide or not between them and whether or not they need an accent.

🎧 **38 Activity 1**

• Tell the students that they are going to listen to a list of words and that they should write the words they hear. Tell them not worry about accent marks at this stage.

• Play the audio and repeat if necessary. Don't write the words on the board just yet. Have students focus their listening.

Audioscript

guion, bonsái, autor, filosofía, huésped, océano, crucial, habláis, veintiún, acuático, raíz, dehesa.

🎧 **38 Activity 2**

Tell the students that this time when they listen they should listen closely to the syllables in each word. Model a few words, clapping to the syllables, so they can understand how to identify them.

Activity 3

• Have students work individually or in pairs to correctly sort and write the words.

ANSWERS

Activity 2

guion, bon-sái, au-tor, fi-lo-so-fí-a, hués-ped, o-cé-a-no, cru-cial, ha-bláis, vein-tiún, a-cuá-ti-co, ra-íz, de-he-sa.

Activity 3

Diptongos: guion, bonsái, autor, huésped, crucial, habláis, veintiún, acuático;
Hiatos: filosofía, océano, raíz, dehesa.

ADVANCED LEARNERS

For additional practice after Activity 4, have students write an email to a teacher from Ecuador, so they can practice the **usted** form as well.

HERITAGE LANGUAGE LEARNERS

For additional practice with writing accent marks, have students look for and make a list of as many *-ia*, *-ía*, *-io*, *-ío* words as possible. Then have them share the file with another student, who will use it for a dictation exercise.

OBJECTIVES FOR SABOR HISPANO

- Learn about a student's gap year experience as a volunteer in Guatemala
- Compare rates of volunteerism in different countries

CORE RESOURCES

- Audio Program: Track 39

STANDARDS

2.1 Practices and perspectives
3.2 Acquire information
4.2 Compare cultures

INSTRUCTIONAL STRATEGIES

 39

- Focus students' attention on the image at the top of the page. Ask where it was taken. Have them guess what they think is happening.
- Then have students look at the picture of Ryan and read the caption and the title of the text. Have them predict what the text is going to be about.
- Put students into pairs. Have them discuss the questions in the **Antes de leer** box. Encourage them to take notes about their partner's responses. Monitor their conversations and assist as needed.
- Have students switch partners and tell their new partners about their previous partner's responses. Monitor their conversations and assist as needed.
- Have students close their books. Tell them you are going to play the audio about Ryan's experience. To focus their listening, ask them to write down three activities that Ryan talks about.
- Play the audio. Then call on volunteers to give examples of Ryan's activities.
- Have students open their books. Play the audio again, this time allowing students to follow along.
- Ask again about the context of the main photo at the top of the page: **¿Qué estaban celebrando?** Have them find the relevant section of the text that reveals the answer.
- Point out the glossary of terms at the bottom of the next page. Have students find and underline those terms in the text.

ADVANCED LEARNERS

If students have lived abroad or have relatives in others countries, invite them to share their experiences and knowledge about volunteer opportunities in those places. Have them discuss the differences between helping strangers versus helping extended family members and neighbors. Which is more common in the US? Which do they think is more common in Spanish-speaking countries? Encourage them to do more research to find out.

HERITAGE LANGUAGE LEARNERS

Have students investigate opportunities to become a volunteer with Spanish speakers in their own community or in a Spanish-speaking country. Have them choose one opportunity, and report back to the class about the organization and why they want to volunteer with them.

SABOR HISPANO

«ME ENCANTA SER VOLUNTARIO»

Una alfombra de flores en Antigua, Guatemala

Antes de leer

¿Adónde te gustaría viajar para hacer un voluntariado internacional? ¡Por qué?

¿Qué tipo de tareas te gustaría hacer?

 39 **Cada vez hay más gente joven que prefiere hacer un voluntariado en el extranjero˚ a ir directamente a la universidad. Ryan, un muchacho norteamericano, habla de su experiencia.**

«Ser voluntario es genial. Mi vida cambió completamente después de pasar un mes en Guatemala», dice Ryan, un muchacho norteamericano de 16 años que viajó al país centroamericano en 2013. «Cuando llegué a Antigua, hablaba muy poco español. Pero una familia me recibió en su casa y hablando con ellos mi español mejoró rápidamente», cuenta. «Después de estar un mes con ellos, me siento parte de la familia. Ojalá pueda verlos pronto otra vez».

«Mis tareas en Antigua eran ayudar a construir casas en un barrio nuevo», explica Ryan. «Allí había también otros voluntarios internacionales. Hice amistad con una muchacha española, Ainhoa, que ya está de vuelta en Madrid. Espero que sigamos en contacto por correo electrónico y Skype».

«Como tenía las tardes libres, me invitaron a dar clases de inglés a la escuela del barrio», dice. «Me tocó˚ una clase de muchachos de ocho años y hablamos muchísimo. Me hicieron preguntas sobre la vida en Illinois, donde yo vivo. También me enseñaron trabalenguas˚ en español, ¡aunque son dificilísimos!», cuenta Ryan. «Me gustaría que vinieran a visitarme».

Además de pasar tiempo con los niños, Ryan recorrió˚ las antiguas ciudades mayas y los parques naturales. «También participé en las fiestas de la Semana Santa, haciendo alfombras enormes de aserrín˚ y flores», dice.

Ryan piensa que ser voluntario es genial.

160

UNIDAD 5

Países con más voluntarios

Estos son los países con más voluntarios que vienen de otros países, en millones de personas.

157
115
52
45
34
27
21

■ India ■ Nigeria
■ EE.UU. ■ Filipinas
■ Indonesia ■ México
■ China

Países solidarios

Existe un *ranking* que mide la cantidad de gente en un país que ayudó a un desconocido durante los últimos 30 días. Estos son los países con la gente más solidaria, en porcentaje de la población.

77%
73%
72%
70%
68%
67%
67%

■ EE.UU. ■ Senegal
□ Qatar ■ Camerún
■ Libia ■ Nueva Zelanda
■ Colombia

Los mexicanos son los latinoamericanos que más voluntariados hacen.

¿COMPRENDISTE?

Decide si las siguientes afirmaciones son verdaderas (V) o falsas (F).

1. Se pueden hacer voluntariados en todo el mundo.   V◯ F◯
2. El país latino con más voluntarios es México.   V◯ F◯
3. Ryan es un muchacho de EE.UU. que habla de las cooperativas.   V◯ F◯
4. Ryan visitó Nicaragua y México.   V◯ F◯
5. Según estadísticas recientes, Colombia es un país solidario.   V◯ F◯

En Colombia, la mayoría de las personas ayudaría a un desconocido.

AHORA TÚ

¿Qué opinas? Contesta las siguientes preguntas y comenta tus ideas con tus compañeros/as.

1. ¿Qué tipos de voluntariado te imaginas que pueden ser interesantes? ¿Por qué?
2. ¿A qué país latinoamericano te gustaría viajar para hacer de voluntario?
3. ¿Qué actividades piensas que forman parte de un voluntariado?
4. ¿Crees que estos programas son realmente beneficiosos para las comunidades donde se llevan a cabo? ¿Por qué?
5. ¿Cuáles crees que son las ventajas y desventajas de un voluntariado? ¿Por qué?

Glosario

el aserrín – sawdust
el extranjero – abroad
llevarse a cabo – to take place
mejorar – to improve
recorrer – to tour
tocar – to be given
el trabalenguas – tongue-twister

VOCES LATINAS ▶
POLÍTICA EN CHILE Y ARGENTINA

Fuentes: Cooperatour, *Lonely Planet*, World Giving Index.

161

Países con más voluntarios

- Call on a volunteer to read the title and description of the chart.
- Ask a question or two to check students' understanding of the chart information, such as: **¿Cuál es el país de Latinoamérica con más voluntarios?**
- Have students write down two questions of their own about the chart and pass them forward. Hold on to them for a moment.

Países solidarios

- Call on a volunteer to read the title and description of the chart.
- Ask a question or two to check students' understanding of the chart information, such as: **¿Qué porcentaje de la población de Camerún ha ayudado a un desconocido durante los últimos 30 días?**
- Have students write down two questions of their own about the chart and pass them forward. Hold on to them for a moment.
- Put students into small groups. Mix up the questions and pass them out the different groups. Have students work together to answer the questions on their papers.

¿Comprendiste?

- Have students work individually to answer the questions.
- Monitor their progress and assist as needed.
- Go over the answers as a class. Have them explain the false answers.

Ahora tú

- Have students work individually to answer the questions.
- Monitor their progress and assist as needed.
- Put students into pairs. Have them take turns asking each other the questions and responding with their written answer. Encourage students to ask follow-up questions for more information.
- Ask each pair to report back to the class on something interesting from their conversation.

ANSWERS

¿Comprendiste?

1. T; 2. T; 3. F; 4. F; 5. T.

SLOWER-PACED LEARNERS

Have students find statistics related to volunteers or volunteer work in the US. Tell them to make a graph or chart that effectively displays that information and present it to the class.

OBJECTIVES FOR RELATO

- Revisit unit themes, grammar, vocabulary and culture in a new context
- Improve reading comprehension skills

CORE RESOURCES

- Audio program: Tracks 40 and 41
- Extension Activities: EA 5.3

STANDARDS

1.2 Understand the language   1.3 Present the language
5.2 Using the language for personal enjoyment and enrichment

INSTRUCTIONAL STRATEGIES

Activity 1

- Before reading the text, write **Pablo Neruda** on the board. Find out what students may already know about him. (You may choose to consult *http://www.neruda.uchile.cl* to find out more information for yourself). Tell them you are going to read about him. Perhaps go over the meaning of some new vocabulary in the text, such as *cónsul*, *natal*, and *oda*. Finally, pose a simple question or two for students to keep in mind while they read.
- Read the text as a class. Then call on volunteers to answer the simple questions you posed before reading.
- Put students into pairs to answer the four questions at the bottom of the reading. Encourage them to refer back to the text.

🎧 40 Activity 2

- Tell students that they are going to listen to an excerpt of one of Neruda's poems. Before playing the audio, give students a chance to read the statements. Perhaps encourage them to underline key words to listen for to help them determine which statement is correct.
- Play the audio. Then take a class poll as to whether they think the correct statement is **a**, **b**, or **c**.
- Play the audio again. After the second listening, take a class poll again. Have students explain the reasons for their answers.
- Confirm the correct answer, clarifying it, if necessary.

Cultural Note

The first part of the poem evokes the Madrid that Neruda experienced when he arrived in 1935, a Madrid with an intense cultural life favored by the liberal and progressive government of the Second Republic (1931–1936). The second part of the poem (verse 36) talks about how that ideal Madrid disappeared with the outbreak of the war, provoked by the uprising of the National Party (verse 43), led by General Franco, who would use the power to install a dictatorship (1936–1975). The poem makes reference (verse 18) to the Spanish poets Rafael Alberti and Federico García Lorca (already assassinated), both part of the Generation of 27.

ANSWERS

Activity 1

a. Pertenece a sus primeros años; **b.** Por el romanticismo, la melancolía y la influencia del modernismo hispanoamericano de autores como Rubén Darío y Gabriela Mistral; **c.** La Guerra Civil española y el asesinato de Federico García Lorca; **d.** En los objetos más cotidianos y aparentemente insignificantes.

Activity 2

b.

Extension

Copy and cut out the sections of the poem in EA 5.3, *Explico algunas cosas*. Have the students work in groups to put the poem in the correct order. To

---

RELATO Pablo Neruda, Soneto LXXXIX

1 Lee el texto sobre el poeta Pablo Neruda y contesta las preguntas.

Ricardo Eliecer Neftalí Reyes Basoalto (Chile, 1904-1973), más conocido como Pablo Neruda, ha sido uno de los poetas más influyentes en la literatura del siglo XX y así se le reconoció cuando en 1971 ganó el Premio Nobel de Literatura. Su obra es muy variada y extensa. En sus primeros años se caracteriza por el romanticismo y la melancolía, influenciado por el modernismo hispanoamericano de Rubén Darío y de su gran amiga, la poetisa Gabriela Mistral. De esta época es quizá (*possibly*) una de sus obras más famosas: *Veinte poemas de amor y una canción desesperada* (1924).

En 1927 empieza a trabajar como cónsul (*diplomat*). Gracias a esto, viaja por todo el mundo y conoce a los políticos y artistas más importantes de la época, convirtiéndose en un hombre culto y comprometido (*committed*) socialmente. Entre otros, conoce a Federico García Lorca en Buenos Aires, a Picasso en Barcelona y a los autores de la Generación del 27 en Madrid. Al estallar la guerra civil española en 1936, Neruda tiene que regresar a su país natal. Allí, impresionado por la guerra y el asesinato de Federico García Lorca, del que se había hecho muy amigo, escribió su obra *España en el corazón* (1937), un libro de poemas sobre el horror de la guerra y el dolor de las víctimas.

Pero Neruda siguió escribiendo bellos poemas de amor como los recogidos en *Cien sonetos de amor* (1959). Y no solo escribió sobre temas profundos, también los objetos más cotidianos (*everyday*) fueron fuentes (*sources*) de su inspiración. Ejemplo de ello son sus famosas *Odas elementales*: "Oda a la cebolla", "Oda al tomate", "Oda a los calcetines"... Neruda decía que él escribía para gente sencilla, incluso para los que no sabían leer.

a. ¿A qué época de la obra del autor pertenece *Veinte poemas de amor y una canción desesperada*?
b. ¿Por qué se caracteriza dicha época?
c. ¿Qué hechos mueven al autor a escribir *España en el corazón*?
d. ¿En qué se inspiran las *Odas elementales*?

2 🎧 40 Lee parte de un poema de Neruda y di cuál de estas afirmaciones crees que es la correcta.

a. El poema se llama "Oda a Madrid". Neruda primero hace una descripción de Madrid antes y después de la guerra y, más tarde, lo compara con su país natal.
b. El poema se llama "Explico algunas cosas", pertenece a su obra *España en el corazón* y habla de cómo vivió Neruda el estallido de la guerra civil española y por qué cambió su estilo.
c. El poema se llama "Yo vivía en un barrio", pertenece a la primera época de Neruda y trata sobre la nostalgia que Neruda siente por Madrid.

---

check that their answers are correct, have them listen to a recording of the poem, spoken by Pablo Neruda himself, available online by searching "Pablo Neruda, Explico algunas cosas". You may choose to further analyze the poem together as a class, which will serve to teach students more about the history of Spain.

ADVANCED LEARNERS

After reading about Pablo Neruda in Activity 1, have students write a reaction to the text. Why do they think he's in this book and that they are learning about him? Did any of the information surprise or impress them? What else do they want to find out about him or any of the people or time periods mentioned in the text?

[...]
Yo vivía en un barrio
de Madrid, con campanas,
con relojes, con árboles.

Desde allí se veía
5 el rostro seco de Castilla
como un océano de cuero.
Mi casa era llamada
la casa de las flores, porque por todas partes
estallaban geranios: era
10 una bella casa
con perros y chiquillos.

[...]
Y una mañana todo estaba ardiendo
y una mañana las hogueras
salían de la tierra
devorando seres,
15 y desde entonces fuego,
pólvora desde entonces,
y desde entonces sangre.

[...]
Preguntaréis por qué su poesía
no nos habla del sueño, de las hojas,
20 de los grandes volcanes de su país natal.

3 El siguiente poema pertenece a *Cien sonetos de amor,* que Neruda dedicó a su tercera esposa, Matilde Urrutia, su gran amor, su musa y su compañera hasta la muerte. Con tu compañero/a, selecciona palabras de la lista para completar el poema.

amé ○ arena ○ luz ○ manos ○ mar ○ muera ○ oídos ○ pelo ○ viento ○ vivas

Cuando yo .... quiero tus .... en mis ojos:
quiero la .... y el trigo de tus manos amadas
pasar una vez más sobre mí su frescura:
sentir la suavidad que cambió mi destino.
Quiero que .... mientras yo, dormido, te espero,
quiero que tus .... sigan oyendo el ....,
que huelas el aroma del .... que amamos juntos
y que sigas pisando la .... que pisamos.
Quiero que lo que amo siga vivo
y a ti te .... y canté sobre todas las cosas,
por eso sigue tú floreciendo, florida,
para que alcances todo lo que mi amor te ordena,
para que se pasee mi sombra por tu ....,
para que así conozcan la razón de mi canto.

4 🎧 41 Escucha el audio y comprueba tus respuestas.

5 Escribe un poema usando la misma estructura que Neruda.

Cuando yo ....
quiero ....

Quiero que ....
quiero que ....
que ....

y que ....
Quiero que ....

por eso ....
para que ....
para que ....
para que ....

163

INSTRUCTIONAL STRATEGIES

Activity 3

Read the instructions aloud. Have students work in pairs to complete the poem.

🎧 41 Activity 4

- Play the audio so that students can check their answers to Activity 3.
- Confirm any responses that students may have missed in the audio.
- Encourage students to share their opinions about the poem and pick out their favorite verses.

Activity 5

- Go over the instructions. Allow students to spend a few minutes thinking about a moment in their future that they want to write about. Encourage them to jot down ideas first before completing the template.
- Direct students' attention back to the template. Ask them to identify where they need to use the subjunctive. Then give them time to write their poems.
- Monitor their progress and assist as needed.
- Have students take turns presenting their poems to the class or in small groups. If you have students present the poems to the entire class, consider having them vote and choose a winner for the following categories: the most original, the most fun, and the best presentation.

ANSWERS

Activity 3

muera, manos, luz, vivas, oídos, viento, mar, arena, amé, pelo.

HERITAGE LANGUAGE LEARNERS

Have students search on YouTube one of Neruda's poems read in his own voice, for example, **Poema De Amor**. Have them follow along with the lyrics and indicate the words they recognize. Have them discuss their impressions of Neruda's voice, his delivery of the poem, and any of the themes or ideas that they may have understood. An interpretation of the poem sung by Alberto Cortez can be found on YouTube for *Alberto Cortez Neruda*.

OBJECTIVES FOR EVALUACIÓN

- Review grammar, vocabulary and culture from the unit
- Complete self-assessment

CORE RESOURCES

- Interactive Online Materials - ELEteca

STANDARDS

- 1.2 Understand the language
- 4.1 Compare languages

INSTRUCTIONAL STRATEGIES

- Have students complete the activities individually.
- Go over the answers as a class. Encourage students to learn from each other by asking if they agree with the answers given. Provide explanations as needed.
- You may wish to assign point value to each activity as a way for students to monitor their progress.
- Direct students to the indicated pages in **En resumen** if they make more than one or two mistakes in any one section.

ANSWERS

Activity 1

Answers will vary. Possible answers might include the following:

a. Yo lo llevo fatal, la Física nunca ha sido lo mío, espero que no sea muy difícil; **b.** ¡Hala, qué suerte! Pues espero que te diviertas; **c.** Bueno, de aquí al fin de semana quedan unos días, espero que te haga buen tiempo; **d.** ¡Vaya, qué mala suerte! Pues dile a tu hermano de mi parte que se mejore; **e.** Pues, ¡que aproveche!

Activity 2

Answers will vary. Possible answers might include the following:

a. me guste el instituto y mis profesores y compañeros; **b.** aprenda a hablar perfectamente en español; **c.** conocer la ciudad y a la gente de allí; **d.** ir a ver un partido del América en el estadio Azteca; **e.** mis amigos vengan a verme muy pronto.

Activity 3

a. En cuanto; **b.** Al; **c.** hasta que; **d.** Después de; **e.** Después de que; **f.** hasta que; **j.** Cuando.

Activity 4

a. para que sepan; **b.** para hacer; **c.** para que veamos; **d.** para que pienses; **e.** para hacer.

EVALUACIÓN

EXPRESSING WISHES

1 **Estás chateando con un/a amigo/a. Completa la conversación usando algunas de las expresiones que has aprendido.**

» ¡Hola! ¿Cómo llevas el examen de Física? ¿Tú crees que será muy difícil?

» ....

» Uf, yo no puedo concentrarme, porque estoy pensando en el fin de semana. ¡Me voy a Puerto Rico!

» ....

» Lo malo es que he visto en la tele que está lloviendo mucho.

» ....

» Mi hermano también iba a venir, pero se ha roto el brazo, así que no va a poder ser.

» ....

» Gracias, bueno, te dejo que me voy cenar.

» ....

2 **El año que viene te vas a mudar a México D.F. Completa las frases.**

a. Espero que ....
b. Ojalá ....
c. Quiero ....
d. Deseo ....'.
e. Quiero que ....

EXPRESSING THE TIME WHEN AN EVENT OCCURS

3 **Elige la opción correcta.**

a. **En cuanto / Hasta que** llegues al aeropuerto, lo primero que debes hacer es facturar la maleta.
b. **Al / Después** llegar la primavera los campos se llenan de flores.
c. Me quedaré en casa **hasta que / antes de** pare de llover.
d. **Después de / Después** irnos, llegó Pedro.
e. **Antes de / Después de** que salgamos del cine, iremos a tomar algo.
f. Si quieres, puedes ver la tele **después / hasta que** sea la hora de cenar.
g. **Cuando / Después de** cumpla los dieciocho, podré votar.

EXPRESSING A PURPOSE

4 **Completa con *para* o *para que* y la forma correcta del verbo entre paréntesis.**

a. El profesor les ha mandado hacer un trabajo sobre las ONG (saber, ustedes) .... más cosas acerca de ellas.
b. He comprado pan (hacer, yo) .... unos bocadillos.
c. He venido (ver, nosotros) .... una película.
d. Te he hecho esta bufanda (pensar, tú) .... en mí en Irlanda.
e. Este aparato sirve (hacer, el aparato) .... helados.

164

INDICATIVE, SUBJUNCTIVE, INFINITIVE

5 Completa las frases usando la forma correcta del verbo.

a. ¿Cuándo (venir, tú) .... a visitarnos? Tenemos muchas ganas de verte.

b. Quiero (beber, yo) .... algo fresco.

c. Hasta que no (irse) .... Juan no voy a decir nada.

d. Cuando mis abuelos (jubilarse) ...., se fueron a vivir a Florida.

e. Mi hermana me ha dado un libro para que no (aburrirse, yo) .... durante el viaje.

f. Espero que hoy (salir, nosotros) .... puntuales de la clase de español.

g. Me voy antes de que (llover) ....

h. Cuando (terminar, yo) .... la universidad, espero (trabajar, yo) .... en una buena empresa.

i. Espero que no (dormirse, nosotros) .... con la película. Dicen que es un rollo.

j. ¡Ojalá (aprobar, yo) .... todos los exámenes!

k. He venido para que me (contar, tú) .... lo que pasó ayer.

l. Deseo que Pablo y tú (ser) .... muy felices y (tener) .... muchos hijos.

m. ¿Quieres que (empezar, nosotros) .... ya a cenar o prefieres esperar?

n. Su padre no quiere que (ver, ustedes) .... el regalo que les ha comprado.

ñ. Este bolígrafo no sirve para (corregir) ...., necesitas otro de diferente color.

o. No te levantes hasta que yo te lo (decir) ....

p. En cuanto (traer, ellos) .... mi equipaje, me iré de este hotel.

DIPHTHONGS, HIATUS

6 Observa la vocal subrayada y pon una tilde si hace falta. Después, busca diptongos o hiatos.

boina ○ Eugenio ○ estadounidense ○ anciano ○ buho ○ aullar ○ copia ○ acentua ○ orquidea ○ coreografo ○ barbacoa ○ actuo ○ adios ○ violencia ○ buitre ○ diurno ○ buey

CULTURA

7 Contesta las siguientes preguntas con la información que has aprendido en *Me encanta ser voluntario*.

a. ¿Qué beneficios experimentaron algunos jóvenes después de hacer un voluntariado internacional?

b. ¿En qué tipo de actividades participaban los voluntarios?

c. ¿Fue todo trabajo o pudieron hacer otras cosas? Da ejemplos.

d. ¿Te sorprende que EE. UU. sea el primer país con el mayor número de gente que ayuda a los demás? ¿Por qué (no)?

 MORE IN ELETECA: EXTRA ONLINE PRACTICE

ANSWERS

Activity 5

a. vendrás; **b.** beber; **c.** se vaya; **d.** se jubilaron; **e.** me aburra; **f.** salgamos; **g.** llueva; **h.** termine, trabajar; **i.** nos durmamos; **j.** apruebe; **k.** cuentes; **l.** sean, tengan; **m.** empecemos; **n.** vean; **o.** corregir; **p.** diga; **q.** traigan.

Activity 6

Diptongos: boina, Eugenio, estadounidense, anciano, aullar, copia, actuó, adiós, violencia, buitre, diurno, buey.

Hiatos: búho, acentúa, orquídea, coreógrafo, barbacoa, actúo.

Activity 7

Answers will vary. Possible answers might include the following:

a. Los jóvenes mejoraron su español y aprendieron costumbres nuevas; **b.** Construir casas, dar clases de inglés; **c.** Pudieron participar en fiestas, viajar por el país y hacer amistades con otros jóvenes; **d.** Answers will vary.

OBJECTIVES FOR EN RESUMEN: VOCABULARIO

- Review unit vocabulary and expressions
- Practice communicative skills

STANDARDS

1.2 Understand the language
1.3 Present the language

INSTRUCTIONAL STRATEGIES

- Have students role-play scenarios similar to what they see in the images and practice using the correct **Expresiones de deseo**.
- Have students write sentences with the words and phrases in the other vocabulary sections. Call on students to write their sentences on the board —but leaving a blank line where the vocabulary word or phrase should be. Then have the rest of the class write down the answers. Go over the answers as a class.
- Index cards can be used as flashcards with the Spanish term on one side and the English term, a picture, or a drawing on the other.
- Working in pairs or groups, students can use the flashcards to help each other practice unit vocabulary.
- Have students write a dialogue or monologue based on each of the images on the page. Challenge them to integrate as many of the vocabulary words as they can.

EN RESUMEN: Vocabulario

Expresiones de deseo
Cuídate. *Take care.*
Enhorabuena. *Congratulations.*

Felicidades. *Congratulations.*

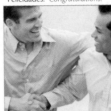

Lo siento mucho. *I'm so sorry.*

ojalá *I hope, let's hope (that)*
Que aproveche. *Enjoy your meal, Bon appétite.*

Que disfrutes. *Have fun.*

Que duermas bien. *Sleep well.*

Que lo pases bien. *Have a good time.*

Que te mejores. *Get well.*

Que tengas buen viaje. *Have a good trip.*

Que tengas suerte. *Good luck.*

Expresiones temporales
dentro de un rato *in a moment*
dentro de… (periodo de tiempo) *within a (period of time)*
el mes que viene *next month*
pasado mañana *day after tomorrow*

Hacer conjeturas y promesas
al *upon*
cuando *when*

en cuanto *as soon as*
hasta (que) *until*
mientras (que) *while*

Las ONG
la ayuda desinteresada *selfless aid*
la campaña de sensibilización *awareness campaign*
la catástrofe natural *natural disaster*
el comercio justo *fair trade*
el conflicto bélico *armed conflict*
los derechos humanos *human rights*
los discapacitados *handicapped people*

el donativo *donation*
la labor social *social work*
las labores humanitarias *humanitarian relief*
la orientación laboral *workforce readiness*
la protección del medioambiente *environmental protection*
sin ánimo de lucro *non-profit*

Verbos
defender (e>ie) *to defend*
desatender *to neglect*
desear *to wish, desire*
esperar *to hope, to wait for*
luchar (por, en, a favor de, contra) *to fight (for, in, in favor of, against)*
ofrecer *to offer*
recaudar fondos *to raise money*

EN RESUMEN: Gramática

PRESENT SUBJUNCTIVE: REGULAR VERBS

(See page 154)

	–AR HABLAR	–ER COMER	–IR VIVIR
yo	hable	coma	viva
tú	hables	comas	vivas
usted/él/ella	hable	coma	viva
nosotros/as	hablemos	comamos	vivamos
vosotros/as	habléis	comáis	viváis
ustedes/ellos/ellas	hablen	coman	vivan

PRESENT SUBJUNCTIVE: IRREGULAR VERBS

(See page 155 and 156)

Stem-changing verbs

QUERER e → ie	VOLVER o → ue	JUGAR u → ue	PEDIR e → i (en todas las personas)
quiera	vuelva	juegue	pida
quieras	vuelvas	juegues	pidas
quiera	vuelva	juegue	pida
queramos	volvamos	juguemos	pidamos
queráis	volváis	juguéis	pidáis
quieran	vuelvan	jueguen	pidan

(!) ■ The verbs **dormir** and **morir** have two stem changes in the present subjunctive: **o →ue** and **o → u:**
- d**ue**rma, d**ue**rmas, d**ue**rma, d**u**rmamos, d**u**rmáis, d**ue**rman.
- m**ue**ra, m**ue**ras, m**ue**ra, m**u**ramos, m**u**ráis, m**ue**ran.

Verbs with irregular *yo* forms

poner → **pong-**	traer → **traig-**	-a
tener → **teng-**	hacer → **hag-**	-as
salir → **salg-**	caer → **caig-**	-a
venir → **veng-**	construir → **construy-**	-amos
decir → **dig-**	conocer → **conozc-**	-áis
		-an

Verbs that are completely irregular

HABER	IR	SABER	ESTAR	SER	VER	DAR
haya	vaya	sepa	esté	sea	vea	dé
hayas	vayas	sepas	estés	seas	veas	des
haya	vaya	sepa	esté	sea	vea	dé
hayamos	vayamos	sepamos	estemos	seamos	veamos	demos
hayáis	vayáis	sepáis	estéis	seáis	veáis	deis
hayan	vayan	sepan	estén	sean	vean	den

OBJECTIVES FOR EN RESUMEN: GRAMÁTICA

- Review unit grammar
- Practice communication skills

STANDARDS

1.2   Understand the language
4.1   Compare languages

INSTRUCTIONAL STRATEGIES

- Focus students' attention on the key grammar topics of the unit.
- Have the students review the Learning Outcomes in the unit opener to assess whether they feel they have mastered the main ideas and skills.
- Ask them if they can remember additional examples for each grammar topic.
- Model how to find and go back to the appropriate page in the unit to review any grammar topic they may need help with.
- Invite students to review the grammar activities they completed in this unit.
- Ask them what grammar activities they found easy and which they found challenging. Encourage them to rework any activities they found particularly challenging.
- Along the same lines as Activity 7 on page 156, have students first write a series of sentences in the present or future tense. Then have them switch sentences with a partner who must rewrite and modify them using a structure that requires the present subjunctive. Have students swap papers with a new partner who must add a new modified version of the original sentence using the present subjunctive.

OBJECTIVES FOR UNIT OPENER

- Introduce unit theme: **¡Hoy me siento bien!** about feelings and emotions
- Introduce culture for the unit: Share information about the arts in Hispanic countries

STANDARDS

1.1   Interpersonal communication
1.2   Understand the language
2.1   Practices and perspectives

INSTRUCTIONAL STRATEGIES

- Introduce unit theme and objectives. Talk about the photo and have students state who they think the man is and what he is doing: **¿Dónde está este hombre? ¿Qué está haciendo? ¿Cómo está vestido? ¿Qué expresión lleva en la cara?**, etc.
- Help students formulate their ideas: **Está tocando y cantando una nueva canción de amor**, etc. Encourage students to use their imagination to create various scenarios.
- Have students work individually to write answers to the questions on the page.
- Put students into pairs or small groups to share and discuss their answers.
- Call on volunteers to report back on their responses and discussions. See if you can get the class to reach agreement.

SLOWER-PACED LEARNERS

Have students retrieve their previous knowledge about feelings, descriptions, body parts, and ask them to use them to describe the musician in the picture.

ADVANCED LEARNERS

Have students adopt a different feeling: surprised, sad, excited, happy, horrified, etc. and act it out in front of the class. They can work in pairs and perform a dialogue.

HERITAGE LANGUAGE LEARNERS

Have students make a list of at least five different emotions and write a sentence explaining when they feel that particular emotion: **Me siento triste cuando mis amigos no me llaman, Me siento feliz cuando no hay escuela**, etc.

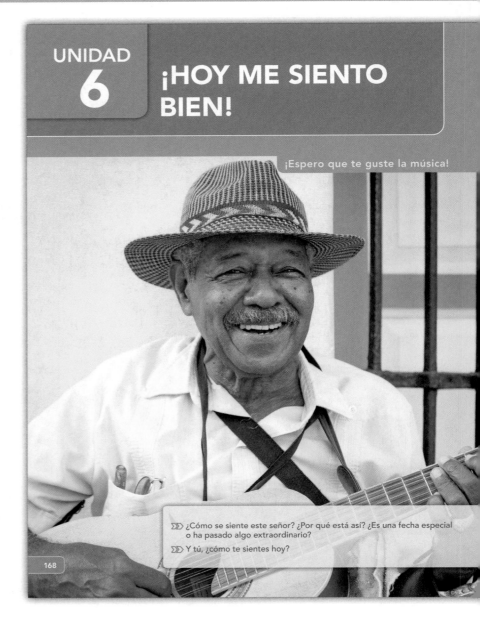

UNIDAD

6 ¡HOY ME SIENTO BIEN!

¡Espero que te guste la música!

¿Cómo se siente este señor? ¿Por qué está así? ¿Es una fecha especial o ha pasado algo extraordinario?

Y tú, ¿cómo te sientes hoy?

168

ADDITIONAL UNIT RESOURCES

Extension Activities (EA) (Photocopiable)	Interactive Whiteboard Lessons (IWB)	Audio	Video	Online ELEteca
EA: 6.1, 6.2, 6.3, 6.4, 6.5, 6.6, 6.7, 6.8	IWB: 6.1	42 to 53	Diálogo 6	EXTENSIÓN DIGITAL

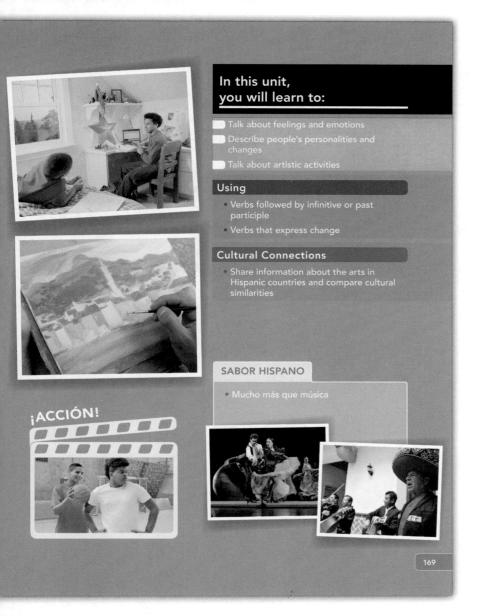

**In this unit,
you will learn to:**

☐ Talk about feelings and emotions
☐ Describe people's personalities and changes
☐ Talk about artistic activities

Using

• Verbs followed by infinitive or past participle
• Verbs that express change

Cultural Connections

• Share information about the arts in Hispanic countries and compare cultural similarities

SABOR HISPANO

• Mucho más que música

¡ACCIÓN!

169

LEARNING OUTCOMES

• Talk about feelings and emotions
• Describe people's personalities and changes
• Talk about artistic activities

INSTRUCTIONAL STRATEGIES

• Use unit opener to preview vocabulary and cultural topics for this unit.
• Have students look at the images on this page and relate them to the objectives listed. Ask questions such as: **¿Quiénes son estas personas? ¿Dónde están? ¿Cómo crees que son? ¿Te gusta la pintura? ¿Quién es tu artista favorito? ¿Qué estilo tiene? ¿Qué otras actividades artísticas pueden nombrar?**
• Invite students to read the topic for **Sabor hispano** and preview that section in the unit. Ask questions such as: **¿Reconocen el tipo de baile y el estilo de música que se presentan en las imágenes?** (el flamenco y la música de los mariachis) **¿Te gusta bailar? ¿Qué tipos de bailes hispanos conoces?**
• Ask students to anticipate what they think the episode for **¡Acción!** will be about.
• Have students work in pairs to talk about the images using the questions you have modeled. Then have volunteers present to the class what they understand this unit to be about.

HERITAGE LANGUAGE LEARNERS

Have students share information about their heritage countries. They can talk about musicians, dances, painters, writers, or any other type of artistic expression they know is important for their families or ancestors. Invite other students to participate. Have them discuss why some people identify all Latinos with **mariachis** or with certain types of music and dances.

	THREE MODES OF COMMUNICATION: UNIT 6		
	INTERPERSONAL	**INTERPRETIVE**	**PRESENTATIONAL**
HABLAMOS DE...	2, 6, 7	1, 3, 4, 5	
COMUNICA	1, 4, 8	2, 3, 5, 6, 7	8
¡ACCIÓN!	1	2, 3, 4, 5	2
PALABRA POR PALABRA	4, 8, 10	1, 2, 3, 5, 6, 9, 11	1, 7, 9, 12, 13
GRAMÁTICA	2, 7	1, 4, 5, 6	3, 6
DESTREZAS		2, 4	
CULTURA		SABOR HISPANO	
RELATO	6, 7	1, 2, 4	3, 5

OBJECTIVES FOR HABLAMOS DE...

- Talk about feelings and emotions
- Preview vocabulary: Feelings, personality, and emotions
- Preview grammatical structures: Verbs followed by infinitive or past participle and verbs that express change

CORE RESOURCES

- Audio Program: Track 42

STANDARDS

1.1	Engage in conversation
1.2	Understand the language
1.3	Present information
4.2	Compare cultures

INSTRUCTIONAL STRATEGIES

Activity 1

- Ask students to talk about the people in the photo and in pairs, ask:
  ¿Quiénes creen que son las personas que ven? ¿Qué relación puede haber entre ellas? ¿Dónde están? ¿Qué llevan? ¿Qué están haciendo? ¿Qué les llama la atención a ustedes?
- Have students complete the activity individually and compare their answers with another student. Remind students that they may not have the same answers and more than one answer can be correct.

Activity 2

- Tell students to compare their answers with the words listed in the word bank. Ask students how well they were able to predict the text completions. Ask students to share other options and confirm whether they are correct.
- Then have students complete the activity again using the words provided.
- Correct the activity with the whole class and be sure they understand the text.

Activity 3

- Introduce the activity by asking students to come up with some ideas about what each person in the image is probably thinking. Record responses on the board.
- In this activity students will review the present subjunctive. Ask students to read the first bubbles and identify the form of the verb. Then have them read the remaining thought bubbles and ask whether they all need the subjunctive. Review the forms as necessary.
- Have students to do the activity individually completing the sentences and writing the name of the person who is probably thinking it.

ANSWERS

Activity 1

a. escuela; **b.** clase; **c.** trabajo; **d.** profesor; **e.** compañero; **f.** gusta; **g.** vergüenza; **h.** nerviosa; **i.** contenta.

Activity 3

a. pase, intentaré / intento: Adrián; **b.** salude, se pondrá / se pone: Antonia; **c.** llegue, tenemos: Raquel; **d.** entre, diré: el profesor.

SLOWER-PACED LEARNERS

Have students remember the forms of the present subjunctive. Refer them to page 154 in Unit 5 for more detailed explanations.

HABLAMOS DE... Los sentimientos

1 **Observa la imagen y completa el texto.**

Antonia y Raquel son dos compañeras de la (a) .... que están en la puerta de (b) .... hablando sobre un (c) .... que tienen que presentar en clase. Esperan a que llegue el (d) .... de Historia para entrar en clase y, mientras hablan, ven a Adrián, que es un (e) .... de clase que le (f) .... a Antonia. Esta, al ver que él para a saludarla, se pone roja como un tomate de la (g) .... Raquel le sonríe a Antonia para animarla a hablar con él. Sabe que Antonia está (h) ...., pero también (i) .... porque Adrián se ha fijado en ella.

2 **Compara tus respuestas con las de tu compañero/a. ¿Tienen respuestas similares? Comprueba con las palabras del cuadro.**

> compañero ○ vergüenza ○ nerviosa ○ escuela ○ gusta ○ profesor
> encantada ○ trabajo ○ clase

3 **Completa las frases con la forma correcta del verbo entre paréntesis. Escribe el nombre de la persona de la Actividad 1 que crees que lo está pensando.**

a. Cuando (pasar) ......_pase_...... por aquí, (intentar) .... hablar con ella.

b. Seguro que cuando lo (saludar) ...., (ponerse) .... rojo.

c. Antes de que (llegar) .... el profesor, (tener) .... que estar sentados.

d. En cuanto (entrar) .... en clase, les (decir) ....que hay examen la semana que viene.

4 Lee la conversación entre Antonia y Raquel y complétala con las palabras del cuadro.

atenta ○ musa ○ vergüenza ○ tonta ○ abierta ○ amor ○ enamorada ○ loca

Raquel: ¡Antonia! ¡Antoooonia!

Antonia: ¡Ay! Hola, Raquel, no te había visto.

R.: ¿Cómo me vas a ver con lo distraída que vas?

A.: Es que estaba pensando en una canción que me encanta y…

R.: ¿Qué canción?

A.: La nueva de *Nerea*, ¿la has escuchado?

R.: Sí, está bien, ella tiene una voz espectacular, pero… es demasiado romántica, ¿no? Bueno, para ti es perfecta porque con lo (a) .... que estás últimamente…

A.: Para nada, ¿pero qué dices?

R.: ¿Que no? Pero si se te nota de lejos que estás (b) .... por Adrián. Cada vez que lo ves, pones una cara de (c) ....

A.: Ok, ok, lo que tú digas. Por cierto, compuse un tema nuevo para el concierto.

R.: ¡Súper! Oye, mira quién viene por ahí, tu (d) ....

A.: ¡Ay, caray, qué (e) ....! Tú ahora no te vayas y no me dejes sola. Es que cuando estoy con él no sé qué me pasa que nunca sé qué decirle y me da rabia que piense que soy

una tonta…

R.: Pues dile, por ejemplo, que le has escrito una canción y que quieres que vaya a nuestro concierto. Seguro que cuando te oiga dedicándole "su" canción subida a un escenario, se queda con la boca (f) ....

A.: ¿Qué dices? No me atrevo *(dare)*… ¿Por qué no se lo dices tú?

R.: ¿Yooo? ¡Pero si a mí no me gusta!

A.: ¡Ay! ¡Qué nervios! Ya viene y me está mirando…

R.: Sí, y acaba de tocar el timbre para entrar en clase. Así que mejor dejas tu declaración de (g) .... para otro momento, que cuando nos vea el profe hablando en la puerta…

A.: Sí, mejor entramos. Por cierto, ¿tienes los apuntes del otro día? Es que no estuve muy (h) ....

R.: Sí, vamos, y a ver si hoy escuchas más al profe y compones menos.

A.: Bueno, es que la inspiración llega cuando menos te lo esperas.

5 🎧 42 Escucha la conversación y comprueba tus respuestas.

6 👥 ¿Y tú? Habla con tu compañero/a de tus experiencias. Usa las siguientes preguntas como guía.

• ¿Cómo reaccionas cuando sientes vergüenza? ¿Te pones rojo/a?
• ¿En qué clases estás menos atento/a? ¿Por qué?
• ¿Te has quedado con la boca abierta en alguna situación? ¿Qué pasó?

7 👥 Observa las frases marcadas en la conversación. ¿Cuáles usan el subjuntivo? Con tu compañero/a, túrnate para completar las frases con ejemplos.

a. Cuando el profe vea a los estudiantes hablando en la puerta…
b. Antonia no quiere que Raquel…
c. Raquel cree que Adrián se va a quedar con la boca abierta cuando…
d. En mi opinión,… llega cuando menos te lo esperas.

INSTRUCTIONAL STRATEGIES

Activity 4

• Review the words in the list and have students identify the ones that describe people. You may want to preteach **descargar**, **descargado**, **componer** and **ensayar** asking students to look and see if they recognize the cognates.

• Ask students to read the conversation and fill in the blanks with the appropriate words. Then, work in pairs to compare their answers.

🎧 42 Alternative activity

Play the audio first and tell students they are going to listen to a conversation between Antonia and Raquel with their books closed. Afterwards, ask questions to see how much they have understood. For example: **¿Por qué Antonia no había visto a Raquel? ¿Qué le pasa a Antonia últimamente? ¿Qué le pasa a Antonia cuando está cerca de Adrián?** After the discussion, they can do Activity 4.

🎧 42 Activity 5

Play the audio so students can check their answers to Activity 4.

Activity 6

• The purpose of the activity is to help students identify with the topic and provide opportunities for them to talk about their own experiences and similar feelings. If they don't feel comfortable talking about their own situations they should feel free to invent their own.

• Have students to work in pairs taking turns to complete the activity.

Activity 7

• Ask students to review the highlighted expressions. Call on volunteers to read one aloud and explain the use for the subjunctive or indicative: **No te vayas / No me dejes sola** (negative commands), **Quieres que vaya** (subjunctive: expressing wishes), **Cuando te oiga / Cuando nos vea** (subjunctive: after **cuando** when the action takes place in the future), **Cuando menos te lo esperas** (indicative: everyday occurrence).

• Then have students complete the sentences with their own examples. Record student responses on the board to ensure correct use of subjunctive or indicative.

Extension

Preview the use of the subjunctive with expressions of emotion. Tell students to look for the following expressions in the conversation: **Me da rabia** and **les encanta que**. Then have students look at the form of the verb after **que** and ask students why they think the subjunctive is used and what type of expression introduces the subjunctive.

ANSWERS

Activity 4

a. enamorada; **b.** loca; **c.** tonta; **d.** inspiración; **e.** vergüenza; **f.** abierta; **g.** amor; **h.** atenta.

Activity 7

Answers will vary but should include the following forms of the verb: **a.** future / *ir a* + infinitive; **b.** subjunctive; **c.** subjunctive; **d.** present indicative.

ADVANCED LEARNERS

Have students write down a list of adjectives used so far to express feelings and emotions: **enamorado/a; distraído/a; atento/a**, etc. Then have them write new sentences with them.

HERITAGE LANGUAGE LEARNERS

Call on volunteers to act out the conversation in Activity 4 for the class.

OBJECTIVES FOR COMUNICA

• Present communicative functions of the unit: Talk about feelings and emotions

STANDARDS

1.1	Engage in conversation	1.3	Present information
1.2	Understand the language	4.1	Compare languages

CORE RESOURCES

• Audio Program: Tracks 43 and 44
• Extension Activities: EA 6.1, 6.2, 6.3, 6.4
• Interactive Online Materials - ELEteca

INSTRUCTIONAL STRATEGIES FOR EXPRESSING FEELINGS AND EMOTIONS (1)

• Use EA 6.1 and 6.2, **Estados de ánimo** to activate vocabulary to describe moods and to introduce the section. Distribute cut up cards to student pairs and have them match the images to the descriptions.
• Review with students the expressions for feelings and emotions in the chart and create a sample sentence for each of the endings to emphasize the different uses with nouns, infinitives, indicative and subjunctive forms. Write the samples sentence on the board.
• Share with students one situation explaining your feelings and emotions. Ask a couple of students to do the same. If you or your students do not feel comfortable sharing real situations, invent one.

Activity 1

• Model some examples to help students get started: **Estoy aburrido/a cuando llueve, Me pongo triste cuando llueve, No soporto los días de lluvia**, etc.
• In pairs, have students to express how they are feeling in each situation and have the other student react.

Activity 2

• Ask students to look at the image and describe the following: **¿Quiénes creen que son las personas que aparecen? ¿Qué relación hay entre ellas? ¿De qué creen que están hablando? ¿Cuál es su estado de ánimo o cómo creen que se sienten?**
• Have students work individually and then compare their answers with a partner. Students will have an opportunity to confirm their answers after listening to the audio.

🎧 43 Activity 3

• Play the audio and have students check their answers.
• Have students practice the conversation with a partner.
• Circulate around the room to check that students are on task and actively participating.

ANSWERS

Activity 2

1. estás; **a.** serio; **2.** estoy; **b.** preocupado; **3.** me pongo; **c.** nervioso; **4.** estás; **d.** tranquilo.

COMUNICA

EXPRESSING FEELINGS AND EMOTIONS (1)

Estoy (estar)	contento/a	con la nueva profesora.	→ noun
	encantado/a	cuando / si juega mi equipo.	→ indicative
	nervioso/a	de estar aquí.	→ infinitive: same subject
	aburrido/a	de que te vayas.	→ subjunctive: different subject

 Estoy preocupado por Álex. Hace dos días que no viene a clase.
I'm worried about Álex. He hasn't been to class for two days.

Me pongo (ponerse) *I get / I become*	furioso/a nervioso/a contento/a	cuando escucho mi música favorita. si me cuentan el final de una película.
Me siento (sentirse) *I feel*	bien / mal / fatal...	

Adoro *I love* No soporto *I can't stand*	los paisajes del Caribe. madrugar (to get up early). que me empujen (shove) en el metro.	→ noun → infinitive: same subject → subjunctive: different subject

1 🗣 Explícale a tu compañero/a cómo te sueles sentir en las siguientes situaciones.

a. un día de lluvia   c. en un concierto   e. en el dentista
b. antes de un examen   d. si ves una pelea (fight)   f. de vacaciones

2 Completa las conversaciones con los adjetivos del cuadro y con los verbos para expresar sentimientos y emociones.

nervioso ○ tranquilo ○ preocupado ○ serio

a. » Pero, ¿qué te pasa? Desde que llegaste, (1) .... muy (a) ....
» Es que (2) .... (b) .... por el examen de mañana. He estudiado mucho, pero ahora creo que estoy hecho un lío y no entiendo nada.
» Bueno, eso es normal, yo también (3) .... (c) .... antes de un examen. Mira, hazte un té y acuéstate temprano, ya verás como mañana, después de descansar, (4) .... más (d) .... y te acuerdas de todo.

3 🎧 43 Ahora, escucha y comprueba.

SLOWER-PACED LEARNERS

Have students remember that **estar** is used to express feelings and states of mind. Also they should become familiar with **ponerse**, which describes the process of getting a feeling: **me pongo nervioso / triste / alegre**...

EXPRESS FEELINGS AND EMOTIONS (2)

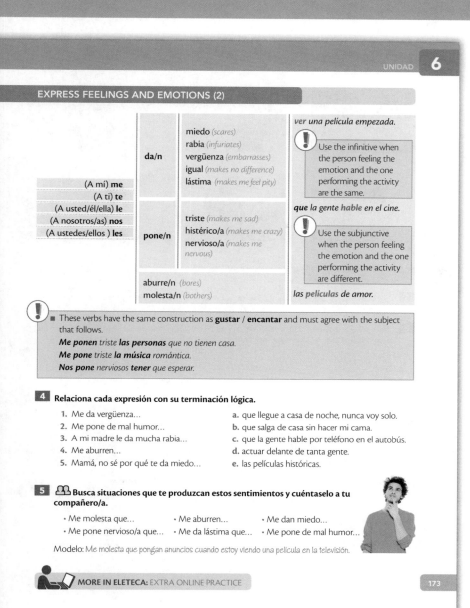

(A mí) me	da/n	miedo *(scares)*	*ver una película empezada.*
(A ti) te		rabia *(infuriates)*	Use the infinitive when the person feeling the emotion and the one performing the activity are the same.
(A usted/él/ella) le		vergüenza *(embarrasses)*	
(A nosotros/as) nos		igual *(makes no difference)*	
(A ustedes/ellos) les		lástima *(makes me feel pity)*	
	pone/n	triste *(makes me sad)*	*que la gente hable en el cine.*
		histérico/a *(makes me crazy)*	Use the subjunctive when the person feeling the emotion and the one performing the activity are different.
		nervioso/a *(makes me nervous)*	
	aburre/n *(bores)*		
	molesta/n *(bothers)*		*las películas de amor.*

■ These verbs have the same construction as **gustar / encantar** and must agree with the subject that follows.

Me ponen triste **las personas** que no tienen casa.

Me pone triste **la música** romántica.

Nos pone nerviosos **tener** que esperar.

4 **Relaciona cada expresión con su terminación lógica.**

1. Me da vergüenza…
2. Me pone de mal humor…
3. A mi madre le da mucha rabia…
4. Me aburren…
5. Mamá, no sé por qué te da miedo…

a. que llegue a casa de noche, nunca voy solo.
b. que salga de casa sin hacer mi cama.
c. que la gente hable por teléfono en el autobús.
d. actuar delante de tanta gente.
e. las películas históricas.

5 **Busca situaciones que te produzcan estos sentimientos y cuéntaselo a tu compañero/a.**

• Me molesta que…   • Me aburren…   • Me dan miedo…
• Me pone nervioso/a que…   • Me da lástima que…   • Me pone de mal humor…

Modelo: Me molesta que pongan anuncios cuando estoy viendo una película en la televisión.

MORE IN ELETECA: EXTRA ONLINE PRACTICE

173

INSTRUCTIONAL STRATEGIES FOR EXPRESSING FEELINGS AND EMOTIONS (2)

• Ask students to describe everything they know about the verb **gustar**. Record responses on the board and provide cues as needed to ensure students cover all aspects of the structure. Then ask students for other verbs like **gustar** (**encantar**, **molestar**, **doler**, etc.).

• Explain to students that the expressions in the chart follow the same pattern as **gustar**. List these on the board separately to help students access meaning. For example, start with **me da rabia**, **me da vergüenza**, and then have students continue calling out the combinations. Move on to **me pone triste**, etc., pausing as needed to clarify meaning, and so on until all expressions have been covered and recorded on the board.

Extension

• For additional practice with meaning, shuffle the cards from EA 6.3, **¿Qué sientes cuando…?** Ask a student to pick a card and formulate a question using **¿Qué sientes cuando…?** and the action pictured in the image. The student then calls on a classmate to match it with one of the expressions listed on the

---

board. You may choose to project the complete set of images to prepare the situations first.

• Next, go over the different ways to express feelings and emotions about something else. Call on students to combine elements to create sample sentences. Make sure they are logical before recording on the board. Go over the uses with infinitives, subjunctive, and nouns.

• Share with students another situation about things that bother you, make you sad, etc., using some of these verbs and a variety of endings. Have students prepare some of their own.

Activity 4

• Have students match the phrases to make logical sentences. Go over the answers as a class.

Activity 5

• Have students work in pairs and express feelings and emotions using the expressions they have learned.

• Observe, provide support, and correct students as needed.

• Call on students to report what their partners said. To liven up the review, ask for volunteers to report back on the strangest, funniest, most surprising things their partners said as well as situations they had in common to practice with **nos**.

Extension

For additional practice with these expressions, distribute copies of EA 6.4, **Expresar sentimientos y estados de ánimo**. Review the instructions with students and have them work individually. Project the answers to self-correct.

ANSWERS

Activity 4

1. d; **2.** c; **3.** b; **4.** e; **5.** a.

EA 6.4

1. a. de; **1.** regresar; **b.** de que; **2.** estemos; **c.** que; **3.** se termine; **d.** cuando; **4.** abrí; **e.** con; **f.** cuando; **5.** tengo; **g.** si; **6.** hay; **7.** volar; **h.** que; **8.** llames; **9.** hacer; **10.** hagas.

2. 1. se pone; **2.** está, me da; **3.** les pone, le dan; **4.** se pone; **5.** Me ponen; **6.** le pone; **7.** se siente; **8.** me pone, le da; **9.** se ponen; **10.** me pongo; **11.** le dan, se pone; **12.** me siento.

OBJECTIVES FOR ¡ACCIÓN!

- Provide students with a structured approach to viewing the video
- Contextualize the content of the unit in a familiar scenario

CORE RESOURCES

- Unit Video 6 - Tu voz es lo más dulce
- Online Materials - ELEteca

STANDARDS

1.1. Interpersonal communication	2.1 Culture: Practices and perspectives
1.2 Interpretive communication	

INSTRUCTIONAL STRATEGIES

Previewing: Antes del video

Activity 1

Put students in small groups to discuss the questions.

Activity 2

Either still in their small groups or working individually, have students discuss the images from the video in more detail and write sentences about them. Tell them to focus on their feelings and emotions to recycle the structures they practiced in **Comunica**.

Activity 3

Have students discuss a possible storyline for the video based on the images. To hold them accountable and keep them focused, suggest that they write down the sequence of main events in their versions of the story. This might be as a bullet list, a timeline, or captions to the images.

Viewing: Durante el video

Activity 4

- Tell students that that they are going to watch the first clip and identify whether Felipe or Sebas said each of the lines. If they need help remembering, point out which character is Felipe (Image 3) and which is Sebas (Image 1). Give students time to skim the sentences before playing the clip.
- Play the segment, pausing where indicated. Go over the answers with the class.

ANSWERS

Activity 4

a. Sebas; **b.** Felipe; **c.** Felipe; **d.** Sebas; **e.** Felipe; **f.** Felipe; **g.** Sebas.

¡ACCIÓN! Tu voz es lo más dulce

1.   2.   3.
4.   5.   6.

ANTES DEL VIDEO

1 Observen a Sebas, Felipe y Alba en la Imagen 6. ¿Dónde están? ¿Qué creen que están haciendo?

2 Observa las Imágenes 1, 2, 3, 4 y 5. ¿Cómo crees que están? ¿Cómo se sienten? Escribe una frase para cada imagen. Basa tu respuesta en lo que crees que puede ocurrir. Usa tu imaginación.

Imagen 1: ....
Imagen 2: ....
Imagen 3: ....
Imagen 4: ....
Imagen 5: ....

3 Con tu compañero/a, observa todas las imágenes e imagina una historia de lo que pasa.

DURANTE EL VIDEO

4 Mira la siguiente secuencia y marca quién dice las siguientes frases.
00:00 - 01:52

	Felipe	Sebas
a. ¡Adoro cuando encesto desde aquí!	☐	☐
b. Pues a mí me da rabia. ¡Hoy no hay manera de ganarte!	☐	☐
c. La verdad es que hoy me aburre estar aquí jugando.	☐	☐
d. Me siento muy bien cuando te estoy ganando al básquet.	☐	☐
e. Ya se te van a quitar las ganas de seguir jugando.	☐	☐
f. ¡Sí, la gran Alba!	☐	☐
g. Tienes razón, yo tampoco tengo más ganas de seguir jugando.	☐	☐

174

5 Haz un breve resumen de lo que pasa en la escena. No olvides explicar cómo se sienten los personajes.

6 Mira el resto del episodio y responde a las siguientes preguntas.

a. ¿Cómo es el primo de Alba?
b. ¿Se llevan mal Alba y su primo?
c. ¿Cómo hablan los españoles?
d. Sebas opina que Alba es muy dulce. ¿Cómo crees que se siente después de decirlo? (Observa la Imagen 5).
e. ¿Está contenta Alba con su nueva vida? ¿Está contenta en la nueva escuela?

7 Completa las frases sobre los sentimientos de Alba. Puedes volver a ver el episodio, si es necesario.

a. Alba se siente bien cuando ....
b. Su primo siempre quiere ....
c. A Alba su primo a veces le ....
d. A ella .... estar sola en su habitación.
e. Alba no soporta ....
f. Y cuando su primo grita ....
g. Porque a ella no le gusta que ....
h. Cuando ...., le gusta dibujar.
i. Se siente muy bien cuando ....

DESPUÉS DEL VIDEO

8 En grupos de cuatro, realicen las siguientes actividades.

a. Recuerden la actividad 3 de *Antes del video.* ¿Se parece la historia del episodio a la de ustedes? ¿Qué historia es la más similar a la del episodio?
b. En la primera parte, cuando Felipe ve a Alba, dice: "*La gran Alba*". ¿Les parece que Alba es una muchacha muy grande? Alba también dice: "*Es una gran ciudad*". ¿Qué quiere decir?

9 Completa la tabla con tus sentimientos y comparte las respuestas con tu compañero/a. ¿Tienen cosas en común ustedes dos?

	Yo	Mi compañero/a
Me encanta estar solo/a en mi habitación.		
Cuando me siento de mal humor...		
Me siento muy bien cuando...		
Me da mucha vergüenza que...		
Me pongo muy nervioso/a cuando...		

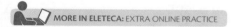 MORE IN ELETECA: EXTRA ONLINE PRACTICE

INSTRUCTIONAL STRATEGIES

Activity 5

• Explain that students should now summarize the scene between Felipe and Sebas and include information about where they are, what they are doing, and how they are feeling. What does each character want, and why? How does the scene end?
• Have students compare their summaries with a partner to confirm that they've both understood the scene in similar ways. Help clarify any major differences between them.

Activity 6

• Before playing the rest of the video, ask students to predict what they are going to talk to Alba about. Then direct their attention to the questions. Allow them to read them before playing the remainder of the video so they know what to listen for.
• After playing the rest of the episode, put students in pairs to discuss what they have understood the answers to be. Instead of resolving any differences between them right away, tell them they'll get a chance to fill in any gaps in their answers when you play the clip again for them in the next activity.

Activity 7

• Working individually, suggest that students complete any of the sentences they know before replaying the clip.
• Replay the segment so that students can complete the sentences and add any notes to their responses in the previous activity.
• Go over the answers as a class.

Post-viewing: Después del video
Activity 8

• Have students compare each other's ideas from Activity 3 against what actually happened in the video and determine whose predictions were the most accurate. You may want to put students back into the same pairs as Activity 3 to discuss what parts of their versions of the story were accurate and which weren't.
• In the second part of the activity, students discuss the different meanings and uses of gran as an adjective. Help them understand the difference between the literal and figurative use of the word. Tell them to work together to interpret what Felipe meant.

Activity 9

• Have students work individually to complete the first column of the chart for themselves. Then have them share their responses with a partner. Tell them to take notes on their partners' responses in the second column of the chart. Encourage them to ask follow-up questions for additional information.
• Have students report back about things they have in common. Alternatively, have students report to new partners about their previous partners' answers.

ANSWERS
Activity 5

Felipe y Sebas están en el gimnasio jugando al básquetbol. Sebas se siente bien porque está ganando. Quiere seguir jugando. Sin embargo, Felipe le da rabia de no puede ganar a Sebas y quiere dejar de jugar. Para convencerle, le muestra que Alba está allí en el gimnasio. Felipe sabe que a Sebas le gusta mucho Alba. Al final, Sebas cambia de opinión y decide dejar de jugar para que puedan saludarla.

Activity 6

a. Es ruidoso, encantador, divertido y cariñoso; b. No, se llevan bien, pero no la deja sola nunca; c. Dicen que hablan fuertemente en voces altas; d. Le da vergüenza. Se pone nervioso; e. Está más o menos contenta con su nueva vida. Está encantada de haber venido a estudiar en la ciudad. Todavía no tiene muchos amigos, pero a ella le da igual no ser una joven muy popular.

Activity 7

a. está sola; b. jugar; c. molesta; d. le encanta; e. que haga tanto ruido; f. le pone muy nerviosa; g. me hable tan fuerte; h. se siente un poco de mal humor; i. esté dibujando.

SLOWER-PACED LEARNERS

You may want to allow students to work with a partner to write their summaries in Activity 5. Play the video again to help them understand more details. Pause it periodically to ask questions to check their understanding.

HERITAGE LANGUAGE LEARNERS

Have students compare their relationships with relatives to those described by Alba and how she feels about her aunt, uncle, and cousin. Tell them to discuss any challenges they've had living with different families members and how they dealt with them.

OBJECTIVES FOR ADJETIVOS CALIFICATIVOS

- Present vocabulary needed to discuss attributes and characteristics
- Describe the qualities of people and things

CORE RESOURCES

- Interactive Online Materials - ELEteca

STANDARDS

1.1	Engage in conversation
1.2	Understand the language
1.3	Present information
4.1	Compare languages and cultures

INSTRUCTIONAL STRATEGIES

- Tell students that in this section they will build vocabulary using adjectives they already know.
- Use the following examples to present the shortened form of adjectives: **Es una buena muchacha / Es un buen muchacho**. Ask students to describe the difference. Then explain that this happens with **bueno** and **malo**.
- Write the following sentence pairs on the board to explain the change in meaning that occur when certain adjectives are placed before the noun: **Es un amigo viejo / Es un viejo amigo**. Ask students to guess at the meanings.
- Finally, write **paciente ≠ impaciente** to show opposites. Then ask students to provide the opposites of **simpático** and **tranquilo** by adding a prefix.
- Walk students through the explanations in the chart to reinforce the information just presented.

Activity 1

- Review the model with students to make sure students understand what they have to do. Ask students to provide other explanations for the model to help them get started. Then work in pairs.
- Call on volunteers to share their answers. Follow up their responses with examples from the sample answers provided below.

Activity 2

- Ask students to work individually and then compare answers with a partner.
- Review as a class.

ANSWERS

Activity 1

Answers will vary. Possible answers include: **a.** Es una empresa grande, en ella trabajan más de 1000 empleados. / Es una gran empresa, su prestigio es conocido a nivel internacional; **b.** Es un alumno viejo, después de jubilarse decidió matricularse en la universidad y volver a estudiar. / Es un viejo alumno y, aunque ya habla español muy bien, sigue viniendo a la escuela para perfeccionarlo; **c.** Es una única obra, al principio pensaron en hacer más, pero el presupuesto no lo permitió. / Es una obra única, según los expertos, ninguna hasta el momento la ha podido igualar.

Activity 2

a. sincero, falso; **b.** tranquilo; **c.** generoso, egoísta; **d.** sociable; **e.** flexible; **f.** tolerante; **g.** preocupado.

SLOWER-PACED LEARNERS

Check that students remember the agreement rules for adjectives and nouns. Ask them to divide the adjectives in Activity 2 in two groups: those that change the ending for masculine and feminine (e.g. **tranquilo**) and those that don't change (e.g. **egoísta**).

PALABRA POR PALABRA Adjetivos calificativos

- Descriptive adjectives describe a trait or quality of the noun they modify.

- In Spanish, descriptive adjectives generally follow the noun, with some exceptions.

- The adjectives **bueno** and **malo** drop the final -o when placed before the noun.
  *Es un **buen hijo**.*
  *No es un **mal ejemplo**.*

- The adjective **grande** becomes **gran** before singular nouns.
  *Es una **gran película**.*

> ! ■ This occurs before masculine, singular nouns only.
> • *Es una **buena** niña.*

- Placing certain adjectives before the noun changes the meaning of the adjective.

Es un **gran** libro.	➡	quality
Es un libro **grande**.	➡	size
Es un **viejo** amigo.	➡	time
Es un amigo **viejo**.	➡	age
Es un **único** ejemplar.	➡	quantity
Es un ejemplar **único**.	➡	without parallel

Impaciente

- Add a prefix, such as **im-**, **in-** or **des-**, to form the opposite of an adjective describing a trait or characteristic: **paciente / impaciente**, **útil / inútil**, **agradable / desagradable**.

1 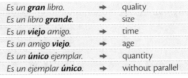 Con tu compañero/a, añade información a las siguientes frases para explicar su significado.

Modelo: Es un hombre **grande**. *Es el más alto y fuerte de la clase.*
Es un **gran** hombre. *Es generoso y todo el mundo lo respeta.*

a. Es una empresa **grande**. / Es una **gran** empresa. ➡ ....
b. Es un alumno **viejo**. / Es un **viejo** alumno. ➡ ....
c. Es una **única** obra. / Es una obra **única**. ➡ ....

2 Completa las frases con los adjetivos del cuadro.

> tranquilo o preocupado o sociable o generoso o tolerante
> sincero o flexible o falso o egoísta

a. Si siempre digo la verdad, soy ...., pero si no digo lo que pienso, soy ....
b. Cuando no estoy nervioso, estoy ....
c. Si me gusta compartir lo mío con los demás, soy ...., pero si lo quiero todo para mí y no pienso en los demás, soy ....
d. Si me gusta relacionarme con las personas, soy ....
e. Cuando me adapto fácilmente a las situaciones y acepto los cambios, soy ....
f. Si acepto otras opiniones y a las personas diferentes a mí, soy ....
g. Cuando tengo un problema, estoy ....

PALABRA POR PALABRA ¡Qué arte! UNIDAD 6

3 🎧 **44** Escribe el contrario de estos adjetivos. ¡Atención! No se forman todos con prefijos. Luego, escucha y comprueba.

a. flexible ➡ ....
b. ordenado ➡ ....
c. educada ➡ ....
d. preocupada ➡ ....
e. responsable ➡ ....
f. tolerante ➡ ....
g. fuerte ➡ ....
h. tranquilo ➡ ....
i. puntual ➡ ....
j. sociable ➡ ....
k. optimista ➡ ....
l. introvertido ➡ ....
m. trabajadora ➡ ....
n. seguro ➡ ....
ñ. paciente ➡ ....

4 👥 Prepara dos descripciones, una tuya y otra de tu compañero/a. Después, intercambia la información. ¿Eran acertadas las descripciones?

5 🎧 **45** Relaciona las palabras de la lista con las imágenes. ¡Atención! Algunas imágenes tienen más de una posibilidad. Después, escucha el audio para comprobar tus respuestas.

1. ☐ acueducto
2. ☐ violín
3. ☐ escultura
4. ☐ estatua
5. ☐ galería de arte
6. ☐ guitarra
7. ☐ guitarrista
8. ☐ museo
9. ☐ músico
10. ☐ orquesta
11. ☐ pintura
12. ☐ poema
13. ☐ poeta
14. ☐ retrato
15. ☐ actuar

177

Activity 4

- Have students prepare a description of themselves and then of their partner. Tell them to include adjectives from the section.
- Have them share the descriptions to check if they were accurate. Discuss together as a class.

OBJECTIVES FOR ¡QUÉ ARTE!

- Present vocabulary needed to talk about the arts
- Talk about artistic activities

CORE RESOURCES

- Audio Program: Track 46
- Extension Activities: EA 6.5

STANDARDS

1.1 Engage in conversation
1.2 Understand the language
3.2 Acquire information

INSTRUCTIONAL STRATEGIES

🎧 **45** Activity 5

After the presentation, have students work individually to match the words and images. Then play the audio for students to check their answers.

Audioscript

a. acueducto; **b.** estatua; **c.** museo; **d.** escultura; **e.** galería de arte; **f.** retrato; **g.** pintura; **h.** guitarrista; **i.** guitarra; **j.** músico; **k.** violín; **l.** actuar; **m.** poeta; **n.** poema; **ñ.** orquesta.

ANSWERS

Activity 3

a. inflexible; **b.** desordenado; **c.** maleducada; **d.** despreocupada / tranquila; **e.** irresponsable; **f.** intolerante; **g.** débil; **h.** intranquilo / nervioso; **i.** impuntual; **j.** insociable; **k.** pesimista; **l.** abierto / extrovertido; **m.** vaga; **n.** inseguro; **ñ.** impaciente.

Activity 5

1. a; **2.** k; **3.** d; **4.** b; **5.** e; **6.** i; **7.** h; **8.** c; **9.** j; **10.** ñ; **11.** g; **12.** n; **13.** m; **14.** f; **15.** l.

ADVANCED LEARNERS

As an alternative to Activity 4, have students prepare descriptions of their partners. Then collect them and share them with the class without using any of their names. The class then tries to guess who is being described.

HERITAGE LANGUAGE LEARNERS

Have students use the adjectives from Activity 3 to describe well-known Spanish-speakers either in contemporary society or from history. Have them share their ideas with a partner, justify their opinions, and see if their partners agree.

INSTRUCTIONAL STRATEGIES

🎧 **44** Activity 3

- Tell students that the prefix *in-* has some variations depending on the first letter of the adjective. Use *irr-* with adjectives starting with *r-* (*regular* / *irregular*), *im-* with adjectives starting with *p-* (*paciente* / *impaciente*).
- Students write individually the opposite of the adjectives from the list. Remind them that not all these adjectives are formed with prefixes.
- Play the audio for students to correct their answers.

Extension

Play charades. Have students write adjectives on separate pieces of paper. Then in groups of 3 or 4, students pick from the cards and act out the adjective for the others to guess. The group with the most correct answers wins.

INSTRUCTIONAL STRATEGIES

Activity 6

- Ask students if they know who the figure in the center is. Explain that Athena (Roman name Minerva) was the goddess of the arts and wisdom. She was the patron goddess of Athens. Her symbol was the owl.
- Have students complete the charts individually and then compare their answers with a partner.
- Review together and clarify meaning as needed.

Activity 7

- In pairs, have students practice with word families to build vocabulary and expand on what they already know.
- Tell students to create two more definitions using the new vocabulary for their partner to guess.
- Call on student volunteers to quiz the class.

Activity 8

- To introduce the activity, present the expression: *Yo creo que soy bueno/a en... porque...* and ask students to talk about themselves. Model some examples to get them started. For example: *Yo creo que soy bueno en fotografía porque dedico mucho tiempo a sacar fotos*.
- Have students ask each other about their talents and interests in the arts.
- Call on students to report back on what they learned about their partners.

Extension

Distribute cards from of EA 6.5, *Pictionary de las artes* to play Pictionary or charades in groups of four. Divide the groups into two teams with each group receiving a set of cards.

ANSWERS

Activity 6

Música: melodía, compositor, violinista, canción, orquesta, guitarrista, ensayar; **Arquitectura:** acueducto, diseñar; **Danza:** baile, ballet, bailarín, ensayar; **Escultura:** estatua, galería de arte, escultor; **Literatura:** obra, novelista, aventuras, poema, poeta, histórica, contar, cuento, tema, novela; **Pintura:** obra, cuadro, retrato, galería de arte, pintar.

Activity 7

a. pintor; **b.** compositor; **c.** arquitecto; **d.** músicos; **e.** escultor; **f.** escritores.

ADVANCED LEARNERS

Have students bring a picture of a painting, sculpture, or building that they like and explain why they consider it a piece of art.

HERITAGE LANGUAGE LEARNERS

Have students present information about a song, dance, or musical instrument from the Hispanic world and discuss its artistic qualities. Encourage them to bring in music, videos, or pictures to use during their presentations.

PALABRA POR PALABRA ¡Qué arte!

6 Clasifica las siguientes palabras según su categoría. *¡Atención!* Algunas palabras pueden colocarse en más de un lugar. ¿Sabes a quién representa la escultura?

> melodía o compositor o obra o cuadro o acueducto o violinista o novelista o ensayar o aventuras o estatua o retrato o canción o poema o galería de arte o pintar o escultor o baile o orquesta o ballet o diseñar o poeta o bailarín o histórica o contar o cuento o tema o guitarrista o novela

MÚSICA	ARQUITECTURA
DANZA	**ESCULTURA**
LITERATURA	**PINTURA**
novela	

7 Practica con las familias de las palabras y completa cada frase con una profesión. Después, inventa dos frases más con el vocabulario de las Actividades 5 y 6 para que las adivine tu compañero/a.

a. Un .... pinta cuadros y retratos de personas famosas.
b. Un .... compone música y melodías.
c. Un .... diseña edificios y otras estructuras como, por ejemplo, puentes.
d. Hay unos cien .... en las orquestas sinfónicas.
e. Un .... crea esculturas de hierro, mármol y otros materiales.
f. Muchos de los .... escriben novelas, poemas y obras de teatro.

8 Túrnate con tu compañero/a haciendo preguntas y respuestas.

a. ¿Has practicado alguna de estas actividades artísticas? ¿Cuál?
b. ¿Hay alguna que te gustaría practicar y aún no lo has hecho?
c. ¿Crees que tienes alguna aptitud artística? ¿Eres bueno haciendo algo?
d. ¿Cuál es tu obra favorita de cada actividad artística? ¿Por qué?

PALABRA POR PALABRA La música

9 **Con tu compañero/a, decide si las siguientes frases son verdaderas (V) o falsas (F). Después, lee el texto sobre la relación entre la música y las emociones. ¿Acertaste en lo que pensabas?**

	V	F
a. La cultura es un sentimiento universal y está por encima de la cultura en la que hemos crecido o que conocemos.	☐	☐
b. La música influye en nuestro estado de ánimo, incluso en nuestro comportamiento.	☐	☐
c. Todas las sociedades poseen escritura, pero algunas no poseen música.	☐	☐
d. La música nos ayuda a comunicarnos y a entender mejor a los demás.	☐	☐

♪♫ La música de las emociones ♪♫

"La música une a las personas y desata (*releases*) emociones allí donde se escucha". Tal vez esta afirmación suena exagerada pero, en realidad, el impacto de la música en nosotros es tan grande que cuando oímos música esta afecta a nuestra memoria, nuestros movimientos y nuestras emociones.

Estudios realizados por científicos, demostraron que, tanto un aborigen como un moderno ingeniero, cuando escuchaban la misma música, reaccionaban de la misma forma. Otra investigación, realizada en Camerún entre personas que no habían oído nunca música occidental antes, demostró que estas eran capaces (*able*) de reconocer en ella la alegría, la tristeza o el terror... Todos son sentimientos comunes que provoca una misma melodía a personas de diferentes culturas. Por eso, hay canciones universales que consiguen ponernos tremendamente tristes y otras que, en cambio, nos contagian (*transmit*) alegría y buen humor, seamos de donde seamos.

Otra de las grandes cualidades de la música es su inmenso poder de unión social. Hay sociedades sin escritura, pero ninguna sin música. Las melodías nos unen, nos hacen compartir estados de ánimo.

A lo largo de la historia los seres humanos nos hemos unido para bailar, cantar y celebrar rituales. De hecho, no hay celebración que no vaya acompañada de música.

10 **¿Y tú?, ¿qué clase de música escuchas en las siguientes situaciones? Habla de tus preferencias musicales con tu compañero/a y menciona los nombres de artistas, compositores y otra información relevante para describir tus emociones.**

Modelo: *Cuando estoy enamorado/a, me gusta escuchar... porque...*

- estás enamorado/a
- te apetece mucho (*feel like*) bailar
- quieres relajarte
- quieres cantar y bailar al mismo tiempo
- estás de mal humor

179

OBJECTIVES FOR LA MÚSICA

- Present vocabulary needed to talk about styles of music
- Talk about musical preferences

STANDARDS

1.1	Engage in conversation
1.2	Understand the language
1.3	Present information
3.2	Acquire information
4.1	Compare languages and cultures

INSTRUCTIONAL STRATEGIES

Activity 9

- Have students read the statements and decide if they are true or false based on what they think they know about the relationship between music and emotions.
- Then have students read the text and check whether their opinions were supported by the reading.
- Find out how many students had the correct answers with a show of thumbs up or down. Encourage students to talk about the ones they got wrong and where the correct information was presented in the text.

Activity 10

- Brainstorm with students different genres of music and list them on the board. Include all types from classical music to show tunes (***melodías de espectáculos musicales***) to give students a broad range from which to choose.
- Have students work in pairs or groups of three. Tell them to use the vocabulary and the expressions they have learned in this section.
- Circulate around the room to check that students are on task and responding with more than just a type of music. Provide support as needed to help students expand on their answers.

ANSWERS

Activity 9

a. T; **b.** T; **c.** F; **d.** T.

SLOWER-PACED LEARNERS

After Activity 10, give students additional practice with the plural forms. Group students according to their likes, for instance, **A estos estudiantes les gusta Lady Gaga**. Have the class say a few more statements in plural about this group of students. Repeat with other students, artists, etc.

ADVANCED LEARNERS

Have students do some research about how music affects people. You can point them to TedTalks, such as The Transformative Power of Classical Music, or have them visit the website Playing for Change: http://playingforchange.com/. Have them report back to the class about what they've learned.

INSTRUCTIONAL STRATEGIES

Activity 11

- Before students begin the activity, go over the meaning of the following words to facilitate comprehension of the text: **seguidor, puntero, encabezar, listas de éxitos, ejercer, imitar, compases, decantarse** (opt for) and **arriesgadas fusiones**. For the words that are already glossed in text, ask students to locate them and explain in their own words using context clues. For the others, explain in Spanish or have students look for familiar words.
- Have students read the text, ignoring the blanks for now. Ask some comprehension questions such as: **¿Qué tipo de música tiene el mayor número de seguidores? ¿Cuándo empezó la música pop a sonar en España? ¿Qué estilo de música ha influido en la música pop?**
- Then in pairs, have students match the missing sentences to their correct spot in the text. After reviewing the answers, call on student volunteers to read a paragraph inserting the new sentences.

Activity 12

- Have students select one of the musical groups mentioned in the reading and research more information about them on Internet or project some of their videos in class.
- Have students discuss their opinions in pairs. Then ask students to share with the class.
- Review the note on **la movida madrileña** and encourage students to seek more information about this transformative period in music.

Extension

As a follow up to Activity 12 and an introduction to Activity 13, have students choose from the following topics: **la Escuela Popular de Música, flamenco-chill, flamenco errante, ska, Alaska y Dinarama**… to do additional research online about what interests them. Encourage students to bring in pictures from the Internet to present and discuss in class.

Activity 13

With a different partner, ask students to discuss these questions.

ANSWERS

Activity 11

a. 2; **b.** 4; **c.** 1; **d.** 5; **e.** 3.

HERITAGE LANGUAGE LEARNERS

Have students do research on contemporary pop musicians from Spain and find the lyrics or a music video of one of their songs. Have them write their impressions of the musicians and their music and post it on a class discussion board.

PALABRA POR PALABRA La música

11 Lee el siguiente texto sobre la evolución de la música pop en España. Después, relaciona las letras del texto con las frases para completarlo de una forma lógica.

> Sin duda, el género que más seguidores (followers) tiene hoy en España es el pop, (a) .... En los 60 y 70, (b) ...., fueron famosos grupos como los Brincos, los Bravos o Fórmula V.
> En los 80, influidos por la conocida movida madrileña, surgen grupos como Alaska y Dinarama, los Secretos o Radio Futura. (c) ....
> Actualmente, grupos pop que destacan (stand out) en el panorama musical español (d) .... son: Maldita Nerea, el Canto del Loco, Amaral o Pereza, entre otros.
> Es importante señalar también que el flamenco ha ejercido una gran influencia en muchos de los grupos y cantantes de la actualidad: así, (e) ...., como es el caso de Chambao y su flamenco-chill, o el Bicho y su flamenco errante.

1. ☐ ➔ Después les seguirán Hombres G, Mecano o Duncan Dhu, líderes indiscutibles de aquella década
2. ⓐ ➔ música que se puede cantar y bailar, y que se desarrolla con la llegada del rock a España en los años 50
3. ☐ ➔ mientras grupos como Ojos de Brujo imitan sus compases, otros se decantan por nuevas y arriesgadas fusiones
4. ☐ ➔ décadas conocidas como la era dorada de los grupos españoles
5. ☐ ➔ y que suelen encabezar (top) las listas de éxitos (hits)

> ■ La movida madrileña fue un movimiento contracultural que surgió (emerged) durante los primeros años de la transición de la España después de la muerte de Franco (1975), y se prolongó hasta mediados de los años ochenta. Fue parte del cambio y liberalización cultural e ideológica que experimentó la gran mayoría de la sociedad española. Flamenco-chill es un subgénero musical derivado de la fusión del flamenco y música electrónica ambiental (background). Se desarrolló con la colaboración de Henrik Takkenberg y el grupo Chambao. El Bicho es un grupo que se conoció en la Escuela Popular de Música de Madrid y en pocas semanas comenzaron a tocar en pequeñas salas (lounges) y por la calle, atrapando a la gente que pasaba con sus canciones de una belleza y sencillez deslumbrante (stunning).

12 🗣 Busca información en Internet sobre estos grupos y mira algunos de sus vídeos musicales. ¿Cuáles te gustaron? Comenta tus opiniones con tu compañero/a.

13 🗣 Túrnate con tu compañero/a haciendo preguntas y respuestas.

a. ¿Conoces alguno de los estilos musicales que se mencionan en el texto?
b. ¿Y los grupos musicales o cantantes?
c. ¿Conoces otros grupos musicales o cantantes hispanos? ¿Qué tipo de música hacen?

 MORE IN ELETECA: EXTRA ONLINE PRACTICE

GRAMÁTICA

UNIDAD **6**

1. VERBS FOLLOWED BY AN INFINITIVE OR PRESENT PARTICIPLE

- To express the beginning point of an activity use **empezar / ponerse a** + infinitive.
  He **empezado a leer** un libro muy interesante. *I have started reading an interesting book.*
  Luis, **¡ponte a hacer** las tareas ahora mismo! *Luis, start doing your homework right now!*

- To express the repetition of an activity use **volver a** + infinitive.
  El año pasado fui a Sevilla y este año **volveré a ir.**
  Last year I went to Sevilla and this year I'm going to go again.

- To express an activity that is ongoing use **seguir / continuar** + present participle.
  Sigo estudiando en la misma escuela que el año pasado.
  I'm still studying in the same school as last year.
  El año pasado iba a clases de teatro y este **continuaré yendo.**
  Last year I was going to acting classes and this year I will continue going.

Plaza de España, Sevilla

- To express an activity that has just finished use **acabar de** + infinitive.
  ¡Acabo de ver al muchacho que conocimos ayer en el concierto!
  I just saw the guy we met yesterday at the concert!

- To express the interruption of an activity use **dejar de** + infinitive.
  He **dejado de ir** a clases de guitarra porque no tengo tiempo.
  I stopped going to guitar classes because I don't have time.

1 Completa con la construcción verbal correcta. ¡Atención! Usa la forma adecuada del pasado.

Asunto: Cosas que pasan

De: Roberto   Para: NachoVela@correoemail.com

Nacho, ¡no te lo vas a creer lo que pasó esta mañana!
(Nosotros) (a) .... de entrar en clase cuando el
profesor (b) .... a escribir en el pizarrón los acordes
(*chords*) de una canción. Todos la reconocimos rápidamente y
(c) .... a cantarla en voz baja. Pero, de pronto, Antonia
(d) .... a cantar en voz alta, mirando hacia Adrián.
Entonces el profesor le mandó callar (*to be quiet*), pero Antonia
(e) .... cantando, mientras Adrián y el resto de la
clase la mirábamos alucinados (*amazed*). Cuando el profesor la
(f) .... a mandar a callar, amenazando con castigarla,
Antonia (g) .... de cantar, pero antes le dijo a Adrián
que quería decirle las palabras de esa canción desde hacía
mucho tiempo.

181

- Present grammatical structures needed to practice communicative functions of the unit: Verbs that are followed by an infinitive or the present participle
- Talk about the beginning, end, continuity, and repetition of an action

CORE RESOURCES

- Interactive Online Materials - ELEteca

STANDARDS

1.1	Engage in conversation
1.2	Understand the language
1.3	Present information
4.1	Compare languages

INSTRUCTIONAL STRATEGIES

1. Verbs Followed by an Infinitive or Present Participle

- To introduce the topic write the following expressions on the board: **empezar a, dejar de, volver a, seguir, acabar de**. Explain to students that you are going to talk about yourself and things that you have started to do or have done again, things you have stopped doing, etc., using the expressions on the board. Ask them to listen for what comes after these expressions in your story and to jot them down. Tell students (pointing to the expressions as you say them): **Empecé a andar cuando tenía 10 meses, Dejé de montar en bicicleta a los 17 años porque empecé a conducir, He vuelto a montar en bicicleta para hacer ejercicio pero todavía sigo conduciendo, Acabo de comprar un coche híbrido que ahorra mucho en gasolina.** Ask students what forms they heard and for which expressions.

- Walk students through the grammatical explanation in the book. Read the examples, review the explanations, and answer any questions they may have.

- Ask personalized questions with each verb so students can give you real examples. Allow students time to write their sentences. Ask: **¿Cuándo empezaste a hablar español / jugar a los videojuegos…? ¿Qué hacías cuando tenías 10 años y qué sigues haciendo ahora? ¿Qué has dejado de hacer?**

Activity 1

- Ask students if they remember the characters Adrián and Antonia from earlier in the unit, and what they know of them.
- Have students complete this activity individually. Then have students compare their answers with a partner.
- Project the activity with the answers inserted. Review with students the expressions: **cantar en voz alta / baja, callar, castigar.**
- Then ask students to describe what happened in class between Adrián and Antonia.

ANSWERS

Activity 1

a. Acabábamos; **b.** empezó; **c.** empezamos; **d.** se puso; **e.** siguió; **f.** volvió; **g.** dejó.

ADVANCED LEARNERS

Have students use the information from Activity 1 to write an email from Antonia's perspective about the incident. Have them notice that they will have to change not only some verbs but also some personal pronouns.

INSTRUCTIONAL STRATEGIES

Activity 2

- Have students walk around the class to find a classmate who has done some of these things. Students will need to write the names next to the appropriate sentence and ask for more information.
- Have three or four students share their findings with the class.

Alternative Activity

Tell students that they need to go around the class and find someone who answers 'yes' to all the questions. The student who completes all the sentences first, wins. Be aware that it is necessary to answer 'yes' to the first question in order to move to the next question.

Activity 3

- Have students write out their sentences on a separate piece of paper, reminding them to include some activities that are not true for them.
- Then in small groups, have students exchange lists with others in the group. Tell them to read their classmate's experiences and try to pick out the facts from fiction, writing **sí** or **no** next to the activities and then return the list to its owner. Take turns responding to false statements using thumbs up or down. Who made the best guesses?

OBJECTIVES FOR GRAMÁTICA 2

- Present grammatical structures needed to practice communicative functions for the unit: Verbs that express change
- Describe changes that can occur in professions, lifestyles, and emotions

CORE RESOURCES

- Audio Program: Track 46
- Interactive Whiteboard Lesson: IWB 6.1

STANDARDS

1.4	Engage in conversation	1.6	Present information
1.5	Understand the language	4.1	Compare languages

INSTRUCTIONAL STRATEGIES

2. Verbs that Express Change

- Project IWB 6.1, **¡Vaya cambio!** to introduce the concept of change. Review each set of images and ask students to think about the type of change depicted: a. a change in profession; b. a change in lifestyle; c. a physical change; d. an emotional change. Then guide students to explain using **antes era…** / **ahora es…** and **antes** (+ imperfect) / **ahora** (+ present) to describe actions.
- Walk the students through the explanation in the book and invite volunteers to read the examples for the class.

ADVANCED LEARNERS

Before beginning the mingling portion of Activity 2, have students add two of their own ideas to the chart so they can find students who have done those as well.

GRAMÁTICA

2 Lee la siguiente lista de actividades. Después, pasea por la clase para encontrar a un/a compañero/a que haya hecho alguna de ellas. Apunta su nombre y pídele más información. Comparte tus resultados con la clase.

	¿Quién?	Más información
Ha empezado a practicar algún deporte nuevo.		¿Cuál?
Alguna vez se ha puesto a llorar viendo una película en el cine.		¿Qué película?
Sigue viviendo en la misma casa en la que nació.		¿En qué lugar?
Acaba de comprar una computadora nueva.		¿Cómo es?
Continúa teniendo un juguete de cuando era pequeño.		¿Qué juguete?
Ha dejado de practicar algún *hobby* que antes practicaba.		¿Qué *hobby*?
Ha empezado a leer un libro recientemente.		¿Cómo se titula?
Ha dejado de colgar *(post)* fotos en su Facebook.		¿Por qué?

3 Haz una lista de actividades que hayas empezado a hacer, que hayas hecho, que piensas volver a hacer o que acabes de hacer. Incluye experiencias verdaderas y algunas que no lo sean.

Modelo: El año pasado fui de vacaciones a China y este año volveré a ir. Acabo de comprar mi boleto de avión.

2. VERBS THAT EXPRESS CHANGE

- To express temporary changes in a person or changes that happen spontaneously use **ponerse** + adjective.
  Se **pone muy nervioso** al hablar en público. *He becomes / gets very nervous when speaking in public.*
  Se **puso rojo** cuando le preguntaron. *He turned / became red when they asked him a question.*

- **Quedarse** shows the result, the final condition.
  Se **quedó muy sorprendido** por la noticia. *He was very surprised by the news (and remained so).*

- **Quedarse** can sometimes express permanent changes.
  - Mi abuelo **se quedó calvo** a los 50 años.
    My grandfather went bald at age 50.

■ To express permanent changes use **volverse** (*not voluntary*) or **hacerse** (*voluntary or gradual change*) + adjective.
Se ha vuelto un antipático. Antes no era así. He has become unlikable. He wasn't like that before.
Jugó a la lotería y se volvió millonario. He played the lottery and became a millionaire.
Con esa situación se hizo fuerte. He became strong.

■ **Hacerse** can be used with adjectives and nouns that describe profession, religion, and ideology.
Antes era abogado y ahora se ha hecho juez. Before he was a lawyer and now he became a judge.
Viajó al Tíbet y se hizo budista. He traveled to Tibet and became a Buddhist.

4 Completa con el verbo de cambio correcto. ¡*Atención!* Ten en cuenta el tipo de cambio que se expresa. Puede haber más de una posibilidad.

a. .... un antipático	d. .... más delgado	g. .... vegetariano	
b. .... blanco	e. .... contento	h. .... un irresponsable	
c. .... guapo	f. .... más sociable	i. .... empresario	

5 Completa las frases con una expresión apropiada de la actividad anterior.

a. Desde que es famoso siempre contesta mal a todo el mundo,..........
b. Los invitaron a la inauguración de una galería de arte,..........
c. Estudió un máster de negocios muy prestigioso y..........
d. Desde que es bailarina..........
e. Cuando le dieron la nota del examen de Literatura..........
f. Desde que trabaja en una ONG en defensa de los animales..........

6 🎧 46 Blanca y Ester han sido amigas desde la escuela. Escucha a Blanca hablando de una reunión de la clase a la que Ester no pudo asistir. Completa con lo que ha cambiado.

	Martín	Carolina	Gustavo	Antonio	Elena	Dani
Aspecto físico						
Carácter						
Profesión						
Ideología						
Vida personal						

7 Ustedes están todos en la reunión de los 10 años de la clase. Paseen por la clase contándose lo que ha cambiado en sus vidas.

MORE IN ELETECA: EXTRA ONLINE PRACTICE ● GRAMMAR TUTORIALS 11 AND 12

Activity 4

Have students complete the activity individually and review as a class.

Activity 5

• Have students do this activity individually and then correct the answers with a partner.
• Ask for a couple of volunteers to ask and respond to each other taking turns: *¿Cuándo fue la última vez que te pusiste nervioso / muy contento / enfermo / rojo...?*

Extension

As a follow-up, project IWB: 6.1, *¡Vaya cambio!* and ask students to describe the changes once again, but this time using the new expressions.

🎧 46 Activity 6

• Explain to students that they will be listening to a conversation between two friends, one of whom attended their high-school reunion.
• Have students review the names and the categories they will need to complete to document changes observed by Blanca at the reunion.
• Play the audio and ask students to complete the chart while listening. Tell them there will be a brief pause between each one. Repeat the audio another time so students can check their answers. Review as a class.

See audioscript on page APP11

Activity 7

• Allow students time to prepare 2 or 3 predictions about how their lives have changed since the last time they were in class. Then tell students to form a circle within a circle to ensure everyone gets a turn.
• Then call on volunteers to share the most drastic changes they heard about their classmates.

ANSWERS

Activity 4

a. Volverse; **b.** Quedarse; **c.** Volverse; **d.** Quedarse; **e.** Ponerse; **f.** Volverse; **g.** Volverse; **h.** Volverse; **i.** Hacerse.

Activity 5

a. se ha vuelto un antipático; **b.** se pusieron contentos; **c.** se hizo empresario; **d.** se ha quedado más delgada; **e.** se puso blanco; **f.** se ha vuelto más sociable.

Activity 6

Martín: Se ha puesto guapísimo; Se ha vuelto mucho más sociable y hablador; No ha dejado de hacer deporte, tiene novia; **Carolina:** Sigue siendo igual de guapa que antes; Se hizo modelo, ahora trabaja para una organización humanitaria; Se hizo budista; Dejó de ser una esclava de la imagen; **Gustavo:** Se puso muy gordo, se está quedando calvo; Sigue siendo tan simpático como siempre; Dejó de hacer deporte, se ha casado y acaba de tener un niño; **Antonio:** Se puso a trabajar en un restaurante, después volvió a estudiar y se hizo profesor de español; Ya no vive en España, dejó de estudiar y se fue a Toronto; **Elena:** Ahora se ha puesto muy guapa, se quedó mucho más delgada; Empezó a llevar un estilo de vida más saludable, se hizo vegetariana; Ya no sale con Dani; **Dani:** Empezó a trabajar por las noches en una discoteca, se ha hecho empresario; Se volvió más irresponsable y despreocupado; Ya no sale con Elena.

HERITAGE LANGUAGE LEARNERS

For additional practice, have students write a paragraph describing changes in their family members with *ponerse*, *quedarse*, *volverse*, or *hacerse*.

OBJECTIVES FOR DESTREZAS

- Anticipate content before listening

CORE RESOURCES

- Audio Program: Tracks 47 and 48

STANDARDS

- Understand the language

INSTRUCTIONAL STRATEGIES

Comprensión auditiva (1)

Activity 1

- Review the strategy with students and give them time to prepare.
- Ask them to look at the images to anticipate the answers to the questions.
- Ask students to discuss it in pairs. They will discover if they were correct after listening the audio (Activity 2).

🎧 **47 Activity 2**

- Tell students that each conversation will be played twice with a pause in between.
- Ask students to give the correct answer.

Audioscript

Conversación 1

≫ Has estado hoy en clase con Juan, ¿no? ¿Le has dicho que hemos quedado en el café de la esquina?

≫ No, no ha venido, ha vuelto a faltar. Se lo diré después en la biblioteca.

Conversación 2

≫ Perdona, me quiero probar estos jeans en la talla 30, esta camiseta y este jersey, pero en verde.

≫ A ver… Es que camisetas solo nos quedan en la talla grande y los jeans no nos quedan en ninguna talla, acaban de llevarse los últimos. El jersey aquí lo tienes y resulta que es el último que hay en la tienda.

INSTRUCTIONAL STRATEGIES

Comprensión auditiva (2)

Activity 3

- Review the strategy with students and give them time to prepare.
- Tell students they will listen to an announcement. In this case, students will hear a longer selection.

ANSWERS

Activity 2

Conversación 1: a; Conversación 2: a.

Remind students about two of the different meanings of the verb **quedar** that will come up in the conversations: **quedar** as in to meet (**Hemos quedado en el café de la esquina**) and **quedar** as in to have left (**No nos quedan en ninguna talla**).

In order to review the meaning of **quedar** for the slower-paced students, have advance students say two sentences or make questions with its two meanings: **¿Cuándo quedas con tus amigos? ¿Cuántas páginas quedan en esta unidad?**

DESTREZAS

COMPRENSIÓN AUDITIVA (1)

1 Antes de escuchar, lee la estrategia en Destrezas y sigue las recomendaciones.

> **Destrezas**
>
> **Anticipating content**
> Read the question carefully before listening to the audio. Look at the interrogative word to determine what type of response is needed. Is it asking for a person, a place, a thing, etc.? Then look at the choice of images and prepare ahead the vocabulary you might expect to hear.
> **Conversación 1:** ¿Dónde creía el muchacho que ella había hablado con Juan?
> **Conversación 2:** ¿Qué prenda está agotada en la tienda?

2 🎧 **47** Escucha dos veces estas conversaciones breves. Después de la segunda vez, elige la opción correcta.

Conversación 1: ¿Dónde creía el muchacho que ella había hablado con Juan?

Conversación 2: ¿Qué prenda está agotada en la tienda?

COMPRENSIÓN AUDITIVA (2)

3 Antes de escuchar este aviso, lee la estrategia en Destrezas y sigue las recomendaciones.

> **Destrezas**
>
> **Listening to longer selections**
> To prepare for longer listening selections, first read the questions you will be asked to answer. Underline or highlight key words you will need to listen for. Say them softly aloud to yourself so you can hear how they are pronounced. Focus on these words and do not be distracted by unfamiliar words.

4 🎧 48 Escucha dos veces un aviso por el sistema de megafonía de una escuela. Después de la segunda vez, decide si las afirmaciones son verdaderas (V) o falsas (F).

	V	F
a. Las bases del concurso se pueden consultar en Internet y en los tablones informativos del centro.	☐	☐
b. El sobre en el que tienen que enviar el escrito se puede recoger en el Departamento de Lengua y Literatura del centro.	☐	☐
c. La modalidad del trabajo es libre.	☐	☐

PRONUNCIACIÓN Los extranjerismos *(foreign words)*

■ En español usamos algunas palabras que proceden de otras lenguas. Se dividen en:

• **Voces adaptadas**
  Se adaptan a la ortografía y pronunciación del español: *estrés, eslogan, cabaré...*

• **Voces no adaptadas**
  Se escriben igual que en la lengua original y su pronunciación es más o menos aproximada a ella: *pizza, rock and roll, jazz, pendrive...*

1 🎧 49 Escucha las siguientes palabras extranjeras que se usan frecuentemente entre los hispanoparlantes, y apúntalas.

_____ _____ _____
_____ _____ _____
_____ _____ _____

2 👥 Compara las palabras que has escrito con tu compañero/a. Decide cuáles han sido adaptadas al español y cuáles no.

3 Completa con la palabra o expresión apropiada aprendida en esta sección.

a. Necesito ir a la .... para comprarme un vestido.
b. A mi hermana le encantan los .... con tomate.
c. Marta y Juan han quedado para jugar al .... esta tarde.
d. Mis padres desayunan un .... y un café con leche.
e. El .... es el equipamiento lógico de un sistema informático.

👤💻 **MORE IN ELETECA:** EXTRA ONLINE PRACTICE

185

INSTRUCTIONAL STRATEGIES

🎧 48 Activity 4

• Tell students that the audio will be played twice with a pause between each one. Correct the activity with the whole class.

See audioscript on page APP11

ANSWERS

Activity 4

a. verdadero; **b.** falso (Los trabajos deberán introducirse en un sobre grande que facilita la Consejería del centro y se entregarán al Departamento de Lengua y Literatura); **c.** falso (Solo se admitirán trabajos en la modalidad de cuento, el tema será libre).

OBJECTIVES FOR PRONUNCIACIÓN

• Learn about foreign words adapted to Spanish and those that stay in the original

CORE RESOURCES

• Audio Program: Track 49
• Interactive Online Materials - ELEteca

STANDARDS

1.2   Understand the language
3.2   Acquire information
4.1   Compare languages

INSTRUCTIONAL STRATEGIES

• Write on the board the following words: **estrés**, **eslogan**, **email**, **iphone**, **pizza**, **espaguetis**, **tenis**, **fútbol**, etc.
• Ask students to tell you which of these words have been adapted to Spanish and which ones remain in their original language.

🎧 49 Activities 1 and 2

• Play the audio and have students write each word.
• Ask students to tell you which words have been adapted to Spanish and which ones have not.
• In pairs, ask students to expand the list. Write the words on the board.

Audioscript

escáner, boutique, máster, stock, marketing, ranking, espaguetis, estatus, yogur, playback, espray, software, ballet, pádel, blus, cruasán.

Activity 3

Ask students to do this activity individually. Correct together as a class.

ANSWERS

Activity 1

See audioscript.

Activity 2

Adapted to Spanish: escáner, máster, espaguetis, estatus, yogur, espray, pádel, blus, cruasán.
Stay in the original: boutique, stock, marketing, ranking, playback, software, ballet.

Activity 3

a. boutique; **b.** espaguetis; **c.** tenis; **d.** cruasán; **e.** software.

HERITAGE LANGUAGE LEARNERS

Discuss ways in which the Spanish language has been modified by Spanish-speakers in the US. Have them consider why Spanish-speakers in the US tend to use words in English when they speak to each other. The words may be borrowed from English (**cool**), adapted from English (**lonchar**), or translated literally based on English grammar structures (**Te llamo para atrás**). Code switching, or switching between languages, is also frequent among Spanish speakers in the US. If appropriate, have them share their experiences speaking Spanish in the US and how people react to this specific variety of Spanish.

OBJECTIVES FOR SABOR HISPANO

- Learn about Hispanic music
- Learn about different type of Hispanic music and dance

CORE RESOURCES

- Audio Program: Track 50

STANDARDS

2.1.	Practices and perspectives
2.2	Products and perspectives
3.2	Acquire information
5.2	Using language for personal enjoyment and enrichment

INSTRUCTIONAL STRATEGIES

🎧 50

- Introduce the topic by asking what the students know about Hispanic music and dance.
- Talk about the images and elicit what they already know and can share.
- Put students in pairs to discuss the questions in the **Antes de leer** box.
- Monitor their conversations and assist as needed.
- Call on volunteers to report back on their discussions.
- Before playing the audio, tell students to listen for the type of stories are told by **los corridos mexicanos**. Either have students close their books while they listen or follow along with the text in the book.
- Elicit responses to the target question. For more detail, ask: **¿Cuándo empezaron los corridos mexicanos? ¿Qué papel tenían en cuanto a la revolución? Y ahora, ¿qué tipo de historias cuentan?**
- To help build vocabulary, have students locate and underline any words from the glossary on the next page in the text. Then have them make and share new sentences with the words. You may choose to have them work individually or in pairs.

SLOWER-PACED LEARNERS

Have students brainstorm a list of topics that might appear in the songs of **Los Tigres del Norte**. Do they know US singers who also use their songs to denounce political and social injustices? What are the advantages and disadvantages of using art for political purposes? For more information about **Los Tigres del Norte**, check http://www.lostigresdelnorte.com/main.

ADVANCED LEARNERS

Have student analyze the lyrics of one **corrido**. They can go to http://lostigresdelnorte.com/main/music and check the album titles first. What do the titles say about the music and the group? Then they can listen to one or two songs. Videos and lyrics of their most popular songs can be found on the web. Make sure you point students to videos that are appropriate for their age. Also, explain that because of the topics preferred by group, their lyrics are not always politically correct.

SABOR HISPANO

MUCHO MÁS QUE MÚSICA

Una banda de mariachis de Puebla, México

Antes de leer

¿Qué música o artistas mexicanos conoces?
¿Piensas que los mariachis son divertidos o están pasados de moda*? ¿Por qué?

🎧 50 **En el mundo hispano hay muchísimos tipos de música y baile. No solamente son expresiones artísticas: a veces, como los corridos mexicanos, son una forma de contar historias de actualidad.**

Los corridos son canciones populares mexicanas que cuentan una historia. La melodía suele ser muy sencilla, y la letra* es fácil de recordar. Eran habituales ya en 1910, en la época de la Revolución mexicana, y cumplían la importante función de diseminar* las noticias en todo el territorio.
Los temas de los corridos son variados: a veces hablan sobre un héroe popular, a veces son divertidos, y otras tienen contenido político. Muchas veces, las bandas de mariachis cantan corridos. Desde 1930, el contenido de los corridos incorpora noticias relacionadas con el narcotráfico. En los últimos años, este género se ha hecho más popular, especialmente en los estados del norte del país como Chihuahua, Nuevo León, Baja California y Sinaloa, donde se concentra la violencia del narcotráfico. En muchos estados, está prohibido reproducir narcocorridos en conciertos, discotecas y bares. «Este tipo de canciones presenta a los narcotraficantes con glamur», dicen las autoridades.

En la actualidad, los Tigres del Norte son una banda muy famosa de música norteña, que incluye los corridos. Son conocidos internacionalmente y han ganado cinco premios Grammy. Sin embargo, varios pueblos les han puesto multas* por cantar narcocorridos en sus conciertos. «La prohibición no es justa», estas canciones son parte de la cultura actual», dicen.

Un edificio público en Culiacán, Sinaloa, tierra del narcocorrido

El tango

Todos los años se celebra un festival internacional de tango en la ciudad de Buenos Aires. Más de 70.000 turistas y bailarines de todo el mundo llegan para participar en el evento. Estos son los principales países representados en el festival, además de Argentina.

- 59%
- 15%
- 8%
- 6%
- 6%
- 6%

- ■ Colombia
- ■ Estados Unidos
- ■ Japón
- ■ Brasil
- ■ Francia
- ■ Argentina

Los top 5 del flamenco

Para muchos turistas, el flamenco es sinónimo de cultura española, aunque proviene* del sur del país. Te contamos cinco cosas que debes saber sobre esta apasionada* danza.

1. Combina la cultura **andaluza**, **sefardí**, **gitana** y **árabe**.
2. Una de sus formas se llama **«cante jondo»**.
3. El bailarín se llama **«bailaor»** y la bailarina, **«bailaora»**.
4. Gran parte del baile es **improvisación**.
5. Los lugares donde se baila flamenco se llaman **«tablaos»**.

El tango nació en Buenos Aires, y siempre se baila en pareja .

¿COMPRENDISTE?

Decide si las siguientes frases son verdaderas (V) o falsas (F).

1. No todos los corridos hablan sobre el narcotráfico. V○ F○
2. Los Tigres del Norte piensan que los narcocorridos son parte de la cultura. V○ F○
3. Colombia es el país extranjero mejor representado en el festival de tango. V○ F○
4. Los pasos del baile flamenco están todos planeados con anticipación. V○ F○
5. El tango se puede bailar de forma individual. V○ F○

El flamenco es la música y baile típicos del sur de España.

AHORA TÚ

¿Qué opinas? Contesta las siguientes preguntas y comenta tus ideas con tus compañeros/as.

1. ¿Qué tipo de música te gusta? ¿Cuál es su atractivo, en tu opinión?
2. ¿Qué tipo de música no escuchas nunca, y por qué?
3. ¿Qué forma musical norteamericana presenta estilos de vida polémicos con glamur?
4. ¿Te gusta bailar? ¿Cuándo fue la última vez que bailaste y qué tipo de música había?
5. ¿Prefieres bailar de forma individual o en pareja? ¿Por qué?
6. Entre el tango y el flamenco, ¿qué estilo musical te parece más interesante? ¿Por qué?

Glosario

apasionado/a – passionate
diseminar – to spread
justo/a – fair
la letra – lyrics
la multa – fine
la pareja – couple
pasado de moda – out of date
provenir – to originate

VOCES ATINAS
LA MÚSICA EN AMÉRICA LATINA

Fuentes: BBC Mundo, Tango BA, Buzzle.

187

INSTRUCTIONAL STRATEGIES

El tango

- Call on a volunteer to read the caption and chart data aloud.
- Have students write three questions about the data.
- Put them into pairs to take turns asking and answering the questions.
- Monitor their conversations and assist as needed. Take note of any common errors that you hear in their discussions.
- Review any common errors with the class, eliciting the corrections.

Los top 5 del flamenco

- Call on a volunteer to read the title and information that follows.
- Check students' understanding of the information by asking questions, such as: **¿Qué culturas están representadas en el flamenco? ¿Qué tipo de baile es? ¿Qué quiere decir?**

¿Comprendiste?

- Have the students say if the statements are true or false.
- Ask for volunteers to point out where in the text they can find the information.
- Discuss any vocabulary that may be unknown, and ask those that have understood to help those that have not.

Ahora tú

- Read the questions with the students and have them think about the answers.
- Have the students answer the questions in pairs and then present to the class. Each student may take a turn at speaking.

ANSWERS

¿Comprendiste?

1. T; **2.** T; **3.** F; **4.** F; **5.** F.

SLOWER-PACED LEARNERS

Have students watch or listen to the music forms introduced on this page. Explain that flamenco is composed of many different types of dances and styles, and for the lay listener, some of those styles are very difficult to enjoy. Have them compare, for instance, a **sevillana** with an example of **cante jondo**, and ask them to discuss the differences and similarities in the music, feelings, melody, etc.

HERITAGE LANGUAGE LEARNERS

Have students share other types of dances they are familiar with. Examples include **cueca** (Chile), **cumbia** (Colombia), **merengue** (República Dominicana), **marinera** (Perú), **tamborito** (Panamá), **jaropo** (Venezuela), **jarabe tapatío** (México), **caporales** and **llamerada** (región de los Andes), and many others. Ask students to reflect on why some of these dances are still very popular among young people while others are just danced during festivals or by older folks.

OBJECTIVES FOR RELATO

- Revisit unit themes, grammar, vocabulary and culture in a new context
- Improve reading comprehension skills

CORE RESOURCES

- Audio Program: Track 51

STANDARDS

- 1.1 Engage in conversation
- 1.2 Understand the language
- 1.3 Present information
- 2.1 Practices and perspectives
- 5.3 Using language for personal enjoyment and enrichment

INSTRUCTIONAL STRATEGIES

Activity 1

- Before doing the activity, ask students to provide the names of famous Hispanic poets or writers they have studied so far, ask them to name different genres, and say which one was their favorite and why.
- The purpose of the activity is to preview the vocabulary that will appear in the text and to facilitate comprehension.
- Ask students to look at the images and match the words with their definitions.
- Help students to access meaning since some of these words are used more in literary texts than in everyday conversations.

🎧 51 Activity 2

- Ask students if they know what animal is pictured. Ask them to talk about its color and why they think its name is **Platero**.
- Before students read the text, review glossed words such as: **peludo**, **blando**, **algodón**, **huesos**, **prado**, **tibiamente**, **celeste**, **naranjas**, **mandarinas**, **uvas moscateles**, **morado**, **cristalino**, **gota** and **miel**.
- Tell students that the sentence **"Tien' asero..."** refers to the way they speak in parts of **Andalucía**.

Activity 3

- Have the students read the questions and skim the text to look for the correct answer.
- Explain what a **comparación** is (a literary device in which a writer compares or contrasts two people, places, things, or ideas) and a **metáfora** (a type of analogy that achieves its effects via association, comparison or resemblance).

ANSWERS

Activity 1

1. d; **2.** a; **3.** i; **4.** b; **5.** f; **6.** c; **7.** g; **8.** e; **9.** h.

Activity 3

a. Un burro; **b.** Físicamente es pequeño, peludo, suave, con los ojos muy negros. De carácter es tierno, y mimoso, alegre, pero también es fuerte; **c.** *Tan blando que se diría todo de algodón; los espejos de azabache de sus ojos son duros como dos escarabajos de cristal negro; Camina con un trotecillo alegre que parece que se ríe; es tierno y mimoso igual que un niño, que una niña; es fuerte y seco como una piedra; tiene acero y plata de luna.*

ADVANCED LEARNERS

Using the text in Activity 2 as a model, have students write a description about an animal or a pet without saying exactly what it is. Then have them share their descriptions with a partner or in small groups to guess the correct animals.

---

1 Relaciona cada palabra con su definición.

1. azabache
2. escarabajo
3. hocico
4. gualdo/a
5. trote
6. cascabeleo
7. higo
8. ámbar
9. despacioso

a. Insecto que busca excremento de otros animales para alimentarse.
b. Amarillo. Se dice así porque hay una flor de ese color con el mismo nombre.
c. Sonido que producen los cascabeles.
d. Tipo de carbón, de color negro, que se usa como adorno en collares, pulseras…
e. Resina fósil de color amarillo, que se emplea en collares, etc.
f. Modo de caminar acelerado de algunos animales, que avanzan saltando.
g. Fruto de la higuera, dulce, de color verde por fuera y blanco o rojo por dentro.
h. Lento, pausado.
i. Parte de la cabeza de algunos animales, en la que están la boca y la nariz.

2 🎧 **51** Lee el siguiente extracto de la novela *Platero y yo* de Juan Ramón Jiménez.

Platero y yo

Platero es pequeño, peludo *(hairy)*, suave; tan blando *(soft)* por fuera, que se diría todo de algodón, que no lleva huesos *(bones)*. Solo los espejos de azabache de sus ojos son duros cual *(like)* dos escarabajos de cristal negro.

Lo dejo suelto y se va al prado, y acaricia *(caresses)* tibiamente con su hocico, rozándolas apenas, las florecillas rosas, celestes y gualdas… Lo llamo dulcemente: "¿Platero?", y viene a mí con un trotecillo alegre que parece que se ríe, en no sé qué cascabeleo ideal…

Come cuanto le doy. Le gustan las naranjas mandarinas, las uvas moscateles, todas de ámbar; los higos morados, con su cristalina gotita de miel…

Es tierno y mimoso *(affectionate)* igual que un niño, que una niña…; pero fuerte y seco por dentro, como una piedra… Cuando paso sobre él, los domingos, por las últimas callejas del pueblo, los hombres del campo, vestidos de limpio y despaciosos, se quedan mirándolo:
- "Tien' asero…".

Tiene acero *(steel)*. Acero y plata de luna, al mismo tiempo.

3 👥 Contesta las siguientes preguntas con tu compañero/a.

a. Según el texto y la imagen, ¿qué animal es Platero?
b. ¿Cómo es físicamente? ¿Y su carácter o personalidad?
c. El autor utiliza metáforas y comparaciones para describir a Platero. ¿Podrías localizarlas en el texto? ¿Sabes qué significan todas?

4 **Ordena los siguientes párrafos para descubrir más sobre el autor, Juan Ramón Jiménez. El primero ya está enumerado.**

○ De carácter hipersensible, la melancolía lo acompañó a lo largo de su vida. En 1913 conoce en Madrid al gran amor de su vida, Zenobia Camprubí, con la que se casó durante su viaje a Estados Unidos en 1916.

○ En 1936, al estallar la Guerra Civil, abandonan España para no regresar nunca. Estados Unidos, Cuba y Puerto Rico fueron sus lugares de residencia a partir de entonces.

○ La primera se caracteriza por ser íntima, emotiva y sentimental, abundan las descripciones del paisaje como reflejo del alma del poeta, y también la melancolía, la música, los recuerdos y los ensueños. El modernismo de Rubén Darío y el simbolismo francés influirán en esta etapa de juventud. Es el tiempo en el que escribió la obra que lo inmortalizó, *Platero y yo*,

① Juan Ramón Jiménez nació en Huelva (España) en 1881, fue un niño solitario y su infancia transcurrió en el pueblo de Moguer, en contacto con la naturaleza.

○ el libro español traducido a más lenguas del mundo, junto con *El Quijote*. Escrito en prosa poética, está inspirado en la amistad del autor con un burro pequeño y peludo que lo acompañó en sus paseos por su pueblo natal.

○ Ya en el colegio se sintió atraído primero por la pintura, después por la música y finalmente por la poesía.

○ Otra de sus obras más conocidas, *Diario de un poeta recién casado* (1917), escrito a partir de su viaje por mar a Estados Unidos, representa una ruptura con la poesía sensitiva, iniciándose así una poesía más intelectual que lo situará en el camino hacia otra más metafísica y depurada en su última etapa.

○ En 1956, tres días antes de la muerte de su esposa, recibió el Premio Nobel de Literatura, él morirá tan solo dos años después. Su obra es muy extensa y su poesía pasa por distintas etapas.

5 **En la primera etapa de su carrera literaria, el autor se centra en la creación de descripciones para provocar ciertos sentimientos. ¿Qué sientes tú al leer la descripción de Platero?**

6 **¿Tienes o has tenido alguna vez una mascota? Escribe una descripción de ella utilizando metáforas y comparaciones como hizo el autor con Platero. Si nunca has tenido una mascota, puedes describir a una persona muy querida por ti.**

Dibuja aquí la mascota
o la persona descrita.

7 👥 **Contesta las preguntas con tu compañero/a.**
- ¿Piensas que el tener animales es bueno para desarrollar algunos sentimientos positivos?
- ¿Crees que puede ayudar a superar otros negativos? ¿Cuáles?

189

INSTRUCTIONAL STRATEGIES

Activity 4
- Tell students to go online and find out more information about Juan Ramón Jiménez and his poetry.
- Ask students to read the text and order the paragraphs to learn more about the author.
- Choose to do this activity individually or in pairs.

Activity 5
- Drawing from the structures and expressions students have learned in this unit, have them discuss their feelings in pairs.
- Ask a couple of volunteers to share their feelings after the reading.

Activity 6
- Have students write a description of their favorite pet using adjectives, comparisons and metaphors as modeled in **Platero y yo**.
- Provide students with the following examples for comparisons: ***Tus ojos se parecen al mar***, ***Tus ojos son como el mar*** and metaphors that connect two nouns in apposition using **ser**: ***Tus ojos son el mar***.
- Ask them to draw their pet to complete the description.
- Ask a couple of students to read their descriptions and draw their pets on the board.
- Have the rest of the students vote for the most interesting / funny / crazy… pet.

Activity 7
- Have students work in pairs to discuss their feelings about pets and what they bring to people's lives.
- You can bring to class articles, texts or some news about animals. You can create a debate with two big groups: one group should be in favor and the other against controversial topics like: bullfights, cockfights, fur coats, etc.

ANSWERS

Activity 4
3, 4, 6, 1, 7, 2, 8, 5.

SLOWER-PACED LEARNERS

As an alternate approach to Activity 6, have students rewrite the text using a feminine pet. Have them name her and use the appropriate adjectives and pronouns in the feminine forms.

HERITAGE LANGUAGE LEARNERS

Instead of just having students talk to each other in Activity 7, have them write their responses in the form of a short essay. Encourage them to ask and answer more questions about the differences between having a pet in the US and having one in another culture. For example, they can discuss what type of pets are most common in different countries and what services available for pets in those countries.

OBJECTIVES FOR EVALUACIÓN

- Review grammar, vocabulary and culture from the unit
- Complete self-assessment

CORE RESOURCES

- Interactive Online Materials - ELEteca

STANDARDS

1.2 Understand the language
2.1 Practices and perspectives
4.1 Compare cultures

INSTRUCTIONAL STRATEGIES

- Activities can be completed individually and then reviewed with the class. Vary by asking students if they agree with the answer given and then writing it on the board. Provide explanations as needed.
- You may wish to assign point value to each activity as a way for students to monitor their progress.
- Direct students to the indicated pages in **En resumen** if they make more than one or two mistakes in any one section.

ANSWERS

Activity 1

a. lleguen; **b.** me despido; **c.** se pone; **d.** tire; **e.** entregar; **f.** hacer; **g.** espero.

Activity 2

Poner: de mal humor; triste; de los nervios; **Dar:** pena; rabia; lástima; igual; miedo.

Activity 3

a. Juan ha vuelto a reprobar el examen de Música; **b.** Ana y Luis dejaron de hablarse; **c.** María sigue estudiando solfeo; **d.** He empezado a ir a clase de guitarra; **e.** Acabo de ver al profesor de Música; **f.** A Carlos le continúa gustando ver caricaturas.

EVALUACIÓN

EXPRESSING FEELINGS AND EMOTIONS

1 **Completa con la forma correcta del verbo entre paréntesis.**

a. Estoy contenta de que (llegar) .... las vacaciones.
b. Estoy triste cuando (despedirse, yo) .... de un amigo por mucho tiempo.
c. Me enfado si mi hermana (ponerse) .... mi ropa sin pedírmela.
d. Me molesta que la gente (tirar) .... papeles al suelo.
e. Nos preocupa no (entregar, nosotros) .... el trabajo a tiempo.
f. Me pongo nervioso cuando (esperar, yo) .... el autobús y tarda mucho en llegar.

2 **Clasifica las palabras de la caja en la columna correspondiente.**

de mal humor ○ pena ○ rabia ○ triste ○ lástima ○ igual ○ nervioso/a ○ miedo

PONER	DAR

Now write a sentence using the following verbs.
a. Poner ....
b. Dar ....

VERBAL CONSTRUCTIONS WITH INFINITIVE OR PRESENT PARTICIPLE

3 **Escribe las siguientes frases usando un verbo en infinitivo o gerundio, como en el modelo.**

a. Juan ha reprobado el examen de Música de nuevo.
   (volver a) *Juan ha vuelto a suspender el examen de Música.*
b. Ana y Luis eran muy amigos, pero hace un mes se enfadaron y ahora no se hablan.
   (dejar de) ....
c. María empezó a estudiar solfeo a los 8 años y ahora con 16 años todavía lo estudia.
   (seguir) ....
d. Me he apuntado a clases de guitarra y voy desde hace una semana.
   (empezar a) ....
e. Vi al profesor de Música hace cinco minutos.
   (acabar de) ....
f. A Carlos le gustaba ver caricaturas de pequeño y ahora también le gusta.
   (continuar) ....

VERBS THAT EXPRESS CHANGE

4 **Elige la opción correcta en cada frase.**

a. Como dejó el deporte, **se puso / se volvió / se quedó** muy gorda.
b. Desde que le robaron **se ha puesto / se ha vuelto / se ha quedado** más desconfiada.
c. Como ya sabe que aprobó, **se ha puesto / se ha vuelto / se ha quedado** tranquila.
d. Como la invitaron a un concierto, **se puso / se volvió / se quedó** muy contenta.
e. Desde que vive sola **se ha puesto / se ha vuelto / se ha quedado** más independiente.

5 **Describe cómo es una persona que tiene estas características. Después, pon el adjetivo contrario.**

a. egoísta ➡ .... ➡ ....
b. sincera ➡ .... ➡ ....
c. vaga ➡ .... ➡ ....
d. tolerante ➡ .... ➡ ....

LAS ARTES

6 **Completa con una palabra del cuadro.**

aventuras ○ paisaje ○ pintor ○ retrato ○ pirámides ○ novela

 Las (a) .... de Chichen Itzá son de origen maya.

 Estuvimos en Costa Rica y el (b) .... era tan bonito que tomé un montón de fotografías.

 Estoy leyendo una (c) .... de (d) .... que trata de tesoros y piratas.

 Los cuadros de ese (e) .... me encantaron, sobre todo el (f) .... de su mujer.

FOREIGN WORDS

7 **Indica las palabras que han adoptado la ortografía y pronunciación del español.**

☐ estrés ☐ pizza ☐ cruasán ☐ cabaré ☐ software
☐ estatus ☐ yogur ☐ pendrive ☐ blus ☐ piercing

CULTURA

8 **Contesta las siguientes preguntas con la información que has aprendido en *Mucho más que música*.**

a. ¿De qué trataban los primeros corridos mexicanos? ¿Qué función tenían?
b. Y ahora, ¿de qué tratan muchos de los corridos modernos?
c. ¿Por qué han recibido multas los Tigres del Norte? ¿Crees que es justo?
d. ¿Qué se celebra cada año en Buenos Aires y qué países participan?
e. Cuenta tres cosas que aprendiste sobre el flamenco.

 MORE IN ELETECA: EXTRA ONLINE PRACTICE

191

ANSWERS

Activity 4

a. se puso; **b.** se ha vuelto; **c.** se ha quedado; **d.** se puso; **e.** se ha vuelto.

Activity 5

a. Persona que piensa en sí misma y no en los demás; solidaria, generosa.
b. Persona que dice lo que piensa; falsa, hipócrita.
c. Persona perezosa, a la que no le gusta trabajar; trabajadora.
d. Persona que respeta las ideas de los demás; intolerante.

Activity 6

a. pirámides; **b.** paisaje; **c.** novela; **d.** aventuras; **e.** pintor; **f.** retrato.

Activity 7

estrés, estatus, yogur, cruasán, cabaré, blus.

Activity 8

a. Los primeros corridos mexicanos trataban de la Revolución mexicana. Su función era diseminar las noticias en todo el territorio; **b.** Muchos corridos modernos tratan del narcotráfico; **c.** Los Tigres del Norte han recibido multas por cantar narcocorridos en sus conciertos; **d.** Se celebra un festival internacional de tango. Participan países del todo el mundo pero especialmente de Colombia, Estados Unidos, Japón, Brasil, Francia y Argentina.

OBJECTIVES FOR EN RESUMEN: VOCABULARIO

- Review unit vocabulary and expressions
- Practice communicative skills

STANDARDS

1.2 Understand the language
1.3 Present information
4.1 Evaluate similarities and differences in language

INSTRUCTIONAL STRATEGIES

- Encourage students to use index cards used as flashcards with the Spanish term on one side and the English term on the other, or a picture or drawing. Tell students to write an example of the use of the word, so they can remember it in context.
- Students work in pairs or groups, using vocabulary flashcards as they would the cards of a board game to help each other practice unit vocabulary.
- Encourage students to write labels or captions for the photos on this page. Remind them to use the vocabulary and expressions they have learned in this unit.
- Working with a partner, have students write a conversation in which they incorporate as many of the target verbs as possible. Then have them perform their conversations in front of the class.
- Have students describe a person based on the words in **Descripciones** but without using them. Their partners have to guess the correct related vocabulary word.
- Have students play a game of pictionary with the words in **Los artes** and **Los instrumentos musicales.**

EN RESUMEN: Vocabulario

Verbos

adorar *to adore*
apetecer *to feel like*
atreverse *to dare*
colarse (o>ue) *to cut in, to sneak in*
colgar (o>ue) *to hang, to post online*
dar igual *to care less*

dar lástima / pena *to feel pity*

dar lo mismo *to be ambivalent*
dar rabia *to infuriate*

dar vergüenza *to feel embarrassed*

diseñar *to design*

ensayar *to rehearse*
hacer cola *to stand in line*
indignar *to anger*
molestar *to bother*
odiar *to hate*

ponerse *to become*
relajarse *to relax*
sentirse (e>ie) *to feel*

Descripciones

agotado/a *sold out, exhausted*
atento/a *attentive*
egoísta *selfish*
falso/a *fake*
gran *great*
histérico/a *crazy*
leal *loyal*
preocupado/a *worried*
seguro/a *assured*
sociable *sociable*
tierno/a *tender*
tolerante *tolerant*
tranquilo/a *calm*

Las artes

el acueducto *aqueduct*
las aventuras *adventures*
el bailarín / la bailarina *ballet dancer*
el compositor *composer*
el cuadro *painting*
la escultura *sculpture*

la estatua *statue*

el género *genre, style*
la galería de arte *art gallery*
el guitarrista *guitarist*
la melodía *melody*
el músico *musician*
el novelista *novelist*
la obra *work*
la orquesta *orchestra*
la pintura *painting*
el poema *poem*
el poeta *poet*
el retrato *portrait*
el violinista *violinist*

Los instrumentos musicales

el arpa *harp*
la flauta *flute*
la guitarra *guitar*
los platillos *cymbals*
el saxofón *saxophone*
el tambor *drum*
el violín *violin*

192

EN RESUMEN: Gramática

UNIDAD **6**

EXPRESSING FEELINGS AND EMOTIONS

(See page 172)

■ To express feelings and emotions use:

· **estar** + adjective + **con** + noun · **estar** + adjective + **de** (**que**)	· **No soportar** (can't stand) · **No aguantar** (can't take) · **Odiar** (to hate) · **Adorar** (to love)	+ noun + infinitive + **que** + subjunctive

· **ponerse / sentirse / estar** + adjective + **cuando / si** + present tense
· **me / te / le / nos...** + **da rabia / pone alegre / molesta** + **que** + subjunctive
· **me / te / le / nos...** + **da rabia / pone alegre / molesta** + infinitive

Mi hermana **está muy contenta con** su profesora de música.
Yo **me pongo furioso cuando** dejo un libro y no me lo devuelven.
Odio que me digan lo que tengo que hacer.
A mí **me da vergüenza** hablar en público.

VERBS FOLLOWED BY INFINITIVE OR PRESENT PARTICIPLE

(See page 181)

■ Some of these constructions are made up of a conjugated verb followed by a preposition and an infinitive. Others are followed by the present participle.

■ Use **empezar / ponerse a** + infinitive to express the start point of an activity.
Empecé a leer una novela muy interesante.
En cuanto llegué a casa **me puse a estudiar** para el examen del día siguiente.

■ Use **volver a** + infinitive to express the repetition of an activity.
El año pasado me apunté a clases de teatro y este año me **volveré a apuntar** de nuevo.

■ Use **seguir / continuar** + present participle to express that an activity is ongoing.
Nos conocimos en la guardería y hoy todavía **seguimos siendo** amigos.
Este verano **continuaré yendo** a clases de inglés, no quiero olvidar lo que he aprendido.

■ Use **acabar de** + infinitive to express that an activity has just finished.
Si quieres pastel, espera a que se enfríe un poco, que **acabo de sacarlo** del horno.

■ Use **dejar de** + infinitive to express the interruption of an activity.
He dejado de ir a clases de guitarra porque este año no tengo tanto tiempo.

VERBS THAT EXPRESS CHANGE

(See page 182)

■ To express spontaneous or temporary changes in a person we use **ponerse** + adjective; **quedarse** shows the result, the final situation.
Se pone muy nervioso al hablar en público.
Se puso rojo cuando le preguntaron.
Se quedó muy sorprendido por la noticia.

■ To express permanent changes use **volverse** (non voluntary) or **hacerse** (voluntary or gradual change).
Se ha vuelto un antipático.
Antes era abogado y ahora **se ha hecho** juez.
Con esa situación **se hizo** fuerte.

193

OBJECTIVES FOR EN RESUMEN: GRAMÁTICA

· Review unit grammar
· Practice communication skills

STANDARDS

1.2 Understand the language
1.3 Present information

INSTRUCTIONAL STRATEGIES

· Model how to review grammar.
· Have the students review the Learning Outcomes in the unit opener to assess whether they feel they have mastered the main ideas and skills.
· Ask them if they can remember additional examples for each grammar topic.
· Model how to find and go back to the appropriate page in the unit to review any grammar topic they may need help with.
· Invite students to review the grammar activities they completed in this unit.
· Ask them what grammar activities they found easy and which they found challenging. Encourage them to rework any activities they found particularly challenging.
· Remind students to complete all of the online grammar activities available.

UNIDAD **6**

193

AHORA COMPRUEBA

OBJECTIVES FOR AHORA COMPRUEBA

- Review and recycle grammar, vocabulary and culture from the last two units
- Complete self-assessment

CORE RESOURCES

- Audio Program: Tracks 52 and 53
- Extension Activities: EA 6.6, 6.7, 6.8

STANDARDS

1.2 Understand the language
1.3 Present information
2.1 Practices and perspectives
4.1 Compare languages and cultures

INSTRUCTIONAL STRATEGIES

Activity 1

- To introduce the theme for the section, ask students to think about the title **Dame vida** and say what they think it means. Go online and search on YouTube for *Dame vida Huecco* so students can check to see if they were on track with their predictions.
- Ask students to look at the images and discuss with a partner what they have in common.

Cultural Note

Huecco es un joven cantante español. Su música es una fusión de estilos muy diversos: rock, hip-hop, rumba y ritmos latinos. Ha saltado a la fama gracias a poner letra y voz a varios proyectos solidarios en los que él mismo ha colaborado. Aunque principalmente se le conoce en España e Hispanoamérica, ha publicado sus discos en varios países de Europa. Para más información consultar su página web: *www.huecco.es*

🎧 52 Activity 2

- Present the expression **hacer ilusión** and tell students it has the same structure as **gustar**.
- Have students review the questions first before listening to the audio. Then play the audio for students to write the answers.

See audioscript on page APP12

Activity 3

Ask students to complete the activity individually. After correcting the activity, review the tenses.

ANSWERS

Activity 1

1. El cantante Huecco; **2.** El futbolista del F.C. Barcelona, David Villa; **3.** El jugador de baloncesto de Los Ángeles Lakers (NBA), Pau Gasol; **4.** Unos niños de un poblado pobre del Sahara; **5.** Un balón que se carga de energía y puede dar luz; **6.** El corredor de motociclismo G.P., Jorge Lorenzo.

Activity 2

a. Porque el público canta y no puede escuchar la música; **b.** Que la gente le pise y le empuje; **c.** Porque lo organiza una ONG; **d.** Para recaudar fondos para fabricar una pelota que se carga de energía; **e.** El balón funciona con el movimiento, se va cargando de energía y después esta se aprovecha en forma de luz eléctrica; **f.** El balón todavía no se puede comprar, antes necesitan recaudar dinero para fabricarlo; **g.** Dos estudiantes americanas; **h.** Porque servirá para dar electricidad a la gente pobre y es bueno para el medioambiente; **i.** Carlos desea que el proyecto tenga éxito y que se puedan fabricar muchos balones; **j.** Sí, porque quiere colaborar en esta causa solidaria.

AHORA COMPRUEBA

1 👥 Observa estas imágenes. ¿Qué crees que tienen en común las personas que aparecen en ellas? Coméntalo con tu compañero/a.

DAME VIDA

2 🎧 52 *Dame vida* no es solo el título de una canción, representa todo un proyecto solidario. Escucha la conversación entre Carlos y Abel y responde las preguntas.

a. ¿Por qué no le gustan los conciertos a Carlos?
b. ¿Qué le molesta a Abel de los conciertos?
c. ¿Por qué le hace ilusión ir al concierto de Raquel?
d. ¿Para qué es el concierto?
e. ¿Cómo funciona el balón?
f. ¿Dónde se puede comprar?
g. ¿Quién lo inventó?
h. ¿Por qué Abel cree que es tan bueno el proyecto del balón?
i. ¿Qué desea Carlos en relación al proyecto y al cantante?
j. ¿Al final irá Carlos al concierto? ¿Por qué?

3 Completa con la forma correcta del verbo entre paréntesis.

a. *Dame vida* es una fundación que desea (recaudar) .... fondos para (ayudar) .... a los necesitados.
b. Jessica Mathews y Julia Silverman son las creadoras del *soccket*, un balón con un acumulador de energía dentro que (recargarse) .... con las patadas que se le dan.
c. Cuando la pelota (cargarse) .... de energía, esta se convertirá en horas de luz para las familias pobres.
d. *Dame vida* quiere que cada hogar sin electricidad (tener) .... un balón con luz.
e. Huecco contactó con varios de los mejores deportistas del mundo para que (colaborar, ellos) .... en la grabación del videoclip de la canción.
f. Vicente del Bosque, seleccionador español de fútbol, ha declarado que le encanta (poder) .... colaborar en el video y que cuando el cantante lo (llamar) .... para (participar) .... no lo dudó un momento.
g. Huecco declaró que quiere (dar) .... las gracias de corazón a todos los que participaron en el videoclip.
h. *Dame vida* quiere que la música (servir) .... para que los más jóvenes (practicar) .... deporte.
i. La fundación también espera que a través de la práctica del deporte (generar) .... energía eléctrica limpia.
j. Huecco declaró que el deporte y la música son las energías más limpias y que este proyecto servirá para (llenar) .... de luz limpia el mundo.

194

Activity 3

a. recaudar, ayudar; **b.** se recarga; **c.** se carga; **d.** tenga; **e.** colaboren; **f.** poder, llamó, participar; **g.** dar; **h.** sirva, practiquen; **i.** se genere; **j.** llenar.

SLOWER-PACED LEARNERS

Have students make a list of the learning objectives noted in the opening spreads of the two previous units. Tell them to ask themselves: *How well can I do this: very well, well, or not well?* Then pair students who can't do an objective well with another student who can; that way, they can teach each other what they know and help each other review.

4 Esta fundación participa también en dos proyectos más. Lee los fragmentos que te va a dar tu profesor y relaciona cada uno con la imagen correspondiente. Después, inventa un título para cada proyecto.

Título: ....

Título: ....

5 🎧 53 Vas a escuchar un programa de radio en el que su locutora habla sobre los tres proyectos en los que participa el cantante Huecco. Relaciona las experiencias que relata con las personas de las imágenes.

Jessica Matthews
Proyecto:

Aganju
Proyecto:

Pau Gasol
Proyecto:

Yveline
Proyecto:

Juan
Proyecto:

6 Completa con la forma correcta de los verbos y aprende más sobre las experiencias de los voluntarios.

acabar de ○ ponerse ○ seguir ○ llevar ○ ponerse a ○ dejar de ○ quedarse ○ volver a ○ empezar a

Todo empezó cuando recibí un correo electrónico en el que buscaban colaboradores para construir escuelas para niños pobres en Guatemala. Al llegar allí (a) .... muy impresionada de ver cómo aquella gente vivía con tan poco. Al principio fue muy duro, yo no estaba acostumbrada a ver tanta pobreza y cuando (b) .... trabajar fue todavía peor, (c) .... muy nerviosa porque había muchas cosas que no sabía hacer y me sentí inútil. (d) .... llegar y ya quería hacer las maletas y regresar a casa… Pero después, un compañero me tranquilizó diciéndome que era normal sentirse así al principio y que ellos también habían tenido que aprender, pero que mi trabajo era importante y que tenía que seguir adelante. Lo pensé mejor y (e) .... trabajar sin preocuparme de si lo hacía bien o mal.

Desde que trabajé codo con codo con ellos me he vuelto más responsable y menos egoísta y (f) .... preocuparme por cosas que en realidad no son importantes. Ya (g) .... tres años colaborando con la organización y estoy deseando que llegue el verano para (h) .... ir a Guatemala y (i) .... ayudando a los niños de allí.

7 Seguro que tú también has colaborado alguna vez en una buena acción. Piensa en esa experiencia y escribe cómo fue y cómo te sentiste.

195

INSTRUCTIONAL STRATEGIES

Activity 4

- Ask students to look at the images and tell them to guess what other two social projects this foundation also participates in.
- Distribute copies of EA 6.6, **Proyectos solidarios**. In pairs, ask students to classify the paragraph according to the project they belong and write a title for each project.
- Explain the following vocabulary words: **granja**, **orfanato**, **potable**, **violencia de género**.

🎧 53 **Activity 5**

- Have student guess who these people are.
- Write on the board: **soccket**, **Haití** and **mujeres**, and have students match the images with these words.
- Play the audio and allow students time to complete this activity individually.

See audioscript on page APP12

Activity 6

Ask students to do this activity individually.

Activity 7

Ask students to write about their experiences and provide as many details as possible.

> **Extension**
>
> - Go to YouTube and play **Se acabaron las lágrimas**. Then distribute copies of EA 6.7 and 6.8, **Se acabaron las lágrimas** de **Huecco**. In pairs, students take turns and one of them gives a definition from his/her card and the other student will guess it.
> - While they are guessing these words, they write the missing words to complete the song.

ANSWERS

Activity 5

Jessica Mathews: soccket; **Aganju:** Haití; **Pau Gasol:** soccket; **Yveline:** Haití; **Juan:** mujeres.

Activity 6

a. me quedé; **b.** empecé a; **c.** me ponía; **d.** Acababa de; **e.** me puse a; **f.** he dejado de; **g.** llevo; **h.** volver a; **i.** seguir.

ADVANCED LEARNERS

For those students who have a good handle on the vocabulary, grammar, and cultural content of the units, encourage them to focus on the development of their listening, speaking, reading, and writing skills prior to quizzes and tests. Challenge them to spend thirty minutes a night for four nights before the assessment focusing on one of each of the four skills each night. In addition to redoing the skills-based activities within the units, encourage them to seek new, related (and fun) material online to help them practice.

HERITAGE LANGUAGE LEARNERS

For students who already have a base of the language, challenge them to put themselves in the position of the teacher prior to assessments. How would they teach a non-native speaker the content of the previous two units? Have them develop worksheets, activities, games, presentations, and lesson plans that could be used to teach other students the material. By putting students in this new role, they will enhance their own knowledge and become masters of the content.

OBJECTIVES FOR UNIT OPENER

• Introduce unit theme: *¡Que no te engañen!* about advertising and Internet
• Introduce culture for the unit: Learn about the role of advertisements and the Internet in Hispanic countries, and compare cultural similarities

STANDARDS

1.1 Engage in conversation
2.2 Products and culture

INSTRUCTIONAL STRATEGIES

• Before students open their books, write the unit title on the board: *¡Que no te engañen!* Give examples of what *engañar* means. For example, *Compras un carro usado y dentro de unos días ya no funciona. Te engañaron; Vas a la tienda y le das al cajero veinte dólares en efectivo y te da el cambio para diez dólares. Te engañaron.* Elicit other ideas from the students and then ask what they think the title means (don't let them fool / trick you) and what content they think they'll encounter in the unit.

• Have students open their books, look at the image, and read the caption. Ask: *¿Dónde están las personas? ¿Qué hacen? ¿Por qué crees que hay tantos jóvenes?*

• Have students work individually to write answers to the questions on the page.

• Monitor their progress and assist as needed.

• Put students into pairs or small groups to share and discuss their answers.

• Call on volunteers to report back on their responses and discussions.

• Help students formulate their ideas using *Están en una tienda de ropa / en unos grandes almacenes*, *Están comprando ropa*, *Hay jóvenes porque hay rebajas y la ropa cuesta menos*, *Creo que las rebajas son un buen momento para comprar las cosas que necesitas / te gustan a buen precio*, etc.

SLOWER-PACED LEARNERS

Have students retrieve their previous knowledge about numbers so they can later talk about prices. Also, have them review verbs needed to talk about buying and selling. Encourage them to use the verbs in the preterite.

ADVANCED LEARNERS

Invite students to talk about some of the things they have bought in the last few weeks and how much they paid for them. Ask them whether they used Internet to buy them or if they bought them in stores. Have them discuss websites they use to look for online bargains.

UNIDAD
7

¡QUE NO TE ENGAÑEN!

De rebajas

40% DESCUENTO

≫≫ ¿Qué están haciendo las personas de la imagen?
≫≫ ¿Qué opinas sobre las rebajas?
≫≫ ¿Qué piensas de los eventos especiales como el Cyber Monday o las rebajas de enero?
≫≫ ¿Sueles aprovechar las rebajas para comprar?

196

ADDITIONAL UNIT RESOURCES

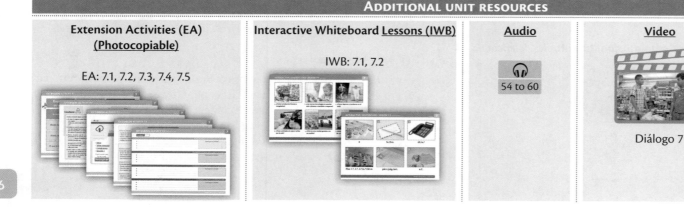

Extension Activities (EA)
(Photocopiable)

EA: 7.1, 7.2, 7.3, 7.4, 7.5

Interactive Whiteboard Lessons (IWB)

IWB: 7.1, 7.2

Audio

54 to 60

Video

Diálogo 7

Online ELEteca

EXTENSIÓN DIGITAL

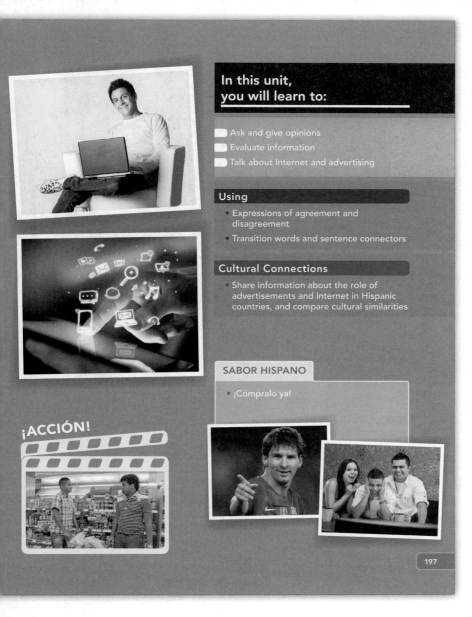

In this unit, you will learn to:

- Ask and give opinions
- Evaluate information
- Talk about Internet and advertising

Using

- Expressions of agreement and disagreement
- Transition words and sentence connectors

Cultural Connections

- Share information about the role of advertisements and Internet in Hispanic countries, and compare cultural similarities

SABOR HISPANO

- ¡Cómpralo ya!

¡ACCIÓN!

197

LEARNING OUTCOMES

- Ask and give opinions
- Evaluate information
- Talk about Internet and advertising

INSTRUCTIONAL STRATEGIES

- Use the unit opener to preview vocabulary and cultural topics for this unit.
- Have students look at the images on this page and try to relate them to the objectives listed.
- Exploit the first main photo a bit further by asking questions, such as: *¿Cuánto tiempo pasan navegando por Internet cada día? ¿Para qué utilizan Internet? ¿Te crees todo lo que lees en Internet? ¿Qué sitios son los más fiables? ¿Y los menos?*
- Exploit the second photo a bit further by asking questions, such as: *¿Qué iconos ven? ¿Qué significan?*
- Invite students to read the topic for **Sabor hispano** and preview that section in the unit. Ask questions, such as: *¿Reconocen al futbolista? ¿Cómo se llama?* (**Lionel Messi**) *¿En qué equipo juega?* (**Barcelona o el Barça**).
- Ask students to anticipate what they think the episode for **¡Acción!** will be about.

HERITAGE LANGUAGE LEARNERS

Have students share their experiences about buying and selling stuff. If they have been to countries where open markets and bargaining is frequent, encourage them to tell the class about how they felt when something had no fixed price.

THREE MODES OF COMMUNICATION: UNIT 7			
	INTERPERSONAL	**INTERPRETIVE**	**PRESENTATIONAL**
HABLAMOS DE...	1, 5	2, 3, 4, 5	
COMUNICA	2, 4, 6, 7	1, 3, 5	6, 7
¡ACCIÓN!	1, 4	2, 3, 4	
PALABRA POR PALABRA	3, 4, 6, 9	1, 2, 4, 5, 7	3, 8
GRAMÁTICA	4	1, 3	2, 4
DESTREZAS		1, 2, 3, 4	
CULTURA		SABOR HISPANO	
RELATO	2, 7	3, 4	1, 5, 6

OBJECTIVES FOR HABLAMOS DE...

- Understand language in context
- Preview vocabulary: Internet and advertising
- Preview grammatical structures: Transition words and phrases and other connectors
- Read and listen to a conversation between four friends about an anticonsumerist advertising campaign

CORE RESOURCES

- Audio Program: Track 54

STANDARDS

- 1.1 Engage in conversation
- 2.2 Products and culture
- 3.2 Acquire information

INSTRUCTIONAL STRATEGIES

Activity 1

- Write the word **publicidad** on the board. Elicit related words from students, such as: **cartel**, **marca**, **anuncio / comercial**, **eslogan**, **consumidores**, **vender**, **convencer**…
- To generate interest, ask questions such as: **¿Les gusta la publicidad? ¿Creen que es necesaria? ¿Cuál es su objetivo? ¿Es honesta?**
- Have students open their books and look at the image at the top of the page. Tell them to focus on the sign and ask: **¿Qué es? ¿Qué representa? ¿Qué significa el texto y la imagen? ¿Les parece raro ver un anuncio así en una tienda o centro comercial? ¿Por qué creen que está? ¿Te parece buena idea tener un día destinado a no comprar?**
- Put students into pairs to ask and answer the questions and discuss their ideas.
- Call on volunteers to report back on their ideas.

Activity 2

- Go over the instructions and review the list of verbs. Ask what kind of verbs they are (like **gustar**) and what that means to the structure (use indirect object pronouns). Model –or elicit– a sample sentence for the class. Remind students that while the first column could be theoretically skipped, the pronoun is always needed: **Me gustan las novedades** is acceptable, but **A mí gustan las novedades** is NOT acceptable.
- Have students work in pairs to make sentences based on the characters in the photo.
- Monitor their progress and assist as needed. Remind them that they can make negative sentences as well.
- Call on volunteers to share their sentences with a class. Encourage students to explain their ideas.

Cultural Note

Share the following information about Adbusters with students. Then ask if they are familiar with the magazine.

Adbusters es una organización anticonsumista que critica y ataca a los medios de comunicación y la filosofía consumista que estos promocionan. Su objetivo es utilizar la publicidad como un medio de comunicación para hacer burla de los productos y compensar así la manipulación que tiene la publicidad sobre la sociedad. La organización aparece en 1989 y en 1994 publican la revista del mismo nombre.

HABLAMOS DE... Las opiniones

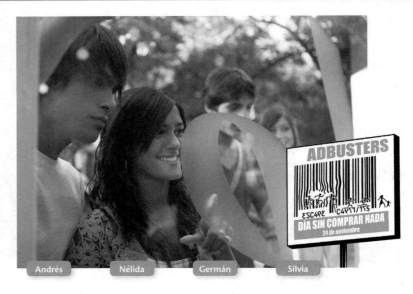

| Andrés | Nélida | Germán | Silvia |

1 🔍 **Observa la imagen y, con tu compañero/a, contesta las preguntas.**

a. ¿Qué crees que están mirando?
b. ¿Qué sensación crees que les provoca ver el cartel de la campaña?
c. ¿Puedes estar un día sin comprar?

2 🔍 **Combina elementos de las columnas para formar frases sobre lo que sienten Andrés y sus amigos acerca de esta campaña publicitaria.**

A mí		encantan	la imagen.
A Nélida y a mí		pone nerviosas	que la gente deje de comprar.
A Germán	le	da miedo	que exista tanta publicidad.
A los cuatro	les	indigna	las novedades.
A Nélida	(no) me	impresiona	ver cosas diferentes.
A Nélida y a Silvia	nos	preocupa	que la gente gaste demasiado.
A Silvia		gusta	que no se entienda el mensaje.

HERITAGE LANGUAGE LEARNERS

While introducing and discussing the topic of the lesson in Activity 1, you can also ask students to identify similarities and differences between advertisements or commercials that they've seen in Spanish-language media to those in English-language media. Do they notice any patterns or stereotypes? Encourage them to give specific examples.

3 🎧 **54** Lee la conversación entre los cuatro amigos y complétala con las palabras del cuadro. Después, escucha y comprueba tus respuestas.

> manipulación o feminidad o iconos o anticonsumista o virilidad o ventanas emergentes o machista

Andrés: ¿Qué les parece el cartel de la campaña? ¡Es una obra de arte!

Nélida: Yo creo que es increíble que esté en un centro comercial, ¿no les parece?

Germán: Pues yo no pienso que sea para tanto. Solo es más publicidad, ¿no?

Silvia: Es terrible que intenten confundirnos. ¿El cartel significa que no compremos? ¡Puf!... No lo entiendo y no me gusta. Por cierto, ¿qué es Adbusters?

A.: ¡¡No los conoces!? Es una organización (a) .... que ataca a los medios de comunicación. Su objetivo es utilizar la publicidad para criticar la (b) .... que esta hace sobre la sociedad. También tienen una revista.

S.: Bueno, en mi opinión, la publicidad trata de informar a un público objetivo sobre lo que hay.

N.: Sí, estoy de acuerdo con que trata de informar, pero para cambiar nuestras opiniones y deseos, ¡claro!

A.: Por supuesto, la publicidad lleva muchos años vendiéndonos el mensaje de la juventud, de la salud, de la (c) ...., de la (d) .... La imagen siempre es la misma: jóvenes, ricos y guapos.

G.: Lo que quiere, desde luego, es provocar. Y tienes razón, a veces incorrectamente, y es racista, sexista, e incluso (e) ....

N.: ¡Ya lo creo! ¿Y qué pasa con la protección de los jóvenes, con el derecho a la intimidad, y con el respeto?

S.: ¡Claro, claro! ¿Y con la libertad de expresión? Pero, de acuerdo, está claro que debe haber límites. En cualquier caso, creo que la gente no le hace tanto caso a la publicidad, hay demasiada: en la calle, en la tele, en los periódicos, en las revistas, en Internet…

A.: ¡Uf! Sí, es ridículo que las redes sociales estén tan llenas de anuncios, no es lo que vas a ver allí. Me preocupa que utilicen nuestra información personal para vender. Y en muchas páginas te atacan las (f) .... que se te abren todo el tiempo.

S.: Pues, a mi modo de ver, no pienso que toda la publicidad sea mala y, como dijiste antes, es arte, creación… Son (g) .... de nuestra cultura, por ejemplo, mira algunas obras de Andy Warhol.

G.: En esto todos estamos de acuerdo, siempre hay cosas bien hechas.

4 Busca en el texto el sinónimo de las siguientes palabras.

a. *Pop-up.* ....
b. Masculinidad, valor, fortaleza. ....
c. Imagen, modelo. ....
d. Femineidad, delicadeza, ternura. ....
e. Cambio que se hace para conseguir algo. ....
f. Prepotencia de hombres sobre mujeres. ....
g. En contra de la compra innecesaria. ....

5 👥 Contesta las siguientes preguntas. Después, compara las respuestas con tu compañero/a. ¿Están de acuerdo?

a. ¿Qué es Adbusters? ....
b. ¿Qué piensa Silvia de la publicidad? ....
c. ¿Están de acuerdo sus amigos con ella? ....

199

INSTRUCTIONAL STRATEGIES

🎧 54 Activity 3

- Tell the students that they are going to listen to a conversation between the four friends in the photo on the previous page. Go over the instructions.
- Give students a moment to read the words in the box before playing the audio. Elicit students' initial ideas about the meanings of the words. Explain that the conversation will provide context to help them determine the meanings.
- Have students read the conversation and try to complete it with the words from the box. Monitor their progress and assist as needed.
- Play the audio and go over the answers as a class.

Activity 4

- Go over the instructions. Have students work individually to find the synonymns in the conversation.
- Then go over the answers as a class.

Activity 5

- Go over the instructions. Have students answer the questions individually.
- Monitor their progress and assist as needed.
- Put students into pairs to compare answers. Encourage them to explain their answers to each other.
- Call on volunteers to share their answers with a class.
- Follow up by asking students for their own opinions on the topic. For example: **¿Qué piensas de la publicidad? ¿Es algo necesario? ¿Por qué? ¿En qué medios de comunicación te molesta más la publicidad?**

ANSWERS

Activity 3

a. anticonsumista; **b.** manipulación; **c.** virilidad; **d.** feminidad; **e.** machista; **f.** ventanas emergentes; **g.** iconos.

Activity 4

a. ventanas emergentes; **b.** virilidad; **c.** icono; **d.** feminidad; **e.** manipulación; **f.** machista; **g.** anticonsumista.

Activity 5

Answers will vary. Possible answers may include the following:
a. Una organización anticonsumista que ataca a los medios de comunicación. Su objetivo es utilizar la publicidad para criticar la manipulación que esta ejerce sobre la sociedad; **b.** Piensa que informa pero que debe haber límites, también cree que hay publicidad que se ha convertido en arte y que es un icono de nuestra cultura; **c.** En parte sí y en parte no. Están de acuerdo en que la publicidad bien hecha es arte, pero Andrés y Nélida, por ejemplo, no piensan que solo trate de informar, sino que creen que esta intenta manipularnos.

SLOWER-PACED LEARNERS

Students may feel overwhelmed by the amount of information provided in this conversation. Encourage students to identify cognates and to anticipate vocabulary.

ADVANCED AND HERITAGE LANGUAGE LEARNERS

While slower-paced students read the text, have advanced students think of specific examples of sexist, racist, homophobic or any other discriminatory advertisement campaigns.

OBJECTIVES FOR COMUNICA

- Present communicative functions of the unit: Expressing opinion
- Practice using different phrases to ask about and share opinions

CORE RESOURCES

- Interactive Online Materials - ELEteca

STANDARDS

3.1 Knowledge of other disciplines

4.1 Compare languages

INSTRUCTIONAL STRATEGIES FOR EXPRESSING OPINION

- Before opening their books, ask students for examples of ways to express opinions (**Creo que**, **Para mí**, etc.). Ask them how to ask for someone's opinion. Write their ideas on the board.
- Have students open their books and read the examples. Ask students which expressions use the indicative and which use the subjunctive. Make sure students understand that **No creo que**, **No pienso que**, **No me parece que** all take subjunctive when used with **no**.
- Model a few questions and answers with volunteers so students can see the language in use. You might ask students for their opinions about celebrities, TV shows, or sports.

Activity 1

- Have students read the text on their own or read it together as a class.
- Put students into pairs to determine the main idea of the text and share their opinions about it. To focus their discussion, consider asking them to come up with an example that demonstrates the use of each of the three main strategies.
- Go over the main idea as a class. Call on volunteers to share the examples of the different strategies they have identified.

Activity 2

- Project the images of the ads and ask students to give their opinion about them. Make sure students understand what is being promoted.
- Put students into pairs to express their opinions about the advertising campaigns.
- Remind them to use the phrases for asking and expressing opinions at the top of the page. Encourage them to give reasons for their opinions.
- Call on volunteers to share their answers with the class.

Extension Activity

Pass out different advertisements, or have students find ads of their own. Have students write about the ways in which their ads do or don't adhere to the blueprint described in the text. Have them present their analyses to the class or share them in small groups.

SLOWER-PACED LEARNERS

Help students prepare for Activity 2 by having the class write a list of words needed to describe the ads: **gafas**, **lengua**, **bigotes**, **orejas**, **chaqueta**, **perro**, **abrazo**, **pan de sándwich**, etc. the colors and some of the verbs.

ADVANCED LEARNERS

Encourage students to use negative statements in Activity 2 as well so they get more practice with the subjunctive form. You might divide students into groups and have them take turns expressing opinions and responding with the opposite points of view. For example, one group might say, **Nos parece que el anuncio es muy efectivo**. Another group responds, **No nos parece que el anuncio sea efectivo**.

COMUNICA

EXPRESSING OPINION

■ Para **pedir opinión** usamos:

¿Qué piensas / crees / opinas de / sobre las compras por Internet?
¿(A ti) qué te parece el blog del que nos habló Carlos?
En tu opinión / Desde tu punto de vista / Según tú, ¿cuál es el anuncio más inteligente?

■ Para **dar opinión** usamos:

En mi opinión / Desde mi punto de vista el blog (no) es muy interesante.
Creo / Pienso / Opino / Me parece que el logo de una marca (no) es muy importante.
No creo / pienso / me parece que el logo sea tan importante como la calidad de sus productos.

1 🔲 Lee este texto que describe algunos elementos de una campaña publicitaria exitosa. Después, con tu compañero/a, apunten las ideas principales y comenten sus opiniones.

> **La publicidad, ¿cómo actúa sobre el público?**
>
> El mensaje publicitario obedece a un esquema de interpretación del comportamiento del público al que se dirige:
> - el anuncio debe llamar la atención, despertar el interés, provocar el deseo y mover a la acción (...);
> - se busca llevar una señal al inconsciente del individuo;
> - el producto o la marca se identifica con un grupo social o una serie de valores admitidos o admirados por una parte de la sociedad. Al comprarlo, se dispone de un símbolo de promoción social.
>
> *http://recursos.cnice.mec.es/media/publicidad/bloque7/pag8.htm*

2 🔲 Estas tres imágenes forman parte de diferentes campañas publicitarias. Con tu compañero/a, contesten las siguientes preguntas:

a. Desde tu punto de vista, ¿cuál es la campaña más original? ¿Y la menos?

b. ¿Estás de acuerdo con tu compañero/a?

c. ¿Crees que los anuncios cumplen (*meet*) con los requisitos que se mencionan en el texto que acabas de leer?

Modelo: E1: Creo que el mejor anuncio es...

E2: No creo que sea el mejor porque...

TO EXPRESS AGREEMENT AND DISAGREEMENT WITH AN OPINION

■ Para **expresar acuerdo o desacuerdo** con una opinión usamos:

	a favor de	*todo **tipo** de anuncios.* (noun)
(No) estoy	estoy en contra de	***ser manipulado** por la publicidad.* (same subject)
	(del todo) de acuerdo con	*que nos **hagan** encuestas.* (different subjects)

3 🗣 Lee las expresiones con tu compañero/a y escríbelas en la columna apropiada.

a. Sí, claro.	g. A mi modo de ver, ese no es el problema / el tema...	l. ¡No, de ninguna manera!
b. Yo pienso lo mismo que tú.	h. Bueno, lo que pasa es que...	m. ¡Y que lo digas!
c. ¡Qué va!	i. ¡A poco!	n. Tienes razón, pero...
d. ¡Desde luego!	j. Yo no diría eso...	ñ. ¡Anda ya!
e. Por supuesto.	k. ¡No, no!	o. Sí, es una idea interesante, pero por otra parte...
f. ¡(Pero) qué dices!		

Expresar acuerdo	Expresar desacuerdo	Suavizar *(soften)* el desacuerdo

4 🗣 Comenta los siguientes temas con tu compañero/a usando las expresiones de la Actividad 3. ¿Están de acuerdo o no?

a. Facebook a cambio *(in exchange for)* de nuestra privacidad.
b. Las descargas *(downloads)* gratuitas y la piratería contra los derechos de autor *(copyright)*.
c. El poder adictivo de las computadoras, Internet o los videojuegos.
d. El peligro de chatear con extraños o colgar nuestras fotos en Internet.
e. Las amistades virtuales y las amistades reales.
f. Las identidades falsas en Facebook y las redes sociales.
g. Las modas y las marcas, ¿estilo o falta de personalidad?

201

INSTRUCTIONAL STRATEGIES FOR EXPRESSING AGREEMENT AND DISAGREEMENT WITH AN OPINION

• To introduce the idea of agreement and disagreement, elicit a student's opinion about something, for example, sushi or some other food. Elicit more students' opinions until one person expresses the same opinion and one expresses a different opinion. After each new opinion, ask: **¿Tienen la misma opinion?** (**Sí/No**). **Entonces, (no) están de acuerdo**. Write **acuerdo** and **desacuerdo** on the board. Go through the examples in the chart.

• Write the following expressions on the board: **Estoy totalmente de acuerdo contigo / con él/ella, No estoy del todo de acuerdo, No estoy nada de acuerdo.** Ask students what they think the purpose of the underlined expressions is (emphasis).

• Distribute copies of EA 7.1, **Expresar acuerdo y desacuerdo** to student pairs and have students sort the expressions under the appropriate categories. Review by having students tape the words to the board. Then ask, **¿Están de acuerdo?** as a way to prompt students to use one of the expressions on the board.

Activity 3
• Put students into pairs to sort the expressions into the appropriate categories.
• Monitor their progress and assist as needed. Go over the answers as a class.

Activity 4
• Put students into pairs to discuss the topics and take turns sharing opinions. To ensure they use a variety of expressions, have them use the cards from EA 7.1, and hold them up to respond to their partner.
• Since there is a long list of topics, you may want to have students switch partners after each topic or after every two topics. This will help add some variety and keep them focused on each new topic.

ANSWERS
Activity 3
Expresar acuerdo: a, b, d, e, m; Expresar desacuerdo: c, f, i, k, l, ñ; Suavizar el desacuerdo: g, h, j, n, o.

SLOWER-PACED LEARNERS
Provide a list of vocabulary related to the topics in EA 7.1 so they are better prepared to discuss them. Alternatively, elicit words from advanced learners list prior to beginning with the exercise.

HERITAGE LANGUAGE LEARNERS
Ask students if they know, have heard, or have used any other expressions that could be added to the lists in Activity 3.

.OBJECTIVES FOR COMUNICA
• Present communicative functions of the unit: Expressing agreement and disagreement with an opinion
• Practice using different expressions for agreeing and disagreeing

CORE RESOURCES
• Extension Activity: EA 7.1

STANDARDS
1.1 Engage in conversation
4.1 Compare languages

COMUNICA COMMUNICATIVE FUNCTIONS

OBJECTIVES FOR COMUNICA

- Present communicative functions of the unit: Making value judgements
- Practice using different expressions to make value judgements

CORE RESOURCES

- Audio Program: Track 55
- Extension Activity: EA 7.2
- Interactive Whiteboard Lesson: IWB 7.1

STANDARDS

1.1 Engage in conversation
1.2 Understand the language
4.1 Compare languages

INSTRUCTIONAL STRATEGIES
FOR MAKING VALUE JUDGEMENTS

- Explain that making value judgements is another way of expressing opinions.
- Review the chart in the book and read aloud different options for explaining how you feel about the topics presented in the sample sentences. Call on students to provide other combinations. Then write these formulas on the board:

Está claro / Es obvio / Es verdad + indicativo
Ser / Parecer + adjetivo + que + subjuntivo
No está claro / No es obvio / No es verdad + subjuntivo

- Put students into pairs to discuss their opinions about the topics presented. Start by calling on students individually and then have them work in pairs. Circulate around the class and take note of common errors to address later as a class.

🎧 55 Activity 5

- Have students work individually first to complete the conversations.
- Monitor their progress and assist as needed. Refer them back to the chart for help.
- Play the audio, and have students listen and check their answers.
- Put students into pairs to practice the conversations. Then have them switch roles and practice the conversations again.

Extension Activity

Have students do the information gap activity EA 7.2, **Opinar y valorar**. Put students into pairs, giving one the card for **Estudiante A** and the other the card for **Estudiante B**. Have them work individually first to correctly conjugate the verbs in their version of the text. Then have them practice the conversation together, checking each other's answers.

COMUNICA

MAKING VALUE JUDGEMENTS

- Para **pedir valoración** usamos:

  *¿**Te parece bien** poder usar buscadores para hacer trabajos de clase?*
  *¿**Te parece mal** el sueldo de un publicista?*
  *¿**Te parece una tontería** (foolish) **que** los publicistas **ganen** mucho dinero?*

- Para **valorar** usamos:

Me parece Es	(parecer) bien / mal (ser) bueno / malo triste / increíble / cómico / justo ridículo / exagerado / preocupante... una tontería / una vergüenza	**que** haya tanta publicidad en Internet.
Está claro Es obvio / verdad	**que** la publicidad es creación.	
¡Qué bien / interesante	este anuncio! poder compartir tanta información a través de Facebook! que nuestra escuela tenga una página web!	

- To form the **present subjunctive**: yo (present) ➜ drop *o* ➜ **add opposite endings**:
  -ar ➜ -e, -es, -e, -emos, -éis, -en   *-er/-ir* ➜ -a, -as, -a, -amos, -áis, -an.

5 🎧 55 **Completa las conversaciones con la forma correcta de los verbos que están entre paréntesis. Usa la tabla de arriba como referencia. Después, escucha y comprueba tus respuestas.**

a. » Me encanta el anuncio del perfume FreeMan.
» Es increíble que tú (a) .... (decir) eso. Hace unos días le decías a Elena que odiabas las marcas y mencionaste precisamente FreeMan.
» Bueno, lo que pasa es que Elena me gusta un montón...
» No, si está claro que tú por Elena (b) .... (hacer) lo que sea, pero me parece un poco triste que (c) .... (tener) que mentir para impresionarla.

b. » Me parece fatal que en la publicidad (a) .... (mostrarse) una imagen tan poco real de los jóvenes: todos frívolos y de fiesta continua.
» Tienes razón, y... ¡¿qué me dices de las muchachas?! ¡Es ridículo que nos (b) .... (reducir) a una cara o a un cuerpo. Y casi siempre anoréxico. ¡Qué triste!
» ¡Ya lo creo! ¿A quién le gusta eso?
» Pues no sé, la verdad, pero es preocupante que nadie (c) .... (hacer) nada por cambiarlo, es una mala influencia para los más jóvenes.

ANSWERS

Activity 5

a) a. diga; **b.** haces; **c.** tengas; **b) a.** se muestre; **b.** reduzcan; **c.** haga.

EA 7.2

Estudiante A: reúna, has estado pensando, podrías, sería, perdería, conozcas.
Estudiante B: sea, pruebes, toques, aparezcan, cambie, preocupe, pruebe.

ADVANCED LEARNERS

When presenting the information about making value judgments, elicit examples of verbs that have irregular subjunctive forms, such as **decir, tener, poner, hacer, ir, haber**, etc. Ask students to write sample sentences making value judgments using these irregular verbs, and have them share their sentences with the class.

6 👥 Con tu compañero/a, contesta las siguientes preguntas. ¿Están de acuerdo?

a. ¿Qué aspectos positivos y negativos piensas que tiene la publicidad?
b. ¿Te parece que la imagen que da de los jóvenes es real?
c. Según tu opinión, ¿cuándo es necesaria la publicidad?
d. ¿Cuál es el último ejemplo de buena publicidad que recuerdas? ¿Y de mala publicidad? ¿Por qué crees que son buenos o malos ejemplos?
e. ¿Qué opinas de la publicidad y el consumismo?

7 👥 Túrnate con tu compañero/a preguntando y describiendo lo que opinan sobre los siguientes temas. Usa las expresiones aprendidas en esta sección.

a. ¿Comer productos frescos o congelados?

b. ¿Las nuevas tecnologías se asocian solo a jóvenes o también a mayores?

c. En el tiempo libre, ¿hacer deporte o relajarse en el sofá?

d. ¿Tener animales en casa o verlos por la tele?

e. ¿Vivir en una ciudad grande o en un pueblo?

f. ¿Hacer turismo cultural o turismo de sol y playa?

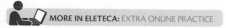

MORE IN ELETECA: EXTRA ONLINE PRACTICE

203

INSTRUCTIONAL STRATEGIES

Activity 6

- Have students work individually first to jot down notes with their ideas.
- Put students into pairs to share and discuss their answers.
- Monitor their progress and assist as needed. Encourage them to explain their opinions and ask each other questions for more information. Remind them to use the expressions they have learned for opinions, agreement, disagreement, and value judgements.
- Invite volunteers to share interesting aspects of their conversations with the class.

Alternative Activity

Put students into groups of five, and arrange them in a circle. Assign each student a different question from the list and have him or her write a complete response to the question. Then have them pass their questions and responses to the person on their right. Have them write a statement agreeing or disagreeing with the original. Have them continue passing the questions and responses to the write until they have all responded to each question.

Activity 7

- Focus students' attention on the images. To activate schema and remind them of relevant vocabulary, invite them to comment on what they see or notice about each image.
- Go over the instructions. Then put students into pairs to ask and answer the questions posed under the images and discuss their opinions.
- Monitor their conversations and assist as needed. Take note of any common errors you hear in their conversations.
- Review any common errors, eliciting corrections from the class.
- Call on volunteers to share any of their partners' opinions that they found interesting.

Alternative Activity

These images are also available for projection in IWB 7.1, **Valorar**. Before going over the activity in the book, you may want to project the images, masking the questions. Have students analyze the images and try to generate the questions themselves.

HERITAGE LANGUAGE LEARNERS

Have students interview Spanish speakers in their communities about one of these topics and report back with their findings. Ask them to compare their opinions with the ones gathered in their interviews. Alternatively, have students share their perception of the concept **pueblo**. Students who have lived or been abroad may have interesting ideas to share.

OBJECTIVES FOR ¡ACCIÓN!

- Provide students with a structured approach to viewing the video
- Contextualize the content of the unit in a familiar scenario

CORE RESOURCES

- Unit Video 7 - Galletas Segismundo
- Online Materials - ELEteca

STANDARDS

1.1 Interpersonal communication
1.2 Interpretive communication
2.1 Culture: Practices and perspectives

INSTRUCTIONAL STRATEGIES

Previewing: Antes del video

Activity 1

Put students in pairs to look at the images from the video and answer the questions. If possible, project the images so they can see the products more clearly. Alternatively, play the first 35 seconds of the video (before any of the characters speak) so they can get a better sense of what's for sale.

Activity 2

Put students in small groups to discuss the reasons for shopping with grocery lists and whether or not they (or their family members) use them. To expand the conversations, ask them to think about how the lists are usually kept (on their phones, on paper, on the refrigerator at home, etc.). They can also discuss how strictly they follow the lists.

Viewing: Durante el video

Activity 3

- Before playing the video, direct students' attention to the title of the video. Point out that *galletas* is used for both cookies and crackers or saltines. To clarify, people often say *galletas saladas* to refer to crackers while *galletas* alone is understood to refer to cookies. Ask students to predict how this might cause a complication in the video.
- Have students read the sentences before playing the video so they are better prepared to select the correct options while they watch.
- After they watch the video for the first time, have students compare their answers with a partner and try to resolve or explain any differences in what they've understood. Don't confirm the correct answers until students have had the chance to watch the video a second time while doing Activity 4 or 5.

ANSWERS

Activity 3

a. no llevan; **b.** una fiesta; **c.** dejó la lista en casa; **d.** saladas; **e.** poco; **f.** bastantes; **g.** escribió.

Have students write an explanation of what's happening in Image 5. Encourage them to be specific and provide context. After watching the video, confirm whose assumptions were most accurate.

¡ACCIÓN! Galletas Segismundo

1.   2.   3.
4.   5.   6.

ANTES DEL VIDEO

1 Mira las imágenes y responde las preguntas. Basa tus respuestas en lo que crees que puede ocurrir. Usa tu imaginación. Trabaja con tu compañero/a.

a. ¿Qué productos podemos comprar en ese supermercado?
b. ¿Qué productos llevan los muchachos en el carro?
c. ¿Por qué crees que fueron a comprar?
d. ¿Por qué crees que discuten en la Imagen 5?

2 En grupos de tres, respondan a estas preguntas.

a. Mucha gente lleva una lista cuando va al supermercado, ¿por qué crees que la llevan?
b. Cuando vas al supermercado, ¿llevas una lista?

DURANTE EL VIDEO

3 Mira el episodio completo y marca la opción correcta.

a. Los muchachos **llevan** / **no llevan** una lista.
b. Están comprando cosas para **una fiesta** / **desayunar**.
c. Sebas **dejó la lista en casa** / **no hizo una lista**.
d. Quieren comprar galletas **dulces** / **saladas**.
e. Tienen **poco** / **suficiente** tiempo para terminar de hacer la compra.
f. Hay **pocas** / **bastantes** marcas de galletas.
g. Lorena **escribió** / **no escribió** la marca de galletas que quería en la lista.

204

4 **Durante el episodio suenan avisos por megafonía. Mira de nuevo el episodio y completa.**

a. Señores clientes, les .... de que nuestras cajas cierran dentro de .... minutos.
b. Señores clientes, les informamos de que nuestro supermercado está a .... de cerrar. Les rogamos vayan pasando por ....
c. Señores clientes, ... cerrando. Pasen .... por caja.
d. Los dos del fondo, los bailarines. ¿Quieren hacer ya el favor de dejar de hacer el tonto y .... ya por las galletas? Que tenemos que ....

5 **Completa. Puedes volver a ver el episodio, si es necesario.**

a. Sebas dice que si vas sin lista al supermercado…
En primer lugar… ....
Y en segundo lugar… ....
b. Esta es la canción de las galletas según Felipe. (Imagen 6)
Galletas Segismundo, galletas Segismundo ....

DESPUÉS DEL VIDEO

6 **En la publicidad de las galletas Segismundo aparece una canción. ¿Recuerdas alguna canción más de algún anuncio de televisión? Trabaja con tu compañero/a, traduzcan la canción al español y escríbanla.**

....
....
....
....

7 **En grupos de cuatro, imaginen que van a hacer una fiesta con toda la clase. Completen esta información.**

Lugares donde podemos hacer nuestra fiesta	¿Qué tipo de música pondremos?	¿Cuántos invitados irán?	¿Qué usaremos para decorar la fiesta?

8 **Solo nos falta ir al supermercado. Preparen una lista con todo lo que necesitarían comprar para esa fiesta.**

10 botellas de refresco de naranja…

MORE IN ELETECA: EXTRA ONLINE PRACTICE

INSTRUCTIONAL STRATEGIES

Activities 4 and 5

• Before playing the video a second time, go over the instructions for both activities. Point out that they will be listening for specific language spoken in the video to complete the sentences.
• Play the video again, pausing after or replaying target lines if necessary.
• Confirm the answers as a class.

Post-viewing: Después del video
Activity 6

• Before putting students into pairs, you may want to brainstorm a few products with popular commercials and jingles. Allow students access to dictionaries while completing this activity.
• Circulate and help students make their translations sound more natural in Spanish.

Activities 7 and 8

• Students work together to share their ideas for a class party. They should first take notes in the chart in Activity 7 and then use those notes to prepare a shopping list in Activity 8.
• Encourage all of the students in the group to take notes on their ideas, and have each group member speak when the group reports back on what they've planned and will buy at the supermarket.

ANSWERS

Activity 4

a. informamos, cinco; **b.** punto, caja; **c.** estamos, inmediatamente; **d.** decidirse, cerrar.

Activity 5

a. seguro que se te olvida algo, seguro que compras más de lo que necesitas;
b. las galletitas saladas que gustan a todo el mundo.

SLOWER-PACED LEARNERS

Have students convert their shopping lists into posters with supporting imagery to help reinforce vocabulary.

HERITAGE LANGUAGE LEARNERS

Have students convert their translations in Activity 6 into commercials. Have students show their commercials in class and vote on the best ones.

OBJECTIVES FOR INTERNET

- Present vocabulary needed to practice communicative and grammatical functions for the unit: Online environments and the Internet
- Understand and use terms related to the Internet

CORE RESOURCES

- Extension Activities: EA 7.3
- Interactive Online Materials - ELEteca

STANDARDS

1.2 Understand the language
1.3 Present information

INSTRUCTIONAL STRATEGIES

Activity 1

- Before students open their books, activate students' schema about online environments and Internet. You may choose to write Internet on the board and invite students to suggest related terms, which they or you can add to the board.
- These might include: **computadora**, **portátil**, **correo electrónico**, **Google**, **contraseña**, **página web**, **YouTube**, **Facebook**…
- Explain to students that they are going to learn the expressions in Spanish for common Internet terms. Have students open their books. Go over the instructions. You may choose to read the definitions aloud as a class. Have students work individually to match the definitions with the images.
- Monitor their progress and assist as needed.
- Go over the answers as a class. Call on students to read the definitions aloud.

ANSWERS

Activity 1

1. a; **2.** g; **3.** c; **4.** e; **5.** d; **6.** f; **7.** b.

HERITAGE LANGUAGE LEARNERS

Have students notice that many words in this unit are very similar to the ones used in English: **portal**, **web**, **Internet**, **computadora**, **blog**, and all the names of web services and apps. Have them notice the different structures of the terms in English and Spanish:

ENGLISH		SPANISH	
username		nombre de usuario	Noun 2 + **de** + Noun 1
video game	Noun 1 + Noun 2	videojuego	Noun 2 + Noun 1
web page		página web	Noun 2 + Noun 1
technology services		servicios tecnológicos	Noun 2 + Adjective

Ask students to look for these patterns in this unit and in other words related to technology. Explain that these patterns apply to other categories of vocabulary as well, and encourage them to find examples.

PALABRA POR PALABRA Internet

1 **Lee la definición de estos términos de Internet y relaciónalos con su imagen correspondiente.**

a. **Usuario:** persona que utiliza una computadora o cualquier sistema informático.

b. **Banner o banderola:** formato publicitario en Internet que consiste en incluir una pieza publicitaria dentro de una página web.

c. **Logo:** representación de una empresa u organización. Puede tener letras e imagen.

d. **Buscador:** sitio especializado para facilitar la búsqueda de información entre los millones de páginas web existentes.

e. **Portal o web portal:** sitio que sirve para ofrecer acceso a una serie de recursos y de servicios relacionados con un mismo tema. Puede incluir: enlaces, buscadores, foros, documentos, aplicaciones, compra electrónica…

f. **Botón:** permite al usuario comenzar una acción, como buscar, aceptar una tarea, interactuar…

g. **Enlace:** conexión de una página web con otra mediante una palabra que representa una dirección de Internet. Generalmente está subrayado y es azul. También sirve para la descarga de ficheros, abrir ventanas, etc.

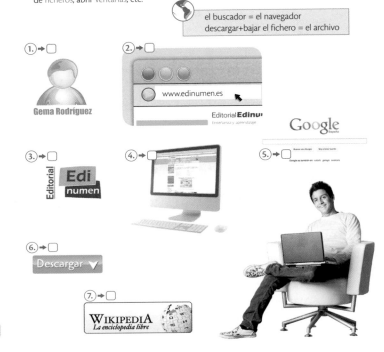

el buscador = el navegador
descargar+bajar el fichero = el archivo

1. → ☐ Gema Rodríguez

2. → ☐ www.edinumen.es Editorial **Edinu**

3. → ☐ Editorial **Edi numen**

4. → ☐

5. → ☐ Google

6. → ☐ Descargar ▼

7. → ☐ WIKIPEDIA La enciclopedia libre

2 Completa las frases con las palabras de la Actividad 1.

a. Mi nombre de .... en Facebook no es mi nombre real. Es necesario proteger la intimidad.

b. Cuando hago un trabajo de investigación, voy a un .... para encontrar lo que necesito.

c. Los .... que encuentro en un artículo del periódico en Internet me dan más información relacionada con la noticia.

d. En la web de mi marca favorita de pantalones el .... de compra es siempre una tentación para mí.

e. Me encantan los diseños de los .... de algunas compañías, dan muy buena imagen.

f. La sofisticación de algunos .... me impresiona, pero también me molesta que aparezcan cuando solo quiero escribir un correo electrónico.

g. La .... de mi centro tiene mucha información útil para los alumnos y es muy fácil de usar.

3 En grupos de tres, creen su propia página web usando el siguiente modelo. Elijan el nombre de su web y una descripción de lo que se puede hacer. Después, preséntenla al resto de la clase.

Crea tu web

[BANNER]

SU WEB [NOMBRE]
Pongan aquí una descripción principal de su web.

[Aquí una frase motivadora]

Aquí su Logo

:: Inicio
:: Sobre nosotros
:: Contáctenos
:: Sección 1
[Aquí botones para las secciones]
Descargar ▼

Bienvenido a su Web [NOMBRE]
[Aquí podrán incorporar texto de bienvenida para sus usuarios. Podrán adjuntar tanto texto como deseen, pero recuerden que no es bueno abusar de contenidos para no agobiar al lector]

Sección Destacada
[imagen]
[Esta sección de inicio puede dedicarse a llamar la atención de algo importante]

4 Lee las siguientes afirmaciones y señala si son verdaderas (V) o falsas (F). Después, compara tus respuestas con un compañero/a. ¿Están de acuerdo?

	V	F
a. Los jóvenes españoles hablan más con sus amigos a través de Internet que en la realidad.	☐	☐
b. Los adolescentes españoles pasan más tiempo viendo la tele que conectados a Internet.	☐	☐
c. La red social preferida de los adolescentes españoles es Facebook.	☐	☐
d. Muchos adolescentes tienen personas que no conocen dentro de sus redes sociales.	☐	☐
e. La mayoría de españoles tiene su primer celular a los 16 años.	☐	☐
f. Las redes sociales son muy seguras.	☐	☐

207

INSTRUCTIONAL STRATEGIES

Activity 2

- Go over the instructions. Have students work individually to complete the sentences with the words from Activity 1.
- Monitor their progress and assist as needed.
- Go over the answers as a class.

Activity 3

- Before beginning the activity, invite students to give examples of their favorite websites and explain what they like about them in terms of both their content and their design.
- Read through the sections and indicate the parts that need to be filled in (indicated by brackets). Distribute copies of EA 7.3, *Crea tu web* and put students into groups of three to create a web page. Tell them to use the model on the page as a guide but to write their information, once the content has been decided, directly on the sheet. Encourage students to be creative and draw their own logo.
- Monitor their progress and assist as needed. Encourage them to think about what makes their website unique or special. Remind them that each member of the group should speak during the presentation and to decide on their parts.
- Have the groups present their webpages to the class.

Activity 4

- Go over the instructions. Have students work individually to answer the questions.
- Put students into pairs to compare answers.
- Monitor their conversations and assist as needed. Remind them to use the expressions they learned for expressing opinions, agreeing, and disagreeing.
- Call on volunteers to report back on their opinions. Encourage them to give reasons for their answers.

ANSWERS

Activity 2

a. usuario; **b.** buscador; **c.** enlaces; **d.** botón; **e.** logos; **f.** banners; **g.** web portal.

Activity 4

Answers will vary. After doing Activity 5, they may reassess their answers as follows:

a. T; **b.** F (Pasan más tiempo conectados a Internet); **c.** F (Tuenti); **d.** T; **e.** T; **f.** F.

ADVANCED LEARNERS

Have students prepare a questionnaire for the class about their Internet use. They may base their questionnaires on some of the ideas expressed in Activity 4. Have them conduct the surveys in class and report back on their findings.

OBJECTIVES FOR LA PUBLICIDAD EN INTERNET

- Present vocabulary needed to practice communicative and grammatical functions for the unit: Online advertising
- Write about and discuss issues related to online advertising

CORE RESOURCES

- Audio Program: Track 56

STANDARDS

1.2 Understand the language

5.1 Spanish in the community

INSTRUCTIONAL STRATEGIES

🎧 56 Activity 5

- Give students time to read items and multiple-choice options before they listen. Encourage them to underline key words to help focus their listening.
- Play the audio. Have students choose the correct options on their own.
- Put them in pairs to compare answers. Encourage them to explain their answers to each other. You may choose to play the audio again for students to resolve any discrepancies in their responses. Go over the answers as a class.

See audioscript on page APP13

Activity 6

- Go over the instructions. Focus students' attention on the prompts in the online forum.
- Before students write, engage them in a prewriting task. For the first prompt, encourage them to make a list of main ideas from the audio. Offer to play the audio from Activity 7 again. To help them along, you may choose to elicit responses to some comprehension questions about the audio, such as: **¿Por qué es gratis el uso de Google y Yahoo? ¿Hay publicidad en las bitácoras / los blogs? ¿Cómo reciben tus datos las compañías que generan la publicidad?**
- For the second prompt, suggest that they make a T-chart to list advantages and disadvantages of online advertising. Encourage them to brainstorm different ideas.
- Have students work individually to write their responses to the forum prompts.
- Put students into pairs and have them exchange their papers. Encourage them to respond to each other orally: asking additional questions, expressing new opinions, agreeing, or disagreeing with each other.

Activity 7

- Put students into pairs to discuss the two questions. Tell students to be prepared to report back on their discussions with the class.
- Have pairs report back with a brief summary or a few interesting ideas from their discussions.
- Go over any common errors you heard, eliciting corrections from the class.

ANSWERS

Activity 5

1. a; **2.** b; **3.** a.

ADVANCED LEARNERS

Have students make an Internet advertisement for their school or perhaps more specifically for the Spanish program at school. Then have students share their ads in small groups and discuss what each ad makes them think and feel about the school / Spanish program.

PALABRA POR PALABRA La publicidad en Internet

5 🎧 56 Escucha el artículo sobre la publicidad en Internet y elige la opción correcta que explica el significado de estos otros términos de Internet.

1. **Entrar y hacer** clic en los enlaces de las páginas web significa…
   a. dinero y publicidad.
   b. que aceptas pagar tú el uso de la página.
   c. ver la información sin ninguna consecuencia económica para los propietarios de la web.

2. Un segundo sistema de publicidad son los **anuncios de texto** que consisten en…
   a. un botón para comprar el producto.
   b. un pequeño recuadro, un título del producto o empresa, un texto corto de descripción, y la **dirección web** con enlace a la página.
   c. un amplio catálogo de productos o servicios disponibles para comprar.

3. Un **blog** (bitácora) en Internet es…
   a. un sitio en el que un autor o autores publican artículos de su interés. Es posible hablar de temas muy variados. Se incluye publicidad en ellos.
   b. una **página web** exclusivamente publicitaria.
   c. algo parecido a un **chat** para presentar temas de interés.

6 El tema de este mes en el sitio web de tu escuela es "la publicidad en Internet". Por eso han creado un foro para conocer la opinión de los alumnos. Entra en el foro y danos tu opinión.

7 🗣 Habla con tu compañero/a de los siguientes temas.
   a. ¿Cómo crees que será en el futuro la publicidad?
   b. ¿Cuáles serán sus canales (*channels*) para llegar a los posibles consumidores?

MORE IN ELETECA: EXTRA ONLINE PRACTICE

GRAMÁTICA

1. TRANSITION WORDS AND PHRASES

1 Lee el siguiente texto y completa las explicaciones con los conectores correspondientes.

En los medios de comunicación, por la calle, en gigantescos espectaculares (*billboards*) o de formas novedosas, muchos rostros (*faces*) conocidos se asoman a la publicidad para aumentar sus beneficios. Por un lado están los deportistas, con un espacio muy importante. Y, sin duda, son los que más dinero generan para las marcas, que se pelean por contar con ellos. Por ejemplo: Cristiano Ronaldo, Messi, Pau Gasol o Rafa Nadal.

Por otro (lado), actrices y modelos. Y es que nadie escapa de la tentación de conseguir dinero extra si su ocupación profesional no pasa por su mejor momento. Sobre eso tendría mucho que contarnos Andie McDowell, que lleva un tiempo alejada de las carteleras y ya es un clásico de los anuncios de cosméticos y productos de belleza. Algo parecido ocurre con Claudia Schiffer. También prestaron su imagen para anunciar todo tipo de productos desde cantantes hasta humoristas, presentadores, antiguas celebridades o hijos de famosos, como es el caso en España de Enrique Iglesias.

Asimismo, podemos recordar grandes personajes que también sucumbieron a la publicidad. Como Mijaíl Gorbachov, que llegó a hacer una campaña para una conocida marca de comida rápida norteamericana. Y es que el dinero que mueve la publicidad es muy goloso (*appetizing*).

Adaptado de www.noticiasterra.es

- Para distinguir dos argumentos:
  - **En primer lugar / En segundo lugar**...
  - *La juventud es muy crítica. **En primer lugar** no acepta cualquier cosa y, **en segundo lugar**, busca lo que quiere.*
- Para **oponer** dos argumentos:
  - .... / ....
  - *Comer es importante. .... es necesario, ... un placer.*

- Para **añadir** argumentos:
  - .... / **además** / .... / ....
  - *La creatividad está presente en la publicidad, **además** de la originalidad, por supuesto.*
- Para **ejemplificar** y **explicar**:
  - .... / **es decir** / **o sea**
  - *El alto nivel de competencia hace necesario invertir en publicidad, **es decir**, hay muchos productos buenos y similares en el mercado, pero algo te hace elegir uno.*
- Para **aludir a un tema** ya planteado (*mentioned*):
  - **(Con) respecto a** (**eso de / eso**) / ....
  - **Con respecto a eso** *que dijiste antes, siento no estar totalmente de acuerdo contigo.*

209

OBJECTIVES FOR GRAMÁTICA 1

- Present grammatical structures needed to practice communicative functions of the unit: Transition words and phrases
- Learn and practice using transitional words and phrases in writing

CORE RESOURCES

- Extension Activity: EA 7.4
- Interactive Online Materials - ELEteca

STANDARDS

1.2   Understand the language
4.1   Compare languages

INSTRUCTIONAL STRATEGIES

1. Transition Words and Phrases

Activity 1

- To introduce the lesson, elicit examples from the class of famous people who have marketed different products in commercials and other forms of advertising. Ask if they can recall the product that the person was promoting, if they liked the advertisement or not, and if they thought the famous person helped to sell the product or not. You may choose to put students into pairs to discuss their favorite advertisements with famous people and explain their preferences. (This will also help them prepare for Activity 2).
- Have students open their books, and go over the instructions. You may choose to read the text as a class or have students read it silently to themselves.
- Have students work invidually to complete the chart with the phrases form the text. Monitor their progress and assist as needed.
- Put students into pairs to compare their answers.
- Go over the answers as a class.

ANSWERS

Activity 1

Para oponer dos argumentos: Por un lado... por otro (lado); Para añadir argumentos: Y, también, asimismo; Para ejemplificar y explicar: Por ejemplo; Para aludir a un tema ya planteado: Sobre eso.

SLOWER-PACED LEARNERS

Have students say names of other celebrities that may make a lot of money in advertising. Have them do some research about celebrity branding. How much do they think an actor or famous basketball player can make for appearing in a commercial?

HERITAGE LANGUAGE LEARNERS

Have students work in groups to write a short story that uses different transition words to connect paragraphs. Have them split the story by paragraphs. Then have them exchange all paragraphs with another group, which will have to put the story back together in the correct order. Alternatively, have students find Spanish-language articles related to the topic of advertising (broadly) and that incorporate transition words and phrases. Have students choose a few places to divide up the article so that can be logically rearranged by others.

INSTRUCTIONAL STRATEGIES

Activity 2

- You may choose to have students work individually or in pairs on the essays.
- Remind them of the three main parts of the essay: the introduction, the body, and the conclusion. Discuss the basic components of each section. Model a possible outline on the board, eliciting examples from the class to complete it together.
- Have students create their own outlines.
- Have students discuss their outlines with a partner or another pair to see to ensure that they have a good plan for their essays.
- Have students write their first drafts.
- Focus students' attention on the first draft questions. Have students exchange papers and markup their first drafts based on the questions provided.
- Have students return the marked up essays and write their second drafts.
- Focus students' attention on the second draft questions. Have students exchange papers and markup their second drafts based on the questions provided.
- Have students write their final drafts, checking their own work based on the final reflection questions in the book.
- If you like, you can distribute copies of EA 7.4, **Guía para escribir y mejorar un texto** to use as a checklist.

OBJECTIVES FOR GRAMÁTICA 2

- Present grammatical structures needed to practice communicative functions of the unit: Other sentence connectors
- Learn new sentence connectors and apply them to appropriate contexts

CORE RESOURCES

- Audio Program: Track 57

STANDARDS

- 1.2 Understand the language
- 4.1 Compare languages

INSTRUCTIONAL STRATEGIES

2. Other Sentence Connectors

- Before students open their books, put the four categories of other sentence connectors on the board. Have them brainstorm examples of each. Discuss their ideas before checking them against the chart in the book.
- Go over the examples of sentence connectors. After each bullet point, elicit new examples of the phrases in context from the class.
- Consider reciting a few new examples of your own. Elicit what the connector is doing in the sentence, e.g. adding a reason, expressing a consequence, etc.

GRAMÁTICA

2 Escribe un texto acerca de un famoso que aparece mucho en los anuncios. Usa los conectores aprendidos para organizar tus ideas. Sigue estas recomendaciones.

Haz un esquema (outline)

- Escribe las ideas principales que le den progreso al tema elegido.
- Marca en cada una de ellas las ideas secundarias, evita las repeticiones.
- Busca y utiliza sinónimos que den coherencia y variedad léxica.
- Organiza y relaciona las partes del texto con los conectores adecuados.
- Finaliza con un resumen o una conclusión.

Primera lectura (first draft)

Comprueba que la información del texto tiene sentido:

- ¿El tipo de texto y el esquema están bien desarrollados?
- ¿Has incluido la información que es más importante para el lector?
- ¿Presentas la información de una forma clara y lógica?
- ¿Has excluido la información no necesaria?

Segunda lectura

Comprueba que las palabras y frases son correctas:

- ¿Puedes cambiar palabras de contenido general por otras más precisas?
- ¿Describes bien y con precisión lo que quieres decir?
- ¿La ortografía, la puntuación y la gramática son correctas?

Reflexión final

- ¿Añadirías o eliminarías algo?
- Como lector, ¿qué crítica le harías al texto?

2. OTHER SENTENCE CONNECTORS

- Para **añadir razones** en un orden de fuerza creciente (increasing):
  - **incluso**

  *María trabaja todos los días, **incluso** los domingos.*

- Para **contraponer** (counter) razones:
  - **bueno** • **no obstante** • **pero** • **en cambio** • **sin embargo**

  *El rojo es mi color preferido, **sin embargo** nunca llevo ropa de ese color.*

- Para expresar **consecuencia**:
  - **así que** • **de ahí que** • **así pues** • **de modo que** • **de manera que** • **pues**

  *Me encantan las películas, **así que** voy al cine siempre que puedo.*

- Para sacar **conclusiones**:
  - **entonces** • **en resumen** • **total que**
  - **por lo tanto** • **para terminar** • **en conclusión**

  *Fuimos a la montaña sin botas ni ropa adecuada, **total que** pasamos muchísimo frío.*

210

SLOWER-PACED LEARNERS

Students may have a difficult time figuring out what to write about the celebrities in Activity 2. If needed, have a brainstorming session about topics related to this subject before asking them to write the actual essay. You can create a mind map to present their ideas on the board.

HERITAGE LANGUAGE LEARNERS

These students may struggle writing their essays in Activity 2, as they may try to transfer their skills in oral discourse organization to written discourse. Discuss some differences between oral and the written discourse so they know what to avoid. Explain that it is very important that ideas are organized in sentences and then in paragraphs, as they are in English-language texts.

3 🎧 57 Un grupo de adolescentes de México D.F. participó en la campaña publicitaria de una famosa marca de zapatillas deportivas. Escucha sus experiencias y ordena las frases de una forma lógica. Después, completa con conectores.

Foro
www.foro_opinion.mx

a. ☐ La clave del éxito de esta campaña fue, ..., el volverse parte de la vida del consumidor y Nike llegó hasta sus propias casas.

b. ☐ Se consiguieron más de 4.000 jóvenes, ... había que implicarlos en el proyecto, ... se crearon las mascotas que representaban a los diferentes barrios de la ciudad. .... aparecieron como grafiti y estaban dibujadas sobre los bancos y en las estaciones de autobuses de todo México.

c. ☐ La campaña de las famosas zapatillas utilizó mercadotecnia (*marketing*) de calle .... de una campaña en redes sociales para conseguir el éxito.

d. ☐ Se empezó con un video que se subió a Youtube donde muchachos de la ciudad jugaban al fútbol en la calle, ... un muchacho hablaba y decía: "El fútbol es diversión, juegues donde juegues".

e. ☐ La idea era organizar un torneo de fútbol con jóvenes de México D.F., ... hubo una convocatoria (*announcement*) en la página Facebook de Nike que tiene 811.000 seguidores allí.

4 👥 Con tu compañero/a, completa las siguientes frases de forma lógica.

a. Las redes sociales llegan a muchísimas personas en cualquier país, **así que** ....
b. Toda la información es muy accesible con Internet. **Total que** ....
c. En los anuncios la música atrae la atención, **pero** ....
d. El tiempo que dura un anuncio cuesta caro, **de modo que** ....
e. Los protagonistas de los anuncios son modelos perfectos, **en cambio** ....
f. Me gustaría participar en un anuncio, **incluso** ....

TU ANUNCIO AQUÍ

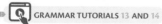

👨‍💻 MORE IN ELETECA: EXTRA ONLINE PRACTICE ➔ 🔍 GRAMMAR TUTORIALS 13 AND 14   211

🎧 **57** Activity 3

• Go over the instructions. Give students time to read the sentences before they listen and anticipate their correct order.
• Play the audio. Have them number the sentences.
• Put students in pairs to compare their answers.
• Then, individually, students complete each sentence with an appropriate connector. Remind them to refer back to the charts on the previous pages to find the appropriate connectors.
• Go over the answers as a class.

See audioscript on page APP13

Activity 4

• Go over the instructions. Model the first example for the class. Ask what the connector *así que* indicates about the type of information that will follow. Elicit a possible ending.
• Put students into pairs to complete the sentences with their own ideas.
• Monitor their progress and assist as needed.
• Have two pairs join each other to share their ideas.
• Call on volunteers to share their examples with the class.

ANSWERS

Activity 3

Answers will vary. Possible answers: **a.** (4) por lo tanto; **b.** (3) sin embargo, así que, Incluso; **c.** (5) además; **d.** (2) entonces; **e.** (1) de modo que.

Activity 4

Answers will vary. Possible answers may include the following:
a. son muy utilizadas por las marcas; **b.** todos podemos conocer qué pasa en cualquier rincón del mundo; **c.** suben demasiado el volumen; **d.** son muy cortos; **e.** la gente real no es así; **f.** hacer cine.

Have students react to the report in Activity 3. Would they like to participate in an ad campaign for a famous sports shoe brand? Why or why not? Which brand would they want to advertise for?

OBJECTIVES FOR DESTREZAS

- Develop grammar and vocabulary comprehension skills
- Learn strategies for preparing for assessments

STANDARDS

1.2   Understand the language

INSTRUCTIONAL STRATEGIES

Comprensión de gramática y vocabulario (1)

Activity 1

- Before beginning the lesson, have a quick discussion about standardized tests and test-taking strategies. Ask questions, such as: **En general, ¿cómo se preparan para los exámenes? ¿Tienen rituales que siguen antes de los exámenes? ¿Cómo se sienten antes, durante y después de los exámenes? ¿Qué hacen cuando no saben la respuesta a una pregunta en un examen?**
- Have students open their books. Go over the strategy.

Activity 2

- Go over the instructions. Have students work individually to select the correct options.
- Put students into pairs to compare their answers. Encourage them to explain their answers by referring back to the questions posed in the **Preparing for assessments (1)** box.
- Go over the answers as a class.

Activity 3

Go over the instructions and strategy as a class.

ANSWERS

Activity 2

1. a; 2. b; 3. a; 4. b; 5. c; 6. c.

ADVANCED LEARNERS

For additional practice after Activity 2, give students cards with new contexts. Have them write three possible options related to each context, two of which are incorrect and one of which is correct. Then have them swap contexts and possible options with a partner who much choose the correct answer.

DESTREZAS

COMPRENSIÓN DE GRAMÁTICA Y VOCABULARIO (1)

1 En algún momento quizá necesites hacer un examen estándar de español. Lee la estrategia en Destrezas y sigue las recomendaciones.

Destrezas

Preparing for assessments (1)

In some testing formats, you may be asked to demonstrate your overall knowledge of the language. In these cases, you will need to identify expressions or sentences that convey the same message. Focus on the message. Is it about something happening now, has it happened in the past or will it happen in the future? Is it a fact, an opinion, a hope, a command, etc.?

2 Elige la opción que corresponde al contexto presentado.

1. Alberto, no es bueno que pierdas tanto tiempo viendo la televisión.
   a. No te parece bien que Alberto vea mucho tiempo la televisión.
   b. No te importa que Alberto vea mucho tiempo la televisión.
   c. Crees que Alberto ve poco la televisión.

2. De segundo, me gustaría tomar pollo rostizado con ensalada.
   a. en un supermercado
   b. en un restaurante
   c. en el cine

3. Es obvio que el atleta ganará este maratón.
   a. Estás convencido de la victoria del atleta.
   b. Crees que el atleta no llegará a la final.
   c. Estás seguro que el atleta participará en el maratón.

4. Encontré mi licencia, de modo que puedo ir a la discoteca esta noche.
   a. Tienes licencia pero no puedes entrar en la discoteca.
   b. No podías ir a la discoteca pero ahora ya sí.
   c. No tienes edad para ir a la discoteca aún.

5. Dime si estás de acuerdo o no.
   a. Pides un deseo.
   b. Pides una acción física.
   c. Pides una opinión.

6. Compré un billete de lotería, sin embargo, creo que he perdido el dinero.
   a. Sé que voy a ganar el primer premio.
   b. Perdí el dinero cuando iba a comprar el billete.
   c. No creo que vaya a ganar ningún premio.

3 El formato de los exámenes incluye la sustitución de palabras en una frase por otra palabra o expresión mejor, basándose en el contexto. Lee la estrategia en Destrezas y sigue las recomendaciones.

Destrezas

Preparing for assessments (2)

In the following group of sentences, a word or expression in boldface does not fit the sentence. You will need to choose from the list of options the word or expression that is not only correct but appropriate in the context provided. To do so, read the item carefully and underline key words. Be sure to identify the structure that needs to be replaced. Is it a verb, a noun, an adjective, an expression?

Next Page

INSTRUCTIONAL STRATEGIES

Comprensión de gramática y vocabulario (2)

Activity 4

- Go over the instructions as a class. Do the first example together. Elicit the part of speech of all the possible answers (verbs). Have students identify all of the verbs in the target sentence. Write the sentence on the board and underline the verbs. Have a volunteer explain which verb is incorrect, what the replacement should be, and why.
- Have students work individually to correct the remaining sentences.
- Monitor their progress and assist as needed. Remind them to underline key words and identify the structure that needs to be replaced.
- Put students in pairs to compare their answers.
- Go over the answers as a class.

ANSWERS

Activity 4

1. b; 2. c; 3. c; 4. d; 5. c; 6. c.

COMPRENSIÓN DE GRAMÁTICA Y VOCABULARIO (2)

4 **En las siguientes frases hay una palabra o expresión equivocada. Sustitúyela por la opción correcta.**

1. Creo que beber en botella de plástico no **es** bien.
  a. funciona   b. está   c. sea   d. bebe   e. sepa

2. **¡A poco!** Yo también creo que el domingo es el mejor día de la semana.
  a. ¿Seguro?   b. Me parece   c. Desde luego   d. No estoy seguro   e. ¿Pero cómo dices?

3. En **el cartel** de perfumes se escucha mi música preferida.
  a. el foro   b. el enlace   c. el anuncio   d. la web   e. el blog

4. No me parece que estudiar **es** lo más aburrido que puedes hacer.
  a. fue   b. era   c. eres   d. sea   e. sería

5. He trabajado duro mucho tiempo, **si** ahora tengo un buen trabajo.
  a. porque   b. sí   c. por lo tanto   d. desde   e. como

6. » La clase de español de hoy ha sido muy divertida.
  » **¡Qué va!** Nunca me había reído tanto.
  a. ¡También!   b. No   c. ¡Y que lo digas!   d. ¡En absoluto!   e. ¡Claro que sí!

PRONUNCIACIÓN Siglas, acrónimos y abreviaturas

SIGLA	ACRÓNIMO	ABREVIATURA
• Palabra formada por el conjunto de letras iniciales de una expresión: **GPS** [ge-pe-ese], **PC** [pe-ce], **FM** [efe-eme]. Su plural es invariable *(does not change)*: *las ONG*.	• Siglas que pueden leerse como palabras. **ONU** (Organización de Naciones Unidas o **UNO** en inglés), **UNESCO** (*United Nations Educational, Scientific and Cultural Organization*).	• Representación reducida de una palabra o grupo de palabras. Al leerlas, leemos la palabra entera: **etc.** (etcétera); **Dña.** (doña); **dcha.** (derecha); **Ud.** (usted); **C.P.** (código postal).

1 🎧 58 **Escucha los siguientes acrónimos y abreviaturas. ¿Sabes lo que representan?**

> PIB ○ Adena ○ ADN ○ TIC ○ VV. AA. ○ UNAM ○ CD ○ FMI ○ FIFA ○ pyme ○ n.º
> VIP ○ Sr. ○ Banxico ○ Láser ○ JJ. OO. ○ NBA ○ GPS ○ DVD

2 **Identifica las letras de la primera columna como *abreviatura* (AB), *acrónimo* (AC) o *siglas* (S). Después, relaciónalas con su significado.**

		AB	AC	S
1. VV. AA.	a. Unión Europea	☐	☐	☐
2. JJ. OO.	b. Varios Autores	☐	☐	☐
3. TIC	c. Pequeña y Mediana Empresa	☐	☐	☐
4. pyme	d. Juegos Olímpicos	☐	☐	☐
5. UE	e. Tecnologías de Información y Comunicación	☐	☐	☐

 MORE IN ELETECA: EXTRA ONLINE PRACTICE

213

OBJECTIVES FOR PRONUNCIACIÓN

• Listening for and pronouncing initials, acronyms, and abbreviations

CORE RESOURCES

• Audio Program: Track 58
• Interactive Whiteboard Lesson: IWB 7.2
• Interactive Online Materials - ELEteca

STANDARDS

1.2   Understand the language
4.1   Compare languages

INSTRUCTIONAL STRATEGIES

🎧 58 **Activity 1**

• To introduce the topic, write **USA** and **EE.UU.** on the board. Elicit what they stand for (*United States, Estados Unidos*).
• Then project IWB 7.2, **Abreviaturas**. Show the photos one at a time, keeping the abbreviations covered. Elicit the abbreviations for each. Ask questions to guide students along as needed.
• Have students open their books. Go over the explanations and examples of **siglas**, **acrónimos**, and **abreviaciones** together.
• Go over the instructions. Play the audio.
• Discuss what the acronyms and abbreviations represent. Practice pronunciations.

Activity 2

• Go over the instructions. Have students work individually or in pairs to select the correct columns and match the meanings.
• Monitor their progress and assist as needed.
• Go over the answers as a class.

ANSWERS

Activity 1

PIB (Producto Interior Bruto, *GDP: Gross Domestice Product*); Adena (Asociación para la Defensa de la Naturaleza); ADN (Ácido Desoxirribonucleico, *DNA*); TIC (Tecnologías de Información y Comunicación); VV.AA. (Varios Autores); UNAM (Universidad Nacional Autónoma de México); CD (Disco Compacto); FMI (Fondo Monetario Internacional, *IMF: International Monetary Fund*); FIFA (Fédération Internationale de Football Association); pyme (Pequeña y Mediana Empresa, *SME: Small and Medium Size Enterprises*); nº (número); VIP (del inglés *Very Important People*, Persona muy importante); Sr. (señor); Banxico (Banco de México); Láser (de la sigla inglesa *Light Amplification by Stimulated Emission of Radiation*); JJ.OO. (Juegos Olímpicos); NBA (Asociación Nacional de Baloncesto); GPS (Sistema de Posicionamiento Global); DVD (del inglés *Digital Video Disc*).

Activity 2

1. b (AB); **2.** d (AB); **3.** e (AC); **4.** C (AC) c; **5.** a (S).

HERITAGE LANGUAGE LEARNERS

Have students do some research on some Internet acronyms and find out whether or not they are used in Spanish. Ask them to share the latest trends in texting shortcuts. What can happen if people interpret the same acronym differently? Encourage them to share examples of when their shortcuts have been misunderstood.

OBJECTIVES FOR SABOR HISPANO

- Learn about the role of advertisements and Internet in Hispanic countries
- Compare cultural similarities about the role of advertisements and Internet around the world

CORE RESOURCES

- Audio Program: Track 59

STANDARDS

2.2   Products and perspectives

4.2   Compare cultures

INSTRUCTIONAL STRATEGIES

🎧 59

- Put students in pairs to discuss the questions in the **Antes de leer** box.
- Monitor their conversations and assist as needed.
- Call on volunteers to report back on their discussions.
- Focus students' attention on the images and their captions. Ask who they are, where they are from, and why they are famous.
- Before playing the audio, tell students to listen for the question posed at the beginning of the audio and be prepared to answer it. Either have students close their books while they listen or follow along with the text in the book.
- Elicit responses to the target question. For more detail, ask: **¿Quiénes tienen más influencia y poder para convencer al consumidor en España: los actores y los cantantes, o los deportistas? ¿Cómo lo saben?**
- To help build vocabulary, have students locate and underline any words from the glossary on the next page in the text. Then have them make and share new sentences with the words. You may choose to have them work individually or in pairs.

Cultural Note

- Lionel Messi's full name is Lionel Andrés Messi Cuccittini, and he often goes by "Leo." He's a professional soccer player from Argentina. He plays on the country's national team as well as for the Spanish club FC Barcelona. He won the Ballon d'Or and FIFA Player of the Year awards in 2009 at the age of 22. He then won the FIFA Ballon d'Or 2010, 2011, and 2012. He was also named UEFA's Best Player in Europe in 2010-2011. By 24, he was Barcelona's all-time top scorer; by 25, he was the youngest player to score 200 goals in **La Liga** (the Spanish soccer league of which FC Barcelona is a part); and by 27, in September 2014, he had scored his 400th goal. He was born on June 24, 2987 in Rosario, Sante Fe, Argentina.
- Shakira is a singer-songwriter from Barranquilla, Colombia. She's also a belly dancer, record producer, choreographer, and model. Her music has Latin and Arabic influences and is a mix of pop and rock and roll. Some of her albums are *Magia* (1991), *Peligro* (1993), *Pies Descalzos* (1996), *Dónde Están los Ladrones?* (1998), *Laundry Service* (2001), *Fijación Oral*, Vol. 1 and *Oral Fixation*, Vol. 2 (2005), *She Wolf* (2009), *Sale el Sol* (2010), and *Shakira* (2014). Some of her most popular songs are "Whenever, Wherever," "Hips Don't Lie," "Waka Waka (This Time for Africa)," (the anthem of the 2010 FIFA World Cup), and "Can't Remember to Forget You." She's been a judge on the television series *The Voice*. She was born on February 2, 1977. She is currently married to Spanish soccer player Gerard Piqué and has one child.

SABOR HISPANO

¡CÓMPRALO YA!

Lionel Messi

Antes de leer

¿Comprarías un producto porque una persona famosa hace la publicidad*? ¿Por qué (no)?

🎧 59 **Muchos famosos usan su imagen y su éxito para vender productos. Pero... ¿funciona esta estrategia en España? ¡Lee para saberlo!**

Lionel Messi es uno de los futbolistas más famosos del mundo. Su fortuna asciende a* 172 millones de dólares. Pero hoy, Lionel está concentrado en convencerte: quiere que compres la tableta de una famosa marca*. Para eso, participa en un video usando el producto. La idea es que, cuando lo veas, te imagines viviendo la glamurosa vida de una estrella de fútbol internacional.

Shakira también quiere que compres algo, y no es solamente la entrada a su último concierto. La cantante colombiana pone su sonrisa* para vender pasta de dientes en videos y publicidades en revistas y periódicos.

Ellos no son los únicos que usan su imagen para comercializar productos: Jennifer López vende celulares, Salma Hayek vende champú y Antonio Banderas vende perfume en publicidades y eventos.

Aunque parezca una receta infalible, en la mayoría de los casos la cara de un famoso deportista o artista no es suficiente para convencer al consumidor. En España, solamente el 5% de la gente compraría un producto porque un actor o cantante hace la publicidad. Los deportistas son, al parecer, más efectivos: el 8% de las personas consultadas en una encuesta* de la empresa Nielsen compraría un producto porque lo recomienda un atleta.

Shakira

214

Before reading and listening to the text, have students brainstorm words and phrases related to the unit theme that they have learned so far. They may relate to advertisement, sponsorship, celebrity branding and other related topics. Model how they can organize the words and phrases in a mind map.

ADVANCED LEARNERS

Find out what students already know about Lionel Messi and Shakira. Put them in small groups to prepare fact sheets about each of them. To create a competition, set a time limit and see which group can produce the most facts about them. For a fact to count toward the team's total, it must be accurate. Check any disputed facts for accuracy online.

Anuncios que más destacan

De acuerdo con su tono o contenido, algunos anuncios quedan en la memoria colectiva. Estas son las estrategias que mejor funcionan.

- 55%
- 30%
- 30%
- 8%
- 50%
- 5%

- ■ con humor
- ■ escenas cotidianas
- ■ valores
- ■ con familias
- ■ con deportistas
- ■ con artistas

¿Quién te convence?

Estas son las razones que llevan a los españoles a consumir un producto o servicio.

- 87%
- 59%
- 56%
- 45%

- ■ mi familia y amigos
- ■ críticas en Internet
- ■ un artículo periodístico
- ■ un anuncio en prensa

Las críticas en Internet son útiles para el consumidor.

¿COMPRENDISTE?

Decide si las siguientes frases son verdaderas (V) o falsas (F).

1. Lionel Messi pone su imagen para vender tecnología. V○ F○
2. Las publicidades con famosos son muy efectivas. V○ F○
3. El humor es la estrategia menos efectiva en los anuncios publicitarios. V○ F○
4. La mayoría de los españoles confía en las recomendaciones de su familia y amigos. V○ F○
5. Para mucha gente, los artículos en prensa escrita son útiles para decidir la compra de un producto. V○ F○

Las anuncios con humor son los más recordados.

AHORA TÚ

¿Qué opinas? Contesta las siguientes preguntas y comenta tus ideas con tus compañeros/as.

1. ¿Qué cosas son importantes para convencerte de comprar un producto? Nombra dos.
2. ¿Por qué crees que los deportistas tienen más éxito en las publicidades que los artistas?
3. Si fueras famoso/a, ¿qué producto no publicitarías nunca? ¿Por qué?
4. ¿Qué famoso norteamericano tiene credibilidad, en tu opinión? ¿Por qué?
5. ¿Cuál es tu publicidad favorita? Descríbela brevemente y explica por qué te parece efectiva.

VOCES LATINAS ▶ LOS FAMOSOS Y LA PUBLICIDAD

Glosario

- **ascender a** – to amount to
- **confiar** – to trust
- **destacar** – to stand out
- **la encuesta** – survey
- **hacer la publicidad** – to promote
- **la marca** – brand
- **la publicidad** – advertising
- **la sonrisa** – smile
- **valores** – value

Fuentes: Nielsen, Msn Latino, *El País.*

215

Anuncios que más destacan

- Call on a volunteer to read the caption and chart data aloud.
- Elicit examples of commercials or advertisements that use some of the strategies described in the charts.
- Have students write three questions about the data.
- Put them into pairs to take turns asking and answering the questions.
- Monitor their conversations and assist as needed. Take note of any common errors that you hear in their discussions.
- Review any common errors with the class, eliciting the corrections.

¿Quién te convence?

- Call on a volunteer to read the title and information that follows.
- Check students' understanding of the information by asking questions, such as: **¿Qué porcentaje de la gente en España consume un producto o servicio según las críticas en Internet?**
- Put students into pairs to discuss whether or not they are influenced the same way as the people in Spain. Have them come up with their own percentages for each category and add any new categories of their own.
- Call on volunteers to report back on their similarities or differences with the data from Spain.

¿Comprendiste?

- Have students work individually to answer the questions.
- Monitor their progress and assist as needed.
- Go over the answers as a class. Have them explain the false answers.

Ahora tú

- Have students work individually to answer the questions.
- Monitor their progress and assist as needed.
- Put students into pairs or small groups to share their ideas. Have them take turns asking and answering the questions. Encourage them to ask each other follow-up questions for more information.
- Ask each pair or group to report back to the class on something interesting from their conversation.

ANSWERS

¿Comprendiste?

1. T; 2. F; 3. F; 4. T; 5. T.

HERITAGE LANGUAGE LEARNERS

Have students name other celebrities that may make a lot of money by appearing in advertisements. Have them do some research about celebrity branding. How much do they think an actor or famous basketball player can make for appearing in a commercial? Alternatively, you can have students share information about celebrities in their countries of origin and discuss what they're famous for, where they live, and what products, services, or organizations they advertise for.

OBJECTIVES FOR RELATO

- Revisit unit themes, grammar, vocabulary and culture in a new context
- Improve reading comprehension skills

CORE RESOURCES

- Audio Program: Track 60

STANDARDS

- 1.3 Present information
- 2.2 Products and perspectives
- 3.1 Knowledge of other disciplines

INSTRUCTIONAL STRATEGIES

Activity 1

- To activate schema, elicit words related to feelings and emotions in Spanish and write them on the board, for example: *alegría*, *pérdida*, *amistad*, *comunicación*, *imaginación*, *fantasía*, *dependencia*, *independencia*, *soledad*, *organización*…
- Go over the instructions. Focus students' attention on the images. Model a possible response based on one of the images using your own experiences and feelings.
- Have students work individually to write their own ideas.
- Monitor their progress and assist as needed. Encourage them to be creative.
- Call on volunteers to share their ideas.

Activity 2

- Go over the instructions. Tell students to be prepared to report back on their partners' responses.
- Put students into pairs to ask and answer the questions.
- Monitor their progress and assist as needed. Encourage them to take notes to focus on what their partner is saying. Listen to any common errors in their discussions.
- Have students' switch partners and report back on their previous partners' responses.
- Go over any common errors you heard, eliciting corrections from the class.

🎧 60 Activity 3

- Read the instructions as a class. Focus students' attention on the title. Ask students what they think the text will include. Elicit ideas and check their understanding of the vocabulary in the title.
- Play the audio, and have students read along.
- Call on volunteers to share their impressions of the text. Ask questions, such as: *Según el texto, ¿creen que el autor piensa que es bueno recibir un reloj de regalo? ¿Por qué sí o por qué no?*
- Put students into pairs to discuss how they can use the ideas in the text in an advertisement.
- Monitor their progress and assist as needed.
- Have volunteers report back on their ideas.

Activity 4

- Go over the instructions. Read the text as a class.
- Have students work individually to find the words in the text with the same meaning.
- Go over the answers as a class.
- Consider asking a few questions to check their comprehension of the text, such as: *¿De dónde es Julio Cortázar? ¿Dónde vivió? ¿Por qué es famoso?*

RELATO *Preámbulo a las instrucciones para dar cuerda a un reloj*

1 Observa estos objetos y escribe qué representan para ti y qué emociones, sentimientos o recuerdos asocias a ellos.

2 👥 Túrnate con tu compañero/a y contesta las siguientes preguntas.

a. ¿Cuál usas con más frecuencia?
b. ¿Cuál es el más indispensable para ti?
c. ¿Imaginas tu vida sin él? ¿Cómo cambiaría tu vida?

3 🎧 60 Imagínate que trabajas para una agencia publicitaria y encuentras el siguiente texto literario. Léelo y comenta con tu compañero/a cómo podrías usarlo en un anuncio.

> ### Preámbulo a las instrucciones para dar cuerda a un reloj
>
> Piensa en esto: cuando te regalan un reloj te regalan un pequeño infierno florido, una cadena (*chain*) de rosas, un calabozo (*jail cell*) de aire. No te dan solamente el reloj, que los cumplas muy felices y esperamos que te dure porque es de buena marca, suizo con áncora (*anchor*) de rubíes; no te regalan solamente ese menudo picapedrero que te atarás a la muñeca (*wrist*) y pasearás contigo. Te regalan —no lo saben, lo terrible es que no lo saben—, te regalan un nuevo pedazo frágil y precario de ti mismo, algo que es tuyo pero no es tu cuerpo, que hay que atar (*tie*) a tu cuerpo con su correa como un bracito desesperado colgándose de tu muñeca. Te regalan la necesidad de darle cuerda (*wind*) todos los días, la obligación de darle cuerda para que siga siendo un reloj; te regalan la obsesión de atender a la hora exacta en las vitrinas de las joyerías, en el anuncio por la radio, en el servicio telefónico. Te regalan el miedo a perderlo, de que te lo roben, de que se te caiga al suelo y se rompa. Te regalan su marca, y la seguridad de que es una marca mejor que las otras, te regalan la tendencia de comparar tu reloj con los demás relojes. No te regalan un reloj, tú eres el regalado, a ti te ofrecen para el cumpleaños del reloj.

4 El texto anterior pertenece a *Historias de cronopios y de famas* (1962) escrito por Julio Cortázar. Lee acerca de este escritor y su obra. Después, busca la palabra en el texto con el mismo significado que estas expresiones.

a. Obra que narra la vivencias personales del autor. ➡ ....
b. Los hechos que se narran no siguen un orden cronológico. ➡ ....
c. La obra del autor que más se ha vendido. ➡ ....
d. Composición de carácter poético no escrita en verso. ➡ ....

ANSWERS

Activity 4

a. Autobiográfica; **b.** No existe la linealidad; **c.** Su mayor éxito editorial; **d.** Prosa poética.

SLOWER-PACED LEARNERS

To help students along with Activity 3, have students write down what they think a watch is for and what things or ideas are associated with having them. You might discuss wearable technology developed by Apple and how some people want the Apple Watch, for instance, because of what it means to have one.

ADVANCED LEARNERS

Discuss the use of parallel structures as a writing technique. Have students try to define what parallel structures are and find examples of them in the text in Activity 3 (the repeated use of sentences beginning with *Te regalan*). Discuss why writers might employ this technique and what effects it has. Why might advertisers want to use parallel structures?

Julio Cortázar nació en Bélgica, el 26 de agosto de 1914 y murió en Francia el 12 de febrero de 1984. Fue un escritor, traductor e intelectual argentino nacionalizado francés. Se le considera uno de los autores más innovadores y originales de su tiempo. Maestro del relato corto, la prosa poética y la narración breve en general, destaca, por ejemplo, su obra autobiográfica *Bestiario*. Fue creador de importantes novelas que inauguraron una nueva forma de hacer literatura en el mundo hispano, rompiendo los moldes clásicos: no existe la linealidad temporal y los personajes tienen autonomía y una profundidad psicológica. Debido a que los contenidos de su obra están en la frontera entre lo real y lo fantástico, se le suele relacionar con el surrealismo. Su mayor éxito editorial, *Rayuela*, la cual le valió el reconocimiento de ser parte del *boom* latinoamericano, se convirtió en un clásico de la literatura argentina. También escribió teatro y poesía. Vivió buena parte de su vida en París, pero también en Argentina, España y Suiza.

5 **Piensa en un objeto especial para ti y escribe un texto similar al de Cortázar sobre ese objeto.**

Piensa en esto:

- Cuando te regalan ....
- Te regalan un ....
- No te dan solamente ....
- No te regalan solamente ....
- Te regalan la necesidad de ....
- Te regalan la obsesión de ....
- Te regalan el miedo de ....
- Te regalan su marca y la seguridad de que ....
- Te regalan la tendencia de ....
- No te regalan un ....
- Tú eres el regalado. A ti te regalan para el cumpleaños del ....

6 **Con esta información, ya has creado el texto para tu anuncio. Elige un eslogan junto con las imágenes y la música que te gustaría utilizar. Después, presenta tu anuncio a la clase.**

7 **Comenta algunos de tus anuncios preferidos con tu compañero/a. Usa las siguientes preguntas como guía.**

a. ¿Cuál es el anuncio publicitario que más te ha llamado la atención?

b. ¿Dónde lo has visto?

c. ¿Por qué te ha impresionado?

217

INSTRUCTIONAL STRATEGIES

Activity 5

- Go over the instructions. Have students work individually or in pairs to brainstorm ideas and complete the sentences.
- Monitor their progress and assist as needed. Encourage them to be creative.

Activity 6

- Go over the instructions. Elicit examples of slogans from current ad campaigns. Discuss the qualities of good slogans; they are often concise, clever, and catchy.
- Have students review their sentences from Activity 5 and come up with a catchy slogan to help sell their object. In addition to the images and music, you may even choose to have students mock up a logo, a rough design of a print ad, or a storyboard for a commercial.
- Have students present their ads to the class.

Activity 7

- Put students into pairs or small groups to discuss the questions.
- Monitor their conversations and assist as needed.
- Call on volunteers to report back on interesting aspects of their conversations.

HERITAGE LANGUAGE LEARNERS

Have students compare ads in Spanish and English for the same product. How are they different? Why? Have them write a paragraph with their own observations and conclusions. Suggest that they searches big brands and multinational corporations to find examples.

EVALUACIÓN SELF-ASSESSMENT

OBJECTIVES FOR EVALUACIÓN

- Review grammar, vocabulary and culture from the unit
- Complete self-assessment

CORE RESOURCES

- Extension Activities: EA 7.5
- Interactive Online Materials - ELEteca

STANDARDS

1.2 Understand the language

4.1 Compare languages

INSTRUCTIONAL STRATEGIES

- Have students complete the activities individually.
- Go over the answers as a class. Encourage students to learn from each other by asking if they agree with the answers given. Provide explanations as needed.
- You may wish to assign point value to each activity as a way for students to monitor their progress.
- Direct students to the indicated pages in **En resumen** if they make more than one or two mistakes in any one section.

Extension

Give students a copy of EA 7.5, **Autoevaluación**. Have them complete the charts with the information they have learned and the mistakes they have made so they may better understand where they need the most improvement.

ANSWERS

Activity 1

a. deben; **b.** se dejen; **c.** pidan; **d.** desarrollan; **e.** hacen; **f.** vayamos / vayan.

Activity 2

a. No es ridículo que; **b.** No es verdad que; **c.** Es una tontería que; **d.** Es increíble que; **e.** Está claro que.

Activity 3

Answers will vary. Possible answers may include the following:

a. Yo no creo que eso sea verdad, pienso que en verano cada uno elige según sus posibilidades; **b.** En mi opinión sucede todo lo contrario, los medios nos bombardean continuamente con ella; **c.** A mí me parece que es totalmente cierto porque es un sector de la población muy influenciable; **d.** Yo no estoy nada de acuerdo porque el arte puede expresarse a través de cualquier medio.

Activity 4

a. ¡Y que lo digas!; **b.** ¡Qué va!; **c.** ¡Desde luego!; **d.** ¡Anda ya!

EVALUACIÓN

EXPRESSING WISHES

1 **Completa con la forma correcta del verbo entre paréntesis.**

a. Me parece que las escenas en los anuncios (deber) .... ser variadas y dinámicas.

b. No pienso que los jóvenes (dejarse) .... influir tanto por la publicidad.

c. No creo que los niños (pedir) .... los productos que ven en la televisión.

d. Opino que los consumidores (desarrollar) .... un espíritu crítico ante tanta información.

e. Desde mi punto de vista, las asociaciones anticonsumo (hacer) .... un buen trabajo en la sociedad.

f. No me parece bien que todos (ir) .... con la misma ropa y los mismos tenis.

MAKING VALUE JUDGEMENTS

2 **Completa las frases con una expresión del cuadro.**

> Está claro que ○ Es increíble que ○ Es una tontería que ○ No es verdad que ○ No es ridículo que

a. .... los padres vigilen cuántas horas de televisión ven sus hijos pequeños.

b. .... los anuncios sean sinceros.

c. .... las personas crean que un perfume las hará perfectas.

d. .... no sepamos elegir por nosotros mismos.

e. .... los medios de comunicación tienen un gran poder sobre la sociedad.

SHOWING AGREEMENT AND DISAGREEMENT

3 **Indica si estás de acuerdo o no con las siguientes opiniones.**

a. En verano somos más influenciables por la publicidad porque queremos tener unas buenas vacaciones.

b. En la actualidad, hay poca publicidad y por eso todos la siguen con mucha atención.

c. En las redes sociales hay mucha publicidad porque los jóvenes las visitan con mucha frecuencia.

d. La fotografía y el diseño gráfico no son arte.

4 **Completa las siguientes conversaciones. Usa una expresión para demostrar, o no, apoyo a cada afirmación.**

a. » Es ridículo que el cine sea tan caro, me gustaría ir más.
   » ¡.................. ! A mí también me gustaría.

b. » Creo que hay fiestas solo comerciales, como San Valentín.
   » ¡..................! Es la fiesta del amor y el romanticismo.

c. » Es impresionante que compres tantos libros digitales. A mí me gustan en papel.
   » ¡..................! Es mucho mejor en papel, pero pesan y ocupan más.

d. » Me he comprado el último libro de Vargas Llosa. ¡Estoy muy contento!
   » ¡..................! Eres un antiguo. Yo lo llevo en mi ebook.

TRANSITION WORDS AND SENTENCE CONNECTORS

5 **Relaciona los elementos de las dos columnas.**

1. El fútbol es un gran deporte. Sin embargo
2. La fotografía en el cine es fundamental. Por ejemplo,
3. Los jóvenes no ven la publicidad, incluso
4. Pienso que seré seleccionado para el comercial de Axo; en la última entrevista que hice les gusté mucho. Además,
5. El gasto de las compañías en publicidad es muy alto. Total que
6. Por un lado, los anuncios me divierten por su fantasía, pero por otro lado,

a. yo diría que no les interesa.
b. sus productos son muy caros.
c. no es el único.
d. me aburre que haya tantos.
e. había muy poca gente.
f. en *Memorias de África* es impresionante, ¿la recuerdas?

INTERNET Y LA PUBLICIDAD EN INTERNET

6 **Completa con las palabras y expresiones del cuadro.**

botón ○ enlaces ○ texto publicitario ○ usuario ○ web portal ○ logo

Mi centro ha creado una (a) .... que es un sitio en Internet que sirve para que podamos acceder a recursos y servicios relacionados con la vida estudiantil. Puede incluir: enlaces, buscadores, libros, documentos, aplicaciones, compra electrónica. Así, el (b) ...., es decir, la persona que utiliza la web portal, podrá acceder a ella y buscar información solo pinchando un (c) .... Además, podemos conectar con otras páginas web, descargar ficheros o abrir ventanas a través de (d) .... Por suerte, no sufriremos los continuos anuncios, porque no está permitido incluir ningún (e) .... Lo que no me gusta de la página es el (f) ...., vamos, la combinación de letras e imagen que representa el centro escolar.

INITIALS, ACRONYMS AND ABBREVIATIONS

7 **Escribe la abreviatura, el acrónimo o las siglas correspondientes.**

a. Unión Europe ➡ ....
b. Pequeña y Mediana Empresa ➡ ....
c. Organización de Naciones Unidas ➡ ....

d. Estados Unidos ➡ ....
e. Tercero izquierda ➡ ....
f. Juegos Olímpicos ➡ ....

CULTURA

8 **Contesta las siguientes preguntas con la información que has aprendido en ¡*Cómpralo ya!***

a. ¿Cuál es la estrategia de poner a un futbolista como Lionel Messi a vender productos?
b. ¿Qué producto promociona Shakira? ¿Crees que han acertado? ¿Por qué?
c. Según los datos presentados, ¿es suficiente tener a un personaje famoso para convencer al consumidor?
d. ¿Qué tipo de anuncio tiene el mayor éxito a la hora de vender?
e. En el caso de los españoles, ¿cómo se les convence mejor para que compren algo?

 MORE IN ELETECA: EXTRA ONLINE PRACTICE

219

ANSWERS

Activity 5

1. c; **2.** f; **3.** a; **4.** e; **5.** b; **6.** d.

Activity 6

1. web portal; **2.** usuario; **3.** botón; **4.** enlaces; **5.** texto publicitario; **6.** logo.

Activity 7

a. UE; **b.** pyme; **c.** ONU; **d.** EE. UU.; **e.** 3.º izq.; **f.** JJ. OO.

Activity 8

Answers will vary. Possible answers might include the following:

a. La idea es que, cuando lo veas, te imagines viviendo la glamurosa vida de una estrella de fútbol internacional; **b.** Shakira promociona pasta de dientes; **c.** No, no es suficiente; **d.** Tienen más éxito los anuncios con humor; **e.** A los españoles les convencen más las recomendaciones de familia y amigos.

OBJECTIVES FOR EN RESUMEN: VOCABULARIO

- Review unit vocabulary and expressions
- Practice communicative skills

STANDARDS

1.2 Understand the language

1.3 Present information

INSTRUCTIONAL STRATEGIES

- Have students write sentences with the words and phrases in the other vocabulary sections.
- Call on students to write their sentences on the board –but leave a blank line (or give multiple choices, in some cases) where the vocabulary word or phrase should be. Then have the rest of the class write down the answers to complete the sentences
- Go over the answers as a class. You may choose to create a competition and keep score by individual or group.

Alternative Activity

Index cards can be used as flashcards with the Spanish term on one side and the English term, a picture, or a drawing on the other. Working in pairs or groups, students can use the flashcards to help each other practice unit vocabulary.

EN RESUMEN: Vocabulario

La publicidad

la campaña *campaign*
el cartel *sign, poster*
el consumidor *consumer*
el derecho a la intimidad *right to privacy*
la encuesta *survey*
el espectacular *billboard*

la libertad de expresión *freedom of expression*
la manipulación *manipulation*
la marca *brand*
la mercadotecnia / el mercadeo *marketing*
la novedad *fad, novelty*
el público *public*

el punto de vista *point of view*
las rebajas *sales*

las redes sociales *social networks*

el respeto *respect*
el valor *value*

Descripciones

anticonsumista *one who opposes consumerism*
machista *chauvinist*
preocupante *worrisome, alarming*

Verbos

abrir ventanas *to open a new window*
atacar *to attack*
consumir *to consume*

cumplir *to accomplish*
descargar *to download*
hacer caso *to pay attention to*
provocar *to provoke*
tratar de *to try to (do something)*
tuitear *to tweet*

utilizar *to use*

Internet

la amistad virtual *virtual friend*
la banderola *banner*

el botón *button*
el buscador *search engine*

la dirección web *web address*
el enlace *link*
el fichero / el archivo *computer file*
el foro *forum*
el icono *icon*
el logo *logo, branding*
la página web *web page*
el perfil *profile*

la piratería *piracy*

el portal *web portal*
el sitio (web) *(web) site*
el usuario *user*
las ventanas emergentes *pop-up windows*

EN RESUMEN: Gramática

EXPRESSING OPINION
(See page 200 and 201)

- To **ask opinion**:

  ¿Qué piensas / crees / opinas de / sobre...?

  ¿(A ti) qué te parece...?

  ¿En tu opinión / Desde tu punto de vista / Según tú + question sentence?

- To **express agreement** and **disagreement** with an opinion:

(No) estoy	a favor de	+ noun
	estoy en contra de	+ infinitive *(same subject)*
	(del todo) de acuerdo con	+ **que** + present subjunctive *(different subjects)*

- To **express opinion**:

  En mi opinión / Desde mi punto de vista... + opinion

  Me parece que / Creo que / Pienso que + indicative

  No me parece que / No creo que + subjunctive

MAKING VALUE JUDGEMENTS
(See page 202)

- To **ask for evaluation or value judgementes** we use:

  ¿Te parece bien / mal + noun / infinitive / que + present subjunctive?

- To **value judgements**:

Me parece Es	(parecer) bien / mal (ser) bueno / malo triste / increíble / cómico / justo ridículo / exagerado / preocupante... una tontería / una vergüenza	**que** + present subjunctive
Está claro **Es obvio / verdad**	**que** + indicative	
¡Qué bien / **interesante**	noun / infinitive / **que** + subjunctive!	

TRANSITION WORDS AND PHRASES TO ORGANIZE THE IDEAS OF A TEXT
(See page 209)

- To **distinguish** two arguments: En primer lugar... / En segundo lugar...
- To **set out** two arguments: Por un lado / una parte... por otro (lado) / por otra (parte)...
- To **add** arguments: Y / además / también / asimismo...
- To **explain and give examples**: Por ejemplo / es decir / o sea...
- To **mention a previously-raised theme**: (Con) respecto a (eso de / eso) / sobre (eso)...

OTHER SENTENCE CONNECTORS
(See page 210)

- To **add reasons** in strength-raising order: Incluso.
- To **oppose reasons**: Bueno / pero / sin embargo / no obstante / en cambio.
- To **express consequence**: Así que / de modo que / de manera que / de ahí que / así pues / pues.
- To draw **conclusions**: Entonces / total que / por lo tanto / en resumen / en conclusión / para terminar.

221

OBJECTIVES FOR EN RESUMEN: GRAMÁTICA

- Review unit grammar
- Practice communication skills

STANDARDS

| 1.2 | Understand the language |
| 4.1 | Compare languages |

INSTRUCTIONAL STRATEGIES

- Focus students' attention on the key grammar topics of the unit.
- Have students review the Learning Outcomes in the unit opener to assess whether they feel they have mastered the main ideas and skills.
- Ask them if they can remember additional examples for each grammar topic.
- Model how to find and go back to the appropriate page in the unit to review any grammar topic they may need help with.
- Invite students to review the grammar activities they completed in this unit.
- Ask them what grammar activities they found easy and which they found challenging. Encourage them to rework any activities they found particularly challenging.

OBJECTIVES FOR UNIT OPENER

- Introduce unit theme: **¿Sueño o realidad?** about expressing real and hypothetical situations and stories
- Introduce culture for the unit: Learn about letter writing and formal correspondence in Hispanic countries

STANDARDS

1.1 Engage in conversation   2.2 Products and culture

INSTRUCTIONAL STRATEGIES

- Before students open their books, write the unit title on the board: **¿Sueño o realidad?** Elicit ideas from the students about the material they think they will encounter in the unit.
- Have students open their books, look at the image, and read the caption. Ask: **¿Cómo se llama el autor? ¿Cómo se titula el libro? ¿Qué significa el título?** Ask students to recall another title by the same author (**La sombra del viento**).
- Have students work individually to write answers to the three questions on the page. Remind them to use the image of the cover to answer the questions.
- Put students into pairs or small groups to share and discuss their answers.
- Call on volunteers to report back on their responses and discussions. See if you can get the class to reach agreement.

Cultural Note

Carlos Ruiz Zafón is a Spanish author. He wrote the fiction novel *El Juego del Ángel* in 2008 as a prequel to his 2001 novel entitled *La Sombra del Viento*. *El Juego del Ángel* is about David Martín, a young writer in Barcelona in the 1920s and 1930s, and his encounters with a mysterious man who wants him to write a book. The novel retains two specific settings from *La Sombra del Viento*: The Cemetery of Forgotten Books and Sempere & Sons bookshop.

SLOWER-PACED LEARNERS

Have students refresh the present subjunctive by using expressions such as **Es fantástico que..., Me gusta que..., No es bueno que...** Begin by asking them questions about their reading habits. For example: **¿Cuántos libros lees al mes?** Model responses that use of the subjunctive: **Es fantástico que leas cinco libros al mes.**

ADVANCED LEARNERS

Put students in pairs or small groups to talk about books they like. Have them describe the main characters and primary conflicts within the stories. They might also discuss whether or not the stories are easy to follow. Encourage them to ask each other questions for additional information about the books.

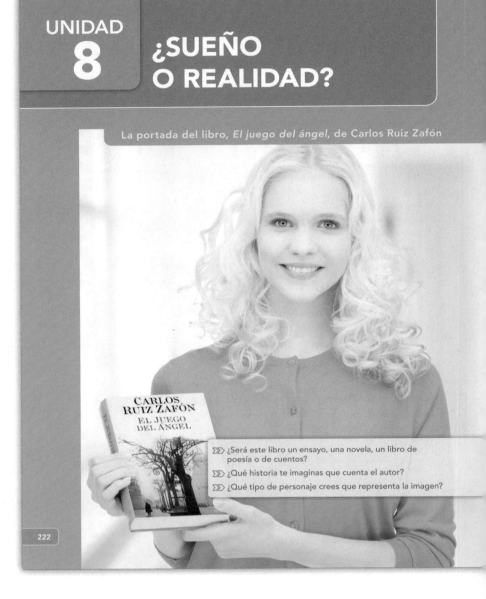

UNIDAD 8 — ¿SUEÑO O REALIDAD?

La portada del libro, *El juego del ángel*, de Carlos Ruiz Zafón

CARLOS RUIZ ZAFÓN
EL JUEGO DEL ÁNGEL

≫ ¿Será este libro un ensayo, una novela, un libro de poesía o de cuentos?

≫ ¿Qué historia te imaginas que cuenta el autor?

≫ ¿Qué tipo de personaje crees que representa la imagen?

222

ADDITIONAL UNIT RESOURCES

Extension Activities (EA) (Photocopiable)	Interactive Whiteboard Lessons (IWB)	Audio	Video	Online ELEteca
EA: 8.1, 8.2, 8.3, 8.4	IWB: 8.1, 8.2, 8.3	61 to 68	Diálogo 8	EXTENSIÓN DIGITAL

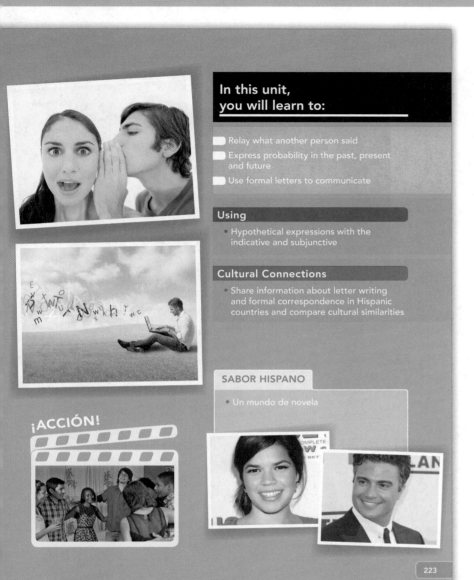

**In this unit,
you will learn to:**

- Relay what another person said
- Express probability in the past, present and future
- Use formal letters to communicate

Using

- Hypothetical expressions with the indicative and subjunctive

Cultural Connections

- Share information about letter writing and formal correspondence in Hispanic countries and compare cultural similarities

SABOR HISPANO

- Un mundo de novela

¡ACCIÓN!

223

LEARNING OUTCOMES

- Relay what another person said
- Express probability in the past, present, and future
- Use formal letters to communicate

INSTRUCTIONAL STRATEGIES

- Use the unit opener to preview vocabulary and cultural topics for this unit.
- Have students look at the images on this page and try to relate them to the objectives listed.
- Exploit the first main photo a bit further by asking questions, such as: **¿Qué le está diciendo el muchacho a la muchacha? ¿Cuál es la reacción de ella? ¿Por qué creen que se siente así?**
- Move on to the second photo and ask questions, such as: **¿Todavía escriben cartas formales? ¿Cuándo? ¿A quiénes escriben cartas formales? ¿Cuáles son las diferencias entre las cartas formales y las cartas informales (o los correos electrónicos)?**
- Invite students to read the topic for **Sabor hispano** and preview that section in the unit. Ask questions, such as: **¿Reconocen a estas personas? ¿Cómo se llaman?** (**América Ferrera**, **Jaime Camil**) **¿Por qué son famosos?** (They are actors who have interpreted leading roles in Hispanic soap operas.)
- Ask students to anticipate what they think the episode for **¡Acción!** will be about.

HERITAGE LANGUAGE LEARNERS

Invite students to talk about any Spanish-language soap operas that they have seen. Tell them to describe the premise of the show, its main characters, and where it takes place. Finally, have them discuss whether or not they like the show and why or why not.

THREE MODES OF COMMUNICATION: UNIT 8		
	INTERPERSONAL	**INTERPRETIVE**	**PRESENTATIONAL**
HABLAMOS DE...	1	1, 2, 3, 4, 5	
COMUNICA	4, 7, 9, 10	1, 2, 3, 5, 6, 8	4, 10
¡ACCIÓN!	5	1, 2, 3, 4	
PALABRA POR PALABRA	5	1, 2, 3, 4, 6, 7, 8, 10	6, 9, 10
GRAMÁTICA	2, 8, 9	1, 2, 3, 4, 5, 7	6, 8, 9
DESTREZAS	3	1, 2, 3	2, 3
CULTURA		SABOR HISPANO	
RELATO	1, 2, 6, 8	3, 4, 5, 7	

OBJECTIVES FOR HABLAMOS DE...

- Understand language in context
- Preview vocabulary: reading fiction
- Preview grammatical structures: Hypothetical expressions with the indicative and the subjunctive
- Read and listen to a conversation between Daniela and José about selecting a birthday gift for a friend

CORE RESOURCES

- Audio Program: Track 61
- Extension Activities: EA 8.1
- Interactive Whiteboard Lesson: IWB 8.1

STANDARDS

- 1.1 Engage in conversation
- 2.2 Products and culture
- 3.2 Acquire information

INSTRUCTIONAL STRATEGIES

Activity 1

- Before students open their books, activate their schema by asking questions, such as: *¿Les gusta leer? ¿Qué cosas leen? ¿Prefieren leer para aprender algo o por diversión? ¿Qué libros pueden recomendar?*
- Have students open their books and look at the images at the top of the page. Put students into pairs to ask and answer the questions and discuss their ideas.
- Monitor their conversations and assist as needed.
- Call on volunteers to report back on their ideas.

Activity 2

- Refer students back to the book covers and have them work individually to answer the questions. Encourage students to make educated guesses if they don't know the answers.
- Go over the answers as a class. Then share the following note with students.

Cultural Note

- **Mafalda** es un personaje argentino, creado por el dibujante Quino, que aparecía en tiras cómicas y que es muy popular en Hispanoamérica y en varios países europeos. Mafalda es una niña que desea que el mundo sea mejor, pero también refleja el pesimismo de la sociedad de los años 60.
- **Don Quijote de la Mancha** es quizás el personaje literario español más popular internacionalmente. Creado en 1605 por Cervantes, es un personaje que ha perdido la razón después de leer muchos libros de caballería. Sale de su pueblo acompañado de Sancho Panza para vivir el tipo de aventuras que ha leído en esos libros.

ANSWERS

Activity 2

El Quijote: b, c, f, g; **Mafalda:** a, d, e, h

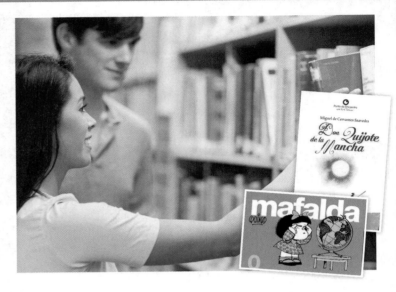

HABLAMOS DE... Libros y cómics

1 👥 Observa la imagen y contesta las preguntas con tu compañero/a.

a. ¿Dónde están los muchachos?
b. ¿Cuál de los dos libros piensas que es más adecuado para un muchacho de tu edad?
c. ¿Cuál comprarías tú?
d. ¿Cuál es el último libro que compraste o leíste?

2 En la imagen aparecen las portadas de dos libros. ¿Puedes imaginar a cuál corresponde la siguiente información?

	El Quijote	Mafalda
a. Es del año 1964.	☐	☐
b. Es del año 1605.	☐	☐
c. Su autor es Cervantes.	☐	☐
d. Su autor es Quino.	☐	☐
e. Otros personajes que aparecen son Felipe, Miguelito y Susanita.	☐	☐
f. Otros personajes que aparecen son Dulcinea, Sancho y Rocinante.	☐	☐
g. Es de origen español.	☐	☐
h. Es de origen argentino.	☐	☐

224

SLOWER-PACED LEARNERS

In Activity 1, students may respond that the people in the image are in a *librería* or *biblioteca*. Have them think about the differences and discuss false cognates (words that sound similar in both languages but have different meanings). Here are some examples: actually is *de hecho* or *en realidad* in Spanish, not actualmente, which means currently; advice is *consejo* in Spanish, not *aviso*, which means notice; *conductor* is director in Spanish, not driver; and contest is *concurso* in Spanish, not *contestar*, which means to answer. Ask students if they have know of any other examples.

HERITAGE LANGUAGE LEARNERS

Have students find comic strips with Mafalda to share with the class. They might work in small groups and read the comic strip aloud. They should then explain it in their own words and make a comment or express their opinions about it.

3 🎧 61 Escucha y contesta verdadero (V) o falso (F).

	V	F
a. Daniela quiere comprar dos libros.	☐	☐
b. Felipe lee solo novelas modernas.	☐	☐
c. Daniela disfrutaba mucho con los cómics de Mafalda cuando era pequeña.	☐	☐
d. A José el cómic no le parece un buen regalo.	☐	☐
e. José ya tiene regalo para Felipe.	☐	☐

4 Lee la conversación y comprueba tus respuestas en la Actividad 3.

Daniela: No sé qué libro comprarle a Felipe para su cumpleaños, ¡estoy hecha bolas!

José: La verdad es que es bastante complicado, tienes razón.

D.: Creo que finalmente voy a regalarle uno de estos dos, pero no sé por cuál decidirme. Son muy diferentes.

J.: Me parece que a Felipe le gusta leer novelas. Pero quizás no le guste *El Quijote*, es un poco antiguo para él.

D.: Es verdad que es un poco antiguo, pero Felipe lee toda clase de libros. En su casa tiene una colección enorme de novelas de todas las épocas. Es increíble que a un muchacho de 17 años le guste tanto leer.

J.: ¿Y sabes si también lee cómics? A lo mejor

el libro de Mafalda es un poquito infantil.

D.: ¿Infantil? Todo lo contrario. En mi opinión deberían leerlo los adultos, es un poco filosófico. En estas historietas aparece una niña preocupada por la paz del mundo y por la humanidad. Yo, cuando era pequeña, tenía un montón de libros de Mafalda, pero no los entendí del todo hasta que no fui adulta.

J.: Pues quizás sea esa una buena opción. Me parece que es más atractivo y más original como regalo.

D.: Pues ya está decidido. ¡Me lo llevo! Le voy a decir al dependiente que me lo envuelva. Oye, ¿y tú qué le vas a comprar?

J.: Ni idea, voy a darme una vuelta por aquí a ver si encuentro algo.

5 Aquí tienes los nombres de algunos cómics españoles. Relaciona cada cómic con su protagonista.

detectives ○ superhéroe ○ niños traviesos ○ trabajador de una editorial

 a.
 b.
 c.
 d.

225

Activity 4

- Put students into pairs. Have them check their answers with a partner. Encourage them to use the transcript to correct any mistakes.
- Monitor their progress and assist as needed.
- Go over the answers as a class. Have students explain the false answers.
- As a follow-up, ask students to suggest gifts José might buy for Felipe based on what you have learned about him.

Activity 5

- Review the instructions and the names of the comic books. Point out that in Spain they are called **tebeos**. The word comes from the name of a magazine published in Barcelona in 1917, TBO.
- Have students match the character descriptions with the covers of the comic books.
- Monitor their progress and assist as needed. Go over the answers as a class.

Alternative Activity

Have students research the comics online to be able to match the characters and covers with more confidence.

Extension

Project the comic strip with the empty speech bubbles from IWB 8.1, **Tebeos** and distribute copies of EA, 8.1, **Tebeos** to each student. Ask some basic questions about the images to activate vocabulary. Then give the students some time to fill in their own speech bubbles for each scene. Put them into small groups to share their comics. Have each group collaborate to produce the best comic strip from the samples provided to be presented to the class. Finally, reveal the speech bubbles in the original comic strip. Compare it to those produced by the students. Discuss its meaning by asking questions, such as: **¿Qué creen que ha querido transmitirnos su autor?**

Answers

Activity 3
a. F; **b.** F; **c.** T; **d.** F; **e.** F.

Activity 5
a. niños traviesos; **b.** detectives; **c.** trabajador de una editorial; **d.** superhéroe.

Advanced Learners

Explain students that manga is very popular in Spanish-speaking countries. Most manga series have been translated into Spanish, and many young people are attracted to reading longer books through exposure to manga when they were younger. Ask students to share their experience reading this type of stories and whether they would like to read manga in Spanish.

Instructional Strategies

🎧 61 **Activity 3**

- Have students close their books. Tell the students that they are going to listen to a conversation between two friends, Daniela and José. Write two questions on the board to focus their attention on the first listening: **¿Dónde creen que están Daniela y José? ¿Por qué?**
- Play the audio. Call on volunteers to offer answers to the target questions.
- Have students open their books. Tell them they are going to listen again to determine whether the sentences are true or false. Give them a little time to read over the sentences and play the audio again.

OBJECTIVES FOR COMUNICA

- Present communicative functions of the unit: Relaying information from others
- Talk about what others said and asked

CORE RESOURCES

- Audio Program: Track 62
- Interactive Online Materials - ELEteca

STANDARDS

- 1.1 Engage in conversation
- 1.2 Understand the language
- 4.1 Compare languages

INSTRUCTIONAL STRATEGIES FOR
RELAYING WHAT ANOTHER PERSON SAID AND ASKED

- Before opening their books, introduce students to the concept of indirect speech. You might ask students if they talked to anyone before class and what that person said. Tell them that relaying what someone else said is called indirect (or reported) speech.
- Have students open their books and walk them through the chart of examples of direct speech converted to indirect speech. Point out that it's important not only to make changes in the verbs but also in the possessives, demonstratives, etc.
- Write an example of direct speech on the board. Elicit how they might convert that to indirect speech. Help them along as needed.
- Next go over the examples of direct speech questions converted into indirect speech statements. Point out the use of **si** in *yes/no* questions and the repetition of the interrogative (still with its accent mark) in information questions.
- Write another example of a *yes/no* question and an information question on the board. Elicit the transformations from the class.

Activity 1

- Put students into pairs to complete the conversation. Encourage them to guess if they are not sure. Students will be able to confirm their answers in Activity 2.

🎧 62 Activity 2

- Play the audio to allow them to check their answers. Ask if they need any clarification; offer to play the audio again, if necessary.
- Put the students in pairs, and have them practice the conversations.

Activity 3

- Put students into groups of three. Have each member of the group ask the others a question and note the responses.
- Then put students into new groups. Have each student report his/her previous group members' responses to the new group.

Alternative Activity

Play a game of "telephone." Have students sit in a circle. Each student whispers a question into the ear of the person on their right and writes down that person's response; each student also answers the question from the person to the left and writes down that person's question. Then, out loud, each student reports back on the answer from the person to their right and the question from the person to their left.

COMUNICA

RELAYING WHAT ANOTHER PERSON SAID OR ASKED

DIRECT SPEECH	INDIRECT SPEECH
"**Eres** lo mejor de **mi** vida". ➡	*Dice que soy* lo mejor de **su** vida.
"**Estuve aquí** comiendo con Ana". ➡	*Dice que estuvo allí* comiendo con Ana.
"**Creo** que **tenemos este libro**". ➡	*Dice que cree* que **tienen ese** libro.
"**Compra** pan". ➡	*Me ordena* que **compre** pan.
"**¿Hicieron** la tarea?". ➡	El profesor **pregunta** si **hicimos** la tarea.
"¿Cuándo **harán** la tarea?". ➡	El profesor **nos pregunta** cuándo **haremos** la tarea.

- To report what was said, use verbs like: **decir**, **comentar** or **confesar** (e ➡ ie).
- To repeat an order or request, use verbs like **ordenar**, **aconsejar**, **sugerir** or **recomendar** plus the present subjunctive.
- To report what was asked, use **preguntar**.

1 👥 **Marta ha visitado esta mañana a Elena, su mejor amiga, y le cuenta a Pedro lo que le ha dicho. Con tu compañero/a, completa la conversación con las palabras del cuadro.**

> ha recomendado o ha dicho o ayer o ha confesado o que o dice o si o ha dicho

Marta: Elena me (a) .... que se va a cambiar de casa. Que está muy contenta porque (b) .... encontró trabajo.
Pedro: Vaya, qué suerte.
M.: Me (c) .... que realmente no está enamorada de su novio y (d) .... quiere dejarlo.
P.: La verdad es que no hacen buena pareja.
M.: Tienes razón. Por lo visto el otro día discutieron en el cine… Por cierto, me (e) .... la película que vio, (f) .... que es muy buena.
P.: Pues si quieres, vamos a verla este viernes.
M.: Bueno… ¡Ah! y también me (g) .... que cree que el mes que viene va a Ámsterdam a visitar a su hermano y a su cuñada, y me preguntó (h) .... quiero ir con ella.

2 🎧 62 **Escucha la conversación y comprueba tus respuestas.**

3 👥 **En grupos de tres, pregúntale algo a un compañero/a y cuéntale la respuesta al otro.**

Modelo: E1: ¿Cuál es tu libro favorito?
E2: *El señor de los anillos.*
E1: Luis dice que *El señor de los anillos* es su libro favorito.

ANSWERS

Activity 1

a. ha dicho; **b.** ayer; **c.** ha confesado; **d.** que; **e.** ha recomendado; **f.** dice; **g.** ha dicho; **h.** si.

ADVANCED LEARNERS

Using the conversation in Activity 2 as a starting point, have students rewrite the conversation with new details. Encourage them to be creative. Have them work in pairs and then role-play their revised versions of the conversation in front of the class.

EXPRESSING PROBABILITY IN THE PAST AND THE PRESENT

Conozco la información		Imagino la información
Está enfermo. (Present)	→	**Estará** enfermo. (Future)
No durmió anoche porque **estaba** nervioso. (Imperfect)	→	No durmió porque **estaría** nervioso. (Conditional)
Ayer **fue** a una fiesta. (Preterit)	→	Ayer **iría** a una fiesta. (Conditional)

■ Para hacer preguntas:

Sabemos que la persona que escucha la pregunta sabe la respuesta:		Sabemos que nadie conoce la respuesta o estamos solos
¿Qué hora **es**? (alguien tiene reloj)	→	¿Qué hora **será**? (nadie tiene reloj)
¿Quién **rompió** el cristal ayer?	→	¿Quién **rompería** el cristal ayer?
¿Cuánta gente **había** ayer en la fiesta?	→	¿Cuánta gente **habría** ayer en la fiesta?

4 Este perro está muy triste. Transforma las frases para hacer suposiciones.

a. Le **duele** el estómago. → ....

b. **Está buscando** a su dueño. → ....

c. Ayer lo **llevaron** al veterinario porque no **se encontraba** bien. → ....

d. Se **perdió**. → ....

5 🗣 Túrnate con tu compañero/a haciendo preguntas y respuestas sobre el perro de la Actividad 4. ¿Qué puedes adivinar sobre su situación?

a. ¿Cómo (llamarse)? → ....

b. ¿(Comer, hoy)? → ....

c. ¿(Tener) dueño? → ....

d. ¿(Escaparse, ayer) de la perrera (dog pound)? → ....

e. ¿(Estar, ayer) con sus dueños (owners) y los (perder) de vista? → ....

f. ¿Sus dueños le (abandonar, hoy) para irse de vacaciones? → ....

6 🗣 Con tu compañero/a, inventa posibles explicaciones para las siguientes imágenes. Describe lo que crees que está pasando ahora y lo que debió haber ocurrido antes.

MORE IN ELETECA: EXTRA ONLINE PRACTICE

227

OBJECTIVES FOR COMUNICA

• Present communicative functions of the unit: Expressing probability in the past, the present, and the future

• Practice expressing probability by speculating and making assumptions

CORE RESOURCES

• Extension Activities: EA 8.2

STANDARDS

1.1	Engage in conversation	4.1	Compare languages
1.2	Understand the language		

INSTRUCTIONAL STRATEGIES FOR EXPRESSING PROBABILITY IN THE PAST AND THE PRESENT

• To introduce the theme of the section, focus students' attention on the image. Have them imagine what happened to Luis and elicit some responses. Explain that

since we don't know for sure, we have to base our answers on assumptions. Write **Está enfermo** and **Estará enfermo** on the board and compare the difference between them. Explain: **En el primer caso conozco esta información y estoy 100% seguro de ella y en el segundo, desconozco la información, pero imagino que puede ocurrir esto**.

• Explain that we have to use a different form of the verb when we speculate about something versus when we know something is true. Direct their attention to the first chart, and walk them through the examples. (After this explanation, you may choose to proceed with Activity 4).

• Explain that the same verb changes apply to questions when you are not sure of the answer. Again ask students to explain the difference between **¿Qué hora es?** and **¿Qué hora será?** Then walk students through the examples in the second chart. (After this explanation, you may choose to proceed with Activity 5).

INSTRUCTIONAL STRATEGIES

Activity 4

• Have students work individually to transform the sentences. Encourage them to refer back to the charts for help.

• Go over the answers as a class.

Activity 5

• To prepare for this activity, you may choose to have students work individually to write the correct forms of questions first, which they can compare with a partner or you can go over as a class.

• Put students into pairs to ask and answer the questions. Have them take notes on their responses.

• Call on volunteers to share the ideas they discussed with their partners.

Activity 6

• Focus students' attention on the images. To activate schema and remind them of relevant vocabulary, ask them what they see or notice about each picture. Encourage them to first share what they *know* about each image, not what they speculate.

• Then put students into pairs to discuss their hypotheses regarding the circumstances behind each image. Have them talk about what they think is happening now and what they think must have happened before.

• Monitor their conversations and assist as needed.

• Have each pair share their favorite hypotheses with the class.

Alternative Activity

These images are also available in EA 8.2, **Hipótesis**. You can divide the class into groups and give each group a different image. Have them write about what is happening using the future, future perfect, and conditional tenses. Then exchange the pictures and descriptions between the groups and have them correct each other's work and add new ideas.

ANSWERS

Activity 4

a. dolerá; **b.** Estará buscando; **c.** llevaría, se encontraría; **d.** perdería.

Activity 5

a. ¿Cómo se llamará?; **b.** ¿Habrá comido?; **c.** ¿Tendrá dueño?; **d.** ¿Se escaparía de la perrera?; **e.** ¿Estaría con sus dueños y los perdería de vista?; **f.** ¿Sus dueños le habrán abandonado para irse de vacaciones?

HERITAGE LANGUAGE LEARNERS

Have students write a paragraph speculating about what a family member or Spanish-speaking celebrity might be doing right now. Then have them swap papers with a partner and correct each other's work.

OBJECTIVES FOR ¡ACCIÓN!

- Provide students with a structured approach to viewing the video
- Contextualize the content of the unit in a familiar scenario

CORE RESOURCES

- Unit Video 8 - ¡Hasta siempre, mis amigos!
- Online Materials - ELEteca

STANDARDS

1.1   Interpersonal communication
1.2   Interpretive communication
2.1   Culture: Practices and perspectives

INSTRUCTIONAL STRATEGIES

Previewing: Antes del video

Activity 1

- Put students in pairs to come up with answers to the questions. Point out that in some cases they will have to use the indicative form of the verb in their responses, while in other cases they'll have to use the subjunctive. Discuss which sentences require which form.
- Have two pairs join together to form groups of four so they can compare their answers.

Viewing: Durante el video

Activity 2

- Play the first 47 seconds of the video to set the scene. Pause the video and have students describe what they saw. Elicit information about the room, the characters, and their behavior.
- Before continuing the video, tell students that the next bit will focus on a conversation between Alba and Sebas. Give students time to read the questions.
- Play the clip while students jot down notes for their answers. Don't go over the answers now. After playing all of the clips for the separate activities once, play the whole video again for students to check and clarify their answers.

ANSWERS

Activity 1

Answers will vary. They should use the indicative form in sentences **a**, **d**, **f**, and **g** but the subjunctive form in sentences b, c, and e.

Activity 2

a. leer y dibujar los comics manga; **b.** de su amigo Felipe; **c.** Igual tuvo que hacer algo.

ADVANCED LEARNERS

Before they watch the video, have students write speech bubbles for each of the characters in the images at the top of the lesson. Encourage them to be creative.

¡ACCIÓN! ¡Hasta siempre, mis amigos!

ANTES DEL VIDEO

1 Observa las imágenes y contesta las preguntas expresando hipótesis. Basa tus respuestas en lo que crees que puede ocurrir. Usa tu imaginación. Luego, compara tus hipótesis con tu compañero/a.

- **a.** ¿Por qué crees que están todos los amigos reunidos? Creo que...
- **b.** Imagen 1. ¿De qué crees que hablan Alba y Sebas? Quizás...
- **c.** Imagen 2. ¿Qué le cuenta Eli sobre su nuevo trabajo? Es probable que...
- **d.** Imagen 3. ¿Qué le dice que recibió? Supongo que...
- **e.** Imagen 4. ¿Qué va a hacer Juanjo a partir de ahora? Quizás...
- **f.** Imagen 5. ¿Por qué le muestra el mensaje? Supongo que...
- **g.** Imagen 6. ¿Qué están haciendo? Creo que...

DURANTE EL VIDEO

2 00:47 - 01:29 Mira la escena y contesta las preguntas. Compara con tu compañero/a.

- **a.** ¿Qué le gusta hacer a Alba?
- **b.** ¿De quién hablan Sebas y Alba?
- **c.** ¿Qué cree Sebas que le ha pasado a Felipe?

3 🎬 **Mira la escena y completa las frases que dice Eli.**
01:39 - 02:35

a. Me dijeron si estaba dispuesta a irme ....
b. Me dijeron que .... y hoy mismo he recibido la carta.
c. ¡Me dicen que ....!

4 🎬 **Mira la escena y copia la carta que recibe Eli, palabra por palabra.**
02:15 - 02:27

....

....

5 🎬 **Mira la escena, ordena las siguientes frases y marca las que dice Lorena.**
03:01 - 04:00

a. ☐ ¡Espero que puedas un día invitarme a conocer la capital!
b. ☐ Es probable entonces que tú también te vayas de la ciudad.
c. ☐ Seguro que vas a tener una experiencia fantástica.
d. ☐ Es probable que aquí no haya cobertura.
e. ☐ ¡Por supuesto, eso sería genial!

6 🎬 👥 **Mira la escena y anota las palabras relacionadas con el celular. Luego, compara**
03:15 - 03:35 **con tu compañero. ¿Entendiste las cuatro expresiones que mencionan?**

....

DESPUÉS DEL VIDEO

7 👥 **Habla con tu compañero/a sobre las siguientes cuestiones.**

a. ¿Alguna vez has ido a una fiesta de final de curso? ¿Dónde fue?
b. ¿Alguna vez has cambiado de escuela y has tenido que despedirte de tus amigos? ¿Cómo fue?
c. ¿Estarías dispuesto a dejar a tu familia y amigos por un buen trabajo?

8 👥 **Lee las siguientes opiniones. ¿Con cuál de ellas te identificas más? ¿Por qué? Discútelo con tus compañeros/as.**

Opinión 1
La amistad es lo más importante para ti. Vivir en la misma ciudad y rodeado de amigos te hace feliz. No te gustan los cambios. Las oportunidades de trabajo no son más importantes que la amistad.

Opinión 2
La amistad es importante, pero no lo más importante. Los cambios son muy positivos. El trabajo es muy importante porque es el futuro.

 MORE IN ELETECA: EXTRA ONLINE PRACTICE

229

Activities 3 and 4

- Explain that the next scene will focus on Alfonso's conversation with Eli. Students will have to listen closely to complete what Eli says in Activity 3 and then transcribe her dictation of a letter she's received in Activity 4.
- Play the clip while students listen and complete the sentences. Pause periodically while Eli is reciting the lines from the letter so that students have time to write it. Tell them not to worry about catching it all now. They will get to hear it again when you replay the video.

Activity 5

- Explain that the next clip moves on to the conversation between Juanjo and Lorena. Students are to number the sentences in the order they are spoken, and they should mark which lines are spoken by Lorena. Suggest that they put an "L" at the end of the sentence for easy reference. Allow them to skim the sentences before you play the clip.
- Play the episode through to the end. Ask them questions about the segment with Felipe to check their comprehension: ***¿Por qué llegó tarde Felipe? ¿Qué trajo a la fiesta y por qué? ¿Que les dice Felipe a sus amigos? ¿Les gustan la canción que toca para ellos?***

Activity 6

- Explain that you are going to play the entire video a second time from beginning to end without stopping. Tell them to check their answers or finish completing Activities 3 through 5. Go over the instructions for Activity 6 so they now listen for vocabulary related to cell phones in the conversation between Lorena and Juanjo. Point out that they should hear four related words or phrases.
- Play the video again. You may want to have students compare their answers with a partner before going over them as a class.

Post-viewing: Después del video
Activity 7

Put students in pairs to ask and answer the questions. Circulate and provide assistance as needed. Call on volunteers to report back on any interesting aspects of their conversations.

Activity 8

- Either have two pairs from Activity 7 join each other or arrange students into new groups. Read the opinions aloud as a class and explain that students should discuss which one they agree with more and why.
- After their discussions, take a class poll to see which opinion was more popular.

ANSWERS

Activity 3

a. a trabajar fuera de la ciudad; **b.** me escribirían pronto; **c.** el trabajo es mío.

Activity 4

Estimada señorita Castañeda: Tenemos el gusto de comunicarle que ha sido usted elegida para el puesto de auxiliar de enfermería en nuestro hospital.

Activity 5

a. 4; **b.** 1; **c.** 3; **d.** 2; **e.** 5. Lorena dice a-d. Juanjo dice e.

Activity 6

mensaje, acceder a internet, cobertura, cargarse.

SLOWER-PACED LEARNERS

Be prepared to replay the clips for Activities 3 and 4 various times. You may want to repeat the lines back more slowly to help students catch them.

HERITAGE LANGUAGE LEARNERS

After discussing the opinions in Activity 8, have students write their own opinions about friendship and work.

- Present vocabulary needed to practice communicative and grammatical functions for the unit: Letter-writing and cell phone issues
- Learn the parts of a formal letter to write a letter of complaint
- Use language associated with cell phones to talk about what can go wrong

CORE RESOURCES

- Audio Program: Track 63
- Interactive Online Materials - ELEteca

STANDARDS

1.2 Understand the language

3.1 Knowledge of other disciplines

INSTRUCTIONAL STRATEGIES

Activity 1

- Before students open their books, activate students' schema about formal letters. Ask questions, such as: *¿Han escrito alguna vez una carta? ¿Cuándo fue y para qué? ¿En qué situación o por qué escribirían una carta formal?*
- Have students open their books. Put them in pairs to work together to try to identify the different parts of a formal letter. Point out the language box as a reminder for where some parts go.
- Monitor their progress and assist as needed.
- Go over the answers as a class. Ask students to explain in Spanish such terms as: *el remitente* (*la persona que escribe la carta*), *el destinatario* (*la persona a quien va dirigida la carta / la persona que va a recibir la carta*), *despedida* (*decir adiós*), and so on.

Activity 2

- Go over the instructions. Encourage students to begin by first writing down the name of the section (using the phrases from Activity 1) and then numbering them in the order in which they should appear. Have students work individually to put the letter in order.
- Monitor their progress and assist as needed.
- Go over the answers as a class, calling on students to read each section of the letter aloud.

ANSWERS

Activity 1

a. 5; **b.** 2; **c.** 7; **d.** 4; **e.** 1; **f.** 6; **g.** 3.

Activity 2

Fecha, 3; Dirección del destinatario, 2; Despedida, 6; Dirección del remitente, 1; Motivo, 5; Saludo, 4; Firma, 7.

HERITAGE LANGUAGE LEARNERS

Ask students what they know about cell phone companies in the Hispanic world. What providers have the best coverage? Which are the most affordable? Encourage them to do research and ask family members for more information. You might also invite them to bring in advertisements by the different companies so that they can make connections between this topic and some of the ideas discussed in the previous unit.

PALABRA POR PALABRA Cartas formales y celulares

1 Relaciona las partes de una carta formal con su lugar correcto.

a. ☐ motivo
b. ☐ dirección del destinatario
c. ☐ firma
d. ☐ saludo
e. ☐ dirección del remitente
f. ☐ despedida
g. ☐ fecha

(1.) (2.) (3.) (4.) (5.) (6.) (7.)

! ■ Remember, the sender's address always goes first in a formal letter, followed by the date.

la batería = la pila
la cobertura = la recepción

2 Ordena la siguiente carta de un cliente a su compañía de telefonía celular. Después, escribe, siguiendo el ejemplo, a qué parte de la carta corresponde cada fragmento.

☐ Bogotá, 13 de enero de 2014

☐ Movilindo
Paseo de la Antena, 33
110988 Bogotá

☐ Atentamente,

Dirección del remitente — ☐ Juan Mora
C/ Cliente, 130
117592 Bogotá

☐ Les escribo esta carta porque llevo varios días teniendo problemas con mi teléfono celular. Hace cinco meses me regalaron un nuevo **aparato** por llevar como cliente en su empresa más de tres años. Pues bien, este **celular** no deja de darme problemas. A continuación les explico punto por punto cada uno de ellos. La **pantalla táctil** no funciona bien. Cada vez que intento marcar un número, el teléfono se apaga.
En muchos lugares no **tiene cobertura**. Es decir, que cuando salgo de la ciudad tengo muy poca señal y no puedo ni **llamar** ni **recibir llamadas**. Cuando puedo llamar, **se corta** la **conversación** después de dos minutos. Además, cuando intento **cargar el teléfono**, la **batería** solo dura cinco horas y, después, tengo que cargarlo otra vez. Al principio pensé que era problema del **cargador**, pero he probado con otro y sigo teniendo el mismo problema. Debido a todos estos inconvenientes, espero que me cambien el **celular** o me regalen uno nuevo. En caso contrario cambiaré de compañía telefónica.

☐ Estimados señores:

☐ *(firma)*

3 Las palabras marcadas en la carta anterior son formas de saludo y despedida en una carta o correo formal. Clasifica estos otros recursos formales en saludos o despedidas.

> Distinguido señor/a o Se despide atentamente o Muy señor/a mío/a
> Reciba un cordial saludo o Señor/a o En espera de sus noticias o Cordialmente

Saludos	Despedidas

4 Relaciona cada expresión con su definición.

1. el aparato
2. la pantalla táctil
3. cobertura
4. recibir llamadas
5. se corta
6. cargar
7. el cargador
8. la batería

a. Acumula electricidad.
b. Instrumento que conecta la electricidad con la batería.
c. Instrumento o mecanismo que tiene una función determinada.
d. Acción de recuperar la batería.
e. Una de las funciones principales de un celular.
f. Extensión geográfica de los servicios de telecomunicaciones.
g. Cuando se pierde una llamada.
h. Parte de algunos aparatos electrónicos que funciona con el contacto.

5 🗫 Comenta con tu compañero/a las siguientes situaciones.

a. ¿Has tenido problemas con tu teléfono celular? ¿Cuáles?
b. ¿Los solucionaste? ¿Cómo?
c. ¿Cuáles son algunas otras quejas (complaints) que tienes con tu celular o el servicio que recibes?
d. ¿Cómo sería tu celular ideal?

6 🎧 63 Ahora, escucha la conversación entre la secretaria y el director de la empresa *Movilindo* y escribe qué decisión toma el director.

INSTRUCTIONAL STRATEGIES

Activity 3

- Direct students' attention to the phrases highlighted in orange in the letter on the previous page. Confirm their understanding as to which one refers to the greeting and which to the closing parts of a letter. Have them write the words in the appropriate columns of the chart.
- Have students work individually to sort the other greetings and closings in the word box.
- Monitor their progress and assist as needed.
- Go over the answers as a class.

Activity 4

- To introduce the vocabulary relating to cell phones, have students search for terms in the letter that fit the following categories: **Sinónimos**, **Acciones**, **Partes**. Start with the first word in boldface (**aparato**) and ask students to select the correct category (**Sinónimos**) and continue to work through the list.
- Then have students work individually to match the phrases in Activity 4. Encourage them to go back to the letter to see the words in context and better deduce their meanings. Go over the answer as a class.

Activity 5

- Before starting the activity, have students turn back to the letter and ask students to explain the customer's reason for writing it.
- Tell students that they are going to have discussions in pairs and that they should be prepared to report back on their partners' responses using indirect speech. Encourage them to take notes.
- Put students into pairs to ask and answer the questions. Then have students change partner's and report on their previous partner's responses.

🎧 63 Activity 6

- Go over the instructions. Point out that Movilindo is the same company that Juan Mora was writing to about his cell phone on the previous page.
- Play the audio. Give students time to write their responses.
- Call on a volunteer to share the director's plan. Have the class confirm whether or not they heard and understood the same course of action. If it seems like many of them did not hear the director's plan, play the audio again.

See audioscript on page APP14

ANSWERS

Activity 3

Saludos: Distinguido señor/a, Muy señor/a mío/a, Señor/a; **Despedidas:** Se despide atentamente, Reciba un cordial saludo, En espera de sus noticias, Cordialmente.

Activity 4

1. c; **2.** h; **3.** f; **4.** e; **5.** g; **6.** d; **7.** b; **8.** a.

Activity 6

Answers will vary. Possible answers might include the following:
El director le dice a la secretaria que no se preocupe, que él mismo se pondrá en contacto con el departamento comercial y que le escribirán un correo disculpándose. También que le ofrecerán un celular más moderno que no dé problemas.

ADVANCED LEARNERS

Put students in groups to draw comparisons and distinctions between their cell phones using the new vocabulary in Activity 4.

OBJECTIVES FOR LOS CORREOS ELECTRÓNICOS

- Present vocabulary needed to practice communicative and grammatical functions for the unit: email language and expressions
- Practice reading and responding to emails
- Learn how to say common electronic symbols

STANDARDS

1.2   Understand the language

1.3   Present information

INSTRUCTIONAL STRATEGIES

Activity 7

- Go over the instructions. Focus students' attention on the email. Ask questions to have them engage with its parts, such as: **¿Cuál es el saludo? ¿Cuál es la despedida? ¿A quién está escribiendo Movilindo? ¿De qué está escribiendo?**
- Before they read, consider posing a question to focus their reading, such as: **¿Qué le pide el director a Juan Mora?**
- Have students read the email quietly to themselves. Elicit a response to the question you posed.

Activity 8

- Have students work individually or in pairs to match the symbols with their meaning and then go over the answers as a class.
- Put students into pairs, if they are not already, to take turns reading the email from Activity 7 aloud to each other, using the correct words for the symbols.

Culture Note

Websites from Spain end in **.es**, which is read aloud as **punto es**. Have students guess the endings of the URLs for websites from other Spanish-speaking countries: **.pe** (Perú), **.mx** (México), etc.

Activity 9

- Go over the instructions. As a class, elicit ideas as to other possible responses that the director of Movilindo might give to Juan Mora.
- Give students some time to brainstorm additional ideas for their own responses. Remind them to refer back to Juan Mora's initial letter in Activity 2 and respond to his specific complaints.
- Have students work individually to write their own responses to Juan Mora.
- Have students exchange emails with a partner.

Activity 10

- Have students read their partner's emails from Activity 9. You may want to have them first correct any errors they notice.
- Put students into small groups to report back on their partner's email using indirect speech.
- Finally, have students return the emails back to the original writers so that they can see any corrections that were made.
- As a class, discuss the most common responses and rank how effective they are from a customer service point of view.

ANSWERS

Activity 8

1. c; 2. e; 3. f; 4. a; 5. g; 6. b; 7. d.

PALABRA POR PALABRA Los correos electrónicos

7 Lee la respuesta de *Movilindo* a su cliente.

Asunto: Nuevo celular

De: movilindo@mundoreal.es   Para: juanmora@edimail.com

Estimado cliente:

Nos dirigimos a usted con la finalidad de expresarle nuestras disculpas por los problemas causados. Comprendemos perfectamente las molestias que puede haber tenido con el último celular que recibió y, por esa razón, ponemos a su disposición un nuevo modelo. Por favor, para recibir este nuevo aparato mándenos un correo electrónico con la dirección donde quiere recibirlo a *movilindo-aparatos@mundoreal.es*. Si desea ver el modelo que le ofrecemos, puede hacer clic en el siguiente enlace: *www.movilesmovilindo/nuevos*.

Atentamente,

Movilindo
Paseo de la Antena, 33
110988 Bogotá

8 Relaciona cada símbolo con su significado.

1. @	a. guion *(hyphen)*
2. /	b. punto com
3. :	c. arroba
4. -	d. triple doble ve
5. _	e. barra
6. .com	f. dos puntos
7. www	g. guion bajo

9 👥 Imagina que eres el director de *Movilindo*. Escribe una respuesta diferente a tu cliente. Después, intercambia tu email con el de tu compañero/a.

Asunto: Nuevo celular

De: movilindo@mundoreal.es   Para: juanmora@edimail.com

Estimado señor Mora:

10 👥 Lee el email de tu compañero/a e informa a la clase de lo que dice.

Modelo: El director de Movilindo dice que...

232   📧 MORE IN ELETECA: EXTRA ONLINE PRACTICE

SLOWER-PACED LEARNERS

Have students discuss what email addresses might tell us about a person and what URLs might tells us about a website. Explain the difference between .org, .com, .gov, and .edu. Also, discuss potential problems with email addresses that incorporate inappropriate or unprofessional names. Ask students share stories related to this topic.

ADVANCED LEARNERS

For additional writing practice, have students write a formal letter to a company that is offering a summer internship opportunity in a field or company that interests them. In their formal letters, they should explain why they want the internship and why they think they should be chosen for it. Have students share their letters in small groups and discuss how effective and convincing their are.

GRAMÁTICA

1. HYPOTHETICAL EXPRESSIONS WITH THE INDICATIVE

■ Other ways to express hypothesis or probability using the indicative:

Creo / Me parece		ese modelo de celular no **es** uno de los mejores.
Me imagino / Supongo	que	si está en la sierra no **tendrá** cobertura, llámalo mañana.
Para mí / Yo diría		**llovió** anoche, las calles están mojadas.

A lo mejor / Lo mismo / Igual (maybe)	**es** un problema de tu compañía porque yo sí tengo cobertura.

> **!** ■ **Suponer** (to suppose) is conjugated like the verb **poner**.

1 Edu ha encontrado una foto de una casa que le gustaría comprar, pero no tiene ninguna información sobre ella. Lee el texto y completa con la forma correcta de los siguientes verbos.

> vivir ○ poder ○ querer ○ tener ○ haber ○ costar ○ pertenecer

Me encantaría comprar esta casa, pero antes me gustaría tener información sobre ella. **Supongo que** (a) .... muchísimo dinero, pero **creo que** mis padres (b) .... ayudarme. Parece una casa grande, **me imagino que** (c) .... más de tres habitaciones y al menos dos baños. **Lo mismo** en algún baño (d) .... un jacuzzi, sería genial. **Yo diría que** antes (e) .... una familia numerosa, **a lo mejor** la (f) .... vender para irse a vivir a otra ciudad. **Igual** la parte de atrás (g) .... también a la casa y hay una piscina y todo, quién sabe.

2 Observa las siguientes imágenes y escribe tres explicaciones para cada situación usando las expresiones que acabas de aprender. Después, en grupos de tres, intercambien sus impresiones.

¿Por qué no hay nadie?	¿Por qué está llorando?	¿Qué le pasa?
a.	a.	a. ....
b.	b.	b. ....
c.	c.	c. ....

OBJECTIVES FOR GRAMÁTICA 1

- Present grammatical structures needed to practice communicative functions of the unit: Hypothetical expressions with the indicative
- Learn and practice using hypothetical expressions with the indicative

CORE RESOURCES

- Audio Program: Track 64
- Interactive Online Materials - ELEteca

STANDARDS

1.1	Understand the language	4.1	Compare languages

INSTRUCTIONAL STRATEGIES

1. Hypothetical Expressions with the Indicative

- Before presenting the grammar, elicit ways to express hypotheses, to speculate, or to imagine that students have already been using and that do not require use of the future or conditional tenses (**creo que, pienso que**, etc.). You may want to write some of their ideas on the board.
- Go over the examples of hypothetical expressions with the indicative in the book. Then have students write down a hypothesis using one of the expressions in the chart. Give students a topic such as the weather (**el tiempo**), an important game coming up (**el partido, el campeonato**), the next episode of a popular series (**el próximo capítulo de la serie**...), etc. Then ask them to share their hypotheses with the class or with a partner. Guide any necessary corrections.

Activity 1

Have students work individually to complete the sentences with the correct forms of the verbs in the word box. Remind them to refer to the chart above for help. Go over the answers as a class.

Activity 2

- Focus students' attention on the images. Elicit descriptions of what they see to help activate relevant vocabulary.
- Put students into small groups. Encourage them to discuss their ideas before writing them.
- Have a member from each group present their ideas to the class. Guide any necessary corrections.

ANSWERS

Activity 1

a. cuesta / costará; **b.** pueden / podrán; **c.** tiene; **d.** hay; **e.** vivía; **f.** quieren; **g.** pertenece.

Activity 2

Answers will vary. Possible answers might include the following:
Imagen 1: Supongo que es la hora del descanso; Igual se ha confundido y es fiesta; Me imagino que llegarán tarde; **Imagen 2:** Creo que el novio la ha dejado plantada; Igual se le ha roto el vestido; Para mí que es la emoción; **Imagen 3:** Creo que está enfermo; Para mí que tiene dolor de tripa; Lo mismo ha comido algo en malas condiciones.

HERITAGE LANGUAGE LEARNERS

After completing Activity 2, have students refer back to the hypotheses they wrote before Activity 1. Tell them to write the opposite hypothesis, or a different point of view: **Yo diría que mañana va a llover. Pues yo diría que mañana va a hacer sol**. You can also follow-up with the weather by asking them to make guesses about the temperature and weather in different parts of the world today and then look up the actual information.

INSTRUCTIONAL STRATEGIES

🎧 64 Activity 3

- Tell students that they are going to listen to the end of three arguments. To focus their listening, have them write down key words or phrases that they hear.
- Play the first part of the audio. Then put students into pairs. Have them share the key words or phrases that they heard with a partner and give them time to write their hypotheses as to the cause of each argument. Remind them to use the expressions they just learned.
- Have a member from each pair write their hypotheses on the board. Go over the hypotheses as a class.
- Play the complete conversations. As a class, discuss which, if any, of the hypotheses on the board were correct.

See audioscript on page APP14

OBJECTIVES FOR GRAMÁTICA 2

- Present grammatical structures needed to practice communicative functions of the unit: Hypothetical expressions with the indicative and the subjunctive
- Use the indicative or subjunctive to express how certain you feel

CORE RESOURCES

- Audio program: Track 65

STANDARDS

1.1	Engage in conversation
1.2	Understand the language
4.1	Compare languages

INSTRUCTIONAL STRATEGIES

2. Hypothetical Expressions with the Indicative and the Subjunctive

🎧 65 Activity 4

- Before playing the audio, explain that there are some expressions for hypothetical situations that can use the indicative or the subjunctive forms of the verbs, but they have different connotations. Tell students that for now just listen to the conversations and fill in the missing expressions in the first column of the chart. Point out that the expressions will be repeated in different conversations in case they miss them the first time.
- Play the audio and go over the answers as a class, listing them on the board.
- Write out the sample sentences with **Probablemente** and the indicative, then with the subjunctive. Ask students to identify which sentence expresses that the speaker is more confident or certain about the outcome than the other.
- Give other examples from the audio (recited aloud), and have students identify whether you feel confident about the outcome based on how you express it.
- Continue going over the examples of hypothetical expressions that must use the subjunctive. Point out that both **quizás** and **quizá** are considered correct.
- Play the conversations again and encourage students to listen for the form of the verb that follows the expressions.

See audioscript on page APP14

Extension

To exploit the audio further, you may choose to develop questions that check students' general and specific comprehension of the conversations – with less emphasis on the target grammar structures and more on the content.

GRAMÁTICA

3 🎧 64 👥 Escucha el final de tres discusiones y, con tu compañero/a, hagan una hipótesis sobre el motivo que las origina. Después, escucha la conversación completa y comprueben.

a. ....

b. ....

c. ....

2. HYPOTHETICAL EXPRESSIONS WITH THE INDICATIVE AND THE SUBJUNCTIVE

4 🎧 65 👥 Escucha las siguientes conversaciones y completa con las expresiones que faltan.

| Probablemente / .... Seguramente / .... Tal vez | la compañía telefónica **se pone** / **se ponga** en contacto conmigo después de mi reclamación. (indicativo/subjuntivo) |
| .... / **Es probable** Puede ser / .... | que | mi celular **tenga** algún defecto de fábrica, me lo compré hace poco y no me dura nada la batería. (subjuntivo) |

■ With the first group of expressions, the use of the indicative or the subjunctive depends on how certain the speaker feels that the action will take place.

- **Probablemente** la compañía telefónica **se pone** en contacto conmigo.
(Speaker feels there's a strong likelihood the company will contact him / her = indicative)

- **Probablemente** la compañía telefónica **se ponga** en contacto conmigo.
(Speaker feels there is less likelihood that the company will contact him / her = subjunctive)

5 Elige la opción correcta para cada frase. En algunas casos las dos opciones son correctas.

a. Es probable que mañana **llueve** / **llueva**.
b. Seguramente **tiene** / **tenga** más de veinte años.
c. Tal vez **viene** / **venga** mi hermana conmigo.
d. Es posible que **consigue** / **consiga** el trabajo.
e. Quizás no **quiere** / **quiera** trabajar con nosotros.
f. Puede ser que **necesitan** / **necesiten** nuestra ayuda.
g. No le hagas caso, posiblemente lo **hace** / **haga** para molestarte.
h. Puede que mañana **vamos** / **vayamos** a la playa.

6 Termina las siguientes frases.

a. ¡Qué raro que no haya llegado Juan! Él es muy puntual. Es posible que...
b. La compañía telefónica me está cobrando un servicio que no utilizo. Seguramente...
c. Me dijo que me iba a llamar esta tarde pero no lo ha hecho todavía. Tal vez...
d. Le he escrito un correo electrónico y no le ha llegado aún. Puede que...
e. He salido de casa y cuando he entrado en el metro no llevaba el monedero. Probablemente...
f. No encuentro mis gafas por ningún sitio. Quizás...

Activity 5

- Have students work individually to select the correct answers. Remind them to think about what the expressions mean rather than having to memorize the chart.
- Go over the answers as a class. Guide any necessary corrections.

Activity 6

- Have students work individually to complete the sentences with their own ideas.
- Put students into small groups to share their ideas. Encourage them to explain the reasoning for their own hypotheses and respond to each other's ideas.

ANSWERS

Activity 4

Posiblemente, Quizás (con indicativo/subjuntivo); Es posible, Puede (con subjuntivo).

Activity 5

a. llueva; **b.** tiene / tenga; **c.** viene / venga; **d.** consiga; **e.** quiere / quiera; **f.** necesiten; **g.** hace / haga; **h.** vayamos.

7 **Según lo que has aprendido para expresar hipótesis y probabilidades, completa las siguientes frases.**

a. Es probable que (ser) .... su cumpleaños porque invitó a cenar a todos sus amigos.

b. Igual (mudarse, él) .... Hace mucho tiempo que quería cambiar de casa.

c. Quizás (comprarse, yo) .... un teléfono celular nuevo. Este ya no funciona.

d. A lo mejor Juan (ser) .... alérgico a los gatos. No para de estornudar.

e. Posiblemente yo (organizar) .... la fiesta. Soy su mejor amigo.

f. Yo diría que Carmen y Sonia (estar) .... enfadadas. Ya nunca van juntas.

g. Seguramente (ganar) .... el premio. Está haciendo un buen trabajo.

h. Me parece que Carlos no (estar) .... contento con su nuevo trabajo.

i. Puede que (saber) .... hablar italiano. Vivió un tiempo en Roma.

j. » ¡Qué raro que Pepe no esté todavía aquí! Es muy puntual.
» Oye, lo mismo (pasarle) .... algo. ¿Lo llamamos al celular?

8 Habla con tu compañero/a sobre tus planes de futuro que todavía no son seguros relacionados con las siguientes situaciones o eventos.

Tu próximo cumpleaños	Tus próximas vacaciones	Tus próximos estudios

9 Prepara una breve descripción de cómo crees que será la vida de tu compañero/a cuando tenga 50 años. Incluye información sobre: profesión, familia, lugar de residencia, aspecto físico, etc. Después, intercambia la descripción con tu compañero/a. ¿Te sorprendió? ¿Crees que la descripción que hizo tu compañero/a de tu vida es acertada?

Modelo: *Cuando tengas 50 años, es probable que / seguramente...*

Activity 7

• Have students work individually to complete the sentences and then compare their answers with a partner. Encourage students to peer correct.

• Go over the answers as a class.

Activity 8

• Before putting students into pairs, give them some time to brainstorm and jot down ideas in each category. Remind them to use appropriate expressions to indicate how certain they are or aren't about their plans.

• Have students report back on one of their partner's plans.

Activity 9

• Model a pre-writing technique on the board: create a mind map (or word web) using the categories in the instructions. Write the name of a famous young person in the center. Have students imagine what he or she will be like at age 50. Elicit their ideas, and write them in the mind map on the board.

• Give students time to create their own mind maps before they write. Monitor their progress and assist as needed.

• Focusing their attention back on the board, discuss how they can use their mind maps to create a paragraph. Call on a volunteer to convert one of the notes on the board into a sentence.

• Give students time to write their descriptions. Monitor their progress and assist as needed.

• Once completed, have students exchange their descriptions with their partners. Then have students report back on whether or not they think their partner's descriptions of them are accurate and explain why or why not.

ANSWERS

Activity 7

a. sea; **b.** se ha mudado / se mudó; **c.** me compre / me compro; **d.** es; **e.** organice / organizo; **f.** están; **g.** gana / gane; **h.** está; **i.** sepa; **j.** le pasa / ha pasado.

- Present grammatical structures needed to practice communicative functions of the unit: Hypothetical expressions with the imperfect subjunctive
- Learn and practice using hypothetical expressions with the imperfect subjunctive

CORE RESOURCES

- Interactive Online Materials - ELEteca

STANDARDS

1.2   Understand the language

4.1   Compare languages

INSTRUCTIONAL STRATEGIES

3. Hypothetical Expressions with the Imperfect Subjunctive

Activity 10

- Write a hypothetical sentence with the imperfect subjunctive on the board: **Si yo ganara la lotería, viajaría por el mundo.** Ask students questions to confirm that the understand the context of the sentence: **¿He ganado la lotería? (no) ¿Estoy viajando por el mundo? (no) ¿Qué parte de la oración es la causa? (ganar la lotería) ¿Que parte es la consecuencia? (viajar por el mundo)** Then ask students to focus their attention on the forms of the verbs. Point out that **viajaría** is in the conditional, which they've already learned. Explain that **ganara** is in the imperfect subjunctive. As a point of comparison, elicit how this sentence would be expressed in English: *If I won the lottery, I would travel the world.*
- Focus students' attention on the speech bubble. Call on a volunteer to read it aloud. Confirm their understanding of the phrases in bold: **¿La mujer está trabajando mucho? (sí) ¿Está siempre de mal humor? (sí)**
- Have students write the clauses with the imperfect subjunctive in the chart and indicate whether or not the outcome was actually realized. Go over the answer and reinforce the idea that each of these sentences is expressing a hypoethetical situation that has not happened.

Activity 11

In this activity, students focus their attention on the forms of the verbs in the target sentences in Activity 10. Looking at the list of verbs in the imperfect subjunctive form all together, elicit students' ideas about how it is formed.

ANSWERS

Activity 10

Si no trabajara tanto, No; Si no estuviera de mal humor, No; Si saliera más, No; Si gastara mucho dinero, No.

Activity 11

a. trabajara, estuviera, saliera, gastara; **b.** condicional: estaría, saldría, necesitaría, tendría.

For additional oral practice, have students read the exchange in Activity 10 aloud twice, once asking the question and once responding. Help them focus on the correct pronunciation of the imperfect subjunctive verb, making sure that they don't put the emphasis on the final syllable.

GRAMÁTICA

3. HYPOTHETICAL EXPRESSIONS WITH THE IMPERFECT SUBJUNCTIVE

10 Lee la conversación entre el director de Movilindo y su secretaria. Después, extrae las estructuras que se usan para expresar hipótesis y contesta las preguntas.

> ¿Cómo está? Lo veo muy muy preocupado.

> Es que el doctor me dijo que necesito hacer algo para combatir el estrés del trabajo. Me dijo que **si no trabajara tanto, no estaría siempre de mal humor**. Y yo pienso que **si no estuviera de mal humor, saldría más con mis amigos**. Y **si saliera más, necesitaría más dinero** para gastar. Y **si gastara mucho dinero, tendría que trabajar más** y... ¡volvería a sufrir de un nuevo estrés!

> Y **si yo aprendiera a no preguntar tanto**... ¡no tendría que escuchar todo esto!

Frases que expresan hipótesis:	¿Se produce la acción?	
	Sí	No
Si		
Si		
Si		
Si		

11 Contesta las preguntas sobre la conversación de la Actividad 10.

a.   En la conversación, cuando el director habla de las cosas que tendría que hacer (pero no las hace), usa un nuevo tiempo verbal que se llama imperfecto de subjuntivo. Escribe las formas.

a.   Cuando el director describe el posible resultado (de estas acciones que no hace), usa un tiempo verbal que ya conoces. Escribe las formas. ¿Cómo se llama?

4. FORMS AND USES OF THE IMPERFECT SUBJUNCTIVE

	-AR	-ER	-IR
yo	practicara	bebiera	saliera
tú	practicaras	bebieras	salieras
usted/él/ella	practicara	bebiera	saliera
nosotros/a	practicáramos	bebiéramos	saliéramos
vosotros/as	practicarais	bebierais	salierais
ustedes/ellos/ellas	practicaran	bebieran	salieran

- Present grammatical structures needed to practice communicative functions of the unit: Forms and uses of the imperfect subjunctive
- Learn the form of the imperfect subjunctive and practice using it

CORE RESOURCES

- Interactive Online Materials - ELEteca

STANDARDS

1.2   Understand the language   4.1   Compare languages

INSTRUCTIONAL STRATEGIES

4. Forms and Uses of the Imperfect Subjunctive

- Go over the chart and explanations in the book. Point out that imperfect subjunctive has the same irregularities as the third person plural of the preterite: **durmieron-durmieran, murieron-murieran, vieron-vieran, supieron-supieran,** etc. Other irregular verbs that do not change in the third person plural preterite do not change in the imperfect: **salieron-salieran, encontraron-encontraran,** etc.

- The imperfect subjunctive is formed using the **ellos** form of the preterit. Drop the **-ron** and add the appropriate endings. This is true for all regular and irregular verbs. Note, the verb **haber** (**hay**) becomes **hubiera**.

- One of the uses of the imperfect subjunctive is in if-clauses to say what would happen if a certain condition was met. These are also known as contrary-to-fact statements because the action never actually took place. Look at some of the examples from Activity 10.

*Si no **estuviera** de mal humor, saldría más.* *If I were not always in a bad mood, I would go out more. (But in reality, I'm always in a bad mood.)*

*Y si **saliera** más, necesitaría más dinero para gastar.* *And if I went out more, I would need more money to spend. (But in reality, I don't go out.)*

- Contrary-to-fact statements have the following constructions:

Si + imperfect subjunctive, conditional.
Conditional, **si** + imperfect subjunctive.

12 Completa la tabla de verbos irregulares en imperfecto de subjuntivo.

INFINITIVO	PRETÉRITO DE INDICATIVO	IMPERFECTO DE SUBJUNTIVO
querer	quisieron	quisiera
hacer	hicieron	hiciera
poder	pudieron	pudiera
tener		
ser / ir		
estar		

Si no hubiera tantos colores, sería más fácil.

13 Relaciona las ideas con sus conclusiones. Compara tus respuesta con un compañero/a.

1. Si tuviera gato,
2. Si todos los jóvenes leyeran más,
3. Si hubiera menos leyes (*laws*),
4. Si escribiera una novela,
5. Si mis padres fueran generosos,
6. Si todas las clases estuvieran en línea,

a. pasarían menos tiempo en internet.
b. nunca iría nunca a la escuela.
c. me comprarían el último teléfono de Apple.
d. lo llamaría Minifus.
e. habría más criminales.
f. sería de ciencia ficción.

14 Usa la primera parte de las frases de la Actividad 13 para hablar de ti mismo. Comparte tus hipótesis con tus compañeros/as en grupos de cuatro. ¿Cuál de ustedes tiene las frases más originales?

15 Pregúntale a tu compañero/a qué haría en las siguientes situaciones.

Estudiante 1
¿Qué harías si...
• conocer a Shakira
• visitar el Polo Norte
• ganar el concurso de *La voz*

Estudiante 2
¿Qué harías si...
• ser el profesor/la profesora de la clase
• no haber videojuegos
• ver un zombi

MORE IN ELETECA: EXTRA ONLINE PRACTICE • **GRAMMAR TUTORIALS** 15 AND 16

INSTRUCTIONAL STRATEGIES

Activity 12

Have students work individually to complete the chart, and go over the answers as a class. Refer them to an online conjugator, such as http://www.onoma.es/, to use as a resource when they're working on their own outside of class.

Activity 13

Have students match the sentences individually and compare answers with a partner. Have them take turns reading the sentences aloud for oral practice.

Activity 14

- Have students write the sentneces with their own ideas before sharing them with the group.

- For additional practice with imperfect subject, have students keep the second part of the sentences in Activity 13 but write new phrases for the first part. Have them share their sentences with a partner and check each other's conjugations of the imperfect subjunctive.

Activity 15

- Point out that students still need to conjugate the verbs in the imperfect subjunctive to correctly ask the questions. You may want to give them a few moments to jot down those conjugations before putting them into pairs.

- Circulate and observe their conversations, taking note of any errors but not correcting them yet. Hold an error-correction session with the class after they've completed the activity.

ANSWERS

Activity 12

tuvieron, tuviera; fueron, fuera; estuvieron, estuviera.

Activity 13

1. d; **2.** a; **3.** e; **4.** f; **5.** c; **6.** b.

ADVANCED LEARNERS

As an extension to Activity 15, give students examples of hypothetical outcomes in the conditional form for which they have to think of hypothetical causes in the imperfect subjunctive. You can write a list on the board for them to use and invite them to add their own ideas: **dormiría todo el día, no volvería a hablar con él, tendríamos menos contaminación, comeríamos más fruta fresca**, etc. Working in pairs they take turns providing the condition(s): **Si no tuviera colegio**, **Si mi amigo me traicionara**, **Si las fábricas fueran más cuidadosas**, **Si supiera mejor**, etc.

HERITAGE LANGUAGE LEARNERS

Ask if students have ever heard or seen the imperfect subjunctive expressed another way and what the context of that usage was. Point out that the imperfect subjunctive is used in the indirect speech when the main verb is in the past. In this case, the imperfect subjunctive may be expressed with an **–ase** or **–iese** ending: **Me dijo que hablase / hablara más alto. Me pidió que fuese / fuera a su casa**. Explain that the **–ra** form is preferred for the conditional sentences but people use the **–se** form as well. You might also point out that some colloquial varieties of Spanish use the conditional in the **Si** clause: **Si tendría dinero, viajaría más**.

OBJECTIVES FOR DESTREZAS

- Simulate multiple choice testing formats in preparation for international testing certificates as the DELE (*Diploma de Español como Lengua Extranjera*) or in preparation for other state and/or national assessments
- Use strategies presented throughout the units

CORE RESOURCES

- Extension Activity: EA 8.4

STANDARDS

1.1 Engage in conversation
1.3 Present information
2.1 Practices and perspectives

INSTRUCTIONAL STRATEGIES

Comprensión de gramática y vocabulario

Activity 1

- Before reading the letter, activate students' schema about parties and party planning by asking questions, such as: *¿Les gustan las fiestas? ¿Les gustan preparar y organizar las fiestas? En su opinión, ¿qué cosas son necesarias para tener una buena fiesta?*
- Go over the instructions. Have students work individually to choose the correct answers.
- Monitor their progress and assist as needed.
- Put students into pairs to compare answers. Have them reach agreement in the cases where they selected different answers.
- Go over the answers as a class. Have students taking turns reading the paragraphs aloud. Guide any necessary corrections.

ANSWERS

Activity 1

a. en; **b.** para; **c.** asistan; **d.** vayas; **e.** Puede que; **f.** buena; **g.** están / estén; **h.** había; **i.** bailen; **j.** seguramente.

INSTRUCTIONAL STRATEGIES

Expresión e interacción orales

Activity 2

- Go over the instructions. Have students work individually to write their own responses to the questions.
- Put students into pairs to share their ideas. Encourage them to take notes on their partner's responses, as they will be asked to report back on them.
- As a model, call on a volunteer to report back on his or her partner's response to the first question. Encourage him or her to use reported speech.
- Then put students into new pairs and have them report on their previous partner's responses.

ADVANCED LEARNERS

For additional writing practice, have students write the original letter from the reader who was asking for advice.

DESTREZAS

COMPRENSIÓN DE GRAMÁTICA Y VOCABULARIO

1 Lee la respuesta que obtuvo un lector a su carta en la que pedía unos consejos. Elige la opción correcta.

Una fiesta inolvidable

Querido amigo Álex:

Si estás pensado (a) **de / en / para** preparar una fiesta para impresionar a tu familia y amigos, a continuación te daremos algunos consejos (b) **para / por / en** convertir esa celebración en algo inolvidable.

En primer lugar, deberás ponerte en contacto con las personas a las que quieres invitar para decidir el día. Un mensaje de texto o un correo electrónico masivo será la forma más rápida de hacerlo. Lo mejor será proponer un día del fin de semana, ya que es más probable que (c) **asisten / asistirán / asistan** más personas si no hay que madrugar al día siguiente.

Al menos un par de días antes del evento deberás ir al supermercado para comprar todo lo que necesitas cuando (d) **ve / irás / vayas** a preparar la comida.

Piensa en sorprender a tus invitados con originales bocadillos. Además, es importante que haya gran variedad de ellos para satisfacer los gustos y exigencias de todos. (e) **Tal vez / Quizás / Puede que** alguno sea vegetariano, que otro no coma ciertos productos o incluso que haya algún alérgico a cualquier alimento.

Otra cosa importante para causar (f) **buen / buena / grande** impresión es la decoración. Igual los globos y las guirnaldas de las tiendas (g) **están / estén / sean** ya muy vistos, así que te recomendamos que crees tú mismo tu propia decoración, no hay nada como un toque personal para impresionarlos.

Y la música, por supuesto; alguien dijo una vez que no (h) **hubo / había / habría** fiesta que mereciera tal nombre sin música. Para que todos (i) **bailan / bailen / bailarán** sin parar, te recomendamos que la música sea movida y sobre todo variada, por aquello de la diversidad de gustos que ya te comentábamos.

Las canciones lentas resérvalas para el final, (j) **igual / seguramente / imaginamos que** sean la excusa perfecta para aquellos que quieran sacar a bailar a alguna muchacha.

¡Ah! y sentimos decirte que, por muy cansado que estés, deberás ser el último en retirarte.

Si sigues todos estos pasos, te convertirás en el rey de las fiestas.

EXPRESIÓN E INTERACCIÓN ORALES

2 Contesta las siguientes preguntas sobre ti.

a. ¿Te gustan las fiestas? ¿Qué tipo de fiestas son las que más te gustan?
b. ¿Prefieres las fiestas en casa, o en locales o discotecas? ¿Por qué?
c. ¿Te gusta invitar a tus amigos a una fiesta o prefieres que te inviten?
d. ¿Cuál es la última fiesta a la que fuiste? ¿Cómo fue?

238

3 👥 **Con tu compañero/a, representa la siguiente situación.**

Te invitaron a una fiesta en un restaurante. Cuando llegas, el portero no te deja entrar porque dice que vas con zapatillas de deporte. En la invitación no se especifica cómo hay que ir vestido. Solicitas hablar con el encargado del restaurante. Cuando salga, exponle tu queja contándole lo que te dijo el portero y lo que no dice la invitación.

PRONUNCIACIÓN Palabras con diferente significado

1 **Lee las conversaciones y después completa los cuadros.**

1. » ¿*A dónde* / *adónde* podemos ir a almorzar?
» *A donde* / *adonde* tú quieras.
» ¿*Dónde* decías que hacían esas quesadillas tan buenas?
» ¡Ah! Te refieres al sitio *donde* te conté que fui con Marcos.

(a) dónde / adónde ○ (a) donde / adonde
• Usamos el adverbio (a) .... para indicar lugar y (b) .... o (c) .... indistintamente cuando indicamos también dirección o destino mediante la preposición *a*.
• Usamos (d) ...., (e) .... o (f) .... cuando las formas anteriores son exclamativas o interrogativas.

2. » No entiendo el *porqué* de su reacción, no me lo explico.
» Pues yo creo que actuó así *porque* no podía más y al final explotó.
» Pero, ¿*por qué* no le dijo a nadie que necesitaba ayuda?
» Es que es muy orgulloso y le da pena reconocerlo.
» Yo voto *por que* hablemos con él y le ofrezcamos nuestra ayuda.

porque / porqué / por que / por qué
• Usamos (a) .... para expresar la causa o motivo de lo que se expresa a continuación y (b) .... para preguntar por esa causa o motivo.
• Usamos (c) .... cuando nos referimos al sustantivo que significa "la causa, el motivo o la razón".
• Usamos (d) .... para referirnos a la preposición *por* seguida del pronombre *que*.

3. » Su *sino* no es quedarse quieto viendo la vida pasar, *sino* llegar muy lejos.
» Tienes razón, no solo es muy decidido, *sino* también muy trabajador.
» *Si no* cambia será alguien muy importante en el futuro, tal vez un político.
» Sí, además sabe escuchar, tiene carisma, es elegante y, *asimismo*, discreto.
» Sí, pues *así mismo* se lo haremos saber cuando lo veamos.

sino / si no
• Usamos (a) .... como sustantivo que significa "destino"; para introducir una información que reemplaza o sustituye a la negada en la oración precedente.
• Usamos (b) .... para referirnos a la conjunción condicional *si* seguida del adverbio negativo *no*.

asimismo / así mismo
• Usamos (c) .... en el sentido de "también" y (d) .... en el sentido de "de la misma manera".

👤💻 **MORE IN ELETECA:** EXTRA ONLINE PRACTICE

239

Activity 3

• Go over the situation with the class.
• Put students into pairs. Instead of role playing the situation right away, you may want to have students write a script together. Encourage them to write a conversation in which each of them speaks at least three times.
• Monitor their progress and assist as needed.
• Have each pair –or volunteers– perform their conversations in front of the class.

Extension

For additional writing practice, pass out copies of EA 8.4, **Expresión e interacción escritas**. Tell students to use the images in part 1 to write a narrative and to respond to the questions in part 2 with their own likes and preferences.

OBJECTIVES FOR PRONUNCIACIÓN

• Distinguish words with similar spellings or pronunciations but with different meanings

CORE RESOURCES

• Interactive Online Materials - ELEteca

STANDARDS

1.2	Understand the language	4.1	Compare languages

INSTRUCTIONAL STRATEGIES

Activity 1

• Explain that there are some words in Spanish that sound very similar –and are sometimes spelled exactly same, apart from a space or an accent mark– but have different meanings.
• Go over the instructions. Read the first group of sentences together. Elicit the answer to item **a**. Have the student explain his or her answer and identify which sample sentence from the group illustrates that usage.
• Have students work individually or in pairs to complete the other items related to the first group only. Monitor their progress and assist as needed. Go over the answers as a class. Guide any necessary corrections.
• Continue the same process of the second and third group of sample sentences.

ANSWERS

Activity 1

1. a. donde; **b.** a donde; **c.** adonde; **d.** dónde; **e.** a dónde; **f.** adónde;
2. a. porque; **b.** por qué; **c.** porqué; **d.** por que; **3. a.** sino; **b.** si no;
4. a. asimismo; **b.** así mismo.

HERITAGE LANGUAGE LEARNERS

Students have challenges with many other words and expressions that sound similar, like **a ser** / **hacer**, **haber** / **a ver**, **allá** / **haya** / **halla**, **ha** / **a**, **sobre todo** / **sobretodo**, etc. Have students check their journals and notes, and see what common spelling mistakes they make. Remind them that some words may be spelled differently in the Spanish-speaking countries (**talvez** / **tal vez**).

OBJECTIVES FOR SABOR HISPANO

- Learn about Hispanic soap operas
- Compare soap operas from the Spanish-speaking world to the United States

CORE RESOURCES

- Audio Program: Track 66

STANDARDS

2.2 Products and perspectives
4.2 Compare cultures

INSTRUCTIONAL STRATEGIES

🎧 66

- Write the word **telenovela** on the board. Elicit a definition and examples from the class.
- Put students in pairs to discuss the questions in the **Antes de leer** box.
- Monitor their conversations and assist as needed.
- Call on volunteers to report back on their discussions.
- Focus students' attention on the image at the top of the page and its captions. Ask who she is, where she is from, and why she is famous.
- Before playing the audio, pose a question or two to the class to focus their listening, such as: **¿Qué reflejan las telenovelas? ¿Cuál es una función importante de las telenovelas?** You can also give students a moment to locate and skim the glossary on the next page to prepare them for unfamiliar vocabulary in the text and throughout the lesson.
- Either have students close their books while they listen or follow along with the text in the book.
- Elicit responses to the target questions. Have them find the answers in the text.

Cultural Note

In addition to being dubbed the Queen of Latin Pop for her wildly successful singing and musical career, Thalía earned herself another title as the Queen of Telenovelas by accruing enormous sucess as an actress as well. Her first major role was in the telenovela **Quinceañera** in 1987, and her first lead role was in the telenovela **Luz y Sombra** in 1989. Her most popular role, however, was in the telenovela **María Mercedes** in 1992, the first of a trilogy of telenovelas which also included **Marimar** in 1994 and **María la del Barrio** in 1995. Her telenovelas have been aired in over 180 countries and seen by over 2 billion people.

ADVANCED LEARNERS

Have students do some research about the latest **telenovelas**, as they may notice that most of the examples here are more than 20 years old. In addition, have them discuss whether **telenovelas** are easy to translate or not and what may be elements that need to be adapted before it is launched in a foreign country.

SABOR HISPANO

UN MUNDO DE NOVELA

Thalia, cantante y actriz mexicana, conocida como «la reina de las telenovelas»

Antes de leer

¿Qué programas de televisión te gustan? ¿Por qué? ¿ Sueles ver alguna telenovela de la televisión norteamericana? ¿Has visto alguna telenovela en español? ¿Qué sabes de estas telenovelas?

🎧 66 **La telenovela es una expresión cultural típica del mundo hispano. En estos programas de televisión no faltan dramas, villanos... ini capítulos!**

Las telenovelas son programas de televisión dramáticos. Pero no son cualquier programa: están estrechamente° conectadas con la forma de ser de los países hispanos. Las historias de las telenovelas reflejan las tradiciones, las aspiraciones y, muchas veces, los temas de actualidad de la sociedad que las mira. «Las telenovelas son exitosas porque generan emoción y entretenimiento», explica Nora Mazziotti, investigadora argentina y autora de libros sobre telenovelas.

Aunque cada telenovela tiene una historia diferente, hay elementos comunes que están presentes en todas ellas. Suelen tener entre 100 y 200 capítulos. Hay un galán° (normalmente, rico) y una heroína (normalmente, pobre). Hay una villana que hace todo lo posible por separarlos. Y hay varios personajes secundarios que aportan° historias divertidas, para equilibrar° el melodrama de la historia central.

Cada país latinoamericano produce telenovelas con un estilo distinto. «Las telenovelas mexicanas son las más tradicionales: son muy conservadoras.

Las brasileñas tienen elementos modernos. Las colombianas tienen historias muy creativas. Las argentinas suelen tener toques de comedia», dice Maziotti.

Además de entretener, una importante función de las telenovelas es educar. Muchas de las historias incorporan personajes que atraviesan° enfermedades graves, o viven situaciones serias como la decisión de adoptar un hijo o la pérdida° de un trabajo.

Las telenovelas son famosas por sus escenas dramáticas.

240

Los mejores finales de las villanas

① **Catalina Creel** (*Cuna de Lobos*, 1987). Tomó veneno, se vistió elegantemente y declaró que, a pesar de usar un parche˚ en el ojo derecho, veía perfectamente con los dos.

② **Soraya Montenegro** de la Vega (*María la del barrio*, 1996). Quiso encerrar a los protagonistas en una casa en llamas˚ y quedó atrapada en el incendio˚.

③ **Valeria del Castillo** (*Rosalinda*, 1999). Después de muchos planes para separar a los protagonistas, esta villana acaba en la cárcel.

La más exitosa

Yo soy Betty, la fea es una telenovela colombiana. Trata sobre una joven lista y culta˚ que asciende profesionalmente gracias a su talento pero es despreciada˚ por su apariencia física. Es la telenovela latinoamericana más exitosa de la historia. Este es un perfil en números de su éxito:

7 millones de personas vieron el primer beso de Betty con Armando, el galán.

100 países emitieron esta telenovela.

15 son los idiomas a los que se tradujo.

338 es el número de capítulos.

2001 es el año en que terminó.

La actriz América Ferrera protagonizó la versión norteamericana de *Yo soy Betty, la fea.*

¿COMPRENDISTE?

Decide si las siguientes frases son verdaderas (V) o falsas (F).

① Las telenovelas son solamente dramáticas. V◯ F◯

② Muchas telenovelas incorporan elementos de actualidad. V◯ F◯

③ Cada país latinoamericano produce telenovelas diferentes. V◯ F◯

④ *Yo soy Betty, la fea* fue un éxito solamente en Colombia. V◯ F◯

⑤ *Yo soy Betty, la fea* tiene más capítulos de lo habitual en las telenovelas. V◯ F◯

AHORA TÚ

¿Qué opinas? Contesta las siguientes preguntas y comenta tus ideas con tus compañeros/as.

① ¿Qué telenovela de las mencionadas te gustaría ver y por qué?

② ¿Qué programas en la televisión norteamericana tienen la función de entretener y educar? Da dos ejemplos.

③ Piensa en tu género televisivo favorito y haz una lista de los elementos que lo componen, según el ejemplo del texto.

④ Las villanas de las telenovelas siempre tienen un final violento. ¿Por qué?

⑤ ¿Por qué crees que las antagonistas de las telenovelas suelen ser mujeres?

El actor Jaime Camil, protagonista de la telenovela *Por ella soy Eva*

VOCES LATINAS ▶ LAS TELENOVELAS EN ARGENTINA

Glosario

ahorrar – to save
aportar – to add
atravesar – to go through
culto – educated
despreciado – despised
en llamas – burning
equilibrar – to balance
estrechamente – closely
el galán – leading man
el incendio – fire
el parche – patch
la pérdida – loss

Fuentes: Terra, Univisión, Página 12.

241

Los mejores finales de las villanas

- Call on a volunteer (or volunteers) to read the text aloud.
- Check students' understanding of the information by asking questions, such as: **¿Cuál de las tres villanas murió en un incendio? ¿La villana de qué telenovela tomó veneno? ¿Quién acabó en la cárcel?**
- Have students think about what happened to the villain in their favorite TV show or movie and share the information with a partner.
- Monitor their conversations and assist as needed.
- Call on volunteers to share their examples with the class.

La más exitosa

- Call on a volunteer to read the title and information that follows.
- Check students' understanding of the information by asking questions, such as: **¿De qué trata la telenovela Yo soy Betty, la fea? ¿De qué país es originaria? ¿Cuántos países emitieron la telenovela? ¿Quién protagonizó la version norteamericana de la telenovela?**

¿Comprendiste?

- Have students work individually to answer the questions.
- Monitor their progress and assist as needed.
- Go over the answers as a class. Have them explain the false answers.

Ahora tú

- Have students work individually to answer the questions.
- Monitor their progress and assist as needed.
- Put students into pairs or small groups to share their ideas. Have them take turns asking and answering the questions. Encourage them to ask each other follow-up questions for more information.
- Ask each pair or group to report back to the class on something interesting from their conversation.

ANSWERS

¿Comprendiste?

1. F; **2.** T; **3.** T; **4.** F; **5.** T.

HERITAGE LANGUAGE LEARNERS

Have students watch part of an episode of any of these *telenovelas*. Have them describe the characters, the situation, the peculiarities of the setting, etc. Then have them prepare a skit similar to what they saw, or have them devise a skit based on what they think will happen next so they can use the grammar concepts presented in this unit.

OBJECTIVES FOR RELATO

- Revisit unit themes, grammar, vocabulary and culture in a new context
- Improve reading comprehension skills

CORE RESOURCES

- Audio Program: Track 67
- Interactive Whiteboard Lesson: IWB 8.2

STANDARDS

2.2   Products and perspectives

3.1   Knowledge of other disciplines

INSTRUCTIONAL STRATEGIES

Activity 1

- Put students into pairs, assigning one to the role of **Estudiante 1** and the other to **Estudiante 2**. Monitor their progress and assist as needed. Possible questions for students to ask each other: **Estudiante 1: a. ¿Cómo se llamaba?; c. ¿En qué año nació?; e. ¿Cuál es el título de una de sus obras más importantes? Estudiante 2: b. ¿Dónde nació?; d. ¿Cuántas obras escribió?**
- Pose *yes/no* questions with incorrect information to the class and call on students to correct you, for example: **¿Calderón de la Barca es de México? ¿Es guionista de películas famosas? ¿Ha escrito solamente dos obras?**

Activity 2

- Have students jot down ideas on their own first. Encourage them to come up with five possibilities, one for each phrase in the box.
- Then put students into pairs to share their ideas. Have each group report back on their favorite hypothesis.

Activity 3

- Explain that the sentences represent the basic plot of the play **La vida es sueño** but that the sentences are out of order.
- Working individually or in pairs, have students put the plot in order.
- Go over the answers as a class to find out if any of the students' original hypotheses were correct.

ADVANCED LEARNERS

Before beginning the lesson, have students share their experiences going to the theater, or even acting in plays. Ask them about the differences between a play and a novel, and what a monologue is. Ask them why actors play monologues. You can look for adaptations of *Life's a Dream* on YouTube or have students watch excerpts or summaries.

RELATO *La vida es sueño*

1 Uno de los autores más importantes de teatro del Siglo de Oro fue Calderón de la Barca. Pregunta a tu compañero/a para conocer algo de este autor.

Estudiante 1

a. Nombre:

b. Lugar de nacimiento: Madrid.

c. Año de nacimiento:

d. N.º de obras escritas: más de 200.

e. Una de sus obras más importantes:

Estudiante 2

a. Nombre: Pedro.

b. Lugar de nacimiento:

c. Año de nacimiento: 1600.

d. N.º de obras escritas:

e. Una de sus obras más importantes: *La vida es sueño*.

2 En la obra *La vida es sueño* el protagonista, Segismundo, es encerrado al nacer en una torre para que no pueda salir nunca de ella. ¿Puedes imaginar las razones? Comparte tus ideas con tu compañero/a.

- Creo que…
- Tal vez…
- Es posible que…
- A lo mejor…
- Puede que…

3 Para confirmar tus hipótesis, ordena estas partes que resumen el argumento principal de la obra *La vida es sueño*.

a. ☐ Para que nadie sepa que existe un príncipe sucesor, lo encierra en una torre.

b. ☐ Segismundo finalmente gana, pero muestra respeto por su padre, porque es el rey. Basilio en ese momento es consciente de que su hijo será un buen rey en el futuro y le deja el trono.

c. ☐ Una vez en libertad, actúa de forma violenta contra todo el mundo y lo encierran otra vez.

d. ☐ El rey Basilio cuando nace su hijo Segismundo cree en una superstición que dice que ese niño no será un buen sucesor del trono.

e. ☐ El pueblo descubre que existe un príncipe heredero y lo liberan. Segismundo lucha contra su padre.

f. ☐ En una ocasión decide darle una oportunidad para comprobar si podrá ser un buen rey y lo saca de la torre.

4 🎧 **67** **Sigue el texto mientras escuchas este extracto en el que Segismundo habla desde su celda en la torre. Después, elige la interpretación correcta.**

¡Ay, mísero[1] de mí, ay infelice!
Apurar[2], cielos[3], pretendo,
ya que me tratáis así
qué delito[4] cometí
contra vosotros naciendo;
aunque si nací, ya entiendo
qué delito[5] he cometido:
bastante causa ha tenido
vuestra justicia[6] y rigor[7],
pues el delito mayor
del hombre es haber nacido.

Solo quisiera saber
para apurar[8] mis desvelos[9]
dejando a una parte, cielos,
el delito de nacer,
qué más os puede ofender
para castigarme más.
¿No nacieron los demás?
Pues si los demás nacieron,
¿qué privilegios[10] tuvieron
que yo no gocé[11] jamás?

1. Wretched; 2. To find out, discover; 3. The Heavens, plea to God; 4. Offense, mistake; 5. Refers to Original Sin; 6. Refers to the Heaven justice; 7. Severity; 8. Finish, conclude; 9. Worry, suffering; 10. Advantage, better luck; 11. Enjoy.

a. Segismundo no puede entender qué hizo para ser encerrado por su padre.

b. Segismundo está preocupado por el medioambiente.

c. Segismundo piensa que nacen muchos niños en el mundo.

5 **Segismundo, durante la obra, piensa que está dormido y que su vida es un sueño. ¿Qué significan las palabras *sueño* o *soñar* para ti? Haz una lista de todas las palabras que te vengan a la mente al pensar en ellas.**

6 👥 **En grupos de 3 o 4, comenta lo siguiente.**

a. ¿Sueñas con frecuencia?

b. ¿Sueles tener sueños agradables o pesadillas?

c. ¿Hay algún sueño que tengas a menudo?

d. ¿Recuerdas tu último sueño?

7 **Relaciona las siguientes palabras y expresiones relacionadas con los sueños con su significado.**

1. No pegar ojo.
2. Dormir como un tronco.
3. Tener sueño.
4. Soñar con los angelitos.
5. Pasar la noche en blanco.
6. Cumplirse un sueño.
7. Tener un sueño.

a. Estar cansado y con ganas de dormir.
b. Hacerse realidad algo muy deseado.
c. No poder dormir.
d. Desear algo con mucha intensidad.
e. En lenguaje infantil, dormir.
f. Dormir muy profundamente.

8 👥 **¿Qué sueño te gustaría ver realizado en la vida real? Comparte tus ideas con tu compañero/a.** 243

INSTRUCTIONAL STRATEGIES

🎧 67 Activity 4

- Before listening to the audio, consider giving students some time to read through the excerpt and footnoted definitions to familiarize themselves with the new vocabulary.
- Play the audio. Then have students read the three interpretations and select the correct one.
- Go over the answer as a class. Encourage students to explain their answers.

Activity 5

- Write the words **sueño** and **soñar** on the board. Elicit a few examples of other words that students relate to these, and write them on the board as well.
- Have students work individually to brainstorm and jot down more ideas.
- Monitor their progress and assist as needed.
- Call on volunteers to share some of their examples. Invite them explain their word associations if the connections are more tenuous.

Alternative Activity

Create a competition. Each student shares his or her list of associated words or phrases. If other students have the same word or phrase on their own lists, they must cross it off. Students only receive points for those words or phrases that no one else has.

Extension

Project IWB 8.2, **Los sueños**. Have the students match the phrases with the images to learn more vocabulary associated with dreaming.

Activity 6

- Put students into small groups to discuss the questions.
- Monitor their conversations and assist as needed.
- Call on volunteers to report back on interesting aspects of their conversations.

Activity 7

- Go over the instructions. Have students work individually to match the expressions with their meanings. Point out that one definition will be used twice.
- Go over the answers as a class.

Activity 8

- Give students some time to jot down their ideas first.
- Then put students into pairs to share their ideas. Encourage students to ask each other questions for more information.
- Have students change partners and report on their previous partner's dreams.
- Ask students if they were surprised by any of the dreams they heard and explain why or why not.

ANSWERS

Activity 4

Segismundo no puede entender qué ha hecho para ser encerrado por su padre.

Activity 7

1. c; **2.** f; **3.** a; **4.** e; **5.** c; **6.** b; **7.** d.

IWB 8.2

1. c; **2.** a; **3.** e; **4.** b; **5.** f; **6.** d.

HERITAGE LANGUAGE LEARNERS

Have students discuss the similarities and differences between classic theater and soap operas. Do they share any of the same elements? To get them started, write some elements of soap operas and classic theater on the board, and have students choose which ones apply to both.

OBJECTIVES FOR EVALUACIÓN

- Review grammar, vocabulary and culture from the unit
- Complete self-assessment

CORE RESOURCES

- Interactive Online Materials - ELEteca

STANDARDS

1.2	Understand the language
4.1	Compare languages

INSTRUCTIONAL STRATEGIES

- Have students complete the activities individually.
- Go over the answers as a class. Encourage students to learn from each other by asking if they agree with the answers given. Provide explanations as needed.
- You may wish to assign point value to each activity as a way for students to monitor their progress.
- Direct students to the indicated pages in **En resumen** if they make more than one or two mistakes in any one section.

ANSWERS

Activity 1

a. Me dice que tiene frío y que necesita un abrigo y que si no le sirve uno mío, va a comprarse uno; **b.** Me pregunta dónde tiene que ir, qué tiene que hacer y cuándo debe volver; **c.** Me confesó que no había hecho nada y que, cuando vuelva de su viaje, me lo demostrará; **d.** Me preguntó si estaba muy lejos la casa de mi primo porque estaba un poco cansado de caminar; **e.** Me pide que le diga la verdad.

Activity 2

1. b; **2.** e; **3.** d; **4.** a; **5.** c.

Activity 3

a. era; **b.** haremos; **c.** fueron; **d.** nació; **e.** está / estará; **f.** cocinan / cocinarán.

Activity 4

a. Lo mismo; **b.** Probablemente; **c.** Puede ser que; **d.** Quizás; **e.** Es posible que; **f.** Quizás.

EVALUACIÓN

RELATING INFORMATION SAID BY OTHERS

1 **Transforma las siguientes frases al estilo indirecto.**

a. Tengo frío y necesito un abrigo. Si no me sirve uno tuyo, voy a comprarme uno.
Me dice ....

b. ¿Dónde tengo que ir? ¿Qué tengo que hacer? ¿Cuándo debo volver?
Me pregunta ....

c. No hice nada y, cuando vuelva de mi viaje, te lo demostraré.
Me confesó ....

d. ¿Está muy lejos la casa de tu primo? Es que estoy un poco cansado de caminar.
Me preguntó ....

e. Dime la verdad.
Me pide ....

HYPOTHETICAL EXPRESSIONS WITH THE INDICATIVE AND THE SUBJUNCTIVE

2 **Relaciona para formar frases con sentido.**

1. ¡Muchas gracias por el regalo de cumpleaños!
2. (¡Riiinnnggg!) Son las doce de la noche y no espero ninguna llamada.
3. No encuentro las llaves de casa por ningún sitio.
4. No sé por qué se escuchan tantas sirenas de policía.
5. Sara me dice que el abrigo que se compró la semana pasada ahora está mucho más barato.

a. ¿Qué habrá pasado?
b. ¿Qué será?
c. ¿Cuánto costaría antes?
d. ¿Dónde las habré puesto?
e. ¿Quién será?

3 **Escribe la forma correcta del verbo entre paréntesis.**

a. Me parece que ayer (ser) .... el cumpleaños de mi primo y se me olvidó llamarlo.

b. Creo que (hacer, nosotros) .... los ejercicios mañana. Ahora no tenemos tiempo.

c. A lo mejor (ir, ellos) .... a clase la semana pasada pero esta semana no vinieron.

d. Yo diría que (nacer, él) .... en el sur de España. Baila flamenco muy bien.

e. Me imagino que (estar, él) .... en casa. Desde aquí veo que hay luz dentro.

f. Suponemos que (cocinar, ustedes) .... bien, pero nunca nos han invitado a comer.

4 **Elige la forma correcta en cada frase.**

a. **Lo mismo / Es posible que** está en la recámara.

b. **Es probable que / Probablemente** sabe dónde trabaja.

c. **Me parece que / Puede ser que** diga la verdad.

d. **Quizás / A lo mejor** haga el pastel para tu cumpleaños.

e. **Igual / Es posible que** cambie de casa en los próximos días.

f. **Es probable que / Quizás** puede llevarte en su carro.

UNIDAD 8

CARTAS FORMALES

5 Relaciona para formar saludos y despedidas.

1. se despide
2. muy
3. reciba
4. en espera
5. estimado

a. de sus noticias
b. un cordial saludo
c. atentamente
d. señor
e. señor mío

CORREOS ELECTRÓNICOS

6 Completa el siguiente email con los símbolos estudiados.

● ● ●	Mensaje nuevo
De: carol.sanz@gmail.com Para: Laural.a@hotmail.com	

Hola Laura (dos puntos) ....
Te envío la dirección de correo electrónico de Pepe para que le envíes las fotos.
Es (Pepe, guión bajo, Cruz, arroba, hotmail, punto, com) ....
Un besito, Carolina.

WORDS WITH DIFFERENT MEANINGS

7 Elige la opción correcta.

a. ¿**Dónde** / **A dónde** vas? No quiero que juegues **adonde** / **donde** / **dónde** no hay valla.
b. No fue Pedro quien me lo dijo, **sino** / **si no** Juan.
c. Déjalo **asimismo** / **a sí mismo**, ya está bien.
d. » ¿**Porqué** / **Por qué** / **Porque** me pasarán estas cosas a mí?
   » **Porque** / **Porqué** / **Por qué** eres un despistado y no te fijas en lo que haces.

CULTURA

8 Contesta las siguientes preguntas con la información que has aprendido en *Un mundo de novela*.

a. ¿De qué manera están conectadas las telenovelas a los países hispanos?
b. ¿Cuáles son algunos de los elementos que tienen en común las telenovelas? ¿Qué elementos tienen en común con las telenovelas en Estados Unidos?
c. Además de entretener, ¿qué intentan hacer las telenovelas? Y las telenovelas en Estados Unidos, ¿qué temas sociales suelen tocar?
d. ¿Cuáles son las características del personaje Betty de la telenovela *Betty la fea*? ¿Piensas que es una exageración u ocurre así en la vida real?

 MORE IN ELETECA: EXTRA ONLINE PRACTICE

245

ANSWERS

Activity 5

1. c; **2.** e; **3.** b; **4.** a; **5.** d.

Activity 6

1. : (dos puntos); **2.** Pepe_Cruz@hotmail.com

Activity 7

a. A dónde, donde; **b.** sino; **c.** así mismo; **d.** Por qué, Porque.

Activity 8

Answers will vary. Possible answers might include the following:
a. Cada país latinoamericano produce telenovelas con un estilo distinto. Las telenovelas reflejan las tradiciones, las aspiraciones, y los temas de actualidad de la sociedad que las mira; **b.** Suelen tener entre 100 y 200 capítulos. Generalmente, hay un galán rico, una heroína pobre, y una villana que hace todo lo posible por separarlos. Como las telenovelas en los Estados Unidos, son melodramáticas; **c.** Intentan educar. Suelen tocar temas sociales, por ejemplo, la pobreza, la homosexualidad, el abuso, la violencia, el cáncer, y mucho más; **d.** Betty es una joven inteligente y capaz que asciende profesionalmente pero es despreciada por su apariencia física.

OBJECTIVES FOR EN RESUMEN: VOCABULARIO

- Review unit vocabulary and expressions
- Practice communicative skills

STANDARDS

1.2 Understand the language

1.3 Present information

INSTRUCTIONAL STRATEGIES

- Have students write sentences with the words and phrases in the other vocabulary sections.
- Call on students to write their sentences on the board –but leave a blank line (or give multiple choices, in some cases) where the vocabulary word or phrase should be. Then have the rest of the class write down the answers to complete the sentences.
- Go over the answers as a class. You may choose to create a competition and keep score by individual or group.

Alternative Activity

Index cards can be used as flashcards with the Spanish term on one side and the English term, a picture, or a drawing on the other. Working in pairs or groups, students can use the flashcards to help each other practice unit vocabulary.

EN RESUMEN: Vocabulario / Gramática

Cartas formales

a continuación *following*
la despedida *closing (of a letter)*
destinatario *addressee, recipient of letter*
las disculpas *apologies*
la fecha *date*
la finalidad *purpose*
la firma *signature*
la molestia *bother*
el motivo *motive, subject*
la queja *complaint*
el remitente *sender (of a letter)*
el saludo *greeting*

Telecomunicaciones

el aparato *mechanical device*
la arroba *at, @*

la barra *slash*

la batería *battery*
el cargador *charger*

cargar *to charge*
dos puntos *colon*
el guion *hyphen*
el guion bajo *underscore*
hacer clic *to click*

la pantalla táctil *touch screen*

punto com *dot com*
se corta *to be cut, dropped (as in a call)*
la señal *signal*
tener cobertura *to have coverage*

la triple doble ve *www*

Verbos

aconsejar *to advise*

comentar *to comment*
confesar (e > ie) *to confess*
durar *to last*
ordenar *to order*
recomendar (e > ie) *to recommend*
suponer *to suppose*

Expresiones para expresar hipótesis

a lo mejor *maybe*
es probable *it's possible*
igual *maybe*
lo mismo *maybe*
posiblemente *possibly*
probablemente *probably*
puede ser / puede que *it can be that*
seguramente *surely*
tal vez *maybe*

REPORTED SPEECH

(See pages 226 and 227)

■ To relate some information we use the verbs **decir**, **comentar** or **confesar** in present tense.
   "**Eres** lo mejor de **mi** vida". ➜ **Dice que soy** lo mejor de **su** vida.
   "**Estuve aquí** comiendo con Pedro". ➜ **Dice que estuvo allí** comiendo con Pedro.
   "**Creo** que **tenemos** este libro". ➜ **Dice que** cree que tienen ese libro.

■ In these cases there are no changes in the verb tenses, but there are changes in:
   - **Personal pronouns**: "*Yo quiero ir*". ➜ *Dice que* **él / ella** *quiere ir.*
   - **Demonstrative adjectives** and **pronouns**: "*Te daré* **este** *libro*". ➜ *Dice que me dará* **ese** *libro.*
   - **Possessive adjectives** and **pronouns**: "*Este es* **mi** *coche*". ➜ *Dice que ese es* **su** *coche.*

246

EN RESUMEN: Gramática

■ When we relate questions:

"¿Hicieron la tarea?". ➡ *El profesor* **pregunta** *si hicimos la tarea.*
"¿Cuándo harán la tarea?". ➡ *El profesor nos* **pregunta cuándo** *haremos la tarea.*

VERBS AND EXPRESSIONS
TO EXPRESS HYPOTHESIS OR PROBABILITIES
(See pages 235 and 236)

Creo / Me parece		*ese modelo de celular no* **es** *uno de los mejores.*
Me imagino / Supongo	**que**	*si está en la sierra no* **tiene** *cobertura, llámalo mañana.*
Para mí / Yo diría		**llovió** *anoche, las calles están mojadas.*
A lo mejor / Lo mismo / Igual *(maybe)*		**es** *un problema de tu compañía porque yo sí tengo cobertura.*
Probablemente / Posiblemente **Seguramente / Quizás** **Tal vez**		*la compañía telefónica* **se pone** */* **se ponga** *en contacto conmigo después de mi reclamación. (indicativo/subjuntivo)*
Es posible / Es probable **Puede ser / Puede**	**que**	*mi celular* **tenga** *algún defecto de fábrica, me lo compré hace poco y no me dura nada la batería. (subjuntivo)*

■ We can also express probability using some tenses:

Present ➡ Simple Future   *Javier no ha llegado,* **estará** *todavía en el metro.*
Simple Past ➡ Conditional   *Si Javier no vino ayer,* **tendría** *algún motivo.*

■ We use the imperfect subjunctive in *if*-clauses to express actions that are contrary to fact, meaning the actions are purely hypothetical and did not occur.

■ Forms of the imperfect subjunctive:

Preterit of **ellos**, drop **-ron**, add endings:		-AR / -ER / -IR	IRREGULARS
-ra	**-´ramos**	viajar ➡ viajaron	tener ➡ tuvieron
-ras	**-rais**	beber ➡ bebieron	ser ➡ fueron
-ra	**-ran**	vivir ➡ vivieron	poder ➡ pudieron
yo		viajara, bebiera, viviera	tuviera, fuera, pudiera
tú		viajaras, bebieras, vivieras	tuvieras, fueras, pudieras
usted/él/ella		viajara, bebiera, viviera	tuviera, fuera, pudiera
nosotros/as		viajáramos, bebiéramos, viviéramos	tuviéramos, fuéramos, pudiéramos
vosotros/as		viajarais, bebierais, vivierais	tuvierais, fuerais, pudierais
ustedes/ellos/ellas		viajaran, bebieran, vivieran	tuvieran, fueran, pudieran

■ Contrary-to-fact statements have the following constructions:

Si + imperfect subjuntive, conditional.	Conditional, **si +** imperfect subjunctive.

- Review unit grammar
- Practice communication skills

STANDARDS

1.2 Understand the language
4.1 Compare languages

INSTRUCTIONAL STRATEGIES

- Focus students' attention on the key grammar topics of the unit.
- Have students review the Learning Outcomes in the unit opener to assess whether they feel they have mastered the main ideas and skills.
- Ask them if they can remember additional examples for each grammar topic.
- Model how to find and go back to the appropriate page in the unit to review any grammar topic they may need help with.
- Invite students to review the grammar activities they completed in this unit.
- Ask them what grammar activities they found easy and which they found challenging. Encourage them to rework any activities they found particularly challenging.

OBJECTIVES FOR AHORA COMPRUEBA

- Review and recycle grammar, vocabulary and culture from the last two units
- Complete self-assessment

CORE RESOURCES

- Audio Program: Track 68
- Interactive Whiteboard Lessons: IWB 8.3

STANDARDS

1.2 Understand the language

4.1 Compare languages

INSTRUCTIONAL STRATEGIES

🎧 68 Activity 1

- Focus students' attention on the image and ask: **¿Conocen la historia? ¿Han visto la película? ¿Recuerdan los nombres de los personajes?** Elicit what they know about the story and its characters.
- Give students time to read the questions before playing the audio. Encourage them to underline key words to listen for and to take notes while they listen.
- Play the audio. Have students compare their notes with a partner and answer the questions in pairs. Play the audio again so they can check their answers. Go over the answers as a class.

See audioscript on page APP15

Activity 2

- Have students work individually to complete the conversation.
- Put students into pairs to compare their answers. Then go over the answers.
- Have the pairs practice the conversation. Then have them switch roles.

Activity 3

Have students work individually to create sentences. Then go over the answers as a class and have students continue telling the rest of the story.

ANSWERS

Activity 1

a. En el teatro Lope de Vega en Madrid, c/ Gran Vía, 57; **b.** En metro: estaciones de Callao y Plaza de España o en coche con parking en la Plaza de España; **c.** A través de la página web: *www.elreyleon.es* o en el teléfono 902 888 788. También en la taquilla todos los días desde las 12 p.m. hasta el inicio de la última función; **d.** Una butaca que ofrece una visita guiada al *backstage* de *El rey León* y la posibilidad de conocer a los actores después de la función; **e.** *El rey León, el musical que conmueve a todo el mundo.*

Activity 2

1. Qué te parece; **2.** impresionante; **3.** ¡Pero qué dices!; **4.** es asombroso que; **5.** No creo que; **6.** Además; **7.** Desde luego; **8.** creo que.

Activity 3

a. 4, B; **b.** 1, D; **c.** 3, A; **d.** 2, C

SLOWER-PACED LEARNERS

Have students make a list of the learning objectives noted in the opening spreads of the two previous units. Tell them to ask themselves: *How well can I do this: very well, well, or not well?* Then pair students who can't do an objective well with another student who can; that way, they can teach each other what they know and help each other review.

AHORA COMPRUEBA

1 🎧 68 Escucha el siguiente anuncio comercial sobre el musical *El Rey León (The Lion King)* y contesta las preguntas.

a. ¿Dónde puedes ver El Rey León?

b. ¿Cómo puedes llegar?

c. ¿Dónde y cómo puedes comprar los boletos?

d. ¿Qué es la "butaca de oro"?

e. ¿Cuál es el eslogan?

2 Completa la conversación entre Nélida y Silvia con las siguientes expresiones.

> creo que ○ además ○ desde luego ○ es asombroso que ○
> no creo que ○ impresionante ○ qué te parece ○ pero qué dices

Nélida: ¿(a) .... ir a ver el musical de *El Rey León*? Vi la película cuando era pequeña y me parece (b) .... poder ver ahora el musical en Madrid.

Silvia: ¡(c) .... ! No me gustan nada los musicales.

N.: ¿No has visto su anuncio en la tele? Creo que (d) .... estén tan bien caracterizados los actores para parecer animales. Ya solo eso me parece increíble... Y las canciones fueron escritas por Elton John y el letrista Tim Rice, que ganaron un Oscar y un Tony.

S.: (e) .... sea el tipo de espectáculo para mí, prefiero una película. (f) ...., el teatro es carísimo.

N.: ¡(g) .... que es caro! Pero lo vale la emoción del directo, los actores cantando y bailando delante de ti, los efectos de iluminación... Es tan espectacular que (h) .... es imposible verla y que no se te pongan los pelos de punta.

S.: ¡¡Imposible?! Hummm...

3 Relaciona los elementos de las tres columnas y construye frases para descubrir el argumento de *El Rey León*.

a. Simba es un cachorro y sucesor al trono,

b. Scar organiza la muerte de Mufasa, el padre de Simba, y le hace creer que es culpa suya,

c. Simba tiene dos nuevos amigos que le adoptan y,

d. Su tío Scar toma el trono,

1. por eso
2. incluso
3. además,
4. sin embargo

A. le enseñan la filosofía de vivir sin preocupaciones: el *Hakuna Matata*.

B. su tío Scar quiere ser el próximo rey y prepara un plan para ocupar el trono.

C. llega a hacer pensar a todos los animales que Simba murió. ¿Volverá a recuperar su reino?

D. se siente culpable y escapa a la selva.

4 Completa la siguiente conversación entre dos amigos. Ninguno de los dos conoce la obra. Lee las respuestas y escribe la pregunta. La primera ya está hecha.

Sandra: ¿Cuánto costarán los boletos?
Mateo: Ni idea, pero imagino que serán caros.
S.: (a) _____
M.: Imagino que en la taquilla del teatro o por Internet, pero no estoy seguro.
S.: (b) _____
M.: Creo que está por el centro de Madrid. Lo podemos mirar en la página web del teatro.
S.: (c) _____
M.: Me imagino que sí ha ganado muchos premios.
S.: (d) _____
M.: Supongo que más de dos horas, como todos los musicales.
S.: (e) _____
M.: Tal vez. Si no, pues buscamos un estacionamiento.
S.: (f) _____
M.: Ya sabes que yo tampoco lo sé, pero normalmente las funciones son sobre las ocho de la tarde, ¿no?
S.: (g) _____
M.: Seguramente. La están representando en muchos países, entonces supongo que sí, que la vieron muchas personas.

5 En la historia de *El Rey León* aparecen muchos animales. Relaciona la imagen con la palabra apropiada en cada caso.

1.
a. ☐ toro
b. ☐ rinoceronte
c. ☐ jabalí

2.
a. ☐ elefante
b. ☐ ciervo
c. ☐ cerdo

3.
a. ☐ pingüino
b. ☐ oso panda
c. ☐ cebra

4.
a. ☐ loro
b. ☐ águila
c. ☐ tucán

6 Escribe tu hipótesis usando diferentes palabras y los conectores aprendidos.

①. _____
②. _____
③. _____
④. _____

INSTRUCTIONAL STRATEGIES

Activity 4
- Go over the instructions and the model. Point out the key bit of information that neither person knows much about the play. Elicit from the students what that suggests about the grammar and kinds of expressions they should use.
- Put students into pairs. Have them work together to write an appropriate question for each response.
- Monitor their progress and assist as needed.
- Call on volunteers to role-play their conversations in front of the class.

Activity 5
- Go over the instructions. Have students work individually to match the pictures with the correct words.
- Monitor their progress and assist as needed. Encourage them to guess if they are not sure.
- Before going over the answers, have students continue with Activity 6.

Activity 6
- Have students write hypotheses that reflect how confident they are or are not in their guesses in Activity 5.
- Put students in pairs to compare their hypotheses.
- Project IWB 8.3, *Animales* to reveal the answers. To create more suspense, consider revealing the images one at a time, piece by piece. Confirm whether or not their hypotheses were correct.

ANSWERS

Activity 4
Answers will vary. Possible answers might include the following:
1. ¿Dónde podremos comprarlas?; **2.** ¿Dónde estará el teatro?; **3.** ¿Habrá ganado algún premio?; **4.** ¿Cuánto durará la obra?; **5.** ¿Podremos aparcar allí?; **6.** ¿A qué hora serán las funciones?; **7.** ¿La habrá visto mucha gente?

Activity 5
1. b; **2.** c; **3.** a; **4.** b.

ADVANCED LEARNERS

For those students who have a good handle on the vocabulary, grammar, and cultural content of the units, encourage them to focus on the development of their listening, speaking, reading, and writing skills prior to quizzes and tests. Challenge them to spend thirty minutes a night for four nights before the assessment focusing on one of each of the four skills each night. In addition to redoing the skills-based activities within the units, encourage them to seek new, related (and fun) material online to help them practice.

HERITAGE LANGUAGE LEARNERS

For students who already have a base of the language, challenge them to put themselves in the position of the teacher prior to assessments. How would they teach a non-native speaker the content of the previous two units? Have them develop worksheets, activities, games, presentations, and lesson plans that could be used to teach other students the material. By putting students in this new role, they will enhance their own knowledge and become masters of the content.

APÉNDICES

- **Resumen y expansión gramatical**
- **Tabla de verbos**

RESUMEN GRAMATICAL

THE FUTURE TENSE

- Regular verbs:

	−AR VIAJAR	−ER COMER	−IR VIVIR
yo	viajar**é**	comer**é**	vivir**é**
tú	viajar**ás**	comer**ás**	vivir**ás**
usted/él/ella	viajar**á**	comer**á**	vivir**á**
nosotros/as	viajar**emos**	comer**emos**	vivir**emos**
vosotros/as	viajar**éis**	comer**éis**	vivir**éis**
ustedes/ellos/ellas	viajar**án**	comer**án**	vivir**án**

- Irregular verbs:

IRREGULAR VERBS			
poder ➡ **podr**–	tener ➡ **tendr**–	hacer ➡ **har**–	**é**
salir ➡ **saldr**–	poner ➡ **pondr**–	decir ➡ **dir**–	**ás**
caber ➡ **cabr**–	venir ➡ **vendr**–		**á**
haber ➡ **habr**–	valer ➡ **valdr**–		**emos**
saber ➡ **sabr**–			**éis**
querer ➡ **querr**–			**án**

The future is often used with the following temporal expressions:

El año / mes / la semana / primavera **que viene**

Dentro de dos años / un rato / unos días

El/la próximo/a semana / mes / año

Mañana / **Pasado mañana**

SI + PRESENT + FUTURE

- To talk about future actions that will occur if a certain condition is met, use the following:

  - **Si**   +   **present**   +   **future**
    Si   no llueve,   iremos a la playa.

AFFIRMATIVE COMMANDS

- Affirmative commands are used to give an order, to invite, give advice, make recommendations, or give permission to someone.

- Verbs ending in −**ar** will use the −**e**/−**en** endings in **usted** and **ustedes** commands. Verbs ending in −**er**/−**ir** will use the −**a**/−**an** endings in **usted** and **ustedes** commands.

REGULAR VERBS

	COMPRAR	COMER	SUBIR
tú	compra	come	sube
usted	compre	coma	suba
ustedes	compren	coman	suban

IRREGULAR VERBS

	DECIR	HACER	PONER	TENER
tú	di	haz	pon	ten
usted	diga	haga	ponga	tenga
ustedes	digan	hagan	pongan	tengan

AFFIRMATIVE COMMANDS + PRONOUNS

■ Direct, indirect, and reflexive pronouns are attached to affirmative commands to form one word.

Pon el queso en la nevera. ➜ **Ponlo**.   *Dime el secreto.* ➜ **Dímelo**.

EXPANSIÓN GRAMATICAL

Other irregular verbs:

	VENIR	IR	SER	SALIR
tú	ven	ve	sé	sal
usted	venga	vaya	sea	salga
ustedes	vengan	vayan	sean	salgan

Stem-changing verbs in the command form maintain their stem change:

	CERRAR e ➜ ie	DORMIR o ➜ ue	JUGAR u ➜ ue	PEDIR e ➜ i	CONSTRUIR i ➜ y
tú	cierra	duerme	juega	pide	construye
usted	cierre	duerma	juegue	pida	construya
ustedes	cierren	duerman	jueguen	pidan	construyan

NEGATIVE COMMANDS

■ Negative commands are used to tell someone what not to do.

■ To form the negative commands:

• For **usted/ustedes**, use the same form as the affirmative command.

(usted) compre ➜ **no compre**   *(ustedes) compren* ➜ **no compren**

• For **tú**, add −**s** to the negative command of **usted**.

(usted) no compre ➜ *(tú)* **no compres**

REGULAR VERBS

	COMPRAR	COMER	SUBIR
tú	no compres	no comas	no subas
usted	no compre	no coma	no suba
ustedes	no compren	no coman	no suban

IRREGULAR VERBS				
	DECIR	HACER	PONER	TENER
tú	no **digas**	no **hagas**	no **pongas**	no **tengas**
usted	no **diga**	no **haga**	no **ponga**	no **tenga**
ustedes	no **digan**	no **hagan**	no **pongan**	no **tengan**

NEGATIVE COMMANDS AND PRONOUNS

■ Direct, indirect, and reflexive pronouns are placed before negative commands.

*No **lo** pongas en la estantería.*　　　　　　　　　　*No **se lo** digas a nadie.*

EXPANSIÓN GRAMATICAL

Other irregular verbs:

	VENIR	IR	SER	SALIR
tú	no **vengas**	no **vayas**	no **seas**	no **salgas**
usted	no **venga**	no **vaya**	no **sea**	no **salga**
ustedes	no **vengan**	no **vayan**	no **sean**	no **salgan**

Stem-changing verbs in the command form maintain their stem change:

	CERRAR	DORMIR	JUGAR	PEDIR	CONSTRUIR
	e ➡ ie	o ➡ ue	u ➡ ue	e ➡ i	i ➡ y
tú	no c**ie**rres	no d**ue**rmas	no j**ue**gues	no p**i**das	no constru**y**as
usted	no c**ie**rre	no d**ue**rma	no j**ue**gue	no p**i**da	no constru**y**a
ustedes	no c**ie**rren	no d**ue**rman	no j**ue**guen	no p**i**dan	no constru**y**an

UNIDAD 3

THE PLUPERFECT (PAST PERFECT)

The pluperfect is formed with the imperfect of **haber** + past participle of the verb.

				Irregular past participles			
yo	había						
tú	habías			abrir ➡ **abierto**		escribir ➡ **escrito**	
usted/él/ella	había	–**ado** (–ar verbs)	lleg**ado**	hacer ➡ **hecho**		ver ➡ **visto**	
nosotros/as	habíamos	–**ido** (–er / ir verbs)	com**ido**	decir ➡ **dicho**		poner ➡ **puesto**	
vosotros/as	habíais		viv**ido**	romper ➡ **roto**		volver ➡ **vuelto**	
ustedes/ellos/ellas	habían						

■ Uses:

• To talk about an action that ended before another past action. Note the use of **todavía** and **ya**:

*Cuando llegué al cine la película no **había comenzado** todavía / la película todavía no **había comenzado**.*
(Llegué al cine a las 17:59, la película comenzó a las 18:00)
*Cuando llegué al cine la película **había comenzado** ya / la película ya **había comenzado**.*
(Llegué al cine a las 18:05 y la película comenzó a las 18:00)

• To talk about an action that took place before another past action, but with a sense of immediacy:

*Le compré un juguete y al día siguiente ya lo **había roto**.*
*Para mi cumpleaños me regalaron una novela y a la semana siguiente ya la **había leído**.*

• To talk about an action that we had never done before. Note the use of **nunca** and **nunca antes**:

*Nunca / Nunca antes **había estado** aquí / No **había estado** aquí nunca / nunca antes.*
*Nunca / Nunca antes **habíamos viajado** en globo / No **habíamos viajado** en globo nunca / nunca antes.*

• To ask if a person had ever done something before. Note the use of **antes** and **alguna vez**:

*¿**Habías estado** en Madrid alguna vez / antes?*
*¿**Habías estado** alguna vez / antes en Madrid?*

UNIDAD 4

THE CONDITIONAL TENSE

■ Regular verbs:

	HABLAR	COMER	ESCRIBIR
yo	hablar**ía**	comer**ía**	escribir**ía**
tú	hablar**ías**	comer**ías**	escribir**ías**
usted/él/ella	hablar**ía**	comer**ía**	escribir**ía**
nosotros/as	hablar**íamos**	comer**íamos**	escribir**íamos**
vosotros/as	hablar**íais**	comer**íais**	escribir**íais**
ustedes/ellos/ellas	hablar**ían**	comer**ían**	escribir**ían**

■ Irregular verbs:

caber ➡ **cabr–**	tener ➡ **tendr–**	hacer ➡ **har–**	**ía**
haber ➡ **habr–**	poder ➡ **podr–**	decir ➡ **dir–**	**ías**
saber ➡ **sabr–**	poner ➡ **pondr–**		**ía**
querer ➡ **querr–**	venir ➡ **vendr–**	+	**íamos**
	salir ➡ **saldr–**		**íais**
	valer ➡ **valdr–**		**ían**

■ Uses:

• To **give advice** or recommendations:
*Yo / yo que tú / yo en tu lugar, **le diría** la verdad, seguro que lo entiende.*
***Deberías** comer menos dulces, no son muy saludables.*
***Podrías** presentarte al casting para el programa de baile, lo haces muy bien.*

• To **ask for permission** and favors:
*¿**Te importaría** acercarme la chaqueta? Es que yo no alcanzo.*

• To express **probability** or **hypothesize** in the past:
***Tendría** 20 años cuando empezó a cantar.*

THE PRESENT SUBJUNCTIVE

■ Regular verbs:

To form the present subjunctive, start with the **yo** form of the present indicative, drop the **o** and switch to the opposite endings. For **–ar** verbs use: **–e**, **–es**, **–e**, **–emos**, **–éis**, **–en**. For **–er** / **–ir** verbs use: **–a**, **–as**, **–a**, **–amos**, **–áis**, **–an**.

	HABLAR	COMER	ESCRIBIR
yo	habl**e**	com**a**	escrib**a**
tú	habl**es**	com**as**	escrib**as**
usted/él/ella	habl**e**	com**a**	escrib**a**
nosotros/as	habl**emos**	com**amos**	escrib**amos**
vosotros/as	habl**éis**	com**áis**	escrib**áis**
ustedes/ellos/ellas	habl**en**	com**an**	escrib**an**

■ Irregular verbs:

Almost all verbs that are irregular in the present indicative will be irregular in the present subjunctive.

Stem-changing verbs

	QUERER	VOLVER	JUGAR	PEDIR
	e ➡ ie	**o ➡ ue**	**u ➡ ue**	**e ➡ i** (en todas las personas)
yo	qu**ie**ra	v**ue**lva	j**ue**gue	p**i**da
tú	qu**ie**ras	v**ue**lvas	j**ue**gues	p**i**das
usted/él/ella	qu**ie**ra	v**ue**lva	j**ue**gue	p**i**da
nosotros/as	queramos	volvamos	juguemos	p**i**damos
vosotros/as	queráis	volváis	juguéis	p**i**dáis
ustedes/ellos/ellas	qu**ie**ran	v**ue**lvan	j**ue**guen	p**i**dan

■ The verbs **dormir** and **morir** have two stem changes in the present subjunctive: **o ➡ ue** and **o ➡ u**:

- d**ue**rma, d**ue**rmas, d**ue**rma, d**u**rmamos, d**u**rmáis, d**ue**rman.
- m**ue**ra, m**ue**ras, m**ue**ra, m**u**ramos, m**u**ráis, m**ue**ran.

Verbs with irregular *yo* forms

poner ➡ **pong**–	traer ➡ **traig**–	**a**
tener ➡ **teng**–	hacer ➡ **hag**–	**as**
salir ➡ **salg**–	caer ➡ **caig**–	**a**
venir ➡ **veng**–	construir ➡ **construy**–	**amos**
decir ➡ **dig**–	conocer ➡ **conozc**–	**áis**
		an

Verbs that are completely irregular

HABER	IR	SABER	ESTAR	SER	VER	DAR
haya	vaya	sepa	esté	sea	vea	dé
hayas	vayas	sepas	estés	seas	veas	des
haya	vaya	sepa	esté	sea	vea	de
hayamos	vayamos	sepamos	estemos	seamos	veamos	demos
hayáis	vayáis	sepáis	estéis	seáis	veáis	deis
hayan	vayan	sepan	estén	sean	vean	den

■ Uses:

• To express **wishes** or **desires**. If there is only one subject in the sentence, use an infinitive. If there are different subjects, use the subjunctive:

(Yo) Quiero (yo) **hablar** *contigo. / (Yo) Quiero que (nosotros)* **hablemos**.

(Yo) Espero (yo) **verte** *pronto. / (Yo) Espero que (nosotros) nos* **veamos** *pronto.*

• To express **purpose** or **goals in the future**. If there is only one subject in the sentence or a subject that is not specified, use an infinitive. If there are different subjects, use the subjunctive:

He hecho una tortilla para **cenar**. / *He hecho una tortilla para que* **cenéis** *Carla y tú.*

• To express **future actions** after **adverbial conjunctions**:

» *¿Cuándo volverá Ana?*   » *Cuando* **salga** *de trabajar.*

EXPANSIÓN GRAMATICAL

Other verbs with irregular forms in the subjunctive:

e ➡ ie (except in the nosotros and vosotros forms)

cerrar	➡ c**ie**rre	encender	➡ enc**ie**nda	mentir	➡ m**ie**nta
comenzar	➡ com**ie**nce	encerrar	➡ enc**ie**rre	querer	➡ qu**ie**ra
despertarse	➡ se desp**ie**rte	entender	➡ ent**ie**nda	recomendar	➡ recom**ie**nde
divertirse	➡ se div**ie**rta	goberna	➡ gob**ie**rne	sentarse	➡ se s**ie**nte
empezar	➡ emp**ie**ce	manifestar	➡ manif**ie**ste	sentir	➡ s**ie**nta

o ➡ ue (except in the nosotros and vosotros forms)

acordarse	➡ se ac**ue**rde	rogar	➡ r**ue**gue
acostarse	➡ se ac**ue**ste	soler	➡ s**ue**la
contar	➡ c**ue**nte	sonar	➡ s**ue**ne
llover	➡ ll**ue**va	soñar	➡ s**ue**ñe
probar	➡ pr**ue**be	volar	➡ v**ue**le
resolver	➡ res**ue**lva	volver	➡ v**ue**lva

e ➡ i (en todas las personas)

competir	➡ comp**i**ta
despedir	➡ desp**i**da
despedirse	➡ se desp**i**da
impedir	➡ imp**i**da
medir	➡ m**i**da
repetir	➡ rep**i**ta

EXPRESSING FEELINGS AND EMOTIONS

■ To express changing moods and feelings use the following structures:
- Verb **estar** + adjective + **con** + noun.

  Mi hermana está muy contenta con su profesora de música.
- Verb **estar** + adjective + **de** + infinitive (if the subject of both verbs is the same).

  Estamos encantadas de asistir al estreno de la nueva película de Mario Casas.
- Verb **estar** + adjective + **de que** + subjunctive (if the subject of both verbs is different).

  Estoy encantada de que te quedes unos días más con nosotros.
- Verbs **ponerse**, **sentirse** o **estar** + adjective + **cuando** / **si** + indicative.

  Yo me pongo furioso cuando dejo un libro y no me lo devuelven.

  Yo me siento mal si veo una noticia triste.

■ Other verbs:

	+ noun
• **Odiar**	*Odio* los lunes.
• **No soportar**	+ infinitive (same subject)
• **No aguantar**	*No soporto* madrugar.
• **Adorar**	+ **que** + subjunctive (different subjects)
	No aguanto que me *empujen* en el metro.

■ Verbs like **gustar**:
- **Me**, **te**, **le**, **nos**... + **da rabia**, **pone alegre/s**, **molesta** + infinitive (if the person experiencing the emotion and carrying out the action is the same).

  A mí me da vergüenza hablar en público.
- **Me**, **te**, **le**, **nos**... + **da rabia**, **pone alegre/s**, **molesta** + **que** + subjunctive (if the person experiencing the emotion and the person carrying out the action are different).

  A mí me da rabia que la gente toque los cuadros en los museos.
- Remember that adjectives must agree with the subject in number and gender.

  *A mi **madre** le pone **enferma** que no recoja mi habitación.*

VERBS FOLLOWED BY INFINITIVES OR PRESENT PARTICIPLES

■ In some of these constructions, the first verb, which is always conjugated, may be followed by a preposition.
- **Empezar** / **ponerse a** + infinitive expresses the beginning of an action.

  He empezado a leer una novela muy interesante.

  En cuanto llegué a casa me puse a estudiar para el examen del día siguiente.
- **Volver a** + **infinitive** expresses the repetition of an action.

  El año pasado me apunté a clases de teatro y este año he vuelto a apuntarme.
- **Seguir** / **continuar** + **present participle** expresses an action that continues.

  Nos conocimos en la guardería y hoy todavía seguimos siendo amigas.

  Este verano continuaré yendo a clases de inglés, no quiero olvidar lo que he aprendido.

- **Acabar de** + **infinitive** expresses an action that just occurred.

  Si quieres pastel espera a que se enfríe un poco, que acabo de sacarlo del horno.

- **Dejar de** + **infinitive** expresses the interruption of an action (to stop doing something).

  He dejado de ir a clases de guitarra porque este año no tengo tanto tiempo.

VERBS THAT EXPRESS CHANGE

■ To express **spontaneous** or **temporary changes** in a person, use:

- **Ponerse** + adjective.

  Al hablar se ha puesto muy nervioso.   *Se ha puesto rojo cuando le han preguntado.*

- **Quedarse** (describes the end result).

  Se ha quedado muy sorprendido por la noticia.   *¡Mi madre se ha quedado embarazada!*

  Quedarse *can sometimes express permanent changes: Mi abuelo* **se quedó calvo**.

■ To express **permanent changes**, use:

- **Volverse** + adjective / noun (not voluntary)

  Se ha vuelto un antipático. Antes no era así.   *Desde su divorcio, se ha vuelto más reservada.*
  Jugó a la lotería y se volvió millonario.

- **Hacerse** (gradual or voluntary change).

  Antes era abogado y ahora se ha hecho juez.

  Hacerse *can be used with adjectives and nouns that express* **profession**, **religion** *and* **ideology**.
  Estudió Medicina y **se hizo médico**.   *Con esa situación* **se hizo fuerte**.
  Viajó al Tíbet y **se hizo budista**.

UNIDAD 7

EXPRESSING OPINIONS

■ To **ask for an opinion**:

- **¿Qué piensas / crees / opinas de / sobre…?**

  ¿Qué piensas de este periódico?

- **¿(A ti)** qué **te parece…?**

  ¿A ti qué te parece lo que está pasando con la organización de la fiesta?

- **En tu opinión / Desde tu punto de vista / Según tú** + question.

  Desde tu punto de vista, ¿cuál es el anuncio más inteligente?

■ To **give an opinion**:

- **En mi opinión / Desde mi punto de vista**…

  En mi opinión el blog no es muy interesante.

- **Me parece que / Creo que / Pienso que** + indicative.

  Nos parece que la marca es muy importante.

- **No me parece que / No creo que** + present subjunctive.

  No nos parece que la marca sea tan importante.

■ To show agreement and disagreement:

• **(No) estoy a favor de**	+ noun
• **(No) estoy en contra de**	+ infinitive (same subject)
• **(No) estoy (del todo) de acuerdo con**	+ que + present subjunctive (different subjects)

No estoy de acuerdo con todo tipo de anuncios.
Estoy en contra de ser manipulado por la publicidad.

Estoy a favor de que nos pidan opinión antes de vendernos sus productos.

■ Other ways to express:

AGREEMENT	SOFTEN A DISAGREEMENT	DISAGREEMENT
• Sí, claro.	• Yo no diría eso…	• ¡No, no!
• ¡Desde luego!	• Tienes razón, pero…	• ¡No, de ninguna manera!
• ¡Claro, claro!	• Sí, es una idea interesante, pero por otra parte…	• ¡Qué va!
• Yo pienso lo mismo que tú.	• A mi modo de ver, ese no es el problema / el tema…	• ¡(Pero) qué dices! (coloquial)
• Por supuesto.	• Lo que pasa es que…	• ¡Anda ya! (coloquial)
• ¡Y que lo digas! (coloquial)		

MAKING VALUE JUDGEMENTS

■ To **ask**:

• **¿Te parece bien / mal** /… + noun / infinitive / **que** + present subjunctive?

¿Te parece mal el sueldo de un publicista?
¿Te parece bien poder usar buscadores para hacer trabajos de clase?
¿Te parece una tontería que los publicistas ganen mucho dinero?

■ To **respond**:

• **Me parece bien / mal**	
• **Me parece / Es triste / increíble / cómico**…	+ **que** + present subjunctive
• **Me parece / Es una tontería / una vergüenza**…	
• **Es bueno / malo**	

Es increíble que se gasten tanto en anunciar sus productos.
Me parece bien que se entienda como una inversión y no como un gasto.
Creo que es una tontería que siempre veas los anuncios.

• **Está claro**	+ **que** + indicative
• **Es obvio / verdad**	

Está claro que la publicidad es creación.

• **¡Qué + bien / interesante**… + sentence!

¡Qué interesante este artículo!
¡Qué bien poder compartir tanta información a través de Facebook!
¡Qué guay que nuestro instituto tenga una página web!

TRANSITION WORDS AND SENTENCE CONNECTORS

- To present a **series** of reasons or points in an **argument**: **En primer lugar**… **en segundo lugar**…
  La juventud es muy crítica. En primer lugar no acepta cualquier cosa y en segundo lugar busca lo que quiere.

- To present **opposing views**: **Por un lado / una parte**… **por otro (lado) / por otra (parte)**…
  Comer bien es importante. Por un lado es necesario, por otro un placer.

- To **add points** or arguments: **Y / además / también / asimismo**
  La creatividad está presente en la publicidad, además de la originalidad por supuesto.

- To provide **examples** and **explanations**: **Por ejemplo / es decir / o sea**
  El alto nivel de competencia hace necesario invertir en publicidad, es decir, hay muchos productos buenos y similares en el mercado, pero algo te hace elegir uno.

- To refer to a topic **previously presented**: **(Con) respecto a (eso de / eso) / Sobre (eso)**…
  Con respecto a eso que has dicho antes, siento no estar totalmente de acuerdo contigo.

- To **add reasons** to an argument: **Incluso**
  María trabaja todos los días, incluso los domingos.

- To **contrast reasons**: **Bueno / pero / sin embargo / no obstante / en cambio**
  El rojo es mi color preferido, sin embargo nunca llevo ropa de ese color.

- To express **consequence**: **Así que / de modo que / de manera que / de ahí que / así pues / pues**
  Me encantan las películas, así que voy al cine siempre que puedo.

- To draw **conclusions**: **Entonces / total que / por lo tanto / en resumen / en conclusión / para terminar**
  Fuimos a la montaña sin botas ni ropa adecuada, total que pasamos muchísimo frío.

UNIDAD 8

INDIRECT SPEECH

- To repeat information use verbs like **decir**, **comentar** or **confesar** in the present or present perfect tenses:
  "Eres lo mejor de mi vida". ➡ *Dice / Ha dicho **que soy** lo mejor de **su** vida.*
  "Estuve aquí comiendo con Pedro". ➡ *Dice / Ha dicho **que estuvo allí** comiendo con Pedro.*
  "Cree que tenemos este libro". ➡ *Dice / Ha dicho **que** cree que **tienen ese** libro.*

- While the verb tenses in these cases do not change, other changes will take place in the following:
  - Subject Pronouns
    "**Yo** quiero ir". ➡ *Dice que **él/ella** quiere ir.*
    "**Tú** quieres hablar siempre". ➡ *Dice que **yo** quiero hablar siempre.*
  - Demonstrative Adjectives and Pronouns
    "**Te** daré **este** libro". ➡ *Dice que **me** dará **ese** libro.*

- When repeating questions, use the interrogative word in the question (**cómo**, **dónde**, **qué**, **cuándo**…) or **preguntar** + **si** (for questions without interrogatives):
  "¿Han hecho la tarea?". ➡ *El profesor nos ha preguntado si hemos hecho la tarea.*
  "¿Cuándo van a hacer la tarea?". ➡ *El profesor nos ha preguntado cuándo vamos a hacer la tarea.*

HYPOTHETICAL EXPRESSIONS WITH THE INDICATIVE AND THE SUBJUNCTIVE

• **Creo / me parece que** • **Me imagino / aupongo que** • **Para mí / yo diría que**	+ indicative	*Creo que ese modelo de móvil **es** uno de los mejores.*

• **A lo mejor** / **lo mismo** / **igual** + indicative
   *Igual **es** un problema de tu compañía.*

• **Probablemente** / **posiblemente** / **seguramente** / **quizás** / **tal vez** + indicative / subjunctive
   *Quizás la compañía se **pone** / **ponga** en contacto conmigo después de mi reclamación.*

• **Es posible** / **es probable** / **puede (ser)** + **que** + subjunctive
   *Puede que mi teléfono **tenga** algún defecto de fábrica, me lo compré hace poco y no me dura nada la batería.*

■ We can also express probability with the following verb tenses:

• Present ➡ Future
   ≫ *¿Sabes dónde está Javier?*
   ≫ *No sé, **estará** todavía en el metro.*

• Preterit ➡ Conditional
   ≫ *¿Sabes cómo vino ayer a clase?*
   ≫ *No lo sé. **Vendría** andando.*

■ We use the imperfect subjunctive in *if*-clauses to express actions that are contrary to fact, meaning the actions are purely hypothetical and did not occur.

■ Forms of the imperfect subjunctive:

Preterit of *ellos*, drop -**ron**, add endings: -ra -ramos -ras -rais -ra -ran	-AR / -ER / -IR	IRREGULARS
	viajar ➡ viajaron	tener ➡ tuvieron
	beber ➡ bebieron	ser ➡ fueron
	vivir ➡ vivieron	poder ➡ pudieron
yo	viaj**ara**, beb**iera**, viv**iera**	tuv**iera**, fu**era**, pud**iera**
tú	viaj**aras**, beb**ieras**, viv**ieras**	tuv**ieras**, fu**eras**, pud**ieras**
usted/él/ella	viaj**ara**, beb**iera**, viv**iera**	tuv**iera**, fu**era**, pud**iera**
nosotros/as	viaj**áramos**, beb**iéramos**, viv**iéramos**	tuv**iéramos**, fu**éramos**, pud**iéramos**
vosotros/as	viaj**arais**, beb**ierais**, viv**ierais**	tuv**ierais**, fu**erais**, pud**ierais**
ustedes/ellos/ellas	viaj**aran**, beb**ieran**, viv**ieran**	tuv**ieran**, fu**eran**, pud**ieran**

■ Contrary-to-fact statements have the following constructions:

Si + imperfect subjuntive, conditional.	Conditional, **si +** imperfect subjunctive.

TABLA DE VERBOS

Affirmative Commands

Regular verbs

CANTAR	COMER	VIVIR
canta	come	vive
cante	coma	viva
canten	coman	vivan

Irregular verbs

CAER	CONDUCIR	CONOCER	CONSTRUIR	CONTAR
cae	conduce	conoce	construye	cuenta
caiga	conduzca	conozca	construya	cuente
caigan	conduzcan	conozcan	construyan	cuenten

DECIR	DORMIR	ELEGIR	EMPEZAR	HACER
di	duerme	elige	empieza	haz
diga	duerma	elija	empiece	haga
digan	duerman	elijan	empiecen	hagan

HUIR	IR	JUGAR	LLEGAR	OÍR
huye	ve	juega	llega	oye
huya	vaya	juegue	llegue	oiga
huyan	vayan	jueguen	lleguen	oigan

PEDIR	PENSAR	PONER	SABER	SALIR
pide	piensa	pon	sabe	sal
pida	piense	ponga	sepa	salga
pidan	piensen	pongan	sepan	salgan

SER	TENER	VENIR	VESTIR	VOLVER
sé	ten	ven	viste	vuelve
sea	tenga	venga	vista	vuelva
sean	tengan	vengan	vistan	vuelvan

Future Tense

Regular verbs

CANTAR	COMER	VIVIR
cantaré	comeré	viviré
cantarás	comerás	vivirás
cantará	comerá	vivirá
cantaremos	comeremos	viviremos
cantaréis	comeréis	viviréis
cantarán	comerán	vivirán

Irregular verbs

CABER	DECIR	HABER	HACER
cabré	diré	habré	haré
cabrás	dirás	habrás	harás
cabrá	dirá	habrá	hará
cabremos	diremos	habremos	haremos
cabréis	diréis	habréis	haréis
cabrán	dirán	habrán	harán

PODER	PONER	QUERER	SABER
podré	pondré	querré	sabré
podrás	pondrás	querrás	sabrás
podrá	pondrá	querrá	sabrá
podremos	pondremos	querremos	sabremos
podréis	pondréis	querréis	sabréis
podrán	pondrán	querrán	sabrán

SALIR	TENER	VALER	VENIR
saldré	tendré	valdré	vendré
saldrás	tendrás	valdrás	vendrás
saldrá	tendrá	valdrá	vendrá
saldremos	tendremos	valdremos	vendremos
saldréis	tendréis	valdréis	vendréis
saldrán	tendrán	valdrán	vendrán

The pluperfect (past perfect)

yo	había
tú	habías
usted/él/ella	había
nosotros/as	habíamos
vosotros/as	habíais
ustedes/ellos/ellas	habían

–**ado** (–ar verbs)
–**ido** (–er / ir verbs)

lleg**ado**
com**ido**
viv**ido**

Irregular past participles			
abrir	➜ **abierto**	escribir	➜ **escrito**
hacer	➜ **hecho**	ver	➜ **visto**
decir	➜ **dicho**	poner	➜ **puesto**
romper	➜ **roto**	volver	➜ **vuelto**

The conditional

Regular verbs

	HABLAR	COMER	ESCRIBIR
yo	hablar**ía**	comer**ía**	escribir**ía**
tú	hablar**ías**	comer**ías**	escribir**ías**
usted/él/ella	hablar**ía**	comer**ía**	escribir**ía**
nosotros/as	hablar**íamos**	comer**íamos**	escribir**íamos**
vosotros/as	hablar**íais**	comer**íais**	escribir**íais**
ustedes/ellos/ellas	hablar**ían**	comer**ían**	escribir**ían**

Irregular verbs

caber ➡ **cabr–**	tener ➡ **tendr–**	hacer ➡ **har–**	**ía**
haber ➡ **habr–**	poder ➡ **podr–**	decir ➡ **dir–**	**ías**
saber ➡ **sabr–**	poner ➡ **pondr–**		**ía**
querer ➡ **querr–**	venir ➡ **vendr–**	+	**íamos**
	salir ➡ **saldr–**		**íais**
	valer ➡ **valdr–**		**ían**

The present subjunctive

Regular verbs

	HABLAR	COMER	ESCRIBIR
yo	habl**e**	com**a**	escrib**a**
tú	habl**es**	com**as**	escrib**as**
usted/él/ella	habl**e**	com**a**	escrib**a**
nosotros/as	habl**emos**	com**amos**	escrib**amos**
vosotros/as	habl**éis**	com**áis**	escrib**áis**
ustedes/ellos/ellas	habl**en**	com**an**	escrib**an**

Irregular verbs

Stem-changing verbs

	QUERER	VOLVER	JUGAR	PEDIR
	e ➡ ie	o ➡ ue	u ➡ ue	e ➡ i (en todas las personas)
yo	qu**ie**ra	v**ue**lva	j**ue**gue	p**i**da
tú	qu**ie**ras	v**ue**lvas	j**ue**gues	p**i**das
usted/él/ella	qu**ie**ra	v**ue**lva	j**ue**gue	p**i**da
nosotros/as	queramos	volvamos	juguemos	p**i**damos
vosotros/as	queráis	volváis	juguéis	p**i**dáis
ustedes/ellos/ellas	qu**ie**ran	v**ue**lvan	j**ue**guen	p**i**dan

■ The verbs **dormir** and **morir** have two stem changes in the present subjunctive: **o** ➡ **ue** and **o** ➡ **u**:
• d**ue**rma, d**ue**rmas, d**ue**rma, d**u**rmamos, d**u**rmáis, d**ue**rman.
• m**ue**ra, m**ue**ras, m**ue**ra, m**u**ramos, m**u**ráis, m**ue**ran.

APÉNDICES

- Audioscripts
- Lesson plans

UNIT 0: VOLVEMOS A VERNOS

TRACK 1

Carlos: ¡Hola, Lucía! ¿Qué tal tus vacaciones?

Lucía: ¡Genial! Estuve en las playas de California haciendo surf.

Carlos: ¡No me digas! ¿Surf? No sabía que practicabas surf.

Lucía: Sí, estuvo bastante bien. Las playas son fantásticas y lo mejor es que conocí a un montón de gente joven de muchos países.

Carlos: ¡Qué suerte!

Lucía: ¿Y tú? Cuéntame. Fuiste a Colorado, ¿no? ¿Qué tal te fue?

Carlos: Bueno, ¡lo pasé de miedo! Pero terminé cansadísimo. Ya sabes que fui con Luis y Javier y no descansamos nada. Hacer senderismo con ellos fue una experiencia un poco peligrosa. Incluso, nos perdimos una noche. No vuelvo a ir con ellos.

Lucía: ¡Vaya, hombre!, ¡qué aventura!

Carlos: Sí, creo que las próximas vacaciones las voy a pasar en las playas de California sin hacer nada.

TRACK 2

1. Al acabar la escuela secundaria, empecé a ir a la universidad.
2. De pequeño, jugaba mucho al fútbol con mis amigos.
3. Me casé con la mujer de mi vida.
4. Ahora estoy jubilado.
5. De joven tenía muchas novias.
6. Trabajaba muchas horas para mantener a mi familia.
7. Con 5 años aprendí a montar en bici.
8. Esta mañana he ido al parque y ahí he leído el periódico tranquilo.
9. A esa edad me afeité por primera vez.

TRACK 3

¿Buscas hacer un viaje diferente? Te invitamos a conocer tres de los sitios más interesantes de Latinoamérica por su originalidad, historia y toque de misterio.

«Es como estar en la cima del mundo. Es increíble. ¡Pero lleva zapatos cómodos!», dice Devyn, un turista de Nueva York, después de su visita al sitio arqueológico de Teotihuacán en México.

Es un sitio donde los aztecas construyeron una gran ciudad entre los siglos II y VII. Armando, un visitante de California, dice: «Era el lugar número uno que quería visitar en México. Recomiendo llegar bien temprano y subir a la Pirámide del Sol y a la Pirámide de la Luna para tener un panorama completo», sugiere en el sitio de viajes Tripadvisor.

Hoy, Teotihuacán es el segundo sitio arqueológico con más visitas del mundo. Más de dos millones y medio de turistas llegan para admirar las pirámides, los templos y las avenidas.

También pueden ver la recreación de un antiguo ritual azteca, la Danza de los Voladores. Consiste en cinco personas (los voladores) que, a gran altura, hacen impresionantes acrobacias. Originalmente, se trataba de una ceremonia asociada a las cosechas y a la fertilidad.

UNIDAD 1: CONSTRUYENDO UN FUTURO

TRACK 4

Marta: Todavía no sé qué quiero estudiar cuando empecemos la universidad. ¿Tú ya sabes qué vas a estudiar?

Víctor: Me encanta la música, así que me imagino que estudiaré Bellas Artes, como mi hermana mayor. Ella está muy contenta y dice que la universidad es genial.

Marta: Pero tu hermana estudia en Barcelona, ¿verdad?

Víctor: Sí, le encanta la ciudad y está muy contenta.

Marta: ¿Y tú también quieres irte a estudiar allí?

Víctor: Bueno, supongo que iré a Barcelona o quizás a Salamanca. La universidad de Salamanca es preciosa y muy antigua y la ciudad tiene mucha marcha, porque hay mucha gente joven.

Marta: Yo creo que me quedaré aquí en Zaragoza y estudiaré Medicina o Enfermería. Víctor, si te vas… ¡qué pena!

Víctor: Bueno, bueno, que solo estoy haciendo conjeturas Todavía no es nada seguro, ¡y faltan unos años! Además, si me voy, te prometo que vendré a verte cada fin de semana.

Marta: ¿Me lo prometes?

Víctor: ¡Prometido!

TRACK 5

a. **Madre:** ¡El próximo fin de semana estás castigado! Ayer llegaste tardísimo.
   Hijo: Te juro que no volverá a pasar, de verdad.
   Madre: Siempre dices lo mismo y nunca haces caso. ¡No hay más que hablar!
   Hijo: ¡Pero, mamá…!

b. **Luis:** ¡Estuve media hora esperándote y la película ya ha empezado! La próxima vez entro yo solo al cine y no te espero.

Sandra: Anda, no te enfades. He llamado para avisarte… Te prometo que no volverá a pasar.

Luis: ¡Pero si desde que te conozco siempre llegas tarde!

c. **Pedro:** Tu fiesta ha estado genial. Nos hemos divertido muchísimo.
   Daniel: Me alegro. A ver si celebramos otra para tu cumpleaños.
   Pedro: ¡Prometido!

TRACK 6

- cuéntamelo
- corazón
- sábado
- pensar
- salió
- joven
- historia
- carácter
- música
- cómic
- fábrica
- canción
- ciudad
- después
- dáselo
- devuélvemelo
- gracias
- palo
- lápiz
- verano
- maravilla
- jardín
- dímelo
- difícil
- aquí
- rápido
- político
- casa
- envíanoslas
- genial

TRACK 7

Naturaleza espectacular, flora única y fauna salvaje. Estos son algunos de los elementos de los parques nacionales. ¡Visítalos!

«Es nuestro mayor tesoro», dice Humberto Gutiérrez, Jefe de Medioambiente de Tenerife, «el Parque Nacional del Teide es el que recibe más visitas de toda Europa y el segundo del mundo. Además, en él está el volcán más grande del mundo». El Parque Nacional del Teide, en las Islas Canarias, España, es uno de los 15 parques nacionales de este país.

Los parques nacionales se caracterizan por su impresionante naturaleza y su fauna. A menudo están formados por cordilleras o montañas, volcanes, lagos, desiertos, cascadas, bosques, rocas, barrancos, calderas o glaciares.

«No es suficiente con tener hectáreas de terreno. Para que una extensión sea declarada Parque Nacional, esta debe tener una belleza, fauna y flora especiales. El gobierno de un país la acota y protege para que no se construya en ella», dicen desde el Ministerio de Agricultura, Alimentación y Medioambiente de España. Otros parques nacionales importantes son el Parque Nacional de Doñana, el Parque Nacional de Sierra Nevada, el Parque Nacional Marítimo-Terrestre del Archipiélago de Cabrera y el Parque Nacional de los Picos de Europa.

Muchos de estos parques han sido declarados Patrimonio de la Humanidad por la UNESCO.

TRACK 8

Alberto llegó de la escuela, comió, encendió la tele, agarró el mando a distancia y se tumbó en el sofá. ¡ZAP!

—Si quiere disfrutar de unas vacaciones de ensueño, Florida es su destino. ¡ZAP!

—Siempre te querré a ti, mi amor. ¡ZAP!

—Quiero hacerle una pregunta; usted, al recibir el Premio Nobel de Energía afirmó que el futuro que nos espera es mucho más negro de lo que pensamos —interesante, pensó Alberto.

—Sí, efectivamente. Las grandes ciudades del futuro provocarán el efecto invernadero y una megapolución si no hacemos algo. Habrá tanta superpoblación que tendremos que cultivar en grandes huertos urbanos para alimentarnos. Para no terminar con los combustibles fósiles, tendremos que reducir el número de carros y los kilómetros recorridos por los aviones. Habrá islas-vertedero para eliminar los residuos. Se tendrá que ahorrar energía utilizando los elementos de la naturaleza como el sol, el viento o la lluvia. ¡ZAP!

—Buenos días, les presento a William Mitchell, del Instituto Tecnológico de Massachusetts. ¿Cómo piensa usted que serán las ciudades del futuro?

—Bueno, yo pienso que estarán diseñadas como organismos vivos, con inteligencia propia. Las calles y edificios tendrán luces inteligentes que cambiarán de color e intensidad dependiendo de la hora del día. Tanto dentro como fuera de la casa, habrá sensores que nos informarán de todo lo que sucede, como, por ejemplo, tener información de los edificios o monumentos de una ciudad solo con enfocarlos con un celular. ¡ZAP!

—Necesito montar en una nave para teletransportarme en una milésima de segundo a mi planeta, si no, se cerrarán los accesos y no podré entrar. ¡¡Necesito ayuda!! —gritó Alberto.

—Despierta, hijo. Has tenido una pesadilla.

Alberto miró primero a su madre, luego a su alrededor, y se sintió feliz de encontrarse en el siglo XXI.

UNIDAD 2: COSAS DE CASA

TRACK 9

Ernesto: ¡Últimamente mis padres se quejan por todo!

Daría: ¿Por qué dices eso? Tus padres son encantadores.

E.: Pues ahora se han vuelto superestrictos con todo. Me han dicho que entre semana no puedo llegar a casa más tarde de las seis. Bueno, menos los días que tengo tenis, que tengo que estar en casa a las ocho de la noche. Me han dicho que si llego un minuto más tarde, me castigarán sin salir.

D.: ¡Pero si salimos de entrenar a las siete y media! ¡Tendrás que irte corriendo a casa! ¡Y sin ducharte!

E.: Además, ahora dicen que no hacemos nada en casa y que tenemos que colaborar más.

D.: ¡Uf! ¡Qué pesados! Mi madre el año pasado hizo una lista con las tareas que tenía que hacer cada uno, ¡y fue un desastre!

E.: ¿Y eso?

D.: Mi abuelo era el encargado de hacer la compra, pero lo que hacía era pagar 270 pesos a mi hermano Fernando si iba él. Él me pagaba 180 pesos a mí y mientras él "estaba haciendo la compra" se iba de paseo. Y como yo odio ir al supermercado, pues le pagaba 90 pesos a mi hermano Marcos, ¡y él encantado!

E.: ¿Y tus padres no se enteraban?

D.: Al principio no, pero un día vieron a Marcos salir del súper y lo descubrieron.

E.: ¿Y cómo reaccionaron?

D.: Pues decidieron que con los 270 pesos del abuelo, los 180 de Fernando y mis 90, podían pagar a alguien para limpiar la casa varias horas a la semana. ¡Pero nosotros tenemos que seguir haciendo nuestra parte!, ¡y además nos cuesta dinero!

E.: ¡Ja, ja! ¡Tus padres sí que saben!TRACK 10

a. Emilio: Mamá, ya sé que estás leyendo, pero… ¿Puedo poner la tele?

Mamá: Sí, claro, ponla. A mí no me molesta el ruido mientras leo.

Emilio: Vale, gracias, es que ahora hay un programa que me encanta.

b. Marcos: ¿Quieres probar la pizza que he hecho?

Anabel: No, gracias, es que acabo de comer.

Marcos: Anda, come un poco, solo para probarla. Ya verás qué rica me sale.

Anabel: Bueno, la probaré, pero solo un poquito.

TRACK 11

1. Carlos: ¡Uf! ¡Qué calor!

Paco: Pues abre la ventana.

Carlos: ¿De verdad no te importa?

Paco: Claro, ábrela, ábrela sin problemas.

2. Celia: ¿Te vienes con nosotros a casa de Mercedes? Tiene el último videojuego de…

Mario: No, gracias, es que tengo mucho que estudiar.

Celia: Anda, solo un rato, nos lo pasaremos bien.

Mario: Bueno, iré, pero tengo que estar en casa antes de las 7.

3. Carmen: ¿Puedo ponerme tu camiseta?

Juanjo: No, lo siento, es que luego te echas perfume y se queda el olor y no me gusta.

Carmen: De acuerdo.

4. Carolina: Toma, ¿quieres un poco? Es una tarta que he hecho.

Pepe: No, muchas gracias.

Carolina: Venga, pruébala, que está muy buena.

Pepe: Seguro, pero es que no me gusta mucho el dulce.

TRACK 12

1. ≫ A mí, la tarea que menos me gusta hacer es barrer.
≫ A mí tampoco me gusta nada, es un rollo.

2. ≫ ¡Jaime! Pon la mesa, por favor.
≫ Sí, ya voy. Ahora la pongo.

3. ≫ Luisa, ¿vienes a ver la tele?
≫ Sí, un momento que termino de lavar los platos y voy.

4. ≫ Laura, ya que sales, tira también la basura.
≫ Vale.

5. »» Ya veo que eres muy buen cocinero.
   »» Bueno, me gusta mucho la cocina. En casa siempre soy yo el que hace la comida.

6. »» ¿Quieres que planche tu blusa?
   »» Sí, genial. Muchas gracias.

7. »» No entres ahora en la cocina, que estoy fregando el suelo.
   »» Pero mamá, tengo hambre.

8. »» No puedo escuchar la tele con el ruido de la aspiradora.
   »» Entonces, ¿por qué no la pasas tú y ves tu programa después?

9. »» Mi madre no me deja bajar a desayunar si no he hecho la cama.
   »» ¿Sí? Pues yo siempre la hago después del desayuno.

10. »» ¿Puedes echar esto a lavar cuando pongas la lavadora?
    »» Sí, claro.

11. »» ¡Qué rollo! Tengo que tender la ropa.
    »» ¡Venga!, si es solo un momento. Si quieres, te ayudo.

12. »» ¿Siempre paseas tú al perro? Pensé que era de tu hermano.
    »» Bueno, yo lo paseo por las mañanas porque mi hermano tiene que ir a clases, ¿verdad Charlie?

TRACK 13

Estudio español.
Está duchándose.
¡Qué interesante!
¡Ya he terminado!

¿Dónde vives?
¿Tienes un diccionario?
Pues si no lo sabe él…
¡Es tan cursi…!

TRACK 14

a. ¡Ya ha venido!
b. ¿No lo quiere?
c. Habla español.
d. Es que no puede…

TRACK 15

»» ¿Cuándo vendrá Marcos?
»» Supongo que el domingo.
»» Pues si viene el domingo…
»» ¿Acaso te viene mal?

»» ¡Cómo dices eso!
»» ¿Quieres hablar claro?
»» Déjame que te explique…
»» ¡Pues habla ya!

TRACK 16

Hablar alto, tocarse la nariz, empezar a comer antes que otros, llegar tarde… Mucha gente piensa que estos son malos modales pero, ¿son típicos de una persona maleducada o de una cultura?

«Cuando me mudé a España me invitaron a una fiesta. La fiesta era a las 8 de la tarde. En Alemania la puntualidad es importante así que llegué a las 8 en punto. Pero mis amigos españoles no llegaron hasta las 8 y media… ¡Qué vergüenza!», dice Sebastian Rohde, una chico de 21 años de Berlín.

La experiencia de Sebastian no es única. En España no se considera de mala educación llegar tarde a una fiesta. «Si quedo con amigos a una hora determinada, se sobreentiende que llegar algo más tarde es lo normal», dice Marisa López, una chica de Valencia.

«Pero en el ambiente laboral la actitud es muy distinta: con cosas relacionadas con el trabajo, la gente es muy profesional», dice Marisa.

«La primera vez que visité el Reino Unido, me chocó mucho que la gente empezara a cenar antes que el resto de comensales. En España eso se considera de mala educación», dice Samantha Borrás, una estudiante de Madrid que vive en el Reino Unido. «Preferimos comer la comida cuando está caliente», dice su novio inglés.

«¿Que si los españoles son maleducados? A veces sí lo parecen», dice Soroya Conti, una chica argentina que vive en España, «En mi país la gente que trabaja de cara al público utiliza muchas palabras de cortesía. En España se habla de forma más directa. Por eso, a algunos extranjeros les puede parecer que los españoles son maleducados».

«Creo que los españoles hablan muy alto. En Finlandia hablamos mucho más bajo. Allí se considera de mala educación hablar alto. Por eso algunas personas pueden pensar que los españoles son groseros», dice Karen Laatvala, una estudiante que vive en Salamanca.

TRACK 17

No sé si creer en las casualidades. Pero resulta que hoy, en el autobús, mientras iba a la escuela, alguien se había dejado olvidado un libro. Ya su portada me atraía a leerlo y a devorarlo. Fíjate si estaba entusiasmada con la historia, que me pasé la parada de la escuela. El libro se llamaba *Como agua para chocolate* y cuenta la vida de Tita y su historia de amor con Pedro. La madre de Tita tuvo a su hija en la cocina, entre los olores de lo que estaba cocinando. Por eso, ya desde el principio, Tita sentía un gran amor por la cocina. Cuando cocinaba, su estado de ánimo influía en los platos que preparaba. Así, si hacía un plato estando alegre, cuando la gente lo comía, también se ponía contenta.

Ahora estoy en mi habitación y sigo leyéndolo sin parar. Quizás también me gusta esta historia porque me recuerda a mi abuela. Ella pasaba mucho tiempo en la cocina y le encantaba cocinar. Además, al igual que Tita, creía que era muy importante cómo te sentías cuando cocinabas. Siempre que podíamos, mi hermano y yo, a la vuelta de la escuela, pasábamos toda la tarde con ella. Cuando nos veía asomar la cabeza por la puerta siempre nos decía:

– Entren, entren. Miren qué estoy preparando.

Nosotros entrábamos hipnotizados. Dejábamos las mochilas en el suelo y nos poníamos manos a la obra.

– Manuela, ayúdame a cortar esta cebolla, y Tomás, lava las papas para cocerlas.

A mi hermano y a mí nos encantaba ser sus ayudantes en la cocina e imaginar que estábamos en uno de los mejores restaurantes de París.

– No, mira, si quieres que esté dulce, recítale un poema. Sí, así… Muy bien… En la vida hay que poner el corazón en lo que haces. Si no, no sirve para nada… Eso es, ponle alegría, que es para la familia…

Daba igual si no lo hacíamos perfecto, ella siempre nos sonreía. Claro, que eso no era muy difícil, porque todo le parecía bien y casi siempre estaba de buen humor. Creo que solamente se enfadaba y se quejaba cuando cortaba la cebolla y le lloraban los ojos.

– Seguro que esto no es bueno. Si lloro ahora cocinando, ¿qué pasará cuando lo coman los invitados? Yo no quiero llorar cocinando. ¿Y si se me caen las lágrimas encima de la comida?

Un día, por su cumpleaños, se nos ocurrió regalarle unas gafas de buceo para cortar cebollas y así perder el miedo a cocinar algo triste. Todavía recuerdo su sonrisa cuando se las puso. Nos dijo que era el mejor regalo del mundo.

TRACK 18

»» ¡Qué temprano vienes!
»» ¡Tú sí que has venido temprano!
»» Es que hoy no he perdido el bus. Por cierto, ¿qué hora es?
»» ¿Es que no tienes reloj?
»» Lo he olvidado en casa. ¿A qué hora viene el jefe?
»» No lo sé.
»» ¿Y si vamos a tomar un café?
»» ¿Otro café?
»» Es que no he desayunado.
»» Bueno, te acompaño.

AHORA COMPRUEBA. REPASO UNIDADES 1-2

TRACK 19

a. ≫ ¿Puedo bajar después de comer a la piscina?
≫ No, lo siento, es que después de comer vamos a ir a comprar.

b. ≫ ¿Qué te pasa, Andrés?
≫ Es que esta noche hay una fiesta y me gustaría ir. ¿Puedo ir, mamá?

c.: ≫ ¿Quieres más papas?
≫ No gracias, ¡estoy lleno!

d. ≫ ¿Qué transporte es el mejor para moverme por la ciudad, papá?
≫ Lo mejor es comprar el abono transporte. Cómpralo el primer día del mes, cuesta 40 euros. Puedes tomar el metro, el autobús y el tren todas las veces que quieras.

e. ≫ ¡Andrés! ¡Sal ya de la piscina y ven a comer!
≫ ¡Ya voy!

f. ≫ Perdone, ¿para ir a la estación de Atocha?
≫ Siga todo recto, al final de la calle gire a la derecha y después tome la primera a la izquierda.
≫ Gracias.

g. ≫ ¿Te importa si uso tu computadora? Es que quiero escribirles un email a mis amigos.
≫ No, claro, hazlo.

h. ≫ Andrés, ¿por qué no vamos a patinar esta tarde?
≫ ¡Vale! ¡Buena idea!

TRACK 20

Las ventanas, la compra, la mesa, los platos, el suelo, la cama, la habitación, la lavadora, el polvo de los muebles.

UNIDAD 3: DE CINE

TRACK 21

Ricardo: ¿Te has enterado de los talleres de este curso? He oído que van a ser totalmente diferentes.
Daniela: ¿Y eso?
R.: Pues parece que han contratado a dos famosos para organizar un taller con el Departamento de Literatura.
D.: ¡No me lo puedo creer! Dos famosos trabajando en una escuela…
R.: Ya, pero, según dicen, a estos los han elegido por su relación con la cultura y por su carrera profesional. He oído que son amigos del nuevo profesor de Literatura, parece que se conocieron cuando trabajaban juntos en una escuela de idiomas, creo que enseñaban español.
D.: ¡Anda ya! Dos profesores famosos, ¡imposible! Pero, dime, dime, que estoy intrigadísima. ¿De qué es el taller? ¿Quién lo va a impartir?
R.: Al parecer, es un taller de cine y teatro…
D.: ¡Qué chévere!
R.: La parte de cine la va a impartir la directora y guionista Anamar Orson y la parte de teatro el actor Cristian Pascual.
D.: ¿En serio? Pero si los dos son conocidísimos… ¡Cristian Pascual en la escuela! ¡Qué fuerte! ¿Hablas en serio?
R.: Sí, Daniela, sí, hablo en serio, aunque si quieres, llamamos para preguntar al Departamento de Literatura, porque no estoy demasiado seguro.

TRACK 22

¡Anamar! Te he llamado mil veces esta semana. ¿Todavía no has vuelto de Berlín? Mira, te llamo para contarte que el otro día quedé con Paco para tomar un café y me propuso colaborar en un taller de cine y teatro en su escuela. Yo acepté y entonces me pidió hablarlo contigo. En ese momento dije que estabas muy ocupada, pero luego pensé: "Solo van a ser cuatro semanas y siempre te ha encantado trabajar con jóvenes…". Ah, otra cosa, la respuesta tiene que ser urgente. Paco necesita confirmar nuestra colaboración para empezar a organizarlo.

TRACK 23

1. habitual; **2.** helicóptero; **3.** había; **4.** hidroeléctrico; **5.** hiedra; **6.** hielo; **7.** hipersensible; **8.** homologar; **9.** honrado; **10.** hormonas; **11.** huele; **12.** huésped.

TRACK 24

a. Mónica ha vuelto a Madrid.
b. ¿Ves estos libros de cine tan bonitos? Creo que los van a vender todos y no va a haber más hasta el próximo mes.
c. ¡Ay, Isaac! Quita la computadora de ahí, ¿no ves que no hay espacio suficiente?
d. ¡Hola, Sergio! ¿Has visto qué olas tan buenas hay para hacer surf?
e. Otra vez he hecho una tortilla horrible, siempre le echo demasiada sal.

TRACK 25

El cine en español, y en especial el mexicano, tiene cada vez más presencia en los festivales y cines internacionales. Lee estos extractos de entrevistas al director Guillermo del Toro.

¿Cuándo supo que se quería dedicar al cine?
De niño crecí viendo películas de animación japonesas. Todas eran de monstruos japoneses y robots pilotados por humanos. Desde entonces quise contar historias a través de imágenes.

¿Cuándo comenzó?
Cuando estudiaba en el Instituto de Ciencias de Guadalajara comencé a filmar y a los 21 años filmé mi primera película. En esa época también fundé el Festival de Cine de Guadalajara.

¿Cuál es su especialidad?
La verdad es que no tengo ninguna. He filmado películas basadas en cómics, películas de terror, películas históricas, de fantasía, de ciencia ficción…

¿Cuáles son sus películas más importantes?
Sin duda, *El laberinto del fauno* y *El espinazo del diablo*.

¿Por qué?
Porque me dieron a conocer en muchos países. A partir de ese momento comencé a trabajar en proyectos más ambiciosos e interesantes. Esas dos películas son muy queridas por mí… Tienen una temática que me interesa: en ellas hablo de la niñez y de la política, y utilizo elementos fantásticos.

¿A qué otros directores mexicanos admira?
Admiro mucho a Luis Mandoqui porque tiene personalidad.

¿Dónde vive?
Ahora vivo en Los Ángeles, Estados Unidos. México es mi hogar pero Los Ángeles es la cuna del cine.

¿Qué proyectos futuros tiene?
Estoy estudiando una propuesta para desarrollar *El increíble Hulk*, una historia basada en los cómics de Marvel.

TRACK 26

Bernarda: Niña, dame un abanico.

Amelia: Tome usted.

Bernarda: ¿Es este el abanico que se da a una viuda? Dame uno negro y aprende a respetar el luto de tu padre.

Martirio: Tome usted el mío.

Bernarda: ¿Y tú?

Martirio: Yo no tengo calor.

Bernarda: Pues busca otro, que te hará falta. En ocho años que dure el luto no ha de entrar en esta casa el viento de la calle. Haceros cuenta que hemos tapiado con ladrillos puertas y ventanas. Así pasó en casa de mi padre y en casa de mi abuelo.

Yerma: ¡María! ¿Por qué pasas tan deprisa por mi puerta?

María: Cuando voy con el niño, lo hago… ¡Como siempre lloras…!

Yerma: Tienes razón.

María: Me da tristeza que tengas envidia.

Yerma: No es envidia lo que tengo; es pobreza.

María: No te quejes.

Yerma: ¡Cómo no me voy a quejar cuando te veo a ti y a las otras mujeres llenas por dentro de flores, y viéndome yo inútil en medio de tanta hermosura!

UNIDAD 4: ¡SUPERESPACIO!

TRACK 27

Lucía: Mira, Carla, las fotos que trae esta semana *SuperEspacio*. Hay una entrevista a Maxi Castro.

Carla: ¿Maxi Castro? ¡Ay!, Lucía, déjame ver… Yo estoy enamoradísima de ese actor… Es tan guapo y tan simpático.

Lucía: Mira… también viene un test para saber si conoces bien la vida de Maxi… Y si aciertas todas las preguntas, participas en el sorteo de un viaje a París, la ciudad del amor. ¿Podrías ayudarme?

Carla: Claro, yo conozco todos los secretos de la vida de Maxi. De todos modos, yo que tú primero leería la entrevista y después contestaría el test. Seguro que esa entrevista contiene mucha información.

Lucía: ¿Has visto que parece que Mario Medina y Mónica Pérez están juntos?

Carla: ¿Mónica Pérez es la actriz de la película *La soga*?

Lucía: Carla, deberías estar más informada… Es la actriz de la serie *Sombras*. Es la que hace el papel de mala.

Carla: Bueno, vale. También sale la cocinera esa de *Salud al día*, el programa de televisión… A mi madre le encanta y en casa nos lo pone todos los días.

Lucía: A mí no me saques de las hamburguesas y las papas fritas. Odio las verduras.

Carla: ¿En serio? No me lo puedo creer. Pues deberías comer más verdura. Es muy buena para la salud.

TRACK 28

Carlos: Maruchi, te veo todos los días en la tele y me encanta tu programa. Mi problema es que últimamente estoy engordando mucho, ¿tú qué harías para adelgazar?

Maruchi: Yo que tú comería con moderación y prepararía las comidas con aceite de oliva, preferentemente crudo. También disminuiría el consumo de azúcar y de sal.

Carlos: ¡Uf!… todo eso ya lo hago, pero engordo…

Maruchi: A lo mejor consumes más calorías de las que necesitas. En ese caso, yo en tu lugar, practicaría ejercicio diariamente.

Alicia: Hola, Maruchi, me encanta tu programa. Mira, mi problema es que últimamente me encuentro muy cansada y, a veces, me duele la cabeza. El médico dice que estoy sanísima, pero yo me siento sin energías, ¿podrías darme algunos consejos?

Maruchi: Alicia, querida, ¿seguro que te alimentas bien? En primer lugar, deberías incluir legumbres y frutos secos en tu dieta. Para el dolor de cabeza, yo que tú tomaría abundante cantidad de agua durante todo el día.

TRACK 29

a. aceite de girasol	**e.** aceite de oliva
b. berenjena	**f.** calabacín
c. espinacas	**g.** bizcocho
d. piña	**h.** garbanzos

i. cereza	**p.** magdalena
j. chorizo	**q.** mantequilla
k. carne picada	**r.** pechuga de pollo
l. guisantes	**s.** yogur natural / desnatado / con
m. kiwi	futas
n. lentejas	**t.** salchichón
ñ. chuleta de cerdo	**u.** bistec
o. frijoles	**v.** leche entera / desnatada

TRACK 30

a. Isabel: Sí, si eso lo sabemos todas las madres, pero, ¿qué harías si a tu hijo no le gusta el sabor de casi ninguna?

Maruchi: Entonces, amiga mía, deberías usar tu imaginación, hay muchas salsas que disimulan el sabor de los alimentos. ¿Has probado con el kétchup, la mayonesa o la mostaza con miel? A ellos les encanta…

b. Luz: Bueno, sería la primera vez que venía a la tele y le daría muchísima vergüenza, pero eso no significa que no te quiera conocer.

Benjamin: ¿Y tú qué harías entonces, Luz?

Luz: Mira, yo esperaría. Hemos tenido muchos casos de invitados que no vienen al primer programa y que después se lo piensan mejor y cambian de opinión.

c. Isabel: Eso quiere decir que casi empezaste a actuar antes que a hablar.

Maxi: ¡Ja! ¡ja! Sí, podríamos decir que sí.

Isabel: ¿Y no te cansa tener que ensayar y filmar durante tantas horas?

Maxi: Bueno, forma parte de mi trabajo, es verdad que es la parte menos divertida, pero creo que no sabría hacer otra cosa, provengo de una familia de actores y para mí la vida sin el cine es inimaginable.

Isabel: ¿Te importaría firmarme un autógrafo para mi hija?

Maxi: Sí, claro, cómo no.

Isabel: Es que si le digo que te he entrevistado y llego sin un autógrafo… ¡no entro en casa!

Maxi: ¡Ja, ja, ja!

d. Luz: Entonces… ¿podrías decirnos cuándo empezó esa bonita amistad?

Mónica: Mira, de verdad, es que no me gusta hablar de mi vida privada.

Luz: Pero entonces reconoces que Mario Medina formaría parte de tu vida privada…

Mónica: No, yo no he dicho eso, deberías limitarte a escribir lo que digo y no buscar dobles sentidos a mis palabras.

Luz: Bueno, no te enfades, pero piensa que los lectores quieren saber más de tu vida y, si realmente no hay nada serio entre ustedes, yo que tú lo dejaría claro de una vez.

TRACK 31

La comida mediterránea es típica de los países que rodean el mar Mediterráneo. España es uno de ellos. Pero, ¿esta dieta existe o es un mito?

«El clima es el factor más importante de la dieta mediterránea, ya que produce una serie de ingredientes típicos de esta gastronomía», dice el Doctor José Ordovas. Hay muchos platos típicos de los países mediterráneos que tienen ingredientes en común, como los vegetales, las aceitunas, el pescado, el marisco, las frutas, el aceite de oliva y algunos condimentos.

«Culturalmente, los países del Mediterráneo pueden ser muy distintos. Y, claro, su gastronomía también puede diferir, pero los ingredientes son los mismos», dice el doctor.

España es uno de estos países. Sin embargo, solo una parte del país está en el Mediterráneo y disfruta de este clima cálido. El norte de España, por ejemplo, tiene un clima más frío y lluvioso.

«En España, al hablar de los hábitos alimentarios, no se puede generalizar. El clima y la dieta varían mucho de norte a sur, o de este a oeste. En el norte se come marisco, pero también mucha carne y patatas. En el centro son típicos los guisos», asegura Mariona Coslada, nutricionista.

Además, la dieta está cambiando. Las familias ya no tienen tanto tiempo para cocinar y suelen preparar platos rápidos, a menudo no muy saludables.

Una encuesta reciente reveló que muchos jóvenes ahora prefieren la comida rápida, o comida basura, a la dieta mediterránea. «A mí me encanta la comida rápida, la verdad. Hamburguesas, papas fritas, aros de cebolla… », dice Mario Velázquez, un estudiante de 20 años.

TRACK 32

Los mayores solo probaron algunas lascas del pavo, pero no perdonaron el relleno que estaba elaborado con unas almendras que se deshacían y con unas ciruelas que parecían crecer de nuevo con la provocada segregación del paladar. Los garzones, un poco huidizos aún al refinamiento del soufflé, crecieron su gula habladora en torno al almohadón de la pechuga, donde comenzaron a lanzarse tan pronto el pavón dio un corto vuelo de la mesa de los mayores a la mesita de los niños, que cuanto más comían, más rápidamente querían ver al pavón todo plumado, con su pachorra en el corralón.

Al final de la comida, doña Augusta quiso mostrar una travesura en el postre. Presentó en las copas de champagne la más deliciosa crema helada. Después que la familia mostró su más rendido acatamiento al postre sorpresivo, doña Augusta regaló la receta: "Son las cosas sencillas, que podemos hacer en la cocina cubana, la repostería más fácil, y que enseguida el paladar declara incomparables. Un coco rallado en conserva, más otra conserva de piña rallada, unidas a la mitad de otra lata de leche condensada, y llega entonces el hada, es decir, la viejita Marie Brizard, para rociar con su anisete la crema olorosa. Al refrigerador, se sirve cuando está bien fría".

Luego la vamos saboreando, recibiendo los elogios de los otros comensales que piden con insistencia el bis, como cuando oímos alguna pavana de Lully.

Al mismo tiempo que se servía el postre, doña Augusta le indicó a Baldovina que trajese el frutero, donde mezclaban sus colores las manzanas, peras, mandarinas y uvas.

AHORA COMPRUEBA. REPASO UNIDADES 4-5

TRACK 33

1. He suspendido otra vez Matemáticas…, no sé cómo voy a aprobar esta asignatura, estudio un montón pero es que soy muy malo para los números.

2. ¡Qué horror! ¡¡¡Esta fotografía queda fatal!!! Se la ve desde muy lejos y borrosa, casi no se reconoce que es ella.

3. No sé qué hacer… Por un lado, quiero seguir con la tradición familiar de ser médico y no quitarles la ilusión a mis padres, pero por otro pienso que es mi futuro lo que está en juego y que a mí lo que me apasiona es el periodismo.

4. Estoy aburrida de hacer siempre lo mismo el fin de semana: o película o discoteca. ¿Es que a nadie se le ocurre algún plan más interesante?

5. Nunca conseguiré que me seleccionen para el papel, cuando estoy en el escenario se me olvida todo y no me salen ni las palabras.

6. No sé qué hacer para aprobar Historia: es demasiada información y no retengo nada.

TRACK 34

1. ≫ He suspendido otra vez Matemáticas…, no sé cómo voy a aprobar esta asignatura, estudio un montón pero es que soy muy malo para los números.
≫ No te preocupes, tu problema tiene solución. Es evidente que te esfuerzas, pero creo que no estás dando los pasos acertados. Yo en tu lugar buscaría un profesor particular.

2. ≫ ¡Qué horror! ¡Esta fotografía queda fatal! Se la ve desde muy lejos y borrosa, casi no se reconoce que es ella.
≫ ¿Y si le pedimos una suya? Es tan maja que seguro que nos da alguna.

3. ≫ No sé qué hacer… Por un lado, quiero seguir con la tradición familiar de ser médico y no quitarles la ilusión a mis padres, pero por otro pienso que es mi futuro lo que está en juego y que a mí lo que me apasiona es el periodismo.
≫ ¿Por qué no hablas sinceramente con ellos? Seguro que te entenderán.

4. ≫ Estoy aburrida de hacer siempre lo mismo el fin de semana: o película o discoteca. ¿Es que a nadie se le ocurre algún plan más interesante?
≫ ¿Por qué no echas un vistazo a las sugerencias para el finde de la revista? Proponen un montón de planes alternativos: desde rutas turísticas por la ciudad, hasta intercambios de idiomas, excursiones a la sierra… Seguro que encuentras algo interesante.

5. ≫ Nunca conseguiré que me seleccionen para el papel, cuando estoy en el escenario se me olvida todo y no me salen ni las palabras.
≫ Eso se llama pánico escénico. Yo que tú intentaría aprender algunas técnicas de relajación y centraría mis esfuerzos en prepararme bien el guion.

6. ≫ No sé qué hacer para aprobar Historia: es demasiada información y no retengo nada.
≫ Deberías organizarte, estudiar un poco todos los días y hacerte resúmenes y esquemas, porque si lo dejas todo para antes del examen, te agobiarás más.

UNIDAD 5: ¡OJALÁ!

TRACK 35

Irene: ¡Hola, Paula! Oye, ¿has hablado ya con Ana? Es que esta mañana me ha dicho que quiere que vayamos este verano a la casa que tienen sus tíos en la Costa Brava, y que si queremos podemos pasar todo el mes de julio allí. Ellos ya no van nunca y la casa está vacía.

Paula: Sí, precisamente te llamo por eso. Es que me han ofrecido la posibilidad de ir a Guatemala para ayudar a construir un colegio. Así que yo no podré ir con ustedes.

I.: ¡Qué me dices! Eso es estupendo, Paula. ¿Y vas tú sola?

P.: Bueno, voy a través de una ONG que se llama *Ayuda en Acción*. La verdad es que no conozco mucho a la gente pero, antes de irnos, nos van a dar un curso durante dos semanas para saber lo que tenemos que hacer allí, conocer la situación, su cultura… y también para que nos conozcamos entre nosotros. ¡Vamos a estar un mes conviviendo y trabajando! Espero llevarme bien con todos.

I.: Ya verás como sí. ¿Y cuándo te vas?

P.: En cuanto terminemos las clases. De hecho, el avión sale el mismo día por la noche.

¡Ay, Irene! Son doce horas de avión y ¡odio volar! ¡Ojalá me quede dormida pronto en el avión!

I.: ¡Uf! ¡Doce horas! Bueno, tú llévate el libro que nos ha recomendado el profesor de Filosofía y seguro que te duermes enseguida. Yo lo intenté empezar el otro día pero, en cuanto lo abrí, me quedé dormida. Oye, ahora en serio, me parece genial tu idea de ir a Guatemala, creo que va a ser toda una experiencia y te deseo de todo corazón que te vaya muy bien y ojalá tu esfuerzo sirva para que esos niños puedan vivir mejor.

P.: Muchas gracias. Ya te contaré cuando vuelva. ¡Ah! y yo también espero que se lo pasen muy bien en la Costa Brava. Dense un bañito en la playa por mí.

I.: ¡Eso seguro! Pero, bueno, nos veremos antes de que te vayas para despedirnos, ¿no?

P.: ¡Claro! ¡Faltaría más!

TRACK 36

a. Jorge: ¡Oh! ¡Qué colgante tan bonito!
   Ruth: Gracias, me lo ha regalado Marina. Dice que si me lo pongo cuando haga el examen de Química, me dará suerte.
   Jorge: Uf… yo no creo en esas supersticiones. Lo que tienes que hacer es estudiar antes de hacer el examen.

b. Alicia: ¡Que tengas buen viaje, cariño! ¡No te olvides de llamarme al llegar al hotel!
   Diego: Descuida. Te llamaré en cuanto llegue.
   Alicia: Eso espero, porque la última vez no me llamaste.
   Diego: ¡Cómo que no! Sí te llamé.
   Alicia: Sí, me llamaste, pero tres días después de llegar.
   Diego: No, también te llamé antes, pero no contestaste. De todas formas, no te preocupes, esta vez no dejaré de llamarte hasta que me contestes.

TRACK 37

≫ Pedro, vamos a pedir unas pizzas para cenar y a ver una película, ¿te unes?

≫ ¡Uf!, qué va, me voy a la cama, estoy supercansado y, además, mañana tengo un examen y me quiero levantar pronto para repasar.

≫ Bueno, pues que descanses.

Madre: ¡Hola, Daniel! ¿Qué tal las clases?
Daniel: Bien, bien, mamá. Ha venido Carlos para que le deje unos apuntes.
Madre: Vale, pero no tarden mucho que la comida está ya lista.
Carlos: Hola, señora Carmen. Ummm, ¡qué bien huele!
Madre: Hola, Carlos. ¿Te quieres quedar a comer?

Carlos: No, gracias, que mi madre también me estará esperando.
Daniel: Toma, Carlos, aquí están.
Carlos: Bueno, gracias, nos vemos luego. Adiós, señora Carmen, y que aproveche.

Hija: Adiós, mamá, me voy a clase.
Madre: Pero si todavía es muy pronto, ¿no?
Hija: Sí, pero es que hoy tenemos una presentación y hemos quedado un rato antes para organizarnos.
Madre: Bueno, pues que te vaya bien.
Hija: Gracias, mamá. Adiós.

≫ ¡Cómo me duele la cabeza!

≫ ¿Te has tomado algo?

≫ Sí, unas pastillas que me recomendó el médico, pero, por ahora, no me han hecho nada…

≫ ¡Vaya! Bueno… me tengo que ir, que te mejores.

≫ ¡Hola, Irene! Te llamo para despedirme.

≫ ¡Ay! Hola, Pedro.

≫ ¿Qué?, ¿ya tienes todo preparado?

≫ Sí, más o menos, solo me falta poner unas cosas en la maleta y ¡poder cerrarla!

≫ Las chicas, siempre igual. Seguro que te llevas media casa para solo dos semanas… Oye, ¿cuándo sale el avión?

≫ A las 7. Ahora cuando venga mi padre, me lleva al aeropuerto.

≫ Bueno, pues un beso y ¡que te diviertas!

María: Mira, por ahí viene Lucas, pobrecillo, está muy triste porque acaba de morir su perro.
Lucas: Hola, chicos.
Álex: Hola, Lucas, oye, que María me acaba de contar lo de Toby, lo siento mucho.
Lucas: Gracias, Álex.

≫ ¡Chicos! ¡Me han admitido en el conservatorio! ¡No me lo puedo creer!

≫ Bueno, ¡felicidades! ¡Esto hay que celebrarlo por todo lo alto!

≫ ¡Enhorabuena! ¿Lo ves? ¡Si es que eres la mejor!

≫ Bueno, aprende mucho inglés y aprovecha tu año en Michigan, pero no te olvides de nosotros. Cuelga muchas fotos y conéctate al Facebook, anda.

≫ Claro, eso seguro. Además, hasta que no empiece a conocer a gente me voy a sentir muy sola.

≫ Te voy a echar mucho de menos, sobre todo de camino la escuela.

≫ Yo también. Bueno, ya tengo que entrar. ¡Adiós!

≫ Adiós y ¡cuídate!

TRACK 38

guion, bonsái, autor, filosofía, huésped, océano, crucial, habláis, veintiún, acuático, raíz, dehesa.

TRACK 39

Cada vez hay más gente joven que prefiere hacer un voluntariado en el extranjero a ir directamente a la universidad. Ryan, un chico norteamericano, habla de su experiencia.

«Ser voluntario es genial. Mi vida cambió completamente después de pasar un mes en Guatemala», dice Ryan, un muchacho norteamericano de 16 años que viajó al país centroamericano en 2013. «Cuando llegué a Antigua, hablaba muy poco español. Pero una familia me recibió en su casa y hablando con ellos mi español mejoró rápidamente», cuenta. «Después de estar un mes con ellos, me siento parte de la familia. Ojalá pueda verlos pronto otra vez».

«Mis tareas en Antigua eran ayudar a construir casas en un barrio nuevo», explica Ryan. «Allí había también otros voluntarios internacionales. Hice amistad con una muchacha española, Ainhoa, que ya está de vuelta en Madrid. Espero que sigamos en contacto por correo electrónico y Skype».

«Como tenía las tardes libres, me invitaron a dar clases de inglés a la escuela del barrio», dice. «Me tocó una clase de muchachos de ocho años y hablamos muchísimo. Me hicieron preguntas sobre la vida en Illinois, donde yo vivo. También me enseñaron trabalenguas en español, ¡aunque son dificilísimos!», cuenta Ryan. «Me gustaría que vinieran a visitarme».

Además de pasar tiempo con los niños, Ryan recorrió las antiguas ciudades mayas y los parques naturales. «También participé en las fiestas de la Semana Santa, haciendo alfombras enormes de aserrín y flores», dice.

TRACK 40

[…]
Yo vivía en un barrio
de Madrid, con campanas,
con relojes, con árboles.
Desde allí se veía
el rostro seco de Castilla
como un océano de cuero.
Mi casa era llamada
la casa de las flores, porque por todas partes
estallaban geranios: era
una bella casa
con perros y chiquillos.
[…]

Y una mañana todo estaba ardiendo
y una mañana las hogueras
salían de la tierra
devorando seres,
y desde entonces fuego,
pólvora desde entonces,
y desde entonces sangre.
[…]
Preguntaréis por qué su poesía
no nos habla del sueño, de las hojas,
de los grandes volcanes de su país natal.

TRACK 41

Cuando yo muera quiero tus manos en mis ojos:
quiero la luz y el trigo de tus manos amadas
pasar una vez más sobre mí su frescura:
sentir la suavidad que cambió mi destino.
Quiero que vivas mientras yo, dormido, te espero,
quiero que tus oídos sigan oyendo el viento,
que huelas el aroma del mar que amamos juntos
y que sigas pisando la arena que pisamos.
Quiero que lo que amo siga vivo
y a ti te amé y canté sobre todas las cosas,
por eso sigue tú floreciendo, florida,
para que alcances todo lo que mi amor te ordena,
para que se pasee mi sombra por tu pelo,
para que así conozcan la razón de mi canto.

UNIDAD 6: ¡HOY ME SIENTO BIEN!

TRACK 42

Raquel: ¡Antonia! ¡Antoooonia!
Antonia: ¡Ay! Hola, Raquel, no te había visto.
R.: ¿Cómo me vas a ver con lo distraída que vas?
A.: Es que estaba pensando en una canción que me encanta y…
R.: ¿Qué canción?
A.: La nueva de *Nerea*, ¿la has escuchado?
R.: Sí, está bien, ella tiene una voz espectacular, pero… es demasiado romántica, ¿no? Bueno, para ti es perfecta porque con lo enamorada que estás últimamente…
A.: Para nada, ¿pero qué dices?
R.: ¿Que no? Pero si se te nota de lejos que estás loca por Adrián. Cada vez que lo ves, pones una cara de tonta…
A.: Ok, ok, lo que tú digas. Por cierto, compuse un tema nuevo para el concierto.
R.: ¡Súper! Oye, mira quién viene por ahí, tu inspiración.
A.: ¡Ay, caray, qué vergüenza! Tú ahora no te vayas y no me dejes sola. Es que cuando estoy con él no sé qué me pasa que nunca sé qué decirle y me da rabia que piense que soy una tonta…
R.: Pues dile, por ejemplo, que le has escrito una canción y que quieres que vaya a nuestro concierto. Seguro que cuando te oiga dedicándole "su" canción subida a un escenario, se queda con la boca abierta.
A.: ¿Qué dices? No me atrevo… ¿Por qué no se lo dices tú?
R.: ¿Yooo? ¡Pero si a mí no me gusta!

A.: ¡Ay! ¡Qué nervios! Ya viene y me está mirando…
R.: Sí, y acaba de tocar el timbre para entrar en clase. Así que mejor dejas tu declaración de amor para otro momento, que cuando nos vea el profe hablando en la puerta…
A.: Sí, mejor entramos. Por cierto, ¿tienes los apuntes del otro día? Es que no estuve muy atenta.
R.: Sí, vamos, y a ver si hoy escuchas más al profe y compones menos.
A.: Bueno, es que la inspiración llega cuando menos te lo esperas.

TRACK 43

≫ Pero, ¿qué te pasa? Desde que llegaste, estás muy serio…
≫ Es que estoy preocupado por el examen de mañana. He estudiado mucho, pero ahora creo que estoy hecho un lío y no entiendo nada.
≫ Bueno, eso es normal, yo también me pongo nervioso antes de un examen.
≫ Mira, hazte un té y acuéstate temprano, ya verás como mañana, después de descansar, estás más tranquilo y te acuerdas de todo.

TRACK 44

a. inflexible; **b.** desordenado; **c.** maleducada; **d.** despreocupada, tranquila; **e.** irresponsable; **f.** intolerante; **g.** débil; **h.** intranquilo, nervioso; **i.** impuntual; **j.** insociable; **k.** pesimista; **l.** abierto, extrovertido; **m.** vaga; **n.** inseguro; **ñ.** impaciente.

TRACK 45

a. acueducto; b. estatua; c. museo; d. escultura; e. galería de arte; f. retrato; g. pintura; h. guitarrista; i. guitarra; j. músico; k. violín; l. actuar; m. poeta; n. poema; ñ. orquesta.

TRACK 46

Esther: Bueno, cuenta, cuenta… ¿Qué tal la reunión?

Blanca: ¡Buah!, genial. Nos lo pasamos superbién. Qué pena que no pudiste venir.

Esther: Ya… Bueno, ¿y quién fue?

Blanca: Pues prácticamente todos. Bueno, menos tú, Antonio y alguno más.

Esther: Y Antonio, ¿por qué no fue?

Blanca: Pues es que ya no vive aquí. Parece que dejó de estudiar y se fue a Toronto. Al principio se puso a trabajar en un restaurante, pero después, volvió a estudiar y se hizo profesor de español allí.

Esther: ¿Profesor de español? Pero si él quería ser abogado, ¿no?

Blanca: Sí, pero todos dicen que está encantado con su nueva profesión.

Esther: ¡Qué bien! Oye, ¿viste a Gustavo, ¿sigue siendo tan guapo como en el colegio?

Blanca: ¡Que va, hija! Si lo ves, no lo reconoces.

Esther: ¿Y eso?

Blanca: Pues nos contó que tuvo una lesión y dejó de hacer deporte, así que está más gordo y, además, está casi calvo.

Esther: ¡No me digas! Con lo guapo que era…

Blanca: Eso sí, sigue siendo tan simpático como siempre, fue la alegría de la fiesta. ¡Ah! y ¿sabes? Se ha casado y acaba de tener un niño.

Esther: ¡Qué bien! Me alegro por él.

Blanca: ¡Ah!, pero, ¿sabes quién sí se ha puesto guapísimo?

Esther: ¿Quién?

Blanca: Martín.

Esther: ¡¡Martín!?

Blanca: Sí, chica, Martín… Se ve que él no ha dejado de hacer deporte. Cuando lo vimos, ¡nos quedamos con la boca abierta! ¡Qué guapo!

Esther: Bueno, ¿y él está casado?

Blanca: Casado no, pero tiene novia. Nos contó muchas cosas. Se ha vuelto mucho más sociable y hablador que en la escuela.

Esther: Vaya… ¡Ah! ¿Y Carolina?

Blanca: Bueno, ella también ha cambiado mucho.

Esther: ¿Sí?

Blanca: A ver, está tan guapa como antes, lo que pasa es que se fue unos años al Tíbet y se hizo budista. Ahora trabaja para una organización humanitaria y, claro, dejó de ser una esclava de la moda como antes.

Esther: Pues si ella quería ser modelo…

Blanca: Sí, sí, se hizo modelo. Estuvo trabajando en Nueva York y todo, pero le cansó ese mundo y decidió cambiar de vida de forma radical.

Esther: ¡Qué interesante…! Oye, ¿y fue Elena?

Blanca: ¡Claro!

Esther: ¿Sigue saliendo con Dani?

Blanca: Qué va, rompieron hace un año. Elena me contó que Dani empezó a trabajar por las noches en una discoteca y que cambió mucho, que se volvió más irresponsable y despreocupado y que al final rompieron. Creo que él se ha hecho empresario y tiene varias discotecas.

Esther: ¿Sí? No me lo imagino, pero…, y Elena, ¿cómo está?

Blanca: Ella muy bien. Me contó que empezó a llevar un estilo de vida más saludable y se hizo vegetariana y que, a partir de entonces, se quedó más delgada y se ha puesto muy guapa.

Esther: Qué bien, oye y…

TRACK 47

Conversación 1

≫ Has estado hoy en clase con Juan, ¿no? ¿Le has dicho que hemos quedado en el café de la esquina?

≫ No, no ha venido, ha vuelto a faltar. Se lo diré después en la biblioteca.

Conversación 2

≫ Perdona, me quiero probar estos jeans en la talla 30, esta camiseta y este jersey, pero en verde.

≫ A ver… Es que camisetas solo nos quedan en la talla grande y los jeans no nos quedan en ninguna talla, acaban de llevarse los últimos. El jersey aquí lo tienes y resulta que es el último que hay en la tienda.

TRACK 48

Atención a todos los alumnos. Recuerden que el 19 de abril nuestra escuela celebrará, en colaboración con la editorial Edinumen, su tradicional concurso para jóvenes escritores. Las bases del concurso, que estarán colgadas tanto en los tablones informativos del centro como en nuestro portal de Internet, son las siguientes: podrán participar todos los alumnos de la escuela, solo se admitirán trabajos en la modalidad de cuento, el tema será libre y las composiciones deberán ir firmadas con un pseudónimo.

Además, los trabajos deberán introducirse en un sobre grande que estará disponible en la oficina principal del centro y se entregará al Departamento de Lengua y Literatura. El plazo de presentación de los trabajos finalizará el día 19 de marzo, un mes antes de la votación del jurado, que dará a conocer el nombre del ganador y de los finalistas del concurso el mismo día de la celebración. Además de la entrega de premios, se realizarán actividades como la lectura de fragmentos de las obras participantes y diferentes talleres de creación literaria impartidos por miembros de la editorial.

TRACK 49

escáner, boutique, máster, stock, marketing, ranking, espaguetis, estatus, yogur, playback, espray, software, ballet, pádel, blus, cruasán.

TRACK 50

En el mundo hispano hay muchísimos tipos de música y baile. No solamente son expresiones artísticas: a veces, como los corridos mexicanos, son una forma de contar historias de actualidad.

Los corridos son canciones populares mexicanas que cuentan una historia. La melodía suele ser muy sencilla, y la letra es fácil de recordar. Eran habituales ya en 1910, en la época de la Revolución mexicana, y cumplían la importante función de diseminar las noticias en todo el territorio.

Los temas de los corridos son variados: a veces hablan sobre un héroe popular, a veces son divertidos, y otras tienen contenido político. Muchas veces, las bandas de mariachis cantan corridos.

Desde 1930, el contenido de los corridos incorpora noticias relacionadas con el narcotráfico. En los últimos años, este género se ha hecho más popular, especialmente en los estados del norte del país como Chihuahua, Nuevo León, Baja California y Sinaloa, donde se concentra la violencia del narcotráfico.

En muchos estados, está prohibido reproducir narcocorridos en conciertos, discotecas y bares. «Este tipo de canciones presenta a los narcotraficantes con glamur», dicen las autoridades.

En la actualidad, los Tigres del Norte son una banda muy famosa de música norteña, que incluye los corridos. Son conocidos internacionalmente y han ganado cinco premios Grammy. Sin embargo, varios pueblos les han puesto multas por cantar narcocorridos en sus conciertos. «La prohibición no es justa, estas canciones son parte de la cultura actual», dicen.

TRACK 51

Platero es pequeño, peludo, suave; tan blando por fuera, que se diría todo de algodón, que no lleva huesos. Solo los espejos de azabache de sus ojos son duros cual dos escarabajos de cristal negro.

Lo dejo suelto y se va al prado, y acaricia tibiamente con su hocico, rozándolas apenas, las florecillas rosas, celestes y gualdas…: Lo llamo dulcemente: "¿Platero?", y viene a mí con un trotecillo alegre que parece que se ríe, en no sé qué cascabeleo ideal…

Come cuanto le doy. Le gustan las naranjas mandarinas, las uvas moscateles, todas de ámbar; los higos morados, con su cristalina gotita de miel…

Es tierno y mimoso igual que un niño, que una niña…; pero fuerte y seco por dentro, como una piedra… Cuando paso sobre él, los domingos, por las últimas callejas del pueblo, los hombres del campo, vestidos de limpio y despaciosos, se quedan mirándolo:

- "Tien' asero

Tiene acero. Acero y plata de luna, al mismo tiempo.

AHORA COMPRUEBA. REPASO UNIDADES 5-6

TRACK 52

Abel: ¡Oye, Carlos! ¿Te apetece ir este sábado al concierto de Huecco con Raquel y conmigo?

Carlos: Uf, no sé, es que a mí los conciertos no me gustan mucho. Odio que la gente empiece a cantar, ahí, gritando… Prefiero oír el disco tranquilamente en mi casa.

Abel: ¡Hombre, pero no es lo mismo! A mí no me importa que la gente cante. Lo que sí me molesta es que la gente me pise y me empuje, pero los concierto son así. Además, es un concierto benéfico, y ya sabes que a Raquel le encanta todo lo relacionado con las ONG, así que le hace mucha ilusión que vayamos.

Carlos: ¿Y para qué ONG es?

Abel: No lo sé muy bien, solo sé que es para recaudar fondos para fabricar unos balones que producen electricidad y llevarlos después a los países pobres.

Carlos: ¿¿Qué?! ¿Un balón que produce electricidad?

Abel: Sí, es un balón que dentro tiene una batería. Al jugar con él, el movimiento del balón produce energía y esta energía se guarda dentro de la batería. Después puedes enchufar cualquier tipo de aparato y ¡ya funciona!

Carlos: ¿En serio? Entonces el balón funciona como una batería, ¿no?

Abel: Exactamente.

Carlos: Pero tendrás que jugar durante mucho rato para que produzca energía, ¿no?

Abel: No, con 15 minutos es suficiente para tener unas cuantas horas de luz.

Carlos: ¿Y este balón se puede comprar en las tiendas?

Abel: Todavía no, porque lo han inventado unas estudiantes americanas y necesitan dinero para poder fabricarlo. Yo, en cuanto esté en las tiendas, me compro uno; porque además de ayudar a la gente, la verdad es que es algo muy práctico.

Carlos: ¡Qué buena idea! Ojalá inventen más aparatos como estos. ¿Te imaginas? ¡Podríamos tener energía gratis!

Abel: Sí, esta idea es genial, porque no solo van a ayudar a personas sino que además es bueno para el medioambiente… y para que la gente haga deporte.

Carlos: Estoy completamente de acuerdo contigo. Espero que este proyecto tenga mucho éxito y ojalá Huecco venda muchos discos para que gane mucho dinero y se puedan fabricar muchos balones.

Abel: Bueno, entonces, ¿vienes al concierto?

Carlos: Pues mira, sí, ¡todo sea por una buena causa!

TRACK 53

Buenos días, queridos radioyentes. Hoy tenemos el placer de hablarles de un gran proyecto solidario que conseguirá que familias de todo el mundo puedan tener luz eléctrica en sus hogares.

El proyecto, *Dame vida*, cuenta con la colaboración de numerosos rostros famosos del mundo del deporte como nuestro querido bicampeón del baloncesto de la NBA con Los Ángeles Lakers, quien declaró que los deportistas, además de ganar partidos, tienen otra obligación más allá del deporte que es la de ayudar y colaborar con los que más lo necesitan. Por eso, los deportistas, admirados por tantos jóvenes, deben dar ejemplo con acciones solidarias como la de este fantástico balón. Por su parte, una de las inventoras del *soccket*, nos confesó que, cuando recibió la llamada del cantante y le propuso colaborar con su invento, fue tal su sorpresa que tardó unos minutos en reaccionar, claro que después contestó que sí inmediatamente.

Pero *Dame vida* no es solo el nombre de este fantástico proyecto, es también una fundación que colabora en otros proyectos sociales como, por ejemplo, el de la *lucha contra la violencia de género*, donde llevan una activa labor en contra de los malos tratos y diversos programas de integración social. Un joven madrileño de 23 años nos contaba que, por desgracia, este es un tema del que se habla casi todos los días en las noticias y que tenemos que ayudar a estas personas para que recuperen su vida anterior lo antes posible.

Otro de los proyectos en los que trabaja es el de la *Ayuda a Haití*, donde tanto queda por hacer a pesar de haber pasado ya varios años desde aquel terrible terremoto que conmocionó al mundo.

Claro que no podíamos cerrar este programa sin acordarnos de los principales protagonistas de estos proyectos, aquellos para los que su vida sería todavía mucho más difícil sin la acción solidaria de personas como Huecco.

Nos referimos a personitas como esta niña de 11 años, que nos contaba que después del terremoto estaba muy triste, porque este destruyó su casa y también su escuela, pero que ahora, gracias a la ayuda de personas buenas, ha podido volver a estudiar.

O el testimonio de un chico de 13 años, quien nos contaba que todos están muy contentos en su pueblo porque haciendo deporte, lo que más les gusta, pueden ayudar en casa para tener luz por las noches.

UNIDAD 7: ¡QUE NO TE ENGAÑEN!

TRACK 54

Andrés: ¿Qué les parece el cartel de la campaña? ¡Es una obra de arte!

Nélida: Yo creo que es increíble que esté en un centro comercial, ¿no les parece?

Germán: Pues yo no pienso que sea para tanto. Solo es más publicidad, ¿no?

Silvia: Es terrible que intenten confundirnos. ¿El cartel significa que no compremos? ¡Puf!… No lo entiendo y no me gusta. Por cierto, ¡qué es Adbusters?

A.: ¡¿No los conoces!? Es una organización anticonsumista que ataca a los medios de comunicación. Su objetivo es utilizar la publicidad para criticar la manipulación que esta hace sobre la sociedad. También tienen una revista.

S.: Bueno, en mi opinión, la publicidad trata de informar a un público objetivo sobre lo que hay.

N.: Sí, estoy de acuerdo con que trata de informar, pero para cambiar nuestras opiniones y deseos, ¡claro!

A.: Por supuesto, la publicidad lleva muchos años vendiéndonos el mensaje de la juventud, de la salud, de la virilidad, de la feminidad… La imagen siempre es la misma: jóvenes, ricos y guapos.

G.: Lo que quiere, desde luego, es provocar. Y tienes razón, a veces incorrectamente, y es racista, sexista, e incluso machista.

N.: ¡Ya lo creo! ¿Y qué pasa con la protección de los jóvenes, con el derecho a la intimidad, y con el respeto?

S.: ¡Claro, claro! ¿Y con la libertad de expresión? Pero, de acuerdo, está claro que debe haber límites. En cualquier caso, creo que la gente no le hace tanto caso a la publicidad, hay demasiada: en la calle, en la tele, en los periódicos, en las revistas, en Internet…

A.: ¡Uf! Sí, es ridículo que las redes sociales estén tan llenas de anuncios, no es lo que vas a ver allí. Me preocupa que utilicen nuestra información personal para vender. Y en muchas páginas te atacan las ventanas emergentes que se te abren todo el tiempo.

S.: Pues, a mi modo de ver, no pienso que toda la publicidad sea mala y, como dijiste antes, es arte, creación… Son iconos de nuestra cultura, por ejemplo, mira algunas obras de Andy Warhol.

G.: En esto todos estamos de acuerdo, siempre hay cosas bien hechas.

TRACK 55

a. ≫ Me encanta el anuncio del perfume FreeMan.

≫ Es increíble que tú digas eso. Hace unos días le decías a Elena que odiabas las marcas y mencionaste precisamente FreeMan.

≫ Bueno, lo que pasa es que Elena me gusta un montón…

≫ No, si está claro que tú por Elena haces lo que sea, pero me parece un poco triste que tengas que mentir para impresionarla.

b. ≫ Me parece fatal que en la publicidad se muestre una imagen tan poco real de los jóvenes: todos frívolos y de fiesta continua.

≫ Tienes razón, y… ¡¿qué me dices de las muchachas?! Es ridículo que nos reduzcan a una cara o a un cuerpo. Y casi siempre anoréxico. ¡Qué triste!

≫ ¡Ya lo creo! ¿A quién le gusta eso?

≫ Pues no sé, la verdad, pero es preocupante que nadie haga nada por cambiarlo, es una mala influencia para los más jóvenes.

TRACK 56

En la actualidad, *Yahoo* y *Google* tienen un sistema propio de publicidad en Internet. Los enlaces a las páginas web de las empresas se colocan en los buscadores y por cada *clic* del usuario la empresa paga un precio al buscador; por eso, el uso de estas páginas es gratis para los usuarios. El entrar y hacer clic en los enlaces supone publicidad para la empresa y dinero para el buscador. Como segundo sistema tienen los anuncios de textos. Estos consisten en un pequeño recuadro, con un título del producto o empresa, un texto corto de descripción, y la dirección web con enlace a la página. Puede aparecer tanto en las barras a los lados, como en la superior e inferior de la web. Por lo tanto, la publicidad en Internet está en los *clics* que realiza el usuario y la información de imagen y texto que recibe.

Existen otros muchos fenómenos que se suelen aprovechar, por ejemplo, el blog o la bitácora, páginas en las que se publica desde un diario hasta artículos sobre cualquier tema de interés para su autor o autores. A veces permiten conversaciones a través de comentarios entre los lectores y el autor. Aquí aparecen a menudo anuncios Google, banners, botones y logos, que llevan a la página en promoción. Por lo tanto, la publicidad en Internet puede existir en todo sitio. En los últimos años, las grandes protagonistas han sido las redes genéricas, tipo Facebook, en las que el usuario comparte todo tipo de información con sus contactos, y sin ser muy conscientes, con las compañías que utilizan y acceden a estos datos para generar su publicidad en estas mismas páginas.

Internet es un gran mundo lleno de posibilidades para todos, y para la publicidad es barato, atractivo, fácil y con un alcance extraordinario. Si nos molesta, tenemos que recordar que nos permite acceder a muchos servicios e información gratis.

TRACK 57

La campaña *City Cup* de Nike fue más que un anuncio publicitario; logró comunicarse con los jóvenes apasionados del fútbol de México D.F., poniéndolos a competir en un torneo para que defendieran la bandera de su barrio. Así, Nike alcanzó el 9% de conocimiento de marca y se convirtió en uno de los 13 monstruos de la mercadotecnia de la revista *Expansión* en 2011.

El vídeo que Nike subió a YouTube para promocionar su torneo *City Cup* mostraba, en un primer momento, a un par de adolescentes que jugaban en la calle y entonces uno de ellos decía: "El fútbol es diversión, juegues donde juegues".

A través de las redes sociales, convocaron a los chicos del D.F. a participar en el torneo y defender a su barrio. En tres días reclutaron a 4.000 jóvenes de entre 16 y 19 años. La razón de hacer una campaña con enfoque digital era obvia, pues Nike es la marca de productos de consumo en México con más seguidores en Facebook, casi 811.000.

Como los adolescentes son leales a su barrio, se crearon 32 mascotas inspiradas en la cultura prehispánica que representaban las 32 casas en que fue dividido el México D.F. para esta competición. Además de los contenidos en redes sociales, el *branding* de calle, por medio de las mascotas oficiales del torneo, apareció en grafiti sobre 144 m² de muros y en 32.000 plantillas plasmadas sobre bancos, bases de postes de luz y en estaciones de autobuses en todo México. "El joven encontró identidad inmediata con una marca global que le rinde tributo directamente a su cuadra", comenta Reynoso, publicista de la campaña. La mejor estrategia para destacar es volverse parte de la vida del consumidor, y Nike llegó hasta la puerta de su casa.

El *mix* de medios incluye mercadotecnia de calle y redes sociales. No solo fue digital, sino que hubo un torneo detrás. "Lo interesante es que lo *online* se fue a lo *offline*, es decir, al mundo real, para intensificar la experiencia de la marca", dice Reynoso.

TRACK 58

PIB, Adena, A-De-Ene, TIC, Varios Autores, UNAM, Ce De, Efe-Eme-i, FIFA, Pyme, Número, VIP, señor, Banxico, Láser, Juegos Olímpicos, Ene-Be-A, Ge-pe-ese, De-Uve-de.

TRACK 59

Muchos famosos usan su imagen y su éxito para vender productos. Pero… ¿funciona esta estrategia en España? ¡Lee para saberlo!

Lionel Messi es uno de los futbolistas más famosos del mundo. Su fortuna asciende a 172 millones de dólares. Pero hoy, Lionel está concentrado en convencerte: quiere que compres la tableta de una famosa marca. Para eso, participa en un video usando el producto. La idea es que, cuando lo veas, te imagines viviendo la glamurosa vida de una estrella de fútbol internacional.

Shakira también quiere que compres algo, y no es solamente la entrada a su último concierto. La cantante colombiana pone su sonrisa para vender pasta de dientes en videos y publicidades en revistas y periódicos.

Ellos no son los únicos que usan su imagen para comercializar productos: Jennifer López vende celulares, Salma Hayek vende champú y Antonio Banderas vende perfume en publicidades y eventos.

Aunque parezca una receta infalible, en la mayoría de los casos la cara de un famoso deportista o artista no es suficiente para convencer al consumidor. En España, solamente el 5% de la gente compraría un producto porque un actor o cantante hace la publicidad. Los deportistas son, al parecer, más efectivos: el 8% de las personas consultadas en una encuesta de la empresa Nielsen compraría un producto porque lo recomienda un atleta.

TRACK 60

Piensa en esto: cuando te regalan un reloj te regalan un pequeño infierno florido, una cadena de rosas, un calabozo de aire. No te dan solamente el reloj, que los cumplas muy felices y esperamos que te dure porque es de buena marca, suizo con áncora de rubíes; no te lo regalan solamente ese menudo picapedrero que te atarás a la muñeca y pasearás contigo. Te regalan –no lo saben, lo terrible es que no lo saben–, te regalan un nuevo pedazo frágil y precario de ti mismo, algo que es tuyo pero no es tu cuerpo, que hay que atar a tu cuerpo con su correa como un bracito desesperado colgándose de tu muñeca. Te regalan la necesidad de darle cuerda todos los días, la obligación de darle cuerda para que siga siendo un reloj; te regalan la obsesión de atender a la hora exacta en las vitrinas de las joyerías, en el anuncio por la radio, en el servicio telefónico. Te regalan el miedo a perderlo, de que te lo roben, de que se te caiga al suelo y se rompa. Te regalan su marca, y la seguridad de que es una marca mejor que las otras, te regalan la tendencia de comparar tu reloj con los demás relojes. No te regalan un reloj, tú eres el regalado, a ti te ofrecen para el cumpleaños del reloj.

UNIDAD 8: ¿SUEÑO O REALIDAD?

TRACK 61

Daniela: No sé qué libro comprarle a Felipe para su cumpleaños, ¡estoy hecha bolas!

José: La verdad es que es bastante complicado, tienes razón.

D.: Creo que finalmente voy a regalarle uno de estos dos, pero no sé por cuál decidirme. Son muy diferentes.

J.: Me parece que a Felipe le gusta leer novelas. Pero quizás no le guste *El Quijote*, es un poco antiguo para él.

D.: Es verdad que es un poco antiguo, pero Felipe lee toda clase de libros. En su casa tiene una colección enorme de novelas de todas las épocas. Es increíble que a un muchacho de 17 años le guste tanto leer.

J.: ¿Y sabes si también lee cómics? A lo mejor el libro de Mafalda es un poquito infantil.

D.: ¿Infantil? Todo lo contrario. En mi opinión deberían leerlo los adultos, es un poco filosófico. En estas historietas aparece una niña preocupada por la paz del mundo y por la humanidad. Yo, cuando era pequeña, tenía un montón de libros de Mafalda, pero no los entendí del todo hasta que no fui adulta.

J.: Pues quizás sea esa una buena opción. Me parece que es más atractivo y más original como regalo.

D.: Pues ya está decidido. ¡Me lo llevo! Le voy a decir al dependiente que me lo envuelva. Oye, ¿y tú qué le vas a comprar?

J.: Ni idea, voy a darme una vuelta por aquí a ver si encuentro algo.

TRACK 62

Marta: Elena me ha dicho que se va a cambiar de casa. Que está muy contenta porque ayer encontró trabajo.

Pedro: Vaya, qué suerte.

M.: Me ha confesado que realmente no está enamorada de su novio y que quiere dejarlo.

P.: La verdad es que no hacen buena pareja.

M.: Tienes razón. Por lo visto el otro día discutieron en el cine… Por cierto, me ha recomendado la película que vio, dice que es muy buena.

P.: Pues si quieres, vamos a verla este viernes.

M.: Bueno… ¡Ah! y también me ha dicho que cree que el mes que viene va a Ámsterdam a visitar a su hermano y a su cuñada, y me preguntó si quiero ir con ella.

TRACK 63

Secretaria: Con permiso, Señor Marín.

Director: Dígame.

Secretaria: Hemos recibido una carta de uno de nuestros mejores clientes, se llama Juan Mora y dice que el nuevo teléfono que le regalamos no para de darle problemas. Dice que la pantalla táctil no funciona bien, que en muchos lugares no tiene cobertura y no puede llamar, que cuando llama, la conversación siempre se corta en el minuto 2. También dice que la batería no dura más de cinco horas.

Director: Muy bien, no se preocupe. Yo mismo me pondré en contacto con el departamento comercial. Le escribiremos un correo electrónico para pedirle disculpas. Además le ofreceremos un nuevo teléfono celular mucho más moderno. Yo lo tengo y no creo que con él tenga problemas. Gracias por la información.

TRACK 64

a. Marta: ¡Pero bueno! ¿Se puede saber dónde están la ensalada de papa y los bocadillos que había en la cocina?

Nacho: Ejem… ¿La ensalada de papa y los bocadillos?

Marta: Sí, los estuve preparando ayer por la noche porque hoy nos vamos de excursión al campo, ¿no te acuerdas que te lo comenté? A ver si alguien los ha metido en el refrigerador…

Nacho: Ejem… No, en el refrigerador no busques que no están.

Marta: ¿No? pero entonces, ¿dónde están?, ¿tú lo sabes?, ¿los has puesto en algún sitio?

Nacho: No, es que…

Marta: ¡Ay, Nacho! ¡Es que ¿qué?!

Nacho: Pues… es que… yo no sabía que eran tuyos y ayer cuando llegamos del partido teníamos mucha hambre y…

Marta: ¡¿Qué!? ¡¿Que te has comido la ensalada entera y todos los bocadillos!?

Nacho: No, yo solo no, es que vine con Carlos y con Armando y…

Marta: ¡No me lo puedo creer, Nacho! ¡Eres lo peor y me parece terrible lo que has hecho! ¿Es que no sabías que lo había preparado todo para hoy?

b. Hija: Por favor, papá, vamos a comprar uno, si son un amor.

Padre: Que no, Carmen, que ya te he dicho que no quiero animales en casa.

Hija: Pero mira qué bonito es, además seguro que no da apenas trabajo, ¿no ves lo pequeñito que es? Si casi ni se ve…

Padre: Desde luego… si casi lo pisan al pobre.

Hija: Anda, papá, te prometo que lo cuido yo.

Padre: ¡Que no! ¡Ya te he dicho mil veces que no! No me importa si es grande o pequeño o si se ve o no, cuando tú seas mayor haces lo que quieras, pero mientras vivas en casa no.

c. Toni: Tengo que conseguir rescatar a la princesa del castillo antes de que se derrumbe.

Mónica: Sí, pero necesitamos la llave, si no, no podemos entrar en el castillo.

Toni: Pero es que cada vez que intento agarrar la llave sale el dragón y me lanza bolas de fuego, no sé cómo esquivarlas.

Mónica: Es que no tienes que saltar cuando lanza las bolas sino cuando las tienes más cerca.

Toni: A ver, lo intento.

Mónica: ¡No! ¡Todavía no saltes! ¡Te he dicho que saltes cuando la bola de fuego esté más cerca! Si saltas antes, caes justo encima de la bola. Déjame a mí y yo te lo paso.

Toni: No, lo tengo que conseguir yo.

Mónica: Bueno, pues hazlo justo cuando te digo, solo te queda una vida.

Toni: A ver…

Mónica: ¡No! ¡Aún no! Se acabó. Te dije que si volvías a hacerlo no tendrías más oportunidades.

TRACK 65

a. ≫ ¿Has visto mis gafas? Es que las estoy buscando por todas partes y no las encuentro.

>> Pero, ¿estás seguro de que has vuelto a casa con ellas? Posiblemente te las dejaste en la oficina.

>> Pues me parece que sí, ahora que lo dices creo que me las quité para lavarme la cara y seguramente estén en el baño de la oficina.

b. >> No me funciona Internet en el celular.

>> A ver…, pues a mí sí me funciona, quizás sea un problema de conexión de tu compañía.

>> No, yo creo que es mi celular, me da problemas desde que me lo compré.

>> Pero es bastante nuevo, está en garantía aún, ¿no?

>> Sí.

>> Pues llévalo a la tienda, posiblemente sea una tontería y si no, seguramente te lo cambien por otro celular.

c. >> Qué raro, Juan no está en la biblioteca.

>> Bueno, quizás se ha quedado estudiando en casa.

>> No creo, me dijo que vendría a estudiar aquí si yo venía también, que tenía algunas dudas y que así las comentábamos juntos.

>> No sé, puede que llegue más tarde, todavía es pronto.

>> Voy a llamarlo.

>> ¿Qué?

>> Salta el contestador, dice que no tiene cobertura, probablemente esté en el metro y viene de camino.

d. >> ¿Oíste lo de Santi?

>> No…

>> Pues me contó que es posible que a su padre lo manden a trabajar a Hong Kong.

>> ¿Es verdad? Y si lo mandan ahí, ¿él que haría?

>> Pues me dijo que lo están pensando en casa y que tal vez se vaya toda la familia con él.

>> ¡Pero si él no sabe chino!

>> Bueno, irse allí es una buena forma de aprenderlo, ¿no? Además en Hong Kong todo el mundo habla inglés.

>> Sí, seguramente, pero ¿y en la escuela? Las clases serán en chino, digo yo…

>> Pues es verdad…, no sé, puede que se tenga que matricular en un curso intensivo antes de irse.

>> Pero el chino es muy difícil…

TRACK 66

La telenovela es una expresión cultural típica del mundo hispano. En estos programas de televisión no faltan dramas, villanos… ¡ni capítulos!

Las telenovelas son programas de televisión dramáticos. Pero no son cualquier programa: están estrechamente conectadas con la forma de ser de los países hispanos. Las historias de las telenovelas reflejan las tradiciones, las aspiraciones y, muchas veces, los temas de actualidad de la sociedad que las mira. «Las telenovelas son exitosas porque generan emoción y entretenimiento», explica Nora Mazziotti, investigadora argentina y autora de libros sobre telenovelas. Aunque cada telenovela tiene una historia diferente, hay elementos comunes que están presentes en todas ellas. Suelen tener entre 100 y 200 capítulos. Hay un galán (normalmente, rico) y una heroína (normalmente, pobre). Hay una villana que hace todo lo posible por separarlos. Y hay varios personajes secundarios que aportan historias divertidas, para equilibrar el melodrama de la historia central.

Cada país latinoamericano produce telenovelas con un estilo distinto. «Las telenovelas mexicanas son las más tradicionales: son muy conservadoras. Las brasileñas tienen elementos modernos. Las colombianas tienen historias muy creativas. Las argentinas suelen tener toques de comedia», dice Maziotti. Además de entretener, una importante función de las telenovelas es educar. Muchas de las historias incorporan personajes que atraviesan enfermedades graves, o viven situaciones serias como la decisión de adoptar un hijo o la pérdida de un trabajo.

TRACK 67

¡Ay, mísero de mí, ay infelice!
Apurar, cielos, pretendo,
ya que me tratáis así
qué delito cometí
contra vosotros naciendo;
aunque si nací, ya entiendo
qué delito he cometido:
bastante causa ha tenido
vuestra justicia y rigor,
pues el delito mayor
del hombre es haber nacido.
Solo quisiera saber
para apurar mis desvelos
dejando a una parte, cielos,
el delito de nacer,
qué más os puede ofender
para castigarme más.
¿No nacieron los demás?
Pues si los demás nacieron,
¿qué privilegios tuvieron
que yo no gocé jamás?

AHORA COMPRUEBA. REPASO UNIDADES 7-8

TRACK 68

El rey León, el musical que conmueve a todo el mundo.

El rey León transporta al espectador al exotismo africano, con evocadoras músicas y un diseño artístico extraordinario. Representa un nuevo hito en el mundo del espectáculo y es, sin duda alguna, un musical que a nadie deja indiferente.

El rey León es un espectáculo único, cargado de valores familiares, que demuestra la conexión de cada uno de nosotros con nuestras raíces. Nos hace pensar sobre la importancia de todas nuestras acciones y el efecto que causan en nuestro entorno. Además, es un canto al respeto y al amor por la naturaleza. ¿Dónde? En el Teatro Lope de Vega, calle Gran Vía, 57.

Con una duración de 2h y 30 minutos, incluido el descanso.

¿Cómo puedes llegar? Recomendamos el transporte público, porque la zona es de mucho tráfico. Si vas en metro, las estaciones son Callao y Plaza de España.

Encontraréis parking público en Plaza de España.

El horario de la función es: martes, miércoles y jueves a las ocho y media de la tarde, viernes y sábados a las seis y a las ocho, y los domingos a las siete.

El precio de la entrada va desde los 20 a los 80 euros, dependiendo de la zona del teatro y del día de la semana. Puedes comprarla en la siguiente página web: *www. elreyleon*.es o en el teléfono 902 888 788. También en la taquilla todos los días desde las 12 del mediodía hasta el inicio de la última función.

Descubre con la Butaca de Oro los secretos que esconde este extraordinario musical detrás del escenario. Disfrutarás de una asombrosa visita guiada al *backstage* de *El rey León* y del encuentro con los actores después de la función. ¡No esperes más! Ya están disponibles las entradas para los meses de marzo, abril y mayo.

TRACK 1

Habla con tu pareja, tienes que ser más cuidadoso y todo mejorará. Podrás conseguir todos tus proyectos, además una persona de tu familia te ayudará mucho.

Si no tienes novia, será por poco tiempo. Pronto conocerás a una persona muy especial en tu vida y te volverás loco de amor. Llegará también un buen cambio en tu trabajo, las cosas irán mejor y ganarás más dinero.

Vivirás el amor intensamente, pero no tendrás la suerte de tu parte. Los problemas en tu trabajo te pondrán nervioso. Encontrarás muchas dificultades. Si pones flores amarillas en casa, te darán mucha suerte.

TRACK 2

Ana: ¿Friego el suelo?
Sergio: No, no lo friegues, ya lo hago yo.
Sergio: ¿Paso la aspiradora?
Ana: Sí, pásala por favor.
Sergio: ¿Hago la cama?
Ana: No, no la hagas, ya la hago yo.
Ana: ¿Plancho la ropa?
Sergio: No, no la planches, ya la plancho yo.
Ana: ¿Limpio el polvo?
Sergio: Sí, por favor, límpialo.
Sergio: ¿Pongo la lavadora?
Ana: Sí, ponla.
Sergio: ¿Barro el suelo?
Ana: No, no lo barras, ya lo hago yo.
Ana: ¿Lavo los platos?
Sergio: Sí, lávalos, por favor.

TRACK 3

1. ¡Qué risa en el cine! Gracias por recomendármela. ¡Me ha encantado! No he parado de reírme en toda la película.
2. He trabajado con muchos directores internacionales, pero todavía no he trabajado con Pedro Almodóvar. Creo que es el director que mejor dirige a los personajes femeninos, el que mejor refleja la sociedad española actual.
3. Cuando era pequeño estaba todo el día jugando con mis amigos a películas de acción. Pensaba que iba a ser un famoso actor y que todo sería muy fácil. Ahora que estoy estudiando interpretación, sé lo difícil que es interpretar algunos papeles.
4. Para mí hacer cine significa crear obras de arte. No hago una película pensando en el éxito, ese no es mi objetivo.

TRACK 4

1. Deberías estudiar en tu habitación.
2. Yo en tu lugar no la compraría por Internet, tendrías que verla y probarla.
3. Te aconsejo dormir más.
4. ¿Por qué no te haces socio de la biblioteca?
5. Yo la llamaría antes por teléfono.
6. Tendrías que consultarlo antes con tus padres.

TRACK 5

El apadrinamiento es una forma de colaboración que junta a los padrinos con los niños de países donde Global Humanitaria realiza su trabajo. Esta colaboración nos permite realizar proyectos de desarrollo que benefician a la población infantil, muy vulnerable, pero también a toda la comunidad en la que viven.

Las cuotas de apadrinamiento son las cantidades de dinero que financian, por ejemplo, la construcción de escuelas y el mantenimiento de comedores escolares, la formación de adultos, los hogares de acogida para niños de la calle y las iniciativas comunales. Esta cuota mensual es de 21 euros. Como padrino vas a recibir en tu domicilio una fotografía del niño o la niña apadrinados y una ficha con sus datos personales. A partir de ese momento, puedes establecer correspondencia con ellos.

TRACK 6

Locutora: Hoy se cumple un año del nacimiento del movimiento 15-M y volvemos al lugar en el que este se originó para comprobar que el espíritu que lo hizo nacer sigue vivo. Entonces, muchos jóvenes decidieron unirse y manifestarse pacíficamente en las calles para mostrar su disconformidad con una clase política que les ignoraba y no entendían la serie de medidas y recortes que se estaban realizando y deterioraban el estado del bienestar… Y vamos a hablar con algunos de los jóvenes que están concentrados en la plaza. Hola, Buenos días.
Chica 1: Hola.
Locutora: ¿Cómo te llamas?
Chica 1: Laura.
Locutora: ¿Te importa que te haga unas preguntas?
Chica 1: No, claro.
Locutora: ¿Piensas que después de un año y no conseguir nada, volver a salir a las calles servirá para algo?
Chica 1: Bueno, no sabemos si servirán o no nuestras protestas, lo que sí sabemos es que no podemos quedarnos en casa mientras estos políticos recortan en educación. Me da mucha pena que nosotros, los jóvenes, tengamos que pagar por los errores la mala gestión del gobierno. Nos suben las tasas universitarias, el precio del material escolar, recortan en los programas de estudio…
Locutora: Bueno, vemos que tienes motivos para protestar…. Y aquí vemos a otro chico. ¿Nos podrías decir tu nombre?
Chico 1: Sí, me llamo Carlos.
Locutora: ¿Qué pides tú, Carlos?
Chico 1: Principalmente, el poder acceder a una vivienda. Como consecuencia de la subida de los precios, muchas familias y los jóvenes que quieren independizarse no podrán nunca comprar una vivienda.
Locutora: Y la señora que está contigo, ¿es tu madre, por casualidad?
Madre: Sí, yo soy su madre.
Locutora: ¿Y qué protesta usted, señora?
Madre: Estoy aquí para poder tener una jubilación digna y para que mis hijos puedan vivir como lo hemos hecho nosotros. Me pongo histérica cuando oigo a estos políticos decir que hay que hacer recortes y que no tienen más remedio, si quieren recortar que empiecen por bajarse el sueldo ellos.
Locutora: Ahora vemos a otra chica. Hola, ¿cómo te llamas?
Chica 2: Daniela.
Locutora: Y tú, ¿por qué estás aquí?
Chica 2: Pues para protestar por la situación actual de los jóvenes en nuestro país. No es justo que tengamos que irnos a otro país porque aquí no hay trabajo ni oportunidades. Yo estudié Química, he hecho un máster en Ciencias medioambientales y, si en unos meses no encuentro trabajo, sí, me iré. Me da mucha pena dejar aquí amigos, familiares y el lugar en el que me gustaría seguir viviendo…
Locutora: Bueno, como vemos, el espíritu del 15-M sigue muy vivo y los motivos para protestar, desgraciadamente, siguen siendo muchos…

TRACK 7

Los empresarios están incorporando, cada vez más, las redes sociales en sus negocios. Esto hace que los consumidores puedan registrarse en la cuenta de Facebook o Twitter de la empresa, en vez de hacerlo en la página web.

Este tipo de registros permite a los empresarios obtener una información mucho más amplia de sus consumidores y así llegar a su público objetivo de una forma más directa.

Un estudio recoge los beneficios que los comerciantes obtienen del registro de los consumidores en sus redes sociales. En primer lugar, se encuentra el aumento del compromiso con la marca; en segundo lugar, la información del perfil del consumidor es mucho más completa para saber exactamente qué le interesa; y en tercer lugar, supone una mayor facilidad para el envío de recomendaciones de productos, e-mails, promociones y cupones.

Pero los empresarios deben tener cuidado con esta forma de hacer publicidad, por ejemplo, cuando hace recomendaciones personalizadas. Esto puede hacer que los consumidores sientan que su privacidad on-line está en peligro y genere una reacción negativa, o sea, que el consumidor potencial deje de serlo.

TRACK 8

Mónica: Hola Marta, qué mala cara tienes, ¿te pasa algo?

Marta: ¡Qué tal! Pues es que no funciona mi computadora y la necesito para hacer los trabajos de la universidad.

Mónica: ¡Oh, no! ¿Y qué le ha pasado?

Marta: Ni idea. Ayer funcionaba con normalidad. Estuve mirando mi correo electrónico y mirando algunas fotos, y sin problema. Pero esta mañana cuando quería encenderlo no podía. Estoy desesperada porque no sé qué le pasa.

Mónica: Es posible que tenga un virus. A lo mejor dejó de funcionar al instalar algún programa nuevo.

Marta: No creo. No he instalado nada últimamente. Igual es un problema con la pantalla, porque al intentar encenderlo se escuchan sonidos pero no se ve nada.

Mónica: Seguramente ya sea muy vieja. ¿Cuántos años tiene?

Marta: Pues no sé, porque antes era de mi hermano, me imagino que tiene siete años como mínimo.

Mónica: Pues quizás sea el momento para comprar otra, ¿no?

Marta: Eso dice mi hermano. Esta mañana he hablado con él y me ha dicho que mañana va a intentar repararla, pero cree que va a ser complicado. Me ha recomendado que me compre una nueva en una tienda de informática que él conoce donde los precios son un poco más bajos. Pero creo que voy a comprar una de segunda mano por Internet.

Mónica: Ah, pues yo necesito algunas cosas, quiero comprar un ratón, un nuevo monitor y una memoria externa, me tienes que dar la dirección de esa tienda y la semana que viene voy a ver qué hay.

EPISODIO 1: UNA CITA CON MORGANA

Sebas: ¡No puedo creer que esté aquí!

Felipe: Tranquilo, no tengas miedo, Sebas.

Sebas: ¡Yo no tengo miedo! Lo que pasa es que no creo en estas cosas.

Felipe: Pues creerás. Mi madre vino a esta adivina una vez y le dijo todo su futuro. Le ayudó mucho. Es una adivina muy buena.

Sebas: ¡Yo no necesito a una adivina!

Felipe: Sí la necesitas. Es el principio de un nuevo curso y tú tienes muchas dudas sobre lo que debes estudiar, ¿verdad?

Sebas: Sí, eso es cierto. No sé muy bien qué hacer… ni en qué voy a trabajar cuando termine de estudiar. ¡Estoy muy confuso!

Felipe: Pues por eso es muy importante que tengas claro tu futuro, para elegir correctamente lo que vas a estudiar. Así que por eso estamos aquí: para que sepas cosas sobre tu futuro.

Sebas: Pero a mí no me gustan esas cosas. Nunca antes estuve en una adivina.

Felipe. Pues es el momento perfecto para preguntar sobre tu futuro.

Sebas: A mí todo esto me pone muy nervioso.

Felipe: Tranquilo, Sebas, verás que todo va a salir bien…

Adivina: Bienvenidos a la casa de la Señora Doña Morgana, adivinadora de todas las preguntas. El futuro se mostrará a través de mis cartas. Abran la mente. Todos los misterios serán resueltos. La magia guiará todas mis palabras… ¿Quién de ustedes dos necesita preguntar por su futuro?

Sebas: ¿Ella no lo sabe? ¡Pero qué clase de adivina es que no sabe quién de los dos…!

Felipe: Calla, tonto… Es mi amigo Sebas. Él necesita hacerle a usted algunas preguntas sobre su futuro.

Adivina: Muy bien, Sebas, pues ahora mira fijamente a los ojos de Doña Morgana y dime qué es lo que necesitas saber… ¿Sobre la salud? ¿Sobre la familia? ¿Sobre el amor?

Sebas: Necesito saber en qué trabajaré. No sé qué estudiar y quiero aclarar mis planes de futuro.

Adivina: Divide la baraja en dos y deja que Doña Morgana mire tu futuro… ¡Sí! ¡Sí! ¡Veo tu futuro con mucha luz, muchacho!

Sebas: ¿Sí? ¿Qué es lo que está usted viendo?

Adivina: Tu trabajo será cuidar de este planeta. Mira este árbol en la carta, ¿lo ves? Es el Árbol de la Vida. Tu destino está muy claro: trabajarás cuidando el medioambiente.

Sebas: ¿Yo? ¿Cuidaré el medioambiente?

Adivina: Sí, las cartas están hablando muy claro. Pero, ¡atención!, mira esta otra carta.

Sebas: ¿Qué es? ¿Qué pasa?

Adivina: ¡El Cruce de Caminos!

Sebas: ¿Eso es algo malo?

Adivina: Tendrás que enfrentarte a una decisión. Tu futuro tiene dos caminos para llegar al mismo lugar, pero tendrás que elegir solo uno de los dos.

Sebas: ¿Qué dos caminos son esos?

Adivina: El primero, serás político. Estarás en un importante partido político. Serás elegido candidato. Prometerás hacer muchas cosas para cuidar el medioambiente. Las encuestas te serán muy favorables durante tu campaña. La gente te admirará por tu lucha contra la contaminación. Tendrás muchos votos en todo el país y ganarás unas importantes elecciones. Lo veo con total claridad.

Felipe: ¡Mi mejor amigo presidente!

Adivina: Pero recuerda: ese es solo uno de los dos caminos. ¿Ves esta carta? Marca otro de los modos en que cumplirás tu destino…

Sebas: ¿Cuál, Doña Morgana? ¿Cuál es mi otro camino?

Adivina: ¡Serás guardabosques!

Sebas: ¿Yo? ¿Trabajaré de guardabosques?

Adivina: Sí, estudiarás Ciencias de la Naturaleza. Tendrás unas notas impresionantes, te será muy fácil comenzar a trabajar en un parque nacional. Cuidarás de toda la riqueza de los animales y plantas, serás especialista en especies salvajes y harás un importante estudio sobre el efecto invernadero. Viajarás por todo el país y darás conferencias sobre la necesidad de cuidar los bosques y las especies. Amarás tu trabajo. Y serás muy feliz…

Sebas: ¡Guardabosques! ¡Trabajaré con la naturaleza!

Felipe: ¡Qué bien! Te imagino perfectamente, Sebas. ¡Es un trabajo maravilloso para ti!

Sebas: ¡Sí, nunca antes lo pensé! Lo de ser político no me gusta, pero acabo de descubrir por fin lo que quiero estudiar. ¡Por fin lo tengo claro! ¡Seré guardabosques! ¡Es el trabajo más hermoso del mundo! ¡Muchas gracias, Doña Morgana! ¡Voy corriendo a decírselo a mis padres! ¡Les va a encantar! Te veo luego, Felipe. ¡Adiós! ¡Gracias, gracias!

Lorena: Creo que se lo creyó todo, ¿verdad?

Felipe: Sí, has estado estupenda, Lorena. ¡Y por fin ya tiene claro lo que va a estudiar!

Lorena: ¡Las cosas que hacemos por los amigos!

EPISODIO 2: EL SEÑOR DON LIMPIO

Eli: ¡Hola!

Sebas: Hola, hermana.

Eli: ¡Ay, por fin en casa!

Sebas: Terminaste hoy las clases antes, ¿no?

Eli: Sí, pero es que además necesitaba hoy llegar antes a casa.

Sebas: ¿Por qué?

Eli: Porque voy a preparar una cena. ¡Esta noche tenemos invitados en casa!

Sebas: ¿Ah, sí? ¿Quién viene?

Eli: Invité a cenar a Alfonso y a Juanjo.

Sebas: Ah, qué interesante.

Eli: Ya tenía ganas de invitar a mis amigos a cenar a casa, así que ahora que papá y mamá salieron de viaje y estamos solos… ¡Es la ocasión perfecta!

Sebas: Sí, claro…

Eli: Tengo pensado un plato muy especial… Oye, ¿tú vas a cenar con nosotros? Es que necesito saber cuántos vamos a ser exactamente.

Sebas: ¿Yo? No. No me apetece una cena con tres universitarios…

Eli: No seremos tres, seremos cuatro.

Sebas: Alfonso, Juanjo, tú y… ¿quién más?

Eli: Alba, la hermana pequeña de Juanjo. Hace poco llegó a la ciudad y la invité a casa a cenar también.

Sebas: ¿Alba? ¿La hermana de Juanjo?

Eli: ¿La conoces?

Sebas: Sí, claro que la conozco.

Eli: Pues también viene a casa esta noche. ¡Lástima que no te quedes a cenar con nosotros!

Sebas: Pues… creo que mejor me quedo a cenar con ustedes…

Eli: ¿Sí? Por mí no lo hagas. Si no te apetece cenar con unos universitarios, no es necesario que…

Sebas: ¡No, no, no! ¡Qué va! Si a mí me gustan mucho tus amigos. Me encantará cenar con ellos.

Eli: Muy bien, perfecto. ¿Podrías ayudarme a hacer la comida?

Sebas: Ok, te ayudaré… pero… La casa está muy desordenada. Tenemos que hacer algo…

Eli: ¿Desordenada?

Sebas: Sí, y además está sucia. ¡No podemos tener la casa así con invitados! ¿Qué van a pensar?

Eli: ¡Pero la casa está bien! Además, son amigos de confianza. No hay problema…
Sebas: No, tenemos que limpiar todo esto antes de que lleguen… ¡Tenemos que darles una buena impresión!
Eli: Pero, Sebas, ¿desde cuándo te has preocupado de la limpieza? ¿Por qué te preocupas ahora?
Sebas: ¡Porque tenemos invitados! A ver… hay que limpiar el polvo, ¿desde cuándo no limpiamos el polvo?
Eli: ¿Pero a ti cuándo te ha preocupado tanto el polvo?
Sebas: Hay que ponerse en marcha… vamos, barre tú la cocina mientras yo voy a pasar la aspiradora por todo el salón.
Eli: Yo no voy a hacer nada de eso, Sebas…
Sebas: Y luego, hacemos las camas, y después, sacar la basura.

Eli: Sebas, por favor. Estás loco…
Sebas: ¡Tiene que estar todo perfecto! Y mientras tú pones el lavaplatos, yo voy a poner una lavadora… ¡tenemos demasiada ropa sucia!
Felipe: ¡Hola, familia!
Eli: Hola, Felipe. Me alegro de que llegues. A ver si eres capaz de tranquilizar al "señor Don Limpio".
Felipe: ¿Están de limpieza o qué?
Sebas: Hola, Felipe, escucha, necesito que me ayudes. Es algo muy importante.
Felipe: ¿Qué te pasa, amigo?
Sebas: Mientras mi hermana hace la cena, yo voy a tener que tender la ropa. Felipe, necesito tu ayuda… ¿Podrías sacar a pasear al perro?
Eli y Felipe: ¡Pero si tú no tienes perro!

EPISODIO 3: LA CASA DE LAS PAREDES NEGRAS

Alba: Gracias, chicas, por haberme invitado a venir con ustedes al cine.
Eli: De nada, mujer, eres nueva en la ciudad. Solo nos conoces a nosotras.
Lorena: Cuando yo llegué a la ciudad, Eli me ayudó mucho a no sentirme sola.
Alba: ¡Qué guay!
Lorena: ¿Te gusta el cine, Alba?
Alba: Claro. Pero, sobre todo, me gustan las películas de terror.
Eli: ¿De terror? A mí no me gustan nada las de terror. Ese tipo de cine le gusta mucho a mi hermano Sebas. Pero yo lo odio.
Lorena: Pues la película que vamos a ver no es de terror.
Alba: No sé nada sobre esta película. No la conozco.
Eli: Es una comedia.
Lorena: He leído algo sobre ella. Al parecer, tiene un guion muy bueno, y los actores son muy cómicos. Hacen una interpretación muy divertida.
Alba: ¿Tiene efectos especiales? Me encantan las películas con mucha fantasía…
Lorena: Creo que no. Ayer vi el tráiler por la tele y no parece que sea muy espectacular. ¡Pero creo que nos reiremos mucho!
Felipe: A ver, Sebas, recordemos el plan…
Sebas: Nos acercamos a las chicas y nos quedamos con ellas.
Felipe: ¿Y después?
Sebas: A continuación, tú te pondrás a hablar con Lorena y con mi hermana, y entonces yo puedo hablar con Alba.
Felipe: Es tu oportunidad para acercarte a ella.
Sebas: No sé, Felipe, esto… esto es muy raro, no estoy seguro…
Felipe: Pero, Sebas, chico, ¿no dices que te gusta Alba?
Sebas: Sí… ¡Me encanta!
Felipe: ¿Y no dices que te encantaría salir con ella?
Sebas: Bueno, al menos ir un día juntos al cine, hablar un poco con ella, no sé…
Felipe: Pero eres demasiado tímido para decírselo, ¿verdad?
Sebas: Sí, me da mucha vergüenza pedírselo.
Felipe: Pues para eso está aquí tu amigo Felipe, para ayudarte… Yo te llevé a la adivina para decidir tu futuro y eso te ayudó mucho. Así que deja que te consiga una cita con Alba…
Sebas: No sé, pero hacer todo este teatro… Todo esto es muy raro…
Felipe: ¡Tú confía en mí! Pero sigamos recordando el plan: yo hablo con las chicas y tú te acercas y empiezas a hablar con Alba.
Sebas: Sí, le hablo de la película…
Felipe: Sí, y dile que te encantan las comedias. Di que te gusta mucho el cine, ¡pero no le digas que te gusta el cine de terror! Eso no funciona con las chicas…
Sebas: ¡Pero a mí me encanta el cine de terror!
Felipe: Pero eso no tienes que decirlo en tu primera conversación. Créeme, ¡yo entiendo mucho de chicas! Di que te gustan las comedias. O mejor, las películas románticas…

Sebas: De acuerdo, como quieras.
Felipe: ¿Y qué harás entonces?
Sebas: Le compro un refresco y palomitas de maíz.
Felipe: Muy bien. No dejes de hablarle de lo que te gustan las comedias. Recuerda: ¿cuál es el objetivo principal?
Sebas: Entrar en el cine hablando con Alba para sentarme a su lado.
Felipe: No lo olvides. Eso es lo que hay que conseguir. Yo hablaré con tu hermana y con Lorena hasta que tú te sientes al lado de Alba. ¿Entendido?
Sebas: Creo que sí…
Felipe: ¡Pues vamos!
Sebas: ¿Y entonces a ti te gusta mucho venir al cine?
Alba: Sí, bastante.
Sebas: A mí también. A mí me encantan las comedias, y las películas románticas… Lo que no me gusta es el cine de terror… ¡Lo odio! ¿Qué clase de películas te gustan a ti?
Alba: Las películas de terror.
Sebas: Bueno, algunas películas de terror sí me gustan…
Alba: Mira, Sebas, yo sé que te encanta el cine de terror. No es necesario que lo ocultes. ¿Te da vergüenza decírmelo, o qué?
Sebas: Es que pensé que no te gustaba el cine de terror.
Alba: Pues me encanta, que lo sepas…
Sebas: Pues entonces para qué hacerme el romántico… ¡Me encantan las películas de terror! ¡Y cuanto más miedo den, mejor!
Alba: ¡Y a mí! ¡Me encanta pasar mucho miedo! Una bolsa de palomitas y un refresco, por favor.
Sebas: No, no, déjame que yo te las…
Alba: Mira, Sebas. Yo, en realidad, odio las palomitas… y también odio las comedias.
Sebas: A mí me pasa lo mismo.
Alba: En la sala 10 ponen La casa de las paredes negras. Me han dicho que es terrorífica. ¿Ya la has visto?
Sebas: No, pero también oí que da mucho miedo.
Alba: Pues mira: dejemos a esta gente que vaya a ver la comedia, y vámonos tú y yo solos a ver la de terror. ¿Te parece bien?
Sebas: ¡Me encantaría hacer eso! Pero déjame que te invite yo al refresco, ya que dices que odias las palomitas…
Alba: ¡Por supuesto! ¡Tú invitas al refresco y yo te invito a las palomitas! Chicas, Sebas y yo nos vamos mejor a ver la película de terror de la sala 10. ¡Nos vemos a la salida!

EPISODIO 4: PAELLA CON CURRY

Felipe: Entonces, primero, hay que cocinar las verduras y luego, poner el arroz. ¡Justo al revés de como decías, Sebas!

Sebas: Bueno, yo nunca he hecho una paella...

Felipe: Yo tampoco, pero hay que tener cuidado. Cada paso es importante. Tenemos que hacerlo todo en su orden...

Sebas: ¡Pues vamos allá! Voy a empezar a cortar.

Felipe: Espera, hay que chequear antes. ¿Tenemos toda la verdura?

Sebas: Creo que sí.

Felipe: ¿Seguro? A ver... Tomates...

Sebas: ¡Tomates!

Felipe: Cebolla...

Sebas: ¡Cebolla!

Felipe: Pimientos...

Sebas: ¡Pimientos!

Felipe: Ajo...

Sebas: ¡Ajo! ¡Está todo!

Felipe: ¡Pues adelante, a lavar y a cortar! Recuerda: en trozos muy pequeños.

Sebas: Sé cómo tengo que hacerlo. Preocúpate tú por el marisco.

Felipe: ¡Todo tiene que salir perfecto!

Sebas: No sé si ha sido una buena idea invitar a cenar a Alba...

Felipe: Claro que sí. Tienes que impresionarla...

Sebas: Pues mejor sería hacer algo más simple, ¡no una paella!

Felipe: Si queremos impresionarla, tenemos que hacer algo fuera de lo normal... ¿Tú qué harías? ¡No vas a sorprenderla con unos tacos!

Sebas: Yo preferiría tacos. ¡Los tacos me salen muy ricos!

Felipe: A todo el mundo le salen ricos los tacos. Una paella es mucho más sorprendente.

Sebas: ¡Pues espero que nos salga bien!

Felipe: Nada puede fallar. Oye, pon a calentar el aceite de oliva, que la verdura ya está cortada.

Sebas: Este aceite de oliva es muy caro.

Felipe: Hay que usar ingredientes de primera calidad. Ese es el secreto para la buena cocina.

Sebas: He gastado mis pocos ahorros en los ingredientes para esta cena...

Felipe: Lo sé, pero tiene que ser así... Los mejores ingredientes son el secreto para los mejores platos. ¡Esto va a estar delicioso! No hay que pensar en el dinero.

Sebas: ¡Claro, como no lo has pagado tú!

Felipe: Yo solo quiero ayudar a mi amigo para que impresione a la chica que le gusta.

Sebas: Sí, sí, claro. Vamos, pon la verdura, que el aceite ya está caliente...

Felipe: ¿Le ponemos mantequilla?

Sebas: Pero, ¿cómo vas a poner mantequilla? ¿No leíste la receta? ¡Es aceite de oliva!

Felipe: Bueno, no hay que seguir la receta literalmente... Hay que ser creativo.

Felipe: Yo voy a ponerle mantequilla.

Sebas: No sé, no sé...

Felipe: Y vamos a poner también frijoles...

Sebas: ¿Frijoles en la paella? ¡Eso tampoco viene en la receta!

Felipe: Relájate, Sebas, tú confía en mí... Los frijoles siempre saben bien... y, mira... ¡Curry! Seguro que le sienta bien un poco de curry... ¿Y esto qué es?... Bah, no sé qué es esto, ¡pero seguro que mejora la receta!

Sebas: A ver cómo termina todo esto...

Felipe: Dale, dale..., ahora te vas a enterar...

Sebas: ¿Estará ya la paella?

Felipe: No, aún le queda un poco... ¡Sigue jugando!

Sebas: ¿Seguro? Alba vendrá pronto.

Alba: ¡Hola! Espero no haber llegado tarde.

Sebas: No, llegas justo a tiempo.

Felipe: Sí, estamos a punto de servir la mesa.

Alba: ¿Y qué ese olor tan extraño?

Sebas: Es la paella, que ya está preparada...

Alba: ¿Paella? Pues huele como a quemado...

Sebas: ¡No!

Alba: Me lo imaginé. Chicos, creo que voy a pedir unas pizzas. Yo invito...

Sebas: ¡No!

EPISODIO 5: CASTING EN SOMALIA

Alfonso: Hola, buenas tardes.

Juanjo: Tengo que contarte una cosa.

Alfonso: ¿Qué te pasa? ¿Estás nervioso?

Juanjo: Sí. Mucho. Esta mañana me llamaron por teléfono. Tengo que... que... prepararme urgentemente para un casting.

Alfonso: ¿Un casting? ¿Para una película?

Juanjo: No, para un comercial en televisión.

Alfonso: ¿Un comercial? ¿Un comercial de qué?

Juanjo: De una ONG. Están haciendo una campaña por televisión para buscar voluntarios y me han llamado para que me prepare para una audición. Si lo hago bien, me contratan. ¡Saldré en televisión!

Alfonso: ¡Eso es una noticia estupenda!

Juanjo: Sí, pero tengo que aprender el guion.

Alfonso: ¿Cuándo es el casting?

Juanjo: ¡Pasado mañana!

Alfonso: ¡Pasado mañana! ¡Pero tendrás que ensayar mucho!

Juanjo: Sí, aquí tengo el guion. Tengo que memorizarlo. Lo he estudiado un poco entre clase y clase, pero no me lo sé muy bien.

Alfonso: ¿Te ayudo?

Juanjo: Sí, por favor. Necesito ensayar con alguien delante.

Alfonso: Pues... ándale, dame el guion y comienza.

Alfonso: Okey, comencemos... Tres, dos, uno... ¡Acción!

Juanjo: ¿Alguna vez pensaste en dedicar tu tiempo en ayudar a los demás? ¿Te gustaría proteger el medioambiente? ¿Te interesan el comercio justo y los trabajos humanitarias...?

Alfonso: Aquí dice "las labores humanitarias"...

Juanjo: Sí, claro, labores, labores... ¡Uf! Al salir de clase estudié un poco, pero está caro que tengo que estudiar más.

Alfonso: Continúa, por favor...

Juanjo: ¿Te interesan el comercio justo y las labores humanitarias? En "Madre Tierra" estamos buscando gente como tú: valiente, creativa, solidaria... ¿Te parece bien?

Alfonso: Me parece un poco exagerado... No estás natural.

Juanjo: Es que estoy nervioso...

Alfonso: Pues, tranquilízate. No tengas prisa, es importante que pronuncies bien.

Juanjo: Ojalá me den el papel...

Alfonso: No pienses ahora en eso. Ahora es momento de ensayar duro. Continúa...

Juanjo: Ahora tienes la oportunidad de unirte a un gran equipo de gente que trabaja de forma voluntaria en diferentes países de África y unirte a algunos de nuestros proyectos. Puedes ayudar a construir un colegio en... en... en... ¿Dónde es?

Alfonso: En Somalia.

Juanjo: Eso... Somalia, Somalia...

Alfonso: Continúa...

Juanjo: Puedes ayudar a construir colegios en Somalia o trabajar de voluntario en un hospital infantil en... ¿Dónde está el hospital?

Alfonso: En Burkina Faso.

Juanjo: ¡Burkina Faso! ¡Nunca voy a conseguir aprender el nombre de ese país!

Alfonso: Continúa...

Juanjo: "Madre Tierra" pagará tu viaje y te conseguirá el alojamiento en el país. Podrás vivir con la gente de allí…

Alfonso: Aquí no dice exactamente eso… "Tendrás la experiencia de vivir con familias nativas…".

Juanjo: ¡No! ¡Horror! ¡Tengo que estudiar más!

Alfonso: Me parece que sí.

Juanjo: Pero no soporto estudiar el guion. ¡Es tan aburrido!

Alfonso: Bueno, continúa…

Juanjo: Tendrás la experiencia de vivir con familias nativas… y cumplir tus sueños más solidarios. Esta es tu gran oportunidad. Ven y vive con nosotros una experiencia que nunca olvidarás.

Alfonso: Esa última frase es importante. Yo que tú la diría con más energía…

Juanjo: ¿Más energía? Vale… ¡Esta es tu gran oportunidad! ¡Ven y vive una experiencia que nunca olvidarás!

Alfonso: Más, más… ¡Más energía!

Juanjo: ¡Esta es tu gran oportunidad! ¡Ven y vive una experiencia que nunca olvidarás!

Alfonso: ¡Más!

Juanjo: ¡Esta es tu gran oportunidad! ¡Ven y vive una experiencia que nunca olvidarás!

Alfonso: ¡Más!

Juanjo: ¡Esta es tu gran oportunidad! ¡Ven y vive una experiencia que nunca olvidarás! Creo que será mejor que ensayemos en casa…

EPISODIO 6: TU VOZ ES LO MÁS DULCE

Sebas: ¡Adoro cuando encesto desde aquí!

Felipe: Pues a mí me da rabia. ¡Hoy no hay manera de ganarte!

Sebas: Sí, te estoy machacando, Felipe.

Felipe: La verdad es que hoy me aburre estar aquí jugando…

Sebas: Eso lo dices porque vas perdiendo. Si estuvieras ganando, seguro que estarías más contento.

Felipe: Pues yo no tengo muchas ganas de seguir jugando más, Sebas.

Sebas: ¡Vamos, amigo! Seguimos otro rato. Me siento muy bien cuando te estoy ganando al básquet… ¡Yo quiero seguir jugando!

Felipe: Vaya, pero… ¡quién está ahí!

Sebas: ¿Qué pasa?

Felipe: ¡Perfecto! Ya se te van a quitar las ganas de seguir jugando.

Sebas: ¿A mí? ¿Por qué?

Felipe: ¿Sabes a quién estoy viendo allí?

Sebas: No, ¿a quién?

Felipe: Mira allí…, en la grada.

Sebas: ¡Es Alba!

Felipe: ¡Sí, la gran Alba!

Sebas: Um… esto… ¿Sabes? Tienes razón, yo tampoco tengo más ganas de seguir jugando… ¡Vamos a saludarla!

Felipe: ¡Lo sabía!

Sebas: Hola, Alba.

Felipe: ¡Hola!

Alba: Hola, chicos, ¿ya terminaron de jugar?

Felipe: Sí. Yo quería seguir, pero como Sebas iba perdiendo, no quería jugar más, ¿verdad, campeón?

Sebas: Yo era quien iba ganando, pero es que no tengo más ganas de jugar.

Felipe: ¿Y tú? ¿Qué haces por aquí?

Alba: Nada. Solo me apetecía estar sola.

Sebas: ¿Te ocurre algo?

Alba: No, solo es que a veces me siento bien cuando estoy sola. Tenía ganas de salir un rato de casa.

Felipe: Tú vives en casa de tus tíos, ¿verdad?

Alba: Sí. Y la casa de mis tíos no es una casa muy tranquila…

Felipe: ¿Por qué? ¿Tus tíos son muy nerviosos?

Alba: No, mi tío está siempre fuera de casa, en el restaurante. Y mi tía es muy amable y cariñosa. El problema es mi primo. Mis tíos tienen un hijo pequeño. Tiene 8 años, y es muy ruidoso…

Sebas: Pero, ¿te llevas mal con él o qué?

ALBA: ¡No! Realmente es encantador. Muy divertido y cariñoso. Pero siempre quiere que juegue con él, ¡a todas horas! Y a mí me gusta jugar con él, pero a veces me pone un poco nerviosa, sobre todo cuando está en mi habitación. A mí me encanta estar sola en mi habitación, pero él siempre quiere estar conmigo.

Sebas: Y nunca te deja sola.

Alba: Sí. A veces, no soporto que haga tanto ruido. Mi primo siempre habla gritando. Me pone muy nerviosa cuando grita. ¡No me gusta que me hablen tan fuerte!

Felipe: ¡Pero es que ustedes los españoles siempre hablan muy fuerte!

Alba: Yo no…

Sebas: Eso es cierto, tú no. Tú eres mucho más dulce siempre… Oye, ¿cómo te va en la ciudad? ¿Te estás adaptando bien a tu nueva vida?

Alba: Sí, más o menos. Estoy contenta con mi nueva vida. En realidad, estoy encantada de haber venido a estudiar a la ciudad. Es una gran ciudad.

Felipe: ¿Y en la escuela?

Alba: Bueno, aunque aún no conozco a mucha gente. ¡Acabo de llegar! Todavía no tengo muchos amigos en clase, aunque a mí me da igual no ser una chica muy popular…

Sebas: Nosotros somos tus amigos…

Alba: Sí, eso es verdad…

Felipe: Oye, te vi de lejos que estabas dibujando. ¿Qué hacías?

Alba: No, nada, una tontería…

Sebas: ¿Te gusta dibujar?

Alba: Bueno… Cuando me siento un poco de mal humor, me gusta dibujar. Me siento muy bien cuando estoy dibujando.

Sebas: ¿Nos lo muestras?

Alba: ¡No! ¡Me da vergüenza!

Felipe: ¡Por favor! ¡Muéstranoslo!

Sebas: ¡Vamos, Alba! ¡Dijiste que somos tus amigos!

Alba: Bueno, vale… ¿Les gusta?

Sebas y Felipe: ¡Somos nosotros!

EPISODIO 7: GALLETAS SEGISMUNDO

Voz: Señores clientes, les informamos de que nuestras cajas cierran dentro de cinco minutos.

Sebas: Tenemos que acabar. ¿Llevamos ya todo?

Felipe: Me parece que sí.

Sebas: ¿Te parece? Tenemos que estar seguros de que no falte nada.

Felipe: No creo que falte nada.

Sebas: Nos mandaron hacer la compra para la fiesta. Somos los responsables. ¡No puede faltar nada!

Felipe: No te preocupes, llevamos todo.

Sebas: Pues, en mi opinión, se nos está olvidando algo. A ver… ¿Servilletas?

Felipe: Están.

Sebas: Platos pequeños.

Felipe: Están. Mira, Sebas, te digo que ya está todo, así que deja de preocuparte.

Sebas: Pero te olvidaste la lista. Nunca hay que venir al supermercado sin la lista. ¡Es una ley universal! Si vienes sin lista, en primer lugar seguro que se te olvida algo. Y en segundo lugar, seguro que compras más de lo que necesitas.

Felipe: Ya te dije que dejé la lista en casa. Pero no te preocupes, que ya está todo.

Sebas: Me pone muy nervioso venir de compras sin la lista.

Felipe: ¡Espera! ¡Sí! ¡Se nos olvidan las galletas saladas!

Sebas: ¿Lo ves? Te dije que se nos olvidaba algo…

Voz: Señores clientes, les informamos de que nuestro supermercado está a punto de cerrar. Les rogamos vayan pasando por caja.

Sebas: No, al final, no nos da tiempo a comprar todo.

Felipe: Tranquilo, las galletas están aquí mismo.

Sebas: Vamos, corre…

Felipe: ¡Cuántas marcas de galletas diferentes! ¿Alguna marca en especial?

Sebas: Me parece que en la lista estaba anotada la marca que quería Lorena.

Felipe: Entonces tendremos que decidir nosotros. A mí me gustan… a ver… ¡Estas!

Sebas: Ok, agarra un par de cajas y vámonos ya.

Felipe: No, espera, mejor esta.

Sebas: Vale, pues esa.

Felipe: No, espera, mejor esta… No, espera, ¡esta!

Sebas: Felipe, por favor, decídete, que están cerrando…

Felipe: ¡Es que me gustan todas!

Sebas: No seas bruto, ¡estas mismas!

Felipe: No, espera, acabo de recordar lo que había escrito en la lista.

Sebas: O sea, que Lorena sí que las quería de una marca especial.

Felipe: Sí. ¿Cómo he podido olvidarlo? ¡Si son las mejores galletas!

Sebas: ¿Y cuáles son?

Felipe: ¡Estas! "Galletas Segismundo,/galletas Segismundo,/las galletitas saladas/ que gustan a todo el mundo…".

Sebas: Eso no es así…

Felipe: Me encanta ese anuncio. Lo he visto mil veces. ¿Cómo que no es así?

Sebas: No, las galletas Segismundo son galletas dulces, no saladas…

Voz: Señores clientes, estamos cerrando. Pasen IN-ME-DI-A-TA-MEN-TE por caja…

Felipe: Pero, ¡qué dices! Galletas Segismundo son galletas saladas, eso lo sabe todo el mundo…

Sebas: Pues te equivocas. Dame… "Galletas Segismundo,/galletas Segismundo,/las galletitas más dulces/que gustan a todo el mundo…" ¿Ves? Son dulces, no saladas… Así que estás recordando mal la canción del anuncio.

Felipe: ¡De eso nada! Me indigna que seas tú quien no recuerde ese anuncio. ¡Dame, te voy a demostrar que eres tú quien está equivocado! "Galletas Segismundo,/galletas Segismundo,/las galletitas ¡SALADAS!,/que gustan a todo el mundo…" ¿Ves? ¡Saladas, son saladas…! ¡SA-LA-DAS!

Sebas: ¡Claro que no es así! ¡Dame otra vez esa caja…! ¡Voy a demostrarte que…!

Voz: ¡Hey, los dos del fondo! ¡Los bailarines! ¿Quieren hacer ya el favor de dejar de hacer el tonto y decidirse ya por las galletas? ¡Que tenemos que cerrar!

EPISODIO 8: ¡HASTA SIEMPRE, MIS AMIGOS!

Sebas: A mí me gustan más los cómics de Marvel que los Manga, la verdad…

Alba: Pues mis cómics favoritos, sin duda, son los de Manga.

Sebas: Sí, además te gusta dibujarlos. ¡Me encantó el que nos hiciste a Felipe y a mí jugando al básquetbol!

Alba: Sí, gracias. A mí me encantó dibujarlos… Oye, y ahora que mencionas a

Felipe: ¿Qué hora será?

Sebas: No sé…

Alba: ¡Qué extraño! Felipe aún no ha llegado. ¿Qué le habrá pasado?

Sebas: No sé… Igual… tuvo algo que hacer.

Alba: Es raro, habría avisado por teléfono, ¿no?

Sebas: Sí, ¡pero siempre llega tarde a todo!

Alba: Sí, eso será…

Alfonso: ¿Entonces te fue bien la entrevista de trabajo?

Eli: Sí, chévere.

Alfonso: ¿Qué te preguntaron?

Eli: Muchas cosas. Lo más difícil fue cuando me dijeron si estaba dispuesta a irme a trabajar fuera de la ciudad.

Alfonso: Y tú les dijiste que estabas dispuesta, ¿no?

Eli: Claro, aunque al principio mi idea no era irme a trabajar fuera de la ciudad. Pero es un buen trabajo. No lo puedo rechazar…

Alfonso: ¿Y entonces te dijeron que estabas contratada o qué?

Eli: Me dijeron que me escribirían pronto y hoy mismo he recibido la carta.

Alfonso: ¿Y qué te dicen?

Eli: Estimada señorita Castañeda: Tenemos el gusto de comunicarle que ha sido usted elegida para el puesto de auxiliar de enfermería en nuestro hospital…

Alfonso: ¿Pero qué dices? ¿En serio?

Eli: ¡Me dicen que el trabajo es mío!

Alfonso: ¡Eso es una noticia genial!

Eli: Sí. ¡Estoy superfeliz!

Alfonso: Me alegro mucho por ti, aunque me da un poco de tristeza…

Eli: ¿Por qué?

Alfonso: Porque vas a estar lejos de… quiero decir… de nosotros…

Eli: Pero podrán ustedes venir a visitarme cuando quieran.

Alfonso: Sí, lo sé, pero te echaré mucho de menos.

Eli: Yo también a ti, Alfonso.

Lorena: Es probable entonces que tú también te vayas de la ciudad, ¿verdad, Juanjo?

Juanjo: Sí. Me admitieron en el curso y estaré varios meses en la capital.

Lorena: ¿Cuándo recibiste la noticia?

Juanjo: Hoy mismo. Mira, aquí, en el teléfono, aún tengo el mensaje. Vaya, no puedo acceder a Internet…

Lorena: Es probable que aquí no haya cobertura.

Juanjo. No hace falta… ¡Ah!, mira, espera, sí, ya se ha cargado… mira.

Lorena: ¡Enhorabuena! Seguro que vas a tener una experiencia fantástica.

Juanjo: ¡Sí, cierto! Esta beca era seguramente la más interesante para continuar con mis estudios. ¡Y, además, voy a poder pagar mi propio apartamento!

Lorena: ¡Qué bien! ¡Espero que puedas un día invitarme a conocer la capital!

Juanjo: ¡Por supuesto, eso sería genial!

Lorena: Vaya, al final no hay galletas saladas.

Juanjo: Pues…, parece que no.

Lorena: Bueno, es igual… ¿Te apetece que bailemos?

Juanjo: ¡Claro!

Alba: ¡Eh! ¡Por fin llegaste!

Sebas: ¡Estábamos preocupados! ¿Dónde te metiste?

Felipe: Estaba en casa buscando este disco. Es de mis padres… ¡No lo encontraba!

Sebas: ¿Llegaste tarde a la fiesta porque estabas buscando un disco?

Felipe: Sí, un disco especial. Muchachos, ustedes saben que el curso terminó y llega el verano. Vamos a pasar una temporada sin vernos. Algunos de ustedes incluso es probable que se vayan de la ciudad para el curso próximo. Así que no quería venir a esta fiesta sin este disco. Hay aquí una canción muy especial que quiero compartir con ustedes. Es mi mejor forma de agradecerles su amistad. Es una canción bien viejita, pero creo que les va a gustar.

Eli: ¡Pero esta canción es maravillosa!

Felipe: Sabía que les iba a gustar. Es mi pequeño homenaje a esta gran ciudad… ¡y a todos ustedes!

UNIDAD 0: VOLVEMOS A VERNOS

	OBJECTIVES / TOPIC	PRESENT/PRACTICE/COMMUNICATE	ADDITIONAL TEACHER RESOURCES	HOMEWORK	ELETECA ONLINE PRACTICE

DAY 1	• Introduce unit theme: **Volvemos a vernos**, activities in the past and vacation time
	• Introduce culture for the unit: Learn about vacation time in Hispanic countries
	• Review vocabulary related to travel and free-time activities
		• **Unit Opener** (15 minutes)
		• *Las vacaciones* (30 minutes)
		  – Activity 1
		  – Activity 2 (Audio 1)
		  – Activity 3
		  – Activity 4
		  – Activity 5
		• **Wrap-up/Assess** (5 minutes)
			• IWB 0.1, 0.2		

DAY 2	• Review grammatical structures: Present progressive tense; preterit, and present perfect
	• Talk about past vacations and what you did
		• **Warm-up** (10 minutes)
		• *Las vacaciones* (35 minutes)
		  – Activity 6
		  – Activity 7
		  – Activity 8
		  – Activity 9
		  – Activity 10
		  – Activity 11
		• **Wrap-up/Assess** (5 minutes)			

DAY 3	• Talk about activities in the past
	• Relate a story or anecdote
		• **Warm-up** (10 minutes)
		• *Recuerdos de la escuela* (35 minutes)
		  – Activity 1
		  – Activity 2 (Audio 2)
		  – Activity 3 (Audio 2)
		• **Wrap-up/Assess** (5 minutes)
			• EA 0.1		

DAY 4	• Talk about activities in the past
	• Relate a story or anecdote
		• **Warm-up** (10 minutes)
		• *Recuerdos de la escuela* (35 minutes)
		  – Activity 4
		  – Activity 5
		  – Activity 6
		• **Wrap-up/Assess** (5 minutes)			

DAY 5	• Describe physical characteristics and personality traits in the past
	• Review verbs **ser / estar**
	• Review informal commands
		• **Warm-up** (10 minutes)
		• *Recuerdos de la escuela* (35 minutes)
		  – Activity 7
		  – Activity 8
		  – Activity 9
		• Un poco más
		  – Activities 1-6			

DAY 6	• Learn about Hispanic treasures
	• Compare similarities
		• **Warm-up** (10 minutes)
		• **Sabor Hispano** (35 minutes)
		Tesoros Latinoamericanos (Audio 3)
		  – Las líneas de Nazca
		  – Rapa Nui
		  – Activities
		• **Wrap-up/Assess** (5 minutes)			

	OBJECTIVES / TOPIC	PRESENT/PRACTICE/COMMUNICATE	ADDITIONAL TEACHER RESOURCES	HOMEWORK	ELETECA ONLINE PRACTICE

DAY 7	• Review unit vocabulary and expressions
	• Practice communicative skills
		• **Wrap-up** (10 minutes)
		• **En resumen** (30 minutes)
		  – Vocabulario
		  – Gramática
		• **Wrap-up/Assess** (10 minutes)			

UNIDAD 1: CONSTRUYENDO UN FUTURO

	OBJECTIVES / TOPIC	PRESENT/PRACTICE/COMMUNICATE	ADDITIONAL TEACHER RESOURCES	HOMEWORK	ELETECA ONLINE PRACTICE

DAY 1	• Introduce unit theme: ***Construyendo un futuro***, making plans for the future
	• Introduce culture for unit: Learn about politics and the environment in Hispanic countries and compare cultural similarities
	• Preview vocabulary: Talking about what people plan to do in the future
		• **Unit Opener** (15 minutes)
		• **Hablamos de...** (30 minutes)
		El futuro
		  – Activity 1
		  – Activity 2
		• **Wrap-up/Assess** (5 minutes)
					• Hablamos de...
					  – Activity 1
					    (10 minutes)
					  – Activity 2
					    (10 minutes)
					  – Activity 3
					    (10 minutes)

DAY 2	• Preview grammatical structures: Future of regular and irregular verbs; Time expressions; ***Si*** + present + future	• **Warm-up** (10 minutes)
		• **Hablamos de...** (35 minutes)
		El futuro
		  – Activity 3 (Audio 4)
		  – Activity 4 (Audio 4)
		  – Activity 5
		  – Activity 6
		• **Wrap-up/Assess** (5 minutes)			

DAY 3	• Present communicative functions of the unit: Making assumptions or conjectures	• **Warm-up** (10 minutes)
		• **Comunica** (35 minutes)
		Making assumptions
		  – Presentation
		  – Activity 1
		  – Activity 2
		  – Activity 3
		  – Activity 4
		  – Activity 5
		• **Wrap-up/Assess** (5 minutes)
			• EA 1.1
			• IWB 1.1, 1.2
					• Comunica
					  – Activity 1
					    (10 minutes)
					  – Activity 2
					    (10 minutes)
					  – Activity 3
					    (10 minutes)

DAY 4	• Present the communicative functions of the unit: Making promisesPresent communicative	• **Warm-up** (10 minutes)
		• **Comunica** (35 minutes)
		Making promises
		  – Presentation
		  – Activity 6 (Audio 5)
		  – Activity 7
		  – Activity 8
		• **Wrap-up/Assess** (5 minutes)			

	OBJECTIVES / TOPIC	PRESENT/PRACTICE/COMMUNICATE	ADDITIONAL TEACHER RESOURCES	HOMEWORK	ELETECA ONLINE PRACTICE

DAY 5	• Contextualize the content of the unit: *¡Acción!* Video
	• Provide students with a structured approach to viewing the video
		• **¡Acción!** (50 minutes)
		Una cita con Morgana
		  Antes del video
		  – Activity 1
		  Durante el video
		  – Activity 2
		  Después del video
		  – Activity 3
			• DVD Episodio 1: *Una cita con Morgana*		• Video 1: *Una cita con Morgana* (10 minutes)
					• Extra activity (16 minutes)

DAY 6	• Present the vocabulary needed to practice the communicative and grammatical functions for the unit: The environment and the future	• **Warm-up** (10 minutes)
		• **Palabra por palabra** (35 minutes)
		El medioambiente
		  – Activity 1
		  – Activity 2
		  – Activity 3
		• **Wrap-up/Assess** (5 minutes)
			• EA 1.2
			• IWB 1.3
				• WB Online practice: Vocabulario 1.1 - 1.3	• Palabra por palabra
					  – Activity 1 (10 minutes)
					  – Activity 2 (10 minutes)
					  – Activity 3 (10 minutes)

DAY 7	• Talk about ways to preserve natural resources	• **Warm-up** (10 minutes)
		• **Palabra por palabra** (35 min)
		El medioambiente
		  – Activity 4
		  – Activity 5
		  – Activity 6
		• **Wrap-up/Assess** (5 minutes)			

DAY 8	• Present vocabulary needed to practice communicative and grammatical functions for the unit: Politics and elections
	• Talk about candidates and campaign promise
		• **Warm-up** (10 minutes)
		• **Palabra por palabra** (35 minutes)
		La política
		  – Activity 7
		  – Activity 8
		  – Activity 9
		• **Wrap-up/Assess** (5 minutes)			

DAY 9	• Present the grammatical structures needed to practice the communicative functions of the unit: The future tense of regular and irregular verbs
	• Use the future tense to make predictions and talk about what will happen
		• **Warm-up** (10 minutes)
		• **Gramática** (35 minutes)
		1. The future tense
		  – Presentation
		  – Activity 1
		  – Activity 2
		• **Wrap-up/Assess** (5 minutes)
				• WB Online practice: Gramática 1.4 - 1.7	• Grammar tutorials
					  – Tutorial 1 (8 minutes)
					  – Extra activity (14 minutes)
					  – Tutorial 2 (8 minutes)
					• Extra activity (14 minutes)

DAY 10	• Present the grammatical structures needed to practice the communicative functions of the unit: *Si* + present + future
	• Make predictions about what will happen under certain conditions
		• **Warm-up** (10 minutes)
		• **Gramática** (35 minutes)
		2. *Si* + present + future
		  – Presentation
		  – Activity 3
		  – Activity 4
		  – Activity 5
		  – Activity 6
		  – Activity 7
		• **Wrap-up/Assess** (5 minutes)			

	OBJECTIVES / TOPIC	PRESENT/PRACTICE/COMMUNICATE	ADDITIONAL TEACHER RESOURCES	HOMEWORK	ELETECA ONLINE PRACTICE

DAY 11	• Scan for specific information
	• Organize information in a logical order
		• **Destrezas** (45 minutes)
		Comprensión de lectura
		  – Activity 1
		  – Activity 2
		
		Expresión e interacción escritas
		  – Activity 3
		  – Activity 4
		• **Wrap-up/Assess** (5 minutes)
				• WB Online practice: Destrezas 1.8 - 1.11	• Destreza lectora (15 minutes)
					• Destreza escrita (15 minutes)
					• Destreza oral (15 minutes)

DAY 12	• Practice separating syllables and using stress correctly	• **Wrap-up** (10 minutes)
		• **Pronunciación** (35 minutes)
		  – Presentation
		  – Activity 1 (Audio 6)
		  – Activity 2
		  – Activity 3
		• **Wrap-up/Assess** (5 minutes)
					• Pronunciación
					  – Activity 1 (10 minutes)
					  – Activity 2 (10 minutes)
					  – Activity 3 (10 minutes)

DAY 13	• Learn about Spanish national parks
	• Activate vocabulary connected with the environment
		• **Warm-up** (10 minutes)
		• **Sabor Hispano** (35 minutes)
		¡Bienvenidos a los parques nacionales de España! (Audio 7)
		  – Parques nacionales
		  – Atractivos
		  – Activities
		• **Wrap-up/Assess** (5 minutes)
			• Voces latinas video: *El misterio de Rapa Nui*	• WB Online practice: Cultura 1.12	• Voces latinas video: *El misterio de Rapa Nui*
					• Extra activity (10 minutes)

DAY 14	• Revisit unit themes, grammar, vocabulary, and culture in a new context
	• Improve reading comprehension skills
		• **Warm-up** (5 minutes)
		• **Relato** (40 minutes)
		Viaje al futuro
		  – Activity 1
		  – Activity 2 (Audio 8)
		  – Activity 3
		  – Activity 4
		  – Activity 5
		  – Activity 6
		• **Wrap-up/Assess** (5 minutes)			

DAY 15	• Review grammar, vocabulary, and culture from the unit
	• Complete self-assessment
		• **Warm-up** (5 minutes)
		[Option 1]
		• **Evaluación** (35 minutes)
		  – Activities 1-8
		[Option 2]
		• **Casa del español-videos** (35 minutes)
		  – Videos 1 and 2
		  – Extra activities
		• **En resumen** (10 minutes)
		  – Vocabulario
		  – Gramática
			• EA 1.3		• Evaluación
					• Casa del español videos
					  – Video 1 (5 minutes)
					  – Extra activity (10 minutes)
					  – Video 2 (5 minutes)
					• Extra activity (10 minutes)

	OBJECTIVES / TOPIC	PRESENT/PRACTICE/COMMUNICATE	ADDITIONAL TEACHER RESOURCES	HOMEWORK	ELETECA ONLINE PRACTICE
DAY 16	• Assessment	• **Warm-up** (5 minutes) • **Online test Unit 1** (30 minutes)	• Unit 1 assessment		
DAY 17	• Gamification project				

UNIDAD 2: COSAS DE CASA

	OBJECTIVES / TOPIC	PRESENT/PRACTICE/COMMUNICATE	ADDITIONAL TEACHER RESOURCES	HOMEWORK	ELETECA ONLINE PRACTICE

DAY 1	• Introduce unit theme **Cosas de casa**, families and household chores
	• Introduce culture for the unit: Learn about what is considered polite in Spanish culture and what is not
	• Preview vocabulary: Talking about what people do in the family context
		• **Unit Opener** (15 minutes)
		• **Hablamos de...** (30 minutes)
		Las tareas de la casa
		  – Activity 1
		  – Activity 2
		• **Wrap-up/Assess** (5 minutes)
					• Hablamos de...
					  – Activity 1
					  (10 minutes)
					  – Activity 2
					  (10 minutes)
					  – Activity 3
					  (10 minutes)

DAY 2	• Preview grammatical structures: Affirmative and negative commands; Commands and pronouns	• **Wrap-up/Assess** (5 minutes)
		• **Hablamos de...** (30 minutes)
		Las tareas de la casa
		  – Activity 3 (Audio 9)
		  – Activity 4
		• **Wrap-up/Assess** (5 minutes)			

DAY 3	• Present communicative functions of the unit:
	  – Ask and give permission
	  – Offer and encourage others to accept
		• **Warm-up** (10 minutes)
		• **Comunica** (35 minutes)
		Asking, giving and denying permission
		  – Presentation
		Offering and encouraging others to accept
		  – Presentation
		  – Activity 1 (Audio 10)
		  – Activity 2 (Audio 11)
		  – Activity 3
		• **Wrap-up/Assess** (5 minutes)
			• EA 2.1
			• IWB 2.1		

DAY 4	• Present the communicative functions of the unit: Asking for and giving instructions	• **Warm-up** (10 minutes)
		• **Comunica** (35 minutes)
		Asking for and giving instructions
		  – Presentation
		  – Activities 4 - 6
		• **Wrap-up/Assess** (5 minutes)
					• Comunica
					  – Activity 1
					  (10 minutes)
					  – Activity 2
					  (10 minutes)
					  – Activity 3
					  (10 minutes)

DAY 5	• Contextualize the content of the unit: *¡Acción!* Video
	• Provide students with a structured approach to viewing the video
		• **¡Acción!** (50 minutes)
		El señor Don Limpio
		  Antes del video
		  – Activity 1
		  Durante el video
		  – Activity 2
		  Después del video
		  – Activities 3 and 4
			• DVD
			Episodio 2:
			El señor Don Limpio
					• Video 2: *El señor Don Limpio* (10 minutes)
					• Extra activity (16 minutes)

	OBJECTIVES / TOPIC	PRESENT/PRACTICE/COMMUNICATE	ADDITIONAL TEACHER RESOURCES	HOMEWORK	ELETECA ONLINE PRACTICE
DAY 6	• Present vocabulary needed to practice communicative and grammatical functions for the unit: Household chores	• **Warm-up** (10 minutes) • **Palabra por palabra** (35 minutes) *Las tareas domésticas* — Activity 1 (Audio 12) — Activity 2 • **Wrap-up/Assess** (5 minutes)	• EA 2.2	• WB Online practice: Vocabulario 2.1 - 2.7	• Palabra por palabra — Activity 1 (10 minutes) — Activity 2 (10 minutes) — Activity 3 (10 minutes)
DAY 7	• Talk about how to organize family members to do household chores	• **Warm-up** (10 minutes) • **Palabra por palabra** (35 minutes) *Las tareas domésticas* — Activity 3 — Activity 4 — Activity 5 • **Wrap-up/Assess** (5 minutes)			
DAY 8	• Present vocabulary needed to practice communicative and grammatical functions for the unit: Sports • Describe how to play certain sports and games	• **Warm-up** (10 minutes) • **Palabra por palabra** (35 minutes) *Los deportes* — Activity 6 — Activity 7 — Activity 8 — Activity 9 — Activity 10 • **Wrap-up/Assess** (5 minutes)			
DAY 9	• Present grammatical structures needed to practice communicative functions of the unit: Affirmative commands of regular and irregular verbs • Use affirmative command forms to tell different people what to do	• **Warm-up** (10 minutes) • **Gramática** (35 minutes) 1. Affirmative commands — Presentation — Activity 1 — Activity 2 — Activity 3 • **Wrap-up/Assess** (5 minutes)	• EA 2.3 • IWB 2.2	• WB Online practice: Gramática 2.8 - 2.11	• Grammar tutorials — Tutorial 3 (8 minutes) — Extra activity (14 minutes) — Tutorial 4 (8 minutes) • Extra activity (14 minutes)
DAY 10	• Present grammatical structures needed to practice communicative functions of the unit: — Negative commands of regular and irregular verbs — Use negative command forms to tell different people what not to do	• **Warm-up** (10 minutes) • **Gramática** (35 minutes) 2. Negative commands — Presentation — Activity 4 — Activity 5 — Activity 6 — Activity 7 • **Wrap-up/Assess** (5 minutes)			
DAY 11	• Learn to skim a brochure for information • Asking the right questions	• **Destrezas** (45 minutes) *Comprensión de lectura* — Activity 1 — Activity 2 *Expresión e interacción orales* — Activity 3 • **Wrap-up/Assess** (5 minutes)		• WB Online practice: Destrezas 2.12 - 2.15	• Destreza lectora (15 minutes) • Destreza escrita (15 minutes) • Destreza oral (15 minutes)

	OBJECTIVES / TOPIC	PRESENT/PRACTICE/COMMUNICATE	ADDITIONAL TEACHER RESOURCES	HOMEWORK	ELETECA ONLINE PRACTICE

DAY 12	• Practice correct intonation
	• Listen and identify meaning through pronunciation
		• **Warm-up** (10 minutes)
		• **Pronunciación** (35 minutes)
		  – Presentation
		  – Activity 1 (Audio 13)
		  – Activity 2 (Audio 14)
		  – Activity 3 (Audio 15)
		• **Wrap-up/Assess** (5 minutes)
					• Pronunciación
					  – Activity 1
					    (10 minutes)
					  – Activity 2
					    (10 minutes)
					  – Activity 3
					    (10 minutes)

DAY 13	• Learn about manners in Spanish society
	• Learn how other cultures have different norms
		• **Warm-up** (10 minutes)
		• **Sabor Hispano** (35 minutes)
		Buenos y malos modales (Audio 16)
		  – *¿Qué suelen pensar los extranjeros del comportamiento social de los españoles?*
		  – *5 comportamientos de buena educación en España*
		  – Activities
		• **Wrap-up/Assess** (5 minutes)
			• Voces latinas video: *¿Cómo son tus modales?*	• WB Online practice: Cultura 2.16 - 2.18	• Voces latinas video: *¿Cómo son tus modales?*
					• Extra activity (10 minutes)

DAY 14	• Revisit unit themes, grammar, vocabulary and culture in a new context
	• Improve reading comprehension skills
		• **Warm-up** (5 minutes)
		• **Relato** (40 minutes)
		Mi abuela Eva
		  – Activity 1
		  – Activity 2 (Audio 17)
		  – Activity 3
		  – Activity 4
		  – Activity 5
		• **Wrap-up/Assess** (5 minutes)			

DAY 15	• Review grammar, vocabulary, and culture from the unit	• **Warm-up** (5 minutes)
		[Option 1]
		• **Evaluación** (35 minutes)
		  – Activity 1
		  – Activity 2
		  – Activity 3
		  – Activity 4
		  – Activity 5 (Audio 18)
		  – Activity 6
		[Option 2]
		• **Casa del español-videos** (35 minutes)
		  – Videos 1 and 2
		  – Extra activities
		• **En resumen** (10 minutes)
		  – Vocabulario
		  – Gramática
					• Evaluación
					• Casa del español videos
					  – Video 3
					    (5 minutes)
					  – Extra activity
					    (10 minutes)
					  – Video 4
					    (5 minutes)
					• Extra activity (10 minutes)

DAY 16	• Assessment	• **Warm-up** (5 minutes) • **Online test Unit 2** (30 minutes)	• Unit 2 assessment		
DAY 17	• Gamification project				

	OBJECTIVES / TOPIC	PRESENT/PRACTICE/COMMUNICATE	ADDITIONAL TEACHER RESOURCES	HOMEWORK	ELETECA ONLINE PRACTICE

DAY 18	• Review grammar, vocabulary, and culture from the last two units
	• Complete self-assessment
		• **Ahora comprueba** (50 minutes)
		  – Activity 1
		  – Activity 2 (Audio 19)
		  – Activity 3 (Audio 20)
		  – Activity 4
		  – Activity 5
		  – Activity 6			

UNIDAD 3: DE CINE

	OBJECTIVES / TOPIC	PRESENT/PRACTICE/COMMUNICATE	ADDITIONAL TEACHER RESOURCES	HOMEWORK	ELETECA ONLINE PRACTICE

DAY 1	• Introduce unit theme **De cine**, about movies and theater
	• Introduce culture for the unit: Learn about movies and Theater
	• Preview vocabulary: Words and colloquial expressions relating to movies and theater
		• **Unit Opener** (15 minutes)
		• **Hablamos de...** (30 minutes)
		Cines y teatros
		  – Activity 1
		  – Activity 2 (Audio 35)
		  – Activity 3
		• **Wrap-up/Assess** (5 minutes)
			• IWB 3.1		• Hablamos de...
					  – Activity 1
					    (10 minutes)
					  – Activity 2
					    (10 minutes)
					  – Activity 3
					    (10 minutes)

DAY 2	• Preview grammatical structures: Imperfect and preterit; Pluperfect; Time expressions; Prepositions **por** and **para**	• **Warm-up** (10 minutes)
		• **Hablamos de...** (35 minutes)
		Cines y teatros
		  – Activity 4 (Audio 21)
		  – Activity 5 (Audio 21)
		  – Activity 6
		• **Wrap-up/Assess** (5 minutes)			

DAY 3	• Present communicative functions of the unit:
	  – Express surprise, skepticism, curiosity and give information
	  – React to information you hear
		• **Warm-up** (10 minutes)
		• **Comunica** (35 minutes)
		Expressing surprise, skepticism, curiosity, and giving information
		  – Presentation
		  – Activity 1
		  – Activity 2
		  – Activity 3
		  – Activity 4
		• **Wrap-up/Assess** (5 minutes)
			• EA 3.1		• Comunica
					  – Activity 1
					    (10 minutes)
					  – Activity 2
					    (10 minutes)
					  – Activity 3
					    (10 minutes)

DAY 4	• Present communicative functions of the unit: Expressing purpose or motive of an action	• **Warm-up** (10 minutes)
		• **Comunica** (35 minutes)
		Expressing purpose or motive of an action
		  – Presentation
		  – Activity 5
		  – Activity 6
		  – Activity 7
		• **Wrap-up/Assess** (5 minutes)			

	OBJECTIVES / TOPIC	PRESENT/PRACTICE/COMMUNICATE	ADDITIONAL TEACHER RESOURCES	HOMEWORK	ELETECA ONLINE PRACTICE
DAY 5	• Contextualize the content of the unit: **¡Acción!** Video • Provide students with a structured approach to viewing the video	• **¡Acción!** (50 minutes) *La casa de las paredes negras* Antes del video – Activity 1 Durante el video – Activities 2 and 3 Después del video – Activity 4	• DVD Episodio 3: *La casa de las paredes negras*		• Video 3: *La casa de las paredes negras* (10 minutes) • Extra activity (16 minutes)
DAY 6	• Present vocabulary needed to practice communicative and grammatical functions for the unit: Expressions relating to movies and theater • Talk about the movie and theater industry and what people do	• **Warm-up** (10 minutes) • **Palabra por palabra** (35 minutes) *El cine y el teatro* – Activity 1 – Activity 2 – Activity 3 • **Wrap-up/Assess** (5 minutes)	• EA 3.2	• WB Online practice: Vocabulario 3.1 - 3.13	• Palabra por palabra – Activity 1 (10 minutes) – Activity 2 (10 minutes) – Activity 3 (10 minutes)
DAY 7	• Present vocabulary needed to practice communicative and grammatical functions for the unit: Movie types • Talk about the types of movies you prefer	• **Warm-up** (10 minutes) • **Palabra por palabra** (35 minutes) *Géneros de cine* – Activity 4 – Activity 5 – Activity 6 • **Wrap-up/Assess** (5 minutes)			
DAY 8	• Present grammatical structures needed to practice communicative functions of the unit: – Review of past tenses (preterit, imperfect and present perfect) – Distinguish between the tenses and their uses	• **Warm-up** (10 minutes) • **Gramática** (35 minutes) 1. Review of past tenses – Presentation – Activity 1 – Activity 2 (Audio 22) • **Wrap-up/Assess** (5 minutes)		• WB Online practice: Gramática 3.14 - 3.20	• Grammar tutorials – Tutorial 5 (8 minutes) – Extra activity (14 minutes) – Tutorial 6 (8 minutes) • Extra activity (14 minutes)
DAY 9	• Present grammatical structures needed to practice communicative functions of the unit: Time expressions associated with past tenses • Sequence actions in the past	• **Warm-up** (10 minutes) • **Gramática** (35 minutes) 2. Narrating in the past – Activity 3 – Activity 4 • **Wrap-up/Assess** (5 minutes)			
DAY 10	• Present grammatical structures needed to practice communicative functions of the unit: The pluperfect tense • Describe actions that took place before other actions in the past	• **Warm-up** (10 minutes) • **Gramática** (35 minutes) 3. The Pluperfect – Presentation – Activity 5 • **Wrap-up/Assess** (5 minutes)	• EA 3.3 • IWB 3.2		

	OBJECTIVES / TOPIC	PRESENT/PRACTICE/COMMUNICATE	ADDITIONAL TEACHER RESOURCES	HOMEWORK	ELETECA ONLINE PRACTICE
DAY 11	• Focus on relevant information	• **Destrezas** (45 minutes) *Comprensión de lectura* — Activity 1 — Activity 2 — Activity 3 • **Wrap-up/Assess** (5 minutes)		• WB Online practice: Destrezas 3.21 - 3.24	• Destreza lectora (15 minutes) • Destreza escrita (15 minutes) • Destreza oral (15 minutes)
DAY 12	• Practice pronouncing and spelling words containing the letter *h*	• **Warm-up** (5 minutes) • **Pronunciación** (35 minutes) — Activity 1 — Activity 2 (Audio 23) — Activity 3 (Audio 24) • **Wrap-up/Assess** (5 minutes)			• Pronunciación — Activity 1 (10 minutes) — Activity 2 (10 minutes) — Activity 3 (10 minutes)
DAY 13	• Learn about the Mexican movie world • Activate vocabulary connected with movies	• **Warm-up** (10 minutes) • **Sabor Hispano** (35 minutes) *El cine mexicano... ¡está de moda!* ((Audio 25) — *Estas son las películas más taquilleras del cine moderno mexicano* — *Estos son los actores mexicanos más famosos* — *Activities* • **Wrap-up/Assess** (5 minutes)	• Voces latinas video: *El México de Frida Kahlo*	• WB Online practice: Cultura 3.25 - 3.27	• Voces latinas video: *El México de Frida Kahlo* • Extra activity (10 minutes)
DAY 14	• Revisit unit themes, grammar, vocabulary, and culture in a new context • Improve reading comprehension skills	• **Warm-up** (5 minutes) • **Relato** (40 minutes) *Lorca y la Generación del 27* — Activity 1 — Activity 2 — Activity 3 (Audio 26) — Activity 4 • **Wrap-up/Assess** (5 minutes)			
DAY 15	• Review grammar, vocabulary, and culture from the unit • Complete self-assessment • Review unit vocabulary and expressions • Practice communicative skills	• **Warm-up** (5 minutes) [Option 1] • **Evaluación** (35 minutes) — Activities 1-8 [Option 2] • **Casa del español-videos** (35 minutes) — Videos 1 and 2 — Extra activities • **En resumen** (10 minutes) — Vocabulario — Gramática			• Evaluación • Casa del español videos — Video 5 (5 minutes) — Extra activity (10 minutes) — Video 6 (5 minutes) • Extra activity (10 minutes)
DAY 16	• Assessment	• **Warm-up** (5 minutes) • **Online test Unit 3** (30 minutes)		• Unit 3 assessment	
DAY 17	• Gamification project				

UNIDAD 4: ¡SUPERESPACIO!

	OBJECTIVES / TOPIC	PRESENT/PRACTICE/COMMUNICATE	ADDITIONAL TEACHER RESOURCES	HOMEWORK	ELETECA ONLINE PRACTICE

DAY 1	• Introduce unit theme: **¡Superespacio!**, healthy lifestyles and giving advice
	• Introduce culture for the unit: Learn about pop culture and teen magazines in the Hispanic world
	• Preview vocabulary: Talking about pop culture, food and health
		• **Unit Opener** (15 minutes)
		• **Hablamos de...** (30 minutes)
		Revistas juveniles
		  – Activity 1
		  – Activity 2
		• **Wrap-up/Assess** (5 minutes)
					• Hablamos de...
					  – Activity 1
					    (10 minutes)
					  – Activity 2
					    (10 minutes)
					  – Activity 3
					    (10 minutes)

DAY 2	• Preview grammatical structures: The conditional	• **Warm-up** (10 minutes)
		• **Hablamos de...** (35 minutes)
		Revistas juveniles
		  – Activity 3 (Audio 27)
		  – Activity 4
		  – Activity 5
		  – Activity 6
		• **Wrap-up/Assess** (5 minutes)			

DAY 3	• Present communicative functions of the unit: Asking for and giving advice	• **Warm-up** (10 minutes)
		• **Comunica** (35 minutes)
		Asking for and giving advice
		  – Presentation
		  – Activity 1
		  – Activity 2
		  – Activity 3 (Audio 28)
		  – Activity 4
		• **Wrap-up/Assess** (5 minutes)
			• EA 4.1		• Comunica
					  – Activity 1
					    (10 minutes)
					  – Activity 2
					    (10 minutes)
					  – Activity 3
					    (10 minutes)

DAY 4	• Present communicative functions of the unit:
	  – Ask for favors and permission
	  – Express probability in the past
		• **Warm-up** (10 minutes)
		• **Comunica** (35 minutes)
		Asking for favors and permission
		  – Presentation
		  – Activity 5
		  – Activity 6
		Expressing probability in the past
		  – Presentation
		  – Activity 7
		  – Activity 8
		• **Wrap-up/Assess** (5 minutes)
			• IWB 4.1	• WB	

DAY 5	• Contextualize the content of the unit: **¡Acción!** video
	• Provide students with a structured approach to viewing the video
		• **¡Acción!** (50 minutes)
		Paella con curry
		Antes del video
		  – Activities 1 and 2
		Durante el video
		  – Activity 3
		Después del video
		  – Activity 4
			• DVD Episodio 4: *Paella con curry*		• Video 4: *Paella con curry*
					  (10 minutes)
					• Extra activity
					  (16 minutes)

DAY 6	• Present vocabulary needed to practice communicative and grammatical functions for the unit: Foods and healthy eating
	• Talk about foods and following a healthy diet
		• **Warm-up** (10 minutes)
		• **Palabra por palabra** (35 minutes)
		La comida
		  – Activity 1 (Audio 29)
		  – Activity 2
		  – Activity 3
		  – Activity 4
		• **Wrap-up/Assess** (5 minutes)
			• IWB 4.2
			• IEA 4.2
				• WB
				Online practice: Vocabulario 4.1 - 4.5
					• Palabra por palabra
					  – Activity 1
					    (10 minutes)
					  – Activity 2
					    (10 minutes)
					  – Activity 3
					    (10 minutes)

	OBJECTIVES / TOPIC	PRESENT/PRACTICE/COMMUNICATE	ADDITIONAL TEACHER RESOURCES	HOMEWORK	ELETECA ONLINE PRACTICE
DAY 7	• Present vocabulary needed to practice communicative and grammatical functions for the unit: – Cooking – Talk about food preparation and recipes	• **Warm-up** (10 minutes) • **Palabra por palabra** (35 minutes) *¡A cocinar!* – Activity 5 – Activity 6 – Activity 7 • **Wrap-up/Assess** (5 minutes)	• EA 4.3	• WB Online practice: Vocabulario 4.1 - 4.5	• Palabra por palabra – Activity 1 (10 minutes) – Activity 2 (10 minutes) – Activity 3 (10 minutes)
DAY 8	• Present grammatical structures needed to practice communicative functions of the unit: The conditional tense of regular verbs • Use the conditional to give advice	• **Warm-up** (10 minutes) • **Gramática** (35 minutes) 1. The conditional tense: regular verbs – Presentation – Activity 1 – Activity 2 • **Wrap-up/Assess** (5 minutes)		• WB Online practice: Gramática 4.6 - 4.15	• Grammar tutorials – Tutorial 7 (8 minutes) – Extra activity (14 minutes) – Tutorial 8 (8 minutes) • Extra activity (14 minutes)
DAY 9	• Present grammatical structures needed to practice communicative functions of the unit: The conditional tense of irregular verbs	• **Warm-up** (10 minutes) • **Gramática** (35 minutes) 2. The conditional tense: irregular verbs – Presentation – Activity 3 – Activity 4 • **Wrap-up/Assess** (5 minutes)			
DAY 10	• Use the conditional to ask for favors and express probability	• **Warm-up** (10 minutes) • **Gramática** (35 minutes) 3. The conditional tense: irregular verbs – Presentation – Activity 5 (Audio 30) – Activity 6 (Audio 30) – Activity 7 – Activity 8 • **Wrap-up/Assess** (5 minutes)			
DAY 11	• Identify the format of a text	• **Destrezas** (45 minutes) *Comprensión de lectura* – Activity 1 – Activity 2 (Audio 49) • **Wrap-up/Assess**	• WB Online practice: Destrezas 4.16 - 4.19		• Destreza lectora (15 minutes) • Destreza escrita (15 minutes) • Destreza oral (15 minutes)
DAY 12	• Practice pronouncing and spelling words containing the letters **y** and **x**	• **Warm-up** (10 minutes) • **Pronunciación** (35 minutes) – Presentation – Activity 1 – Activity 2 • **Wrap-up/Assess** (5 minutes)			• Pronunciación – Activity 1 (10 minutes) – Activity 2 (10 minutes) – Activity 3 (10 minutes)
DAY 13	• Learn about the Mediterranean diet and healthy eating • Activate vocabulary connected with food and cooking	• **Warm-up** (10 minutes) • **Sabor Hispano** (35 minutes) *La dieta mediterránea... ¿mito o realidad?* (Audio 31) – *Estos fueron los alimentos más consumidos en España en 2013* – *Gasto en comida rápida en el mundo (euros por habitante)* – Activities • **Wrap-up/Assess** (5 minutes)	• Voces latinas video: *La dieta mediterránea... ¿mito o realidad?*	• WB Online practice: Cultura 4.20 - 4.22	• Voces latinas video: *La dieta mediterránea... ¿mito o realidad?* • Extra activity (10 minutes)

	OBJECTIVES / TOPIC	PRESENT/PRACTICE/COMMUNICATE	ADDITIONAL TEACHER RESOURCES	HOMEWORK	ELETECA ONLINE PRACTICE

DAY 14	• Revisit unit themes, grammar, vocabulary, and culture in a new context
	• Improve reading comprehension skills
		• **Warm-up** (5 minutes)
		• **Relato** (40 minutes)
		Paradiso
		  – Activity 1
		  – Activity 2
		  – Activity 3 (Audio 32)
		  – Activity 4
		  – Activity 5
		• **Wrap-up/Assess** (5 minutes)			

DAY 15	• Review unit vocabulary, expressions, and grammar
	• Practice communicative skills
		• **Warm-up** (5 minutes)
		[Option 1]
		• **Evaluación** (35 minutes)
		  – Activities 1-7
		[Option 2]
		• **Casa del español-videos** (35 minutes)
		  – Videos 1 and 2
		  – Extra activities
		• **En resumen** (10 minutes)
		  – Vocabulario
		  – Gramática
					• Evaluación
					• Casa del español videos
					  – Video 7
					    (5 minutes)
					  – Extra activity
					    (10 minutes)
					  – Video 8
					    (5 minutes)
					• Extra activity
					  (10 minutes)

DAY 16	• Assessment	• **Warm-up** (5 minutes) • **Online test Unit 4** (30 minutes)	• Unit 4 assessment		
DAY 17	• Gamification project				

DAY 18	• Review and recycle grammar, vocabulary, and culture from the last two units
	• Complete self-assessment
		• **Ahora comprueba** (50 minutes)
		  – Activity 1
		  – Activity 2
		  – Activity 3
		  – Activity 4 (Audio 33)
		  – Activity 5 (Audio 34)
		  – Activity 6
		  – Activity 7			

UNIDAD 5: ¡OJALÁ!

	OBJECTIVES / TOPIC	PRESENT/PRACTICE/COMMUNICATE	ADDITIONAL TEACHER RESOURCES	HOMEWORK	ELETECA ONLINE PRACTICE

DAY 1	• Introduce unit theme: **¡Ojalá!**, expressing wishes and emotional reactions to events
	• Introduce culture for unit: Learn about opportunities for volunteering in Hispanic countries
	• Preview vocabulary: Expressing wishes
		• **Unit Opener** (15 minutes)
		• **Hablamos de…**(30 minutes)
		Expresar deseos
		  – Activity 1
		  – Activity 2
		  – Activity 3 (Audio 35)
		• **Wrap-up/Assess** (5 minutes)
					• Hablamos de…
					  – Activity 1
					    (10 minutes)
					  – Activity 2
					    (10 minutes)
					  – Activity 3
					    (10 minutes)

DAY 2	• Preview grammatical structures: The present subjunctive	• **Warm-up** (10 minutes)
		• **Hablamos de…** (35 minutes)
		Expresar deseos
		  – Activity 4
		  – Activity 5
		  – Activity 6
		• **Wrap-up/Assess** (5 minutes)			

	OBJECTIVES / TOPIC	PRESENT/PRACTICE/COMMUNICATE	ADDITIONAL TEACHER RESOURCES	HOMEWORK	ELETECA ONLINE PRACTICE

DAY 3	• Present communicative functions of the unit: Expressing wishes and desires
	
	• Recognize and practice expressions of purpose, objective, and wishes
		• **Warm-up** (10 minutes)
		
		• **Comunica** (35 mi tes)
		Expressing the moment when an action takes place
		  – Presentation
		  – Activity 1
		  – Activity 2 (Audio 36)
		Expressing wishes and desires
		  – Activities 3 and 4
		
		• **Wrap-up/Assess** (5 minutes)
			• IWB 5.1
			• IWB 5.2
					• Comunica
					  – Activity 1
					    (10 minutes)
					  – Activity 2
					    (10 minutes)
					  – Activity 3
					    (10 minutes)

DAY 4	• Present communicative functions of the unit: Other expressions of wishes and social responses
	
	• Practice using appropriate social responses in a variety of situations
		• **Warm-up** (10 minutes)
		
		• **Comunica** (35 minutes)
		Other expressions and social responses
		  – Activity 5 (Audio 37)
		  – Activity 6
		
		• **Wrap-up/Assess** (5 minutes)			

DAY 5	• Contextualize the content of the unit: **¡Acción!** Video
	
	• Provide students with a structured approach to viewing the video
		• **¡Acción!** (50 minutes)
		Casting en Somalia
		  Antes del video
		  – Activity 1
		  Durante el video
		  – Activity 2
		  Después del video
		  – Activities 3 and 4
			• DVD Episodio 5: *Casting en Somalia*		• Vídeo 5: *Casting en Somalia* (10 minutes)
					
					• Extra activity (16 minutes)

DAY 6	• Present vocabulary needed to practice communicative and grammatical functions for the unit: Non-governmental organizations or NGOs	• **Warm-up** (10 minutes)
		
		• **Palabra por palabra** (35 minutes)
		Las ONG y el voluntariado
		  – Activity 1
		  – Activity 2
		  – Activity 3
		  – Activity 4
		  – Activity 5
		  – Activity 6
		
		• **Wrap-up/Assess** (5 minutes)
			• IWB 5.3	• WB Online practice: Vocabulario 5.1 - 5.6	• Palabra por palabra
					  – Activity 1
					    (10 minutes)
					  – Activity 2
					    (10 minutes)
					  – Activity 3
					    (10 minutes)

DAY 7	• Identify and discuss different causes for which people often volunteer	• **Warm-up** (10 minutes)
		
		• **Palabra por palabra** (35 minutes)
		Las ONG
		  – Activitiy 7
		  – Activity 8
		  – Activity 9
		
		• **Wrap-up/Assess** (5 minutes)			

DAY 8	• Present grammatical structures needed to practice communicative functions of the unit:
	  – The present subjunctive: regular verbs
	  – Learn to conjugate regular verbs in the present subjunctive
		• **Warm-up** (10 minutes)
		
		• **Gramática** (35 minutes)
		1. The present subjunctive: regular verbs
		  – Presentation
		  – Activity 1
		  – Activity 2
		
		• **Wrap-up/Assess** (5 minutes)
			• EA 5.1	• WB Online practice: Gramática 5.7 - 5.12	• Grammar tutorials
					  – Tutorial 9
					    (8 minutes)
					  – Extra activity
					    (14 minutes)
					  – Tutorial 10
					    (8 minutes)
					
					• Extra activity (14 minutes)

	OBJECTIVES / TOPIC	PRESENT/PRACTICE/COMMUNICATE	ADDITIONAL TEACHER RESOURCES	HOMEWORK	ELETECA ONLINE PRACTICE

DAY 9	• Present grammatical structures needed to practice communicative functions of the unit: The present subjunctive: irregular verbs	• **Warm-up** (10 minutes)
		• **Gramática** (35 minutes)
		2. The present subjunctive: irregular verbs
		  – Presentation
		  – Activity 3
		  – Activity 4
		  – Activity 5
		  – Activity 6
		  – Activity 7
		• **Wrap-up/Assess** (5 minutes)
			• EA 5.2	• WB Online practice: Gramática 5.7 - 5.12	• Grammar tutorials
					  – Tutorial 9 (8 minutes)
					  – Extra activity (14 minutes)
					  – Tutorial 10 (8 minutes)
					• Extra activity (14 minutes)

DAY 10	• Learn to conjugate irregular verbs in the present subjunctive.	• **Warm-up** (10 minutes)
		• **Gramática** (35 minutes)
		2. The present subjunctive: irregular verbs
		  – Activity 8
		  – Activity 9
		  – Activity 10
		  – Activity 11
		• **Wrap-up/Assess** (5 minutes)			

DAY 11	• Develop writing skills by learning how to use a chart to organize information	• **Destrezas** (45 minutes)
		Expresión e interacción escritas I
		  – Activity 1
		  – Activity 2
		• **Wrap-up/Assess** (5 minutes)
			• IWB 5.4	• WB Online practice: Destrezas 5.13 - 5.16	• Destreza lectora (15 minutes)
					• Destreza escrita (15 minutes)
					• Destreza oral (15 minutes)
					• Pronunciación
					  – Activity 1 (10 minutes)
					  – Activity 2 (10 minutes)
					  – Activity 3 (10 minutes)

DAY 12	• Learn strategies for writing an email
	• Practice the correct pronunciation of diphthongs and hiatuses
		• **Destrezas** (45 minutes)
		Expresión e interacción escritas II
		  – Activity 3
		  – Activity 4
		• **Pronunciación**
		  – Presentation
		  – Activity 1 (Audio 38)
		  – Activity 2 (Audio 38)
		  – Activity 3
		• **Wrap-up/Assess** (5 minutes)			

DAY 13	• Learn about a student's gap year experience as a volunteer in Guatemala
	• Compare rates of volunteerism in different countries
		• **Warm-up** (10 minutes)
		• **Sabor Hispano** (35 minutes)
		Me encanta ser voluntario (Audio 39)
		  – *Países con más voluntarios*
		  – *Países solidarios*
		  – Activities
		• **Wrap-up/Assess** (5 minutes)
			• Voces latinas video: *Política en Chile y Argentina*	• WB Online practice: Cultura 5.17	• Voces latinas video: *Política en Chile y Argentina*
					• Extra activity (10 minutes)

DAY 14	• Revisit unit themes, grammar, vocabulary, and culture in a new context
	• Improve reading comprehension skills
		• **Warm-up** (5 minutes)
		• **Relato** (40 minutes)
		Pablo Neruda, Soneto LXXXIX
		  – Activity 1
		  – Activity 2 (Audio 40)
		  – Activity 3
		  – Activity 4 (Audio 41)
		  – Activity 5
		• **Wrap-up/Assess** (5 minutes)
			• EA 5.3		

	OBJECTIVES / TOPIC	PRESENT/PRACTICE/COMMUNICATE	ADDITIONAL TEACHER RESOURCES	HOMEWORK	ELETECA ONLINE PRACTICE

DAY 15	• Review grammar, vocabulary, and culture from the unit
	• Complete self-assessment
		• **Warm-up** (5 minutes)
		[Option 1]
		• **Evaluación** (35 minutes)
		  – Activities 1-7
		[Option 2]
		• **Casa del español-videos** (35 minutes)
		  – Videos 1 and 2
		  – Extra activities
		• **En resumen** (10 minutes)
		  – Vocabulario
		  – Gramática
					• Evaluación
					• Casa del español videos
					  – Video 9
					    (5 minutes)
					  – Extra activity
					    (10 minutes)
					  – Video 10
					    (5 minutes)
					• Extra activity
					  (10 minutes)

DAY 16	• Assessment	• **Warm-up** (5 minutes) • **Online test Unit 5** (30 minutes)	• Unit 5 assessment		
DAY 17	• Gamification project				

UNIDAD 6: ¡HOY ME SIENTO BIEN!

	OBJECTIVES / TOPIC	PRESENT/PRACTICE/COMMUNICATE	ADDITIONAL TEACHER RESOURCES	HOMEWORK	ELETECA ONLINE PRACTICE

DAY 1	• Introduce unit theme: *¡Hoy me siento bien!* , feelings and emotions
	• Introduce culture for the unit: Share information about the arts in Hispanic countries
	• Talk about feelings and emotions
		• **Unit Opener** (15 minutes)
		• **Hablamos de...** (30 minutes)
		Los sentimientos
		  – Activity 1
		  – Activity 2
		  – Activity 3
		• **Wrap-up/Assess** (5 minutes)
					• Hablamos de...
					  – Activity 1
					    (10 minutes)
					  – Activity 2
					    (10 minutes)
					  – Activity 3
					    (10 minutes)

DAY 2	• Preview vocabulary: Feelings, personality, and emotions
	• Preview grammatical structures: Verbs followed by infinitive or past participle and verbs that express change
		• **Warm-up** (10 minutes)
		• **Hablamos de...** (35 minutes)
		Los sentimientos
		  – Activity 4
		  – Activity 5 (Audio 42)
		  – Activity 6
		  – Activity 7
		• **Wrap-up/Assess** (5 minutes)			

DAY 3	• Present communicative functions of the unit: Talk about feelings and emotions	• **Warm-up** (10 minutes)
		• **Comunica** (35 minutes)
		Expressing feelings and emotions (1)
		  – Presentation
		  – Activity 1
		  – Activity 2
		  – Activity 3 (Audio 43)
		  – Activity 4
		• **Wrap-up/Assess** (5 minutes)
			• EA 6.1, 6.2, 6.3, 6.4		• Comunica
					  – Activity 1
					    (10 minutes)
					  – Activity 2
					    (10 minutes)
					  – Activity 3
					    (10 minutes)

DAY 4	• Present communicative functions of the unit: Talk about feelings and emotions	• **Warm-up** (10 minutes)
		• **Comunica** (35 minutes)
		Express feelings and emotions (2)
		  – Presentation
		  – Activity 5
		  – Activity 6
		• **Wrap-up/Assess** (5 minutes)			

	OBJECTIVES / TOPIC	PRESENT/PRACTICE/COMMUNICATE	ADDITIONAL TEACHER RESOURCES	HOMEWORK	ELETECA ONLINE PRACTICE

DAY 5	• Contextualize the content of the unit: **¡Acción!** Video
	• Provide students with a structured approach to viewing the video
		• **¡Acción!** (50 minutes)
		Tu voz es lo más dulce
		   Antes del video
		   – Activities 1 and 2
		   Durante el video
		   – Activities 3 and 4
		   Después del video
		   – Activity 5
		• **Wrap-up/Assess** (5 minutes)
			• DVD Episodio 6: *Tu voz es lo más dulce*		• Video 6: *Tu voz es lo más dulce* (10 minutes)
					• Extra activity (16 minutes)

DAY 6	• Present vocabulary needed to discuss attributes and characteristics: Describe the qualities of people and things	• **Warm-up** (10 minutes)
		• **Palabra por palabra** (35 minutes)
		Adjetivos calificativos
		   – Presentation
		   – Activity 1
		   – Activity 2
		• **Wrap-up/Assess** (5 minutes)
				• WB Online practice: Vocabulario 6.1 - 6.9	• Palabra por palabra
					   – Activity 1 (10 minutes)
					   – Activity 2 (10 minutes)
					   – Activity 3 (10 minutes)

DAY 7	• Present vocabulary needed to talk about the arts: Talk about artistic activities	• **Warm-up** (10 minutes)
		• **Palabra por palabra** (35 minutes)
		¡Qué arte!
		   – Activity 3 (Audio 44)
		   – Activity 4
		   – Activity 5 (Audio 45)
		   – Activity 6
		   – Activity 7
		   – Activity 8
		• **Wrap-up/Assess** (5 minutes)
			• EA 6.5		

DAY 8	• Present vocabulary needed to talk about styles of music: Talk about musical preferences	• **Warm-up** (10 minutes)
		• **Palabra por palabra** (35 minutes)
		La música
		   – Activity 9
		   – Activity 10
		   – Activity 11
		   – Activity 12
		   – Activity 13
		• **Wrap-up/Assess** (5 minutes)			

DAY 9	• Present grammatical structures needed to practice communicative functions of the unit:
	   – Verbs that are followed by an infinitive or the present participle
	   – Talk about the beginning, end, continuity, and repetition of an action
		• **Warm-up** (10 minutes)
		• **Gramática** (35 minutes)
		1. Verbs followed by an infinitive or present participle
		   – Presentation
		   – Activity 1
		   – Activity 2
		   – Activity 3
		• **Wrap-up/Assess** (5 minutes)
				• WB Online practice: Vocabulario 6.10 - 6.14	• Grammar tutorials
					   – Tutorial 13 (8 minutes)
					   – Extra activity (14 minutes)
					   – Tutorial 14 (8 minutes)
					• Extra activity (14 minutes)

DAY 10	• Present grammatical structures needed to practice communicative functions of the unit:
	   – Verbs that express change
	   – Describe changes that can occur in professions, lifestyles, and emotions.
		• **Warm-up** (10 minutes)
		• **Gramática** (35 minutes)
		2. Verbs that express changev
		   – Presentation
		   – Activity 4
		   – Activity 5
		   – Activity 6 (Audio 46)
		   – Activity 7
		• **Wrap-up/Assess** (5 minutes)
			• IWB 6.1		

	OBJECTIVES / TOPIC	PRESENT/PRACTICE/COMMUNICATE	ADDITIONAL TEACHER RESOURCES	HOMEWORK	ELETECA ONLINE PRACTICE
DAY 11	• Anticipate content before listening	• **Destrezas** (45 minutes) *Comprensión auditiva I* – Activity 1 – Activity 2 (Audio 47) *Comprensión auditiva II* – Activity 3 – Activity 4 (Audio 48) • **Wrap-up/Assess** (5 minutes)		• WB Online practice: Destrezas 6.15 - 6.18	• Destreza lectora (15 minutes) • Destreza escrita (15 minutes) • Destreza oral (15 minutes)
DAY 12	• Learn about foreign words adapted to Spanish and those that stay in the original	• **Warm-up** (10 minutes) • **Pronunciación** – Presentation – Activity 1 (Audio 49) – Activity 2 – Activity 3 • **Wrap-up/Assess** (5 minutes)			• Pronunciación – Activity 1 (10 minutes) – Activity 2 (10 minutes) – Activity 3 (10 minutes)
DAY 13	• Learn about Hispanic music • Learn about different type of Hispanic music and dance	• **Warm-up** (10 minutes) • **Sabor Hispano** (35 minutes) *Mucho más que música* (Audio 50) – El tango – Los top 5 del flamenco – Activities • **Wrap-up/Assess** (5 minutes)	• Voces latinas video: *La música en América Latina*	• WB Online practice: Cultura 6.19 - 6.20	• Voces latinas video: *La música en América Latina* • Extra activity (10 minutes)
DAY 14	• Revisit unit themes, grammar, vocabulary, and culture in a new context • Improve reading comprehension skills	• **Warm-up** (5 minutes) • **Relato** (40 minutes) *Platero y yo* – Activity 1 – Activity 2 (Audio 51) – Activity 3 – Activity 4 – Activity 5 – Activity 6 – Activity 7 • **Wrap-up/Assess** (5 minutes)			
DAY 15	• Review unit vocabulary, grammar, and culture from the unit • Practice communicative skills	• **Warm-up** (5 minutes) [Option 1] • **Evaluación** (35 minutes) – Activities 1-8 [Option 2] • **Casa del español-videos** (35 minutes) – Videos 1 and 2 – Extra activities • **En resumen** (10 minutes) – Vocabulario – Gramática			• Evaluación • Casa del español videos – Video 11 (5 minutes) – Extra activity (10 minutes) – Video 12 (5 minutes) • Extra activity (10 minutes)
DAY 16	• Assessment	• **Warm-up** (5 minutes) • **Online test Unit 6** (30 minutes)		• Unit 6 assessment	
DAY 17	• Gamification project				

	OBJECTIVES / TOPIC	PRESENT/PRACTICE/COMMUNICATE	ADDITIONAL TEACHER RESOURCES	HOMEWORK	ELETECA ONLINE PRACTICE
DAY 18	• Review grammar, vocabulary, and culture from the last two units • Complete self-assessment	• **Ahora comprueba** (50 minutes) – Activity 1 – Activity 2 (Audio 52) – Activity 3 – Activity 4 – Activity 5 (Audio 53) – Activity 6 – Activity 7	• EA 6.6, 6.7, 6.8		

UNIDAD 7: ¡QUE NO TE ENGAÑEN!

	OBJECTIVES / TOPIC	PRESENT/PRACTICE/COMMUNICATE	ADDITIONAL TEACHER RESOURCES	HOMEWORK	ELETECA ONLINE PRACTICE
DAY 1	• Introduce unit theme: *¡Que no te engañen!*, advertising and Internet • Introduce culture for the unit: Learn about the role of advertisements and the Internet in Hispanic countries, and compare cultural similarities • Preview vocabulary: Internet and advertising	• **Unit Opener** (15 minutes) • **Hablamos de...** (30 minutes) *Las opiniones* – Activity 1 – Activity 2 • **Wrap-up/Assess** (5 minutes)			• Hablamos de... – Activity 1 (10 minutes) – Activity 2 (10 minutes) – Activity 3 (10 minutes)
DAY 2	• Preview grammatical structures: Transition words and phrases and other connectors	• **Warm-up** (10 minutes) • **Hablamos de...** (35 minutes) *Las opiniones* – Activity 3 (Audio 54) – Activity 4 – Activity 5 • **Wrap-up/Assess** (5 minutes)			
DAY 3	• Present communicative functions of the unit: – Expressing opinion – Practice using different phrases to ask about and share opinions • Present communicative functions of the unit: Expressing agreement and disagreement with an opinion • Practice using different expressions for agreeing and disagreeing	• **Warm-up** (10 minutes) • **Comunica** (35 minutes) Expressing opinion – Presentation – Activity 1 – Activity 2 To express agreement and disagreement with an opinion – Presentation – Activity 3 – Activity 4 • **Wrap-up/Assess** (5 minutes)	• EA 7.1		• Comunica – Activity 1 (10 minutes) – Activity 2 (10 minutes) – Activity 3 (10 minutes)
DAY 4	• Present communicative functions of the unit: Making value judgements • Practice using different expressions to make value judgements	• **Warm-up** (10 minutes) • **Comunica** (35 minutes) Making value judgements – Presentation – Activity 5 (Audio 55) – Activity 6 – Activity 7 • **Wrap-up/Assess** (5 minutes)	• EA 7.2 • IWB 7.1		

	OBJECTIVES / TOPIC	PRESENT/PRACTICE/COMMUNICATE	ADDITIONAL TEACHER RESOURCES	HOMEWORK	ELETECA ONLINE PRACTICE
DAY 5	• Contextualize the content of the unit: *¡Acción!* Video • Provide students with a structured approach to viewing the video	• **¡Acción!** (45 minutes) *Galletas Segismundo* 　Antes del video 　– Activities 1 and 2 　Durante el video 　– Activity 3 　Después del video 　– Activity 4 • **Wrap-up/Assess** (5 minutes)	• DVD Episodio 7: *Galletas Segismundo*		• Video 7: *Galletas Segismundo* (10 minutes) • Extra activity (16 minutes)
DAY 6	• Present vocabulary needed to practice communicative and grammatical functions for the unit: Online environments and the Internet	• **Warm-up** (10 minutes) • **Palabra por palabra** (35 minutes) *Internet* 　– Activity 1 　– Activity 2 • **Wrap-up/Assess** (5 minutes)	• EA 7.3	• WB Online practice: Vocabulario 7.1 - 7.9	• Palabra por palabra 　– Activity 1 (10 minutes) 　– Activity 2 (10 minutes) 　– Activity 3 (10 minutes)
DAY 7	• Understand and use terms related to the Internet	• **Warm-up** (10 minutes) • **Palabra por palabra** (35 minutes) *Internet* 　– Activity 3 　– Activity 4 • **Wrap-up/Assess** (5 minutes)			
DAY 8	• Present vocabulary needed to practice communicative and grammatical functions for the unit: Online advertising • Write about and discuss issues related to online advertising	• **Warm-up** (10 minutes) • **Gramática** (35 minutes) *La publicidad en Internet* 　– Activity 5 (Audio 56) 　– Activity 6 　– Activity 7 • **Wrap-up/Assess** (5 minutes)			
DAY 9	• Present grammatical structures needed to practice communicative functions of the unit: Transition words and phrases • Learn and practice using transitional words and phrases in writing	• **Warm-up** (10 minutes) • **Gramática** (35 minutes) 1. Transition words and phrases 　– Activity 1 　– Activity 2 • **Wrap-up/Assess** (5 minutes)	• EA 7.4	• WB Online practice: Gramática 7.10 - 7.13	• Grammar tutorials 　– Tutorial 13 (8 minutes) 　– Extra activity (14 minutes) 　– Tutorial 14 (8 minutes)
DAY 10	• Present grammatical structures needed to practice communicative functions of the unit: Other sentence connectors • Learn new sentence connectors and apply them to appropriate contexts	• **Warm-up** (10 minutes) • **Gramática** (40 minutes) 2. Other sentence connectors 　– Presentation 　– Activity 3 (Audio 57) 　– Activity 4 • **Wrap-up/Assess** (5 minutes)			• Extra activity (14 minutes)
DAY 11	• Develop grammar and vocabulary comprehension skills • Learn strategies for preparing for assessments	• **Warm-up** (10 minutes) • **Destrezas** *Comprensión de gramática y vocabulario I* 　– Activity 1 　– Activity 2 　– Activity 3 *Comprensión de gramática y vocabulario II* 　– Activity 4 • **Wrap-up/Assess** (5 minutes)	• IWB 7.2	• WB Online practice: Destrezas 7.14 - 7.17	• Destreza lectora (15 minutes) • Destreza escrita (15 minutes) • Destreza oral (15 minutes)

	OBJECTIVES / TOPIC	PRESENT/PRACTICE/COMMUNICATE	ADDITIONAL TEACHER RESOURCES	HOMEWORK	ELETECA ONLINE PRACTICE

DAY 12	• Listening for and pronouncing initials, acronyms, and abbreviations	• **Warm-up** (10 minutes)
		• **Pronunciación** (35 minutes)
		   – Presentation
		   – Activity 1 (Audio 58)
		   – Activity 2
		• **Wrap-up/Assess** (5 minutes)
					• Pronunciación
					   – Activity 1
					   (10 minutes)

DAY 13	• Learn about the role of advertisements and Internet in Hispanic countries
	• Compare cultural similarities about the role of advertisements and Internet around the world
		• **Warm-up** (10 minutes)
		• **Sabor Hispano** (35 minutes)
		Cómpralo ya (Audio 59)
		   – *Anuncios que más destacan*
		   – *¿Quién te convence?*
		   – Activities
		• **Wrap-up/Assess** (5 minutes)
			• Voces latinas video: *Los famosos y la publicidad*	• WB Online practice: Cultura 7.18	• Voces latinas video: *Los famosos y la publicidad*
					• Extra activity (10 minutes)

DAY 14	• Revisit unit themes, grammar, vocabulary and culture in a new context
	• Improve reading comprehension skills
		• **Warm-up** (10 minutes)
		• **Relato** (35 minutes)
		Preámbulo a las instrucciones para dar cuerda a un reloj
		   – Activity 1
		   – Activity 2
		   – Activity 3 (Audio 60)
		   – Activity 4
		   – Activity 5
		   – Activity 6
		   – Activity 7
		• **Wrap-up/Assess** (5 minutes)			

DAY 15	• Review unit vocabulary, expressions, and grammar
	• Practice communicative skills
		• **Warm-up** (5 minutes)
		[Option 1]
		• **Evaluación** (35 minutes)
		   – Activities 1-8
		[Option 2]
		• **Casa del español-videos** (35 minutes)
		   – Videos 1 and 2
		   – Extra activities
		• **En resumen** (10 minutes)
		   – Vocabulario
		   – Gramática
			• EA 7.5		• Evaluación
					• Casa del español videos
					   – Video 13
					   (5 minutes)
					   – Extra activity
					   (10 minutes)
					   – Video 14
					   (5 minutes)
					• Extra activity
					   (10 minutes)

DAY 16	• Assessment	• **Warm-up** (5 minutes) • **Online test Unit 7** (30 minutes)		• Unit 7 assessment	
DAY 17	• Gamification project				

	OBJECTIVES / TOPIC	PRESENT/PRACTICE/COMMUNICATE	ADDITIONAL TEACHER RESOURCES	HOMEWORK	ELETECA ONLINE PRACTICE

DAY 1	• Introduce unit theme: **¿Sueño o realidad?**, expressing real and hypothetical situations and stories
	• Introduce culture for the unit: Learn about letter writing and formal correspondence in Hispanic countries
	• Preview vocabulary: Reading fiction
		• **Unit Opener** (15 minutes)
		• **Hablamos de…** (30 minutes)
		Libros y cómics
		  – Activity 1
		  – Activity 2
		• **Wrap-up/Assess** (5 minutes)
			• EA 8.1
			• IWB 8.1
					• Hablamos de…
					  – Activity 1
					    (10 minutes)
					  – Activity 2
					    (10 minutes)
					  – Activity 3
					    (10 minutes)
					  – Activity 4
					    (10 minutes)

DAY 2	• Preview grammatical structures: Hypothetical expressions with the indicative and the subjunctive	• **Warm-up** (10 minutes)
		• **Hablamos de…** (35 minutes)
		Libros y cómic
		  – Activity 3 (Audio 61)
		  – Activity 4
		  – Activity 5
		• **Wrap-up/Assess** (5 minutes)			

DAY 3	• Present communicative functions of the unit: Relaying information from others
	• Talk about what others said and asked
		• **Warm-up** (10 minutes)
		• **Comunica** (35 minutes)
		Relaying what another person said or asked
		  – Presentation
		  – Activity 1
		  – Activity 2 (Audio 62)
		  – Activity 3
		• **Wrap-up/Assess** (5 minutes)
					• Comunica
					  – Activity 1
					    (10 minutes)
					  – Activity 2
					    (10 minutes)
					  – Activity 3
					    (10 minutes)

DAY 4	• Present communicative functions of the unit: Expressing probability in the past, the present, and the future	• **Warm-up** (10 minutes)
		• **Comunica** (35 minutes)
		Expressing probability in the past and the present
		  – Presentation
		  – Activity 4
		  – Activity 5
		  – Activity 6
		• **Wrap-up/Assess** (5 minutes)
			• EA 8.2
			• EA 8.3		

DAY 5	• Contextualize the content of the unit: **¡Acción!** Video
	• Provide students with a structured approach to viewing the video
		• **¡Acción!** (50 minutes)
		¡Hasta siempre, mis amigos!
		Antes del video
		  – Activities 1 and 2
		Durante el video
		  – Activity 3
		Después del video
		  – Activities 4 and 5
		• **Wrap-up/Assess** (5 minutes)
			• DVD Episodio 8: *¡Hasta siempre, mis amigos!*		• Video 8: 30 *¡Hasta siempre, mis amigos!* (10 minutes)
					• Extra activity (16 minutes)

DAY 6	• Present vocabulary needed to practice communicative and grammatical functions for the unit: Letter-writing and cell phone issues
	• Learn the parts of a formal letter to write a letter of complaint
	• Use language associated with cell phones to talk about what can go wrong
		• **Warm-up** (10 minutes)
		• **Palabra por palabra** (35 minutes)
		Cartas formales y celulares
		  – Activity 1
		  – Activity 2
		  – Activity 3
		  – Activity 4
		  – Activity 5
		  – Activity 6 (Audio 63)
		• **Wrap-up/Assess** (5 minutes)
				• WB Online practice Vocabulario 8.1 - 8.6	• Palabra por palabra
					  – Activity 1
					    (10 minutes)
					  – Activity 2
					    (10 minutes)
					  – Activity 3
					    (10 minutes)

	OBJECTIVES / TOPIC	PRESENT/PRACTICE/COMMUNICATE	ADDITIONAL TEACHER RESOURCES	HOMEWORK	ELETECA ONLINE PRACTICE

DAY 7	• Present vocabulary needed to practice communicative and grammatical functions for the unit: Email language and expressions
	• Practice reading and responding to emails
	• Learn how to say common electronic symbols
		• **Warm-up** (10 minutes)
		• **Palabra por palabra** (35 minutes)
		Los correos electrónicos
		  – Activity 7
		  – Activity 8
		  – Activity 9
		  – Activity 10
		• **Wrap-up/Assess** (5 minutes)			

DAY 8	• Present grammatical structures needed to practice communicative functions of the unit: Hypothetical expressions with the indicative
	• Learn and practice using hypothetical expressions with the indicative
		• **Warm-up** (10 minutes)
		• **Gramática** (35 minutes)
		1. Hypothetical expressions with the indicative
		  – Presentation
		  – Activity 1
		  – Activity 2
		  – Activity 3 (Audio 64)
		• **Wrap-up/Assess** (5 minutes)
				• WB Online practice: Gramática 8.7 - 8.18	• Grammar tutorials
					  – Tutorial 15 (8 minutes)
					  – Extra activity (14 minutes)
					  – Tutorial 16 (8 minutes)
					• Extra activity 14 minutes)

DAY 9	• Present grammatical structures needed to practice communicative functions of the unit:
	  – Hypothetical expressions with the indicative and the subjunctive
	  – Use the indicative or subjunctive to express how certain you feel
		• **Warm-up** (10 minutes)
		• **Gramática** (35 minutes)
		2. Hypothetical expressions with the indicative and the subjunctive
		  – Presentation
		  – Activity 4 (Audio 65)
		  – Activity 5
		  – Activity 6
		  – Activity 7
		  – Activity 8
		  – Activity 9
		• **Wrap-up/Assess** (5 minutes)			

DAY 10	• Present grammatical structures needed to practice communicative functions of the unit:
	  – Hypothetical expressions with the imperfect subjunctive
	  – Forms and uses of the imperfect subjunctive
		• **Warm-up** (10 minutes)
		• **Gramática** (10 minutes)
		3. Hypothetical expressions with the imperfect subjunctive
		  – Activity 10
		  – Activity 11
		• **Gramática** (25 minutes)
		4. Forms and uses of the imperfect subjunctive
		  – Presentation
		  – Activity 12
		  – Activity 13
		  – Activity 14
		  – Activity 15
		• **Wrap-up/Assess** (5 minutes)			

DAY 11	• Simulate multiple choice testing formats in preparation for international testing certificates as the DELE (*Diploma de Español como Lengua Extranjera*) or in preparation for other state and/or national assessments
	• Use strategies presented throughout the units
	• Distinguish words with similar spellings or pronunciations but with different meanings
		• **Warm-up** (10 minutes)
		• **Destrezas**
		Comprensión de gramática y vocabulario
		  – Activity 1
		Expresión e interacción orales
		  – Activities 2 and 3
		• **Pronunciación**
		  – Activity 1
		• **Wrap-up/Assess** (5 minutes)
			• EA 8.4	• WB Online practice Destrezas 8.19 - 8.22	• Destreza lectora (15 minutes)
					• Destreza escrita (15 minutes)
					• Destreza oral (15 minutes)
					• Pronunciación
					  – Activity 1 (10 minutes)

	OBJECTIVES / TOPIC	PRESENT/PRACTICE/COMMUNICATE	ADDITIONAL TEACHER RESOURCES	HOMEWORK	ELETECA ONLINE PRACTICE
DAY 12	• Learn about Hispanic soap operas • Compare soap operas from the Spanish-speaking world to the United States	**Warm-up** (5 minutes) **Sabor Hispano** (40 minutes) *Un mundo de novela* (Audio 66) – *Los mejores finales de las villanas* – *La más exitosa* – Activities **Wrap-up/Assess** (5 minutes)	• Voces latinas video: *La telenovela en América Latina*	• WB Online practice: Cultura 8.23 - 8.24	• Voces latinas video: *La telenovela en América Latina* • Extra activity (10 minutes)
DAY 13	• Revisit unit themes, grammar, vocabulary and culture in a new context	**Warm-up** (10 minutes) **Relato** (35 minutes) *La vida es sueño* – Activity 1 – Activity 2 – Activity 3 **Wrap-up/Assess** (5 minutes)	• IWB 8.2		
DAY 14	• Improve reading comprehension skills	**Warm-up** (10 minutes) **Relato** (35 minutes) *La vida es sueño* – Activity 4 – Activity 5 – Activity 6 – Activity 7 – Activity 8 **Wrap-up/Assess** (5 minutes)			
DAY 15	• Review unit vocabulary, expressions, and grammar • Practice communicative skills	**Warm-up** (5 minutes) [Option 1] **Evaluación** (35 minutes) – Activities 1-8 [Option 2] **Casa del español-videos** (35 minutes) – Videos 1 and 2 – Extra activities **En resumen** (10 minutes) – Vocabulario – Gramática			• Evaluación • Casa del español videos – Video 15 (5 minutes) – Extra activity (10 minutes) – Video 16 (5 minutes) • Extra activity (10 minutes)
DAY 16	• Assessment	**Warm-up** (5 minutes) **Online test Unit 8** (30 minutes)	• Unit 8 assessment		
DAY 17	• Gamification project				
DAY 18	• Review grammar, vocabulary, and culture from the last two units • Complete self-assessment	**Ahora comprueba** (50 minutes) – Activity 1 (Audio 68) – Activity 2 – Activity 3 – Activity 4 – Activity 5 – Activity 6			